Fodors®

New EDITION

Florence, Tuscany, and Umbria

The complete guide, thoroughly up-to-date

Packed with details that will make your trip

The must-see sights, off and on the beaten path

What to see, what to skip

Mix-and-match vacation itineraries

City strolls, countryside adventures

Smart lodging and dining options

Essential local do's and taboos

Transportation tips, distances and directions

Key contacts, savvy travel tips

When to go, what to pack

Clear, accurate, easy-to-use maps

Books to read, videos to watch

Fodor's Travel Publications, Inc.
New York • Toronto • London • Sydney • Auckland
www.fodors.com

PRAIANO AMALFI

Fodor's Florence, Tuscany, and Umbria

EDITOR: Caragh Rockwood

Editorial Contributors: Robert Andrews, Barbara Walsh Angelillo, Robert Blake, David Brown, Bernard Burt, Jon Eldan, Candice Gianetti, Valerie Hamilton, Nancy Hart, Christina Knight, Carla Lionello, Patricia Rucidlo, Helayne Schiff, M. T. Schwartzman (Gold Guide editor)

Editorial Production: Melissa Klurman

Maps: David Lindroth, *cartographer*; Steven K. Amsterdam and Robert Blake, *map editors*

Design: Fabrizio La Rocca, *creative director*; Guido Caroti, *associate art director*; Jolie Novak, *photo editor*

Production/Manufacturing: Robert Shields

Cover Photograph: Robert Gill; Papilio/Corbis

Copyright

Special Sales

Fodor's Travel Publications are available at special discounts for bulk purchases for sales promotions or premiums. Special editions, including personalized covers, excerpts of existing guides, and corporate imprints, can be created in large quantities for special needs. For more information, contact your local bookseller or write to Special Markets, Fodor's Travel Publications, 201 East 50th Street, New York, NY 10022. Inquiries from Canada should be directed to your local Canadian bookseller or sent to Random House of Canada, Ltd., Marketing Department, 2775 Matheson Boulevard East, Mississauga, Ontario L4W 4P7. Inquiries from the United Kingdom should be sent to Fodor's Travel Publications, 20 Vauxhall Bridge Road, London SW1V 2SA, England.

PRINTED IN THE UNITED STATES OF AMERICA

10 9 8 7 6 5 4 3 2 1

CONTENTS

Maps

ON THE ROAD WITH FODOR'S

WHEN I PLAN A VACATION, the first thing I do is cast around among my friends and colleagues to find someone who's just been where I'm going. That's because there's no substitute for a recommendation from a good friend who knows your tastes, your budget, and your circumstances, someone who's just been there. Unfortunately, such friends are few and far between. So it's nice to know that there's *Fodor's Florence, Tuscany, and Umbria.*

In the first place, this book won't stay home when you hit the road. It will accompany you every step of the way, steering you away from wrong turns and wrong choices and never expecting a thing in return. Most important of all, it's written and assiduously updated by the kind of people you *would* hit up for travel tips if you knew them. They're as choosy as your pickiest friend, except they've probably seen a lot more of Florence, Tuscany, and Umbria. In these pages, they don't send you chasing down every town and sight in the regions, but have instead selected the best ones, the ones that are worthy of your time and money. To make it easy for you to put it all together in the time you have, they've created short, medium, and long itineraries and, in cities, neighborhood walks that you can mix and match in a snap. Will this be the vacation of your dreams? We hope so.

About Our Writers

Our success in helping to make your trip the best of all possible vacations is a credit to the hard work of our extraordinary writers. Fodor's would also like to thank Alitalia for its ever-superb service and generosity.

The first time veteran Fodorite **Barbara Walsh Angelillo** arrived in Rome, she was traveling on a tight schedule; still, she had time to fall in love with both the city and a dark-eyed Italian—simultaneously. Within a year, Barbara said *arrivederci* to her native New York City to settle, marry, and raise three children in Italy. Barbara unwinds in what she calls "two of Italy's most special places," Umbria and the Amalfi Coast.

Jon Eldan studied European history in Berkeley, California, before packing his bags in 1994 to see the real thing. He now lives and bakes bread in Rome, and goes back to visit the old country from time to time. **Carla Lionello** grew up in Venice. Seven years ago she traded Piazza San Marco for the Spanish Steps and moved to Rome. Although she still hasn't learned to drive, it doesn't stop her from traveling all over Italy in search of endangered pastry.

After a decade's long-distance love affair with Rome, **Valerie Hamilton** recently settled in the city permanently, working in television—covering topics from wine making to heli-rescue dogs—in between stints for Fodor's. While classic Italian specialties have charmed her since adolescence, it is Italy's subtle side that has captured her heart: the creative yet calculated twist of a *tortello,* or the gentle curve of an Italian shoe. In two Close-Up essays, Valerie explores two of Tuscany's pleasures: *terme* and vino.

Nancy Hart, a former U.S. newspaper and television feature reporter, came to Italy in 1991, expecting to stay the proverbial one year, but failed. Based in Rome, she now travels to the Third World to create documentary videos (among other things) dealing with developmental issues. Her time spent writing the Chianti chapter was interrupted by travels to Ouagadougou, Abidjan, and Gangtok—interesting places to visit, but the wine isn't nearly as good.

Patricia Rucidlo lives in Florence with her dog, Tillie, who occasionally accompanies her on the Tuscan art history and food beat. Though she has masters degrees in Italian Renaissance history and art history, Patti's true love is Italian food (as is Tillie's). Patti has also taught Italian cooking classes and ran her own catering business in the United States.

New This Year

We are thrilled that this edition of *Fodor's Florence, Tuscany, and Umbria* has been expanded for more in-depth coverage of the regions of Tuscany and Umbria. Chapters 3–9 are revised and expanded, offering you more of everything—enchanting hill towns, great local restaurants, lodging finds for every pocketbook, churches and abbeys, fun sports, insider shopping, and helpful tips. We've also added some essays on the wines of Chianti, the Palio, and thermal baths to enhance your travels—check them out.

Connections

We're pleased that the American Society of Travel Agents continues to endorse Fodor's as its guidebook of choice. ASTA is the world's largest and most influential travel trade association, operating in more than 170 countries, with 27,000 members pledged to adhere to a strict code of ethics reflecting the Society's motto, "Integrity in Travel." ASTA shares Fodor's devotion to providing smart, honest travel information and advice to travelers, and we've long recommended that our readers—even those who have guidebooks and traveling friends—consult ASTA member agents for the experience and professionalism they bring to your vacation planning.

On Fodor's Web site (www.fodors.com), check out the new Resource Center, an online companion to the Gold Guide section of this book, complete with useful hot links to related sites. In our forums, you can also get lively advice from other travelers and more great tips from Fodor's experts worldwide.

How to Use This Book

Organization

Up front is the **Gold Guide,** an easy-to-use section arranged alphabetically by topic. Under each listing you'll find tips and information that will help you accomplish what you need to in Florence, Tuscany, and Umbria. You'll also find addresses and telephone numbers of organizations and companies that offer destination-related services and detailed information and publications.

The first chapter in the guide, Destination: Florence, Tuscany, and Umbria, helps get you in the mood for your trip. New and Noteworthy cues you in on trends and happenings, What's Where gets you oriented, Pleasures and Pastimes describes the activities and sights that make Florence,

Tuscany, and Umbria unique, Fodor's Choice showcases our top picks, and Festivals and Seasonal Events alerts you to special events you'll want to seek out.

Chapters in *Fodor's Florence, Tuscany, and Umbria* are arranged by logical areas within each region. The Florence city chapter begins with Exploring information, which is divided into neighborhood sections; it recommends a walking or driving tour and lists sights in alphabetical order. Each regional chapter is divided by geographical area; within each area, towns are covered in logical geographical order, and attractive stretches of road and minor points of interest between them are indicated by the designation *En Route*. And within town sections, all restaurants and lodgings are grouped.

To help you decide what to visit in the time you have, all chapters begin with our recommended itineraries. The A to Z section that ends all chapters covers getting there and getting around. It also provides helpful contacts and resources.

At the end of the book you'll find Portraits, with a chronology about Florence, Tuscany, and Umbria, followed by a glossary of useful art terms and suggestions for pretrip research, from recommended reading to movies that use Florence, Tuscany, and Umbria as a backdrop.

Icons and Symbols

★　　Our special recommendations
✕　　Restaurant
🏠　　Lodging establishment
✕🏠　Lodging establishment whose restaurant warrants a special trip
⚓　　Good for kids (rubber duck)
☞　　Sends you to another section of the guide for more information
✉　　Address
☎　　Telephone number
◷　　Opening and closing times
💶　　Admission prices

Numbers in white and black circles ③ ❸ that appear on the maps, in the margins, and within the tours correspond to one another.

Dining and Lodging

The restaurants and lodgings we list are the cream of the crop in each price range. Price charts appear in the Pleasures and Pastimes section that follows each chapter introduction.

Hotel Facilities

We always list the facilities that are available—but we don't specify whether you'll be charged extra to use them: When pricing accommodations, always ask what's included. In addition, assume that all rooms have private baths unless noted otherwise. In addition, when you book a room, be sure to mention if you have a disability or are traveling with children, if you prefer a private bath or a certain type of bed, or if you have specific dietary needs or other concerns.

Assume that hotels operate on the **European Plan** (EP, with no meals) unless we specify that they use the **Continental Plan** (CP, with a Continental breakfast daily), **Modified American Plan** (MAP, with breakfast and dinner daily), or the **Full American Plan** (FAP, with all meals).

Restaurant Reservations and Dress Codes

Reservations are always a good idea; we mention them only when they're essential or are not accepted. Book as far ahead as you can, and reconfirm as soon as you arrive. Unless otherwise noted, the restaurants listed are open daily for lunch and dinner. We mention dress only when men are required to wear a jacket or a jacket and tie. Look for an overview of local dining-out habits in the Gold Guide.

Credit Cards

The following abbreviations are used: **AE,** American Express; **DC,** Diners Club; **MC,** MasterCard; and **V,** Visa.

Don't Forget to Write

You can use this book in the confidence that all prices and opening times are based on information supplied to us at press time; Fodor's cannot accept responsibility for any errors. Time inevitably brings changes, so always confirm information when it matters—especially if you're making a detour to visit a specific place.

Were the restaurants we recommended as described? Did our hotel picks exceed your expectations? Did you find a museum we recommended a waste of time? Keeping a travel guide fresh and up-to-date is a big job, and we welcome your feedback, positive *and* negative. If you have complaints, we'll look into them and revise our entries when the facts warrant it. If you've discovered a special place that we haven't included, we'll pass the information along to our correspondents and have them check it out. So send us your thoughts via e-mail at editors@fodors.com (specifying the name of the book on the subject line) or on paper in care of the Florence, Tuscany, and Umbria editor at Fodor's, 201 East 50th Street, New York, New York 10022. In the meantime, have a wonderful trip!

Karen Cure

Karen Cure
Editorial Director

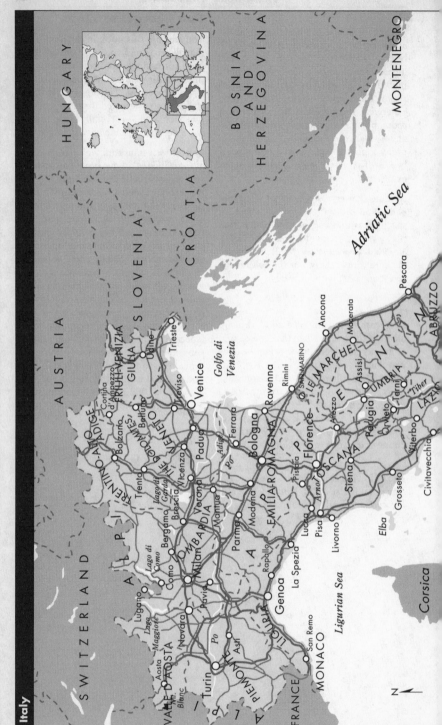

Italy

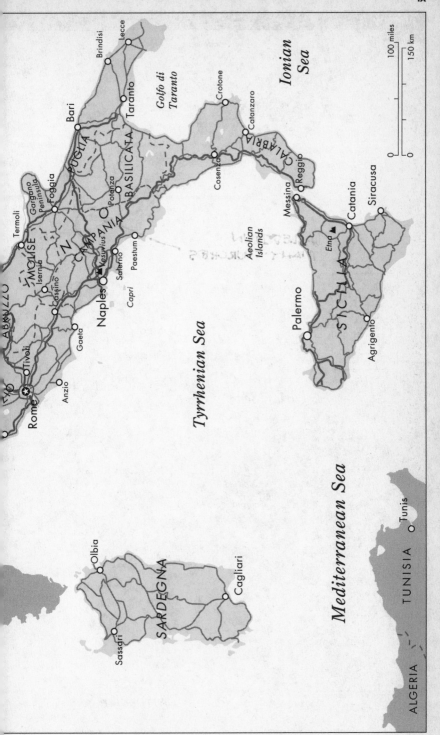

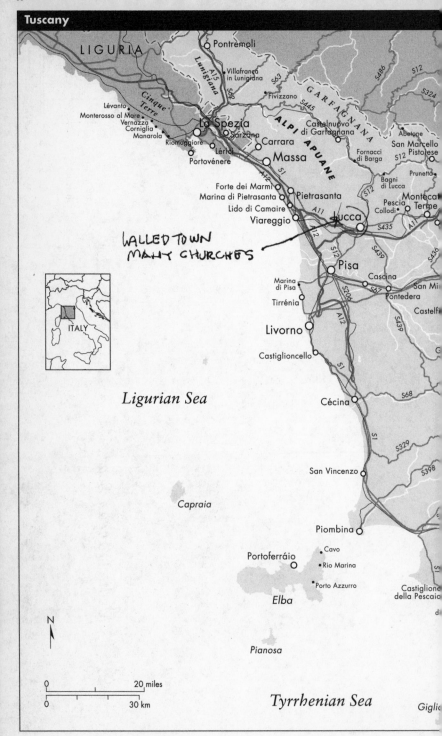

Tuscany

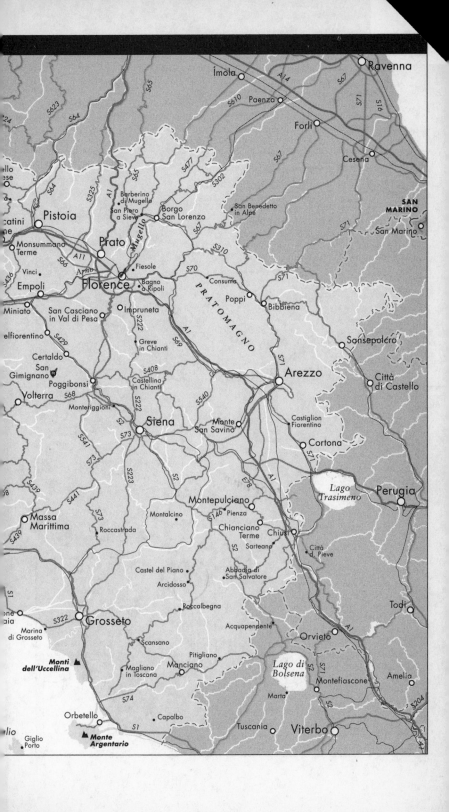

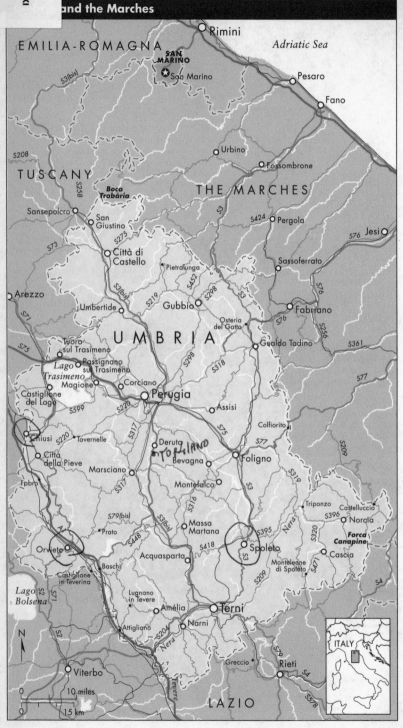

EMILIA-ROMAGNA

Adriatic Sea

Rimini

SAN MARINO

San Marino

Pesaro

Fano

S3(bis)

S208

Urbino

Fossombrone

TUSCANY

THE MARCHES

S258

Boca Trabária

Sansepolcro

San Giustino

Pergola

S424

Jesi

S76

S275

S73

Città di Castello

Pietralunga

Sassoferrato

S452

Arezzo

S3(bis)

S219

S298

Gubbia

S76

Fabriano

Umbertide

S71

Osteria del Gatto

S256

S361

U M B R I A

Gualdo Tadino

S75

Ìvoro sul Trasimeno

S3

S77

Passignano sul Trasimeno

Lago Trasimeno

S298

S318

Magione

Corciano

Perugia

Castiglione del Lago

S599

S226

Assisi

Chiusi

S220

Tavernelle

Colfiorito

S317

S75

Deruta

S77

S209

Città della Pieve

STO-MIANO

Bevagna

Foligno

Fabro

Marsciano

Montefalco

S319

S317

S316

S3

Triponzo

Castelluccio

S79(bis)

S3(bis)

Massa Martana

S396

Norcia

Prato

S448

Nera

S320

S418

S395

Spoleto

Forca Canapine

Orvieto

Acquasparta

S3

Cascia

Baschi

Castiglione in Teverina

Monteleone di Spoleto

S471

Lugnano in Tevere

S209

S4

Lago Bolsena

S2

S71

Amélia

Terni

Narni

Attigliano

Nera

S204

Greccio

Rieti

S4

N

Viterbo

S2

Tevere

S578

LAZIO

0   10 miles

0   15 km

ITALY

SMART TRAVEL TIPS A TO Z

Basic Information on Traveling in Italy, Savvy Tips to Make Your Trip a Breeze, and Companies and Organizations to Contact

AIR TRAVEL

BOOKING YOUR FLIGHT

Price is just one factor to consider when booking a flight: frequency of service and even a carrier's safety record are often just as important. Major airlines offer the greatest number of departures. Smaller airlines—including regional and no-frills airlines—usually have a limited number of flights daily. On the other hand, so-called low-cost airlines usually are cheaper, and their fares impose fewer restrictions, such as advance-purchase requirements. Safety-wise, low-cost carriers as a group have a good history—about equal to that of major carriers.

When you book, **look for nonstop flights** and **remember that "direct" flights stop at least once.** Try to **avoid connecting flights,** which require a change of plane. Two airlines may jointly operate a connecting flight, so ask if your airline operates every segment—you may find that your preferred carrier flies you only part of the way. International flights on a country's flag carrier are almost always nonstop; U.S. airlines often fly direct.

Ask your airline if it offers electronic ticketing, which eliminates all paperwork. There's no ticket to pick up or misplace. You go directly to the gate and give the agent your confirmation number. There's no worry about waiting on line at the airport while precious minutes tick by.

CARRIERS

When flying internationally, you must usually choose between a domestic carrier, the national flag carrier of the country you are visiting, and a foreign carrier from a third country. You may, for example, choose to fly Alitalia to Italy. National flag carriers have the greatest number of nonstops. Domestic carriers may have better connections to your home town and serve a greater number of gateway cities. Third-party carriers may have a price advantage.

Alitalia—in addition to other major European airlines and smaller, privately run companies such as Meridiana and Air One—complete an extensive network of internal flights in Italy. Ask your domestic or Italian travel agent about discounts, which include a 50% family reduction and up to 30% off certain night flights.

➤ MAJOR AIRLINES: **Alitalia** (☎ 800/223–5730) to Rome, Milan, and Venice. **American Airlines** (☎ 800/433–7300) to Milan. **Continental Airlines** (☎ 800/231–0856) to Rome and Milan. **Delta Air Lines** (☎ 800/241–4141) to Rome and Milan. **Northwest Airlines** (☎ 800/225–2525) to Milan. **TWA** (☎ 800/892–4141) to Rome and Milan. **United Airlines** (☎ 800/538–2929) to Milan. **US Airways** (☎ 800/428–4322) to Rome.

➤ FROM THE U.K.: Direct service from Heathrow is provided by **Alitalia** (☎ 0171/602–7111 or 0990/448–259) and **British Airways** (☎ 0345/222–111). From Manchester there are one or two direct flights daily to Milan, and at least three weekly to Rome. Privately run **Meridiana** (☎ 0171/839–2222) has direct flights between London and Olbia on Sardinia on Tuesday and Saturday in summer, and daily flights to Cagliari via Florence throughout the year. Lower-priced charter flights to a range of Italian destinations are available throughout the year.

➤ WITHIN ITALY: **Alitalia** (☎ 06/65621 or 06/65643 for main Rome office; ☎ 02/62811 for main Milan office). **Meridiana** (☎ 0789/4745057 for main Olbia office). **Air One** (☎ 1478/48880 for reservations and information).

CHARTERS

Charters usually have the lowest fares but are the least dependable. Departures are infrequent and seldom on time, flights can be delayed for up to 48 hours or can be canceled for any reason up to 10 days before you're scheduled to leave. Itineraries and prices can change after you've booked your flight.

In the U.S., the Department of Transportation's Aviation Consumer Protection Division has jurisdiction over charters and provides a certain degree of protection. The DOT requires that money paid to charter operators be held in escrow, so if you can't pay with a credit card, **always make your check payable to a charter carrier's escrow account.** The name of the bank should be in the charter contract. If you have any problems with a charter operator, contact the DOT (☞ Airline Complaints, *below*). If you buy a charter package that includes both air and land arrangements, remember that the escrow requirement applies only to the air component.

CHECK IN & BOARDING

Airlines routinely overbook planes, assuming that not everyone with a ticket will show up, but sometimes everyone does. When that happens, airlines ask for volunteers to give up their seats. In return these volunteers usually get a certificate for a free flight and are rebooked on the next flight out. If there are not enough volunteers, the airline must choose who will be denied boarding. The first to get bumped are passengers who checked in late and those flying on discounted tickets, so **get to the gate and check in as early as possible,** especially during peak periods.

Although the trend on international flights is to drop reconfirmation requirements, many airlines still ask you to reconfirm each leg of your international itinerary. Failure to do so may result in your reservation being canceled.

Always **bring a government-issued photo ID to the airport.** You may be asked to show it before you are allowed to check in.

CONSOLIDATORS

Consolidators buy tickets for scheduled international flights at reduced rates from the airlines, then sell them at prices that beat the best fare available directly from the airlines, usually without restrictions. Sometimes you can even get your money back if you need to return the ticket. Carefully read the fine print detailing penalties for changes and cancellations, and **confirm your consolidator reservation with the airline.**

➤ CONSOLIDATORS: **Cheap Tickets** (☎ 800/377–1000). **Up & Away Travel** (☎ 212/889–2345). **Discount Travel Network** (☎ 800/576–1600). **Unitravel** (☎ 800/325–2222). **World Travel Network** (☎ 800/409–6753).

COURIERS

When you fly as a courier, you trade your checked-luggage space for a ticket deeply subsidized by a courier service. It's all perfectly legitimate, but there are restrictions: You can usually book your flight only a week or two in advance, your length of stay may be set for a certain number of days, and you probably won't be able to book a companion on the same flight.

CUTTING COSTS

The least-expensive airfares to Italy are priced for round-trip travel and usually must be purchased in advance. It's smart to **call a number of airlines, and when you are quoted a good price, book it on the spot**—the same fare may not be available the next day. Airlines generally allow you to change your return date for a fee. If you don't use your ticket, you can apply the cost toward the purchase of a new ticket, again for a small charge. However, most low-fare tickets are nonrefundable. To get the lowest airfare, **check different routings.** Compare prices of flights to and from different airports if your destination or home city has more than one gateway. Also price off-peak flights, which may be significantly less expensive.

Travel agents, especially those who specialize in finding the lowest fares (☞ Discounts & Deals, *below*), can be especially helpful when booking a plane ticket. When you're quoted a price, **ask your agent if the price is likely to get any lower.** Good agents know the seasonal fluctuations of airfares and can usually anticipate a sale or fare war. However, waiting can be risky: The fare could go *up* as seats become scarce, and you may wait so long that your preferred flight sells out. A wait-and-see strategy works best if your plans are flexible. If you must arrive and depart on certain dates, don't delay.

ENJOYING THE FLIGHT

For more legroom, **request an emergency-aisle seat.** Don't sit in the row in front of the emergency aisle or in front of a bulkhead, where seats may not recline.

If you don't like airline food, **ask for special meals when booking.** These can be vegetarian, low-cholesterol, or kosher, for example.

When flying internationally, try to maintain a normal routine, to help fight jet-lag. At night, **get some sleep.** By day, **eat light meals, drink water (not alcohol), and move around the cabin** to stretch your legs.

Many carriers have prohibited smoking on all of their international flights; others allow smoking only on certain routes or certain departures, so **contact your carrier regarding its smoking policy.**

FLYING TIMES

Flying time is 8½ hours from New York, 10–11 hours from Chicago, and 12–13 hours from Los Angeles.

HOW TO COMPLAIN

If your baggage goes astray or your flight goes awry, complain right away. Most carriers require that you **file a claim immediately.**

➤ AIRLINE COMPLAINTS: U.S. Department of Transportation Aviation Consumer Protection Division (✉ C-75, Room 4107, Washington, DC 20590, ☎ 202/366–2220). Federal Aviation Administration Consumer Hotline (☎ 800/322–7873).

AIRPORTS

The major gateways to Italy include Rome's **Aeroporto Leonardo da Vinci,** better known as **Fiumicino,** and

Milan's **Aeroporto Malpensa.** If you are going directly to Florence and landing at Rome's Fiumicino, you can make connections at the airport for a flight to Florence. Smaller, minor gateways (☞ *below*) are served by domestic and some international flights).

➤ MAJOR AIRPORTS: Rome's **Aeroporto Leonardo da Vinci,** also called Fiumicino (✉ 30 km/19 mi southeast of Rome, ☎ 06/65953640). Milan's **Aeroporto Malpensa** (☎ 02/38011172). Milan's **Aeroporto Linate** (✉ 10 km/6 mi east of Milan, ☎ 02/74852200).

➤ MINOR AIRPORTS: Florence's **Aeroporto A. Vespucci** called Peretola (✉ 10 km/6 mi northwest of Florence, ☎ 055/333498) and **Aeroporto Galileo Galilei** (✉ Pisa, 80 km/50 mi west of Florence, ☎ 050/500707). Bologna's **Aeroporto Guglielmo Marconi** (✉ Borgo Panigale, 7 km/4 mi from Bologna, ☎ 051/6479615).

BIKE TRAVEL

BIKES IN FLIGHT

Most airlines will accommodate bikes as luggage, provided they are dismantled and put into a box. Call to see if your airline sells bike boxes (about $5; bike bags are at least $100), although you can often pick them up free at bike shops. International travelers can sometimes substitute a bike for a piece of checked luggage for free; otherwise, it will cost about $100. Domestic and Canadian airlines charge a $25–$50 fee.

BOAT & FERRY TRAVEL

Ferries connect the mainland with all major islands. There is frequent daily ferry and hydrofoil service between towns and lakes in the lake district. Car ferries operate to Sicily, Sardinia, Elba, Ponza, Capri, Ischia, the Lido near Venice, and other islands.

➤ FERRY LINES: Tirrenia (☎ 06/4814779 in Rome, 010/258041 in Genoa; 081/7613688 in Naples) operates ferries to Sicily and Sardinia. SNAV (☎ 081/7612348), operates high-speed ferries between Naples and Palermo. Lauro (☎ 081/5522838) has hydrofoils and car ferries to Capri and Ischia. Adriatica

(☎ 06/4818341) connects Italy with Greece. FS ferries (☎ 0766/23273) sail from Civitavecchia to Golfo Aranci, near Olbia. **Navarma** (✉ Piazzale Premuda, Elba, ☎ 0565/225211), **Elba Ferries** (✉ Viale Regina Margherita, Elba, ☎ 0565/220956), and **Toremar** (✉ Piazzale Premuda 13, Elba, ☎ 0565/31100) serve Elba from Piombino. For the lake district contact **Navigazione Laghi** (✉ Via Ariosto 21, Milan, ☎ 02/4812086).

BUS TRAVEL

Italy's bus network—particularly in Tuscany and Umbria—is extensive, although not as attractive as those in other European countries, partly because of the low cost of train travel. Schedules are often drawn up with commuters and students in mind and may be sketchy on weekends. Regional bus companies often provide the only means of getting to out-of-the-way places. Even when this is not the case, buses can be faster and more direct than local trains, so it's a good idea to **compare bus and train schedules.** You should **buy your ticket before you board.**

Most of Tuscany's and Umbria's major cities have urban bus services, usually operating on a system involving the purchase of tickets before you board (from a machine, newsstand, or tobacco store) and stamping the ticket in the machine on the bus. These buses are inexpensive, but they can become unbearably jammed at rush hours. Remember that there are also lunchtime rush hours in the hotter periods, particularly in the south, when people go home for a siesta.

➤ BUS LINES: **SITA** (✉ Viale Cadorna 105, Florence, ☎ 055/278611) operates throughout the country. **Lazzi** (✉ Via Mercadante 2, Florence, ☎ 055/363041) operates in Tuscany and central Italy. Bus information is available at local tourist offices and travel agencies.

FROM THE U.K.

If you're traveling by bus from the United Kingdom, **bring a few French francs to spend en route.** And be sure to consider the train (☞ Train Travel, *below*), as bus fares are quite high,

especially when you take the long and tiring overnight journey into account. Eurolines runs a weekly bus service to Rome that increases to three times a week between June and September.

➤ INFORMATION: **Eurolines** (✉ 52 Grosvenor Gardens, London SW1W 0AU, ☎ 0171/730–8235 or 0171/730–3499; or contact any National Express agent).

BUSINESS HOURS

BANKS

Banks are open weekdays 8:30–1:30 and 2:45–3:45. Most churches are open from early morning until noon or 12:30, when they close for two hours or more; they open again in the afternoon, closing about 7 PM or later.

CHURCHES

Major cathedrals and basilicas, such as the Duomo in Florence, are open all day. Note that sightseeing in churches during religious rites is usually discouraged.

MUSEUMS

Museum hours vary and may change with the seasons. Many important national museums are closed one day a week, often on Monday. Always check locally. Most shops are open from 9:30 to 1 and from 3:30 or 4 to 7 or 7:30, but they may stay open until 10 according to a new national ordinance. In all but resorts and small towns, shops close on Sunday and one half-day during the week. Some tourist-oriented shops are open all day, also on Sunday, as are some department stores and supermarkets.

POST OFFICES

Post offices are open 8–2; central and main district post offices stay open until 6 or 8 PM for some operations. The main post office in major cities is open on Sunday 8:30–7. Barbers and hairdressers, with some exceptions, are closed Sunday and Monday.

CAMERAS & COMPUTERS

EQUIPMENT PRECAUTIONS

Always **keep your film, tape, or computer disks out of the sun.** Carry an extra supply of batteries, and **be prepared to turn on your camera, camcorder, or laptop** to prove to security personnel that the device is real. Always **ask for hand inspection of film,** which becomes clouded after successive exposure to airport X-ray machines, and **keep videotapes and computer disks away from metal detectors.**

TRAVEL PHOTOGRAPHY

➤ PHOTO HELP: **Kodak Information Center** (☎ 800/242–2424). *Kodak Guide to Shooting Great Travel Pictures,* available in bookstores or from Fodor's Travel Publications (☎ 800/533–6478; $16.50 plus $4 shipping).

CAR RENTAL

Rates in Florence begin at $49 a day and $167 a week for an economy car with air-conditioning, a manual transmission, and unlimited mileage. This does not include the 19% tax on car rentals. Note that Italian legislation now permits certain rental wholesalers, such as Auto Europe, to drop the VAT (☞ Taxes, *below*). Many companies impose mandatory theft insurance on all rentals; coverage costs $12–$18 a day.

➤ MAJOR AGENCIES: **Avis** (☎ 800/331–1084, 800/879–2847 in Canada, 008/225–533 in Australia). **Budget** (☎ 800/527–0700, 0800/181181 in the U.K.). **Dollar** (☎ 800/800–4000; 0990/565656 in the U.K., where it is known as Eurodollar). **Hertz** (☎ 800/654–3001, 800/263–0600 in Canada, 0345/555888 in the U.K., 03/9222–2523 in Australia, 03/358–6777 in New Zealand). **National InterRent** (☎ 800/227–3876; 0345/222525 in the U.K., where it is known as Europcar InterRent).

CUTTING COSTS

To get the best deal, **book through a travel agent who is willing to shop around.**

Be sure to **look into wholesalers,** companies that do not own fleets but rent in bulk from those that do and often offer better rates than traditional car-rental operations. Prices are best during off-peak periods. Rentals booked through wholesalers must be paid for before you leave the United States.

➤ RENTAL WHOLESALERS: **Auto Europe** (☎ 207/842–2000 or 800/223–5555, FAX 800–235–6321). **Europe by Car** (☎ 212/581–3040 or 800/223–1516, FAX 212/246–1458). **DER Travel Services** (✉ 9501 W. Devon Ave., Rosemont, IL 60018, ☎ 800/782–2424, FAX 800/282–7474 for information or 800/860–9944 for brochures). **Kemwel Holiday Autos** (☎ 914/835–5555 or 800/678–0678, FAX 914/835–5126).

INSURANCE

When driving a rented car you are generally responsible for any damage to or loss of the vehicle. Before you rent, **see what coverage you already have** under the terms of your personal auto-insurance policy and credit cards.

Collision policies that car-rental companies sell for European rentals typically do not cover stolen vehicles. Before you buy additional coverage for theft, check with your credit-card company and personal auto insurance—you may already be covered. All car-rental companies operating in Italy require that you buy theft-protection policies.

REQUIREMENTS

In Italy your own driver's license is acceptable. An International Driver's Permit is a good idea; it's available from the American or Canadian automobile association, and, in the United Kingdom, from the Automobile Association or Royal Automobile Club. These international permits are universally recognized, and having one in your wallet may save you a problem with the local authorities.

SURCHARGES

Before you pick up a car in one city and leave it in another, **ask about drop-off charges or one-way service fees,** which can be substantial. Note, too, that some rental agencies charge extra if you return the car before the time specified in your contract. To avoid a hefty refueling fee, **fill the tank just before you turn in the car,** but be aware that gas stations near the rental outlet may overcharge.

CAR TRAVEL

There is an extensive network of *autostrade* (toll highways), complemented by equally well-maintained

THE GOLD GUIDE / SMART TRAVEL TIPS

but free *superstrade* (expressways). All are clearly signposted and numbered. The ticket you are issued upon entering an autostrada must be returned when you exit and pay the toll; on some shorter autostrade, mainly connecting highways, the toll is paid upon entering. Viacard cards, on sale at many autostrada locations, make paying tolls easier and faster. A *raccordo* is a connecting expressway. *Strade statali* (state highways, denoted by *S* or *SS* numbers) may be single-lane roads, as are all secondary roads; directions and turnoffs are not always clearly marked.

AUTO CLUBS

➤ IN AUSTRALIA: **Australian Automobile Association** (☎ 06/247–7311).

➤ IN CANADA: **Canadian Automobile Association** (CAA, ☎ 613/247–0117).

➤ IN NEW ZEALAND: **New Zealand Automobile Association** (☎ 09/377–4660).

➤ IN THE U.K.: **Automobile Association** (AA, ☎ 0990/500–600), **Royal Automobile Club** (RAC, ☎ 0990/722–722 for membership, 0345/121–345 for insurance).

➤ IN THE U.S.: **American Automobile Association** (☎ 800/564–6222).

➤ BREAKDOWNS: **ACI Emergency Service** (✉ Servizio Soccorso Stradale, Via Solferino 32, 00185 Roma, ☎ 06/44595) offers 24-hour road service. Dial 116 from any phone, 24 hours a day, to reach the nearest ACI service station.

GASOLINE

Only a few gas stations are open on Sunday, and most close for a couple of hours at lunchtime and at 7 PM for the night. Self-service pumps may be few and far between outside major cities. Gas stations on autostrade are open 24 hours. Gas costs about 2,500 lire per liter.

PARKING

In most cities, parking space is at a premium; historic town centers are closed to most traffic, and peripheral parking areas are usually full. Parking in an area signposted ZONA DISCO is allowed for limited periods (from 30 minutes to 2 hours or more—the limit is posted); if you don't have the cardboard disk to show what time you parked, you can use a piece of paper. The *parcometro*, the Italian version of metered parking, has been introduced in some cities. It's advisable to **leave your car only in guarded parking areas.** Unofficial parking attendants can help you find a space but offer no guarantees. In major cities your car may be towed away if illegally parked.

ROAD CONDITIONS

Autostrade are well maintained, as are most interregional highways. The condition of provincial (county) roads varies, but road maintenace at this level is generally good in Italy. Italians drive fast, and are impatient with those who don't. Traffic is heaviest around cities in morning and late afternoon commuter hours, and on weekends.

RULES OF THE ROAD

Driving is on the right, as in the United States. Regulations are largely as in Britain and the United States, except that the police have the power to levy on-the-spot fines. In most Italian towns the use of the horn is forbidden in certain, if not all, areas; a large sign, ZONA DI SILENZIO, indicates where. Speed limits are 130 kph (80 mph) on autostrade and 110 kph (70 mph) on state and provincial roads, unless otherwise marked. Fines for driving after drinking are heavy, with the additional possibility of six months' imprisonment.

CHILDREN & TRAVEL

CHILDREN IN ITALY

Although Italians love children and are generally very tolerant and patient with them, they provide few amenities for them. In restaurants and trattorias you may find a high chair or a cushion for the child to sit on, but rarely do they offer a children's menu. Order a *mezza porzione* (half-portion) of any dish, or ask the waiter for a *porzione da bambino* (child's portion).

Discounts do exist. Always ask about a *sconto bambino* (child's discount) before purchasing tickets. Children under a certain height ride free on municipal buses and trams. Children under 18 who are EU citizens are admitted free to state-run museums and galleries, and there are similar privileges in many municipal or private museums.

Be sure to plan ahead and **involve your youngsters** as you outline your trip. When packing, include things to keep them busy en route. On sightseeing days try to schedule activities of special interest to your children. If you are renting a car don't forget to **arrange for a car seat** when you reserve.

FLYING

If your children are two or older, **ask about children's airfares.** As a general rule, infants under two not occupying a seat fly at greatly reduced fares or even for free.

In general the adult baggage allowance applies to children paying half or more of the adult fare. When booking, **ask about carry-on allowances for those traveling with infants.** In general, for babies charged 10% of the adult fare you are allowed one carry-on bag and a collapsible stroller, which may have to be checked; you may be limited to less if the flight is full.

Experts agree that it's a good idea to use safety seats aloft for children weighing less than 40 pounds. Airlines, however, can set their own policies: U.S. carriers allow FAA-approved models but usually require that you buy a ticket, even if your child would otherwise ride free, since the seats must be strapped into regular seats. Airline rules vary, so it's important to **check your airline's policy about using safety seats during takeoff and landing.** Safety seats cannot obstruct the movement of other passengers in the row, so get an appropriate seat assignment as early as possible.

When making your reservation, **request children's meals or a free-standing bassinet** if you need them; the latter are available only to those seated at the bulkhead, where there's enough legroom. Remember, however, that bulkhead seats may not have their own overhead bins, and there's no storage space in front of you—a major inconvenience.

GROUP TRAVEL

When planning to take your kids on a tour, look for companies that specialize in family travel.

➤ FAMILY-FRIENDLY TOUR OPERATORS: **Grandtravel** (⊠ 6900 Wisconsin Ave., Suite 706, Chevy Chase, MD 20815, ☎ 301/986–0790 or 800/247–7651) for people traveling with grandchildren ages 7–17. **Families Welcome!** (⊠ 92 N. Main St., Ashland, OR 97520, ☎ 541/482–6121 or 800/326–0724, FAX 541/482–0660). **Rascals in Paradise** (⊠ 650 5th St., Suite 505, San Francisco, CA 94107, ☎ 415/978–9800 or 800/872–7225, FAX 415/442–0289).

HOTELS

Most hotels allow children under a certain age to stay in their parents' room at no extra charge, but others charge them as extra adults; be sure to **ask about the cutoff age for children's discounts.**

➤ BEST CHOICES: **ITT-Sheraton Hotels** (☎ 800/221–2340). **Club Med** (⊠ 40 W. 57th St., New York, NY 10019, ☎ 800/258–2633). **Valtur** (⊠ Via Milano 42, Roma, ☎ 06/4821000, FAX 06/4706334).

CONSUMER PROTECTION

Whenever possible, **pay with a major credit card** so you can cancel payment or get reimbursed if there's a problem, provided that you can provide documentation. This is the best way to pay, whether you're buying travel arrangements before your trip or shopping at your destination.

If you're doing business with a particular company for the first time, **contact your local Better Business Bureau and the attorney general's offices** in your state and the company's home state, as well. Have any complaints been filed?

Finally, if you're buying a package or tour, always **consider travel insurance** that includes default coverage (☞ Insurance, *below*).

➤ LOCAL BBBs: **Council of Better Business Bureaus** (⊠ 4200 Wilson Blvd., Suite 800, Arlington, VA 22203, ☎ 703/276–0100, FAX 703/525–8277).

THE GOLD GUIDE / SMART TRAVEL TIPS

CUSTOMS & DUTIES

When shopping, **keep receipts** for all of your purchases. Upon reentering the country, **be ready to show customs officials what you've bought.** If you feel a duty is incorrect, appeal the assessment. If you object to the way your clearance was handled, get the inspector's badge number. In either case, first ask to see a supervisor, then write to the appropriate authorities, beginning with the port director at your point of entry.

IN ITALY

Of goods obtained anywhere outside the EU or goods purchased in a duty-free shop within an EU country, the allowances are: (1) 200 cigarettes or 100 cigarillos or 50 cigars or 250 grams of tobacco; (2) 2 liters of still table wine or 1 liter of spirits over 22% volume or 2 liters of spirits under 22% volume or 2 liters of fortified and sparkling wines; and (3) 50 milliliters of perfume and 250 milliliters of toilet water.

Of goods obtained (duty and tax paid) within another EU country, the allowances are: (1) 800 cigarettes or 400 cigarillos or 400 cigars or 1 kilogram of tobacco; (2) 90 liters of still table wine plus (3) 10 liters of spirits over 22% volume plus 20 liters of spirits under 22% volume plus 60 liters of sparkling wines plus 110 liters of beer.

IN AUSTRALIA

Australia residents who are 18 or older may bring back $A400 worth of souvenirs and gifts (including jewelry), 250 cigarettes or 250 grams of tobacco, and 1,125 ml of alcohol (including wine, beer, and spirits). Residents under 18 may bring back $A200 worth of goods.

➤ INFORMATION: **Australian Customs Service** (Regional Director, ✉ Box 8, Sydney, NSW 2001, ☎ 02/9213–2000, FAX 02/9213–4000).

IN CANADA

Canadian residents who have been out of Canada for at least 7 days may bring in C$500 worth of goods duty-free. If you've been away less than 7 days but more than 48 hours, the duty-free allowance drops to C$200; if your trip lasts 24–48 hours, the allowance is C$50. You may not pool allowances with family members. Goods claimed under the C$500 exemption may follow you by mail; those claimed under the lesser exemptions must accompany you. Alcohol and tobacco products may be included in the 7-day and 48-hour exemptions but not in the 24-hour exemption. If you meet the age requirements of the province or territory through which you reenter Canada, you may bring in, duty-free, 1.14 liters (40 imperial ounces) of wine or liquor *or* 24 12-ounce cans or bottles of beer or ale. If you are 16 or older you may bring in, duty-free, 200 cigarettes and 50 cigars.

You may send an unlimited number of gifts worth up to C$60 each duty-free to Canada. Label the package UNSOLICITED GIFT—VALUE UNDER $60. Alcohol and tobacco are excluded.

➤ INFORMATION: **Revenue Canada** (✉ 2265 St. Laurent Blvd. S, Ottawa, Ontario K1G 4K3, ☎ 613/993–0534, 800/461–9999 in Canada).

IN NEW ZEALAND

Although greeted with a "Haere Mai" ("Welcome to New Zealand"), homeward-bound residents with goods to declare must present themselves for inspection. If you're 17 or older, you may bring back $700 worth of souvenirs and gifts. Your duty-free allowance also includes 4.5 liters of wine or beer; one 1,125-ml bottle of spirits; and either 200 cigarettes, 250 grams of tobacco, 50 cigars, or a combo of all three up to 250 grams.

➤ INFORMATION: **New Zealand Customs** (✉ Custom House, ✉ 50 Anzac Ave., Box 29, Auckland, New Zealand, ☎ 09/359–6655, FAX 09/309–2978).

IN THE U.K.

If you are a U.K. resident and your journey was wholly within the European Union (EU), you won't have to pass through customs when you return to the United Kingdom. If you plan to bring back large quantities of alcohol or tobacco, check EU limits beforehand.

➤ INFORMATION: **HM Customs and Excise** (✉ Dorset House, ✉ Stamford St., London SE1 9NG, ☎ 0171/202–4227).

IN THE U.S.

U.S. residents may bring home $400 worth of foreign goods duty-free if they've been out of the country for at least 48 hours (and if they haven't used the $400 allowance or any part of it in the past 30 days).

U.S. residents 21 and older may bring back 1 liter of alcohol duty-free. In addition, regardless of your age, you are allowed 200 cigarettes and 100 non-Cuban cigars. Antiques, which the U.S. Customs Service defines as objects more than 100 years old, enter duty-free, as do original works of art done entirely by hand, including paintings, drawings, and sculptures.

You may also send packages home duty-free: up to $200 worth of goods for personal use, with a limit of one parcel per addressee per day (and no alcohol or tobacco products or perfume worth more than $5); label the package PERSONAL USE, and attach a list of its contents and their retail value. Do not label the package UNSOLICITED GIFT, or your duty-free exemption will drop to $100. Mailed items do not affect your duty-free allowance on your return.

➤ INFORMATION: **U.S. Customs Service** (Inquiries, ✉ Box 7407, Washington, DC 20044, ☎ 202/927–6724; complaints, Office of Regulations and Rulings, ✉ 1301 Constitution Ave. NW, Washington, DC 20229; registration of equipment, Resource Management, ✉ 1301 Constitution Ave. NW, Washington DC 20229, ☎ 202/927–0540).

DINING

MEALTIMES

Lunchtime lasts from 12:30 to about 2, though you won't be turned away if hunger strikes shortly after noon or close to 2:30. Dinner is served from 7:30 to 9:30 or 10, though some places stay open later.

DISABILITIES & ACCESSIBILITY

ACCESS IN ITALY

Italy has only recently begun to provide facilities such as ramps, telephones, and rest rooms for people with disabilities; such things are still the exception, not the rule. Travelers' wheelchairs must be transported free of charge, according to Italian law, but the logistics of getting a wheelchair on and off trains and buses can make this requirement irrelevant. Seats are reserved for people with disabilities on public transportation, but few buses have lifts for wheelchairs. High, narrow steps for boarding trains create additional problems. In many monuments and museums, even in some hotels and restaurants, architectural barriers make it difficult, if not impossible, for those with disabilities to gain access. In Florence, the Galleria degli Uffizi is accessible by wheelchair.

Contact the nearest Italian consulate regarding bringing a Seeing Eye dog into Italy; this requires an import license, a current certificate detailing the dog's inoculations, and a letter from your veterinarian certifying the dog's health.

➤ LOCAL RESOURCES: **The Italian Government Travel Office** (ENIT, ☞ Visitor Information, *below*) can provide a list of hotels that provide access and addresses of Italian associations for travelers with disabilities.

MAKING RESERVATIONS

When discussing accessibility with an operator or reservations agent, **ask hard questions.** Are there any stairs, inside *or* out? Are there grab bars next to the toilet *and* in the shower/tub? How wide is the doorway to the room? To the bathroom? For the most extensive facilities meeting the latest legal specifications, **opt for newer accommodations**, which are more likely to have been designed with access in mind. Older buildings or ships may have more limited facilities. Be sure to **discuss your needs before booking.**

➤ COMPLAINTS: **Disability Rights Section** (✉ U.S. Department of Justice, Civil Rights Division, ✉ Box 66738, Washington, DC 20035–

6738, ☎ 202/514–0301 or 800/514–0301, TTY 202/514–0383 or 800/514–0383, FAX 202/307–1198) for general complaints. **Aviation Consumer Protection Division** (☞ Air Travel, *above*) for airline-related problems. **Civil Rights Office** (✉ U.S. Department of Transportation, Departmental Office of Civil Rights, S-30, ✉ 400 7th St. SW, Room 10215, Washington, DC, 20590, ☎ 202/366–4648, FAX 202/366–9371) for problems with surface transportation.

TRAVEL AGENCIES & TOUR OPERATORS

As a whole, the travel industry has become more aware of the needs of travelers with disabilities. In the United States, the Americans with Disabilities Act requires that travel firms serve the needs of all travelers. Note, though, that some agencies and operators specialize in making travel arrangements for individuals and groups with disabilities.

➤ TRAVELERS WITH MOBILITY PROBLEMS: **Access Adventures** (✉ 206 Chestnut Ridge Rd., Rochester, NY 14624, ☎ 716/889–9096), run by a former physical-rehabilitation counselor. **Accessible Journeys** (✉ 35 W. Sellers Ave., Ridley Park, PA 19078, ☎ 610/521–0339 or 800/846–4537, FAX 610/521–6959), for escorted tours exclusively for travelers with mobility impairments. **CareVacations** (✉ 5019 49th Ave., Suite 102, Leduc, Alberta T9E 6T5, ☎ 403/986–6404, 800/648–1116 in Canada) has group tours and is especially helpful with cruise vacations. **Flying Wheels Travel** (✉ 143 W. Bridge St., Box 382, Owatonna, MN 55060, ☎ 507/451–5005 or 800/535–6790, FAX 507/451–1685), a travel agency specializing in customized tours and itineraries worldwide. **Hinsdale Travel Service** (✉ 201 E. Ogden Ave., Suite 100, Hinsdale, IL 60521, ☎ 630/325–1335), a travel agency that benefits from the advice of wheelchair traveler Janice Perkins.

DISCOUNTS & DEALS

Be a smart shopper and **compare all your options** before making any choice. A plane ticket bought with a promotional coupon may not be cheaper than the least expensive fare from a discount ticket agency. For high-price travel purchases, such as packages or tours, keep in mind that what you get is just as important as what you save. Just because something is cheap doesn't mean it's a bargain.

CLUBS & COUPONS

Many companies sell discounts in the form of travel clubs and coupon books, but these cost money. You must use participating advertisers to get a deal, and only after you recoup the initial membership cost or book price do you begin to save. If you plan to use the club or coupons frequently, you may save considerably. Before signing up, find out what discounts you get for free.

➤ DISCOUNT CLUBS: **Entertainment Travel Editions** (✉ 2125 Butterfield Rd., Troy, MI 48084, ☎ 800/445–4137; $20–$51, depending on destination). **Great American Traveler** (✉ Box 27965, Salt Lake City, UT 84127, ☎ 801/974–3033 or 800/548–2812; $49.95 per year). **Moment's Notice Discount Travel Club** (✉ 7301 New Utrecht Ave., Brooklyn, NY 11204, ☎ 718/234–6295; $25 per year, single or family). **Privilege Card International** (✉ 237 E. Front St., Youngstown, OH 4450˝, ☎ 330/746–5211 or 800/236–9732; $74.95 per year). **Sears's Mature Outlook** (✉ Box 9390, Des Moines, IA 50306, ☎ 800/336–6330; $19.95 per year). **Travelers Advantage** (✉ CUC Travel Service, ✉ 3033 S. Parker Rd., Suite 1000, Aurora, CO 80014, ☎ 800/548–1116 or 800/648–4037; $59.95 per year, single or family). **Worldwide Discount Travel Club** (✉ 1674 Meridian Ave., Miami Beach, FL 33139, ☎ 305/534–2082; $50 per year family, $40 single).

CREDIT-CARD BENEFITS

When you use your credit card to make travel purchases you may get free travel-accident insurance, collision-damage insurance, and medical or legal assistance, depending on the card and the bank that issued it. American Express, MasterCard, and Visa provide one or more of these services, so **get a copy of your credit card's travel-benefits policy.** If you are a member of an auto club, always **ask** hotel and car-rental reservations agents about auto-club discounts. Some clubs offer additional discounts on tours, cruises, and admission to attractions.

DISCOUNT RESERVATIONS

To save money, **look into discount-reservations services** with toll-free numbers, which use their buying power to get a better price on hotels, airline tickets, even car rentals. When booking a room, always **call the hotel's local toll-free number** (if one is available) rather than the central reservations number—you'll often get a better price. Always ask about special packages or corporate rates.

When shopping for the best deal on hotels and car rentals, **look for guaranteed exchange rates,** which protect you against a falling dollar. With your rate locked in, you won't pay more, even if the price goes up in the local currency.

➤ AIRLINE TICKETS: ☎ **800/FLY–4–LESS.**

➤ HOTEL ROOMS: **Hotels Plus** (☎ 800/235–0909). **International Marketing & Travel Concepts** (☎ 800/790–4682). **Steigenberger Reservation Service** (☎ 800/223–5652). **Travel Interlink** (☎ 800/888–5898).

PACKAGE DEALS

Packages and guided tours can save you money, but don't confuse the two. When you buy a package, your travel remains independent, just as though you had planned and booked the trip yourself. Fly/drive packages, which combine airfare and car rental, are often a good deal. If you **buy a rail/drive pass,** you'll save on train tickets and car rentals. All Eurail- and Europass holders get a discount on Eurostar fares through the Channel Tunnel.

ELECTRICITY

To use your U.S.-purchased electric-powered equipment, **bring a converter and adapter.** The electrical current in Italy is 220 volts, 50 cycles alternating current (AC); wall outlets take Continental-type plugs, with two round prongs.

If your appliances are dual-voltage, you'll need only an adapter. Don't use 110-volt outlets, marked FOR SHAVERS ONLY, for high-wattage appliances such as blow-dryers. Most laptops operate equally well on 110 and 220 volts and so require only an adapter.

EMERGENCIES

➤ EMERGENCIES: **Carabinieri** (militarized police; ☎ 112). **Fire** (☎ 115). **Italian Automobile Club** (☎ 116). **Medical emergency and ambulance** (☎ 118; not yet operational in all areas; alternatively call 113). **Police** (☎ 113).

GAY & LESBIAN TRAVEL

➤ GAY- AND LESBIAN-FRIENDLY TOUR OPERATORS: **Hanns Ebensten Travel** (✉ 513 Fleming St., Key West, FL 33040, ☎ 305/294–8174, FAX 305/292–9665), one of the oldest operators in the gay market.

➤ GAY- AND LESBIAN-FRIENDLY TRAVEL AGENCIES: **Corniche Travel** (✉ 8721 Sunset Blvd., Suite 200, West Hollywood, CA 90069, ☎ 310/854–6000 or 800/429–8747, FAX 310/659–7441). **Islanders Kennedy Travel** (✉ 183 W. 10th St., New York, NY 10014, ☎ 212/242–3222 or 800/988–1181, FAX 212/929–8530). **Now Voyager** (✉ 4406 18th St., San Francisco, CA 94114, ☎ 415/626–1169 or 800/255–6951, FAX 415/626–8626). **Yellowbrick Road** (✉ 1500 W. Balmoral Ave., Chicago, IL 60640, ☎ 773/561–1800 or 800/642–2488, FAX 773/561–4497). **Skylink Travel and Tour** (✉ 3577 Moorland Ave., Santa Rosa, CA 95407, ☎ 707/585–8355 or 800/225–5759, FAX 707/584–5637), serving lesbian travelers.

HEALTH

The Centers for Disease Control and Prevention (CDC) in Atlanta caution that most of Southern Europe is in the "intermediate" range for risk of contacting traveler's diarrhea. Part of this risk may be attributed to an increased consumption of olive oil and wine, which can have a laxative effect on stomachs used to a different diet. The CDC also advises all international travelers to swim only in chlorinated swimming pools, unless they are absolutely certain the local beaches and freshwater lakes are not contaminated.

MEDICAL PLANS

No one plans to get sick while traveling, but it happens, so **consider signing up with a medical-assistance company.** Members get doctor referrals, emergency evacuation or repatriation, 24-hour telephone hot lines for medical consultation, cash for emergencies, and other personal and legal assistance. Coverage varies by plan, so **review the benefits of each carefully.**

➤ MEDICAL-ASSISTANCE COMPANIES: **International SOS Assistance** (✉ 8 Neshaminy Interplex, Suite 207, Trevose, PA 19053, ☎ 215/245–4707 or 800/523–6586, ℻ 215/244–9617; ✉ 12 Chemin Riantbosson, 1217 Meyrin 1, Geneva, Switzerland, ☎ 4122/785–6464, ℻ 4122/785–6424; ✉ 10 Anson Rd., 14-07/08 International Plaza, Singapore, 079903, ☎ 65/226–3936, ℻ 65/226–3937).

HOLIDAYS

National holidays include January 1 (New Year's Day); January 6 (Epiphany); April 4 and 5 (Easter Sunday and Monday, 1999) and April 23 and 24 (2000); April 25 (Liberation Day); May 1 (Labor Day or May Day); August 15 (Assumption of Mary, also known as Ferragosto); November 1 (All Saints' Day); December 8 (Immaculate Conception); December 25 and 26 (Christmas Day and Boxing Day).

The feast days of patron saints are observed locally. Many businesses and shops may be closed in Florence on June 24 (St. John the Baptist). Also *see* Festivals and Seasonal Events *in* Chapter 1.

INSURANCE

Travel insurance is the best way to **protect yourself against financial loss.** The most useful plan is a comprehensive policy that includes coverage for trip cancellation and interruption, default, trip delay, and medical expenses (with a waiver for preexisting conditions).

Without insurance, you will lose all or most of your money if you cancel your trip, regardless of the reason. Default insurance covers you if your

tour operator, airline, or cruise line goes out of business. Trip-delay covers unforeseen expenses that you may incur due to bad weather or mechanical delays. It's important to compare the fine print regarding trip-delay coverage when comparing policies.

For overseas travel, one of the most important components of travel insurance is its medical coverage. Supplemental health insurance will pick up the cost of your medical bills should you get sick or injured while traveling. U.S. residents should note that Medicare generally does not cover health-care costs outside the United States, nor do many privately issued policies. Residents of the United Kingdom can buy an annual travel-insurance policy valid for most vacations taken during the year in which the coverage is purchased. If you are pregnant or have a preexisting condition, make sure you're covered. British citizens should buy extra medical coverage when traveling overseas, according to the Association of British Insurers. Australian travelers should buy travel insurance, including extra medical coverage, whenever they go abroad, according to the Insurance Council of Australia.

Always **buy travel insurance directly from the insurance company**; if you buy it from a cruise line, airline, or tour operator that goes out of business you probably will not be covered for the agency or operator's default, a major risk. Before you make any purchase, **review your existing health and home-owner's policies** to find out whether they cover expenses incurred while traveling.

➤ TRAVEL INSURERS: In the United States, **Access America** (✉ 6600 W. Broad St., Richmond, VA 23230, ☎ 804/285–3300 or 800/284–8300). **Travel Guard International** (✉ 1145 Clark St., Stevens Point, WI 54481, ☎ 715/345–0505 or 800/826–1300). In Canada, **Mutual of Omaha** (✉ Travel Division, ✉ 500 University Ave., Toronto, Ontario M5G 1V8, ☎ 416/598–4083, 800/268–8825 in Canada).

➤ INSURANCE INFORMATION: In the U.K., **Association of British Insurers**

(✉ 51 Gresham St., London EC2V 7HQ, ☎ 0171/600–3333). In Australia, the **Insurance Council of Australia** (☎ 613/9614–1077, FAX 613/9614–7924).

HE GOLD GUIDE / SMART TRAVEL TIPS

LANGUAGE

In cities, language is not a big problem. You can always find someone who speaks at least a little English, albeit with a heavy accent; remember that the Italian language is pronounced exactly as it is written (many Italians try to speak English by enunciating every syllable, with disconcerting results). You may run into a language barrier in the countryside, but a phrase book and close attention to the Italians' astonishing use of pantomime and expressive gestures will go a long way.

Try to **master a few phrases for daily use** and familiarize yourself with the terms you'll need to decipher signs and museum labels. To get the most out of museums, you'll need English-language guidebooks to exhibits; look for them in bookstores and on newsstands, as those sold at the museums are not necessarily the best.

LANGUAGES FOR TRAVELERS

A phrase book and language tape set can help get you started.

➤ PHRASE BOOKS AND LANGUAGE-TAPE SETS: *Fodor's Italian for Travelers* (☎ 800/733–3000, 800/668–4247 in Canada, FAX 212/5722–6045 international orders; audio set $16.95, $23.50 in Canada).

LODGING

Options are numerous, from hotels to camping grounds to short-term rentals in city or country.

APARTMENT & VILLA RENTALS

If you want a home base that's roomy enough for a family and comes with cooking facilities, **consider a furnished rental.** These can save you money, especially if you're traveling with a large group of people. Home-exchange directories list rentals (often second homes owned by prospective house swappers), and some services search for a house or apartment for you (even a castle if that's your fancy)

and handle the paperwork. Some se[nd] an illustrated catalog; others send photographs only of specific properties, sometimes at a charge. Up-front registration fees may apply.

➤ RENTAL AGENTS: **At Home Abroad** (✉ 405 E. 56th St., Suite 6H, New York, NY 10022, ☎ 212/421–9165, FAX 212/752–1591). **Drawbridge to Europe** (✉ 5456 Adams Rd., Talent, OR 97540, ☎ 541/512–8927 or 888/268–1148, FAX 541/512–0978). **Europa-Let/Tropical Inn-Let** (✉ 92 N. Main St., Ashland, OR 97520, ☎ 541/482–5806 or 800/462–4486, FAX 541/482–0660). **Hometours International** (✉ Box 11503, Knoxville, TN 37939, ☎ 423/690–8484 or 800/367–4668). **Interhome** (✉ 124 Little Falls Rd., Fairfield, NJ 07004, ☎ 973/882–6864 or 800/882–6864, FAX 973/808–1742). **Property Rentals International** (✉ 1008 Mansfield Crossing Rd., Richmond, VA 23236, ☎ 804/378–6054 or 800/220–3332, FAX 804/379–2073). **Rent-a-Home International** (✉ 7200 34th Ave. NW, Seattle, WA 98117, ☎ 206/789–9377 or 800/488–7368, FAX 206/789–9379). **Vacation Home Rentals Worldwide** (✉ 235 Kensington Ave., Norwood, NJ 07648, ☎ 201/767–9393 or 800/633–3284, FAX 201/767–5510). **Villas and Apartments Abroad** (✉ 420 Madison Ave., Suite 1003, New York, NY 10017, ☎ 212/759–1025 or 800/433–3020, FAX 212/755–8316). **Villas International** (✉ 605 Market St., San Francisco, CA 94105, ☎ 415/281–0910 or 800/221–2260, FAX 415/281–0919). **Hideaways International** (✉ 767 Islington St., Portsmouth, NH 03801, ☎ 603/430–4433 or 800/843–4433, FAX 603/430–4444; membership $99) is a club for travelers who arrange rentals among themselves.

➤ ITALY-ONLY AGENCIES: **Cuendet USA** (✉ 165 Chestnut St., Allendale, NJ 07041, ☎ 201/327–2333; ✉ Suzanne T. Pidduck, c/o Rentals in Italy, 1742 Calle Corva, Camarillo, CA 93010, ☎ 800/726–6702). **Vacanze in Italia** (✉ 22 Railroad St., Great Barrington, MA 01230, ☎ 413/528–6610 or 800/533–5405).

➤ IN THE U.K.: **CV Travel** (✉ 43 Cadogan St., London SW3 2PR,

England, ☎ 0171/581–0851). **Magic of Italy** (✉ 227 Shepherds Bush Rd., London W6 7AS, England, ☎ 0181/748–7575).

CAMPING

Camping is a good way to find accommodations in otherwise overcrowded resorts, and camper rental agencies operate throughout Italy; contact your travel agent for details. Make sure you **stay only on authorized campsites** (camping on private land is frowned upon), and **get an international camping** *carnet* **(permit)** from your local camping association before you leave home. The Touring Club Italiano publishes a multilingual *Guida Camping d'Italia* (Guide to the Camping in Italy), available in bookstores in Italy for about 30,000 lire, with more detailed information on sites. Camp rates for two people, with car and tent, average about 50,000 lire a day.

➤ DIRECTORY OF CAMPGROUNDS: Write to the **Federazione Italiana del Campeggio e del Caravanning** (✉ Federcampeggio, Casella Postale 23, 50041 Calenzano, Firenze, FAX 055/8825918) and request *Campeggiare in Italia;* send three international reply coupons to cover mailing. It's also available through the ENIT office in the United States and at tourist information offices in Italy (☞ Visitor Information, *below* and *in* individual chapters).

FARM HOLIDAYS & AGRITOURISM

Rural accommodations in the Agritourism category are increasingly popular with both Italians and tourists.

➤ AGENCIES: **Italy Farm Holidays** (✉ 547 Martling Ave., Tarrytown, NY 10591, ☎ 914/631–7880, FAX 914/631–8831). **Essentially Tuscany**(✉ 30 York St., Nantucket, MA 02554, ☎ FAX 508/2282514). **Agriturist** (✉ Piazza San Firenze 3, 50122 Florence, ☎ 055/295163). **Terranostra** (✉ Via dei Magazzini 2, 50122 Florence, ☎ 055/280539). **Turismo Verde** (✉ Via Verdi 5, 50127 Florence, ☎ 055/2344925).

HOME EXCHANGES

If you would like to exchange your home for someone else's, **join a home-exchange organization,** which will send you its updated listings of available exchanges for a year and will include your own listing in at least one of them. It's up to you to make specific arrangements.

➤ EXCHANGE CLUBS: **HomeLink International** (✉ Box 650, Key West, FL 33041, ☎ 305/294–7766 or 800/638–3841, FAX 305/294–1148; $83 per year).

HOSTELS

No matter what your age, you can **save on lodging costs by staying at hostels.** In some 5,000 locations in more than 70 countries around the world, Hostelling International (HI), the umbrella group for a number of national youth hostel associations, offers single-sex, dorm-style beds and, at many hostels, "couples" rooms and family accommodations. Membership in any HI national hostel association, open to travelers of all ages, allows you to stay in HI-affiliated hostels at member rates (one-year membership is about $25 for adults; hostels run about $10–$25 per night). Members also have priority if the hostel is full; they're eligible for discounts around the world, even on rail and bus travel in some countries.

➤ HOSTEL ORGANIZATIONS: **Hostelling International–American Youth Hostels** (✉ 733 15th St. NW, Suite 840, Washington, DC 20005, ☎ 202/783–6161, FAX 202/783–6171). **Hostelling International—Canada** (✉ 400-205 Catherine St., Ottawa, Ontario K2P 1C3, ☎ 613/237–7884, FAX 613/237–7868). **Youth Hostel Association of England and Wales** (✉ Trevelyan House, ✉ 8 St. Stephen's Hill, St. Albans, Hertfordshire AL1 2DY, ☎ 01727/855215 or 01727/845047, FAX 01727/844126); membership in the U.S. $25, in Canada C$26.75, in the U.K. £9.30).

HOTELS

Italian hotels are classified from five-star (deluxe) to one-star (very basic hotels and small inns). Stars are assigned according to standards set by regional boards (there are 20 in Italy), but rates are set by each hotel. During slack periods, or when a hotel is not full, it is often possible to negotiate a discounted rate. In the major cities, room rates are on a par with other European capitals: Deluxe and four-star rates can be downright extravagant. In those categories, **ask for one of the better rooms,** since less desirable rooms—and there usually are some—don't give you what you're paying for. Except in deluxe and some four-star hotels, rooms may be very small compared to U.S standards.

In all hotels there is a rate card inside the door of your room, or inside the closet door; it tells you exactly what you will pay for that particular room (rates in the same hotel may vary according to the location and type of room). On this card, breakfast and any other optionals must be listed separately. Any discrepancy between the basic room rate and that charged on your bill is cause for complaint to the manager and to the local tourist office.

Although, by law, breakfast is supposed to be optional, most hotels quote room rates including breakfast. When you book a room, specifically **ask whether the rate includes breakfast** (*colazione*). You are under no obligation to take breakfast at your hotel, but in practice most hotels expect you to do so. It is encouraging to note that many of the hotels we recommend are offering generous buffet breakfasts instead of simple, even skimpy "continental breakfasts." Remember, if the latter is the case, you can **eat for less at the nearest coffee bar.**

Hotels that we list as ($$) and ($)—moderate to inexpensively priced accommodations—may charge extra for optional air-conditioning. In older hotels the quality of the rooms may be very uneven; if you don't like the room you're given, request another. This applies to noise, too. Front rooms may be larger and have a view, but they also may have a lot of street noise. If you're a light sleeper, **request a quiet room when making reservations.** Rooms in lodgings listed in this guide have a shower and/or bath, unless noted otherwise. Remember **to specify whether you care to have a bath or shower** since not all rooms, especially lodgings outside major cities, have both.

Major cities have no official off-season as far as hotel rates go, though some hotels will reduce rates during the slack season upon request. Always **inquire about special rates.** You can save considerably on hotel rooms in Florence during their off-seasons.

➤ BEST-KNOWN CHAINS: **ITT-Sheraton/The Luxury Collection** (✉ 745 5th Ave., New York, NY 10151, ☎ 800/221–2340, 1678/835035 toll-free in Italy, ⒻⒶⓍ 212/421–5929), has more than 20 Italian properties, almost all five-star deluxe; **Jolly** (☎ 800/247–1277 in New York state, 800/221–2626 elsewhere, 800/237–0319 in Canada, 1670/17703 toll-free in Italy), with 32 four-star hotels in Italy; **Atahotels** (✉ Via Lampedusa 11/A, 20141 Milano, ☎ 02/895261, 1678/23013 toll-free in Italy, ⒻⒶⓍ 02/8465568; some bookable through E&M Associates, ☎ 212/599–8280 or 800/223–9832), with 20 mostly four- and five-star hotels; and **Starhotels** (✉ Via Belfiore 27, 50144 Firenze; ☎ 055/36921, 1678/60200 toll-free in Italy, 800/448–8355 for bookings, ⒻⒶⓍ 055/36924), with 14 mainly four-star hotels. **Space Hotels** (☎ 1678/13013 toll-free in Italy; or book through **Supranational**, ☎ 416/927–1133 or 800/843–3311) has about 50 independently owned four- and five-star (some three-star) hotels. **Italhotels** (☎ 1678/01004 toll-free in Italy) also has about 50 independently owned four- and five-star hotels.

AGIP Motels (☎ 06/4440183 reservations in Italy) is a chain of about 50, mostly four-star motels on main highways; the motels are commercial, functional digs for traveling salespeople and tourists needing forty winks, but they—and the Jolly hotels—can be the best choice in many out-of-the-way places. The Forte group has taken over some top-of-the-line AGIP properties throughout Italy. **Best Western** (☎ 800/528–1234 for reservations), an international association of independently owned hotels, has some 75 mainly three- and four-star hotels in Italy; call to request the *Europe and Middle East Atlas* that lists them.

Family Hotels (✉ Via Faenza 77, 50123 Firenze, ☎ 055/217975,

THE GOLD GUIDE / SMART TRAVEL TIPS

FAX 055/2381905; for information, not booking), which groups about 75 independently owned, family-run two- and three-star hotels (some one-star), offers good value. A spin-off of this group, the **Sun Rays Pool** (☎ 055/4620080) comprises three- and four-star hotels.

MAIL

POSTAL RATES

Airmail letters (lightweight stationery) to the United States and Canada cost 1,300 lire for the first 19 grams and an additional 600 lire for every additional unit of 20 grams. Airmail postcards cost 1,100 lire if the message is limited to a few words and a signature; otherwise, you pay the letter rate. Airmail letters to the United Kingdom cost 800 lire; postcards, 650 lire. You can buy stamps at tobacconists.

RECEIVING MAIL

Mail service is generally slow; allow up to 10 days for mail from Britain, 15 days from North America. Correspondence can be addressed to you care of the Italian post office. Letters should be addressed to your name, "c/o Ufficio Postale Centrale," followed by "Fermo Posta" on the next line, and the name of the city (preceded by its postal code) on the next. You can **collect it at the central post office** by showing your passport or photo-bearing ID and paying a small fee. American Express also has a general-delivery service. There's no charge for cardholders, holders of American Express Traveler's checks, or anyone who booked a vacation with American Express.

MONEY

COSTS

Prices in Florence, Tuscany, and Umbria are in line with those in the rest of Europe, with costs in its main cities comparable to those in other major capitals, such as Paris and London. The days when the country's high-quality attractions came with a comparatively low Mediterranean price tag are long gone. With the cost of labor and social benefits rising and an economy weighed down by the public debt, Italy is therefore not a bargain, but there is an effort to hold the line on hotel and restaurant prices that had become inordinately expensive by U.S. standards. Depending on season and occupancy, you may be able to obtain unadvertised lower rates in hotels; always inquire. If you want the luxury of four- and five-star hotels, be prepared to pay top rates.

As in most countries, prices vary from region to region and are a bit lower in the countryside than in the cities.

When you make hotel reservations, ask explicitly whether breakfast is included in the rate. By law, breakfast is optional, but some hotels pressure guests to eat breakfast on the premises—and then charge a whopping amount for it. Find out what breakfast will cost at the time you book, or at least when you check in, and if it seems high, avoid misunderstanding by clearly stating that you want a room without breakfast.

Admission to the Uffizi Gallery is 12,000 lire; a movie ticket is 12,000 lire. A daily English-language newspaper is 2,500 lire. A taxi ride (1⅓ km, or 1 mi) costs 10,000 lire.

CREDIT & DEBIT CARDS

Should you use a credit card or a debit card when traveling? Both have benefits. A credit card allows you to delay payment and gives you certain rights as a consumer (☞ Consumer Protection, *above*). A debit card, also known as a check card, deducts funds directly from your checking account and helps you stay within your budget. When you want to rent a car, though, you may still need an old-fashioned credit card. Although you can always *pay* for your car with a debit card, some agencies will not allow you to *reserve* a car with a debit card.

Otherwise, the two types of plastic are virtually the same. Both will get you cash advances at ATMs worldwide if your card is properly programmed with your personal identification number (PIN). (For use in Italy, your PIN must be four digits long.) Both offer excellent, wholesale exchange rates. And both protect you against unauthorized use if the card is lost or stolen. Your liability is limited to $50, as long as you report the card missing.

➤ ATM LOCATIONS: **Cirrus** (☎ 800/424–7787). **Plus** (☎ 800/843–7587) for locations in the United States and Canada, or visit your local bank.

CURRENCY

The unit of currency in Italy is the lira. There are bills of 500,000 (practically impossible to change outside of banks), 100,000, 50,000, 10,000, 5,000, 2,000, and 1,000 lire. Coins are 500, 200, 100 and 50 lire. At press time, the exchange rate was about 1,780 lire to the U.S. dollar, 1,210 lire to the Canadian dollar, and 2,900 lire to the pound sterling. It is possible that in 1999 the euro unit of currency will exist alongside the lire, but everyday business will still be conducted in lire.

EXCHANGING MONEY

For the most favorable rates, **change money through banks.** Although fees charged for ATM transactions may be higher abroad than at home, Cirrus and Plus exchange rates are excellent, because they are based on wholesale rates offered only by major banks. You won't do as well at exchange booths in airports or rail and bus stations, in hotels, in restaurants, or in stores, although you may find their hours more convenient. To avoid lines at airport exchange booths, **get a bit of local currency before you leave home.**

➤ EXCHANGE SERVICES: **Chase** *Currency To Go* (☎ 800/935–9935; 935–9935 in NY, NJ, and CT). **International Currency Express** (☎ 888/842–0880 on the East Coast, 888/278–6628 on the West Coast). **Thomas Cook Currency Services** (☎ 800/287–7362 for telephone orders and retail locations).

TRAVELER'S CHECKS

Do you need traveler's checks? It depends on where you're headed. If you're going to rural areas and small towns, go with cash; traveler's checks are best used in cities. Lost or stolen checks can usually be replaced within 24 hours. To ensure a speedy refund, buy your own traveler's checks—don't let someone else pay for them:

irregularities like this can cause delays. The person who bought the checks should make the call to request a refund.

PACKING

LUGGAGE

How many carry-on bags you can bring with you is up to the airline. Most allow two, but the limit is often reduced to one on certain flights. Gate agents will take excess baggage—including bags they deem oversize—from you as you board and add it to checked luggage. To avoid this situation, make sure that everything you carry aboard will fit under your seat. Also, get to the gate early, and request a seat at the back of the plane; you'll probably board first, while the overhead bins are still empty. Since big, bulky baggage attracts the attention of gate agents and flight attendants on a busy flight, make sure your carry-on is really a carry-on. Finally, a carry-on that's long and narrow is more likely to remain unnoticed than one that's wide and squarish.

If you are flying internationally, note that baggage allowances may be determined not by piece but by weight—generally 88 pounds (40 kilograms) in first class, 66 pounds (30 kilograms) in business class, and 44 pounds (20 kilograms) in economy.

Airline liability for baggage is limited to $1,250 per person on flights within the United States. On international flights it amounts to $9.07 per pound or $20 per kilogram for checked baggage (roughly $640 per 70-pound bag) and $400 per passenger for unchecked baggage. You can buy additional coverage at check-in for about $10 per $1,000 of coverage, but it excludes a rather extensive list of items, shown on your airline ticket.

Before departure, **itemize your bags' contents** and their worth, and label the bags with your name, address, and phone number. (If you use your home address, cover it so that potential thieves can't see it readily.) Inside each bag, **pack a copy of your itinerary.** At check-in, **make sure that each bag is correctly tagged** with the destination rt's three-letter code. If your bags arrive damaged or fail to arrive at all, file a written report with the airline before leaving the airport.

PACKING LIST

The weather is considerably milder in Italy than in the north and central United States or Great Britain. In summer, stick with clothing that is as light as possible, although a sweater may be necessary for cool evenings, especially in the mountains even during the hot months. Brief summer afternoon thunderstorms are common in inland cities, so an umbrella will come in handy. In winter bring a medium-weight coat and a raincoat for Rome and farther south; northern Italy calls for heavier clothes, gloves, hats, and boots. Even in milder areas, central heating may not be up to your standards, and interiors can be cold and damp; take wools or flannel rather than sheer fabrics. Bring sturdy shoes for winter, and comfortable walking shoes in any season.

Italians dress exceptionally well. They do not usually wear shorts in the city, unless longish Bermudas happen to be in fashion. Men aren't required to wear ties or jackets anywhere, except in some of the grander hotel dining rooms and top-level restaurants, but are expected to look reasonably sharp—and they do. Formal wear is the exception rather than the rule at the opera nowadays, though people in expensive seats usually do get dressed up.

Dress codes are strict for visits to churches. Women must cover bare shoulders and arms, and short skirts are not accepted. Shorts are taboo for both men and women.

For sightseeing, **pack a pair of binoculars**; they will help you get a good look at painted ceilings and domes. If you stay in budget hotels, **take your own soap**; many such hotels do not provide it or give guests only one tiny bar per room.

In your carry-on luggage **bring an extra pair of eyeglasses or contact lenses** and **enough of any medication you take** to last the entire trip. You may also want your doctor to write a spare prescription using the drug's generic name, since brand names may vary from country to country. **Never put prescription drugs or valuables in luggage to be checked.** To avoid customs delays, carry medications in their original packaging. And don't forget to copy down and carry addresses of offices that handle refunds of lost traveler's checks.

PASSPORTS & VISAS

When traveling internationally, **carry a passport even if you don't need one** (it's always the best form of I.D.), and make **two photocopies of the data page** (one for someone at home and another for you, carried separately from your passport). If you lose your passport, promptly call the nearest embassy or consulate and the local police.

ENTERING ITALY

U.S. CITIZENS

All U.S. citizens, even infants, need only a valid passport to enter Italy for stays of up to 90 days.

CANADIANS

You need only a valid passport to enter Italy for stays of up to 90 days.

U.K. CITIZENS

Citizens of the United Kingdom need only a valid passport to enter Italy for stays of up to 90 days.

AUSTRALIAN CITIZENS

Citizens of Australia need only a valid passport to enter Italy for stays of up to 90 days.

NEW ZEALAND CITIZENS

Citizens of New Zealand need only a valid passport to enter Italy for stays of up to 90 days.

PASSPORT OFFICES

The best time to apply for a passport or to renew is during the fall and winter. Before any trip, be sure to check your passport's expiration date and, if necessary, renew it as soon as possible. (Some countries won't allow you to enter on a passport that's due to expire in six months or less.)

➤ AUSTRALIAN CITIZENS: **Australian Passport Office** (☎ 13–1232).

➤ CANADIAN CITIZENS: **Passport Office** (☎ 819/994–3500 or 800/567–6868).

➤ NEW ZEALAND CITIZENS: **New Zealand Passport Office** (☎ 04/494–0700 for information on how to apply, 0800/727–776 for information on applications already submitted).

➤ U.K. CITIZENS: **London Passport Office** (☎ 0990/21010), for fees and documentation requirements and to request an emergency passport.

➤ U.S. CITIZENS: **National Passport Information Center** (☎ 900/225–5674; calls are charged at 35¢ per minute for automated service, $1.05 per minute for operator service).

SAFETY

The best way to **protect yourself against purse snatchers and pickpockets** is to wear a money belt or a pouch on a string around your neck, both concealed. If you carry a bag or camera, be absolutely sure it has straps; you should sling it across your body bandolier-style. Always be astutely aware of stealthy pickpockets, especially when in jam-packed big-city buses and subways, when making your way through train corridors, and in busy piazzas.

SENIOR-CITIZEN TRAVEL

EU citizens over 60 are entitled to free admission to state museums, as well as to many other museums—always ask at the ticket office. Older travelers may be eligible for special fares on Alitalia. When renting a car, **ask about promotional car-rental discounts,** which can be cheaper than senior-citizen rates.

To qualify for age-related discounts, **mention your senior-citizen status up front** when booking hotel reservations (not when checking out) and before you're seated in restaurants (not when paying the bill). Note that discounts may be limited to certain menus, days, or hours. When renting a car, **ask about promotional car-rental discounts,** which can be cheaper than senior-citizen rates.

➤ ADVENTURES: **Overseas Adventure Travel** (✉ Grand Circle Corporation, ✉ 625 Mt. Auburn St., Cambridge,

MA 02138, ☎ 617/876–0533 or 800/221–0814, ℻ 617/876–0455).

➤ EDUCATIONAL PROGRAMS: **Elderhostel** (✉ 75 Federal St., 3rd floor, Boston, MA 02110, ☎ 617/426–8056). **Interhostel** (✉ University of New Hampshire, ✉ 6 Garrison Ave., Durham, NH 03824, ☎ 603/862–1147 or 800/733–9753, ℻ 603/862–1113). **Folkways Institute** (✉ 14600 Southeast Aldridge Rd., Portland, OR 97236-6518, ☎ 503/658–6600 or 800/225–4666, ℻ 503/658–8672).

SHOPPING

The notice PREZZI FISSI (fixed prices) means just that; in shops displaying this sign it's a waste of time to bargain unless you're buying a sizable quantity of goods or a particularly costly object. Always bargain, however, at outdoor markets (except food markets) and when buying from street vendors. For a comprehensive introduction to the joys of shopping, Italian style, *see* Pleasures & Pastimes *in* Chapter 1. For information on VAT refunds, *see* Taxes, *below.*

STUDENT TRAVEL

Florence is a popular student destination, and in the major art cities there are plenty of facilities (information, lodging) geared to students' needs. A student's card may obtain discounts at museums, galleries, exhibitions, and entertainment venues, and on some transportation.

LOCAL RESOURCES

The Centro Turistico Studentesco (CTS; *see* Travel Agencies, *below*) is a student and youth travel agency with offices in major Italian cities; CTS helps its clients find low-cost accommodations and bargain fares for travel in Italy and elsewhere. CTS is also the Rome representative for EuroTrain International.

TRAVEL AGENCIES

To save money, **look into deals available through student-oriented travel agencies.** To qualify you'll need a bona fide student I.D. card. Members of international student groups are also eligible.

SMART TRAVEL TIPS / THE GOLD GUIDE

➤ STUDENT I.D.s & SERVICES: **Centro Turistico Studentesco** (CTS; ⊠ Via Genova 16, Roma, ☎ 06/4679271). **Council on International Educational Exchange** (⊠ CIEE, ⊠ 205 E. 42nd St., 14th floor, New York, NY 10017, ☎ 212/822–2600 or 888/268–6245, FAX 212/822–2699), for mail orders only, in the United States. **Travel Cuts** (⊠ 187 College St., Toronto, Ontario M5T 1P7, ☎ 416/979–2406 or 800/667–2887) in Canada.

➤ STUDENT TOURS: **Contiki Holidays** (⊠ 300 Plaza Alicante, Suite 900, Garden Grove, CA 92840, ☎ 714/740–0808 or 800/266–8454, FAX 714/740–2034). **AESU Travel** (⊠ 2 Hamill Rd., Suite 248, Baltimore, MD 21210-1807, ☎ 410/323–4416 or 800/638–7640, FAX 410/323–4498).

TAXES

HOTEL

The service charge and the 9% IVA, or VAT tax, are included in the rate except in five-star deluxe hotels, where the IVA (12% on luxury hotels) may be a separate item added to the bill at departure.

RESTAURANT

A service charge of about 15% is added to all restaurant bills; in some cases the menu may state that the service charge is already included in the menu prices.

VALUE-ADDED TAX (V.A.T.)

Value-added tax (IVA) is 19% on clothing, and luxury goods. On most consumer goods, it is already included in the amount shown on the price tag, whereas on services, it may not be.

To **get an IVA refund,** when you are leaving Italy take the goods and the invoice to the customs office at the airport or other point of departure and have the invoice stamped. (If you return to the United States or Canada directly from Italy, go through the procedure at Italian customs; if your return is, say, via Britain, take the Italian goods and invoice to British customs.) Under Italy's IVA-refund system, a non-EU resident can obtain a refund of tax paid after spending a total of 300,000 lire in one store (before tax—and note that price tags and prices quoted, unless otherwise

stated, include IVA). Shop with your passport and ask the store for an invoice itemizing the article(s), price(s), and the amount of tax. Once back home—and within 90 days of the date of purchase—mail the stamped invoice to the store, which will send the IVA rebate to you. A growing number of stores in Italy (and Europe) are members of the Tax-Free Shopping System, which expedites things by providing an invoice that is actually a Tax-Free Cheque in the amount of the refund. Once stamped, it can be cashed at the Tax-Free Cash refund window at major airports and border crossings, or you can also opt to have the refund credited to your credit card or bank account, or sent directly home. To save a step at the airport or border, you can send the Cheque to a Tax-Free Shopping address.

TELEPHONES

COUNTRY AND LOCAL CODES

The country code for Italy is 39. When dialing an Italian number from abroad, you no longer drop the initial 0 from the local area code. For example, a call from New York City to Rome would be dialed as 011 + 39 + 06 + local number.

To make a local call, you must now dial the prefix of the area you are in; for example, if you are in Florence and calling the Uffizi, you will have to dial 055 + Uffizi phone number. Here are area codes for major cities: Bologna, 051; Brindisi, 0831; Florence, 055; Genoa, 010; Milan, 02; Naples, 081; Palermo, 091; Perugia, 075; Pisa, 050; Rome, 06; Siena, 0577; Turin, 011; Venice, 041; Verona, 045.

DIRECTORY & OPERATOR INFORMATION

For general information in English, dial 176. To place international telephone calls via operator-assisted service, dial 170 or long-distance access numbers (☞ International Calls *below*).

INTERNATIONAL CALLS

Since hotels tend to overcharge, sometimes exorbitantly, for long-distance and international calls, it is best to make such calls from public phones, using telephone cards. At Telefoni offices, operators sell international telephone cards and will help you place your call. There are Telefoni offices, designated TELECOM, in all cities and towns, usually in major train stations and in the center business districts. You can **make collect calls from any phone by dialing 172–1011,** which will get you an English-speaking operator. Rates to the United States are lowest 'round the clock on Sunday and 10 PM–8 AM (Italian time) on weekdays.

From major Tuscan and Umbrian cities, you can place a direct call to the United States by reversing the charges or using your phone credit card number. When calling from pay telephones, insert a 200-lire coin that will be returned upon completion of your call. You automatically reach an operator in the country of destination and thereby avoid all language difficulties.

AT&T, MCI, and Sprint international access codes make calling the United States relatively convenient, but you may find the local access number blocked in many hotel rooms. First ask the hotel operator to connect you. If the hotel operator balks, ask for an international operator, or dial the international operator yourself. One way to improve your odds of getting connected to your long-distance carrier is to travel with more than one company's calling card (a hotel may block Sprint, for example, but not MCI). If all else fails, call from a pay phone in the hotel lobby.

➤ ACCESS CODES: **AT&T USADirect** (☎ 172–1011). **MCI Call USA** (☎ 172–1022). **Sprint Express** (☎ 172–1877).

PUBLIC PHONES

Pay phones accept a 200-lire coin, two 100-lire coins, or a 500-lire coin, but **consider buying a** *carta telefonica* **(prepaid calling card).** Scheda phones are common everywhere. You buy the card (values vary—5,000 lire, 10,000 lire, etc.) at Telefoni offices, post offices, and tobacconists. Tear off the corner of the card, and insert it in the slot. When you dial, its value appears in the window. After you hang up, the card is returned so you can use it until its value runs out.

TIPPING

Tipping practices vary, depending on where you are. The following guidelines apply in major cities, but Italians tip smaller amounts in smaller cities and towns. Tips may not be expected in cafés and taxis north of Rome.

In restaurants a service charge of about 15% usually appears as a separate item on your check. A few restaurants state on the menu that cover and service charge are included. Either way, it's customary to leave an additional 5%–10% tip for the waiter, depending on the service. Tip checkroom attendants 500 lire per person, rest room attendants 200 lire; in both cases tip more in expensive hotels and restaurants. Tip 100 lire for whatever you drink standing up at a coffee bar, 500 lire or more for table service in cafés. At a hotel bar tip 1,000 lire and up for a round or two of cocktails.

Railway and airport porters charge a fixed rate per bag. Tip an additional 500 lire per person, but more if the porter is very helpful. Theater ushers expect 500 lire per person, and more for very expensive seats. Give a barber 2,000–3,000 lire and a hairdresser's assistant 3,000–8,000 lire for a shampoo or cut, depending on the type of establishment.

On sightseeing tours, tip guides about 2,000 lire per person for a half-day group tour, more if they are very good. In museums and other places of interest where admission is free, a contribution is expected; give anything from 500 to 1,000 lire for one or two persons, more if the guard or caretaker has been especially helpful. Service station attendants are tipped only for special services, for example, 1,000 lire for checking your tires.

In hotels, give the *portiere* (concierge) about 15% of his bill for services, or 5,000–10,000 lire if he has been generally helpful. For two people in a double room, leave the chambermaid about 1,000 lire per day, or about 4,000–5,000 a week, in a moderately priced hotel; tip a minimum of 1,000 lire for valet or room service. Increase these amounts by one-half in an expensive hotel, and double them in a very expensive hotel. In very expensive hotels, tip doormen 1,000 lire for calling a cab and 2,000 lire for carrying bags to the check-in desk, bellhops 3,000–5,000 lire for carrying your bags to the room and 3,000–5,000 lire for room service. One-third to one-half of these amounts is acceptable in moderately priced hotels.

TOUR OPERATORS

Buying a prepackaged tour or independent vacation can make your trip to Florence, Tuscany, and Umbria less expensive and more hassle-free. Because everything is prearranged, you'll spend less time planning.

Operators that handle several hundred thousand travelers per year can use their purchasing power to give you a good price. Their high volume may also indicate financial stability. But some small companies provide more personalized service; because they tend to specialize, they may also be more knowledgeable about a given area.

BOOKING WITH AN AGENT

Travel agents are excellent resources. In fact, large operators accept bookings made only through travel agents. But it's a good idea to **collect brochures from several agencies,** because some agents' suggestions may be influenced by relationships with tour and package firms that reward them for volume sales. If you have a special interest, **find an agent with expertise in that area**; ASTA (☞ Travel Agencies, *below*) has a database of specialists worldwide.

Make sure your travel agent knows the accommodations and other services. Ask about the hotel's location, room size, beds, and whether it has a pool, room service, or programs for children, if you care about these. Has your agent been there in person or sent others you can contact?

Do some homework on your own, too: Local tourism boards can provide information about lesser-known and small-niche operators, some of which may sell only direct.

BUYER BEWARE

Each year consumers are stranded or lose their money when tour operators—even very large ones with excellent reputations—go out of business. So **check out the operator.** Find out how long the company has been in business, and ask several travel agents about its reputation. If the package or tour you are considering is priced lower than in your wildest dreams, **be skeptical.** Try to **book with a company that has a consumer-protection program.** If the operator has such a program, you'll find information about it in the company's brochure. If the operator you are considering does not offer some kind of consumer protection, then ask for references from satisfied customers.

In the U.S., members of the National Tour Association and United States Tour Operators Association are required to set aside funds to cover your payments and travel arrangements in case the company defaults. It's also a good idea to choose a company that participates in the American Society of Travel Agent's Tour Operator Program (TOP). This gives you a forum if there are any disputes between you and your tour operator; ASTA will act as mediator.

➤ TOUR-OPERATOR RECOMMENDATIONS: **American Society of Travel Agents** (☞ Travel Agencies, *below*). **National Tour Association** (✉ NTA, ✉ 546 E. Main St., Lexington, KY 40508, ☎ 606/226–4444 or 800/755–8687). **United States Tour Operators Association** (✉ USTOA, ✉ 342 Madison Ave., Suite 1522, New York, NY 10173, ☎ 212/599–6599 or 800/468–7862, ℻ 212/599–6744).

COSTS

The more your package or tour includes, the better you can predict the ultimate cost of your vacation. Make sure you know exactly what is covered, and **beware of hidden costs.** Are taxes, tips, and service charges included? Transfers and baggage handling? Entertainment and excursions? These can add up.

Prices for packages and tours are usually quoted per person, based on two sharing a room. If traveling solo, you may be required to pay the full double-occupancy rate. Some operators eliminate this surcharge if you agree to be matched with a roommate of the same sex, even if one is not found by departure time.

GROUP TOURS

Among companies that sell tours to Florence, Tuscany, and Umbria, the following have a proven reputation and offer plenty of options. The classifications used below represent different price categories, and you'll probably encounter these terms when talking to a travel agent or tour operator. The key difference is usually in accommodations, which run from budget to better, and better-yet to best.

➤ SUPER-DELUXE: **Abercrombie & Kent** (✉ 1520 Kensington Rd., Oak Brook, IL 60521-2141, ☎ 630/954–2944 or 800/323–7308, FAX 630/954–3324). **Travcoa** (✉ Box 2630, 2350 S.E. Bristol St., Newport Beach, CA 92660, ☎ 714/476–2800 or 800/992–2003, FAX 714/476–2538).

➤ DELUXE: **Central Holidays** (✉ 206 Central Ave., Jersey City, NJ 07307, ☎ 201/798–5777 or 800/935–5000). **Donna Franca Tours** (✉ 470 Commonwealth Ave., Boston, MA 02215, ☎ 617/375–9400 or 800/225–6290). **Globus** (✉ 5301 S. Federal Circle, Littleton, CO 80123-2980, ☎ 303/797–2800 or 800/221–0090, FAX 303/347–2080). **Maupintour** (✉ 1515 St. Andrews Dr., Lawrence, KS 66047, ☎ 785/843–1211 or 800/255–4266, FAX 785/843–8351). **Perillo Tours** (✉ 577 Chestnut Ridge Rd., Woodcliff Lake, NJ 07675, ☎ 201/307–1234 or 800/431–1515). **Tauck Tours** (✉ Box 5027, 276 Post Rd. W, Westport, CT 06881-5027, ☎ 203/226–6911 or 800/468–2825, FAX 203/221–6866).

➤ FIRST-CLASS: **Annemarie Victory Organization** (✉ 136 E. 64th St., New York, NY 10021, ☎ 212/486–0353, FAX 212/751–3149). **Brendan Tours** (✉ 15137 Califa St., Van Nuys, CA 91411, ☎ 818/785–9696 or 800/421–8446, FAX 818/902–9876). **Caravan Tours** (✉ 401 N. Michigan Ave., Chicago, IL 60611, ☎ 312/321–9800 or 800/227–2826, FAX 312/321–9845). **Collette Tours** (✉ 162 Middle St., Pawtucket, RI 02860, ☎ 401/728–3805 or 800/832–4656, FAX 401/728–1380). **Gadabout Tours** (✉ 700 E. Tahquitz Canyon Way, Palm Springs, CA 92262-6767, ☎ 760/325–5556 or 800/952–5068, FAX 760/325–5127). **Insight International Tours** (✉ 745 Atlantic Ave., #720, Boston, MA 02111, ☎ 617/482–2000 or 800/582–8380, FAX 617/482–2884 or 800/622–5015). **Trafalgar Tours** (✉ 11 E. 26th St., New York, NY 10010, ☎ 212/689–8977 or 800/854–0103, FAX 800/457–6644).

➤ BUDGET: **Cosmos** (☞ Globus, *above*). **Trafalgar** (☞ *above*).

PACKAGES

Like group tours, independent vacation packages are available from major tour operators and airlines. The companies listed below offer vacation packages in a broad price range.

➤ AIR/HOTEL: **DER Tours** (✉ 9501 W. Devon St., Rosemont, IL 60018, ☎ 800/937–1235, FAX 847/692–4141 or 800/282–7474, 800/860–9944 for brochures). **4th Dimension Tours** (✉ 7101 S.W. 99th Ave., #105, Miami, FL 33173, ☎ 305/279–0014 or 800/644–0438, FAX 305/273–9777). **TWA Getaway Vacations** (☎ 800/438–2929). **US Airways Vacations** (☎ 800/455–0123).

➤ FROM THE U.K.: **British Airways Holidays** (✉ Astral Towers, Betts Way, London Rd., Crawley, West Sussex RH10 2XA, ☎ 01293/722–727, FAX 01293/722–624). **Carefree Italy** (✉ Allied Dunbar House, East Park, Crawley, West Sussex RH10 6AJ, ☎ 01293/552277) offers accommodations in apartments, castles, and farmhouses. **Italian Escapades** (✉ 227 Shepherds Bush Rd., London W6 7AS, ☎ 0181/748–2661). **Page and Moy Holidays** (✉ 136–140 London Rd., Leicester, LE2 1EN, ☎ 0116/250–7676).

THEME TRIPS

Travel Contacts (✉ Box 173, Camberley, GU15 1YE, England, ☎ 01276/677217, FAX 01276/63477) represents more than 150 tour operators in Europe.

➤ ART & ARCHITECTURE: **Amelia Tours International** (✉ 28 Old Country Rd., Hicksville, NY 11801, ☎ 516/433–0696 or 800/742–4591, FAX 516/822–6220). **Endless Beginnings Tours** (✉ 9285 Dowdy Dr., San Diego, CA 92126, ☎ 619/566–4166 or 800/822–7855, FAX 619/544–9655).

➤ BALLOONING: **Buddy Bombard European Balloon Adventures** (✉ 333 Pershing Way, West Palm Beach, FL 33401, ☎ 561/837–6610 or 800/862–8537, FAX 561/837–6623).

➤ BICYCLING: **Backroads** (✉ 801 Cedar St., Berkeley, CA 94710-1800, ☎ 510/527–1555 or 800/462–2848, FAX 510/527–1444). **Bike Riders** (✉ Box 130254, Boston, MA 02113, ☎ 617/723–2354 or 800/473–7040, FAX 617/723–2355). **Butterfield & Robinson** (✉ 70 Bond St., Toronto, Ontario, Canada M5B 1X3, ☎ 416/864–1354 or 800/678–1147, FAX 416/864–0541). **Ciclismo Classico** (✉ 13 Marathon St., Arlington, MA 02174, ☎ 781/646–3377 or 800/866–7314, FAX 781/641–1512). **Classic Adventures** (✉ Box 153, Hamlin, NY 14464-0153, ☎ 716/964–8488 or 800/777–8090, FAX 716/964–7297). **Euro-Bike Tours** (✉ Box 990, De Kalb, IL 60115, ☎ 800/321–6060, FAX 815/758–8851). **Himalayan Travel** (✉ 110 Prospect St., Stamford, CT 06901, ☎ 203/359–3711 or 800/225–2380, FAX 203/359–3669). **The International Kitchen** (☞ *below*). **Progressive Travels** (✉ 224 W. Galer Ave., Ste. C, Seattle, WA 98119, ☎ 206/285–1987 or 800/245–2229, FAX 206/285–1988). **Rocky Mountain Worldwide Cycle Tours** (✉ 333 Baker St., Nelson, BC, Canada V1L 4H6, ☎ 250/354–1241 or 800/661–2453, FAX 250/354–2058). **Uniquely Europe** (✉ 2819 1st Ave., Ste. 280, Seattle, WA 98121-1113, ☎ 206/441–8682 or 800/426–3615, FAX 206/441–8862). **Vermont Bicycle Touring** (✉ Box 711, Bristol, VT, 05443-0711, ☎ 800/245–3868 or 802/453–4811, FAX 802/453–4806).

➤ FOOD & WINE: **Amelia Tours** (☞ *Art and Architecture, above*). **Annemarie Victory Organization** (☞ *Group Tours, above*). **Cuisine International** (✉ Box 25228, Dallas, TX 75225, ☎ 214/373–1161 or FAX 214/373–1162). **Donna Franca Tours** (☞ *Group Tours, above*). **The International Kitchen** (✉ 1209 N. Astor, #11-N, Chicago, IL 60610, ☎ 847/295–5363 or 800/945–8606, FAX 847/295–0945).

➤ HOMES & GARDENS: **Coopersmith's England** (✉ Box 900, Inverness, CA 94937, ☎ 415/669–1914, FAX 415/669–1942). **Endless Beginnings Tours** (☞ *Art and Architecture, above*).

➤ HORSEBACK RIDING: **Cross Country International Equestrian Vacations** (✉ Box 1170, Millbrook, NY 12545, ☎ 800/828–8768, FAX 914/677–6077). **Equitour Worldwide Riding Holidays** (✉ Box 807, Dubois, WY 82513, ☎ 307/455–3363 or 800/545–0019, FAX 307/455–2354).

➤ LEARNING: **Earthwatch** (✉ Box 9104, 680 Mount Auburn St., Watertown, MA 02272, ☎ 617/926–8200 or 800/776–0188, FAX 617/926–8532) organizes research expeditions. **IST Cultural Tours** (✉ 225 W. 34th St., New York, NY 10122-0913, ☎ 212/563–1202 or 800/833–2111, FAX 212/594–6953). **Smithsonian Study Tours and Seminars** (✉ 1100 Jefferson Dr. SW, Room 3045, MRC 702, Washington, DC 20560, ☎ 202/357–4700, FAX 202/633–9250).

➤ SPAS: **Great Spas of the World** (✉ 55 John St., New York, NY 10038, ☎ 212/267–5500 or 800/772–8463, FAX 212/571–0510). **Spa-Finders** (✉ 91 5th Ave., #301, New York, NY 10003-3039, ☎ 212/924–6800 or 800/255–7727). **Spa Trek Travel** (✉ 475 Park Ave. S., New York, NY 10016, ☎ 212/779–3480 or 800/272–3480, FAX 212/779–3471).

➤ VILLA RENTALS: **Eurovillas** (✉ 1398 55th St., Emeryville, CA 94608, ☎ FAX 707/648–2066). **Rentals in Italy** (✉ 1742 Calle Corva, Camarillo, CA 93010-8428, ☎ 805/987–5278 or 800/726–6702, FAX 805/482–7976). (Also ☞ *Lodging, above*).

➤ WALKING/HIKING: **Abercrombie & Kent** (☞ *Group Tours, above*). **Above the Clouds Trekking** (✉ Box 398, Worcester, MA 01602-0398, ☎ 508/799–4499 or 800/233–4499, FAX 508/797–4779). **Adventure Center**

(✉ 1311 63rd St., #200, Emeryville, CA 94608, ☎ 510/654–1879 or 800/227–8747, FAX 510/654–4200). **Backroads** (☞ Bicycling, *above*). **Butterfield & Robinson** (☞ Bicycling, *above*). **Ciclismo Classico** (☞ Bicycling, *above*). **Country Walkers** (✉ Box 180, Waterbury, VT 05676-0180, ☎ 802/244–1387 or 800/464–9255, FAX 802/244–5661). **The International Kitchen** (☞ *above*). **Mountain Travel-Sobek** (✉ 6420 Fairmount Ave., El Cerrito, CA 94530, ☎ 510/527–8100 or 888/687–6235, FAX 510/525–7710). **Progressive Travels** (☞ Bicycling, *above*). **Uniquely Europe** (☞ Bicycling, *above*). **Walking the World** (✉ Box 1186, Fort Collins, CO 80522, ☎ 970/498–0500 or 800/340–9255, FAX 970/498–9100) specializes in tours for ages 50 and older. **Wilderness Travel** (✉ 1102 Ninth St., Berkeley, CA 94710, ☎ 510/558–2488 or 800/368–2794).

TRAIN TRAVEL

All Italian trains have first and second classes. On local trains the higher first-class fare gets you little more than a clean doily on the headrest of your seat, but on long-distance trains you get wider seats and more legroom and better ventilation and lighting. At peak travel times, first-class train travel is worth the difference. Remember to **always make seat reservations in advance,** for either class.

The fastest trains on the Ferrovie dello Stato (FS), the Italian State Railways, are the Eurostar trains, operating on several main lines, including Rome–Milan, via Florence and Bologna; seat reservations and supplement are included in the fare. Some of these (the ETR 460 trains) have little aisle and luggage space (though there is a space near the door where you can put large bags). To avoid having to squeeze through narrow aisles, board only at your car (look for the number on the reservation ticket). Car numbers are displayed on their exterior. Next-fastest trains are the Intercity (IC) trains, for which you pay a supplement and for which seat reservations may be required and **are always advisable.** *Interregionale* trains usually make more stops and are a little slower. *Regionale* and *locale* trains are the slowest; many serve commuters.

To avoid long lines at station windows, **buy tickets and make seat reservations up to two months in advance** at travel agencies displaying the FS emblem. Agencies cannot make same-day seat reservations, but can sell tickets for the same day. If you have to reserve at the last minute, reservation offices at the station accept reservations up to three hours before departure. You may be able to get a seat assignment just before boarding the train; look for the conductor on the platform. Trains can be very crowded on weekends and during holiday and vacation seasons; reserve seats in advance or, if the train originates where you get on, get to the station early to find a seat. A card just outside the compartment or over the seat indicates whether it has been reserved. Carry compact bags for easy overhead storage.

All **tickets must be date-stamped in the small yellow or red machines near the tracks before you board.** Once stamped, your ticket is valid for six hours if your destination is within 200 km, for 24 hours for destinations beyond that. You can get on and off at will at stops in between for the duration of the ticket's validity. If you don't stamp your ticket in the machine, you must actively seek out a conductor to validate the ticket on the train, paying 10,000 lire extra for the service. If you merely wait in your seat for him to collect your ticket, you must pay a 30,000 lire fine in addition. You also pay a hefty penalty if you purchase your ticket on board the train. You can buy train tickets for destinations within a 100-km (62-mi) range at tobacconists and at ticket machines in stations.

Note that in some Italian cities (including Milan, Turin, Genoa, Naples, and Rome) there are two or more main-line stations, although one is usually the principal terminal or through-station. Be sure of the name of the station at which your train will arrive, or from which it will depart.

There is refreshment service on all long-distance trains, with mobile carts and a cafeteria or dining car. Tap water on trains is not drinkable.

➤ FROM THE U.K.: **British Rail** (☎ 0171/834–2345). **French Railways** (☎ 0891/515–477); calls charged at 49p a minute peak rate, 39p all other times.

DISCOUNT PASSES

To save money, **look into rail passes.** But be aware that if you don't plan to cover many miles, you may come out ahead by buying individual tickets.

If Italy is your only destination in Europe, **consider purchasing an Italian Railpass,** which allows unlimited travel on the entire Italian Rail network. Prices begin at $132 for four days of travel in second class within a one-month period and $194 in first class. Passes that are good for longer periods of time are also available, as are Flexipasses, which allow a limited amount of train travel within a certain period.

Once in Italy, **inquire about the Carta Verde if you're under 26** (40,000 lire for one year), which entitles the holder to a 20% discount on all first- and second-class tickets. Those under 26 should also inquire about discount travel fares under the Billet International Jeune (BIJ) scheme. The special one-trip tickets are sold by EuroTrain International at its offices in various European cities and by travel agents, mainline rail stations, and youth travel specialists.

You can **purchase the Carta d'Argento if you're over 60** (40,000 lire for one year), good for a 20% discount on all first- and second-class tickets, except for travel June 26–August 14 and December 18–28.

Italy is one of 17 countries in which you can **use EurailPasses,** which provide unlimited first-class rail travel, in all of the participating countries, for the duration of the pass. If you plan to rack up the miles, get a standard pass. These are available for 15 days ($538), 21 days ($698), one month ($864), two months ($1,224), and three months ($1,512). If your plans call for only

limited train travel, **look into a EuroPass,** which costs less money than a EurailPass. Unlike EurailPasses, however, you get a limited number of travel days, in a limited number of countries, during a specified time period. For example, a two month pass ($326) allows five days of rail travel (additional days $42 each) and is good only in France, Germany, Italy, Spain, and Switzerland; rail travel to Austria, Hungary, Portugal, Greece, Holland, Luxembourg, and Belgium can be added to the pass for additional fees.

In addition to standard EurailPasses, **ask about special rail-pass plans.** Among these are the Eurail Youthpass (for those under age 26), the Eurail Saverpass (which gives a discount for two or more people traveling together), a Eurail Flexipass (which allows a certain number of travel days within a set period), the Euraildrive Pass and the Europass Drive (which combines travel by train and rental car).

Whichever pass you choose, remember that you must **purchase your EurailPass or EuroPass before you leave** for Europe.

Many travelers assume that rail passes guarantee them seats on the trains they wish to ride. Not so. You need to **book seats ahead even if you are using a rail pass;** seat reservations are required on some European trains, particularly high-speed trains; and are a good idea on trains that may be crowded—particularly in summer on popular routes. You will also need a reservation if you purchase sleeping accommodations.

➤ DISCOUNT PASSES: Eurail- and EuroPasses are available through travel agents and **Rail Europe** (✉ 226-230 Westchester Ave., White Plains, NY 10604, ☎ 914/682–5172 or 800/438–7245; ✉ 2087 Dundas E., Suite 105, Mississauga, Ontario L4X 1M2, ☎ 416/602–4195), **DER Tours** (✉ Box 1606, Des Plaines, IL 60017, ☎ 800/782–2424, FAX 800/282–7474), or **CIT Tours Corp.** (✉ 342 Madison Ave., Suite 207, New York, NY 10173, ☎ 212/697–2100, 800/248–8687, 800/248–7245 in western U.S.). Italian rail passes can be purchased through DER Tours or CIT Tours as well.

➤ UNIQUE GUIDEBOOK: *Italy by Train* by Tim Jepson (Fodor's Travel Publications, ☎ 800/533–6478 or from bookstores); $16.

TRANSPORTATION

Driving is the best mode of transportation in the region, if not essential. Buses (☞ Bus Travel, *above*), somewhat less comfortable than trains and slightly less expensive, usually offer more frequent service in Tuscany and Umbria. Trains, usually secondary lines, connect the major cities and villages in the region, but do not reach many far-flung areas. Ferries and hydrofoils provide service to Elba, Capraia, and Giglio islands.

Tuscany and Umbria have an intricate network of autostrade routes, superstradas, and local roads, making renting a car (☞ Car Rental *and* Car Travel, *above*) a better but expensive alternative to public transportation. A car can be a good investment for carefree countryside rambles, offering time to explore more remote towns. Having a car in major cities, however, often leads to parking and traffic headaches, plus additional expense in the form of garage and parking fees.

Italy's cities are served by an extensive public railway system, with fast trains offering a speedy and relatively inexpensive alternative. Reliable private train lines radiate to smaller towns. Buses, if somewhat less comfortable than trains and slightly more expensive, are better relied upon in some areas like Tuscany, but infrequent in others.

TRAVEL AGENCIES

A good travel agent puts your needs first. Look for an agency that has been in business at least five years, emphasizes customer service, and has someone on staff who specializes in your destination. In addition, **make sure the agency belongs to a professional trade organization,** such as ASTA in the United States. If your travel agency is also acting as your tour operator, *see* Buyer Beware in Tour Operators, *above*).

➤ LOCAL AGENT REFERRALS: **American Society of Travel Agents** (ASTA, ☎ 800/965–2782 24-hr hot line, FAX 703/684–8319). **Association of Canadian Travel Agents** (✉ Suite 201, 1729 Bank St., Ottawa, Ontario K1V 7Z5, ☎ 613/521–0474, FAX 613/521–0805). **Association of British Travel Agents** (✉ 55–57 Newman St., London W1P 4AH, ☎ 0171/637–2444, FAX 0171/637–0713). **Australian Federation of Travel Agents** (☎ 02/9264–3299). **Travel Agents' Association of New Zealand** (☎ 04/499–0104).

TRAVEL GEAR

Travel catalogs specialize in useful items, such as compact alarm clocks and travel irons, that can **save space when packing.** They also offer dual-voltage appliances, currency converters, and foreign-language phrase books.

➤ CATALOGS: **Magellan's** (☎ 800/962–4943, FAX 805/568–5406). **Orvis Travel** (☎ 800/541–3541, FAX 540/343–7053). **TravelSmith** (☎ 800/950–1600, FAX 800/950–1656).

VISITOR INFORMATION

➤ AT HOME: **Italian Government Tourist Board** (ENIT; ✉ 630 5th Ave., New York, NY 10111, ☎ 212/245–4822, FAX 212/586–9249; ✉ 401 N. Michigan Ave., Chicago, IL 60611, ☎ 312/644–0990, FAX 312/644–3019; ✉ 12400 Wilshire Blvd., Suite 550, Los Angeles, CA 90025, ☎ 310/820–0098, FAX 310/820–6357; ✉ 1 Pl. Ville Marie, Ste 1914, Montréal, Québec H3B 3M9, ☎ 514/866–7667, FAX 514/392–1429; ✉ 1 Princes St., London W1R 8AY, ☎ 0171/408–1254, FAX 0171/493–6695).

➤ TOURIST OFFICES ABROAD: **Florence** (✉ Via Cavour 1/r, next to Palazzo Medici–Riccardi, ☎ 055/290832).

U.S. GOVERNMENT

Government agencies can be an excellent source of inexpensive travel information. When planning your trip, **find out what government materials are available.**

➤ ADVISORIES: **U.S. Department of State** (✉ Overseas Citizens Services Office, ✉ Room 4811 N.S., Wash-

20520; ☎ 202/647–
202/647–3000 for inter-
ine; ☎ 301/946–4400 for
ulletin board); enclose a
sed, stamped, business-size
envelope.

➤ PAMPHLETS: **Consumer Information Center** (⊠ Consumer Information Catalogue, Pueblo, CO 81009, ☎ 719/948–3334 or 888/878–3256) for a free catalog that includes travel titles.

WEB SITES

Do check out the World Wide Web when you're planning. You'll find everything from up-to-date weather forecasts to virtual tours of famous cities. Fodor's Web site, www.fodors.com, is a great place to start your on-line travels.

➤ SUGGESTED WEB SITES: For more information about all of Italy, visit the Italian Government Tourist Board's site at www.italiantourism.com, In Italy Online at www.initaly.com, and Welcome to Italy at www.wel.it. For Florence-specific information, check out Firenze.net at www.firenze.net and Florence*OnLine* at www.fol.it.

WHEN TO GO

The main tourist season runs from April to mid-October. For serious sightseers the best months are from fall to early spring. The so-called low season may be cooler and inevitably

rainier, but it has its rewards: less time waiting on lines and closer-up, unhurried views of what you want to see.

Tourists crowd the major art cities at Easter, when Italians flock to resorts and to the country. From March through May, busloads of eager schoolchildren on excursions take cities of artistic and historical interest by storm.

CLIMATE

Weatherwise, the best months for sightseeing are April, May, June, September, and October—generally pleasant and not too hot. The hottest months are July and August, when brief afternoon thunderstorms are common in inland areas. Winters are relatively mild in most places on the main tourist circuit but always include some rainy spells.

If you can avoid it, don't travel at all in Italy in August, when much of the population is on the move, especially around Ferragosto, the August 15 national holiday, when cities are deserted and many restaurants and shops are closed. (Of course, with residents away on vacation, this makes crowds less of a bother for tourists.) Except for a few year-round resorts, coastal resorts usually close up tight from October or November to April; they're at their best in June and September, when everything is open but uncrowded.

FLORENCE

Jan.	48F	9C	May	73F	23C	Sept.	79F	26C
	36	2		54	12		59	15
Feb.	52F	11C	June	81F	27C	Oct.	68F	20C
	37	3		59	15		52	11
Mar.	57F	14C	July	86F	30C	Nov.	57F	14C
	41	5		64	18		45	7
Apr.	66F	19C	Aug.	86F	30C	Dec.	52F	11C
	46	8		63	17		39	10

➤ FORECASTS: **Weather Channel Connection** (☎ 900/932–8437), 95¢ per minute from a Touch-Tone phone.

1 Destination: Florence, Tuscany, and Umbria

INTRODUCTION

JUST AS TUSCANY AND UMBRIA straddle the boot, so their contribution to the Italian jigsaw is massive and inescapable. Their influence pervades Italian culture and percolates far beyond, to the extent that their impact has been felt throughout European and even world history. Tuscany—and to a lesser extent Umbria—saw the birth of humanism, that classically leaning, secular-tending current that effloresced in the Renaissance and to which the West owes its cultural complexion. In the graphic arts, architecture, astronomy, sculpture, engineering, art history, poetry, political theory, biography . . . in every field of human endeavor the people of these regions have loomed large. The Italian language itself is Tuscan, due largely to Dante's use of his local dialect to compose his *Divine Comedy*. When Italy became a modern state in 1865, Florence was the natural choice for the national capital until Rome's entry six years later.

It is hard to think of any other area that has seen such a dense concentration of human achievement as Tuscany and Umbria, but it is equally difficult to find anywhere so riven by conflict and factions. The strange thing is how neatly the periods of maximum creativity and bellicosity coincided. Was the restless, innovative impulse a consequence of the social turmoil, or the principal cause of it? It is surely no accident that Tuscany and Umbria in general and Florence in particular contain the most quarrelsome elements ever thrown together, as a cursory flip through some of the names in the local annals can testify: the Florentine Niccolò Machiavelli, who became a very synonym for the Devil (Old Nick); Savonarola, whose energetic career pitched church and state into headlong confrontation, igniting the famous "Bonfire of Vanities" in Florence's main square, site of the Dominican friar's own incineration not long afterwards; the town of Pistoia, from which the word "pistol" is derived; Perugia, populated, according to the historian Sigismondo, by "the most warlike people in Italy, who always preferred Mars to the Muse" . . . the very street-names of Florence and Siena recall the clash of medieval factions. Outside the towns, there is hardly a hill, stream, or mountain pass whose name does not evoke some siege, battle, or act of treachery. The historic rivalry of Guelph and Ghibelline never reached such intense acrimony as in these seemingly tranquil hills, and nowhere was allegiance worn so lightly, with communes and families swapping sides whenever their rivals changed theirs.

The sense of opposition is alive in Tuscany and Umbria today just as strongly as it ever was. You can witness it on every two-toned marble church front. Blacks and whites imperial, feudal and commercial, Renaissance and Gothic—the antagonism is embedded in art history, revived in every discussion of the background of every great work. It is a fixed feature of the local scene: the Sienese are still suspicious of the Florentines, the Florentines disdainful of the Sienese, while Siena itself seems to live in a permanent state of warfare within its own city walls, as any spectator of the Palio and the months of preparation that precede it can testify. Outsiders contribute to the debate: for Mary McCarthy, Florence was manly, Siena feminine, and tourists take sides whenever they lay down their reasons for preferring Florence to Siena or vice versa, as if there had to be a dualistic appreciation of the two.

Walking through the city streets of present-day Florence, you can't fail to be struck by the contrast between the austere and unwelcoming external appearance of the palaces and the sumptuous comforts within, or by the 1990s elegance and modernity of the Florentines in the midst of the thoroughly medieval churches and piazzas. Florence is a modern industrial city, and the Florentines themselves perennial modernists, their eyes fixed firmly in front. This helps to explain both their past inventiveness and the ambivalent attitude they hold toward that same past, composed of roughly equal parts of ennui and fierce pride. To its inhabitants, that the city of Florence stands on a par with Athens and Rome is self-evident: To them tourism, which feeds on the past, is reactionary, decadent, and often intrusive, making a burden of the historical heritage. It is tolerated as a business, in a city that has a high regard for business . . . but it is only one of many. In Italy, Florentines are reckoned the most impenetrable, cautious, and circumspect of Italians, a reputation they have held since the days of the Medicis. Nevertheless, Italians have coined a word—*fiorentinità*—to refer to the good taste and fine workmanship that are flaunted here, in a city renowned for its leather goods, handbags, shoes, jewelry, and a host of famous brandnames. Pucci, Gucci, Ferragamo, Cellerini are just four of the high-profile craft-turned-fashion designers that exude *fiorentinità*. Neither are the region's cuisine and fine wines to be taken lightly. Talk to any Florentines about these present-day aspects of their civilization, and they will perk up and debate enthusiastically; mention their past glories and they will stifle a yawn.

Other Tuscan cities possess the same compelling mix of elements: What Tuscany's older centers share is an immaculate medieval setting, modern life taking place within the shell of the past; what divides them is a complex mental set. Needless to say, all of them were rivals at one time or another, and each prevailed in distinct spheres. Pisa, for example, was one of Italy's four great maritime republics, its architectural style visible wherever its ships touched port. Once the most powerful force in the Tyrrhenian, it lost its hegemony on the sea to its trading rival, Genoa, and, land, to Florence. Pisa owed its prestige to a university that bequeathed a scholarly, scientific, and legal tradition to the town, and to its location on the River Arno, though this position much later was responsible for its being one of the most devastated cities in World War II. Skillful rebuilding has ensured a relatively harmonious appearance, however, and the city would still hold plenty of interest if the Torre Pendente (Leaning Tower) had never been built.

Livorno, on the other hand, the main Tuscan port of today, is the Pisa that never was. By Tuscan standards it is a recent affair, developed as a sea outlet for Florence after Pisa's port had silted up. Livorno reveals a highly un-Tuscan cosmopolitan character, a result of 16th-century growth that brought immigra-tion. Livorno's most famou[s] sculptor Amedeo Modigliani, [for exam]ple, was brought up speaking French, Italian, English, and Hebrew, though in other ways this hard-drinking Bohemian did not typify the soberly respectable citizens for whom Livorno is best known. Also heavily bombed in the war, the port was not restored as tastefully as Pisa, though it can at least boast a vigorous culinary tradition, with its range of fresh seafood.

SOUTH FROM LIVORNO stretches a riviera of varying degrees of summer saturation, including numerous select spots where sun- and sea-bathing can be enjoyed in relative peace. The island of Elba—scene of Napoléon's nine-month incarceration—is today more likely to be somewhere to escape to rather than from, and together with the islands of Giglio and Capraia offers everything from absurd overdevelopment to true isolation.

Lucca, the principal enemy of Pisa during the Middle Ages, has been called "the most enchanting walled town in the world." The city's formidable girdle of walls has resisted the intrusions of modern life better than any other Tuscan center and contains within a wealth of palaces and churches wildly out of proportion to the size of what is, after all, a small provincial town. Much of Lucca's present-day success is based on, of all things, the manufacture of lingerie.

A much weightier substance—gold—forms, together with antique furniture, the basis of the wealth of the less imposing town of Arezzo. Such worldly items again form a counterpoint to the fact that this town has produced more than its fair share of pioneers in literature (Petrarch, Pietro Aretino), art (Vasari), and music (Guido d'Arezzo, also called Guido Monaco, inventor of notation and the musical scale).

Arezzo shares a university with Siena, another Tuscan town preserved in the aspic of its medieval past. It is said that there are three subjects you should avoid if you're in a hurry while in Siena: wild pigs (a prized quarry for hunters), the Palio (an object of fanatical zeal), and the battle of Montanerti (Siena's moment of military glory—a perennial obsession). To the rest of Italy, Siena is best known for its banks and its mystics—a characteristically incompatible duo—though foreign visitors are more enchanted by the city's artworks, its easy pace of life, and the pleasing hue of its rose-colored buildings.

Prato and Pistoia, a short roll up the autostrada from Florence, have traditionally fallen within the sphere of that city's influence. Prato combines some choice examples of Renaissance art and architecture with a strong industrial identity, mainly based on its wool exports; Pistoia, on the other hand, was renowned for its ironwork, and its citizens for their murderous propensities.

A CROSS THE REGIONAL boundary in Umbria, the hilltop town of Perugia is dominated by the cold gothic stone of its major monuments, its secretive alleys and steps, yet its animating spirit is among the most progressive and trend-setting in Italy. Within its medieval walls the town hosts one of Europe's prime jazz festivals, a modern tradition that has taken its lead from the international Festa dei Due Mondi (Festival of Two Worlds) at nearby Spoleto. As in Tuscany, modernity lives alongside medievalism in Umbria, a case not so much of collision as coexistence. In the same spirit, the imposing monuments of its towns were built by a new wealthy mercantile class in the teeth of almost uninterrupted warfare throughout the Middle Ages. Spoleto, Gubbio, and Orvieto owed their influence not so much to their continual brawling as to their interchange of goods and ideas. A university was founded in Perugia as early as 1308, and it was the small Umbrian town of Foligno that published the first edition of Dante's *Divine Comedy*. The belligerence of the age paralleled an intense spiritual activity, championed by such towering religious figures as St. Francis, St. Clare, St. Benedict, and the locally venerated St. Rita (as well as the more worldly St. Valentine)— a legacy nowhere so apparent as in the town of Assisi.

Although many of the urban centers of Tuscany and Umbria have cleanly defined boundaries beyond which the countryside abruptly begins, the towns harmonize with the surrounding landscape more closely than anywhere else in Italy. Even if devoid of museums or souvenir shops, the hinterland holds as much of the region's quintessential character as the cities of Tuscany and Umbria, and such unsung treasures as Todi and Bevagna are as revealing as anything seen in the galleries. This is your chance to immerse yourself in the region's less tangible pleasures, to rest your eyes on the gentle ochre stone of villages artfully situated above vine-strung, neatly terraced slopes. From the wine-producing hills of Chianti to the Carrara mountains where Michelangelo quarried to the soft contours of the Vale di Spoleto, the tidy cypress-speared landscape displays a weird inertia like some illustration from a fable. It has a geometric precision that underlines the strict rural economy practiced by the Tuscan and Umbrian peasants, for whom every tree has its purpose. The Tuscans in particular have long been considered the most skilled and intelligent of Italian farmers, having created for themselves a region that is largely self-sufficient, producing a little of everything, and excelling in certain areas, not least in wine-production, for which the Tuscans have nurtured one of the most dynamic wine regions of Italy.

Like the great examples of urban architecture, the country in Tuscany and Umbria presents, for the most part, an ordered, rational, controlled appearance. It is the crust of civilization concealing the greatest paradox of all in this heartland of reason and classical elegance. For buried underneath lies a much older, earthier civilization of which most visitors to the region are oblivious. In every respect the ancient Etruscan civilization that flourished here was opposed to the values of the Renaissance, its vital, animistic spirit murky, dark, and mysterious to us, mainly known from subterranean tombs and wall-paintings. Almost erased from the face of the earth by the Romans, the Etruscan culture—its centers scattered throughout Tuscany and Umbria (Perugia, Orvieto, Chiusi, Roselle, Vetulonia, Volterra, Cortona, Arezzo, Fiesole were the main ones)— was central to the history of Tuscany and Umbria. Like the Hermes Trimegistus incongruously placed on the marble pavement of Siena's cathedral, the Etruscans are a mischievous element amid the harmony of Renaissance Tuscany and Umbria. Their precise influence is unclear, but it may well turn out to have been the contentious and destructive spirit ever-present in the golden age of these regions, harassing, hindering, entangling. Alternatively, it may have been the restless worm of invention, the defiant individuality that brought about the triumph of art in the face of adversity—which is, after all, the greatest achievement of Tuscany and Umbria.

— Robert Andrews

Born and educated in England, writer/journalist Robert Andrews inherited his interest in Italy from his Italian mother. He contributes to *Harpers & Queen, Time Out,* and other magazines as well as to travel books.

NEW AND NOTEWORTHY

Both Tuscany and Umbria are gearing up for the **Jubilee** celebration in Rome. Art restoration projects are furiously being completed with an eye toward 2000. This is especially apparent in **Assisi** and environs, which are struggling to dig out from the rubble left in the wake of a series of earthquakes in the fall of 1997. At least one good thing has resulted from the quakes: A sparkling fresco of the *Crucifixion,* thought to be by Perugino, was found hiding under several layers of paint in the Porziuncola of the basilica of Santa Maria degli Angeli in Assisi. Dating from around 1486, it's a joy to behold for its swoonish Virgin and a Magdalen draped in warm oranges and greens.

For museum goers, the most welcome news in light of the Jubilee has been the **extension of opening hours** of a number of major museums throughout Italy, which are now open roughly from 9 AM to 10 PM on weekdays (except for one day closed) and from 9 to 8 or so on Sunday. It is expected that the hours will alleviate overcrowding and long waits for entrance at the major galleries. In Florence, the list includes the Galleria degli Uffizi, Galleria dell'Accademia, and the Galleria Palatina in Palazzo Pitti. You can also get advance tickets to the Uffizi through the Consorzio ITA (⊠ Viale Gramsca 9a, 50121, ☎ 055/2347941).

The **telephone dialing system** in Italy has changed. Even for local calls, you must dial the regional area code: for example, if dialing within Florence you still have to dial 055 + the local number. The system of calling Italy from outside the country has also changed; you no longer drop the first 0 in the regional area code. For example, to call Rome, you dial 39 + 06 + the local number. No area code is required for emergency numbers such as 112 (carabinieri) or 118 (ambulance or emergency) dialed within Italy.

The Old Sacristy in San Lorenzo in **Florence** is no longer under wraps: You can now see the small, perfectly proportioned 1420s building designed by Filippo Brunelleschi for the Medici. It's a model of Renaissance rationality with strict attention to spatial relations and a heavy reliance on numbers and numerology. On another artful note, most of the scaffolding is gone from another Renaissance gem, Piero della Francesca's *Legend of the True Cross* in the church of San Francesco in **Arezzo.** It's a brilliant display of 15th-century Renaissance perspective and a feast for the eyes.

Several **small airlines** have elbowed in on the former Alitalia monopoly of air routes in Italy and Europe. Among them are Virgin, Debonair, and Air Europe. They offer competitive rates and often use airports that are closer to the city centers than the big hub airports.

WHAT'S WHERE

Like a Santa Claus stocking, the boot of Italy overflows with unsurpassable sights—from top to toe. Here is a sampling of the infinite variety of the Florence, Tuscany, and Umbria's many regions and attractions.

Florence

Florence, the "Athens of Italy" and the key to the Renaissance, hugs the banks of the Arno River where it lies folded among the emerald cypress-studded hills of north-central Tuscany. Elegant and somewhat aloof, as if set apart by its past greatness, this historic center of European civilization still shares with Rome the honor of first place among Italian cities for the magnitude of its artistic works, among them Botticelli's goddess and Michelangelo's powerful *David*. Down every street and *vicolo* (alley) and in every piazza you'll make new discoveries of Romanesque, Gothic, or Renaissance architecture; sheltered within these churches, cloisters, and towers are masterful paintings and sculptures of the Quattrocento and Cinquecento periods. Equally as splendid are the magnificent chapels and palaces of the Medici—whose patronage rocketed Florence to the forefront of the Renaissance—which stand unabashed amid the city's vibrant modern pulse.

North of Florence

North and west of Florence are hills and mountains, snow-capped peaks, thermal waters, and miles of Mediterranean coast. The Apuan Alps split this area nearly in half, with the Lunigiana and the Garfagnana on either side: east of the Alps you're in Tuscany's Rockies; west of them the land flattens out to meet the Tyrrhenian Sea. Michelangelo, not to mention men 1,500 years his senior, quarried marble in Carrara. The Ligurian coast, with the Cinque Terre and Forte dei Marmi, dazzles with its panoramic vistas.

Cities West of Florence

Nestled in valleys and fed along the Arno, the cities west of Florence were coveted by Florence: they provided access to the sea (Pisa) and were rich industrial centers (Prato). San Miniato al Monte, crowned high on a hill, commands views of two valleys. Though the landscape is not the most majestic of Tuscany, the area is rich with superb Renaissance art and gurgling thermal waters, such as in Montecatini Terme.

Chianti

The vineyard-quilted lands spreading south from Florence to Siena—Greve, Radda, Castellina—make up the heart of Chianti. The magical landscape is dotted with ilex and cypress, castles and wineries, and sleepy hill towns. The market town Greve, just 20 minutes south of Florence, is the gateway to sublime Chianti wine and splendid views. Montepulciano and Montalcino, south of Siena, produce some of Italy's most esteemed wines.

Siena and the Hill Towns

The time traveler will be entranced by medieval Siena, "the Pompeii of the Middle Ages," as it was called by the philosopher Taine. Radiating from the Gothic bastion are ocher and emerald lands teeming with olive groves, vineyards, and rolling hills nurtured by the Elsa and the Arbia. Perched dramatically above a fertile valley, San Gimignano—with its Manhattanlike skyline of medieval towers—may jettison you into a Who-turned-back-the-clock? sensation of Mark Twain's Connecticut Yankee when he arrived in King Arthur's court. With a glass of Vernaccia di San Gimignano in hand, you'll feel like lingering long. But the old Etruscan hill town of Volterra, with sweeping views of two valleys, is not to be overlooked.

Arezzo, Cortona, and Southern Tuscany

Heading south from Florence towards Rome to the heart of southern Tuscany, you'll find Arezzo, with its treasures by Piero della Francesca. Compact, perfect Pienza, a fusion of Renaissance and Gothic styles planned by Pope Pius II, overlooks a golden valley. In mystical Cortona, with sweeping views of Lago Trasimeno, you can take pleasure in the scattering of churches and medieval art, but street scenes revealing an old-fashioned way of life are just as essential. Mountainous Elba is rimmed with seductive beaches; Giglio, its sister island to the south, is tinier and rockier.

Perugia and Northern Umbria

Nestled east of Florence and stretching to the Adriatic, Perugia and Northern Umbria—including the eastern Marches region—boast dramatically rolling, checkerboarded hills in hues of green and gold, ablaze with sunflowers and poppies with the sun's nod. The area encompasses the valley cradling the Tiber, exceptionally lush and rich. Undiscovered splendor awaits in the cities: Perugia, a magnet for visitors since the Middle Ages, has a magnificent piazza; Gubbio, to the northeast, is a tiny jewel built against a steep hill; and the beauty of the Renaissance court comes alive in Urbino.

Assisi, Spoleto, and Southern Umbria

There's magic in the air around here in this noble area just east of the Tiber. Assisi, birthplace of St. Francis, is surrounded by wheat fields and olive groves, and the tufa plateau of Orvieto—with its own magnificent Duomo—gives the hallowed town a warm, reddish glow. Hilltop Deruta has been making ceramics for more than 600 years, and Middle-Aged Todi seems nearly celestial behind its three sets of walls.

PLEASURES AND PASTIMES

The Art of Enjoying Art

Travel veterans will tell you that the endless series of masterpieces in Italy's churches, palaces, and museums can cause first-time visitors—eyes glazed over from a heavy downpour of images, dates, and names—to lean, Pisa-like, on their companions for support. After a surfeit of Botticellis and Bronzinos and the 14th Raphael, even the miracle of the High Renaissance may begin to pall. The secret, of course, is to act like a turtle—not a hare—and take your sweet time. Instead of trotting after briskly efficient tour guides, allow the splendors of the age to unfold—slowly. Get out and explore the actual settings—medieval chapels, Rococo palaces, and Romanesque town squares—for which these marvelous examples of Italy's art and sculpture were conceived centuries ago and where many of them may still be seen in situ.

Museums are only the most obvious places to view art; there are always the trompe l'oeil renderings of Assumptions that float across Baroque church ceilings and piazza scenes that might be Renaissance paintings brought to life. Instead of studying a Gothic statue in Florence's Bargello, spend an hour in the medieval cloisters of the nearby convent of San Marco; by all means, take in Michelangelo's *David* and *Slaves* in Florence's Accademia, but then meander down the 15th-century street, a short bus ride away, where he was born. You'll find that after three days trotting through museums, a walk through a quiet neighborhood will act as a much-needed restorative of perspective.

Of course, there may be many art treasures that will not quicken your pulse, but one morning you may see a Caravaggio so perfect, so beautiful, that your knees will buckle.

Il Dolce Far Niente

The idea of vacation was probably invented by some hardworking Roman emperor and, ever since, the Italians have been fine-tuning what they call *il dolce far niente*—the sweet art of idleness. Today, even relaxing can feel like a chore, but thanks to Italy's opulent villas, picture-perfect coastal resorts, and dreamy hill towns, you can idle here more successfully than anywhere else. But it takes more than trading in a silk tie for a T-shirt; you have to adjust to the deeper, subtler rhythms of leisure, Italian style. Hours spent over a Campari in a sun-splashed café; days spent soaking up the sun on the Amalfi Coast; an afternoon spent painting a watercolor on the shores of Lake Como: You may be pleasantly surprised to find that such pursuits prove more beneficial than forced marches through the obligatory sights. The luxury is often in the lingering.

Dining

In Italy, cookery is civilization. In the days of the Roman legions, pundits used to say, *"Ubi Roma ibi allium"* (Where there are Romans, there is garlic). Ever since the days of the Caesars—when emperors quickly learned the wisdom of *"Stomaco pieno, anima consolata"* (Full stomach, satisfied soul)—Italian chefs have taken one of life's sensory pleasures and made it into an art, and today you can feast on an incredible array of culinary delights. Of course, Italian food has come a long way since the days when Horace, the great poet of ancient Rome, feasted on lamprey boiled in five-year-old wine, the liver of a goose fattened on figs, and apples picked by the light of the waning moon. But you can still enter restaurants in Bologna, enjoy a dish of tortellini, and be told, *"Anche Dante le ha mangiate cósi"* (Dante also ate them this way). In fact, the newest trend in Italian cooking is to serve up the old—the simple, rustic, time-honored forms of cucina *simpatica, rustica,* and *trattoria*—with a nouvelle flair.

Dining is a marvelous part of the total Italian experience, a chance to enjoy authentic specialties and ingredients. You have a choice of eating places, ranging from a *ristorante* (restaurant) to a trattoria, *tavola calda*, or *rosticceria*. The line separating ristoranti from trattori have blurred of late, but a trattoria is usually a family-run place, simpler in decor, menu, and service than a ristorante, and slightly less expensive. Some rustic-looking spots call themselves *osterie* but are really restaurants. (A true osteria is a basic, down-to-earth tavern.) At a tavola calda or rosticceria, prepared food is sold to be consumed on the spot or taken out; you choose what you want at the counter, and pay at the cashier. An *enoteca* is a wine bar where you can order wine by the glass or bottle; most have tables, and many serve savory, light meals and nibbles. A *caffè* (coffee bar) serves those beloved coffee drinks replicated abroad, plus sandwiches, pastries, and other snacks. Tell the cashier what you want, pay for it, and then take the stub to the counter, where you restate your order, and then drink and eat standing at the counter. Remember that table service is extra, almost double; don't sit at a table unless you want to be served.

Lunch is served in Florence from 12:30 to 3:30, dinner from 7:30 to 10:30, or later in some restaurants. Service begins an hour earlier in smaller towns. Almost all eating places close one day a week and for vacations in summer and/or winter. *Buon appetito!*

Shopping

"Made in Italy" has become synonymous with style, quality, and craftsmanship whether it refers to high fashion or Maserati automobiles. The best buys are leather goods of all kinds—from gloves to bags to jackets—silk goods, knitwear, gold jewelry, ceramics, and local handicrafts. The most important thing to keep in mind when shopping in Italy is that every region has its specialties: Florence is known for leather, straw goods, gold jewelry, antiques, and paper products; Assisi produces wonderful embroidery; and Deruta and Gubbio have for centuries been centers for ceramics. Unless your purchases are too bulky, avoid having them shipped home for fear of getting lost in the mail (or never sent!); if the shop appears to be reliable about shipping, get a written statement of what will be sent, when, and how.

Thermal Baths

Thanks to its location in the Mediterranean region—one of the world's most active volcano belts—Italy is rich in thermo-mineral springs. Consequently, the Italians have developed a special attitude about what we call spas since the ancient Romans advanced the idea of *"mens sana in corpore sano"* (a sound mind in a healthy body). Perhaps old-fashioned today, taking the waters remains a unique part of Italian culture; it is state-supported and medically supervised. Never mind Greco-Roman worship of the body in templelike baths, choices now range from antiaging cures to American-style aerobic workouts to fangotherapy (medicinal mud therapy). Today, more and more travelers are taking vacations from their vacations by visiting one of Italy's sybaritic spas.

But don't say spa (in Italian, s.p.a. denotes a business corporation). Forget the Roman origins: The term in Italy is *terme* (baths). A peek into a typical Italian health resort can present an image worthy of Dante: a host of monkishly clad and mud-caked figures moving through mists of steam; these are health- and beauty-conscious aficionados enjoying a dizzying range of curative techniques. At these centers, drinking and bathing cures are based on naturally produced thermal mineral waters, with mornings devoted to sipping and strolling as well as occasional forays into espresso bars. Then come hot mud packs, muscle massage, anticellulite treatments, and sinus-targeted steam inhalations.

Cura means "treatment," not miracle(s). After the obligatory evaluation by a staff doctor, a regimen is designed which allows plenty of time for sightseeing, jogging, and post-lunch shopping. If staying at a terme in places like Abano and Montecatini, you can add outings to nearby Etruscan ruins, country inns, and wineries.

Health Italian-style comes in a variety of health, beauty, and antistress packages. Many of the new offerings at terme are based on old methods. Among them: therapeutic skin-care treatments using natural ingredients—flowers, fruits, muds, herbs, honey—in sophisticated salons devoted to *"benessere e bellezza"* (health and beauty); acupuncture, reflexology, shiatsu, facials, and colonic irrigations; longevity cures; and for *la buona figura* (healthy body), *dietetico* meals—based on light but delicious regional cuisine.

Vineyards surround hillside terme where Tuscan food and wine can restore your spirits just in case the waters don't. Diversions range from golf to horse races, but hiking the unspoiled countryside—dotted with castles and Roman ruins—is the best way to discover the region's riches. For more info on spas, *see* Close-Up Terme: Wrath of the Gods *in* Chapter 7.

—by Bernard Burt

FODOR'S CHOICE

No two people agree on what makes a perfect vacation, but it's fun and helpful to know what others think. Here's a compendium drawn from the must-see lists of hundreds of Italian tourists. For detailed information about these memories-in-the-making, refer to the appropriate chapters in this book.

Dining Gems

⭐ **Ristorante Arnolfo, Colle di Val d'Elsa.** Foodies should not miss Arnolfo, arguably one of Tuscany's finest restaurants. Sublime dishes on the two featured fixed-price menus daringly ride the line between innovation and tradition, almost always with spectacular results. *$$$–$$$$*

⭐ **Cibrèo, Florence.** In one of Florence's best restaurants, chef Fabrio Picci reinterprets Tuscan classics, served in Tuscan surroundings gone upscale. It's off the beaten path, but its location next to a marketplace promises the freshest of ingredients—and imagination. *$$$*

⭐ **Da Delfina, Artimino (Prato).** This haven of Tuscan cooking nestled amid vineyards and olive trees started as a refuge for hungry area hunters. Now Delfina has four comfortably rustic farmhouse dining rooms where she oversees cooking centered around pure ingredients, seasonal vegetables, and savory meats accented with herbs. *$$$*

⭐ **Farfarello, Marina di Massa.** This 25-seat trattoria at Massa's port is always crowded with diners hungry for the exceptional fresh seafood dishes and savory pastas. Desserts are fresh interpretations of Italy's classics. *$$*

⭐ **Osteria dei Cavalieri, Pisa.** This charming white-walled *osteria* in Piazza dei Cavalieri, serving excellent seafood, meat, and vegetarian dishes at reasonable prices, is reason enough to explore Pisa. *$$*

Lodging Gems

⭐ **Certosa di Maggiano, Siena.** A former 14th-century monastery replete with a working chapel and bucolic garden has been converted into this exquisite country hotel 1½ km (1 mi) from Siena. Rooms are a study in understated luxury and comfort, trimmed with fine woods, leathers, and traditional prints. *$$$$*

⭐ **Locanda dell'Amorosa, Sinalunga.** The "inn" is actually a stunning four-star hotel in a 14th-century stone-and-brick hamlet, approached by a lane lined with stately cypress, replete with a little stone church. The rooms are antiques repositories and the bathrooms seem like little sitting rooms. *$$$$*

⭐ **Loggiato dei Serviti, Florence.** This hotel in a 16th-century monastery across from the Ospedale degli Innocenti might as well have been designed by Brunelleschi. Vaulted ceilings, tasteful antiques, canopy beds, and rich Florentine fabrics adorn a handsomely spare Renaissance building. *$$–$$$*

⭐ **San Luca, Spoleto.** A brand new hotel built to old-world standards, the San Luca prides itself on attention to details: rooms are spacious, bathrooms elegantly appointed, and an ample breakfast buffet with homemade cakes is served in a pretty room facing the central courtyard. Prices are surprisingly modest. *$$–$$$*

Quintessential Tuscany and Umbria

⭐ **Piazza del Campo, Siena.** Even if you miss the Palio, Siena's shell-shaped central piazza is a must-see. Take a coffee on the Campo while admiring the austere Palazzo Pubblico, then climb the Torre del Mangia for unparalleled views of Siena's red roofs and surrounding countryside.

⭐ **San Gimignano.** In this classic Tuscan town, stand on the steps of the Collegiata church at sunset as the swallows swoop in and out of the famous medieval towers, twittering softly as they coast on the air.

⭐ **Truffles, Umbria.** After a long walk through the narrow, winding streets of an Umbrian town—the air rich with the smell of hearth fires and simmering pots—there is nothing like sitting down to a plate of homemade pasta dressed with the prized truffles that are found in the area.

Special Memories

★ **Piazza del Duomo, Spoleto.** Descending the stairs toward Spoleto's medieval cathedral, you see the the broad piazza, flanked by low medieval buildings, fan out as it spills down toward the pale stone sanctuary, studded with rose-color windows and mosaics set against the verdant green backdrop of Umbria's hills.

★ **Ponte delle Torri, Spoleto.** Spanning the gorge from Spoleto to Monteluco, the 14th-century bridge built by architect Gattapone is an enchanting sight. Make a point of strolling out to its central lookout point and across to the paths along Monteluco, and then return at night to see it majestically lit from below.

★ **San Gimignano.** A guided walk in the countryside just outside town provides a precious opportunity to explore Tuscan scenery so appreciated from windows and the town ramparts. When you have had your fill, return to the town of San Gimignano to taste the wines and see the towers for which the town is famous.

Where Art Comes First

★ **Cappelle Medicee, San Lorenzo, Florence.** This grandiose complex is a Michelangelan tour de force: The earthy marble slabs in the Cappella dei Principi resonate in architectural equilibrium; the allegorical sculptural figures in the Sagrestia Nuova have such an impact, his contemporaries invented a word for the phenomenon—*terribilità* (dreadfulness).

★ **Cupola, Duomo, Florence.** Filippo Brunelleschi's dome presides over the neo-Gothic cathedral—and Florence—with powerful dignity and grace. Employing new building methods, an ancient Roman–herringbone bricklaying pattern, and equipment of his own design, the artist created an engineering breakthrough. When a Florentine is "homesick," they're afflicted with *nostalgia del cupolone* (homesickness for the dome).

★ **Duomo, Orvieto.** Few cathedrals can claim masterpieces inside and out, but in Orvieto you'll find Italy's most perfect Gothic facade matched by the phenomenal intensity and variety of Luca Signorelli's frescoes—among the best in Umbria—in the Cappella di San Brizio.

★ **Palazzo Ducale, Urbino, The Marches.** If the Renaissance was, in ideal form, a celebration of the nobility of man and his works, of the light and purity of the soul, then in no other palace in Italy are these tenets better illustrated.

★ **Museo Etrusco Guarnacci, Volterra.** Tuscany was home to more than just the Renaissance; it was once the land of the Etruscans, the ingenious forerunners to the ancient Romans. Dozens of burial sites yielded the hundreds of artifacts on display in Volterra's museum which helped unlock the mysteries of these ancient people.

★ **San Francesco, Arezzo.** A portion of Piero della Francesca's frescoes depicting *The Legend of the True Cross,* executed on three walls of the choir of this 14th-century church, were called "the most perfect morning light in all Renaissance painting" by Sir Kenneth Clark.

FESTIVALS AND SEASONAL EVE

Contact the **Italian Government Travel Office** (☞ Visitor Information *in* The Gold Guide) for exact dates and further information.

JAN. 5–6➤ **Epiphany Celebrations.** Roman Catholic Epiphany celebrations are held throughout Italy.

FEB. 4–16 (1999)➤ During **Carnevale in Viareggio,** masked pageants, fireworks, a flower show, and parades are among the festivities on the Tuscan Riviera. **Carnevale in San Gimignano** is smaller, with locals, dressed up in colorful costumes, marching through the streets. The biggest fete is, of course, held in Venice.

SPRING

APRIL 4 (1999)➤ The Easter Sunday **Scoppio del Carro,** or "Explosion of the Cart," in Florence, is the eruption of a cartful of fireworks in the Piazza del Duomo, set off by a mechanical dove released from the altar during High Mass.

LATE APR.–JUNE➤ The **Maggio Musicale Fiorentina** (Florence May Music Festival) is a series of internationally acclaimed concerts and recitals.

MID-MAY➤ During the **Festa dei Ceri** (Race of the Candles), the procession of bearers, in local costume, carrying towering wooden pillars, leads to the top of Mt. Ingino in Gubbio.

LATE MAY➤ The **Palio della Balestra** (Palio of the Archers) is a medieval crossbow contest in Gubbio.

SUMMER

EARLY AND MID-JUNE➤ The **Battle of the Bridge** in Pisa is a medieval parade and contest. The **Luminaria** feast day on June 16 honors St. Ranieri, the patron saint of the Pisa. Palaces along the Arno glow with white lights and fireworks.

JUNE 24➤ **Calcio in Costume,** soccer games in 16th-century costume representing Florence's six neighborhoods, are held in Florence on the feast day of St. John the Baptist, commemorating a match played in 1530.

LATE JUNE–EARLY JULY➤ The **Festa dei Due Mondi** (Festival of Two Worlds), in Spoleto, is a famous performing arts festival.

JULY➤ **Pistoia Blues** draws international blues artists who perform in the city's main square. **La Giostra**

dell'Orso (Bear Joust), July 25, celebrates St. James, patron saint of Pistoia. The July **Jazz Festival of Umbria** draws jazz performers and aficionados alike to Perugia.

LATE JULY–EARLY AUGUST➤ Lucca's **Puccini Festival** in late July–early August celebrates the city's native son. **Estate Musicale Lucchese** runs throughout the summer in Lucca.

JUNE–AUGUST➤ **Estate Fiesolana** is a festival of theater, music, dance, and film that takes place in the churches and the archaeological area of Fiesole.

JULY 2 AND AUGUST 16➤ The **Palio** horse race, in Siena, is a colorful bareback horse race with participants competing for the *palio* (banner).

LATE AUG.–EARLY SEPT.➤ The **Siena Music Week** features opera, concerts, and chamber music.

AUTUMN

EARLY SEPT.➤ The **Giostra del Saracino** (Joust of the Saracen) is a tilting contest with knights in 13th-century armor in Arezzo.

MID-SEPT.➤ The **Giostra della Quintana** is a 17th-century-style joust and historical procession in Foligno.

OCT. 4➤ The **Festa di San Francesco** (Feast of St. Francis) is celebrated in Assisi, his birthplace.

Florence

Birthplace of the Renaissance, Florence has been a mecca for travelers since the 19th century, when English ladies flocked here to stay in charming pensiones and paint watercolors. They were captivated by a wistful Botticelli smile, impressed by the graceful dignity of Donatello's bronze David, *and moved by Michelangelo's provocative* Slaves *twisting restlessly in their marble prisons.*

Updated by
Nancy Hart

FLORENCE IS ONE OF THE PREEMINENT TREASURES of Europe, and it is a time-honored mecca for sightseers from all over the world. But as a city, Florence (Firenze in Italian) can be surprisingly forbidding—at first glance. Its architecture is predominantly Early Renaissance and retains many of the implacable, fortresslike features of pre-Renaissance palazzi, whose facades were mostly meant to keep intruders out rather than to invite sightseers in. With the exception of a very few buildings, the classical dignity of the High Renaissance and the exuberant invention of the Baroque are not to be found here. The typical Florentine exterior gives nothing away, as if obsessively guarding secret treasures within.

The treasures, of course, are very real. And far from being a secret, they are famous the world over. The city is a veritable museum of unique and incomparable proportions. A single historical fact explains the phenomenon: Florence gave birth to the Renaissance. In the early 15th century the study of antiquity—of the glory that was Greece and the grandeur that was Rome—became a Florentine passion, and with it came a new respect for learning and a new creativity in art and architecture. In Florence, that remarkable creativity is everywhere in evidence.

Though there had been a town here since Roman times, it wasn't until the 11th and 12th centuries that Florence started to make its mark. At this time Florentine cloth began to do particularly well in foreign markets, the various trades organized themselves in powerful guilds (or *arti*), and the Florentines took over as the most important bankers in Europe, thanks to their florin-based currency. They were perpetually at loggerheads with other Tuscan towns, such as Pisa and Siena, and this is why Florence has such a defensive air, and why its cathedral—the town's symbol—is so huge: It had to be bigger and more splendid than anyone else's. They kept expanding, despite periodic devastating plagues, and equally destructive civil strife. (One of the victims of the internal rift was the great poet Dante, author of the *Divine Comedy,* who happened to be on the losing side; he died in exile, cursing his native town.)

Meanwhile the banking families became more and more powerful, and in the early 15th century one of them, the Medicis, began to outstrip all others. The most famous of them, Lorenzo de' Medici (1449–1492), was not only an astute politician, he was also a highly educated man and a great patron of the arts. "Il Magnifico" gathered around him, in the late 15th century, a court of poets, artists, philosophers, architects, and musicians, and organized all kinds of cultural events, festivals, and tournaments. It was Florence's golden period of creativity, when art made great leaps toward a new naturalism through the study of perspective and anatomy, when architects forged a new style based on the techniques used by the ancient Romans. The Renaissance man was born, a man who, like Leonardo da Vinci, could design a canal, paint a fresco, or solve a mathematical problem with equal ease.

Things changed with Lorenzo's death in 1492. First, his successor handed over most of Florence's key territories to the invading French king, Charles VIII, and then the city was sacked by the French army. A "republic" was set up, and one of its most vocal citizens was a charismatic, hellfire-preaching Dominican monk, Girolamo Savonarola (1452–1498), who activated a moral cleanup operation to which the Florentines took with fanatical enthusiasm. He himself was accused of heresy and executed (his corpse was burned on a pyre in Piazza della

Signoria). After a decade or so of internal unrest, the republic fell and the Medicis were recalled to power. But even with the Medicis back, Florence never regained its former prestige. By the 1530s all the major artistic talent had left the city—Michelangelo, for one, had settled in Rome. The now ineffectual Medicis, calling themselves grand dukes, remained nominally in power until the line died out in 1737, and thereafter Florence passed from the Austrians to the French and back again, until the mid-19th-century unification of Italy, when for seven years it was the capital of Italy under King Vittorio Emanuele II.

Florence was "discovered" in the 19th century by the first art historians. It became a mecca for travelers, particularly the Romantics, including Keats and Shelley, who were inspired by the grandeur of its classicism and the elegance of its child, the Renaissance. Today, millions of modern visitors follow in their footsteps. As the sun sets over the Arno and, as Mark Twain described it, "overwhelms Florence with tides of color that make all the sharp lines dim and faint and turn the solid city to a city of dreams," it's hard not to fall under the city's magic spell.

Pleasures and Pastimes

Dining
Florentines are justifiably proud of their robust food, claiming that it became the basis for French cuisine when Catherine de' Medici took a battery of Florentine chefs with her when she reluctantly relocated to become Queen of France in the 16th century. You can sample such specialties as creamy *fagioli al fiasco* (slow-cooked beans) and *ribollita* (a thick soup of white beans, bread, cabbage, and onions) in bustling trattorias where you share long wooden tables set with paper place mats. The casual, convivial atmosphere in these places puts you in the Florentine mode. Like the Florentines, take a break at an *enoteca* (wineshop and/or wine bar) during the day and discover some little-known but excellent types of Chianti.

Lodging
Whether you are in a five-star hotel or a more modest establishment, you may have one of the greatest pleasures of all: a room with a view. Florence has so many famous landmarks that it's not hard to find lodgings with a vista to remember. And the equivalent of the genteel pensiones of yesteryear still exist, though they are now officially classified as hotels. Usually small and intimate, they often have a quaint appeal that fortunately does not preclude modern plumbing.

Shopping
Since the days of the medieval guilds, Florence has been synonymous with fine craftsmanship and good business. Such time-honored Florentine specialties as antiques (and reproductions), bookbinding, jewelry, lace, leather goods, silk, and straw attest to that. More recently, the Pitti fashion shows and the burgeoning textile industry in nearby Prato have added fine clothing to the long list of merchandise available in the shops of Florence. Another medieval feature is the distinct feel of the different shopping areas, a throwback to the days when each district supplied a different product.

EXPLORING FLORENCE

Sightseeing in Florence is space intensive. Everything that you probably want to see is concentrated in the relatively small historic core of the city. But there is so much packed into the area that you may find yourself slogging from one mind-boggling sight to another and feeling overwhelmed. If you are not an inveterate museum enthusiast, take it easy. Don't try to absorb every painting or fresco that comes into view. There is second-rate art even in the Galleria degli Uffizi and the Palazzo Pitti (*especially* the Pitti), so find some favorites and enjoy them at your leisure.

Walking through the streets and alleyways in Florence is a discovery in itself, but to save time and energy (especially on your third or so day in the city), make use of the efficient bus system. Buses also provide the least-fatiguing way to reach Piazzale Michelangelo, San Miniato, and the Fortezza Belvedere. It is easy to make excursions to, say, Fiesole or the Medici villas by city bus. Most churches are usually open from 8 or 9 until noon or 12:30, and from 3 or 4 until about 7. Usually the Duomo in larger towns and cities is open all day throughout the year.

In between your blitzes into the Renaissance and beyond, stop to breathe in the city, the marvelous synergy between history and modern Florentine life. Firenze is a living, bustling metropolis that has managed to preserve its predominantly medieval street plan and mostly Renaissance infrastructure while successfully adapting to the insistent demands of 20th-century life. During the Guelph-Ghibelline conflict of the 13th and 14th centuries, Florence was a forest of towers—more than 200 of them, if the smaller three- and four-story towers are included. Today only a handful survive, but if you look closely you'll find them as you explore the city's core.

Numbers in the text correspond to numbers in the margin and on the Florence map.

Great Itineraries

You can see most of Florence's outstanding sights in three days. Plan your day around the opening hours of museums and churches; to gain a length on the tour groups in high season, go very early in the morning or around closing time. If you can, allow a day to explore each neighborhood.

IF YOU HAVE 3 DAYS

Spend day one exploring the historic core of Florence, which will give you an eyeful of such masterpieces as Ghiberti's renowned bronze doors at the Battistero, Giotto's Campanile, Brunelleschi's cupola hovering atop the Duomo, Botticelli's mystical spring muse at the Galleria degli Uffizi. On day two, wander north of the Duomo and take in the superb treasury of works ranging from Michelangelo's *David* at the Galleria dell'Accademia to the lavish frescoes at the Cappella dei Magi and the Museo di San Marco (don't miss San Lorenzo, and Michelangelo's Biblioteca Laurenziana and the Cappelle Medicee). On this afternoon (or on the afternoon of day three) head southeast to Santa Croce or west to Santa Maria Novella. On the third day, cross the Ponte Vecchio to the Arno's southern bank and explore the Oltrarno district, being sure not miss the Brunelleschi-designed church of Santo Spirito, Masaccio's frescoes in the church of Santa Maria del Carmine, and the effusion of local color.

IF YOU HAVE 5 DAYS

Break down the tours in the above itinerary into shorter ones, adding a few optional sites, such as Piazzale Michelangelo, halfway up a hill on the Arno's southern bank—where the expansive view of the city is yours to savor—and San Miniato, farther up the same hill, or the Cenacolo di Sant'Apollonia, on the northern part of the city center, near the Museo di San Marco. Climb Giotto's Campanile, which rewards with sweeping views of the city and hills beyond. Take Bus 7 from the station or Piazza del Duomo to enchanting Fiesole. Spend more time in the Galleria degli Uffizi and Bargello or one of the smaller museums such as the Museo dell'Opificio delle Pietre Dure, around the corner from the Galleria dell'Accademia, or the excellent Arno-side Museo di Storia della Scienza, and the Museo di Santa Maria Novella.

IF YOU HAVE 8 DAYS

Add an all-day excursion to Siena or a couple of half-day trips to the Medici villas around Florence (☞ Side Trips, *below*). Visit more of Florence's interesting smaller churches, including Oltrarno's Santa Felicita and Santa Maria Maddalena dei Pazzi to see Pontormo and Perugino masterpieces. On the trail of additional and little-known artistic gems, see Andrea del Castagno's (1421–1457) fresco of *The Last Supper* in the Cenacolo di Sant'Apollonia, northwest of the Museo di San Marco. There are similar treasures in the Chiostro dello Scalzo, just north of the Museo di San Marco, and the Cenacolo di Santo Spirito, west of Piazza Pitti.

Centro Storico: From the Duomo to the Ponte Vecchio

To say that Florence's historic center, stretching from the Piazza del Duomo in the north to the Giardini Boboli across the Arno to the south, is beautiful could be misconstrued as an understatement. Indeed, this relatively small area is home to some of the most important artistic treasures in the world. This smorgasbord of churches, medieval towers, Renaissance palazzi (palaces), and world-class museums and galleries is not a static testimony to the artistic and architectural genius of the past millennium, but a shrine to some of the most outstanding aesthetic achievements of Western history.

A Good Walk

Start at the **Duomo** ① and **Battistero** ②, climbing the **Campanile** ③ if you wish, then visit the **Museo dell'Opera del Duomo** ④, behind the Duomo. You can go directly south from in front of the Duomo to the Piazza della Signoria by way of Via dei Calzaiuoli (from here you can take a quick detour west on Via Speziali to **Piazza della Repubblica** ⑤), passing **Orsanmichele** ⑥, or go instead directly south from the Museo dell'Opera del Duomo along Via del Proconsolo to the **Bargello** ⑦ (opposite the ancient **Badia Fiorentina** ⑧, built in 1285). From the Bargello head west on Via della Condotta to Via Calzauioli, then south to discover the architectural splendors of the **Piazza della Signoria** ⑨, including the Loggia dei Lanzi and the **Palazzo Vecchio** ⑩. The **Palazzo degli Uffizi** ⑪, Italy's most important art gallery, is off the south side of the piazza. Leave the piazza from the southwest corner along Via Vacchereccia. To the left, at the corner with Via Por Santa Maria (lined with stores), is the **Mercato Nuovo** ⑫. Follow Via Por Santa Maria to the river; walk east along the north side of the Arno to Piazza dei Giudici to see the **Museo di Storia della Scienza** ⑬. Backtrack west along the Arno to the **Ponte Vecchio** ⑭.

TIMING

Before much of the *centro storico* (historic center) of Florence was closed to traffic, you had to keep dodging passing cars and mopeds as you walked the narrow streets. Now you have to elbow your way through moving masses of fellow tourists, especially in the neighborhood delimited by the Duomo, Piazza Signoria, Uffizi, and Ponte Vecchio. It takes about 40 minutes to walk the route, with 45 minutes to one hour each for the Museo dell'Opera del Duomo and for Palazzo della Signoria; one to 1½ hours for the Bargello, and a minimum of two hours for the Uffizi (reserve tickets in advance to avoid long lines).

A special museum ticket valid for six months at seven city museums, including the Palazzo Vecchio, the Museo di Firenze Com'Era (Museum of Florentine History), and the Museo di Santa Maria Novella, costs 15,000 lire and is a good buy if you're planning to visit some of these museums. Inquire at any city museum.

Sights to See

❽ Badia Fiorentina. This ancient church was built in 1285; its graceful bell tower—best seen from the interior courtyard—is one of the most beautiful in Florence. The interior of the church proper was half-heartedly remodeled in the Baroque style during the 17th century; its best-known work of art is Filippino Lippi's (1457–1504) delicate *Vision of St. Bernard,* on the left as you enter. The painting—one of Lippi's finest—is in superb condition; take a look at the Virgin's hands, perhaps the most beautiful in the city. ⊠ *Via del Proconsolo.*

★ ❼ Bargello. During the Renaissance this building was used as a prison, and the exterior served as a "most wanted" billboard: Effigies of notorious criminals and Medici enemies were painted on its walls. Today, it houses the **Museo Nazionale,** home to what is probably the finest collection of Renaissance sculpture in Italy. Michelangelo (1475–1564), Donatello (circa 1386–1466), and Benvenuto Cellini (1500–1571) are the preeminent masters here, and the concentration of masterworks is remarkable, though they stand among an eclectic array of arms, ceramics, and enamels. For Renaissance art lovers, the Bargello is to sculpture what the Uffizi is to painting.

One particular display, easily overlooked, should not be missed. In 1401 Filippo Brunelleschi (1377–1446) and Lorenzo Ghiberti (1378–1455) competed to earn the most prestigious commission of the day: the decoration of the north doors of the baptistery in Piazza del Duomo. For the competition, each designed a bronze bas-relief panel on the theme of the Sacrifice of Isaac; both panels are on display, side by side, in the room devoted to the sculpture of Donatello on the upper floor. The judges chose Ghiberti for the commission; you can decide for yourself whether or not they were right. ⊠ *Via del Proconsolo 4,* ☎ *055/2388606.* ☞ *8,000 lire.* ☼ *Daily 8:30–1:50. Closed 1st, 3rd, 5th Sun. and 2nd, 4th Mon. of month.*

★ ❷ Battistero (Baptistery). The octagonal baptistery is one of the supreme monuments of the Italian Romanesque and one of Florence's oldest. Local legend has it that it was once a Roman temple of Mars; modern excavations, however, suggest its foundation was laid in the 4th–5th and 7th–8th centuries AD, well after the collapse of the Roman Empire. The round-arched Romanesque decoration on the exterior probably dates from the 11th or 12th century. The interior ceiling mosaics (finished in 1297) are justly famous, but—glitteringly beautiful as they are—they could never outshine the building's most renowned feature: its bronze Renaissance doors decorated with panels crafted by Lorenzo Ghiberti. The doors, on which Ghiberti spent most of his adult life, from 1403 to 1452, are on the north and east sides of the baptistery—at least copies are—and the Gothic south door panels were designed by Andrea Pisano (1270–circa 1348) in 1330. The originals of the Ghiberti doors were removed to protect them from the effects of pollution and acid rain and have been beautifully restored; some of the panels are now on display in the Museo dell'Opera del Duomo.

Ghiberti's north doors depict scenes from the life of Christ; his later east doors, facing the Duomo facade, render scenes from the Old Testament. They merit close examination, for they are very different in style and illustrate with great clarity the artistic changes that marked

18

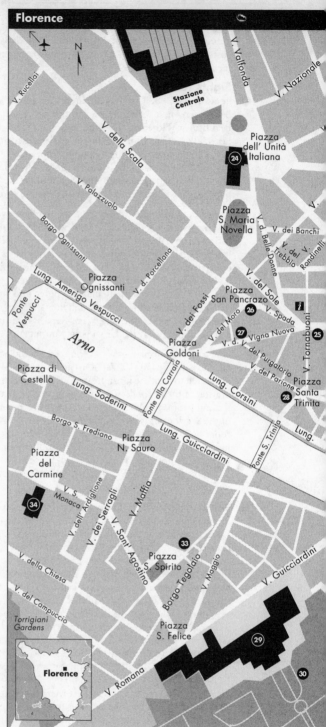

Florence

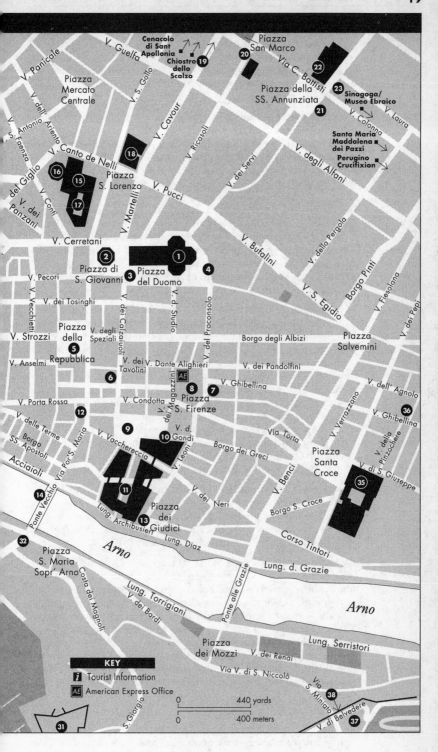

Cenacolo di Sant Apollonia

V. Guelfa

Piazza San Marco

Via C. Battisti

V. Panicale

V. S. Gallo

Chiostro dello Scalzo

Piazza Mercato Centrale

V. dell' Ariento

V. Faenza

V. S. Antonio

Piazza della SS. Annunziata

Sinagoga/ Museo Ebraico

V. Colonna

V. Laura

del Giglio

V. Canto de Nelli

V. Cavour

V. Ricasoli

V. dei Servi

V. degli Alfani

Santa Maria Maddalena dei Pazzi

Perugino Crucifixion

Piazza S. Lorenzo

V. Pucci

V. dei Conti

V. dei Panzani

V. Martelli

V. Cerretani

V. Bufalini

V. della Pergola

Borgo Pinti

V. S. Egidio

V. Fiesolana

Piazza di S. Giovanni

Piazza del Duomo

V. Pecori

V. dei Tosinghi

V. dei Calzaiuoli

V. d. Studio

V. del Proconsolo

V. dei Pepi

V. Vecchietti

Piazza della Repubblica

V. degli Speziali

Borgo degli Albizi

Piazza Salvemini

V. Strozzi

V. Anselmi

V. dei Tavolini

V. Dante Alighieri

V. dei Pandolfini

V. dell' Agnolo

V. Porta Rossa

V. Condotta

V. Ghibellina

V. Ghibellina

Piazza S. Firenze

Acciaioli

Borgo SS. Apostoli

V. delle Terme

V. Vacchereccia

V. Por S. Maria

V. d. Gondi

Via Torta

V. Verrazzano

V. della Pinzochere

V. di S. Giuseppe

V. Leoni

Borgo dei Greci

Piazza Santa Croce

V. Benci

Piazza dei Giudici

V. dei Neri

Borgo S. Croce

Lung. Archibusieri

Lung. Diaz

Corso Tintori

Ponte Vecchio

Arno

Piazza S. Maria Sopr' Arno

Lung. d. Grazie

Costa dei Magnoli

Lung. Torrigiani

V. dei Bardi

Ponte alle Grazie

Arno

Lung. Serristori

Piazza dei Mozzi

V. dei Renai

Via V. di S. Niccolò

Via S. Miniato

V. di Belvedere

S. Giorgio

KEY

i Tourist Information

AE American Express Office

0   440 yards

0   400 meters

the beginning of the Renaissance. Look at the far right panel of the middle row on the earlier north doors (*Jesus Calming the Waters*). Ghiberti here captured the chaos of a storm at sea with great skill and economy, but the artistic conventions he used are basically pre-Renaissance: Jesus is the most important figure, so he is the largest; the disciples are next in size, being next in importance; the ship on which they founder looks like a mere toy.

The panels on the east doors are larger, more expansive, more sweeping, and more convincing. Look at the middle panel on the left-hand door. It tells the story of Jacob and Esau, and the various episodes of the story (the selling of the birthright, Isaac ordering Esau to go hunting, the blessing of Jacob, and so forth) have been merged into a single beautifully realized street scene. A perspective grid is employed to suggest depth, the background architecture looks far more credible than on the north door panels, the figures in the foreground are grouped realistically, and the naturalism and grace of the poses (look at Esau's left leg) have nothing to do with the sacred message being conveyed. Although the religious content remains, man and his place in the natural world are given new prominence and are portrayed with a realism not seen in art since the fall of the Roman Empire, more than a thousand years before.

As a footnote to Ghiberti's panels, one small detail of the east doors is worth a special look. Just to the lower left of the Jacob and Esau panel, Ghiberti placed a tiny self-portrait bust. From either side, the portrait is extremely appealing—Ghiberti looks like everyone's favorite uncle—but the bust is carefully placed so that there is a single spot from which you can make direct eye contact with the tiny head. When that contact is made, the impression of intelligent life—of *modern* intelligent life—is astonishing. It is no wonder that when these doors were completed, they received one of the most famous compliments in the history of art, from a competitor known to be notoriously stingy with praise: Michelangelo himself declared them so beautiful that they could serve as the Gates of Paradise. ⊠ *Piazza del Duomo,* ☎ *055/ 2302885.* 🎟 *5,000 lire.* ☉ *Mon.–Sat. 1:30–6:30, Sun. 8:30–1:30.*

❸ **Campanile.** Giotto's (1266–1337) bell tower is a shaft of multicolor marble decorated with reliefs now in the Museo dell'Opera del Duomo. A climb of 414 steps rewards you with a close-up of Brunelleschi's dome and a sweeping view of the city. ⊠ *Piazza del Duomo.* 🎟 *10,000 lire.* ☉ *Apr.–Oct., daily 9–7:30; Nov.–Mar., daily 9–5.*

★ ❶ **Duomo** (Cattedrale di Santa Maria del Fiore). In 1296 Arnolfo di Cambio (1245–1302) was commissioned to build "the loftiest, most sumptuous edifice human invention could devise" in the newest Romanesque style on the site of the old church of Santa Reparata. The immense Duomo was not completed until 1436, the year when it was consecrated. The imposing facade dates only from the 19th century; it was added in the neo-Gothic style to complement Giotto's genuine Gothic 14th-century campanile. The real glory of the Duomo, however, is Filippo Brunelleschi's dome, presiding over the cathedral with a dignity and grace that few domes, even to this day, can match.

Brunelleschi's **cupola** was epoch-making as an engineering feat. The space to be enclosed by the dome was so large and so high above the ground that traditional methods of dome construction—wooden centering and scaffolding—were of no use whatever. So Brunelleschi developed entirely new building methods, which he implemented with equipment of his own device (including the modern crane). Beginning work in 1420, he built not one dome but two, one inside the other, and connected them with common ribbing that stretched across the intervening empty space, thereby considerably lessening the crushing weight of the structure. He also employed a new method of bricklaying, based on an ancient Roman herringbone pattern, interlocking each new course of bricks with the course below in a way that made the growing structure self-supporting. The result was one of the great engineering breakthroughs of all time: Most of Europe's great domes, including St. Peter's in Rome, were built employing Brunelleschi's methods, and today the Duomo has come to symbolize Florence in the same way that the Eiffel Tower symbolizes Paris. The Florentines are justly proud, and to this day the Florentine phrase for "homesick" is *nostalgia del cupolone* (homesick for the dome).

The interior is a fine example of Florentine Gothic. Much of the cathedral's best-known art has been moved to the nearby Museo dell'Opera del Duomo (☞ *below*). Notable among the works that remain, however, are two equestrian frescoes honoring famous soldiers: Andrea del Castagno's *Niccolò da Tolentino,* painted in 1456, and Paolo Uccello's (1397–1475) *Sir John Hawkwood,* painted 20 years earlier; both are on the left-hand wall of the nave. *Niccolò da Tolentino* is particularly impressive: He rides his fine horse with military pride and wears his even finer hat—surely the best in town—with panache. Restorers worked from 1983 to 1995 to repair the structure of Brunelleschi's dome and clean the vast and crowded fresco of the *Last Judgment*—painted by Vasari and Zuccaro—on its interior. Originally, Brunelleschi wanted mosaics to cover the interior of the great ribbed cupola, but by the time the Florentines got around to commissioning the decoration, 150 years later, tastes had changed.

You can explore the upper and lower reaches of the cathedral. Ancient remains have been excavated beneath the nave; the stairway down is near the first pier on the right. The climb to the top of the dome (463 steps) is not for the faint of heart, but the view is superb; the entrance is on the left wall just before the crossing. ⊠ *Piazza del Duomo,* ☎ *055/2302885.* ☺ *Weekdays 10–5, 1st Sat. of month 10–3:30, Sun. 1–5. Excavation:* ☜ *3,000 lire.* ☺ *Mon.–Sat. 10–5. Ascent to dome:* ☜ *10,000 lire.* ☺ *Weekdays 9:30–7 and Sat. 8:30–5 (1st Sat. of month 8:30–3:20).*

⑫ Mercato Nuovo (New Market). This open-air loggia was new in 1551. Today it hosts mostly souvenir stands; its main attraction is Pietro Tacca's bronze *Porcellino* (Little Pig) fountain on the south side, dating from around 1612 and copied from an earlier Roman work now in the Uffizi. Rubbing its drooling snout is a Florentine tradition, said to bring good luck. ⊠ *Corner of Via Por San Maria and Via Porta Rossa.* ☺ *Tues.–Sat. 8–7, Mon. 1–7.*

★ **❹ Museo dell'Opera del Duomo** (Cathedral Museum). The major attractions here—other than Ghiberti's original Baptistery door panels and the *cantorie* (choir loft) reliefs by Donatello and Luca della Robbia (1400–1482)—are Donatello's *Mary Magdalen* and Michelangelo's *Pietà* (not to be confused with his more famous *Pietà* in St. Peter's). The Renaissance in sculpture is in part defined by its revolutionary realism, but Donatello's *Magdalen* goes beyond realism: It is suffering incarnate. Michelangelo's heart-wrenching *Pietà* was unfinished at his death; the female figure supporting the body of Christ on the left was added by one Tiberio Calcagni, and never has the difference between competence and genius been manifested so clearly. ⊠ *Piazza del Duomo 9,* ☎ *055/2302885.* ☜ *10,000 lire.* ☺ *Mar.–Oct., Mon.–Sat. 9–7:30; Nov.–Feb., Mon.–Sat. 9–7.*

⑬ **Museo di Storia della Scienza** (Museum of Science History). Though it tends to be obscured by the glamour of the neighboring Uffizi, this science museum has a wealth of interest: Galileo's own instruments, a collection of antique armillary spheres, some of them real works of art, and a host of other reminders that the Renaissance made not only artistic but also scientific history. ⊠ *Piazza dei Giudici 1,* ☎ *055/2398876.* ☜ *10,000 lire.* ☉ *Tues., Thurs., Sat. 9:30–1; Mon., Wed., Fri. 9:30– 1 and 2–5.*

⑥ **Orsanmichele.** This church, containing a beautifully detailed 14th-century Gothic tabernacle by Andrea Orcagna (1308–1368), was originally a granary. The building was transformed in 1336 into a church with 14 exterior niches. Each of the major Florentine trade guilds was assigned its own niche and paid for the sculpture the niche was to contain. The niches soon held works by Florence's most talented sculptors. Unfortunately, the best have been removed and replaced with copies. The originals will eventually be placed in a museum, perhaps even in Orsanmichele. Even so, all the statues are worth examining. One of those removed—Andrea del Verrocchio's (1435–1488) *Doubting Thomas* (circa 1470)—was particularly deserving of attention. Were the niche not empty, you would see Christ, like the building's other figures, entirely framed within the niche, and St. Thomas standing on its bottom ledge, with his right foot outside the niche frame. This one detail, the positioning of a single foot, brought the whole composition to life. Appropriately, this is the only niche to be topped with a Renaissance pediment. ⊠ *Via dei Calzaiuoli,* ☎ *055/284944.* ☜ *Free.* ☉ *Daily 9–noon and 4–6. Closed 1st and last Mon. of month.*

★ ⑪ **Palazzo degli Uffizi** (Uffizi Palace). The **Galleria degli Uffizi** (Uffizi Gallery) occupies the top floor of this U-shape building fronting on the Arno, designed by Giorgio Vasari (1511–1574) in 1559 to hold the administrative offices of Medici Grand Duke Cosimo I (1519–1574)— *uffizi* means offices in Italian. And here later Medicis installed their art collections, creating what was Europe's first modern museum, open to the public (at first only by request, of course) since 1591. Today the palazzo houses the finest collection of paintings in Italy. If you're a hard-core museum aficionado, you might want to pick up a complete guide to the collections, sold in bookshops and on newsstands.

The collection's highlights include Paolo Uccello's *Battle of San Romano* (its brutal chaos of lances is one of the finest visual metaphors for warfare ever committed to paint); Fra Filippo Lippi's (1406–1469) *Madonna and Child with Two Angels* (the foreground angel's bold, impudent eye contact would have been unthinkable prior to the Renaissance); Sandro Botticelli's (1445–1510) ethereal interpretation of the *Birth of Venus* and *Primavera* (its nonrealistic fairy-tale charm exhibits the painter's idiosyncratic genius at its zenith); Leonardo da Vinci's (1452–1519) *Adoration of the Magi* (unfinished and perhaps the best opportunity in Europe to investigate the methods of a great artist at work); Raphael's (1483–1520) *Madonna of the Goldfinch* (darkened by time, but the tenderness with which the figures in the painting touch each other is undimmed); Michelangelo's *Holy Family* (one of the very few easel works in oil he ever painted, clearly reflecting his stated belief that draftsmanship is a necessary ingredient of great painting); Rembrandt's (1606–1669) *Self-Portrait as an Old Man*; Titian's (circa 1488–1576) *Venus of Urbino*; and Caravaggio's (1573–1610) *Bacchus* (two very great paintings whose attitudes toward myth and sexuality are—to put it mildly—diametrically opposed). If panic sets in at the prospect of absorbing all this art at one go, bear in mind that the Uffizi is, except on Sunday, open late and isn't usually crowded in the late afternoon. The coffee bar inside the Uffizi has a terrace with a fine close-up view of Palazzo Vecchio. Advance tickets can be purchased from Consorzio ITA. ⊠ *Piazzale degli Uffizi 6,* ☎ *055/23885. Advance tickets:* ⊠ *Consorzio ITA, Viale Gramsca 9a, 50121,* ☎ *055/ 2347941.* ☞ *12,000 lire.* ⊙ *Tues.–Sat. 8:30–10, Sun. 8:30–6.*

⑩ Palazzo Vecchio (Old Palace). Looming over Piazza della Signoria is Florence's forbidding, fortresslike city hall. The palazzo was begun in 1299 and designed (probably) by Arnolfo di Cambio, and its massive bulk and towering campanile dominate the piazza. It was built as a meeting place for the heads of the seven major guilds that governed the city at the time; over the centuries it has served lesser purposes, but today it is once again the City Hall of Florence. The interior courtyard is a good deal less severe, having been remodeled by Michelozzo (1396–1472) in 1453; the copy of Verrocchio's bronze *puttino* (little putto), topping the central fountain, softens the effect considerably.

The main attraction is on the second floor: two adjoining rooms that supply one of the most startling contrasts in Florence. The first is the vast **Sala dei Cinquecento** (Room of the Five Hundred), named for the 500-member Great Council, the people's assembly established by Savonarola, that met here. The Sala was decorated by Giorgio Vasari, around 1570, with huge—almost grotesquely huge—frescoes celebrating Florentine history; depictions of battles with nearby cities predominate. Continuing the martial theme, the Sala also contains Michelangelo's *Victory* group, intended for the never-completed tomb of Pope Julius II, plus other sculptures of decidedly lesser quality.

The second room is the little **Studiolo,** to the right of the Sala's entrance. The study of Cosimo de' Medici's son, the melancholy Francesco I (1541–1587), it was designed by Vasari and decorated by Vasari and Agnolo Bronzino. It is intimate, civilized, and filled with complex, questioning, allegorical art. It makes the vainglorious proclamations next door ring more than a little hollow. ⊠ *Piazza della Signoria,* ☎ *055/2768465.* ☞ *10,000 lire.* ⊙ *Mon.–Wed. and Fri.–Sat. 9–7, Sun. 8–1.*

⑤ Piazza della Repubblica. This square marks the site of the ancient forum that was the core of the original Roman settlement. The street plan in the area around the piazza still reflects the carefully plotted orthogonal grid of the Roman military encampment. The Mercato Vecchio (Old Market), located here since the Middle Ages, was demolished at the end of the last century, and the current piazza was constructed between 1885 and 1895 as a neoclassical showpiece. Nominally the center of town, it has yet to earn the love of most Florentines.

★ ⑨ Piazza della Signoria. This is by far the most striking square in Florence. It was here, in 1497, that the famous "bonfire of the vanities" took place, when the fanatical monk Savonarola induced his followers to hurl their worldly goods into the flames; it was also here, a year later, that he was hanged as a heretic and, ironically, burned. A bronze plaque in the piazza pavement marks the exact spot of his execution.

The statues in the square and in the 14th-century **Loggia dei Lanzi** on the south side vary in quality. Cellini's famous bronze *Perseus Holding the Head of Medusa* is his masterpiece; even the pedestal is superbly executed. Other works in the loggia include *The Rape of the Sabine Women* and *Hercules and the Centaur,* both late 16th-century works by Giambologna (1529–1608), and, in the back, a row of sober matrons that date from Roman times.

In the square, Bartolomeo Ammannati's (1511–1592) Neptune Fountain, dating from 1550 to 1575, takes something of a booby prize. Even

Ammannati himself considered it a failure, and the Florentines call it *Il Biancone,* which may be translated as "the big white man" or "the big white lump," depending on your point of view. Giambologna's equestrian statue, to the left of the fountain, pays tribute to the Medici Grand Duke Cosimo I. Occupying the steps of the Palazzo Vecchio are a copy of Donatello's proud heraldic lion of Florence, known as the *Marzocco* (the original is now in the Bargello); a copy of Donatello's *Judith and Holofernes* (the original is inside the Palazzo Vecchio); a copy of Michelangelo's *David* (the original is now in the Galleria dell'Accademia); and Baccio Bandinelli's *Hercules.*

★ ⑭ **Ponte Vecchio** (Old Bridge). This elegant bridge is to Florence what Tower Bridge is to London. It was built in 1345 to replace an earlier bridge that was swept away by flood, and its shops housed first butchers, then grocers, blacksmiths, and other merchants. But in 1593 the Medici Grand Duke Ferdinando I, whose private corridor linking the Medici palace (Palazzo Pitti) with the Medici offices (the Uffizi) crossed the bridge atop the shops, decided that all this plebeian commerce under his feet was unseemly. So he threw out all the butchers and blacksmiths and installed 41 goldsmiths and eight jewelers. The bridge has been devoted solely to these two trades ever since.

Take a moment to study the **Ponte Santa Trinita,** the next bridge downriver. It was designed by Bartolomeo Ammannati in 1567 (possibly from sketches by Michelangelo), blown up by the retreating Germans during World War II, and painstakingly reconstructed after the war ended. By virtue of its graceful arc and delicate curves, Florentines like to claim it is the most beautiful bridge in the world. Given its simplicity, this may sound like idle Tuscan boasting.

Michelangelo Country: From San Lorenzo to the Accademia

Poet, painter, sculptor, and architect, Michelangelo was a consummate genius. His prodigious energy and virtuoso technique overcame the political and artistic vicissitudes of almost a century to produce some of the greatest sculpture of his—or any—age. The Biblioteca Laurenziana is perhaps his most intuitive work of architecture. The key to understanding Michelangelo's genius is in the magnificent Cappelle Medicee sculptures. The towering and beautiful *David,* his most recognized work, resides in the Galleria dell'Accademia.

A Good Walk

Start at the church of **San Lorenzo** ⑮, visiting the **Biblioteca Laurenziana** ⑯ and its famous anteroom, before circling the church to the northwest and making your way through the San Lorenzo outdoor market on Via del Canto de' Nelli to the entrance of the **Cappelle Medicee** ⑰. Retrace your steps through the market and take Via dei Gori east to Via Cavour and the **Palazzo Medici-Riccardi** ⑱, home to Florence's most important family throughout the Renaissance. Follow Via Cavour two blocks north to Piazza San Marco and the church of the same name, attached to which is the **Museo di San Marco** ⑲, a memorial to the pious and exceptionally talented painter-monk, Fra Angelico. If you have time, go northwest from Piazza San Marco to the Cenacolo di Sant'Apollonia and then north to the Chiostro dello Scalzo. From Piazza San Marco, walk a half block south down Via Ricasoli (which runs back toward the Duomo) to the **Galleria dell'Accademia** ⑳. If you have time to make a detour, return to the east side of Piazza San Marco and take Via Cesare Battisti east into Piazza della Santissima Annunziata, one of Florence's prettiest squares, site of the **Ospedale degli Innocenti** ㉑ and, at the north end of the square, the church of **Santissima Annun-**

ziata ㉒. One block southeast of the entrance to Santissima Annunziata, through the arch and on the left side of Via della Colonna, is the **Museo Archeologico** ㉓.

TIMING
The walk alone takes about one hour; add another two hours to see the sights. Note that Cappelle Medicee and the Museo di San Marco close at 2. After visiting San Lorenzo, resist the temptation to explore the clothes market that surrounds the church before going to the Palazzo Medici-Riccardi; you can always come back later, when the churches and museums have closed; the market is open until 7 PM.

Sights to See

⑯ **Biblioteca Laurenziana** (Laurentian Library). Michelangelo the architect was every bit as original as Michelangelo the sculptor. Unlike Brunelleschi (the architect of San Lorenzo), however, he was not bent on ordered harmony of the spheres in his architecture. He was interested in experimentation and invention and in expressing a personal vision at times highly idiosyncratic.

It was never more idiosyncratic than in the Laurentian Library and its famous **vestibolo** (anteroom). This strangely shaped anteroom has had scholars scratching their heads for centuries. In a space more than two stories high, why did Michelangelo limit his use of columns and pilasters to the upper two-thirds of the wall? Why didn't he rest them on strong pedestals instead of on huge, decorative curlicue scrolls, which rob them of all visual support? Why did he recess them into the wall, which makes them look weaker still? The architectural elements here do not stand firm and strong and tall, as inside the church next door; instead, they seem to be pressed into the wall as if into putty, giving the room a soft, rubbery look that is one of the strangest effects ever achieved by classical architecture. It is almost as if Michelangelo purposely set out to defy his predecessors—intentionally to flout the conventions of the High Renaissance in order to see what kind of bizarre, mannered effect might result. His innovations were tremendously influential and produced a period of architectural experimentation, the Mannerist era, that eventually evolved into the Baroque. As his contemporary Giorgio Vasari put it, "Artisans have been infinitely and perpetually indebted to him because he broke the bonds and chains of a way of working that had become habitual by common usage."

Nobody has ever complained about the anteroom's staircase (best viewed head-on), which emerges from the library with the visual force of an unstoppable lava flow. In its highly sculptural conception and execution, it is quite simply one of the most original and elegant staircases in the world. ⊠ *Piazza San Lorenzo 9, entrance to the left of San Lorenzo,* ☎ *055/213440.* ⊡ *Free.* ☼ *Mon.–Sat. 8:30–1.*

★ ⑰ **Cappelle Medicee** (Medici Chapels). This magnificent complex includes the **Cappella dei Principi,** the Medici chapel and mausoleum that was begun in 1605 and kept marble workers busy for several hundred years, and the **Sagrestia Nuova** (New Sacristy) designed by Michelangelo, so called to distinguish it from Brunelleschi's Sagrestia Vecchia (Old Sacristy).

Michelangelo received the commission for the New Sacristy in 1520 from Cardinal Giulio de' Medici, who later became Pope Clement VII and who wanted a new burial chapel for his father, Giuliano, his uncle Lorenzo the Magnificent, and two recently deceased cousins. The result was a tour de force of architecture and sculpture. Architecturally, Michelangelo was as original and inventive here as ever, but it is—quite properly—the powerful sculptural compositions of the side wall tombs that dominate the room. The scheme is allegorical: On the wall tomb to the right are figures representing day and night, and on the wall tomb to the left are figures representing dawn and dusk; above them are idealized portraits of the two cousins, usually interpreted to represent the active life and the contemplative life. But the allegorical meanings are secondary; what is most important is the intense presence of the sculptural figures, the force with which they hit the viewer. Michelangelo's contemporaries were so awed by the impact of this force (in his sculpture here and elsewhere) that they invented an entirely new word to describe the phenomenon: *terribilità* (dreadfulness). To this day it is used only when describing his work, and it is in evidence here at the peak of its power. During his stormy relations with the Medicis, Michelangelo once hid out in a tiny subterranean room that is accessed from the left of the altar. Ever the artist, he drew some charcoal sketches on the wall. If you want to see them, tell the ticket vendor and pay 1,000 lire extra; guided visit only. ⊠ *Piazza di Madonna degli Aldobrandini,* ☎ *055/2388602.* ▣ *10,000 lire.* ☉ *Daily 8:30–1:50. Closed 1st, 3rd, 5th Mon. of month.*

★ ⑳ **Galleria dell'Accademia** (Accademia Gallery). The collection of Florentine paintings, dating from the 13th to the 18th centuries, is notable, but the statues by Michelangelo are renowned. The unfinished *Slaves,* fighting their way out of their marble prisons, were meant for the tomb of Michelangelo's malevolent benefactor Pope Julius II. But the focal point is the original *David,* moved here from Piazza della Signoria in 1873. The *David* was commissioned in 1501 by the Opera del Duomo (Cathedral Works Committee), which gave the 26-year-old sculptor a leftover block of marble that had been ruined by another artist. Michelangelo's success with the block was so dramatic that the city showered him with honors, and the Opera del Duomo voted to build him a house and a studio in which to live and work.

Today the *David* is beset not by Goliath but by tourists, and seeing the statue at all—much less really studying it—can be a trial. After a 1991 attack upon it by a hammer-wielding artist who, luckily, inflicted only a few minor nicks on the toes, the sculpture is surrounded by a Plexiglas barrier. The statue is not quite what it seems. It is so poised and graceful and alert—so miraculously alive—that it is often considered the definitive embodiment of the ideals of the High Renaissance in sculpture. But its true place in the history of art is a bit more complicated.

As Michelangelo well knew, the Renaissance painting and sculpture that preceded his work were deeply concerned with ideal form. Perfection of proportion was the ever-sought Holy Grail; during the Renaissance, ideal proportion was equated with ideal beauty, and ideal beauty was equated with spiritual perfection. But the *David,* despite its supremely calm and dignified pose, departs from these ideals. Michelangelo did not give the statue perfect proportions. The head is slightly too large for the body, the arms are too large for the torso, and the hands are dramatically large for the arms. By High Renaissance standards these are defects, but the impact and beauty of the *David* are such that it is the *standards* that must be called into question, not the statue. Michelangelo, revolutionary because he brought a new expressiveness to art, created the "defects" of the *David.* He knew exactly what he was doing, calculating that the perspective of the viewer would be such that, in order for the statue to appear proportioned, the upper body, head, and arms would have to be bigger as they are farther away from the viewer's line of vision. But he also did it to express and embody, as powerfully as possible in a single figure, an entire biblical story. *David*'s hands *are* too big, but so was Goliath, and these are the hands that slew him. ⊠ *Via Ricasoli 60,* ☎ *055/2388609.* 🎫 *12,000 lire.* ⊙ *Tues.–Sat. 8:30–10, Sun. 8:30–6.*

OFF THE BEATEN PATH **MUSEO DELL'OPIFICIO DELLE PIETRE DURE –** This fascinating small museum is attached to an Opificio, or workshop, established by Ferdinando I de' Medici (1503–1564) to train craftsmen in the art of working with precious and semiprecious stones and marble. It is internationally renowned as a center for the restoration of mosaics and inlays in semiprecious stones. Informative exhibits include some magnificent antique examples of this highly specialized craft. ⊠ *Via degli Alfani 78,* ☎ *055/210101.* 🎫 *4,000 lire.* ⊙ *Tues.–Sat. 9–2.*

㉓ **Museo Archeologico** (Archaeological Museum). Of the Etruscan, Egyptian, and Greco-Roman antiquities here, the Etruscan collection is particularly notable—the largest in northern Italy. The famous bronze *Chimera* was discovered (without the tail, a reconstruction) in the 16th century. ⊠ *Via della Colonna 36,* ☎ *055/23575.* 🎫 *8,000 lire.* ⊙ *Tues.–Sat. 9–2, Sun. 9–2, 1st, 3rd, and 5th Mon. of month 9–1. Closed 1st, 3rd, and 5th Sun. of month.*

OFF THE BEATEN PATH **SANTA MARIA MADDALENA DEI PAZZI –** One of Florence's hidden treasures, Perugino's cool and composed *Crucifixion,* is in the chapter hall of the monastery adjacent to this church. ⊠ *Borgo Pinti 58.* 🎫 *Donation requested.* ⊙ *Daily 9–noon and 5–7.*

CHIOSTRO DELLO SCALZO – Often overlooked, this small, peaceful 16th-century cloister was frescoed in monochrome by Andrea del Sarto (1486–1531) with scenes from the life of St. John the Baptist, Florence's patron saint. ⊠ *Via Cavour 69.* 🎫 *Free.* ⊙ *Mon.–Thurs. 9–1.*

TORRE DEI CORBIZI – The tower at the south end of the small Piazza San Pier Maggiore dates from the Middle Ages, when, during the Guelph-Ghibelline conflict of the 13th and 14th centuries, Florence was awash with such towers—more than 200 of them. Today only a handful survive. From the Museo Archeologico, follow Via della Colonna east to Borgo Pinti and turn right, following Borgo Pinti through the arch of San Piero into the piazza. ⊠ *Piazza San Pier Maggiore.*

⑲ **Museo di San Marco.** A former Dominican monastery adjacent to the church of San Marco now houses this museum, which is a memorial to Fra Angelico, the Dominican monk as famous for his piety as for his painting. When the monastery was built in 1437, he decorated it with his frescoes, which were meant to spur religious contemplation. His paintings are simple and direct and furnish a compelling contrast to the Palazzo Medici-Riccardi chapel. Fra Angelico probably would have considered the glitter of Benozzo Gozzoli's (1420–1497) work there worldly and blasphemous. The entire monastery is worth exploring, for Fra Angelico's paintings are everywhere, including the Chapter House, at the top of the stairs leading to the upper floor (the famous *Annunciation*), in the upper-floor monks' cells, and in the gallery just off the cloister as you enter. The latter room contains, among many other works, his beautiful *Last Judgment;* as usual, the tortures of the damned are far more inventive than the pleasures of the redeemed. ⊠ *Piazza San Marco 1,* ☎ *055/2388608.* 🎫 *8,000 lire.* ⊙ *Daily 8:30–1:40. Closed 1st, 3rd, 5th Sun. and 2nd, 4th Mon. of month.*

OFF THE BEATEN PATH **CENACOLO DI SANT'APOLLONIA –** The frescoes of this refectory of a former Benedictine monastery were painted in sinewy style by Andrea del Castagno, a follower of Masaccio (1401–1428). The *Last Supper* is a powerful version of this typical refectory theme. From the Cenacolo entrance, walk around the corner to Via San Gallo 25 and take a peek at the lovely 15th-century cloister that belonged to the same monastery but is now part of the University of Florence. ⊠ *Via XXVII Aprile 1.* 🎟 *Free.* ⊙ *Daily 8:30–2. Closed 1st, 3rd, 5th Sun. and 2nd, 4th Mon. of month.*

㉑ Ospedale degli Innocenti. Built by Brunelleschi in 1419 to serve as a foundling hospital, it takes the historical prize as the very first Renaissance building. Brunelleschi designed the building's portico with his usual rigor, building it out of the two shapes he considered mathematically (and therefore philosophically and aesthetically) perfect: the square and the circle. Below the level of the arches, the portico encloses a row of perfect cubes; above the level of the arches, the portico encloses a row of intersecting hemispheres. The whole geometric scheme is articulated with Corinthian columns, capitals, and arches borrowed directly from antiquity. At the time he designed the portico, Brunelleschi was also designing the interior of San Lorenzo, using the same basic ideas. But since the portico was finished before San Lorenzo, the Ospedale degli Innocenti can claim the honor of ushering in Renaissance architecture. The 10 ceramic medallions depicting swaddled infants that decorate the portico are by Andrea della Robbia (1435–1525), done in about 1487. ⊠ *Piazza di Santissima Annunziata 1.*

★ ⑱ Palazzo Medici-Riccardi. The main attraction of this palace, begun in 1444 by Michelozzo for Cosimo de' Medici, is the interior chapel, the so-called **Cappella dei Magi** on the upper floor. Painted on its walls is Benozzo Gozzoli's famous *Procession of the Magi,* finished in 1460 and celebrating both the birth of Christ and the greatness of the Medici family. Like his contemporary Domenico Ghirlandaio (1449–1494), Gozzoli was not a revolutionary painter and is today considered less than first rate because of his technique, old-fashioned even for his day. Gozzoli's gift, however, was for entrancing the eye, not challenging the mind, and on those terms his success here is beyond question. The paintings are full of activity yet somehow frozen in time in a way that fails utterly as realism, but succeeds triumphantly as soon as the demand for realism is set aside. Entering the chapel is like walking into the middle of a magnificently illustrated child's storybook, and this beauty makes it one of the most unpretentiously enjoyable rooms in the entire city. ⊠ *Via Cavour 1,* ☎ *055/2760340.* 🎟 *6,000 lire.* ⊙ *Mon.–Tues. and Thurs.–Sat. 9–1 and 3–6, Sun. 9–1.*

⑮ San Lorenzo. The facade of this church was never finished. Like Santo Spirito on the other side of the Arno, the interior of San Lorenzo was designed by Filippo Brunelleschi in the early 15th century. The two church interiors are similar in design and effect and proclaim with ringing clarity the beginning of the Renaissance in architecture. San Lorenzo possesses one feature that Santo Spirito lacks, however, which considerably heightens the dramatic effect of the interior: the grid of dark, inlaid marble lines on the floor. The grid makes the rigorous regularity with which the interior was designed immediately visible and offers an illuminating lesson on the laws of perspective. If you stand in the middle of the nave at the church entrance, on the line that stretches to the high altar, every element in the church—the grid, the nave columns, the side aisles, the coffered nave ceiling—seems to march inexorably toward a hypothetical vanishing point beyond the high altar, exactly as in a single-point-perspective painting. Brunelleschi's **Sagrestia Vecchia** has stucco decorations by Donatello; it's at the end of the left transept. ⊠ *Piazza San Lorenzo,* ☎ *055/216634.* ⊙ *Daily 7–noon and 3:30–6:30.*

OFF THE
BEATEN PATH

MERCATO CENTRALE – In this huge, two-story market hall, food is every-where, some of it remarkably exotic. At the Mercato Nuovo (☞ *above*), near the Ponte Vecchio, you will see tourists petting the snout of the bronze piglet for good luck; here you will see Florentines petting the snout of a very real one. There is a coffee bar upstairs among the mountains of vegetables. ⊠ *Piazza del Mercato Centrale.*

㉒ **Santissima Annunziata.** This church was designed in 1447 by Miche-lozzo, who gave it an uncommon (and lovely) entrance cloister. The interior is an extreme rarity for Florence: a sumptuous example of the Baroque. But it is not really a fair example, since it is merely 17th-century Baroque decoration applied willy-nilly to an earlier structure—exactly the sort of violent remodeling exercise that has given the Baroque a bad name ever since. The **Tabernacle of the Annunziata,** immediately inside the entrance to the left, illustrates the point. The lower half, with its stately Corinthian columns and carved frieze bearing the Medici arms, was built at the same time as the church; the upper half, with its erupting curves and impish sculpted cherubs, was added 200 years later. Each is effective in its own way, but together they serve only to prove that dignity is rarely comfortable wearing a party hat. ⊠ *Piazza di Santis-sima Annunziata.* ⏱ *Daily 7:30–12:30 and 4–6:30.*

Santa Maria Novella to the Arno

Piazza Santa Maria Novella is near the train station, and like the train stations of most other European cities, it is an area pervaded by a certain squalor, especially at night. Nevertheless, the streets in and around the piazza are an architectural treasure trove, lined with some of Florence's most elegant palazzi.

A Good Walk

Start in the Piazza Santa Maria Novella, its north side dominated by the church of **Santa Maria Novella** ㉔, then take Via delle Belle Donne, which leads from the east side of Piazza Santa Maria Novella to a minuscule square, at the center of which a curious shrine, known as the Croce al Trebbio, stands. Take Via del Trebbio east and turn right onto **Via Tornabuoni,** Florence's finest shopping street. At the intersection of Via Tornabuoni and Via Strozzi is the classical **Palazzo Strozzi** ㉕. If you want a dose of contemporary art, head straight down Via Spada to the **Museo Marino Marini** ㉖. One block west from Via Tornabuoni and Palazzo Strozzi, down Via della Vigna Nuova, is Alberti's High Renaissance–style **Palazzo Rucellai** ㉗. Follow the narrow street opposite the palazzo (Via del Purgatorio) east almost to its end, then zigzag right and left, turning east on Via Parione to reach Piazza di Santa Trinita, where, in the middle, stands the **Colonna della Giustizia,** erected by Cosimo de' Medici in 1537. Halfway down the block to the south (toward the Arno) is the church of **Santa Trinita** ㉘, home to Ghirlandaio's glowing frescoes. Then go east on Borgo Santi Apostoli, a typical medieval street flanked by tower houses, to Via Por Santa Maria. Alternatively, from Piazza Santa Trinita you can cross Ponte Santa Trinita and head into the Oltrarno neighborhood.

TIMING
The walk takes about 30 minutes, plus 30 minutes for Santa Maria Novella and 15 minutes for Santa Trinita. A visit to the Santa Maria Novella museum and cloister takes about 30 minutes.

Sights to See
Croce al Trebbio. This little street shrine was erected in 1338 by the Dominican friars (near Santa Maria Novella is a Dominican church) to commemorate a victory famous locally: It was here that they de-

feated their avowed enemies, the Patarene heretics, in a bloody street brawl. ⊠ *Via del Trebbio.*

㉖ Museo Marino Marini. The dates of Marino Marini (1901–1980) are not a misprint. This is the only museum in Italy dedicated to a contemporary artist. One of Marini's major works, a 21-ft-tall bronze horse and rider, dominates the space of the main gallery. The museum itself is an eruption of contemporary space in a deconsecrated 10th-century church, designed with a series of open stairways, walkways, and balconies that allow you to peer at Marini's work from all angles. In addition to Marini's Etruscanesque sculpture, the museum houses Marini's paintings, drawings, and engravings. ⊠ *Piazza San Pancrazio,* ☎ *055/ 219432.* 🎟 *8,000 lire.* ☽ *Wed.–Mon. 10–5.*

㉗ Palazzo Rucellai. Architect Leon Battista Alberti (1404–1472) designed perhaps the very first private residence done in Renaissance style—which goes a step further than the Palazzo Strozzi. A comparison between the two is illuminating. Evident on the facade of the Palazzo Rucellai is the ordered arrangement of windows and rusticated stonework seen on the Palazzo Strozzi, but Alberti's facade is far less forbidding. Alberti devoted a far larger proportion of his wall space to windows, which soften the facade's appearance, and filled in the remainder with rigorously ordered classical elements borrowed from antiquity. The end result, though still severe, is less fortresslike, and Alberti strove for this effect purposely (he is on record as stating that only tyrants need fortresses). Ironically, the Palazzo Rucellai was built some 30 years *before* the Palazzo Strozzi. Alberti's civilizing ideas here, it turned out, had little influence on the Florentine palazzi that followed. To the Renaissance Florentines, power—in architecture, as in life—was just as impressive as beauty. ⊠ *Via della Vigna Nuova.*

㉕ Palazzo Strozzi. This is the most imposing palazzo on Via Tornabuoni. Designed (probably) by Giuliano da Sangallo around 1489 and modeled after Michelozzo's earlier Palazzo Medici-Riccardi (☞ Michelangelo Country, *above*), the exterior of the palazzo is simple and severe; it is not the use of classical detail but the regularity of its features, the stately march of its windows, that marks it as a product of the early Renaissance. The interior courtyard (entered from the rear of the palazzo) is another matter altogether. It is here that the classical vocabulary—columns, capitals, pilasters, arches, and cornices—is given uninhibited and powerful expression. Unfortunately, the courtyard's effectiveness is all but destroyed by the addition of a severe metal fire escape. Its introduction here is one of the most disgraceful acts of 20th-century vandalism in the entire city. ⊠ *Via Tornabuoni.*

㉔ Santa Maria Novella. The facade of this church looks distinctly clumsy by later Renaissance standards, and with good reason: It is an architectural hybrid. The lower half of the facade was completed mostly in the 14th century; its pointed-arch niches and decorative marble patterns reflect the Gothic style of the day. About a hundred years later (around 1456), architect Leon Battista Alberti was called in to complete the job. The marble decoration of his upper story clearly defers to the already existing work below, but the architectural features he added evince an entirely different style. The central doorway, the four ground-floor half-columns with Corinthian capitals, the triangular pediment atop the second story, the inscribed frieze immediately below the pediment—these are classical features borrowed from antiquity, and they reflect the new Renaissance era in architecture, born some 35 years earlier at the Ospedale degli Innocenti. Alberti's most important addition, however, the S-curve scrolls that surmount the decorative circles on either side of the upper story, had no precedent whatever in antiquity. The problem was to soften the abrupt transition between wide ground floor and narrow upper story. Alberti's solution turned out to be definitive. Once you start to look for them, you will find scrolls such as these (or sculptural variations of them) on churches all over Italy, and every one of them derives from Alberti's example here.

The architecture of the interior is, like the Duomo, a dignified but somber example of Italian Gothic. Exploration is essential, however, because the church's store of art treasures is remarkable. Highlights include the 14th-century stained-glass rose window depicting *The Coronation of the Virgin* (above the central entrance); the Cappella Filippo Strozzi (right of the altar), containing late 15th-century frescoes and stained glass by Filippino Lippi; the chancel (the area around the altar), displaying frescoes by Domenico Ghirlandaio (1485); and the Cappella Gondi (to the left of the altar), containing Filippo Brunelleschi's famous wooden crucifix, carved around 1410 and said to have so stunned the great Donatello when he first saw it that he dropped a basket of eggs.

Of special attention, for its great historical importance and beauty, is Masaccio's *Holy Trinity with Two Donors*, on the left-hand wall, almost halfway down the nave. Painted around 1425 (at the same time Masaccio was working on his frescoes in Santa Maria del Carmine), it unequivocally announced the arrival of the Renaissance era. The realism of the figure of Christ was revolutionary in itself, but what was probably even more startling to contemporary Florentines was the coffered ceiling in the background. The mathematical rules for employing perspective in painting had just been discovered (probably by Brunelleschi), and this was one of the first paintings to employ them with utterly convincing success. ⊠ *Piazza Santa Maria Novella,* ☎ *055/ 210113.* ☉ *Sun.–Fri. 7–12:15 and 3–6, Sat. 7–12:15 and 3–5.*

The **Museo di Santa Maria Novella,** to the left of Santa Maria Novella, includes church's cloisters, interesting for the faded fresco cycle by Paolo Uccello depicting tales from Genesis, with a dramatic vision of the Deluge. Earlier and better-preserved frescoes painted by Andrea da Firenze in the 1360s are in the chapter hall, or Cappella degli Spagnoli, off the cloisters. ⊠ *Piazza Santa Maria Novella,* ☎ *055/282187.* ▨ *5,000 lire.* ☉ *Mon.–Thurs. and Sat. 9–2, Sun. 8–1.*

㉘ Santa Trinita. Originally Romanesque in style, the church underwent a Gothic remodeling during the 14th century (remains of the Romanesque construction are visible on the interior front wall). Its major work is the fresco cycle and the altarpiece in the Cappella Sassetti, the second to the high altar's right, painted by Ghirlandaio, around 1485. Ghirlandaio was a conservative painter for his day, and generally his paintings exhibit little interest in the investigations into the rigorous laws of perspective that had been going on in Florentine painting for more than 50 years. But his work here possesses such graceful decorative appeal it hardly seems to matter. The wall frescoes illustrate the life of St. Francis, and the altarpiece, *The Adoration of the Shepherds,* nearly glows. ⊠ *Piazza Santa Trinita,* ☎ *055/216912.* ☉ *Mon.–Sat. 8–noon and 4–6, Sun. 4–6.*

In the center of Piazza Santa Trinita is a column from Rome's Terme di Caracalla, given to the Medici Grand Duke Cosimo I by Pope Pius IV in 1560. The column was raised here by Cosimo in 1565, to mark the spot where he heard the news, in 1537, that his exiled Ghibelline enemies had been defeated at Montemurlo, near Prato; the victory made his power in Florence unchallengeable and all but absolute. The column is called, with typical Medici self-assurance, the **Colonna della Giustizia,** the Column of Justice.

Oltrarno: Palazzo Pitti, Giardini Boboli, Santo Spirito

A walk through the Oltrarno takes in two very different aspects of Florence: the splendor of the Medicis, manifest in the riches of the mammoth Palazzo Pitti and the gracious Giardini Boboli; and the charm of the Oltrarno, literally "beyond the Arno," a now-gentrified, fiercely proud working-class neighborhood with artisans and antiques shops.

A Good Walk

If you start from Santa Trinita, cross the Arno over Ponte Santa Trinita and continue south down Via Maggio until you reach the crossroads of Sdrucciolo dei Pitti (on the left) and the short Via Michelozzi (on the right). Turn left onto the Sdrucciolo dei Pitti. **Palazzo Pitti** ㉙, Florence's largest architectural monument, lies before you as you emerge onto Piazza Pitti. Behind the palace are the **Giardini Boboli** ㉚. If you have time, walk through the gardens. At the top, the adjacent **Fortezza Belvedere** ㉛ commands a wonderful view and sometimes has art exhibits but is not always open to the public. If you want to see the Pontormo fresco cycle at **Santa Felicità** ㉜, head northeast from Palazzo Pitti on Via Guicciardini back toward the Ponte Vecchio. Return to Via Maggio off Piazza Pitti, take Via Michelozzi west to Piazza Santo Spirito, dominated at its north end by the unassuming facade of the church of **Santo Spirito** ㉝. After your visit to perhaps Italy's most important architectural interior, and to the Cenacolo di Santo Spirito, next door, take Via Sant'Agostino, diagonally across the square from the church entrance, and follow it west to Via dei Serragli. Cross and follow Via Santa Monaca west through the heart of the Oltrarno neighborhood—the equivalent of Rome's Trastevere—to Piazza del Carmine and the church of **Santa Maria del Carmine** ㉞, where, in the attached Cappella Brancacci, is the Masaccio cycle famous throughout the world. Go to the far end of Piazza del Carmine and turn right onto Borgo San Frediano, then follow Via di Santo Spirito and Borgo San Jacopo east to reach the Ponte Vecchio.

TIMING

The walk alone takes about 45 minutes; allow one hour to visit the Galleria Palatina in Palazzo Pitti, or more if you visit the other galleries. Spend at least 30 minutes to an hour savoring the graceful elegance of the Giardini Boboli. When you reach the crossroads of the Sdrucciolo dei Pitti and Via Michelozzi, you have a choice. If the noon hour approaches, you may want to postpone the next stop temporarily to see the churches of Santo Spirito, Santa Felicità, and Santa Maria del Carmine before they close for the afternoon. Otherwise, proceed to Palazzo Pitti. The churches can be visited in 15 minutes each.

Sights to See

㉛ **Fortezza Belvedere** (Belvedere Fortress). This impressive structure was built in 1590 to help defend the city against siege. But time has effected an ironic transformation, and what was once a first-rate fortification is now a first-rate exhibition venue. Farther up the hill is Piazzale Michelangelo, but, as the natives know, the best views of Florence are right here. To the north, all the city's monuments are spread out in a breathtaking cinemascopic panorama, framed by the rolling Tuscan hills beyond. To the south, the nearby hills furnish a complementary rural view, in its way equally memorable. The fortress, occasionally a setting for art exhibitions, is adjacent to the top of the Giardini Boboli. ⊠ *Porta San Giorgio.* ☞ *Varies per exhibit.*

㉚ **Giardini Boboli** (Boboli Gardens). The main entrance to these landscaped gardens is in the right wing of Palazzo Pitti. The gardens began to take shape in 1549, when the Pitti family sold the palazzo to Eleanor of Toledo, wife of the Medici Grand Duke Cosimo I. The initial landscaping plans were laid out by Niccolò Pericoli Tribolo. After his death in 1550 development was continued by Bernardo Buontalenti, Giulio, and Alfonso Parigi, and, over the years, many others, who produced the most spectacular backyard in Florence. The Italian gift for landscaping—less formal than the French but still full of sweeping drama—is displayed here at its best. The famous *Bacchino,* near the main entrance, is a copy of the original fountain, showing Pietro Barbino, Cosimo's favorite dwarf, astride a particularly unhappy tortoise. It seems to be illustrating—very graphically, indeed—the perils of too much pasta. ⊠ *Enter through Palazzo Pitti (☞ below),* ☎ *055/213440.* ☞ *4,000 lire.* ⊙ *Daily 9 AM–1 hr before sunset. Closed 1st and last Mon. of each month.*

㉙ Palazzo Pitti. This enormous palace is one of Florence's largest—if not one of its best—architectural set pieces. The original palazzo, built for the Pitti family around 1460, comprised only the middle cube (the width of the middle seven windows on the upper floors) of the present building. In 1549 the property was sold to the Medicis, and Bartolomeo Ammannati was called in to make substantial additions. Although he apparently operated on the principle that more is better, he succeeded only in producing proof that more is just that—more.

Today it houses several museums: the former **Apartamenti Reali** (Royal Apartments), containing furnishings from a remodeling done in the 19th century; the **Museo degli Argenti,** displaying a vast collection of Medici household treasures; the **Galleria del Costume,** a showcase of the fashions of the past 300 years; the **Galleria d'Arte Moderna,** holding a collection of 19th- and 20th-century paintings, mostly Tuscan; and, most famous of all, the **Galleria Palatina,** containing a broad collection of 16th- and 17th-century paintings. The rooms of the latter remain much as the Medici family left them. Their floor-to-ceiling paintings are considered by some as Italy's most egregious exercise in conspicuous consumption, aesthetic overkill, and trumpery. Still, the collection possesses high points, including a number of portraits by Titian and an unparalleled collection of paintings by Raphael, such as the famous *Madonna of the Chair.* ⊠ *Piazza Pitti,* ☎ *055/210323. Museo degli Argenti:* ☞ *8,000 lire (also valid for Galleria del Costume).* ⊙ *Daily 8:30–1:50; closed 2nd, 4th Sun. and 1st, 3rd, 5th Mon. of month. Galleria del Costume:* ☞ *8,000 lire.* ⊙ *Tues.–Sun. 8:30–1:50. Galleria d'Arte Moderna:* ☞ *4,000 lire.* ⊙ *Daily 8:50–1:50. Closed 2nd, 4th Sun. and 1st, 3rd, 5th Mon. of month. Galleria Palatina:* ☞ *12,000 lire.* ⊙ *Tues.–Sat. 8:50–10, Sun. 8:50–6.*

㉜ Santa Felicità. This diminutive late Baroque church (its facade was remodeled 1736–1739) contains the Mannerist Jacopo Pontormo's (1494–1557) tour de force, the Deposition altarpiece, which is regarded as a masterpiece of 16th-century Florentine art. The remote figures, which transcend the realm of Renaissance classical form, are portrayed in an array of tangled shapes and intense pastel colors (well preserved because of the low lights in the church), in space and depth that defy reality. The granite column in the piazza was erected in 1381, and marks a Christian cemetery. ⊠ *Piazza Santa Felicità, Via Guicciardini.* ⊙ *Weekdays 9–6, Sun. 9–11 AM.*

㉞ Santa Maria del Carmine. The **Cappella Brancacci,** at the end of the right transept of this church, houses a masterpiece of Renaissance painting: a fresco cycle that changed the course of art forever. Fire almost destroyed the church in the 18th century; miraculously, the Cappella Brancacci survived almost intact. The cycle is the work of three artists: Masaccio and Masolino, who began it in 1423, and Filippino Lippi, who finished it, after a long interruption during which the sponsoring Brancacci family was exiled, some 50 years later. It was Masaccio's work that opened a new frontier for painting; tragically, he did not live to experience the revolution his innovations caused, as he died in 1428 at the age of 27.

Masaccio collaborated with Masolino on several of the paintings, but by himself he painted *The Tribute Money* on the upper-left wall; *Peter Baptizing the Neophytes* on the upper altar wall; *The Distribution of the Goods of the Church* on the lower altar wall; and, most famous, *The Expulsion of Adam and Eve* on the chapel's upper-left entrance pier. If you look closely at the latter painting and compare it with some of the chapel's other works, you will see a pronounced difference. The figures of Adam and Eve possess a startling presence, primarily due to the dramatic way in which their bodies seem to reflect light. Masaccio here shaded his figures consistently, so as to suggest emphatically a single, strong source of light within the world of the painting but outside its frame. In so doing, he succeeded in imitating with paint the real-world effect of light on mass, and he thereby imparted to his figures a sculptural reality unprecedented in its day.

These matters have to do with technique, but with *The Expulsion of Adam and Eve,* Masaccio's skill went beyond technical innovation, and if you look hard at the faces of Adam and Eve, you will see more than just finely modeled figures. You will see terrible shame and suffering, and you will see them depicted with a humanity rarely achieved in art. ⊠ *Piazza del Carmine,* ☎ *055/2382195.* ⌷ *5,000 lire.* ☉ *Mon. and Wed.–Sat. 10–5, Sun. 1–5.*

🔢 **Santo Spirito.** The plain, unfinished facade gives nothing away, but the interior, although it appears chilly (cold, even) compared with later churches, is one of the most important pieces of architecture in all Italy. One of a pair of Florentine church interiors designed by Filippo Brunelleschi in the early 15th century (the other is San Lorenzo), it was here that Brunelleschi supplied definitive solutions to the two main problems of interior Renaissance church design: how to build a cross-shape interior using classical architectural elements borrowed from antiquity and how to reflect in that interior the order and regularity that Renaissance scientists (of which Brunelleschi was one) were at the time discovering in the natural world around them.

Brunelleschi's solution to the first problem was brilliantly simple: turn a Greek temple inside out. To see this clearly, look at one of the stately arch-topped arcades that separate the side aisles from the central nave. Whereas the ancient Greek temples were walled buildings surrounded by classical colonnades, Brunelleschi's churches were classical arcades surrounded by walled buildings. This brilliant architectural idea overthrew the previous era's religious taboo against pagan architecture once and for all, triumphantly reclaiming that architecture for Christian use.

Brunelleschi's solution to the second problem—making the entire interior orderly and regular—was mathematically precise: He designed the ground plan of the church so that all its parts are proportionally related. The transepts and nave have exactly the same width; the side aisles are precisely half as wide as the nave; the little chapels off the side aisles are exactly half as deep as the side aisles; the chancel and transepts are exactly one-eighth the depth of the nave; and so on, with dizzying exactitude. For Brunelleschi, such a design technique would have been far more than a convenience; it would have been a matter of passionate conviction. Like most theoreticians of his day, he believed that mathematical regularity and aesthetic beauty were opposite sides of the same coin, that one was not possible without the other. The conviction stood unchallenged for a hundred years, until Michelangelo turned his hand to architecture and designed the Cappelle Medicee and the Biblioteca Laurenziana across town (☞ Michelangelo Country, *above*), and thereby unleashed a revolution of his own that spelled the end of the Renaissance in architecture and the beginning of the Baroque. In the **Cenacolo di Santo Spirito** adjacent to the church, you can see Andrea Orcagna's fresco of the Crucifixion. *Church:* ⊠ *Piazza Santo Spirito,* ☎ *055/210030.* ☉ *Thurs.–Tues. 8–noon and 4–6, Wed. 8–noon. Cenacolo:* ⊠ *Piazza Santo Spirito 29,* ☎ *055/287043.* ☞ *4,000 lire.* ☉ *Tues.–Sat. 9–2, Sun. 8–1.*

From Santa Croce to San Miniato al Monte

The Santa Croce neighborhood, on the southwest fringe of the historic center, was built up in the Middle Ages just outside the medieval city walls. The centerpiece of the neighborhood was the church of Santa Croce, which could hold great numbers of worshipers and accommodate the overflow in the vast piazza, which also served as a fairground and playing field for traditional, no-holds-barred football games. A center of leather working since the Middle Ages, the neighborhood is still packed with leather craftsmen and leather shops.

A Good Walk

Begin your walk at the church of **Santa Croce** ㉟; from here you can take a quick jaunt up Via della Pinzochere to **Casa Buonarroti** ㊱ to see an early Michelangelo work. Return to Santa Croce, and at the southeast end of the piazza go south on Via de' Benci and cross the Arno over Ponte alle Grazie. Turn left onto Lungarno Serristori and continue to Piazza Poggi, where a series of ramps and stairs climbs to **Piazzale Michelangelo** ㊲, where the city lies before you like a painting. From Piazzale Michelangelo, climb the stairs behind La Loggia restaurant to the church of San Salvatore al Monte, and go south on the lane leading to the stairs that climb to **San Miniato al Monte** ㊳, cutting through the fortifications hurriedly built by Michelangelo in 1529 when Florence was threatened by Emperor Charles V's troops. If you prefer, you can avoid the long walk by taking Bus 12 or 13 at the west end of Ponte alle Grazie and get off at the stop after Piazzale Michelangelo. You still have to climb the monumental stairs to San Miniato, but then the rest of your itinerary will be downhill. From San Miniato descend to San Salvatore al Monte and then to Piazzale Michelangelo, where you can get a bus back to town center.

TIMING

The walk alone takes about 1½ hours one way, plus 30 minutes in Santa Croce, 30 minutes in the Museo di Santa Croce, and 30 minutes in San Miniato. Depending on the amount of time you have, you can limit your sightseeing to Santa Croce and Casa Buonarroti or continue on to Piazzale Michelangelo. The walk to Piazzale Michelangelo is a long uphill hike, with the prospect of another climb to San Miniato from there. If you decide to take a bus, remember to buy your ticket before you board. Finally, since you go to Piazzale Michelangelo for the view, skip it if it's a hazy day.

Sights to See

㊱ **Casa Buonarroti.** If you are really enjoying walking in the footsteps of the great genius, you may want to complete the picture by visiting Michelangelo's home. Even though he never actually lived in the house (it was given to his nephew and it was the nephew's son, Michelangelo, who began the process of turning it into a gallery dedicated to his great-uncle), his descendents began the process of filling it with art treasures—some by Michelangelo himself (a marble bas-relief, *The*

Madonna of the Steps, carved when he was just a teenager and his ear-liest known work, and his wooden model for the facade of San Lorenzo) and some by other artists that pay homage to him. ⊠ *Via Ghibellina 70,* ☎ *055/241752.* 🎫 *10,000 lire.* ⊘ *Wed.–Mon. 9:30–1:30.*

③⑦ Piazzale Michelangelo. From this lookout, you have a marvelous view of Florence and the hills around it, rivaling the vista from the Belvedere Fortress. It has a copy of Michelangelo's *David* and outdoor cafés packed with tourists during the day and with Florentines in the evening. In May, the Giardino dell'Iris (Iris Garden) off the piazza is abloom with more than 2,500 varieties of the flower that has been Florence's sym-bol since 1251. The Giardino delle Rose (Rose Garden) on the terraces below the piazza is also in full swing May and June.

③⑧ San Miniato al Monte. This church, like the Baptistery, is a fine exam-ple of Romanesque architecture and one of the oldest churches in Flo-rence, dating from the 11th century. The lively green-and-white marble facade has a 12th-century mosaic topped by a gilded bronze eagle, em-blem of San Miniato's sponsors, the Calimala (Wool Merchant's Guild). Inside are a 13th-century inlaid marble floor and apse mosaic. Artist Spinello Aretino covered the walls of the **Sagrestia** with frescoes of the life of St. Benedict. The adjacent **Cappella del Cardinale del Portogallo** (Chapel of the Portuguese Cardinal) is one of the richest Renaissance works in Florence. Built to hold the tomb of a Portuguese cardinal, Prince James of Lusitania, who died young in Florence in 1459, it has a glorious ceiling by Luca della Robbia, a sculptured tomb by Anto-nio Rossellini, and inlaid pavement in multicolor marble. ⊠ *Viale Galileo Galilei, Piazzale Michelangelo,* ☎ *055/2342731.* ⊘ *Daily Apr.–Oct., 8–noon and 2–7, Nov.–Mar., 8–noon and 2:30–6.*

★ ③⑤ Santa Croce. Like the Duomo, this church is Gothic, but also like the Duomo, its facade dates only from the 19th century. The interior is most famous for its art and its tombs. As a burial place, the church is a Flo-rentine pantheon and probably contains more Renaissance-celeb skele-tons than any church in Italy. Among others, the tomb of Michelangelo is immediately to the right as you enter (he is said to have chosen this spot so that the first thing he would see on Judgment Day, when the graves of the dead fly open, would be Brunelleschi's Duomo dome through Santa Croce's open doors); the tomb of Galileo Galilei (1564–1642), who pro-duced evidence that the earth is not the center of the universe (and who was not granted a Christian burial until 100 years after his death be-cause of it), is on the left wall, opposite Michelangelo; the tomb of Nic-colò Machiavelli (1469–1527), the Renaissance political theoretician whose brutally pragmatic philosophy so influenced the Medicis, is halfway down the nave on the right; the grave of Lorenzo Ghiberti, creator of the Gates of Paradise doors to the Baptistery, is halfway down the nave on the left; the tomb of composer Gioacchino Rossini (1792–1868), of "William Tell Overture" fame, is at the end of the nave on the right. The monument to Dante Alighieri (1265–1321), the greatest Italian poet, is a memorial rather than a tomb (he is actually buried in Ravenna); it is on the right wall near the tomb of Michelangelo.

The collection of art within the church and church complex is by far the most important of that in any church in Florence. Historically, the most significant works are probably the Giotto frescoes in the two ad-jacent chapels immediately to the right of the high altar. They illustrate scenes from the lives of St. John the Evangelist and St. John the Bap-tist (in the right-hand chapel) and scenes from the life of St. Francis (in the left-hand chapel). Time has not been kind to them; over the cen-turies, wall tombs were introduced into the middle of them, whitewash and plaster covered them, and in the 19th century they underwent a clumsy restoration. But the reality that Giotto introduced into painting can still be seen. He did not paint beautifully stylized symbols of religion, as the Byzantine style that preceded him prescribed; he instead painted drama—St. Francis surrounded by grieving monks at the very moment of his death. This was a radical shift in emphasis, and it changed the course of art. Before him, the role of painting was to symbolize the attributes of God; after him, it was to imitate life. The style of his work is indeed primitive, compared with later painting, but in the proto-Renaissance of the early 14th century, it caused a sensation that was not equaled for another 100 years. He was, for his time, the equal of both Masaccio and Michelangelo.

Among the church's other highlights are Donatello's *Annunciation,* one of the most tender and eloquent expressions of surprise ever sculpted (on the right wall two-thirds of the way down the nave); Taddeo Gaddi's (circa 1330–1366) 14th-century frescoes illustrating the life of the Virgin, clearly showing the influence of Giotto (in the chapel at the end of the right transept); and Donatello's *Crucifix,* criticized by Brunelleschi for making Christ look like a peasant (in the chapel at the end of the left transept). Outside the church proper, in the **Museo dell'Opera di Santa Croce** off the cloister, is Cimabue's (circa 1240–1302) 13th-century *Triumphal Cross,* badly damaged by the flood of 1966. An epitome of architectural geometry, the **Cappella Pazzi,** at the end of the cloister, is the work of Brunelleschi. ✉ *Piazza Santa Croce 16,* ☎ *055/244619.* ☉ *Church: Apr.–Sept., Mon.–Sat. 8–6:30, Sun. 3–5; Oct.–Mar., Mon.–Sat. 8–12:30 and 3–6:30, Sun. 3–5. Cloister and museum:* 🎫 *4,000 lire.* ☉ *Apr.–Sept., Thurs.–Tues. 10–12:30 and 2:30–6:30; Oct.–Mar., Thurs.–Tues. 10–12:30 and 3–5.*

OFF THE
BEATEN PATH

SINAGOGA – The Synagogue was built around 1874–1882 in a style best defined as an eclectic interpretation of Byzantine-Moorish motifs. The adjacent **Museo Ebraico** charts the history of Florence's Jewish community. Piazza della Repubblica (☞ Centro Storico, *above*) is the site of the Jewish ghetto, where Jews were forced to live from 1571 until 1848; it was torn down in 1885. The only kosher restaurant in Tuscany is next to the synagogue. **Ruth** (✉ Via Farini 2, ☎ 055/2480888), closed Friday dinner, and Saturday lunch, offers inexpensive vegetarian and Mediterranean dishes and a large selection of kosher wines. *Synagogue and museum:* ✉ *Via Farini 4,* ☎ *055/2346654.* 🎫 *6,000 lire.* ☉ *Apr.–Sept., Sun.–Thurs. 10–1 and 2–5, Fri. 10–1; Oct.–Mar., Sun.– Thurs. 10–1 and 2–4, Fri. 10–1.*

DINING

Revised by
Patricia Rucidlo

A typical Tuscan repast starts with an antipasto of *crostini* (grilled bread spread with various savory toppings) or cured meats such as prosciutto *crudo* (cured ham thinly sliced) and *finocchiona* (salami seasoned with fennel). *Primi piatti* (first courses) can consist of local versions of pasta dishes available throughout Italy. Peculiar to Florence, however, are the vegetable-and-bread soups such as *pappa al pomodoro* (bread and tomato soup), ribollita, or, in the summer, a salad called *panzanella* (tomatoes, onions, vinegar, oil, basil, and bread). Before they are eaten, these are often christened with *un "C" d'olio,* a generous C-shape drizzle of the sumptuous local olive oil.

Unparalleled among the *secondi piatti* (main courses) is *bistecca alla fiorentina*—a thick slab of local Chianina beef, grilled over charcoal, seasoned with olive oil, salt, and pepper, and served rare. *Trippa alla fiorentina* (tripe stewed with tomato sauce) and *arista* (roast loin of pork seasoned with rosemary) are also regional specialties, as are many other roasted meats that go especially well with Chianti. A secondo is usually served with a *contorno* (side dish) of white beans, sautéed greens, or artichokes in season, all of which can be drizzled with more of that wonderful olive oil.

Dining hours are earlier here than in Rome, starting at 1 for the midday meal and at 8 for dinner. Many of Florence's restaurants are small, so reservations are a must.

CATEGORY	COST*
$$$$	over 110,000 lire
$$$	80,000–110,000 lire
$$	35,000–80,000 lire
$	under 35,000 lire

Prices are per person, for a three-course meal, including house wine and taxes.

Centro Storico

$$ ✕ **Buca dell'Orafo.** A Florentine *buca*, meaning hole-in-the-wall, Buca dell'Orafo is set in the cellar of a former goldsmith's shop near the Ponte Vecchio. It's the perfect place to lunch either before or after visiting the Uffizi, as it's just around the corner. The food is typical Tuscan. Here you're paying for the atmosphere and the location; it's a shame the place doesn't take plastic. ⊠ *Via dei Girolami 28,* ☎ *055/213619. No credit cards. Closed Sun.–Mon. and Aug.*

$$ ✕ **Il Latini.** As soon as you spy the primary decoration pieces—innumerable slabs of prosciutto on the bone—you realize you're in hog lover's heaven. This is not the place to come if you're a vegetarian. Portions are big—you'll think you won't be able to eat it all. But you will. This place packs them in, tourists and locals alike, with good reason. Meat dishes don't get much better than this. Reservations are advised. It's around the side of Palazzo Rucellai. ⊠ *Via dei Palchetti 6/r,* ☎ *055/ 210916. AE, DC, MC, V. Closed Mon. and 15 days in Aug.*

$$ ✕ **Osteria n. 1.** No pretence, just excellent food, is the draw to this romantic restaurant nestled in the ground floor of an old palazzo in the historic center. The food is expertly handled—try, for example, their delicate artichoke ravioli with olive oil and Parmesan or their *crespelle*, a little package of pasta stuffed with zucchini puree and topped with a subtle walnut sauce, before moving on to any of their grilled specialties. ⊠ *Via del Moro 22,* ☎ *055/284897. AE, DC, MC, V. Closed Sun. and 15 days in Aug. No lunch Mon.*

San Lorenzo and Beyond

$$$ ✕ **Taverna del Bronzino.** Want to have an elegant meal in a 16th-century Renaissance artist's studio? Though it was actually the studio of Santi di Tito, a student of Bronzino, the restaurant—with high ceilings and traces of frescoes on the walls—retains the master's name. The food is classic Tuscan and superb, the presentation often dramatic; try the *carpaccio di cervo* (cured, thinly sliced venison dribbled with olive oil). The only thing better than the food and outstanding service is the wine list, which has solid, affordable choices. Reservations are advised, especially for eating in the wine cellar's only table. ⊠ *Via delle Ruote 27/r,* ☎ *055/495220. AE, DC, MC, V. Closed Sun. and Aug.*

$$ ✕ **Alfredo.** This place is just on the other side of Piazza della Libertà, which happily puts it somewhat off the beaten tourist path. The decor is simple—white walls and white tablecloths—and the atmosphere lively. The cooks spin a fine pizza, but even better are the primi and

secondi—some are atypical Tuscan and pleasant surprises. There's also plenty on the menu for a vegetarian to eat, and even hard-core meat lovers will rave about the *sformato con tartufo* (a type of soufflé with truffles). You'd be wise to reserve ahead. ⊠ *Viale Don Giovanni Minzoni 3/r,* ☎ *055/578291. AE, DC, MC, V. Closed Mon. and 15 days in Aug.*

$$ ✕ **Toscano.** A small table attractively set in a show window identifies this restaurant, about five minutes from Palazzo Medici-Riccardi. It lives up to its name in ambience and cuisine. The cold-cuts counter at the entrance, terra-cotta tile floors, and beamed ceilings typify a Tuscan trattoria, but the pink tablecloths, arty photos on the walls, and a touch of creative cuisine take it out of the ordinary. The kitchen prides itself on top-quality meat; this is the place to try *tagliata* (thin slivers of rare beef) or *spezzatino peposo* (beef stew with lots of black pepper and a wine sauce). ⊠ *Via Guelfa 70/r,* ☎ *055/215475. AE, DC, MC, V. Closed Tues. and Aug.*

$ ✕ **Mario.** Clean and classic, this family-run trattoria on the corner of Piazza del Mercato near San Lorenzo offers genuine Florentine atmosphere and cooking, with no frills, but under a wooden ceiling dated 1536. It's open for lunch only. ⊠ *Via Rosina 2/r (Piazza del Mercato Centrale),* ☎ *055/218550. Reservations not accepted. No credit cards. Closed Sun. No dinner.*

Santa Maria Novella to the Arno

$$$ ✕ **Harry's Bar.** You don't come to Harry's for the food but for the swank atmosphere—it's cozy, with a tiny bar, white tablecloths, and plenty of well-heeled customers captured in rosy lighting. Enjoy a Bellini (peach nectar and Prosecco) or, better yet, Harry's absolutely superb martini before tucking into the menu. The perfectly bilingual staff are more than affable. But don't expect any culinary punches: This is nursery food for the privileged set, and you can eat better elsewhere in Florence. That said, the cheeseburger might be the best on this side of the Atlantic. Reservations are advised. ⊠ *Lungarno Vespucci 22/r,* ☎ *055/2396700. AE, MC, V. Closed Sun. and Dec. 15–Jan. 8.*

$$$ ✕ **Il Cestello.** So named because it is across the Arno from the church of San Frediano in Cestello, the restaurant is part of the Excelsior Hotel. A huge Florentine hearth keynotes the Renaissance tone of the dining room decor, but it's really the only cozy element in an otherwise formal atmosphere. The Tuscan-based menu features delicious risotto and pasta dishes, a rare selection of seafood, and an ever-changing sampling of whatever is fresh from the market. Reservations are advised. ⊠ *Excelsior Hotel, Piazza Ognissanti 3,* ☎ *055/264201. Jacket and tie. AE, DC, MC, V.*

$$ ✕ **Cantinetta Antinori.** Here's the place to lunch after a rough morning of shopping on Via Tornabuoni, Florence's swankiest street. But be prepared to pay: Cantinetta Antinori is the place where Florentine ladies (and men) who lunch come to see and be seen. The food is as elegant as the 15th-century palazzo in which it is served. Try the crostini *di lardo* (toasted bread with hot pork fat) and the *insalata di gamberoni e gamberetti con carciofi freschi* (shrimp salad with raw shaved artichokes). ⊠ *Piazza Antinori 3,* ☎ *055/292234. AE, DC, MC, V. Closed weekends and Aug.*

$$ ✕ **Le Fonticine.** This restaurant is a welcome oasis in a neighborhood
★ near the train station not noted for its fine dining options. Here you dine very well since this place combines the best of two Italian cuisines: Owner Silvano Bruci is from Tuscany and his wife Gianna from Emilia-Romagna. Start with the mixed vegetable antipasto plate, or the delicately deep-fried cauliflower balls before moving on to their *osso buco*

40

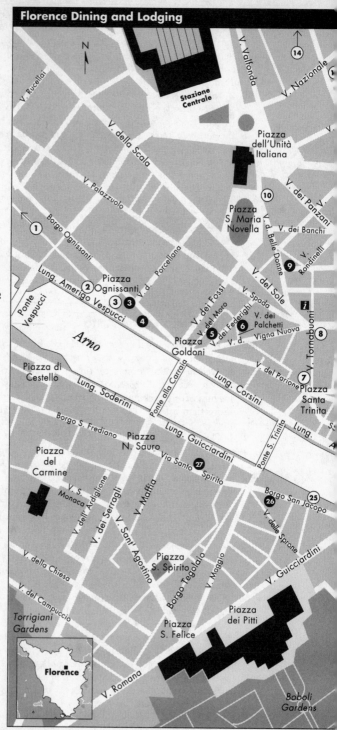

Florence Dining and Lodging

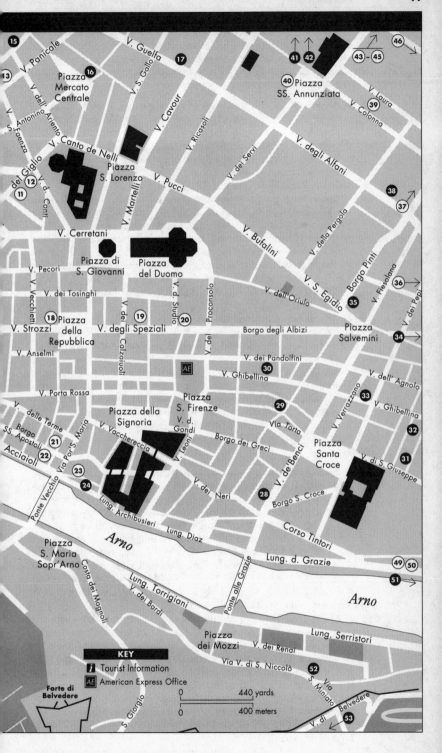

15
V. Panicale
13
V. S. Antonino
V. dell' Ariento
V. Faenza
Piazza Mercato Centrale **16**
V. Guelfa
V. S. Gallo
17
V. Canto de Nelli
del Giglio
V. d. Conti
12
11
Piazza S. Lorenzo
V. Martelli
V. Cavour
V. Ricasoli
V. Pucci
40 Piazza SS. Annunziata
41 **42**
43–**45**
46
V. Laura
V. Colonna
39
V. degli Alfani
V. dei Servi
V. Cerretani
Piazza di S. Giovanni
Piazza del Duomo
V. della Pergola
38
37
V. Pecori
V. Vecchietti
V. dei Tosinghi
18 Piazza della Repubblica
V. Strozzi
V. Anselmi
V. degli Speziali **19**
V. dei Calzaiuoli
V. d. Studio
20
V. del Proconsolo
V. Bufalini
V. dell'Oriolo
V. S. Egidio
Borgo Pinti
V. Fiesolana
V. de' Pepi
36
35
Piazza Salvemini
34
Borgo degli Albizi
V. dei Pandolfini
V. Ghibellina
30
Piazza S. Firenze
V. d. Gondi
V. Leoni
V. dell' Agnolo
33
V. Ghibellina
32
AE
V. Porta Rossa
V. delle Terme
Borgo SS. Apostoli
21
22
Acciaioli
V. Por S. Maria
V. Vacchereccia
Piazza della Signoria
23
24
Ponte Vecchio
Lung. Archibusieri
Lung. Diaz
Borgo dei Greci
V. dei Neri
28
Via Torta
V. de' Benci
V. Verrazzano
Piazza Santa Croce
V. di S. Giuseppe
31
Borgo S. Croce
29
Corso Tintori
Arno
Piazza S. Maria Sopr'Arno
Costa dei Magnoli
Lung. Torrigiani
V. dei Bardi
Ponte alle Grazie
Lung. d. Grazie
49 **50**
51
Arno
Lung. Serristori
Piazza dei Mozzi
V. dei Renai
Via V. di S. Niccolò
52
Via S. Miniato
53
Belvedere
V. di

Forte di Belvedere

S. Giorgio

KEY
i Tourist Information
AE American Express Office

0 ——— 440 yards
0 ——— 400 meters

alla fiorentina (veal shanks in a hearty tomato sauce). The interior of the restaurant, filled with the Brucis' painting collection, is as cheery as the food is satisfying. ⊠ *Via Nazionale 79/r,* ☎ *055/282106. AE, DC, MC, V. Closed Sun.–Mon. and July 25–Aug. 25.*

Oltrarno and Santo Spirito

\$\$ ✕ **Angiolino.** Though some fans have complained recently that standards are slipping here, there's no arguing with their arista served with fresh herbs, or their *acquacotta* (literally cooked water, a delicious Tuscan onion, bread, and tomato peasant soup). This and other good stuff is served in a room with wood-burning stove by a thoroughly wonderful waitstaff. ⊠ *Via Santo Spirito 36/r,* ☎ *055/240 618. AE, DC, MC, V. Closed Mon., and last 3 wks in July. No dinner Sun.*

\$\$ ✕ **Cammillo.** At this bustling trattoria just on the other side of the Arno, many languages are spoken, English included since the place is no longer a secret to travelers. The restaurant has been in the capable hands of the Masiero family for three generations, and in its present location since 1945. Their farm in the country supplies the olive oil and wines for the restaurant, which go along nicely with the wide-ranging list of Tuscan specialties. Reservations are advised. ⊠ *Borgo San Jacopo 57/r,* ☎ *055/212427. AE, DC, MC, V. Closed Wed., 15 days in Aug., and 15 days Dec.–Jan.*

\$ ✕ **Osteria Antica Mescita San Niccolò.** This bustling osteria is directly next to the church of San Niccolò, and if you sit in the lower part of the restaurant, you will find yourself in what was once a chapel dating from the 11th century. Such subtle but dramatic background plays off nicely with the food, which is simple Tuscan style at its very best. The *pollo con limone* is tasty little pieces of chicken in a fragrant lemon-scented broth. In the winter, try the *spezzatino di cinghiale con aromi* (wild boar stew with herbs). Reservations are advised. ⊠ *Via San Niccolò 60/r,* ☎ *055/2342836. No credit cards. Closed Sun.*

Santa Croce

\$\$\$\$ ✕ **Enoteca Pinchiorri.** A sumptuous Renaissance palace with high, fres-
★ coed ceilings and bouquets in silver vases is the setting for this restaurant, one of the most expensive in Italy, and also considered one of the best. The enoteca part of the name comes from its former incarnation as a wineshop under owner Giorgio Pinchiorri, who still keeps a stock of vintage bottles in the cellar. A variety of fish, game, and meat dishes are always on the menu, along with splendid pasta combinations like the *ignudi*—ricotta and cheese dumplings with a lobster and coxcomb fricassee. ⊠ *Via Ghibellina 87,* ☎ *055/242777. Reservations essential. Jacket and tie. AE, MC, V. Closed Sun., Aug., and 1 wk in Dec. No lunch Mon. or Wed.*

\$\$\$ ✕ **Alle Murate.** This sophisticated restaurant features creative versions of classic Tuscan dishes—*anatra alle erbe* (duck with herb and orange sauce)—but also southern Italian specialties such as lasagna *con mozzarella e pomodoro fresco* (with mozzarella and fresh tomatoes). The main dining room has a rich, uncluttered look, with warm wood floors and paneling and soft lights. In a smaller adjacent room called the *vineria,* table settings are simpler, the menu more limited. Since the Murate is known for its wine list, this is the place to splurge on a good bottle. ⊠ *Via Ghibellina 52/r,* ☎ *055/240618. AE, DC, MC, V. Closed Mon. No lunch.*

\$\$\$ ✕ **Cibrèo.** The food here is fantastic, from the first bite of seamless,
★ creamy crostini *di fegatini* (savory Tuscan chicken liver spread on crostini) to the last bite of one of the meltingly good desserts. If you thought you'd never try tripe—let alone like it—this is the place to lay

any doubts to rest: The *trippa in insalata* (cold tripe salad) with parsley and garlic is an epiphany. So is just about everything else on the menu. It's best to construe owner Fabio Picchi's adamantly advising his customers on the A to Zs of Italian eating as a manifestation of his enthusiasm about his food—which is warranted as he has created some of the best, most creative food in town. ⊠ *Via A. del Verrocchio 87,* ☎ *055/2341100. Reservations essential. AE, DC, MC, V. Closed Sun.–Mon., July 25–Sept. 5, and Dec. 31–Jan. 7.*

$$ ✗ **Caffè Concerto.** A short taxi ride from city center takes you to this veranda-style restaurant, all glass and polished wood alongside the Arno. The excellent, creative Tuscan cuisine—and equally fine Tuscan wine list—draws visiting celebrities and a steady Florentine clientele. ⊠ *Lungarno Colombo 7,* ☎ *055/677377. Reservations essential. AE, DC, MC, V. Closed Sun.*

$$ ✗ **La Giostra.** The clubby La Giostra, which means "carousel" in Ital-
★ ian, serves unusually good pastas requiring some explanation from Dimitri or Soldano, the owner's good-looking twin sons. In perfect English they'll describe a favorite dish, delicious *gnocchetti alla tibetana* (little potato dumpling morsels with mint and basil pesto). Try the *spianata* (slices of thinly shaved beef baked quickly and served with fresh rosemary and sage). Leave room for dessert: This might be the only show in town with a sublime tiramisu and a wonderfully gooey Sacher torte. ⊠ *Borgo Pinti 12/r,* ☎ *055/241341. AE, DC, MC, V.*

$$ ✗ **Maximilian.** "This is not fast food" appears on the menu outside the door of this intimate trattoria (make reservations) with long narrow tables and white walls. Until recently, Adele, the chef-owner, was the sole employee. Though she has since hired a waitress, the service is still relaxed—slow, in fact. All complaints immediately dissipate with the first bite. The risotto *al tartufo nero* (with black truffle sauce) is a creamy, heavenly perfumed concoction. The menu is rich with vegetarian primi and secondi, a rarity in Florentine restaurants. ⊠ *Via degli Alfani 10/ r,* ☎ *055/2478080. AE, DC, MC, V. Closed Mon. and 3 wks in Aug.*

$$ ✗ **Pallottino.** With its tiled floor, photograph-filled walls, and wooden tables, Pallottino is the quintessential Tuscan trattoria, with hearty, heartwarming classics like pappa al pomodoro and *peposo alla toscana* (a beef stew laced with black pepper). Their lunch special could be, at 13,000 lire, the best bargain in town. ⊠ *Via Isola delle Stinche 1/r,* ☎ *055/289573. AE, DC, MC, V. Closed Mon. and Aug. 1–20.*

$ ✗ **Baldovino.** This lively, brightly hued trattoria across the street from the church of Santa Croce is the brainchild of David Gardner and Catherine Storrar, expat Scots. In addition to turning out fine, thin-crusted pizzas, Baldovino offers some tasty antipasti (try the plate of smoked salmon and tuna) and *insalatone* (big salads). They also serve various pasta dishes and grilled meat til the wee hours. Save room for dessert; they're all winners. If you're pressed for time, duck into their lovely enoteca just across the street for a quick bite to eat and a glass of wine. ⊠ *Via di S. Giuseppe 22/r,* ☎ *055/241 773. AE, DC, MC, V. Closed Mon. and last wk Nov.–1st wk Dec.*

$ ✗ **La Maremmana.** Owners Benedetto Silenu and Sergio Loria have
★ owned this restaurant for the past 18 years, and their chef has been in place for the same amount of time. It shows. The space is light and cheery—with white walls, tile floor, and pink tablecloths. Dead center is a mixed antipasto table, with a formidable array of choices: cold squid salad, various marinated vegetables, fried whole anchovies, marinated salmon, and more. The spaghetti *alle vongole* (with tiny clams) is a winner, as are their grilled meats. ⊠ *Via dei Macci 77/r,* ☎ *055/ 241226. DC, MC, V. Closed Sun. and Aug.*

$ ✗ **Osteria de'Benci.** Just a few minutes from Santa Croce, this charming osteria serves some of the most eclectic food in Florence at remarkably

low prices. Try the lively spaghetti *degli eretici* (of the heretics), in a
fresh tomato sauce laced with fresh herbs and a dash of *peperoncino*
(hot chile peppers). When it's warm, you can dine outside with a view
of the 13th-century tower belonging to the prestigious Alberti family.
The English-speaking staff shouldn't scare you off: Florentines *do* eat
here. ⊠ *Via de' Benci 11/13/r,* ☎ *055/2344923. AE, DC, MC, V. Closed
Sun.*

Pizzerias

Many pizza aficionados believe that the best pizza is town can be
found at **Il Pizziauolo** (⊠ Via dei Macci 113/r, ☎ 055/241171). In the
Oltrarno, **Borgo Antico** (⊠ Piazza S. Spirito 6/r, ☎ 055/210437) serves
up a good pizza and other trattoria fare. Others insist that the best pizza
in town can be had at **I Tarocchi** (⊠ Via de' Renai 12/14r, ☎ 055/
2343912), also in the Oltrarno.

Enoteche

Just a hop, skip, and a jump from Orsanmichele in the heart of the historic center, the little enoteca (wine bar) **I Fratellini** (⊠ Via dei Cimatori
38/r, San Giovanni, ☎ 055/2396096) has been around since 1875. It sells
wines by the glass and has a list of 27 sandwiches—try the pecorino with
sun-dried tomatoes or the spicy wild boar *salame* with goat cheese if you're
feeling brave. **Le Volpi e l'Uva** (⊠ Piazza de' Rossi 1, Santa Maria
Novella, ☎ 055/2398132), closed Sunday, just off Piazza Santa Trinita,
is an oenophile's dream: They pour significant wines by the glass and
serve equally impressive cheeses and little sandwiches to accompany them.

Caffè

Caffès in Italy serve not only coffee concoctions and pastries, but also
sweets, drinks, and *panini* (sandwiches), and some offer hot pasta and
lunch dishes. They are usually open from early in the morning to late,
and closed all day Sunday.

All bars in Italy ought to be like **Caffetteria Piansa** (⊠ Borgo Pinti
18/r, Santa Croce, ☎ 055/2342362), great for breakfast, lunch, and
drinks at night. After looking at the frescoes in Santissima Annunziata, cross the piazza towards the elegant **Robiglio** (⊠ Via dei Servi 112/
r, San Giovanni, ☎ 055/212784). **Gilli** (⊠ Piazza della Repubblica 39/
r, Centro Storico, ☎ 055/21986), closed Tuesday, has been a caffé, with
all the amenities, since 1733. Try any of their chocolates. **Giacosa** (⊠
Via Tornabuoni 83/r, Santa Maria Novella, ☎ 055/2396226), in the
heart of Florence's ritzy shopping district, serves fancy sandwiches and
sweets. The Negroni (a bombshell of a drink: gin, Campari, and sweet
vermouth) was supposedly invented here before WWII.

Gelaterie and Pasticcerie

Though the *pasticceria* (bakery) **Dolci e Dolcezze** (⊠ Piazza C. Beccaria 8/r, Santa Croce, ☎ 055/2345458), closed Monday, is somewhat
off the beaten path, if you walk down colorful Borgo La Croce, you'll
be rewarded with the prettiest and tastiest cakes, sweets, and tarts in
town. **Gran Caffè** (⊠ Piazza San Marco 11/r, San Giovanni, ☎ 055/
215833) is down the street from the Accademia, so it's a perfect stop
for a marvelous panino or sweet, while raving about the majesty of
Michelangelo's *David*. Most people seem to think **Vivoli** (⊠ Via Isola
delle Stinche 7, Santa Croce, ☎ 055/292334) is the best gelateria in
town. What with their *cioccolata con caffè* (chocolate ice cream heavily dosed with coffee), they're probably right.

Salumerie

Salumerie are gourmet food shops strong on fine fresh ingredients, such as meats and cheeses, and are great for picking up the fixings for a picnic lunch. If you find yourself in the Oltrarno and hungry for lunch or a snack, drop into **Azzarri Delicatesse** (⊠ Borgo S. Jacopo 27/b–27/c, Santo Spirito, ☎ 055/2381714), closed Sunday. They make sandwiches, or you can get the fixings to go. Their list of cheeses, some of which come from France, is rather impressive. Looking for some cheddar cheese to pile in your panino? **Pegna** (⊠ Via dello Studio 8, San Giovanni, ☎ 055/282701, 055/282702), closed Sunday and Saturday afternoon, has been selling Italian food and non-Italian food since 1860. **Perini** (⊠ Mercato Centrale, enter at Via dell'Aretino, near San Lorenzo, San Giovanni, ☎ 055/2398306), closed Sunday, sells everything from prosciutto and mixed meats to sauces for pasta and a wide assortment of antipasti. It's probably the nicest little food shop in all of Florence—bring a lot of money.

LODGING

Florence's importance not only as a tourist city but as a convention center and the site of the Pitti fashion collections throughout the year has guaranteed a variety of accommodations, many in former villas and palazzi. However, these very factors mean that, except during the winter, reservations are a must. If you do find yourself in Florence with no reservations, go to the **Consorzio ITA** office (⊠ Stazione Centrale, ☎ 055/212245, FAX 055/2381226).

CATEGORY	COST*
$$$$	over 450,000 lire
$$$	300,000–450,000 lire
$$	190,000–300,000 lire
$	under 190,000 lire

Prices are for a double room, including service and tax.

Centro Storico

$$$ 🏨 **Brunelleschi.** Architects united a Byzantine tower, a medieval church,
★ and a later building in a stunning structure in the very heart of Renaissance Florence to make this a truly unique hotel. There's even a museum displaying the ancient Roman foundations and pottery shards found during restoration. Medieval stone walls and brick arches contrast pleasantly with the plush, contemporary decor. The comfortable, soundproof bedrooms are done in coordinated patterns and soft colors; the ample bathrooms feature beige travertine marble. ⊠ *Piazza Sant'Elisabetta (Via dei Calzaiuoli), 50122, ☎ 055/290311, FAX 055/219653. 96 rooms, 7 junior suites. Restaurant, bar, meeting rooms, parking (fee). CP. AE, DC, MC, V.*

$$$ 🏨 **Hermitage.** Comfortable and charming are suitable adjectives for this hotel occupying the top six floors of a palazzo next to Ponte Vecchio and the Uffizi. Bright breakfast rooms, a flowered roof terrace, and well-lighted bedrooms have the decor and atmosphere of a well-kept Florentine home. Double glazing and air-conditioning sustain the relaxing ambience. (The hotel has an elevator at the top of a short flight of stairs from the street.) ⊠ *Vicolo Marzio 1 (Piazza del Pesce, Ponte Vecchio), 50122, ☎ 055/287216, FAX 055/212208. 28 rooms. Breakfast room. CP. MC, V.*

$$ 🏨 **Pendini.** The atmosphere of an old-fashioned Florentine pensione is intact at this find in the absolute center of Florence. Public rooms are delightful, complete with a portrait of Signora Pendini, who founded the hotel in 1879, and early 19th-century antiques or reproductions throughout. Most bedrooms have brass or walnut beds, pretty floral wallpaper, and pastel carpeting; baths are modern. Many rooms can accommodate extra beds. Rates are low for the category, and off-season rates are a real bargain. ⊠ *Via Strozzi 2, 50123,* ☎ *055/211170,* FAX *055/281807. 42 rooms. CP. AE, DC, MC, V.*

$$ 🏨 **Torre Guelfa.** Enter this hidden hotel through an immense wooden door on a narrow street, continue through an iron gate, and up a few steps where an elevator will take you to the third floor of this palazzo where the 12 guest rooms are. A few more steps will take you into the 13th-century Florentine *torre* (tower) itself. Each guest room is different, some with canopied beds, some with balconies. The Torre Guelfa once protected the fabulously wealthy Acciaiuoli family. Now it's one of the best-located small hotels in Florence, where you can have breakfast or sunset drinks on a rooftop that offers unmatched Florentine panoramas. ⊠ *Borgo S.S. Apostoli 8, 50123,* ☎ *055/2396338,* FAX *055/2398577. 12 rooms. Bar, breakfast room. CP. AE, MC, V.*

$ 🏨 **Albergo Firenze.** A block from the Duomo, this hotel is in one of the oldest piazzas in Florence. In fact, it is said that Dante's wife lived in one of the medieval houses in the piazza. The hotel is clean and bright, with a large lobby area and breakfast room. No frills but adequate furnishings are found in the guest rooms, some of which have two bathrooms. ⊠ *Piazza Donati 4, 50122,* ☎ *055/214203,* FAX *055/212370. 57 rooms. Breakfast room. CP. No credit cards.*

$ 🏨 **Alessandra.** The location, a block from the Ponte Vecchio, and clean, ample rooms make this a good choice. The English-speaking staff is friendly and helpful. ⊠ *Borgo Santi Apostoli 17, 50123,* ☎ *055/283438,* FAX *055/210619. 25 rooms, 9 without bath. CP. AE, MC, V. Closed Dec. 15–26.*

$ 🏨 **Bellettini.** You couldn't ask for anything more central; this small hotel
★ is on three floors (the top floor has two nice rooms with a view) of a palazzo near the Duomo. The cordial family management takes good care of guests, providing a relaxed atmosphere and attractive public rooms with a scattering of antiques. Breakfast, featuring homemade cakes, and air-conditioning are included in the low room rate. The good-size rooms have Venetian or Tuscan provincial decor; bathrooms are bright and modern. ⊠ *Via dei Conti 7, 50123,* ☎ *055/213561,* FAX *055/283551. 28 rooms. Bar, parking (fee). CP. AE, DC, MC, V.*

$ 🏨 **Burchianti.** This hotel is on the first floor of a regal 15th-century palace in the center of Florence, with large, traditionally decorated rooms, many with frescoes and trompe l'oeil images on the walls, and pretty flowers painted on the wooden ceilings. Most of the 12 rooms have showers and sinks and many have complete baths. Some rooms are near busy streets so there is considerable noise, but this is still a special hotel with a glorious Renaissance feeling if you're looking for a bargain. ⊠ *Via del Giglio 6, 50123,* ☎ *055/212796. 12 rooms. CP. No credit cards.*

San Lorenzo and Beyond

$$ 🏨 **Porta Faenza.** The 12th-century medieval well discovered during renovations has now become a focal point in the lobby. Two small pensiones were combined and a ground floor added to create this new hotel, which offers good value in spacious rooms decorated in Florentine style. The friendly Italian-Canadian owners extend lots of little touches and services, including a no-smoking floor and breakfast room, baby-sitting, modern bathrooms, and an E-mail station. ⊠ *Via Faenza 77, 50123,* ☎ *055/284119,* FAX *055/210101. 25 rooms. Parking (fee). CP. AE, DC, MC, V.*

Near Piazza San Marco and Beyond

$$–$$$ ☆ ★ **Loggiato dei Serviti.** This hotel was not designed by Brunelleschi, Florence's architectural genius, but it might as well have been. A mirror image of the architect's famous Ospedale degli Innocenti across the way, the Loggiato is tucked away on one of the city's quietest and loveliest squares. Occupying a 16th-century former monastery, the building was originally a refuge for traveling priests. Vaulted ceilings, tasteful furnishings (some antique), canopy beds, and rich fabrics make this a find if you want to get the feel of Florence in an attractively spare Renaissance building while enjoying modern creature comforts. ☒ *Piazza Santissima Annunziata 3, 50122,* ☎ *055/289592,* ℻ *055/289595. 29 rooms. Bar, breakfast room, parking (fee). CP. AE, DC, MC, V.*

$$ ☆ ★ **Morandi alla Crocetta.** Near Piazza Santissima Annunziata, this is a charming and distinguished residence in which guests are made to feel like privileged friends of the family. It is close to the sights but very quiet, in a former monastery, and is furnished comfortably in the classic style of a gracious Florentine home. The Morandi is not only an exceptional hotel but also a good value. It's very small, so try to book well in advance. ☒ *Via Laura 50, 50121,* ☎ *055/2344747,* ℻ *055/ 2480954. 10 rooms. CP. AE, DC, MC, V.*

Santa Maria Novella to the Arno

$$$$ ☆ ★ **Excelsior.** Traditional old-world charm finds a regal setting at the Excelsior, built as a convent in the 13th century and once the private residence of Josephine Bonaparte. The neo-Renaissance palace has painted wooden ceilings, stained glass, and acres of Oriental carpets strewn over marble floors in the public rooms. The opulence of 19th-century Florentine antiques and fabrics is set off by charming old prints of the city and long mirrors of the Empire style. ☒ *Piazza Ognissanti 3, 50123,* ☎ *055/264201,* ℻ *055/210278. 168 rooms. Restaurant, piano bar. EP. AE, DC, MC, V.*

$$$$ ☆ **Grand.** Across the piazza from the Excelsior, this Florentine classic provides all the luxurious amenities of its sister. Here most rooms and public areas are decorated in sumptuous Renaissance style with rich fabrics in distinctive Florentine style. Guests can choose between imperial- or Florentine-style rooms, many with frescoes or canopied beds. Baths are all marble. A few rooms have balconies overlooking the Arno. ☒ *Piazza Ognissanti 1, 50123,* ☎ *055/288781,* ℻ *055/217400. 107 rooms. Restaurant, bar, parking (fee). EP. AE, DC, MC, V.*

$$$ ☆ **Beacci Tornabuoni.** This is perhaps *the* classic Florentine pensione. Set in a 14th-century palazzo, it has old-fashioned style and just enough modern comfort to keep you happy. The food is good and can be served in the dining room, the garden, or in the rooms, most of which have views of the red-tile roofs in the neighboring downtown area. ☒ *Via Tornabuoni 3, 50123,* ☎ *055/212645,* ℻ *055/283594. 28 rooms. Restaurant, bar. CP, MAP. AE, DC, MC, V.*

$$$ ☆ **Kraft.** The efficient and comfortable Kraft is modern, but it has many period-style rooms, all with polished wooden floors, some with balconies, and a rooftop terrace café. Its location near the Teatro Comunale (also next to the U.S. consulate) gives it a clientele from the music world. ☒ *Via Solferino 2, 50123,* ☎ *055/284273,* ℻ *055/2398267. 75 rooms, 5 junior suites. Restaurant, bar, pool, parking (fee). EP. AE, DC, MC, V.*

$$ ☆ **La Residenza.** On Florence's fanciest shopping street, on the upper floors of a restored 15th-century building, La Residenza has character and comfort. The roof garden and adjacent sitting room are added attractions. Paintings and etchings add interest to the rooms, which have soundproofing and satellite TV. ☒ *Via Tornabuoni 8, 50123,* ☎

055/218684, FAX *055/284197. 24 rooms, 4 without bath. Restaurant, bar, parking (fee). CP, MAP. AE, DC, MC, V.*

$ 🏨 **Le Vigne.** At this small hotel on one of Florence's most beautiful and central squares, the new owners have created the warm atmosphere of a private home. Complimentary afternoon tea and homemade breakfast jams and cakes are on offer, in addition to many other amenities such as a play area for children and an Internet connection. The spacious, air-conditioned rooms are furnished in 19th-century Florentine style. The caring management and reasonable rates make this a very special place. ✉ *Piazza Santa Maria Novella 24, 50123,* ☎ *055/ 294449,* FAX *055/2302263. 25 rooms. EP. AE, DC, MC, V.*

$ 🏨 **Nuova Italia.** Near the train station and within walking distance of the sights, this hotel is run by a genial English-speaking family. It has a homey atmosphere; rooms are clean and simply furnished and have air-conditioning and triple-glazed windows to ensure restful nights. Some rooms can accommodate extra beds. Low bargain rates include breakfast. ✉ *Via Faenza 26, 50123,* ☎ *055/268430,* FAX *055/210941. 20 rooms. Parking (fee). CP. AE, DC, MC, V.*

Oltrarno

$$$$ 🏨 **Grand Hotel Villa Cora.** Built near the Boboli Gardens in 1750, the Villa Cora retains the opulence of the 18th and 19th centuries. The decor of its remarkable public and private rooms runs the gamut from neoclassical to rococo and even Moorish, and reflects the splendor of such former guests as the Empress Eugénie, wife of Napoleon III, and Madame Von Meck, Tchaikovsky's mysterious benefactress. ✉ *Viale Machiavelli 18, 50125,* ☎ *055/2298451,* FAX *055/229086. 48 rooms. Restaurant, piano bar, pool, parking (fee). CP. AE, DC, MC, V.*

$$$$ 🏨 **Lungarno.** The location couldn't be better—right on the river directly across from the Palazzo Vecchio and the Duomo. Nineteen rooms and suites have private terraces—some big enough for a party—that jut out right over the Arno. Four suites in a 13th-century tower preserve atmospheric details like exposed stone walls and old archways and look out onto a little square with another medieval tower covered in jasmine. The very chic decor approximates a breezily elegant home, with lots of crisp white fabrics trimmed in blue, as well as more than 400 fine paintings and drawings—from Picassos and Cocteaus to important contemporary Italian artists—hung in hallways, bedrooms, even bathrooms. There's more art in the restaurant, with great photographs by Cecil Beaton and others of famous figures like Eleanora Duse and Gabriele D'Annunzio. The lobby bar has a wall of windows and a sea of white couches that makes it one of the nicest places in the city to stop in for a drink, even if you're not staying here. ✉ *Borgo San Jacopo 14, 50125,* ☎ *055/27261,* FAX *268437. 61 rooms, 11 suites. Restaurant, bar, parking (fee). CP. AE, DC, MC, V.*

Santa Croce

$$$$ 🏨 **Plaza Hotel Lucchesi.** Elegant without being ostentatious, this hotel
★ is right on the Arno near Santa Croce. Front bedrooms have views of the river and hills beyond; rear rooms on the top floor have balconies and knockout views of Santa Croce. Spacious, quiet bedrooms (double glazing throughout) are furnished comfortably in mahogany and pastel fabrics against creamy white walls. The roomy, welcoming lounges and piano bar are favorite meeting places for Florentines. ✉ *Lungarno della Zecca Vecchia 38, 50122,* ☎ *055/26236,* FAX *055/ 2480921. 97 rooms. Restaurant, bar. EP. AE, DC, MC, V.*

$$$$ 🏨 **Regency.** In this stylish hotel in a residential district near the synagogue, the noise and crowds of Florence seem far away, though you are less than 10 minutes away from the Accademia and Michelangelo's *David.* The rooms are decorated in richly colored and tasteful fabrics and antique-style furniture faithful to the hotel's 19th-century origins as a private mansion. ⊠ *Piazza Massimo D'Azeglio 3, 50121,* ☎ *055/245247,* 🖷 *055/2346735. 34 rooms. Restaurant, parking (fee). CP. AE, DC, MC, V.*

$$$ 🏨 **J&J.** Away from the crowds, on a quiet street within walking distance of the sights, this unusual hotel is a converted 16th-century monastery. Its large, suitelike rooms are ideal for honeymooners, families, and small groups of friends. Some rooms are on two levels, and all are imaginatively arranged around a central courtyard and decorated with flair. The smaller rooms are more intimate, some opening onto their own little courtyard. The gracious owners chat with guests in the elegant lounge; breakfast is served in a glassed-in Renaissance loggia or in the central courtyard. ⊠ *Via di Mezzo 20, 50121,* ☎ *055/2345005,* 🖷 *055/240282. 20 rooms. Bar. CP. AE, DC, MC, V.*

$$$ 🏨 **Monna Lisa.** Housed in a Renaissance palazzo, the hotel retains its
★ original marble staircase, terra-cotta floors, and painted ceilings. Its rooms still have a rather homey quality, and though on the small side, many have contemplative views of a lovely garden. The ground-floor lounges give you the feel of living in an aristocratic town house. ⊠ *Borgo Pinti 27, 50121,* ☎ *055/2479751,* 🖷 *055/2479755. 30 rooms. Bar. CP. AE, DC, MC, V.*

$$ 🏨 **Ritz.** Set amidst a row of buildings on the Arno, this old hotel has been given new energy by young owners who have worked to give it a comfortable family feeling. They've decorated to make clients feel as if they are guests in a very pretty 19th-century Florentine home with 20th-century amenities. Almost all the rooms have dramatic views of the river or the domed, red-roofed "skyline" of Florence. ⊠ *Lungarno Zecca Vecchia 24, 50122,* ☎ *055/2340650,* 🖷 *055/240863. 30 rooms. Bar, breakfast room. CP. AE, DC, MC, V.*

Fiesole

For exploring information, *see* Side Trips, *below.*

$$$$ 🏨 **Villa San Michele.** The setting for this hideaway is so romantic—nestled in a luxuriant garden—that it once attracted Brigitte Bardot for her honeymoon. The villa was originally a monastery whose facade and loggia have been attributed to Michelangelo. Many of the rooms contain sumptuous statuary, paintings, and whirlpool baths. The restaurant is excellent. This is one of Italy's costliest hotels. ⊠ *Via Doccia 4, Fiesole 50014,* ☎ *055/59451,* 🖷 *055/598734. 41 rooms. Restaurant, piano bar, pool, exercise room. MAP. AE, DC, MC, V. Closed Dec.–mid-Mar.*

$$$ 🏨 **Villa Aurora.** On the main piazza, this attractive hotel takes advantage of its hilltop spot, with beautiful views in many of the rooms, some of which are on two levels with beamed ceilings and balconies. ⊠ *Piazza Mino 39, Fiesole 50014,* ☎ *055/59100,* 🖷 *055/59587. 25 rooms. Bar, restaurant, meeting rooms. EP. AE, MC, DC, V.*

$$ 🏨 **Bencistà.** Below the luxurious Villa San Michele, this hotel has the same tranquil setting and is even two centuries older. The rooms are furnished with antiques, and dinner is included in the price. ⊠ *Via Benedetto da Maiano 4, Fiesole 50014,* ☎ *055/59163,* 🖷 *055/59163. 44 rooms, 12 without bath. Dining room. MAP. No credit cards.*

NIGHTLIFE AND THE ARTS

Nightlife

Unlike the Romans and Milanese, the reserved Florentines do not have a reputation for an active nightlife; however, the following places attract a mixed crowd of Florentines and visitors.

Bars

Rex (⊠ Via Fiesolana 23–25/r, Santa Croce, ☎ 055/2480331) has a hip, trendy atmosphere and an arty clientele. June to September, Rex moves its operations to the courtyard of **Le Murate** (⊠ Via Ghibellina), a former Renaissance convent and 19th-century prison. **Robin Hood's Tavern** (⊠ Via dell'Oriuolo 58/r, Santa Croce, ☎ 055/244579) is the place to come when you're craving a dose of English beer, English chatter, and formidable plates of Buffalo chicken wings, of all things. **Sant'Ambrogio Caffè** (⊠ Piazza Sant'Ambrogio 7–8/r, Santa Croce, ☎ 055/241035) has outdoor summer seating with a view of an 11th-century church (Sant'Ambrogio) directly across the street. If you're all dressed up and in the center of town, **Hotel Brunelleschi** (⊠ Piazza Santa Elisabetta 3, Centro Storico, ☎ 055/290311) is the place to come for a quiet cocktail. You'll be sitting among the refurbished remains of a tower dating from the 9th century.

Nightclubs

Most clubs are closed either Sunday or Monday. **Yab** (⊠ Via Sassetti 5/r, ☎ 055/282018) is one of the largest clubs, with a young clientele. **Hurricane Roxy** (⊠ Via Il Prato 58/r, ☎ 055/210399) serves up a light lunch during the day, but in the evening there's a deejay, good music, and a welcoming atmosphere. **Space Electronic** (⊠ Via Palazzuolo 37, ☎ 055/293082) has two floors with karaoke upstairs, and an enormous disco downstairs. A less frenetic alternative is **Jackie O'** (⊠ Via Erta Canina 24, ☎ 055/2344904).

Full Up (⊠ Via della Vigna Vecchia 21/r, ☎ 055/293006) draws a very young clientele. **Meccanò** (⊠ Viale degli Olmi 1, in Le Cascine park, ☎ 055/331371) is a multimedia experience in a high-tech disco with a late-night restaurant. **River Club** (⊠ Lungarno Corsini 8, ☎ 055/282465) has winter-garden decor and a large dance floor.

The Arts

Film

You can find movie listings in *La Nazione,* the daily Florence newspaper. English-language films are shown at the **Cinema Astro** (⊠ Piazza San Simone near Santa Croce). There are two shows every evening, Tuesday through Sunday (closed in July). On Monday, English-language films are offered at the **Odeon** (⊠ Piazza Strozzi) and on Wednesday at the **Goldoni** (⊠ Via Serragli). The **Festival dei Popoli,** held each November, is devoted to documentaries, and is held in the Fortezza da Basso. An international panel of judges gathers in late spring at the Forte di Belvedere for the **Florence Film Festival** to preside over new releases.

Music

The **Maggio Musicale Fiorentina** series of internationally acclaimed concerts and recitals is held in the Teatro Comunale (⊠ Corso Italia 16, ☎ 055/2779236) from late April through June. From December to early June, there is a concert season of the **Orchestra Regionale Toscana** (⊠ Santo Stefano al Ponte Vecchio church, ☎ 055/210804). **Amici della Musica** organizes concerts at the Teatro della Pergola (⊠ Box office, Via della Pergola 10/r, ☎ 055/2479652).

Opera

Operas are performed in the **Teatro Comunale** (✉ Corso Italia 16, ☎ 055/2779236 or 055/211158) from December through February.

OUTDOOR ACTIVITIES AND SPORTS

Participant Sports

Biking

Bikes are a good way of getting out into the hills, but the scope for biking is limited in town center. **Florence by Bike** (✉ Via della Scala 12/r, ☎ 055/264035) has designed some guided city tours that work quite well. They leave several times a day for one- to three-hour tours of major monuments or for tours with specific themes such as Renaissance Florence or 13th-century Florence. **I Bike Italy** (✉ Borgo degli Albizi 11, ☎ ℻ 055/2342371) offers one-day tours of the Florence countryside. For information on where to rent bicycles, *see* Getting Around *in* Florence A to Z, *below*.

Golf

Golf Club Ugolino (✉ Via Chiantigiana 3, Impruneta, ☎ 055/2301009) is a hilly 18-hole course in the heart of Chianti country just outside town. It is open to the public.

Health Clubs and Gyms

Palestra Riccardi (✉ Borgo Pinti 75, ☎ 055/2478444, 055/2478462), admission daily 20,000 lire, weekly 50,000 lire, has free weights, stretching, aerobics, and body building. **Centro Sportivo Fiorentino Indoor Club** (✉ Via Bardazzi 15, ☎ 055/430275, 430703), admission daily 30,000 lire, weekly 135,000 lire, has all the usual gym amenities plus sauna and pool. The only drawback is that it's far from the city center. **Palestra Gymnasium** (✉ Via Palazzuolo 49/r, ☎ 055/293308), admission daily 20,000 lire, is your basic, run-of-the-mill gym.

Running

Don't even think of running on the skinny city streets, where tour buses and triple-parked Alfa Romeos leave precious little space for pedestrians. Instead, head for **Le Cascine,** the park along the Arno at the western end of the city. You can run to Le Cascine along the Lungarno (stay on the sidewalk), or take Bus 17 from the Duomo. A cinder track lies on the hillside just below **Piazzale Michelangelo,** across the Arno from the city center. The locker rooms are reserved for members, so come ready to run.

Swimming

Bellariva (✉ Lungarno Colombo 6, ☎ 055/677521). **Circolo Tennis alle Cascine** (✉ Viale Visarno 1, ☎ 055/356651). **Costoli** (✉ Viale Paoli, ☎ 055/675744). **Le Pavoniere** (✉ Viale degli Olmi, ☎ 055/367506).

Tennis

Circolo Tennis alle Cascine (✉ Viale Visarno 1, ☎ 055/356651). **Tennis Club Rifredi** (✉ Via Facibeni, ☎ 055/432552). **Il Poggetto** (✉ Via Mercati 24/b, ☎ 055/460127).

Spectator Sport

Soccer

Italians are passionate about *calcio* (soccer), and the Florentines are no exception; indeed, *tifosi* (fans) of the Fiorentina team are fervent supporters. The team plays its home games at the **Stadio Comunale** (Municipal Stadium, ✉ Top of Viale Manfredo Fanti, northeast of the city center). Tickets for all games except those against their biggest rivals—Juventus of Turin and A. C. Milan—are difficult but not impossible to come by. Try the ticket booth **Chiosco degli Sportivi** (⊠ North side of Piazza della Repubblica, ☎ 055/29236388). Games are usually played on Sunday afternoon, from about late August to May. A medieval version of the game, **Calcio Storico,** is played on or around June 24, the feast day of St. John the Baptist, each year by teams dressed in costume representing the six Florence neighborhoods.

SHOPPING

Window shopping in Florence is like visiting an enormous contemporary art gallery, for many of today's greatest Italian artists are fashion designers, and most keep shops in Florence. Except during the two sale seasons (January 7–March 7 and July 10–September 10), Florence is a very expensive shopping city. Discerning shoppers may find bargains in the street markets. Shops are generally open 9–1 and 3:30–7:30 but closed Sunday and Monday morning most of the year. Summer (June–September) hours are usually 9–1 and 4–8, and some shops close Saturday afternoon instead of Monday morning. When looking for addresses of shops, you will see two color-coded numbering systems on each street. The red numbers are commercial addresses and are indicated, for example, as 31/r. The blue or black numbers are residential addresses. Most shops take major credit cards and will ship purchases, but due to possible delays it's wiser to take your purchases with you.

Markets

Those with a tight budget or a sense of adventure may want to take a look at the souvenir stands under the loggia of the **Mercato Nuovo** (⊠ Corner of Via Por San Maria and Via Porta Rossa; ☞ Centro Storico *in* Exploring Florence, *above*), or the clothing and leather goods stalls of the **Mercato di San Lorenzo** in the streets next to the San Lorenzo church. The **Mercato Centrale** (⊠ Piazza del Mercato Centrale; ☞ Michelangelo Country *in* Exploring Florence, *above*) is the huge indoor food market in the midst of the San Lorenzo Market. You can find bargains at the **flea market** on Piazza dei Ciompi on the last Sunday of the month. An **open-air market** is held in Le Cascine park every Tuesday morning.

Shopping Districts

Florence's most elegant shops are concentrated in town center. The fanciest designer shops are mainly on **Via Tornabuoni** and **Via della Vigna Nuova.** The city's largest concentration of antiques shops can be found on **Borgo Ognissanti** and Oltrarno's **Via Maggio.** The **Ponte Vecchio** houses reputable jewelry shops, as it has since the 16th century. The area near **Santa Croce** is the heart of the leather merchants' district.

Specialty Stores

Antiques

At **Alberto Pierini** (⊠ Borgo Ognissanti 22/r, ☎ 055/2398138) the rustic Tuscan furniture is all antique, and much of it dates from the days of the Medicis. Specialties at **Paolo Ventura** (⊠ Borgo Ognissanti 61/r, ☎ 055/214397) are antique ceramics from all periods and places of origin. **Galleria Luigi Bellini** (⊠ Lungarno Soderini 5, Oltrarno, ☎ 055/214031) claims to be Italy's oldest antiques dealer, which may be true, since father Mario Bellini was responsible for instituting Florence's international antiques biennial. **Giovanni Pratesi** (⊠ Via Maggio 13/r,

☎ 055/2396568) specializes in Italian antiques, in this case furniture, with some fine paintings, sculpture, and decorative objects turning up from time to time. Vying with Luigi Bellini as one of Florence's oldest antiques dealers, **Guido Bartolozzi** (✉ Via Maggio 18/r, ☎ 055/215602) deals in predominately period Florentine objects. At **Paolo Paoletti** (✉ Via Maggio 30/r, ☎ 055/214728) look for Florentine antiques with an emphasis on Medici-era objects from the 15th and 16th centuries.

Books and Paper

Pineider (✉ Piazza della Signoria 14/r and Via Tornabuoni 76/r, ☎ 055/284655) now has shops throughout the world, but it began in Florence and still does all its printing here. Personalized stationery and business cards are the mainstay, but the stores also sell fine desk accessories. **Centro Di** (✉ Piazza dei Mozzi 1, Oltrarno, ☎ 055/2342666) publishes art books and exhibition catalogs for some of the most important organizations in Europe. One of Florence's oldest paper-goods stores, **Giannini** (✉ Piazza Pitti 37/r, Oltrarno, ☎ 055/212621) is *the* place to buy the marbleized stock, which come in a variety of forms, from flat sheets to boxes and even pencils. Long one of Florence's best art bookshops, **Salimbeni** (✉ Via Matteo Palmieri 14/r, ☎ 055/2340904) specializes in publications on Tuscany. **FMR** (✉ Via delle Belle Donne 41/r, ☎ 055/283312), the shop of world famous art book editor and tastemaker Franco Maria Ricci, offers exquisite art books, handmade papers, and small works on paper. **Cozzi Alberto** (✉ Via del Parione 35/r, ☎ 055/294963) stocks an extensive line of Florentine papers and paper products, and the artisans in the shop rebind and restore books and works on paper.

Clothing

The surreal window displays at **Luisa Via Roma** (✉ Via Roma 19, ☎ 055/2381810) hint at the trendy yet elegant clothing that can be found inside this fascinating, *alta moda* boutique featuring the world's top designers as well as Luisa's own line. The sleek, classic **Giorgio Armani** (✉ Via della Vigna Nuova 51/r, ☎ 055/209040) boutique is a centerpiece of the dazzling high-end shops clustered in this part of town. Its sister store, **Emporio Armani** (✉ Piazza Strozzi 16/r, ☎ 055/284315) offers more-affordable, funky, nightclub-friendly Armani threads. You can take home a custom-made suit or dress from **Giorgio Vannini** (✉ Via Borgo SS Apostoli 43/r, ☎ 055/293037), who has a showroom for his pret-a-porter designs. **Bernardo** (✉ Via Porta Rossa 87/r, ☎ 055/283333) specializes in men's shirts (with details like mother-of-pearl buttons), trousers, and cashmere sweaters.

Jasmine (✉ Borgo San Jacapo 27/r, ☎ 055/213501) is an unpretentious yet sophisticated shop well worth taking a look at in the Oltrarno. If you're looking for something to turn heads in the Florence clubs, try **Metropole** (✉ P. Stazione 24r, ☎ 055/295022). The aristocratic Marchese di Barsento **Emilio Pucci** (✉ Via dei Pucci 6/r; Via della Vigna Nuova 99/r, ☎ 055/287622) became an international name in the early 1960s, when the stretch ski clothes he designed for himself caught on with the la-dolce-vita crowd—his pseudo-psychedelic prints and "palazzo pajamas" became all the rage. The showroom in the family palazzo and two boutiques still sell the celebrated Pucci prints.

Embroidery and Linens

Signora **Loretta Caponi** (✉ Piazza Antinori 4/r, ☎ 055/213668) is synonymous with Florentine embroidery, and her luxury lace, linens, and lingerie have earned her worldwide renown. **Valmar** (✉ Via Porta Rossa 53/r, ☎ 055/284493) is filled with tangled spools of cords, ribbons, and fringes, plus an array of buttons, tassels, sachets, and hand-embroidered cushions you can take home—or bring in your own fabric, choose the adornments, and you can have your cushion or table runner made.

Gifts and Housewares

The essence of a Florentine holiday is captured in the sachets of the **Officina Profumo Farmaceutica di Santa Maria Novella** (✉ Via della Scala 16/r, ☎ 055/216276), an art nouveau emporium of herbal cosmetics and soaps that are made following centuries-old recipes created by monks. For housewares nothing beats **Bartolini** (✉ Via dei Servi 30/r, ☎ 055/211895) for well-designed practical items. **Sbigoli Terrecotte** (✉ Via Sant'Egidio 4/r, ☎ 055/229706) carries traditional Tuscan terra-cotta and ceramic vases, pots, cups, and saucers. If you want to go one step further, you can even shop in the **Sbigoli Laboratorio** (✉ Via di Camaldoli 10/r, ☎ 055/229706), where the artisans are working on their wheels and glazing the pieces. For outstanding contemporary design housewares, check out **Open House** (✉ Via Barbadori 40/r, ☎ 055/212094).

Jewelry

Della Loggia (✉ Ponte Vecchio 52/r, ☎ 055/2396028) combines precious and semiprecious stones and metals in contemporary settings. **Gherardi** (✉ Ponte Vecchio 5/r, ☎ 055/287211), Florence's king of coral, has the city's largest selection of finely crafted pieces, as well as cultured pearls, jade, and turquoise. Antique jewelry, some of which comes from noble families down on their luck, is the specialty at **Lui Lei** (✉ Piazza del Limbo 8/r, corner of Borgo SS Apostoli, ☎ 055/283318), which also collects period furniture and small objets d'art. The venerable **Piccini** (✉ Ponte Vecchio 23/r, ☎ 055/280479) has literally been crowning the heads of Europe for almost a century, and combines its taste for the antique with contemporary designs. One of Florence's oldest jewelers, **Tiffany-Faraone** (✉ Via Tornabuoni 25/r, ☎ 055/215506) has supplied Italian (and other) royalty with finely crafted gems for centuries. Its selection of antique-looking classics has been updated with a choice of contemporary silver. To reach **C. O. I. Wholesale Jewelry** (✉ Via Por S. Maria 8/r, ☎ 055/283970), you must ring the doorbell at the street and take the elevator to the second floor, where the display cases are filled with handsome handmade Florentine designs.

Shoes and Leather Accessories

In the high tourist season, status-conscious shoppers often stand in line outside **Gucci** (✉ Via Tornabuoni 73/r, ☎ 055/264011), ready to buy anything with the famous designer's initials. **Ugolini** (✉ Via Tornabuoni 20/r, ☎ 055/216664) once made gloves for the Italian royal family, but now anyone can have the luxury of its exotic leathers, as well as silk and cashmere ties and scarves. Born near Naples, the late Salvatore **Ferragamo** (✉ Via Tornabuoni 16/r, ☎ 055/292123) made his fortune custom-making shoes for famous feet, especially Hollywood stars. His palace has since passed on to his wife, Wanda, and displays designer clothing and accessories, but elegant footwear still underlies the Ferragamo success.

Giotti (✉ Piazza Ognissanti 3/r) has a full line of leather goods and its own leather clothing. **Leather Guild** (✉ Piazza Santa Croce 20/r, ☎ 055/241932) is one of many such shops that produce inexpensive, antique-looking leather goods of mass appeal, but here you can see the craftspersons at work. **Lily of Florence** (✉ Via Guicciardini 2/r, ☎ 055/294748) offers high-quality, classic shoe designs at reasonable prices and in American sizes. **Il Bisonte** (✉ Via del Parione 31/r, just off Via della Vigna Nuova, ☎ 055/215722) is known for its natural-looking leather goods, all stamped with the store's bison symbol. The ultimate fine leathers are crafted into classic shapes at **Casadei** (⊠ Via Tornabuoni 33/r, ☎ 055/287240), winding up as women's shoes and bags. **Madova** (⊠ Via Guicciardini 1/r, ☎ 055/210244) has a rainbow array of quality leather gloves.

SIDE TRIPS
Fiesole and Gracious Gardens Around Florence

Fiesole

A half-day excursion to Fiesole, set in the hills 8 km (5 mi) above Florence, gives you a pleasant respite from museums and a wonderful vantage point of the city. From here, the view of Brunelleschi's powerful Duomo cupola will give you a new sense of appreciation of what he—and the Renaissance—accomplished. Fiesole began life as an ancient Etruscan and later Roman village that held some power until it succumbed to the barbarian invasions and eventually gave up its independence in exchange for Florence's protection. The medieval cathedral, some other old churches, the ancient Roman amphitheater, and lovely old villas behind garden walls are clustered on a series of hilltops. A walk around Fiesole can take from one to two or three hours, depending on how far you stroll from the main piazza. For information about hotels in Fiesole, *see* Lodging, *above.*

The **Duomo** reveals a stark medieval interior. In the raised presbytery, the **Cappella Salutati** was frescoed by 15th-century artist Cosimo Rosselli, but it was his contemporary, sculptor Mino da Fiesole, who put the town on the artistic map. The Madonna on the altarpiece and the tomb of Bishop Salutati are his work. ⊠ *Piazza Mino da Fiesole.* ☞ *Free.* ☺ *Daily 9–noon and 3–6.*

The nearby beautifully preserved 2,000-seat **Anfiteatro Romano** (Roman Amphitheater) dates from the 1st century BC and is still used for summer concerts. To the right of the amphitheater are the **Terme Romani** (Roman Baths), where you can see the gymnasium, hot and cold baths, and the rectangular chamber where the water was heated. A beautifully designed **Museo Archeologico,** an intricate series of levels connected by elevators, is built amidst the ruins and contains objects dating from 2000 BC. The nearby **Museo Bandini** is a small venue with a lot to offer. It is filled with the private collection of Canon Angelo Maria Bandini (1726–1803), who fancied 13th- to 15th-century Florentine paintings, terra-cotta pieces, and wood sculpture, which he bequeathed to the Diocese of Fiesole. ⊠ *Via San Francesco 3,* ☎ *055/59477.* ☞ *10,000 lire (1 ticket provides access to the archaeological park and the museums).* ☺ *May–Oct., Wed.–Sun. 9:30–7; Nov.–Apr., Wed.–Sun. 9:30–5.*

Climb the hill to the church of **San Francesco** for a good view of Florence and the plain below enjoyed from terrace and benches. Halfway up the hill, you'll see sloping steps to the right; they lead to a lovely wooded **park** with trails that loop out and back to the church.

OFF THE BEATEN PATH

VIA VECCHIA FIESOLANA – If you really want to stretch your legs, walk 4 km (2½ mi) back toward Florence center along Via Vecchia Fiesolana, a narrow lane dating from the days of the Etruscans, to the church of **San Domenico** (⊠ Piazza San Domenico, off Via Giuseppe Mantellini). Sheltered in the church is *Madonna and Child with Saints* by Fra Angelico (1387–1455), a.k.a. Fra Giovanni da Fiesole, who was the prior of this church. From the church, it's only a five-minute walk northwest to the

Badia Fiesolana (⊠ Via della Badia dei Roccettini), which was the original cathedral of Fiesole. Bus 7 (☞ Fiesole A to Z, *below*) goes from Florence to Fiesole, and also stops in San Domenico; from here you can walk the rest of the way to Fiesole along Via Vecchia Fiesolana.

Nightlife and the Arts

From June through August, **Estate Fiesolana** (⊠ Teatro Romano, Fiesole, ☎ 055/599931) is a festival of theater, music, dance, and film that takes place in the churches and the archaeological area of Fiesole.

Fiesole A to Z

ARRIVING AND DEPARTING

The trip from Florence by car or bus takes 20–30 minutes. Take city Bus 7 from the Stazione Centrale di Santa Maria Novella, Piazza San Marco, or the Duomo. There are several possible routes for the two-hour walk from central Florence to Fiesole. One route begins in a residential area of Florence called Salviatino (Via Barbacane, near Piazza Edison, on Bus 7 route), and after a short time it offers glorious peeks over garden walls of beautiful villas, as well as the opportunity to look over your shoulder at the panorama of Florence nestled in the valley.

BIKING TOURS

If you have well-exercised legs and lungs, you can also take a guided half-day bicycle tour from Florence to Fiesole. For bike rental information, *see* Getting Around *in* Florence A to Z, *below*.

VISITOR INFORMATION

Fiesole (⊠ Piazza Mino da Fiesole, ☎ 055/598720).

Gracious Gardens Around Florence

Like the Medicis you can get away from Florence's hustle and bustle by heading for the hills. Take a break from city sightseeing to enjoy the gardens and villas set like jewels in the hills around the city. Villa di Castello and Villa La Petraia, both just northwest of the center in Castello, can be explored in one trip. The Italian garden at Villa Gamberaia is a quick 8-km (5-mi) jaunt east of the center near Settignano.

Villa di Castello

A fortified residence in the Middle Ages, Villa di Castello was rebuilt in the 15th century by the Medicis. The Accademia della Crusca, a 400-year-old institution that is official arbiter of the Italian language, now occupies the palace, which is not open to the public. The gardens are the main attraction. From the villa entrance, walk uphill through the 19th-century park laid out in Romantic style, set above part of the formal garden. You'll reach the terrace, which affords a good view of the geometric layout of the Italian garden below; stairs on either side descend to the parterre.

Though the original garden design has been altered somewhat over the centuries, the allegorical theme of animals devised by Tribolo in the 1540s to the delight of the Medicis is still evident. The artificial cave, Grotta degli Animali (Animal Grotto), displays an imaginative menagerie of sculpted animals by Giambologna and his assistants. Two bronze sculptures by Ammanati, centerpieces of fountains studding the Italian garden, can now be seen indoors in Villa La Petraia (☞ *below*). Another Ammanati sculpture, a figure of an old man representing the Appenines, is at the center of a pond on the terrace overlooking the Italianate garden. Allow about 45 minutes to visit the gardens; you can easily visit Villa La Petraia (☞ *below*) from here, making for a four-hour trip in total. ⊠ *Via di Castello 47, Castello*, ☎ *055/454791.* ▨

4,000 lire (includes entrance to Villa La Petraia). ⊗ *Gardens: daily 9–1 hr before sunset. Closed 1st and 3rd Mon. of month.*

Villa La Petraia

The splendidly planted gardens of Villa La Petraia sit high above the Arno plain on Castello Hill, allowing a sweeping view of Florence. The villa was built around a medieval tower and reconstructed after it was purchased by the Medicis in 1575. Virtually the only trace of the Medicis having lived here is the 17th-century courtyard frescoes depicting glorious episodes of the clan's history. In the 1800s the villa served as a country residence of King Victor Emmanuel II (who kept his mistress here) while Florence was the temporary capital of the newly united Kingdom of Italy.

An Italian-speaking guide will take you through the 19th-century-style salons. The Italian garden—also altered in the 1800s—and the vast park behind the palace suggest a splendid contrast between formal and natural landscapes. Allow 60–90 minutes to explore the park and gardens, plus 30 minutes for the guided tour of the so-called museum, the villa interior. This property is best visited after the Villa di Castello (☞ *above*). ⊠ *Via della Petraia 40, Castello,* ☎ *050/454791.* ☜ *4,000 lire (includes entrance to Villa di Castello).* ⊗ *Tues.–Sun. 9–1 hr before sunset.*

Villa Gamberaia

Villa Gamberaia, near the village of Settignano on the eastern outskirts of Florence, was the rather modest country home of the Rossellino family, which fostered some great early Renaissance sculptors. In the early 1600s, the villa eventually passed into the hands of the wealthy Capponi family. They spared no expense in rebuilding it and, more importantly, creating the Italian garden, one of the finest near Florence. Festooned with statues and fountains, the garden suffered damage during World War II but has been restored according to the original 17th-century design. This excursion takes about 1½ hours, allowing 45 minutes to visit the garden. ⊠ *Via del Rossellino 72, near Settignano,* ☎ *055/697205.* ☜ *12,000 lire.* ⊗ *Gardens: weekdays 9–noon and 1–6, weekends by appointment. Villa closed to the public.*

Gracious Gardens Around Florence A to Z

VILLA DI CASTELLO

By car, head northwest from Florence on Via Reginaldo Giuliani (also known as Via Sestese) to Castello, about 6 km (4 mi) northwest of city center in the direction of Sesto Fiorentino; follow signs to Villa di Castello. Or take Bus 28 from city center, and tell the driver you want to get off at Villa di Castello; from the stop, walk north about ½ km (¼ mi) up the tree-lined allée from the main road to the villa.

VILLA LA PETRAIA

By car, follow directions to Villa di Castello (☞ *above*), but take the right off Via Reginaldo Giuliani, following the sign for Villa La Petraia. You can walk from Villa di Castello to Villa La Petraia in about 15 minutes; turn left beyond the gate of Villa di Castello and continue straight along Via di Castello to the imposing Villa Corsini; take Via della Petraia uphill to the entrance.¡

VILLA GAMBERAIA

By car, head east on Via Aretina, an extension of Via Gioberti, which is picked up at Piazza Beccaria; follow the sign to the turnoff to the north to Villa Gamberaia, about 8 km (5 mi) from the city center. Take Bus 10 to Settignano. From Settignano's main Piazza Tommaseo walk east on Via di San Romano; the second lane on the right is Via del

Rossellino, which leads southeast to the entrance of Villa Gamberaia. The walk from the piazza takes about 10 minutes.

FLORENCE A TO Z

Arriving and Departing

By Bus

Long-distance buses offer inexpensive if somewhat claustrophobic service between Florence and other cities in Italy and Europe. One operator is **SITA** (⊠ Via Santa Caterina da Siena 15/r, ☎ 055/483651 weekdays, 055/211487 weekends). Also try **Lazzi Eurolines** (⊠ Via Mercadante 2, ☎ 055/215154).

By Car

Florence is connected to the north and south of Italy by the Autostrada del Sole (**A1**). It takes about an hour via scenic roads to get to Bologna (although heavy truck traffic over the Apennines often makes for slower going) and about three to Rome. The Tyrrhenian Coast is an hour away on **A11** west.

By Plane

Although the Aeroporto A. Vespucci Airport, called **Peretola** (⊠ 10 km/6 mi northwest of Florence, ☎ 055/333498), accommodates flights from Milan, Rome, and some European cities, it is still a relatively minor airport. **Aeroporto Galileo Galilei** (⊠ Pisa, 80 km/50 mi west of Florence, ☎ 050/500707) is used by most international carriers, but is also a minor gateway. For flight information, call the **Florence Air Terminal** (⊠ Stazione Centrale di Santa Maria Novella, ☎ 055/216073) or Aeroporto Galileo Galilei.

International travelers flying on Alitalia to Rome's **Aeroporto Leonardo da Vinci** (⊠ 30 km/19 mi southwest of Rome, ☎ 06/65953640), also known as Fiumicino, and headed directly for Florence can make connections at the airport for a flight to Florence (the same holds true for Milan's Malpensa), but if the layover is a long one, consider taking the FS airport train to Termini station in Rome, where fast trains for Florence are frequent during the day.

BETWEEN THE AIRPORTS AND DOWNTOWN

By Bus. There is a local bus service from Peretola to Florence. Buy a ticket at the second-floor café; the bus shelter is beyond the parking lot. There is no direct bus service from Pisa's airport to Florence. Buses do go to Pisa itself, but then you have to change to a slow train service.

By Car. From Peretola take autostrada **A11** directly into the city. Driving from the airport in Pisa, take **S67,** a direct route to Florence.

By Train. A scheduled service connects the station at Pisa's Aeroporto Galileo Galilei with Florence's Stazione Centrale di Santa Maria Novella, roughly a one-hour trip. Trains start running about 7 AM from the airport, 6 AM from Florence, and continue service every hour until about 11:30 PM from the airport, 8 PM from Florence. You can check in for departing flights at the **air terminal** (⊠ Track 5, Galileo Galilei Airport station, ☎ 055/216073).

By Train

Florence is on the principal Italian train route between most European capitals and Rome and within Italy is served quite frequently from Milan, Venice, and Rome by nonstop Intercity (IC) and Eurostar trains. **Stazione Centrale di Santa Maria Novella** (☎ 1478/88088 toll-free) is the most convenient city-center station. Be sure to avoid trains that stop only at the Campo di Marte or Rifredi stations, which are not convenient to the city center.

Getting Around

By Bicycle

Brave souls (cycling in Florence is difficult, at best) may rent bicycles at easy-to-spot locations at Fortezza da Basso, the Stazione Centrale di Santa Maria Novella, and Piazza Pitti. To rent bikes, try **Motorent** (⊠ Via San Zanobi 9/r, ☎ 055/490113) and **Alinari** (⊠ Via Guelfa 85r, ☎ 055/280500).

By Bus

Maps and timetables are available for a small fee at the **ATAF** booth (⊠ Piazza del Duomo 57/r; next to the train station), or for free at visitor information offices (☞ Contacts and Resources, *below*). Tickets must be bought in advance at tobacco stores, newsstands, from automatic ticket machines near main stops, or at ATAF booths. The ticket must be canceled in the small validation machine immediately upon boarding. Two types of tickets are available, both valid for one or more rides on all lines. One costs 1,500 lire and is valid for one hour from the time it is first canceled; the other costs 2,500 lire and is valid for three hours. A multiple ticket—four tickets each valid for 60 minutes—costs 5,800 lire. A 24-hour tourist ticket costs 6,000 lire; there are also two-day (8,000 lire), three-day (11,000 lire), and seven-day (19,000 lire) tickets. Monthly passes (53,000 lire) are also available.

By Car

In the city, abandon all hope of using a car, since most of the downtown area is a pedestrian zone. For assistance or information, call the **ACI** (Italian Automobile Club, ☎ 055/24861).

By Moped

If you want to go native and rent a noisy Vespa (Italian for "wasp") or other make of motorcycle or moped, you may do so at Motorent (☞ By Bicycle, *above*). Helmets can be rented at either place.

By Taxi

Taxis usually wait at stands throughout the city (such as in front of the train station and in Piazza della Repubblica), or you can call for one (☎ 055/4390 or 055/4798). The meter starts at 4,500 lire, with a 7,000 lire minimum, and extra charges for nights, Sunday, or radio dispatch.

Contacts and Resources

Agritourist Agencies

Agriturist (⊠ Piazza San Firenze 3, 50122 Florence, ☎ 055/295163). **Terranostra** (⊠ Via dei Magazzini 2, 50122 Florence, ☎ 055/280539). **Turismo Verde** (⊠ Via Verdi 5, 50127 Florence, ☎ 055/2344925).

Car Rentals

Eurodollar (⊠ Via Il Prato 72/r–82/r, ☎ 055/2382480). **Hertz Italiana** (⊠ Via Finiguerra 33/r, ☎ 055/239-8205, FAX 055/2302011). **Maggiore-Budget Autonoleggio** (⊠ Via Termine 1, ☎ 055/311256).

Consulates

U.S. (⊠ Lungarno Vespucci 38, ☎ 055/2398276). **U.K.** (⊠ Lungarno Corsini 2, ☎ 055/284133). **Canadians** should contact their consulate in Rome (⊠ Via Zara 30, ☎ 06/445981).

Doctors and Dentists

You can get a list of English-speaking doctors and dentists at the U.S. consulate (☞ *above*). Contact the **Tourist Medical Service** (⊠ Viale Lorenzo Il Magnifico, ☎ 055/475411).

Emergencies

Police (⊠ Via Zara 2, near Piazza della Libertà, ☎ 49/771). **Ambulance** (☎ 118). **Emergencies** (☎ 113). **Misericordia** (Red Cross, ⊠ Piazza del Duomo 20, ☎ 055/212222). If you need hospital treatment, and an interpreter, you can call **AVO**, a group of volunteer interpreters (☎ 055/4250126 or 055/2344567), open Monday, Wednesday, and Friday 4–6 PM; Tuesday and Thursday 10–noon.

English-Language Bookstores

Paperback Exchange (⊠ Via Fiesolana 31/r, ☎ 055/2478154). **BM Bookshop** (⊠ Borgo Ognissanti 4/r, ☎ 055/294575). **Seeber** (⊠ Via Tornabuoni 68, ☎ 055/215697).

Guided Tours

BIKING

See Outdoor Activities and Sports, *above*.

ORIENTATION

The major bus operators (☞ Arriving and Departing, By Bus, *above*) offer half-day itineraries, all of which use comfortable buses staffed with English-speaking guides. Morning tours begin at 9, when buses pick visitors up at the main hotels. Stops include the cathedral complex, the Galleria dell'Accademia, Piazzale Michelangelo, and the Palazzo Pitti (or, on Monday, the Museo dell'Opera del Duomo). Afternoon tours stop at the main hotels at 2 PM and take in Piazza della Signoria, the Galleria degli Uffizi (or the Palazzo Vecchio on Monday, when the Uffizi is closed), nearby Fiesole, and, on the return, the church of Santa Croce. A half-day tour costs about 48,000 lire, including museum admissions.

Late-Night Pharmacies

The following are open 24 hours a day, seven days a week. For a **complete listing**, call 192. **Comunale No. 13** (⊠ Stazione Centrale di Santa Maria Novella, ☎ 055/289435). **Molteni** (⊠ Via Calzaiuoli 7/r, ☎ 055/289490). **Taverna** (⊠ Piazza San Giovanni 20/r, ☎ 055/284013).

Travel Agencies

American Express (⊠ Via Guicciardini 49/r, near Piazza Pitti, ☎ 055/288751; ⊠ Via Dante Alighiere 20/r, ☎ 055/50981) is also represented by **Universalturismo** (⊠ Via Speziali 7/r, off Piazza della Repubblica, ☎ 055/217241). **CIT** (⊠ Via Cavour 56, ☎ 055/294306; ⊠ Piazza Stazione 51, ☎ 055/2396963). **Thomas Cook** is represented by **World Vision** (⊠ Via Cavour 154/r, ☎ 055/579294).

Villa Rentals

Florence and Abroad (⊠ Via S. Zanobi 58, Florence 50100, ☎ 055/470603). **Chianti e Terre di Toscana** (⊠ Via S. Maria Macerata 23/a, Montefiridolfi 50020, ☎ 055/8244211, FAX 055/8244382). **Ville e Casali Toscani** (⊠ Via delle Scuole 12, Rosia (Siena) 53010, ☎ 0577/344901, FAX 0577/344800).

Visitor Information

Ufficio Informazione Turistiche Commune di Firenze (Florence Tourist Information Office; ⊠ Via Cavour 1/r, next to Palazzo Medici-Riccardi, 50100, ☎ 055/290832; ⊠ Inside Stazione Centrale di Santa Maria Novella, ☎ 055/212245; ⊠ Piazza della Signoria, Chiasso dei Baroncelli 17/r, 50100, ☎ 055/2302124).

3 North of Florence

The towns and cities north of Florence might be Tuscany's last hidden secret. The sheer wild beauty of the landscape is breathtaking: the dry, untamed land is crisscrossed with craggy, often snowcapped mountains and roads curve and wind up and down incredible heights. Even when it's warm elsewhere it's a little cooler here—this is Tuscan mountain territory that eventually meets the sea at Ligurian beach resorts.

By Patricia
Rucidlo

CITIES NORTHWEST OF FLORENCE in the Garfagnana and Lima valleys such as Castlenuovo di Garfagnana and Barga were often intimately involved with the fate of Lucca, a dominant power during the Middle Ages and the Renaissance, and often at odds with Florence and Pisa. The Mugello, due north of Florence, provided food for the city as well as links with the Emilia-Romagna, which often waged war with Tuscany. Visual reminders of this food link may be seen even today, as much of Florence's milk comes from the pastures of Mugello. Quarries in Carrara, Forte dei Marmi, and Pietrasanta, on the Ligurian coast, have been sources of marble for sculptors—Michelangelo among them—for two millenniums.

The majestic Alpi Apuane mountain chain cuts a swath between the Garfagnagna and the Lunigiana, offering trails through the protected Parco Naturale delle Alpi Apuane and starkly beautiful landscapes. Seductively close to the northwestern edge of Tuscany—beyond the resort town of Viareggio and the marble towns—are the five seaside towns in the region of Liguria called the Cinque Terre, where sleepy pastel houses are stacked on sheer cliffs and fishermen haul in their catch at the day's end.

Pleasures and Pastimes

Dining

In the Mugello, sample the *tortelli di Mugello,* ravioli with potato stuffing sauced in a variety of ways. *Lardo di colonnata,* a deliciously obscene dish of cured pork fat, hails from near Carrara and should be sampled even if you're skeptical—one bite and you could very well be hooked. The Garfagnana valley produces the ancient grain *farro* (emmer wheat), a pearly grain that in some ways resembles barley. It shows up in local dishes, and should definitely be sampled either in *zuppa di farro* (farro and bean soup) or in *farro all contadina,* a *primo piatto* (first course) in which the grain is cooked in water or broth and then tossed with extra-virgin olive oil and chopped fresh tomatoes; it's so simple and so good. Restaurants in the Garfagnana stock Lucca's deep-green, fruity olive oil, which makes practically every dish taste exquisite. The Garfagnana is also a huge chestnut-growing area; sample anything on the menu that has chestnuts, especially *polenta di castagna* (chestnut polenta) in cooler months. Specialities from the sea can be found in the many resort towns dotting the coast such as in Forte dei Marmi and Viareggio.

Restaurants in the Lunigiana and the Mugello are generally less expensive than those in major cities; however, when dining in Forte dei Marmi or Viareggio you would do well to remember that you are in resort towns where resort prices are frequently charged.

CATEGORY	COST*
$$$$	over 110,000 lire
$$$	60,000 lire–110,000 lire
$$	35,000 lire–60,000 lire
$	under 35,000 lire

Prices are per person, for a three course meal, house wine and tax included.

Lodging

Lodging is generally less expensive than in other parts of Italy, beach resort towns excluded. Some real bargains can be found in the off-the-beaten-path towns. Many area hotels have restaurants that offer delicious fare.

CATEGORY	COST*
$$$$	over 350,000 lire
$$$	220,000 lire–350,000 lire
$$	100,000 lire–220,000 lire
$	under 100,000 lire

Prices are for a double room for two, tax and service included.

Outdoor Activities and Sports

Serious hikers and trekkers come to this part of Tuscany for its network of trails and incredible views. The Apennine's Parco dell'Orecchiella in the Garfagnana has extensive woods with trails for hiking, biking, and horseback riding. There is also some great terrain for mountain bikers in the Forte dei Marmi area. For information about area mountains, contact **C.A.I. Sexzione Pistoia** (⊠ Via Antonini 7, Casella Postale n. 1, ☎ 0573/365582).

Exploring North of Florence

Geographically, towns north of Florence are rather spread out. The best way to explore the region is by car, as part of the fun is driving on winding roads and stopping to soak in the scenery. If you have to rely on public transportation, bus service to the region can get you around, and train service is extremely limited.

Numbers in the text correspond to numbers in the margin and on the Mugello and Northwestern Tuscany and the Ligurian Coast maps.

Great Itineraries

You can get a good sense of this part of Tuscany in three or four days. The region is spread out and mountainous, and it takes considerable time to get around the winding roads. It's also geographically diverse: you can be looking at soaring mountain vistas in the morning and lazing on the beach in the afternoon.

IF YOU HAVE 3 DAYS

If you have three days, you might want to pick a specific area and stick to it: otherwise, you'll be spending most of your time in the car. Drive either from Florence or Lucca to the Garfagnana and spend the first night in **Castelnuovo di Garfagnana** ⑪, then head to the Lunigiana and stay in ⊡ **Fivizzano** ⑭ or ⊡ **Equi Terme** ⑮; on the third night, drive to ⊡ **Forte dei Marmi** ⑳ via ⊡ **Carrara** ㉒ and check out the caves.

IF YOU HAVE 5 DAYS

Though there's some wonderful art to be seen in these spots, as well as some wonderful food to be eaten, the scenery takes precedence when touring this area. Drive north from Florence on S302 into the rolling hills of the Mugello: visit the two Medici villas at **Trebbio** ③ and **Cafaggiolo** ② and stop at the **Bosco ai Frati** ⑤ monastery, having lunch along the way. Go south back towards Florence; before hitting Florence, turn west (take the A11 to Montecatini Terme, pick up the S633 to S12) and drive a good hour and a half to **Abetone** ⑨, the mountain resort in the Garfagnana. Spend the night, inhaling fresh mountain breezes and admiring the views. From Abetone, drive south along curving, winding roads to **Bagni di Lucca** ⑬, then go north through to **Barga** ⑫. In Barga stop to see the Duomo and admire the panorama from its little piazza. Stay the second night in ⊡ **Castelnuovo di Garfagnana** ⑪. Head north to ⊡ **Fivizzano** ⑭ or ⊡ **Equi Terme** ⑮ to spend the night. The following day, drive south to ⊡ **Carrara** ㉒ and explore some marble caves. Overnight in **Forte dei Marmi** ⑳, doing nothing except relaxing and eating well. In the morning, explore the splendors of **Pietrasanta** ⑲, especially its marvelous main Renaissance square. Spend the last night in ⊡ **Viareggio** ⑱ before returning to Florence.

When to Tour North of Florence

Summer is the time to be in Forte dei Marmi and Viareggio: the towns are bustling with people and the beaches are crowded. If you want to enjoy the beach—but not the crowds during the height of summer—come on the fringe of the tourist season in June or September, when the water is warm enough to take a swim. Another good time to visit Viareggio is during Carnevale, the period before Lent that culminates in a huge street party on Shrove Tuesday; it's said that Viareggio's celebrations are second only to Venice's. Hiking, trekking, and mountain biking vacations are best taken in the warmer months. If you simply want to drive around and marvel at the gorgeous scenery, anytime from spring to fall is best.

THE MUGELLO

The lands of the Mugello—surrounding the upper reaches of the Sieve River and the vineyard-rich Val di Sieve—were distributed in the 1st century AD to those soldiers who had fought for the Roman general Sulla (138–78 BC); they took over land previously inhabited by the Etruscans. Florence hankered after the area, in part because of its rich agricultural resources, and conquered it in the 14th century. Its native sons include the artists Giotto (1266–1337), Fra Angelico (1387–1455), and Andrea del Castagno (circa 1421–1457). San Piero a Sieve, a small town in the region, was where the Medici originally came from. Now the Mugello is more or less quiet, its days of glory gone. Though parts of it are industrialized, flat, and uninteresting, other parts are extremely beautiful with sharp hills and dramatic sunsets.

Barberino di Mugello

❶ *34 km (21 mi) north of Florence.*

Barberino di Mugello is alternately marked by stupendous views of Tuscan countryside and industrial complexes. It's not unusual to have each vista on either side of the road. Two fine restaurants and a couple of well-priced hotels (☞ Dining and Lodging, *below*) make this an attractive base from which to explore the rest of the region. The historic center has a not-particularly-interesting parish church **San Silvestro,** which dates from the 16th century but was largely refurbished in the 19th century. A copy of Domenico Ghirlandaio's (1449–1494) *Last Supper* from Florence's Ognissanti adorns the interior. ⊠ *Corso Bartolomeo Corsini,* ☏ *no phone.* ▨ *Free.* ☼ *Daily 8–12 and 4–7.*

Next to the church is the **Oratorio Del Ss. Sebastiano e Rocco** (Oratory of Sts. Sebastian and Rocco), which dates from the 18th century. ⊠ *Corso Bartolomeo Corsini,* ☏ *no phone.* ▨ *Free.* ☼ *Mon.–Sat. 4:30–5:30, Sun. 8–9.*

Dining and Lodging

$$ ✕ **Cosimo de' Medici.** There are probably lots more places named for the so-called *pater patriae* in this area, as this is where the Medici hail from. But this would be the Cosimo de' Medici restaurant to eat at—it's right off the highway, so is easy to get to. Don't be put off by the number of trucks parked in the lot—this might be a trucker's stop, and the interior might have the charm of a convenience store, but the food is typical Tuscan and good. Grilled meats are a specialty and the pastas are made in-house—try the *farfalle alla Cosimo,* butterflies of pasta gently sauced with an herbed pesto (the taste of sage lingers). Save room for dessert; when the dessert cart rolls around,

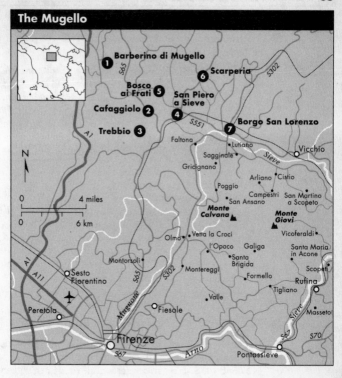

The Mugello

you'll get your second wind, especially for the profiteroles. ☒ *Via del Lago 19,* ☎ *055/8420370. AE, DC, MC, V. Closed Mon. and 10 days in Aug.*

$$ ✕ **Marisa.** Just next door to Cosimo de' Medici, this place serves up Tuscan fare in a light, airy space with white walls. Tuscan products are also for sale—local salami, cheeses, olive oil, and *biscottini* (small hard cookies). If you've got the time, sit down and have the *lombatina alla vitella* (grilled veal) with lemon; it's a great bargain, as are the pastas. If you're in a hurry, you can have them make you a *panini* (sandwich) while you sip a coffee before hitting the road again. ☒ *Exit 18 off the A1,* ☎ *055/842 0045. AE, MC, V.*

$$ ▥ **Hotel Barberino.** The best thing about this place is its convenient location. It's just off the autostrada and a perfect place to stay while exploring the area. Though the front of the hotel looks out onto the autostrada, the back looks out onto gently rolling hills. There's a solarium and two tennis courts. The hotel also has four wheelchair-friendly rooms, which is a rarity in Italian hotels. ☒ *Uscita Autosole 18, 50030,* ☎ *055/8420051 and 055/8420052,* ℻ *055/8420432. 78 rooms. Restaurant, 2 tennis courts. EP. AE, DC, MC, V.*

$$ ▥ **Poggio di Sotto.** Perched on a little hill (*poggio,* in fact, means "hillock"), this agriturismo is a series of small, ocher-color buildings that look on to some pretty Mugellan countryside (and the inevitable view of industry from one side). You can borrow a mountain bike from the proprietor and explore the area if you wish; horseback riding is also nearby. A small restaurant featuring local specialties is attached to the place. The hotel generally operates on a no-meals basis, but half pension is an option (92,000 lire). ☒ *Località Galliano 50030,* ☎ *055/8428447 and 055/8428448,* ℻ *no fax. 9 rooms. Restaurant. EP, MAP. AE, MC, V. Closed weekdays Nov.–Feb.*

Cafaggiolo

② *6 km (4 mi) south of Barberino di Mugello, 26 km (16 mi) north of Florence.*

Cafaggiolo is probably most famous for its **Villa Medicea di Cafaggiolo.** Cosimo de' Medici (the Elder, 1389–1464) commissioned Michelozzo (1396–1472) in 1454 to redo the structure, originally a fortress, which became a favorite hunting spot for the Medici. Unless you're a Medici villa fanatic, it's not worth the trip. If, however, you happen to be in the neighborhood or just driving by, pull over. ⊠ *Via Nazionale,* ☎ *055/8417846.* ⊙ *By appointment Thurs. and Fri. 4–8, weekends 10–noon and 4–8.*

Dining

$ ✕ **Girodibacco Osteria.** About 300 ft down the road from Cafaggiolo, this rustic *osteria* (tavern-style restaurant) serves typical Tuscan dishes such as *ribollita* (a thick soup of white beans, bread, cabbage, and onions), *pappa al pomodoro* (bread and tomato soup), and grilled meats. There's also a bar in front if you want to take a break from the road and have an espresso. ⊠ *Via Nazionale 8, Barberino di Mugello,* ☎ *055/8418173. AE, DC, MC, V. Closed Mon.*

Trebbio

❸ *3 km (2 mi) south of Cafaggiolo, 25 km (16 mi) north of Florence.*

Trebbio is the site of **Castello di Trebbio,** which was transformed from a medieval fortress into an elegant villa by Michelozzo between the years 1427 and 1436. The narrow, serpentine road lined with cypresses leading to the villa creates a sense of drama, as if you're swept back to the Renaissance age. Because the villa is still owner occupied (not, alas, by the Medici!), a visit to the gardens only is accepted by previous appointment, and you must arrange a group of at least 10. Don't bother coming without an appointment—you can't see anything from the street, the trip's tough on the shocks, and it would be terribly impolite to bang on the gate. ⊠ *Via Bandini 6, Borgo San Lorenzo (for information),* ☎ *050/8438793.* 🎫 *20,000 lire/person.* ⊙ *Garden tours by appointment Thur. and Fri. at 11 AM. Villa closed to the public.*

San Piero a Sieve

❹ *4 km (2½ mi) north of Trebbio, 26 km (16 mi) north of Florence.*

This is a sleepy little town. During the Renaissance it belonged first to the Ubaldini before becoming a Florentine possession. The 11th-century parish church of **San Pietro** is worth a stop. It was greatly modified in the late 18th century but nevertheless has some terra-cotta from the early 16th century attributed to the school of Giovanni della Robbia (1469–circa 1529); there's also a panel painting of the *Madonna and Child* that may have been executed by Lorenzo di Credi (circa 1456/1460–1537). ⊠ *Via Provinciale,* ☎ *055/848161.* 🎫 *Free.* ⊙ *Daily 8–7.*

The **Fortezza di San Martino,** just southwest of town, was built as a defensive fortification by Cosimo I (the Great, 1519–1574) in the 1560s and may be visited by appointment. Contact the Commune (☎ 055/848003).

Dining and Lodging

$$ ✕🏨 **Hotel Ristorante Ebe.** Set right along a two-lane highway, this place is brightly hued, from its pink-and-white tiled floors to the sun that streaks through the lobby's atrium. Rooms are immaculately clean and given a great deal of care, even tending to be a bit fussy with neat throw

pillows and wall decoration. The attached restaurant serves only vegetarian food. Both the restaurant and the hotel are run by the Dalle Fabbriche family, six family members devoted to vegetarianism. Want to eat seitan, Italian style? Here's the place to do it. The family also runs the Villa Ebe, a few kilometers from the hotel. ⊠ *Via Provinciale 1, 50027,* ☎ *055/848019,* ⅻ *055/848567. 24 rooms, 4 suites. Restaurant. EP. AE, MC, V.*

Bosco ai Frati

❺ *2 km (1 mi) west of San Piero a Sieve, 28 km (17 mi) north of Florence.*

At this Franciscan monastery set in the countryside, you get the feeling that not much has changed since St. Francis visited in 1212. It was here in 1273 that St. Bonaventure, biographer of St. Francis, was washing dishes when he heard the news that he was made a cardinal. Cosimo de' Medici, a patron of the monastery, commissioned the young Michelozzo in 1420 to redo the facade. The most important work of art remaining in the monastery is a wood sculpture of the *Crucifixion* by Donatello (circa 1386–1466) dating from 1430. According to local legend, it was carved from a pear tree in the monastery's garden. ⊠ *Off S65,* ☎ *055/848111.* ⅻ *Free.* ☉ *Daily 9–12 and 2–6.*

Scarperia

❻ *4 km (2½ mi) north of San Piero a Sieve, 30 km (19 mi) north of Florence.*

Florence founded Scarperia in the early 1300s as a strategic defensive point in the Mugello. It was an active market town in the 16th and 17th centuries, and flourished from a strong local knife-producing industry. The **Oratorio della Madonna dei Terremoti** (Oratory of the Madonna of the Earthquakes) has a 15th-century fresco of the *Madonna and Child;* some believe it's by Fra Filippo Lippi (1406–1469). ⊠ *Viale John F. Kennedy 18,* ☎ *no phone.* ⅻ *Free.* ☉ *Daily 9–7.*

The 13th-century **Palazzo del Vicario** contains 15th-century frescoes. ⊠ *Via Roma 50,* ☎ *no phone.* ⅻ *Free.* ☉ *Check with local tourist office.*

The Augustinian church of **Ss. Jacopo e Filippo,** though dating from the 14th century, was restored in the 19th and early 20th centuries. Inside are frescoes attributed to Bicci di Lorenzo (circa 1373–1452). Note the marble tondo of the *Madonna and Child* by Benedetto da Maino (circa 1442–1497) in the chapel to the left of the main altar. ⊠ *Via San Martino 17,* ☎ *no phone.* ⅻ *Free.* ☉ *Daily 9–7.*

Borgo San Lorenzo

❼ *5 km (3 mi) east of San Piero a Sieve, 17 km (11 mi) east of Barberino di Mugello, 32 km (20 mi) north of Florence.*

Borgo San Lorenzo's biggest claim to fame is that Giotto was born here—though some other towns, including Vespignano, which claims to have the house that Giotto was born in, would dispute this. What is inarguable is that the town can claim Roman origins, and that in the Middle Ages it eventually was taken over by Florence. It saw some heavy fighting during World War II, and the plaque commemorating the heroism of its citizens, which can be seen on the wall of the Palazzo Pretorio, is moving in its strong and unapologetic language. For those of you interested in the so-called minor decorative arts of the early 20th century, lots of Liberty-style buildings have been erected in Borgo San Lorenzo.

Documents refer to a church on the site of **San Lorenzo** as early as 941, and there is evidence to suggest that the foundation was built over a Roman temple dedicated to Bacchus. The 1263 bell tower, rebuilt from one dating to 1193, is a fine example of Roman-Byzantine architecture. Inside the church, which preserves the simplicity of churches of this period, are works of art spanning the centuries, the most important of which is a *Madonna* attributed to Giotto. It is the only work of his still to be found in his native territory. ⊠ *Via San Francesco, off Piazza Garibaldi,* ☎ *no phone.* ⊡ *Free.* ☉ *Daily 9–7.*

There's no real evidence that the **Museo di Casa di Giotto** (Museum of the House of Giotto) was once Giotto's house, but if you are a Giotto aficionado, you just might want to check it out since he could have been born here. Inside the house-museum are reproductions of his major works. There's also a tiny chapel, the **Cappellina della Bruna,** which has some 15th-century fresco fragments. You can get the key to the chapel at the museum. ☎ *055/8448251 for the Biblioteca Comunale, which handles all requests.* ⊡ *2,000 lire.* ☉ *Nov.–Mar., Tues. and Thurs. 4–7 and weekends 10–12 and 4–7; Apr.–Sept., Tues. and Wed. 3–6 and weekends 10–12 and 3–6.*

Dining and Lodging

$ ✕ **La Casa di Prosciutto.** This rustic, small country inn at the foot of a tiny 14th-century bridge is 6 km (4 mi) from Borgo San Lorenzo and worth the detour for lunch. The food is terrific, from *primi piatti* (first courses) to *dolci* (desserts). Try the regional specialty, tortelli di Mugello, pasta stuffed with potatoes, served with a sauce of porcini mushrooms, duck, or *ragù* (tomato sauce with meat). Afterwards you can walk off your lunch by trudging up a hill to the main piazza, with a plaque notes that where Fra Angelico was born. Reservations are advised. ⊠ *Via Ponte a Vicchio 1,* ☎ *055/844031. AE, DC, MC, V. Closed Mon. and most of Jan. and July. No dinner.*

$$$ ⌂ **Park Hotel Ripaverde.** Though this hotel is in what looks like the middle of a parking lot (don't expect pretty scenery) and though the exterior is lots of glass and steel, the interior is clean, comfortable, and offers many amenities. Rooms are contemporary and well furnished. The restaurant, L'O di Giotto, serves regional and typical Italian specialties. The exercise room has a sauna and water massage. ⊠ *Viale Giovanni XXII 36, 50032,* ☎ *055/8496003,* 🖷 *055/8459379. 51 rooms, 6 suites. Bar, sauna, exercise room. CP, MAP, FAP. AE, DC, MC, V. Restaurant closed Mon.*

THE GARFAGNANA AND THE LIMA VALLEY

The heart of the Alpi Apuane (Apuan Alps) might be the most visually stunning in all of Tuscany. Roads marked by constant hairpin turns wind around precipitous, jagged mountains. Cool mountain air tempers even the sultriest summers. Most of the major cities and towns can be found along the Serchio, Italy's third largest river, that runs north–south. The Val di Lima (Lima Valley), formed by the Lima River, has for centuries been known for its curative thermal waters.

San Marcello Pistoiese

❽ *20 km (12 mi) east of Bagni di Lucca, 50 km (31 mi) north of Lucca, 66 km (41 mi) northwest of Florence.*

This little town has a church, **San Marcello,** that dates from the 12th century. The interior was redone in the 18th century, and most of the art inside dates from that period. The main square, right along the road, has plenty of cafés. It's a good stopping point if you're on the road. ⊠ *Piazza Arcangeli,* ☎ *0573/630179.* 🎟 *Free.* ⊙ *Daily 9–7.*

Outdoor Activities and Sports

Rent mountain bikes at **Nonsolovolo** (⊠ Via Marconi 22, ☎ 0573/6224089).

Abetone

⑨ *29 ½ km (18 mi) northwest of San Marcello in Pistoiese, 65 km (40 mi) north of Lucca, 90 km (59 mi) northwest of Florence.*

Abetone is one of the most-visited vacation spots in the Appennines, where Tuscans, Emilia-Romagnans, and others go to ski. It's easily accessible from Florence and offers a number of trails, mostly for beginner and intermediate skiers (expert skiers might be somewhat deterred by the fact that the entire area offers only two expert slopes). In summer, there's ample opportunity to trek or mountain bike in and around its beautiful hills and mountains.

OFF THE
BEATEN PATH

SAN PELLEGRINO IN ALPE – If you're driving from Abetone to Castelnuovo di Garfagnana, San Pellegrino in Alpe will not be off the beaten path but rather right on it. Do stop and enjoy the staggering view. The story has it that a 9th-century Scot, Pellegrino by name, came here to repent. Though that doesn't really explain why he would trade in windswept moors for windswept mountains, don't dwell on that. The Museo Ethnografico Provinciale (Provincial Ethnographic Museum) is mostly devoted to farm objects; check out the vista by the wooden cross.

Lodging

$$ 🏨 **Hotel Bellavista.** Originally a 19th-century villa belonging to a Strozzi (a family that played a major role in Renaissance Florence) nestled against a mountain, the place is now a contemporary inn. It still feels 19th-century in some places—some of the public rooms have a quaint Victorian charm to them—but the rooms themselves feel completely 1990s. It's a perfect place to stay in winter, as you can ski to the slopes. In summer, you can hike in the mountains. ⊠ *Via Brennero 383, 51021,* ☎ *0573/60028, 0573/60245,* 🅵🅰🆇 *0573/60028, 0573/60245. 42 rooms. Restaurant, bar. CP, MAP, FAP. AE, MC, V. Closed May and Nov.*

Outdoor Activities and Sports

BIKING

Rent bikes for exploring area mountain trails of all skill levels at **F. Ballantini** (⊠ Via Brennero 615, ☎ 0573/60482) or **Franceschi** (⊠ Via La Secchia, ☎ 0573/606819).

SKIING

The area has 37 different ski slopes, amounting to about 50 km (31 mi) of ski surface, which are all connected through the purchase of a single Multipass. Contact the Consorzio Impianti (⊠ Via Brennero 429, ☎ 0573/60557).

Parco dell'Orecchiella

⑩ *Southeastern boundary about 35 km (22 mi) northwest of Abetone.*

Parco dell'Orecchiella (Orecchiella Park), some 52 square km of it, is protected parkland dedicated to preserving the local flora and fauna. It's a pretty 30-minute drive on winding two-lane roads from Abetone (20 minutes from Castelnuova di Garfagnana) to San Romano in Garfagnana, the main entrance point to the park. For the avid hiker, there's lots to do here, as there are many trails marked out along with the times that they take to do them—anywhere from 2½ to 5 hours. ☎ *Contact: Visitor's Center and Information Office 0583/619098; National Forest Administration 0583/955525.* 🎟 *Free.* ☉ *Apr.–May., Sun. 9 AM–twilight; June, weekends 9–7; July–Aug., daily 9–7; Sept., daily 9–twilight; Oct.–Nov., weekends 9–twilight. Closed Dec.–Mar.*

Dining

$ ✕ **Bar Ristorante Orecchiella.** You can't get more rustic than this little place. It's in the woods in San Romano in Garfagnana near the main parking lot in Orecchiella Park. You can stop for a coffee, grab some water and hit a trail, or stop for lunch between hikes. It serves Tuscan specialties, grilled meats (*cinghiale*, or wild boar, is often on the menu), and rich pasta dishes. ⊠ *Parco dell'Orecchiella, San Romano in Garfagnana,* ☎ *0583/619010. No credit cards. Closed Fri.*

Castelnuovo di Garfagnana

⓫ *57 km (35 mi) west of Abetone, 47 km (29 mi) north of Lucca, 121 km (75 mi) northwest of Florence.*

Castelnuovo di Garfagnana might be the best place to use as a base while exploring the Garfagnana, as it is more or less centrally located with respect to the other towns. During the Renaissance, the town's fortunes were frequently tied in with those of the powerful d'Este family of Ferrara. The writer Ludovico Ariosto (1474–1533), author of the epic poem *Orlando Furioso*, among other works, served here briefly as commissar general for the d'Este. During Napoleon's supremacy in Europe, Castelnuovo di Garfagnana became part of the Cisalpine republic. In 1814, it once again became a possession of the d'Este.

La Rocca, in Piazza Umberto I, dates from the 12th century and has a plaque commemorating Ariosto's tenure. The **Duomo,** dedicated to St. Peter, was begun in the 11th century and was reconstructed in the early 1500s. Inside is a crucifix dating from the 14th to 15th centuries. There's also an early 16th-century terra-cotta attributed to the school of the della Robbia. ⊠ *Piazza del Duomo,* ☎ *0583/62170.* 🎟 *Free.* ☉ *Daily 9–7.*

Dining and Lodging

$$ ✕🛏 **La Lanterna.** A few minutes' drive from the center of town up a long winding road, this contemporary inn has beautiful mountain views and gracious hosts in Alelmo Bravi and his wife Elena Andreucci. The rooms are modern, with white walls and wall-to-wall carpeting. Their enthusiasm for the splendors of the area is palpable. You might want to plan on having all your meals at the hotel restaurant, where the food is fantastic and inexpensive. It features farro, the local grain, in several guises. The chef also has a gift for sauces—try the pork with a reduced radicchio sauce. ⊠ *Località alle Monache, Piano Pieve 55032,* ☎ *0583/62272,* 📠 *0583/ 62272. 42 rooms. Restaurant. CP, MAP, FAP. AE, DC, MC, V.*

Barga

⓬ *13½ (8 km) southeast of Castelnuovo di Garfagnana, 37 km (23 mi) north of Lucca, 111 km (69 mi) northwest of Florence.*

Barga is a lovely little town with a finely preserved medieval core. It produced textiles—particularly silk—in the Renaissance, and wool in the 18th century. And though there's not a lot to see, it's a lot of fun to wander the narrow streets and sip cappuccino. Do drop in to the **Duomo,** dedicated to St. Christopher. It's an oddly shaped structure that saw four separate building campaigns; the first began in the 9th century. Inside, there's an intricately carved pulpit by an anonymous Lucchese sculptor dating from the second half of the 12th century. From the Duomo you can enjoy the beautiful panorama of the surrounding countryside. It makes the effort to climb the steep path well worth it. ⊠ *Via del Duomo,* ☎ *no phone.* 🎫 *Free.* ⊙ *Daily 9–7.*

Bagni di Lucca

⑬ *18 km (11 mi) southeast of Barga, 27 km (17 mi) north of Lucca, 101 km (63 mi) northwest of Florence.*

Pretty Bagni di Lucca was certainly a fashionable town in days of yore—in part because of its thermal waters. The 16th-century French writer Montaigne (1533–1592) came here twice to take the waters, and on each occasion recorded in great detail the effect that bathing and the waters had on his digestion. The Romantic poet Percy Bysshe Shelley (1792–1822) installed his family here during the summer of 1818. He wrote to a friend in July of that year that the waters here were "exceedingly refreshing": "My custom is to undress and sit on the rocks, reading Herodotus, until perspiration has subsided, and then to leap from the edge of the rock into this fountain." Bagni di Lucca was probably equally as refreshing for the Brownings who, in the summer of 1853, summered in a house on the main square.

Dining

$$ ✕ **Del Sonno.** Did the Brownings eat here? If the story holds—that the place dates from the 14th century—then they certainly could have. The main street restaurant does have a rather antique feel, from its high beamed ceilings to open brickwork; despite the fact that the space is deep, the restaurant manages a bright and breezy feel. The mixed antipasto plate makes for a refreshing starter, with various vegetables *sott'olio* (under oil), beans, and marinated fish. The pastas are good—try the Roman *spaghetti alla carbonara,* as good as it gets in Tuscany. At night, they fire up the pizza oven as well. ⊠ *Viale Umberto 1, 146,* ☎ *0583/805080 or 0583/87240. AE, DC, MC, V. Closed Mon.*

THE LUNIGIANA

The Lunigiana was of strategic importance in pre-Roman times as a commercial center for trading between the Celts and the Ligurians. It maintained its economic strength during the early Middle Ages, serving as a junction between cities north of the Alps and those south. It was also a stopping point for pilgrims en route to Rome. The area was hotly contested territory between the Milanese, the Genovans, and the Florentines during the Renaissance. This is the place to let your medieval fantasies run wild: the hills are steep, the mountains plentiful, and there's lots of castles—more than 100 of them still whole and in pieces that provide testimony to the Lunigiana's tumultuous past. Built in the 13th and 14th centuries, the castles and other defensive structures such as towers guard much of landscape. The effect is powerful.

Fivizzano

⑭ *50 km (31 mi) west of San Romano in Garfagnana, 14 km (7 mi) east of Aulla.*

There's really not much reason to come to this provincial town except for the fact that it's pretty and quiet. It became part of the Florentine Republic in the 15th century. In 1471, Jacopo da Fivizzano was known as one of the first in Italy to have his own printing press (which might explain why nearby Pontremoli became known for its traveling bookstores). Cosimo I built walls 40 ft high with three access doors around

Northwestern Tuscany and the Ligurian Coast

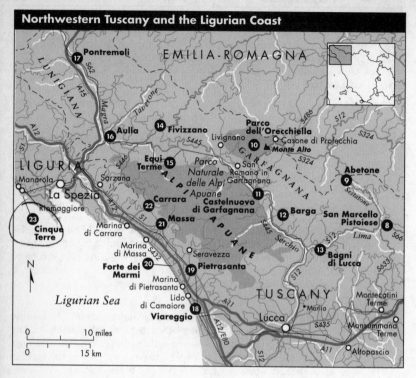

the present-day historic center. In the 1630s Fivizzano became the administrative center of the Lunigiana. **Piazza Medicea,** the main square in town, has a fountain erected by Cosimo III in 1683. Lots of cafés with outdoor seating line this square, making it the perfect place to while away an hour or two. Also in this main square is the church of **Ss. Jacopo e Antonio,** built in the 1370s and embellished in the 15th century. ☒ *Piazza Medicea,* ☏ *no phone.* ☏ *Free.* ☉ *Daily 9–7.*

OFF THE
BEATEN PATH

VERRUCOLA – Just a few minutes' drive from Fivizzano will put you in Verrucola, which has a castle dating from the 11th to 12th centuries. It first belonged to the d'Este, and then in the 15th century it, like Fivizzano, entered into the Florentine orbit. In the mid-16th century, the castle became a monastery. In the 20th it is privately owned and accessible only by prior appointment. Call Pietro Cascella (☏ 0585/92466) for information.

Dining and Lodging

$ ✕ **Ristorante Pizzeria Medicea.** Talk about a nice cheap eat! If you're on the road and feel like stopping, pop in here. You can have a pizza, or a sizable piece of *vitello al limone* (sautéed veal scallops topped with fragrant lemon sauce and butter), along with a plate of pasta and wine for very little. Though the interior decor inexplicably includes an aquarium with an exceedingly large cactus next to it, it's clean and the service is prompt. If you don't eat everything on your plate you might be asked to explain why. In the summer, you can sit outside in the main piazza. ☒ *Piazza Medicea,* ☏ *0585/92085. No credit cards. Closed Wed.*

$ ✕▥ **Il Giardinetto.** You will feel as if you entered a time warp here. The hotel has been around since 1882; Beppino Mercadini, the innkeeper, is the latest in a string of Mercadinis who have run the place. It's quirky. The rooms are small with beds with wooden frames and cotton sheets.

The bathrooms are even smaller. The restaurant feels like a throwback to the '50s—the walls are crammed with portraits done in various media that span the decades. But there's nothing dated about the food: It's terrific Tuscan, from its classic minestrone to the veal sautéed in marsala. Don't be surprised if Beppe hums along to the Rachmaninoff playing in the background—he comes from a long line of musicians. If you plan to stay out past 10:30 PM, let him know as he locks the place up! ⊠ *Via Roma 151, 54013,* ☎ *0585/92060,* FAX *no fax. 19 rooms. Restaurant. EP, MAP. MC, V. Restaurant closed Mon. and Oct.*

Equi Terme

⑮ *15 km (9 mi) southeast of Fivizzano, 45 km (28 mi) east of La Spezia.*

If you're hankering for a spa experience, but are put off by the high prices of many spas, here's a way to do it without breaking the bank. Equi Terme is a pretty, teeny little town nestled in the mountains. The waters clock in at a warm 81°F. Though the Romans first discovered these waters, it wasn't until the end of the 19th century that the thermal waters were a draw. Supposedly the waters helps cure respiratory diseases; even if they don't, this is still a relaxing place to be, with not much else to do but enjoy the waters, hike, and sample the local Tuscan fare.

At the **Stabilimento Termale di Equi Terme** you can linger in a large pool with warm thermal waters and gaze up into the clear blue sky above, or you can treat yourself to any of the spa services—sauna, massage, water therapy, and water massage, among other things—offered within. ⊠ *Via Umberto I 20,* ☎ *0585/949300.* 🎫 *treatments 15,000 lire– 45,000 lire.* ☉ *Mid-May–Oct.*

Dining and Lodging

$ ⤫🏨 **La Posta.** This is a slightly ramshackle, totally fun place to stay
★ and eat. It's directly across the little stream from the Hotel Terme (☞ *below*). The seven basic rooms have high ceilings and baths. The restaurant is a real treat and worth a trip—the *ravioli alle ortiche* (spinach ravioli stuffed with nettles, lightly dressed with a creamy nut sauce) is tasty, and the house special, the *lasagne la spagnola* (a nonsensical name), made—as the proprietor says—with "top secret" ingredients, is definitely made with five different cheeses and tastes as light as a feather. ⊠ *Via Provinciale 26, 54022,* ☎ *0585/97937,* FAX *no fax. 7 rooms. Restaurant. CP, MAP, FAP. AE, DC, MC, V. Closed Jan. and Feb.; restaurant closed Tues.*

$ 🏨 **Hotel Terme.** This is the place to unwind with no distractions. The hotel, which is 100 years old, is cool, comfortable, and directly next door to a spa that offers all sorts of soothing things for body and soul. A small river runs near it, which might be the only noise you hear during your stay. The restaurant offers local specialties and the menu changes frequently. ⊠ *Via Noce Verde, Equi Terme, Massa 54022,* ☎ *0585/97830 and 0585/97831,* FAX *0585/97831. 20 rooms. Restaurant, bar, meeting room. MAP, FAP. AE, DC, MC, V.*

Aulla

⑯ *30 km (19 mi) northwest of Equi Terme, 23 km (14 mi) northeast of La Spezia, 152 km (94 mi) northwest of Florence.*

Aulla is a sleepy town just off the autostrada, and there's not much to see or do here. It was heavily bombed by the United States during World War II, so much of what you see is post-war reconstruction. However, on the outskirts of town is a park with an old castle that offers up some superb views.

The castle **La Brunella** dates from the 16th century, and you can see remnants of a 9th-century abbey dedicated to San Caprasio. It was the English couple Aubrey Waterfield and Linda Duff-Gordon who bought it in the early years of this century and turned it into a country home, feudal style; they also created its garden. D. H. Lawrence (1885–1930), among others, visited them here. Inside the complex is the **Museo di Storia Naturale della Lunigiana** (Museum of Natural History of the Lunigiana). ⊠ *Castello del Piagnaro,* ☎ *0187/400252, 0187/409077.* ▧ *4,000 lire.* ☉ *Castle: daily 9–12 and 3–6; daily 9–12 and 4–7. Park: daily 8:30–7:30.*

Pontremoli

⑰ *17½ km (11 mi) north of Aulla, 40 km (25 mi) northeast of La Spezia, 164 km (102 mi) northwest of Florence.*

Beautifully set where the Magra and Verde rivers meet, Pontremoli has a historic center developed according to a medieval matrix. During the Middle Ages, the city was a point of contact between north and south and economically it flourished. Here originated the *libri ambulenti* (traveling book fair), and a prestigious literary prize, the Premio Bancarella, is still awarded. The town is especially bursting with activity on Wednesday and Saturday, when an open-air market stacked with fruits, vegetables, and clothing takes over the Piazza del Duomo and the adjoining Piazza Repubblica.

The 17th-century **Duomo,** in the midst of Piazza del Duomo, is an exercise in Baroque excess—the lime green walls, accentuated with pale pink on the pilasters, and the white molding throughout look like a gaudy wedding cake. ⊠ *Piazza del Duomo,* ☎ *no phone.* ▧ *Free.* ☉ *Daily 9–7.*

Cross the Magra and to the Via Mazzini to check out the pretty Rococo facade of the **Chiesa di Nostra Donna,** finished in the 1730s. The lovely **Parco della Torre** along the Magra is great for a picnic; it's at the end of the street at the church. **Castello di Pignaro** has been around since the 9th and 10th centuries, but not a whole lot from that period remains. Additions and subtractions occurred between the 15th and 16th centuries. What does remain, however, is a fully formed castle with stupefying views and a **Museo delle Statue Stele Lunigianesi,** which contains prehistoric stele found in the area. ⊠ *Via Garibaldi,* ☎ *0187/831439.* ▧ *5,000 lire.* ☉ *Oct.–Mar., Tues.–Sun. 9–12 and 2–5; Apr.–Sept., Tues.–Sun. 9–12 and 3–6.*

La Chiesetta di San'Ilario. This is a very little—say, 15 ft across at its widest—chapel built 1883–1893. And though it has little art historic merit, it's so cute that it's worth a visit. It's got an almost Disneyesque style with its orange and yellow painted exterior. Inside are ceiling decorations painted after World War II by the members of the Triani family, natives of Pontremoli. It's just a few minutes' walk from the castle. ⊠ *Via Pagnaro 13,* ☎ *no phone.* ▧ *Free. Ask at the Duomo (☞ above) for Corinna Triani, sister of the painters, to open it.*

Dining

$$ ✕ **Da Busse.** Just around the corner from the Duomo, this Mom and Pop eatery serves up solid local fare in a casual, understated way. This is not the place to come for a romantic meal, but rather for when you're hungry for a good lunch. The interior is brightly lighted, the tables are close together, and there's a hum from the kitchen and chatting diners. Reservations are advised weekends. ⊠ *Piazza Duomo 31,* ☎ *0187/831371. No credit cards. Closed Fri. and 3 weeks in July. No dinner (except Sat. and holidays).*

LIGURIAN COAST AND THE ALPI APUANE

Here's where Tuscans and others come to play on long sandy beaches. These beach towns are lively, bustling places in the summer, and somewhat quieter in the off-season.

Viareggio

18 *20 km (13 mi) northwest of Pisa, 97 km (60 mi) west of Florence.*

Tobias Smollett (1721–1771), an English novelist, wrote in the 1760s that Viareggio was "a kind of sea-port on the Mediterranean . . . The roads are indifferent and the accommodation is execrable." Much has changed in Viareggio since Smollett's time: there are lots of accommodations ranging from five-star splendor to one-star simplicity, for this is a beach town that gets very crowded in the summer. It's loud, brassy, and not the place to come to if you're looking for some peace and quiet.

Viareggio also has numerous buildings decorated in the Liberty style and a wide promenade parallel to the sea that resembles, in some ways, American boardwalks where tourists and locals alike come out to stroll. Lining the main drag are bars, cafés, and some very fine restaurants. It's worth a stop or a detour if you like the beach and want to see how middle-class Italians spend their beach vacations. If you can't make it to Venice for **Carnevale** (Carnival), settle for Viareggio, which is nearly as much fun as Venice. The city is packed with revelers from all over Tuscany who come to join in the riot of colorful parades and festivities. Try to book lodging in advance, but beware: Lots of people want to be here to celebrate Carnival, and hotels acknowledge this fact by charging high-season prices.

Dining and Lodging

$$$ ✕ **Romano.** This fine restaurant is run by Romano Franceschini and
★ his family. It's sophisticated dining at its best with superb service. They do fish here and they do it extremely well. There's some odd pairings, like the shrimp with a reduced carrot sauce, but they work. The mixed seafood grill is a delight. Romano, an excellent host, is ebullient and proud of his food and he should be. Reservations are advised. ✉ *Via Mazzini 122,* ☎ *0584/31382. AE, DC, MC, V. Closed Mon. and 3 weeks in Jan.*

$$$ 🏨 **Grand Hotel.** A hotel since the turn of the century, this hotel looks majestic from the outside, and inside sweepingly high ceilings maintain the feeling. The *salone,* where dinner is served in cooler months, has in the past doubled as a ballroom. The ceilings are high and the tablecloths pink: it's terribly romantic. The yellow breakfast room is flooded with light that bounces off the potted palms. Individual rooms have tiled floors, and some have balconies overlooking the sea (additional charge). There is a three-day minimum in high season. The restaurant menu changes daily. ✉ *Viale Carducci 44, 55049,* ☎ *0584/ 45151,* 🖷 *0584/31438. 102 rooms. Breakfast room, dining room, minibars, pool, Ping-Pong, bicycles, meeting room. MAP, FAP. AE, DC, MC, V. Closed Nov.–Mar. (except during Carnival and Easter).*

$$$ 🏨 **Hotel President.** This hotel has a soothing exterior decorated in white and yellow, and its interior bespeaks a quiet elegance. Some of the rooms—with slightly formal decor, high ceilings, and pastel walls— look directly out on to the sea; the only thing between you and it is a street and that famous promenade. The hotel restaurant, Ristorante Gaudi, is open to nonguests. The hotel bar with an outdoor terrace is trimmed with crisp turn-of-the-century furniture. Two suites each have a hot tub. ⊠ *Viale Carducci 5, 55049,* ☎ *0584/962 712,* FAX *0584/963658. 31 rooms, 4 suites, 2 residential suites. Restaurant, in-room safes, minibars, meeting room. MAP, FAP. AE, DC, MC, V. Restaurant closed Nov.–Feb.; no lunch (except during Carnival and Aug.).*

Pietrasanta

⑲ *8 km (5 mi) north of Viareggio, 104 km (65 mi) northwest of Florence.*

Pietrasanta has a gorgeous rectangular Renaissance Piazza del Duomo that gives you a feel for how grandly 15th-century architects conceived of urban planning. It was also known for its marble in the 15th century. Both Donatello and later Michelangelo (1475–1564) used marble quarried nearby.

Piazza del Duomo is a nice square to enjoy a coffee at an outside café and people-watch. The **Porta Pisana** will be on your left, as well as the remains of the **Rocca Arringhina,** a structure dating from the 1320s and rebuilt in the 1480s. On the corner of Via Padre e Barsanti and Piazza del Duomo is a plaque recording that Michelangelo signed a contract in 1518 on this spot to do the facade of San Lorenzo in Florence.

The **Duomo,** dedicated to San Martino and begun in the mid-13th century, is undergoing a lengthy restoration and is at present closed to the public. Most of the art inside dates from the 16th and 17th centuries. ⊠ *Piazza del Duomo,* ☎ *no phone.* ☞ *Free. Closed for renovation.*

The church of **Sant'Agostino** was built in the 14th century by the Augustinians. Some 15th-century frescoes and paintings from the 17th and 18th centuries are contained within. It's no longer a church but is used for special exhibitions. ⊠ *Via Sant'Agostino,* ☎ *no phone.* ☞ *Free.* ☉ *Daily 9:30–12:30 and 5–7.*

The **Museo dei Bozzetti** contains a collection of sculptural sketches and models made by contemporary Italian and foreign artists, including the most important sculptors of this century in the Versilian workshops. ⊠ *Piazza del Duomo,* ☎ *0584/791122.* ☞ *Free.* ☉ *Tues.–Fri. 2:30–7, Sat. 2:30–6.*

The **Civico Museo Archeologico** has objects from the 3rd millennium BC as well as pottery dating from the Renaissance. The collection is housed in the 15th-century **Palazzo Moroni.** At press time, the museum was closed for restoration. ⊠ *Palazzo Moroni, Piazza del Duomo,* ☎ *0584/795288 or 0584/795289.* ☉ *Oct.–Apr., Tues., Wed., and Thurs. 9–12 and Sun. 10–12:30.*

The church of **Sant'Antonio Abate** (also known as the church of San Biagio) dates from the 14th century and is dedicated to San Biagio. Inside are two wood polychromed sculptures of San Biagio and Sant'Antonio Abate dating from the 16th century. Frescoes by Colombian artist Fernando Botero (born 1932) depicting *La Porta del Paradiso* (*The Gates of Heaven*) and *La Porta dell'Inferno* (*The Gates of Hell*), dating from the 1990s, are in the side nave. ⊠ *Via G. Mazzini,* ☎ *0584/70056.* ☞ *Free.* ☉ *Daily 8–12 and 3–6.*

Forte dei Marmi

⑳ *5 km (3 mi) north of Pietrasanta, 14 km (9 mi) north of Viareggio, 104 km (65 mi) west of Florence.*

Forte dei Marmi is a playground for wealthy Italians and equally wealthy tourists. Its wide sandy beaches—strands run for 6 km (4 mi)—have the Apuan Alps as a dramatic background. The town was, from Roman times, the port from which marble from Carrara was quarried and then transported. In the 1920s, it became a fashionable seaside resort and has so remained to this day. During the winter, the town's population is about 10,000; in the summer, it swells seven to eight times that.

Dining and Lodging

$$$ ✕ **Lorenzo.** Even in the dead of winter, this restaurant, which special-
★ izes in fish, is crowded. It's easy to see why. Twice a day fresh ship-
ments of fish arrive and go almost directly to the table. The affable
Lorenzo Viani has owned and run the restaurant for 15 years. There's
not a dud dish on this menu—start with the chilled raw clams and oys-
ters before moving on to any of the terrific primi (starters) and *piatti
secondi* (entrées). If you don't like fish, there's some nonfish offerings
as well. ⊠ *Via Carducci 61,* ☎ *0584/84030,* FAX *0584/89671. Reservations essential. AE, DC, MC, V. Closed Mon. No lunch July and Aug.*

$$ ✕ **Bistrot.** You could go directly from the beach to this fish restaurant,
as it is on the beach, but it's advisable to get a little dressed up. The
place is awash in pastels; the food is as good as the place is pretty. Their
starter of *assaggini* (little tastes) is a great way to begin—the *carpac-
cio di branzino* (sea bass) is quickly seared and then served with fra-
grant local olive oil, basil, and tomatoes. Their pastas are homemade
and their *sauté di frutti di mare,* a cross between a soup and stew, fea-
tures *vongole* (clams), tomatoes, garlic, and oil in a heavenly broth.
Reservations are advised. ⊠ *Viale Franceschi 14,* ☎ *0584/89879. AE,
DC, MC, V. Closed Tues.*

$$$$ 🏨 **Byron.** Put yourself in the lap of luxury in this elegant hotel, cre-
★ ated by joining two Liberty villas dating from 1899 and 1902. The pale
pastel yellow of the exterior hints at the elegance inside. If you don't
feel like walking all the way to the beach, which is directly across the
street, you can linger by the pool. This fine hotel also includes the restau-
rant La Magnolia, which serves regional cuisine served alfresco in
summer. ⊠ *Viale Arthur-Jules Morin 46, 55042,* ☎ *0584/787052,* FAX
*0584/787152. 24 rooms, 6 suites. Restaurant, pool, billiards, meeting
rooms. MAP, FAP. AE, DC, MC, V.*

$$$$ 🏨 **Goya.** This hotel right in the center of town might be described as
neo-Liberty, as it was only finished a little over 10 years ago. Despite
its relative newness, it evokes old-world charm. The rooms have high
ceilings, and some of them have their own little balconies with a view
to the sea. There's also an outdoor hot tub if you feel like unwinding
after a day at the beach. The hotel also includes a restaurant. ⊠ *Via
Carducci 69, 55042,* ☎ *0584/787221,* FAX *0584/787269. 47 rooms, 1
suite. Restaurant, hot tub. MAP, FAP. AE, DC, MC, V.*

$$$$ 🏨 **Ritz.** You might feel like you're in Miami Beach if you stay in this
1920s Liberty villa adorned with palm trees, but the dramatic Apuan
Alps on the horizon will quickly set you straight. It's just one block from
any of the beach clubs, and the center of town is a short walk away. ⊠
Via Flavio Gioia 2, 55042, ☎ *0584/787531,* FAX *0584/787522. 32
rooms, 1 suite. Pool, free parking. CP, MAP, FAP. AE, DC, MC, V.*

Nightlife and the Arts

If you can tear yourself away from the beach, stop in at **Alma Rosa Art
Music and Bar** (⊠ Viale Morin 89/a, ☎ 0584/82503). Don't be sur-
prised if you run into some Italian soccer players or other young,
good-looking Italian celebrities. They've been known to pop in here
during high season. Leonardo, the owner-bartender, is charming and
speaks English.

Outdoor Activities and Sports

BIKING

Claudio Maggi Cicli (⊠ Viale Morin 85, ☎ 0584/89529) and **Maggi-
Coppa** (⊠ Via A. Franceschi 4d, ☎ 0584/83528) rent bicycles.

The **Forte dei Marmi Club Alpino Italiano** (✉ Via Michelangelo 49, ☎ 0584/89808) can provide information on getting vertical.

Massa

㉑ *8 ½ km (5 mi) north of Forte dei Marmi, 22 km (14 mi) north of Viareggio, 115 km (74 mi) northwest of Florence.*

Massa itself is not all that interesting. Should you find yourself here, attempt to visit the **Rocca,** which was built between the 14th and 16th centuries. To get there it's a steep climb. The fortress is currently undergoing restoration, but you can at least peek at the exterior. Things are livelier in Marina di Massa, Massa's port 5 km (3 mi) south, where you can go to the beach and eat well, too.

Dining and Lodging

$$ ✕ **Farfarello.** This tiny trattoria in Marina di Massa seats only about
★ 25, and it's always crowded. There's a good reason: The food is terrific. Start with their mixed antipasto plate, which contains a variety of fish dishes (smoked tuna and swordfish) and a vongole salad served in a scallop cup among other starters. Then follow with any of their pastas—the tagliarini with little shrimp and a hint of *peperoncino* (hot chile peppers) is a treat. Save room for dessert: Their *ciambella*, an often tired Italian dessert, gets a complete rehaul here. Reservations are advised. ✉ *Via Cristoforo Colombo 30, Marina di Massa, ☎ 0585/ 869090. AE, DC, MC, V. Closed Wed. and Oct.–Mar.*

$$$ 🏨 **Hotel Excelsior.** This hotel is as close to being on the beach as you can be—the only thing separating it from the water is a street. There's great views of the Apuan Alps to be had as well. The marble quarries are only 5 km (3 mi) away, and there's an 18-hole golf course only 8 km (5 mi) from here. The rooms are spacious and comfortable. The hotel restaurant, Il Sestante, specializes in local and international dishes. Three of the rooms are wheelchair friendly. ✉ *Lungomare Vespucci, Via Cesare Battisti I, 54037, ☎ 0585/8601, FAX 0585/869795. 71 rooms, 5 suites. Restaurant, pool, meeting room. MAP, FAP. AE, DC, MC, V. Restaurant closed Wed. in winter.*

$$–$$$ 🏨 **Hotel Tirreno** Once a private Liberty villa, the building just about 100 ft from the sea became a hotel in the 1950s. Rooms have high ceilings, which contribute to grand sense of space, and are decorated in cool pastel hues. Full pension is required in July and August. ✉ *Piazza Betti, Marina di Massa, 54037, ☎ 0585/246173, FAX 0585/240827. 28 rooms, 5 suites. Restaurant. MAP, FAP. AE, DC, MC, V.*

Carrara

㉒ *26 km (16 mi) north of Viareggio, 7 km (4½ mi) north of Massa, 126 km (79 mi) northwest of Florence.*

Carrara's history dates to Roman times. In 963, the Holy Roman Emperor Otto I (912–973) donated the land that comprised Carrara to the bishops of Luni. The town faded into obscurity in the Middle Ages, and in the early 15th century it came under domination by the Malaspina family. During the 19th and 20th centuries it became a hotbed for anarchism, and during World War II, the town put up fierce resistance to the Nazis. The town is lively thanks to its art institute. The **Accademia di Belli Arti,** founded by Maria Teresa Cybo Malaspina d'Este in 1769, draws studio art students from all over Italy. Their presence explains the funky atmosphere that's found in some of the piazzas, and most likely explains why Carrara has a macrobiotic shop—something rare in Italy.

Marble has been quarried in the area for the past 2,000 years. Michelangelo, who is perhaps the most famous sculptor of all, quarried his marble here. The art historian Giorgio Vasari (1511–1574) records that Michelangelo came to Carrara with two apprentices to quarry the marble for his ill-fated tomb for Julius II (1443–1513). According to Vasari, he spent eight months among the rocks conceiving fantastical ideas for future works. Carrara has a lot of still-active quarries—well over a hundred at last count. Most of them are not open to the public for safety reasons. However, it is possible to tour specific caves.

For the true gourmand, this is the time to sample lardo di colonnata, the sinfully delicious, cholesterol-be-damned cured pork fat. It hails from this area and can be eaten hot on *crostini* (grilled bread with a drizzle of olive oil and topping) or cold with other mixed meats.

Work began on the **Duomo** in the 11th century and continued into the 14th. The cathedral is dedicated to St. Andrew and is the first church of the Middle Ages constructed entirely of marble. Most of the marble comes from Carrara (the white, light blue gray, black, and red). The tremendous facade is a fascinating blend of Pisan Romanesque architecture and Gothic. Note the human figures and animals on Corinthian capitals. ⊠ *Piazza del Duomo*, ☎ *no phone*. ⊡ *Free*. ⊙ *Daily 9–7*.

The lovely Baroque church of **San Francesco** is worth looking at simply because of its understated elegance. It dates from the 1620s to 1660s, and even though it was built during the peak years of the Baroque, the only excess can be found in the twisting, marble columns embellishing the altars. ⊠ *Piazza XXVII Aprile*, ☎ *no phone*. ⊡ *Free*. ⊙ *Daily 9–7*.

Carrara's history as a marble-producing center is well documented in the **Museo del Marmo** (Museum of Marble), beginning with early works from the AD 2nd century. Exhibits detail the production of marble, from quarrying it, transporting it, and sculpting it. ⊠ *Viale XX Settembre*, ☎ *0585/845746*. ⊡ *6,000 lire*. ⊙ *June–Sept., Mon.–Sat. 10–8; Oct. and May, Mon.–Sat. 10–5; Nov.–Apr., Mon.–Sat. 8:30–7:30*.

NEED A BREAK? If you want to grab a cappuccino or a tasty panini, stop in at **Casanova** (⊠ Just off Piazza Alberica, ☎ 0585/777833), which is always open. While you're there, check out the lovely piazza; though it serves, sadly, as a parking lot, its brightly colored buildings lining the large rectangular area give you a fine idea of the 19th century.

Lodging

$$ 🏨 **Hotel Carrara.** Though the hotel isn't actually in Carrara, it's right down the street from the Avenza-Carrara train station (Carrara is 4 km/2½ mi northwest). It's a small, quiet hotel with simple rooms with tiled floors. It offers an extensive breakfast buffet. ⊠ *Via Petacchi 21, 54031 Avenza*, ☎ *0585/52371*, 𝔽𝔸𝕏 *0585/50344*. *32 rooms. Breakfast room. CP, MAP, FAP. AE, DC, MC, V.*

$$ 🏨 **Hotel Mediterraneo.** A 10-minute drive from Carrara, this hotel in Marina di Carrara, about 8 km (5 mi) south, offers a nice option to staying in Carrara itself (where the hotel options are somewhat grim). The Mediterraneo is just 150 ft from the sea, although you'll have to walk a little farther to get to a beach. Many of the rooms have balconies, and breakfast is served on a terrace flanked by sea and mountain views. The restaurant, where the menu changes daily, derives inspiration from the sea, but there are meat options as well. ⊠ *Via Genova 2/h, Marina di Carrara 54036*, ☎ 𝔽𝔸𝕏 *0585/785222. 42 rooms, 1 suite. Restaurant, bar, meeting room. MAP, FAP. AE, DC, MC, V. Restaurant: no lunch Oct.–Apr.*

Cinque Terre

La Spezia 144 km (90 mi) west of Florence.

The aura of isolation that has surrounded five almost inaccessible coastal villages known as Cinque Terre, together with their dramatic coastal scenery, has made them one of the eastern Riviera's premier attractions. Clinging haphazardly to steep cliffs, they are linked by footpaths, by train, and now by narrow, unasphalted and rather tortuous roads, a fairly recent development. The local train on the Genoa–La Spezia line stops at each town between Levanto and Riomaggiore. The westernmost village is Monterosso, but the easiest to reach by car is Riomaggiore, easternmost of the villages and closest to La Spezia and the A12 autostrada.

All five of the Cinque Terre and the tiny mountain settlements that are linked to them are connected by well-established hiking footpaths (☞ Outdoor Activities and Sports, *below*)—for much of their history, these were the only way to get from town to town on land. Although today the train, and to a certain extent the road, have surpassed the footpaths, they're still well kept and showcase breathtaking ocean views as well as access to rugged, secluded beaches and grottoes that will never have a train station.

The largest of the five fishing towns is **Monterosso,** with a 12th-century church in the Ligurian style, lively markets, and small beaches. To the east is **Vernazza,** a charming village of narrow streets, small squares and arcades, and the remains of forts dating from the Middle Ages. The buildings, narrow lanes, and stairways of **Corniglia,** the middle village, are strung together on a hillside amid vineyards; excellent views of the entire coastal strip can be seen on a clear day. The enchanting pastel houses in **Manarola** are nestled into a steep hill, hugging the rocky shoreline. At the eastern end of the Cinque Terre is **Riomaggiore,** huddled around a tiny harbor dotted with fishing boats and hemmed in by sheer cliffs.

Dining and Lodging

$$ ✕ **Miki.** Have lunch here if in Monterosso—what better reward to give yourself after hiking all or part of the trail? (For the record, dinner here is equally good.) Specialties include anything having to do with fish: The *insalata di mare* (cold squid and fish salad) is more than tasty; so is the grilled fish and any pasta with fish. If you're more in the mood for a pizza, you can order that here as well. Miki has a beautiful little garden in the back. ⊠ *Via Fegina 104, Monterosso al Mare,* ☎ *0187/ 817608. AE, MC, V. Closed Nov. and Dec.; Oct.–Apr., closed Tues..*

$$ ✕ **Trattoria Gianni Franzi.** Things are casual here in Vernazza, so if you're in the middle of hiking, don't worry that you might be underdressed. This is the place to order pesto, a Ligurian specialty that somehow tastes better when you're eating it in Liguria. Here they serve it with green beans. Other options include lots of treats from the sea; you can eat all of this outside with a view on to a tiny port suitable for wading. ⊠ *Piazza Marconi 5, Vernazza,* ☎ *0187/821003. AE, DC, MC, V.*

$$$ ▨ **Porto Roca.** In a panoramic position above the sea, Porto Roca is
★ set slightly apart, blessedly removed from the crowds who visit, especially on weekends. It has the look of a well-kept villa; interiors have authentic antique pieces and there are ample terraces. The rooms are bright, with sea breezes. Porto Roca is on a network of not-too-demanding hill walks and has a faithful American clientele. ⊠ *Via Corone 1, Monterosso al Mare 19016,* ☎ *0187/817502,* FAX *0187/817692. 43 rooms. Restaurant, bar. MAP. AE, MC, V. Closed Nov. 4–Mar. 23.*

Outdoor Activities and Sports
HIKING

The most well-known and easiest hiking trail is the **Via dell'Amore** (Lover's Lane), which—going east to west—links Riomaggiore with Manarola (2 km/1 mi, 30 min) with a flat path cut into the cliff side. The same trail continues to Corniglia (3 km/2 mi, 1 hr), then becomes more difficult between Corniglia and Vernazza (3 km/2 mi, 1½ hrs) and more so still from Vernazza to Monterosso (2 km/1 mi, 1½ hrs). Additionally, trails lead from Monterosso up the mountainside and back down to Vernazza, and into the mountains from Corniglia, Manarola, and Riomaggiore, with historic churches and great views along the way. Trail maps are available at the Monterosso tourist office. Be sure to wear sturdy shoes and a hat, and bring a water bottle, as there is little shade.

NORTH OF FLORENCE A TO Z

Arriving and Departing

By Bus

Most of the Mugello's small towns rely on bus service from COPIT and Lazzi, with erratic connections to Florence. Bus service can get you around the Garfagnana, and should be chosen over trains. Bus service to the Lunigiana is limited. A car is necessary to see Massa and Carrara due to sporadic bus service.

By Car

The east–west A11 autostrada connects Viareggo, Lucca, Montecatini Terma, Pistoia, Prato, and Florence. The A1 runs north–south from Milan through Bologna, Florence, and down to Rome and Naples.

By Plane

The largest airports in the region are Pisa's **Aeroporto Galileo Galilei** (☎ 050/500707) and Florence's **Aeroporto Peretola** (☎ 055/373498).

By Train

The Mugello has train service to Borgo San Lorenzo, but limited service otherwise. In the Garfagnana, train connections are extremely limited. Trains make their way to some parts of the Lunigiana, but it, too, is best explored by car. To properly explore Massa and Carrara, the two marble towns, a car is necessary due to spotty service. Viareggio, because it is on a major train line, is easily reachable from Florence and Rome. To get to the Cinque Terre, take a train to La Spezia, and then take a local train to any of the five towns. For the state-run line (FS) **train information,** call 147/888088 toll-free.

Getting Around

By Bus

Buses connect the towns in the Mugello, though connections are often difficult. Limited bus connections run in the Lunigiana, the Garfagnana, and the coast. It's also possible to take a bus from Pistoia or Florence to get to Abetone.

By Car

Driving is the best way to get around this area. The A11 will take you west from Florence, and the A12 will take you up the coast. Most of these towns are approached by lesser highways and two-lane roads.

By Train

With the exception of Viareggio and Borgo San Lorenzo, which are on a main FS train line, the towns and cities are difficult to get to by train. In some cases, such as Forte dei Marmi and Carrara, the train stations are not anywhere near the center of town.

Contacts and Resources

Agritourist Agencies
☞ Chapter 2.

Car Rentals
☞ Chapter 2.

Emergencies
In an **emergency,** dial 113 for paramedics, police, or the fire department.

Late-Night Pharmacies
All pharmacies post the addresses of the nearest late-night pharmacies outside their doors.

Travel Agencies
☞ Chapter 2.

Visitor Information
Abetone (⊠ Via Pescinone 15, ☎ 0573/607811). **Borgo San Lorenzo** (⊠ Via Togliatti 45, ☎ 055/8495346). **Carrara** (⊠ Viale Galilei 133, Marina di Carrara, ☎ 0585/632218). **Forte dei Marmi** (⊠ Via A. Franceschi 8, ☎ 0584/80091, 0584/83214). **Marina di Massa** (⊠ Viale Amerigo Vespucci 23, ☎ 0585/240 046). **San Marcello Pistoiese** (⊠ Piazza Matteotti, ☎ 0573/62121). **Viareggio** (⊠ Piazza Mazzini 22, ☎ 0584/48881).

4 Cities West of Florence

Of the cities strung along the autostrada west of Florence—Prato, Pistoia, Montecatini Terme, and Lucca—some are sprawling and industrial, but have well-preserved medieval and Renaissance centers. As you head west, the landscape becomes progressively more dramatic, with the craggy Alpi Apuane in the distance. Towards Pisa the land flattens out as it nears the sea.

DURING THE MIDDLE AGES AND THE RENAISSANCE, cities such as Prato, Pistoia, Lucca, and Pisa were the bane of Florence, which, in her struggle to become the dominant force in Tuscany, waged many wars. Eventually these cities—with the exception of Lucca—came under Florentine influence. It's best when traveling to the region to resist the pull of Florence that persists today: the fine churches and museums in these cities are fewer but no less rich. Lucca's charm lies in its medieval walls that surround the historic center, and the beauty of Pisa's Duomo, Battistero, and Torre Pendente (Leaning Tower) complex is unsurpassable. Prato has many works by Fra Filippo Lippi, a native son, and in its Duomo and Battistero, Pistoia preserves its medieval aura.

Revised by
Patricia Rucidlo

Pleasures and Pastimes

Architecture

The Middle Ages left its mark on these cities. Many of their churches bear the green-and-white marble striping typical of churches built during the period, and historic centers have palaces adorned with coats of arms from various prominent families. If your taste leans towards the more recent, you might delight in the distinctive Liberty style, popular in the late 19th and early 20th centuries. It's most evident in Lucca, with its main thoroughfare, the Fillungo, dotted with examples.

Dining

Most restaurants in the region serve dishes that will be familiar to you if you've eaten in Florence: it's still possible to eat *bistecca alla fiorentina* (grilled local Chianina beef) and *ribollita* (a thick soup of white beans, bread, cabbage, and onions). One of the most fun things about eating around Italy is sampling its regional cuisine, and this area offers up some treats. Pistoia and environs are famous for its *maccheroni all'anatra* (macaroni-shape pasta with a duck sauce). Prato can boast of having the most famous biscotti in all of Italy, the exquisite *biscotti di Prato,* a hard cookie made for dunking into a steaming cappuccino or *vin santo,* a sweet dessert wine. Pisa can lay claim to *ceccina,* which is a pancake made of chickpea flour that can be eaten alone or rolled with various toppings. Montecatini has its *cialda,* a thin, sweet wafer usually topped with gelato. Lucca is famous for its *farro,* called emmer or spelt in English. It's been cultivated for a couple thousand years and is unique to the region. You can eat it in soup, or cooked in the manner of risotto (some wags refer to it as *"farrotto"*), or as a cold grain salad. And then there's Lucca's fragrant olive oil, arguably the best in the world.

CATEGORY	COST*
$$$$	over 110,000 lire
$$$	60,000 lire–110,000 lire
$$	35,000 lire–60,000 lire
$	under 35,000 lire

Prices are per person, for a three course meal, house wine and tax included.

Lodging

For a taste of the country, you can stay outside of Florence, particularly in the warmer months when Florence is at its hottest and most crowded, and avail yourself of the excellent train service for day trips into the city. Another option might be to stay in an *agriturismo,* or farm stay, and experience a different kind of Tuscany—one based more in the 19th and early 20th centuries. More lavish accommodations can be found in Montecatini, where it's perfectly permissible to pamper yourself with spa treatments—people have been doing it for more than 100 years.

CATEGORY	COST*
$$$$	over 350,000 lire
$$$	220,000 lire–350,000 lire
$$	100,000 lire–220,000 lire
$	under 100,000 lire

Prices are for a double room for two, tax and service included.

Exploring Cities West of Florence

The best way to see this part of Tuscany is by car, as some of the smaller cities are otherwise hard to get to. However, cities such as Lucca, Pisa, Prato, Pistoia, Empoli, and Montecatini have regular train and bus service, which makes getting around easy. Five days would be ample time to tour the area, as most of the towns are very close to one another and—with the exception of Lucca and Pisa, which demand more time—can be toured relatively quickly.

Numbers in the text correspond to numbers in the margin and on the Cities West of Florence, Lucca, and Pisa maps.

Great Itineraries

Lucca and Pisa are probably the most-visited Tuscan cities west of Florence, and with good reason. Lucca's charm is preserved within the medieval walls that surround the historic center, and Pisa has perhaps the most famous (leaning) tower in the world. Less visited but eminently worthwhile are the smaller cities of Pistoia and Prato, which have fine Romanesque churches, good restaurants, and fewer tourists. A different taste of Tuscany can be had by heading west to Empoli, San Miniato, and other smaller cities. Part of the pleasure of visiting these places comes from being slightly off the well-trod tourist path, and a greater part comes from discovering the smaller treasures that these places offer.

IF YOU HAVE 3 DAYS

Starting from Florence, travel to ▦ **Prato** ① and spend the morning seeing the Filippo Lippi frescoes in the Duomo and the Museo di Pittura Murale before heading off to ▦ **Pistoia** ② for the afternoon. In Pistoia, check out the lovely Catttedrale di San Zeno, with its magnificent silver altar, and the Ospedale del Ceppo, with its multicolored terracotta frieze. Spend the night in ▦ **Montecatini Terme** ③, and take in the sights from the lively and bustling Piazza del Popolo. Travel to ▦ **Lucca** ⑥–⑫ in the morning. Tour the Duomo and see the early 15th-century tomb of Ilaria del Caretto; in the afternoon, go to ▦ **Pisa** ⑬–㉑ and see the Torre Pendente, Duomo, and Battistero. Travel to ▦ **San Miniato** ㉓ and overnight here. Duck into the Museo Diocesano in the morning, and head back to Florence in the afternoon.

IF YOU HAVE 5 DAYS

Using Florence as a starting point, travel to ▦ **San Miniato** ㉓ and book a hotel. Explore the little town in the morning before heading south to **Castelfiorentino** ㉔ to see the tremendous Benozzo Gozzoli tabernacles in the Biblioteca Comunale before moving on to **Certaldo** ㉖ to pay homage to the birthplace (and final resting spot) of Giovanni Boccaccio, Certaldo's most famous son. The next morning, explore ▦ **Empoli** ㉒ and its Collegiata, then go to ▦ **Pisa** ⑬–㉑ to spend the afternoon. Stay in Pisa or a local agriturismo. The next morning go to ▦ **Lucca** ⑥–⑫ and spend the entire day seeing the Duomo, Roman Ampitheater, and the church of San Michele. Pop into the Pinacoteca

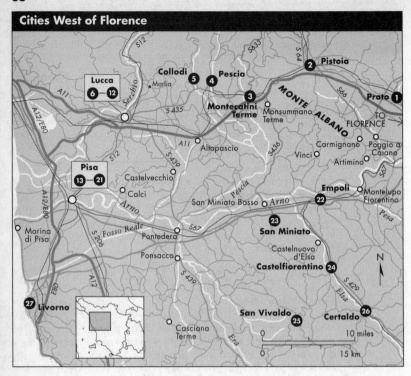

Cities West of Florence

Nazionale and spend some time in the room with portraits of various Medici. Stay over in Lucca that evening, and then drive to ⊠ **Montecatini Terme** ③ in the morning. Spend the day taking the waters, or simply walking through the thermal parkland, and take the funicular up to Montecatini Alto. Overnight in Montecatini Terme, and return to Florence in the morning.

When to Tour Cities West of Florence

The best time to tour these cities—particularly in the cases of Lucca and Pisa—is any time but July and August, when the tourist season is in full swing and the sun is at its hottest. If you visit during July or August, plan to do early-morning or late-afternoon touring when the crowds and the heat are somewhat less oppressive. Stay in one of the hill towns—such as San Miniato—to avoid crowds and heat. Or discover the joys of Empoli and Pistoia, two wonderful but sadly neglected cities teeming with Renaissance art.

There are some enjoyable area events perhaps worth changing your schedule for: If you're in Pisa in June, by all means try to see its Luminaria, which is held on June 16. Blues lovers might want to check out Pistoia Blues in July or Pistoia's La Giostra dell'Orso (Bear Joust) on July 25th. Lucca's famous annual Puccini Festival is held the end of July and early August. For the traveling gourmand, you might want to sample various black truffle celebrations in and around San Miniato in October.

FROM FLORENCE TO COLLODI

The journey from Florence to Collodi takes you north and west of Florence via industrial Prato. Pistoia is a short distance away. After Pistoia, the countryside becomes a little hillier and much prettier. At

Montecatini, wander north along the Pescia River to Pescia, a flower-market town with worthwhile art, and Collodi, with a whole amusement park devoted to Pinocchio.

Prato

❶ *19 km (12 mi) northwest of Florence, 81 km (50 mi) east of Pisa.*

The wool industry in this city, which is one of the world's largest manufacturers of cloth, was known throughout Europe as early as the 13th century. It was further stimulated in the 14th century by a local cloth merchant, Francesco di Marco Datini, who built his business, according to one of his surviving ledgers, "in the name of God and of profit."

Prato's main attraction is its 11th-century **Duomo.** Romanesque in style, it is famous for its **Cappella del Sacro Cingolo** (Chapel of the Holy Girdle) to the left of the entrance, which enshrines the sash of the Virgin. It is said that the girdle was given to the apostle Thomas by the Virgin herself when she miraculously appeared after her Assumption. The Duomo also contains 15th-century frescoes by Prato's most famous son, Fra Filippo Lippi (1406–1469). Included are scenes from the life of St. Stephen on the left wall and scenes from the life of St. John the Baptist on the right in the **Cappella Maggiore** (Main Chapel). Bring a flashlight—no illumination is provided. ⊠ *Piazza del Duomo,* ☎ *0574/26234.* ☞ *Free.* ☉ *Daily 7–12 and 3:30–6:30.*

Sculpture by Donatello (circa 1386–1466) that originally adorned the Duomo's exterior pulpit is now on display in the **Museo dell'Opera del Duomo.** ⊠ *Piazza del Duomo 49,* ☎ *0574/29339.* ☞ *5,000 lire (includes entry to Museo di Pittura Murale, ☞ below).* ☉ *Mon. and Wed.–Sat. 9:30–12:30 and 3–6:30, Sun. 9:30–12:30.*

The **Museo di Pittura Murale** (Museum of Mural Painting) was at press time temporarily housing the fine collection of paintings by Fra Filippo Lippi and other works from the 13th and 14th centuries in a special exhibit called "Treasures of the City." The permanent collection contains frescoes removed from sites in Prato and environs. ⊠ *Piazza San Domenico,* ☎ *0574/29339.* ☞ *5,000 lire (includes entry to Museo dell'Opera del Duomo, ☞ above).* ☉ *Mon. and Wed.–Sat. 10–1 and 3:30–7:30, Sun. 3:30–7:30.*

Prato's **Centro per l'Arte Contemporanea L. Pecci** (L. Pecci Center of Contemporary Art) is acquiring a burgeoning collection of works by Italian and other artists. ⊠ *Viale della Repubblica 277,* ☎ *0574/ 570620.* ☞ *10,000 lire.* ☉ *Mon. and Wed.–Sun. 10–7.*

Who would ever think to put a small but significant collection of paintings from the 15th to the 20th centuries on the second floor of their palatial offices? The Cassa di Risparmio di Prato—that's who—and we have them to thank for opening up their private collection, **Galleria degli Alberti,** which includes such 15th-century gems as Fra Filippo Lippi's *Madonna and Child* and Giovanni Bellini's (circa 1430–1516) *Christ on the Cross,* as well as Caravaggio's (1573–1610) *Christ Crowned with Thorns.* Visits are by appointment; call ahead. ⊠ *c/o Cassa di Risparmio di Prato, Via degli Alberti 2,* ☎ *0574/617 359.* ☞ *Free.* ☉ *By appointment only, weekdays 8:30–1:30 and 3–4.*

Preserved in the **Museo del Tessuto** (Textile Museum) is what made this city a Renaissance economic powerhouse. The collection is composed of clothing, fragments of fabric, samples, and the machines used to make them from the 14th to the 20th centuries. Check out the 15th-century fabrics with pomegranate prints, a virtuoso display of Renaissance tex-

tile wizardry. ⊠ *Piazza del Commune,* ☎ *0574/611503.* ⊡ *5,000 lire.*
⊙ *Mon. and Wed.–Fri. 10–1 and 2:30–7:30, weekends 3:30–7:30.*

<table>
<tr><td>OFF THE
BEATEN PATH</td><td>

POGGIO A CAIANO – For a look at gracious country living, Renaissance style, detour south of Prato to the Medici villa Poggio a Caiano. Lorenzo the Magnificent (1449–1492) commissioned Giuliano da Sangallo (circa 1445–1516) to redo the villa, which was lavished with frescoes by important Renaissance painters such as Andrea del Sarto (1486–1531) and Pontormo (1494–1557). You can take a walk around the lovely grounds while waiting for the mandatory group tour to begin. ⊠ *7 km (4½ mi) south of Prato, follow signs,* ☎ *055/877012.* ⊡ *4,000 lire.* ⊙ *Apr.–May and Sept., Mon.–Sat. 9–5:30; June–Aug., Mon.–Sat. 9–6:30; Mar. and Oct., Mon.–Sat. 9–4:30; Nov.–Feb., Mon.–Sat. 9–3:30. Guided tours only, hourly on the half hr (9:30–1 hr before closing). Closed 2nd and 3rd Mon. of month. Ticket office closes 1 hr before villa and grounds.*

CARMIGNANO – *The Visitation* by Pontormo is a short car ride away from Poggio a Caiano in a small village called Carmignano. The work is in the Franciscan church of **San Michele**, which was dedicated in 1211. The painting, which dates from 1528–1530, may well be Pontormo's masterpiece. The colors are luminous, the drapery is flowing, and the entire effect is breathtaking. ⊠ *15 km (9 mi) south of Prato,* ☎ *055/8712468.* ⊡ *Free.* ⊙ *Daily 9–5.*

ARTIMINO – You might want to consider heading to this small town next door to Carmignano, to visit the **Villa Medicea La Ferdinanda di Artimino.** It was built by Ferdinando I de' Medici (1549–1609) in the 1590s and was used by the Medici as a hunting lodge. You can only visit it by appointment, however, so do plan on booking. ⊠ *15 km (9 mi) south of Prato,* ☎ *055/8792030 or 055/8718081.* ⊡ *Free.* ⊙ *By appointment only Tues. (book in advance). Closed 2 weeks in Aug.*

</td></tr>
</table>

Dining and Lodging

$$$ ✕ **Da Delfina.** Veer off the autostrada to this haven of Tuscan cook-
★   ing nestled amid vineyards and olive trees past Poggio a Caiano in Ar-
         timino. Delfina began cooking for hungry area hunters, and now she
         has four comfortably rustic dining rooms in a farmhouse where you
         can enjoy dishes centered around pure ingredients, seasonal vegetables,
         and savory meats accented with herbs. Everything is good: the *cros-
         tini di fegatini* (grilled Tuscan bread spread with chicken liver); sea-
         sonal pasta—always homemade; and the *secondi* (second courses)
         such as *coniglio con olive e pignoli* (rabbit sautéed with olives and pine
         nuts). Reservations are absolutely essential. ⊠ *Via della Chiesa 1, Ar-
         timino,* ☎ *055/8718074. Reservations essential. No credit cards.
         Closed Mon., Jan., and Aug. No dinner Sun.*

$$$ ✕ **Piraña.** Oddly named for the cannibalistic fish swimming in an
         aquarium with a full view of the diners, this sophisticated restaurant,
         decorated in shades of blue with steely accents, is a local favorite. Seafood
         is the specialty and may take the form of *raviolo di branzino in crema
         di scampi* (ravioli stuffed with sea bass with a creamy shrimp sauce)
         and *rombo al forno* (baked turbot). It's a bit out of the way for sight-
         seers but handy if you have a car, as it's near the Prato Est autostrada
         exit. ⊠ *Via G. Valentini 110,* ☎ *0574/25746. AE, DC, MC, V. Closed
         Sun. and Aug. No lunch Sat.*

$$–$$$ ✕ **Osvaldo Baroncelli.** Please do not come to this restaurant in shorts
★   and sneakers—the food here is elegant and sophisticated, and de-
         mands respect. Polished wooden floors, subtly striped chairs, and pale
         sponged walls bespeak the seriousness of this restaurant, which has been
         in the Baroncelli family for 50 years, and in that time they've perfected

their menu. You'll be tempted to eat all of the perfectly fried olives that arrive warm at the table, but save room for what's to come. Try the *insalata tiepida di gamberi, calametti, e carciofi* (warm salad with shrimp, squid, and artichokes) or the colorful *flan di zucca gialla e ricotta* (yellow squash and ricotta flan) in a light fish sauce. The pastas are house made—the *tortelli di branzino in salsa di seppie and carciofi* (tortelli stuffed with sea bass in a sauce of cuttlefish and artichokes) is wonderful. Reservations are advised. ⊠ *Via Fra Bartolomeo 13,* ☎ *0574/23810. AE, MC, V. Closed Aug. 7–21. No lunch Sat.*

$$ ✕ **Baghino.** In the heart of the historic center, Baghino serves typical Tuscan fare as well as atypical local fare like *spaghetti all'amatriciana* (spaghetti with bacon in a spicy tomato sauce) and penne *con vongole e curry* (with clams and curry). You can dine in the lovely outdoor terrace in the summer. ⊠ *Via dell'Accademia 9,* ☎ *055/27920. AE, DC, MC, V. Closed Sun. (June–Oct.). No dinner Sun.; no lunch Mon. (Nov.–May).*

$$ ✕ **Biagio Pignatta.** What better place to repair to than this lovely restaurant after viewing the Pontormo and touring Artimino? If you come here in summer, you can dine outdoors in a loggia with a beautiful view of Tuscan hills behind you. The food is Tuscan with some unexpected twists—a most sublime carpaccio and pasta with shellfish. The fried vegetables are as delectable as potato chips, and it's hard to stop noshing on them. Try the local wine—the delightful, crisp rosé is made right in the neighborhood. Reservations are advised, especially if you want an outside table. ⊠ *Viale Papa Giovanni XXIII 3, Artimino,* ☎ *055/8718086 or 055/8792030. AE, DC, MC, V. Closed Wed. No lunch Fri.*

$$ ✕ **La Veranda.** A large antipasto buffet greets you as you enter this restaurant near the 13th-century Castello. Though the decor has an elegant touch, with Venetian chandeliers, the atmosphere is friendly. The Tuscan specialties include *agnello alla cacciatora* (lamb with a tangy wine-vinegar sauce). ⊠ *Via dell'Arco 10,* ☎ *0574/38235. AE, DC, MC, V. Closed Sun. and Aug. No lunch Sat.*

$$$ ⌂ **Hotel President.** Though the exterior is about as exciting as 1970s architecture can get, the interior of this hotel, just a five-minute walk from the historic center, is calm, cool, and well furnished. The rooms are spacious, and each of the four floors is decorated in a different color scheme. One of the two bars has a slight art deco feel with its pale green and pink leather couches. ⊠ *Via Simintendi 20 (corner of Via Baldinucci), 59100,* ☎ *0574/30251,* FAX *0574/36064. 78 rooms. 2 bars, business services, meeting rooms, parking (fee). CP, MAP, FAP. AE, DC, MC, V.*

Shopping

Prato's biscotti (literally "twice cooked") have an extra-dense texture, lending themselves to submersion in your caffè or vin santo. The best in town are at **Antonio Mattei** (⊠ Via Ricasoli 20/22).

Pistoia

❷ *18 km (11 mi) northwest of Prato, 61 km (38 mi) east of Pisa, 37 km (23 mi) northwest of Florence.*

The town saw the beginning of the bitter Guelph-Ghibelline conflict of the Middle Ages. Reconstructed after heavy bombing during World War II, it has preserved some fine Romanesque architecture.

The Romanesque **Duomo,** the Cattedrale di San Zeno, dating from as early as the 5th century, houses the *Dossale di San Jacopo,* a magnificent silver altar. The two half-figures on its left side are by Filippo Brunelleschi (1377–1446), better known as the first Renaissance architect (and designer of Florence's magnificent Duomo cupola). The octagonal **Battistero**, with green and white marble panels, dates from the middle of the 14th century. Three of its eight sides have doorways; the main door facing the piazza is crowned with a rose window. Note the lovely little lantern that crowns the top of the building. ⊠ *Piazza del Duomo,* ☎ *0573/25095.* ☷ *Free; illumination of altarpiece 1,500 lire.* ☉ *Daily 9–noon and 4–7.*

The **Palazzo del Comune,** begun in 1295, houses the **Museo Civico,** containing works by local artists from the 14th to 20th centuries. ⊠ *Museo Civico, Piazza del Duomo,* ☎ *0573/371296.* ☷ *5,000 lire; free Sat. 3–7.* ☉ *Tues.–Sat. 10–7, Sun. 9–12:30.*

Founded in the 13th century and still a functioning hospital today, the **Ospedale del Ceppo** reveals a superb early 16th-century exterior terracotta frieze by the workshop of Santi and Benedetto Buglioni; it was completed by Giovanni della Robbia in 1527. ⊠ *Piazza Ospedale, down Via Pacini from Piazza del Duomo.*

In the church of **Sant'Andrea,** the fine pulpit (1298–1301) by Giovanni Pisano (circa 1250–1314) depicts scenes from the life of Christ. ⊠ *Via Pappe to Via Sant'Andrea,* ☎ *0573/21912.* ☷ *Free.* ☉ *Daily 8–1 and 3–5:30.*

The 16th-century Florentine Mannerist **Palazzo Rospigliosi** houses the **Museo Rospigliosi** and the **Museo Diocesano,** with a collection of mostly 17th-century works. In the Museo Rospigliosi is a room referred to as Pope Clement IX's (1600–1669) apartment; though there's no evidence that the Pistoian native, born Giulio Rospigliosi, stayed in these rooms, it lends a certain aura to the place. The Museo Diocesano has liturgical objects and furnishings from the diocese of Pistoia, many of which date from the 13th, 14th, and 15th centuries. ⊠ *Ripa del Sale 3,* ☎ *0573/28740.* ☷ *5,000 lire one museum, 10,000 lire both museums.* ☉ *Mon., Thurs., and Fri, 10–1 and 4–7; Wed. and Sat. 10–1.*

☾ A 20-minute drive out of town is the **Giardino Zoologico,** a small zoo especially laid out to accommodate the wiles of both animals and children. Take Bus 29 from the train station. ⊠ *Via Pieve a Celle 160/a,* ☎ *0573/911219.* ☷ *13,000 lire.* ☉ *Apr.–Sept., daily 9–7; Oct.–Mar., daily 9–5.*

Dining and Lodging

$$ ✕ **Corradossi.** This lovely restaurant is a short walk from Piazza del Duomo, and makes an excellent place to break for lunch or dinner. The food is ornate yet simple, service quick and attentive, and the prices more than reasonable. The menu offers a wide range of options from all over Italy. Start with the *trofie e gamberi* (corkscrew-shape pasta sauced with perfectly cooked shrimp and sliced baby zucchini), then follow with their *fritte miste* (fish and shellfish crisply fried). ⊠ *Via Frosini 112,* ☎ *0573/25683. AE, DC, MC, V. Closed Sun.*

$$ ✕ **Rafanelli.** *Maccheroni all'anatra* (pasta with duck sauce) and other game dishes—the specialties here—have been prepared with attention to tradition and quality for more than half a century by the same family. The restaurant is just outside the old city walls in a garden setting with alfresco dining in summer. ⊠ *Via Sant'Agostino 47,* ☎ *0573/532046. AE, DC, MC, V. Closed Mon. and Aug. No dinner Sun.*

$$ ✕ **S. Jacopo.** This charming restaurant, minutes away from the Piazza
★   del Duomo, has white walls, tiled floors, and a gracious host in Bruno Lottini, a native Pistoian fluent in English. The food is as welcoming as he: Bread, flecked with olives, is baked on the premises and arrives hot to the table. The menu has mostly regional favorites, such as the *maccheroni S. Jacopo,* wide ribbons of house-made pasta with a duck

ragù (sauce), but they can turn out perfectly grilled squid as well. Save room for dessert, especially the apple strudel. ⊠ *Via Crispi 15,* ☎ *0573/ 27786. AE, DC, MC, V. Closed Mon. No lunch Tues.*

$$ 🏨 **Hotel Leon Bianco.** This is a small, family-run hotel in the heart of the historic center. Most everything that you want to see in Pistoia is only a few minutes' walk from here. The hotel has a lobby decorated in chintz, a small bar to enjoy an *aperitivo* (aperitif), and lively innkeepers who speak perfect English. Florence is only a 45-minute train ride away, which makes staying here and doing day trips there a good idea for the budget-conscious traveler. ⊠ *Via Panciatichi 2, 51100,* ☎ FAX *0573/26675 or 0573/26676. 30 rooms. Bar. CP. AE, DC, MC, V.*

Nightlife and the Arts

In mid-July, **Pistoia Blues** draws international blues artists who perform in the main square. **La Giostra dell'Orso** (Bear Joust), on July 25th, celebrates St. James, patron saint of the city.

Montecatini Terme

❸ *15 km (9 mi) west of Pistoia, 49 km (30 mi) west of Florence, 49 km (30 mi) northeast of Pisa.*

Immortalized in Fellini's 8½, Montecatini Terme is home to Italy's premier *terme* (spas), reputed for their curative powers and, at least once upon a time, for their great popularity among the wealthy. It is renowned for its mineral springs, which flow from five sources and are used to treat liver and skin disorders. Those "taking the cure" report each morning to one of the town's **stabilimenti termali** (thermal establishments; information: ⊠ Via Verdi 41, ☎ 0572/778451) to drink their prescribed cupful of water, whose curative effects became known in the 1800s. The town's wealth of Art Nouveau buildings went up during its most active period of development, at the beginning of this century. Like most well-heeled resort towns, Montecatini attracts the leisured traveler, and it's trimmed with a measure of neon and glitz; aside from taking the waters and people-watching in Piazza del Popolo, there's not a whole lot to do here. Of the Art Nouveau structures, the most attractive is the **Terme Tettuccio** (⊠ Viale Verdi 71, ☎ 0572/778501), a neoclassical edifice with colonnades. Here Montecatini's healthful tonic spouts from fountains set up on marble counters, the walls are decorated with bucolic scenes depicted on painted ceramic tiles, and an orchestra plays under a frescoed dome.

Piazza del Popolo, the main square in town, is teeming with cafés and bars. It's an excellent spot to people-watch, as in the evenings and on weekends it seems like everyone from Montecatini and environs is out walking, seeing and being seen. The piazza also offers a view of the basilica of **Santa Maria Assunta,** a rather jarring-looking church and bell tower that were completed in 1962. ⊠ *Piazza del Popolo,* ☎ *no phone.* 🎫 *Free.* ☉ *Daily 8–12 and 3–5:30.*

NEED A BREAK?	*Cialde,* a local specialty, are circular wafers made with flour, sugar, and eggs and are said to have been invented by St. Brigitte. Whether or not this industrious saint had time to do so isn't all that important. What's important rather is to eat the cialda topped with several scoops of the local gelato. Try this local favorite at **Bargilli** (⊠ Viale Grocco 2, ☎ 0572/79459), supposedly the best gelateria in town.

The older town of Montecatini, called **Montecatini Alto,** sits on top of a hill near the spa town and is reached by a funicular (Viale Diaz) that just recently celebrated its 100th birthday. Though there's not much to do once you get up here, you'll find a medieval square lined with restaurants and bars, the air is crisp, and the views of the Nievole, the valley below, are gorgeous.

Lodging

$$$ ⊞ **Croce di Malta.** Elegant and sophisticated are two words to describe this hotel, which has been around since 1911. It's a short walk on tree-lined streets from the center of town and it's even closer to the beautiful thermal parkland. Rooms are spacious, with high ceilings; many of them have deep bathtubs with water jets. You can enjoy an aperitivo in the grand lobby before dining at the hotel restaurant. The menu changes daily and offers Tuscan specialties as well as other options; the food is as elegant as the hotel. ⊠ *Viale IV Novembre 18, 51016,* ☎ *0572/9201,* FAX *0572/767516. 119 rooms, 19 suites. Restaurant, bar, pool, exercise room, meeting rooms. CP, MAP, FAP. AE, DC, MC, V.*

Pescia

❹ *8 km (5 mi) west of Montecatini Terme, 19 km (12 mi) northeast of Lucca, 61 km (38 mi) northwest of Florence.*

Pescia is a sleepy little town that has a large flower market and some lesser known, but rather interesting Renaissance art. During the early Middle Ages, it was dominated by Lucca, but by 1339 it came under Florence's influence, under which it remained throughout the Renaissance.

The **Santuario della Madonna di Pie di Piazza,** built in 1447 and designed by Andrea Cavalcanti, the adopted son of Filippo Brunelleschi, is a little chapel and the only example of Brunelleschi's style outside of Florence. Inside is a 15th-century *Madonna and Child* on wood panel that was transported to the church in a solemn procession in 1605. ⊠ *Piazza Mazzini,* ☎ *no phone.* ▦ *Free.* ◷ *Daily 8–7:30.*

The church of **Santi Stefano e Niccolao** is an odd combination of Romanesque and Baroque. It dates from at least the 11th century and had alterations as late as the 18th. An early 15th-century *Madonna and Child with Angels,* by the school of Orcagna (active 1343/44–1368), and a panel painting of the *Madonna and Child with Sts. Niccolo and John the Baptist* from around 1400 are among the more interesting works in the church, but given their presence on side walls in the presbytery, they are difficult to see. ⊠ *Piazza Stefano,* ☎ *no phone.* ▦ *Free.* ◷ *Daily 8–7:30.*

The **Palazzo del Podesta** presents a lovely 13th-century facade; inside, however, are banal early 20th-century sculpted works by local son Libero Andreotti (1875–1933). ⊠ *Piazza del Palagio,* ☎ *0572/466533.* ▦ *Free.* ◷ *Fri. and last Sun. of the month 3–6, Sat. 10–1.*

The **Museo Civico** holds Tuscan paintings, a Lorenzo Monaco triptych, Etruscan objects, and works attributed to Fra Angelico and Fra Bartolommeo. At present the museum is closed for restoration. ⊠ *Piazza Santo Stefano,* ☎ *0572/490057.* ▦ *5,000 lire.* ◷ *Wed.–Sat. 10–1, also Fri. 3–6 (closed for restoration).*

The tiny church of **Sant'Antonio Abate** contains an amazing wood sculpture of the *Deposition* (in seven pieces) dating from the second half of the 13th century. Early 14th-century frescoes depict scenes from the life of St. Anthony Abbot. ⊠ *Via Battisti,* ☎ *no phone.* ▦ *Free.* ◷ *Daily 8–7:30.*

The church of **San Francesco** has a wood-panel painting by Bonaventura Berlinghieri (active 1228–1274) dating from 1235 that depicts scenes from the life of St. Francis. ⊠ *Piazza San Francesco,* ☎ *no phone.* ▦ *Free.* ◷ *Daily 8–7:30.*

Unless you're fond of the late Baroque, the **Duomo** is a disappointment after seeing the town's other churches. ⊠ *Piazza del Duomo,* ☎ *no phone.* ⌷ *Free.* ☉ *Daily 8–7:30.*

Collodi

❺ *4 km (2½ mi) west of Pescia, 17 km (11 mi) northeast of Lucca, 63 km (39 mi) northwest of Florence.*

Collodi was the pen name of Carlo Lorenzini (1826–1890), author of *Pinocchio.* His mother was born in the little village and he summered here as a child. **Parco di Pinocchio,** a theme park devoted to the puppet, is complete with sculptures illustrating various characters and scenes from the story. It's a fine place to bring children and to have a picnic. The park would make more sense if the story was fresh in your mind—so you might want to reread it beforehand. ⊠ *Via San Gennaro 2,* ☎ *0572/429342.* ⌷ *11,000 lire.* ☉ *Daily 8:30–sunset.*

LUCCA

It was in this picturesque fortress town that Caesar, Pompey, and Crassus agreed to rule Rome as a triumvirate in 56 BC; it was later the first town in Tuscany to accept Christianity. Lucca still has a mind of its own, and when most of Tuscany was voting communist as a matter of course, its citizens rarely followed suit. The town is best explored on foot. Within the city's 16th- to 17th-century ramparts, the famous composer Giacomo Puccini (1858–1924) was born; he is celebrated, along with his peers, during the summer Opera Theater of Lucca Festival.

Exploring Lucca

The historic center of Lucca is walled and traffic, including motorbikes, is restricted. Walking is therefore the best, most enjoyable way to get around. You can rent bicycles (☞ Outdoor Activities and Sports, *below*), and, as the center is quite flat, getting around town on bike without the threat of traffic is easy.

A Good Walk

Start at the **Pinacoteca Nazionale** ⑥ on Via Galli Tassi, just within the walls. Walk down Via del Toro to Piazza del Palazzo Dipinto, and follow Via di Poggio to **San Michele** ⑦. From Piazza San Michele, walk down Via Beccheria through Piazza Napoleone, and make a left through the smaller Piazza San Giovanni, which leads directly to the **Duomo** ⑧. Check out the fun facade before going into the church and looking at the *Volto Santo* and the *Tomb of Ilaria del Caretto.* Walk down Via dell'Arcivescovado, which is behind the Duomo and turns into Via Guinigi. Climb the **Torre Guinigi** ⑨ and admire the view. The **Museo Nazionale Guinigi** ⑩ is a 10- to 15-minute walk east through Piazza San Francesco on Via della Quarquonia. Backtrack to the Palazzo Guinigi; take Via Sant'Andrea to Via Fillungo to see the many Liberty-style buildings. At Via Fontana, make a left and follow it to Via Cesare Battisti. Make a right and head toward the church of **San Frediano** ⑪, with its incredibly mummified Santa Zita, the patron saint of domestic workers. From the church, walk on Via San Frediano back towards the Fillungo; make a right and then a left, and head into the **Piazza del Anfiteatro Romano** ⑫, where the Anfiteatro Romano once stood. Relax and have an apertivo at one of the many sidewalk cafés.

TIMING

The walk will take about three hours, perhaps a little longer if you linger in the museum.

Sights to See

⑧ Duomo. The round-arched facade of the cathedral is a fine example of the rigorously ordered Pisan Romanesque style, in this case happily enlivened by an extremely disordered collection of small carved columns. Take a closer look at the decoration of the facade and that of the portico below; they make this one of the most entertaining church exteriors in Tuscany. The Gothic interior contains a moving Byzantine crucifix (called the Volto Santo, or Holy Face), brought here in the 8th century, and the masterpiece of the Sienese sculptor Jacopo della Quercia (1374–1438), the marble *Tomb of Ilaria del Caretto* (1406). ✉ *Piazza del Duomo,* ☎ *0583/490530.* 🎟 *3,000 lire.* ⊘ *Apr.–Oct., daily 7–7; Nov.–Mar., daily 7–5*

⑩ Museo Nazionale Guinigi. On the eastern end of the historic center, the museum houses an extensive collection of local Romanesque and Renaissance art. ✉ *Villa Guinigi, Via della Quarquonia,* ☎ *0583/46033.* 🎟 *4,000 lire.* ⊘ *May–Sept., Tues.–Sun. 9–7; Oct.–Apr., Tues.–Sun. 9–2.*

⑫ Piazza dell'Anfiteatro Romano. This is the site where the **Anfiteatro Romano,** or Roman Amphitheater, once stood; some of the medieval buildings built over the amphitheater retain its original oval shape and brick arches. ✉ *Off Via Fillungo.*

NEED A BREAK?   **Guido Cimino Ray Bar** (✉ Anfiteatro 37-38-39, ☎ 0583/955927), within the old ramparts of the Roman Amphitheater, offers good drinks, light lunches (including some novel salad combinations), and seating in the piazza when it's warm. It's closed Tuesday.

⑥ Pinacoteca Nazionale. Highlights are the lovely *Portrait of a Youth* by Pontormo as well as portraits of the Medici by Bronzino (1503–1572) and others. ✉ *Palazzo Mansi, Via Galli Tassi 43, near the west walls of the old city,* ☎ *0583/55570.* 🎟 *8,000 lire.* ⊘ *Tues.–Sat. 9–7, Sun. 9–2.*

⑪ San Frediano. The church of San Frediano, just inside the middle of the north town wall, contains mainly works by Jacopo della Quercia (circa 1371/75–1438) and the bizarre lace-clad mummy of Santa Zita, the patron saint of household servants. ✉ *Piazza San Frediano,* ☎ *no phone.* 🎟 *Free.* ⊘ *Daily 7:30–12 and 3–5, holidays 9–1 and 3–6.*

⑦ San Michele. Slightly west of town center is this church with a facade even more fanciful than that of the Duomo. It was heavily restored in the 19th century, however, and somewhat inexplicably displays busts of 19th-century Italian patriots such as Garibaldi and Cavour. ✉ *Piazza San Michele,* ☎ *no phone.* 🎟 *Free.* ⊘ *Daily 7:30–12:30 and 3–6.*

⑨ Torre Guinigi. The tower of this medieval palace contains one of the city's most curious sights: a grove of ilex trees has grown at the top of the tower, and their roots have grown into the room below. From the top, you will have a magnificent view of the city and the surrounding countryside. ✉ *Palazzo Guinigi, Via Guinigi,* ☎ *0583/490530.* 🎟 *4,500 lire.* ⊘ *Daily 10–4:30.*

OFF THE BEATEN PATH   **VILLA REALE** – Eight kilometers (5 miles) north of Lucca in Marlia, this villa was once the home of Napoleon's sister, Princess Elisa. Restored by the Counts Pecci-Blunt, this estate is celebrated for its spectacular gardens, laid out in the 18th and 19th centuries. Gardening buffs adore the legendary *teatro di verdura,* a theater carved out of hedges and topiaries; concerts are occasionally offered here. One of Tuscany's most popular summer events, the Festival di Marlia, is held in Marlia in July

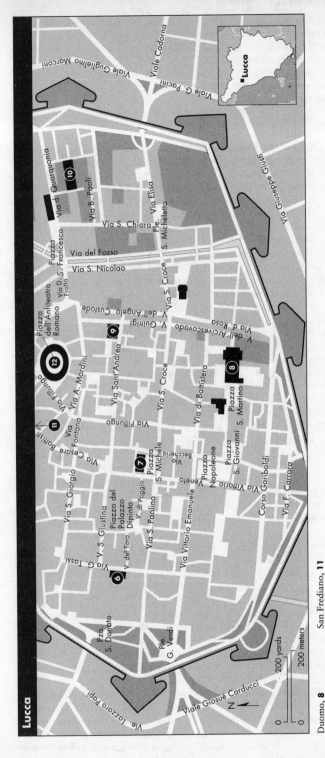

Lucca

Duomo, **8**
Museo Nazionale
Guinigi, **10**
Piazza dell'Anfiteatro
Romano, **12**
Pinacoteca
Nazionale, **6**

San Frediano, **11**
San Michele, **7**
Torre Guinigi, **9**

and August; contact the Lucca tourist office (✉ Piazzale Verdi, ☎ 0583/419689) for details. ✉ *Villa Reale,* ☎ *0583/30108.* ☞ *8,000 lire.* ⊙ *Guided tours July–Sept., Tues.–Sun. at 10, 11, 4, 5, 6; Oct.–Nov. and Mar.–June, Tues.–Sun. at 10, 11, 3, 4, 5. Closed Dec.–Feb.*

Dining and Lodging

$$$ ✗ **Solferino.** About 6 km (4 mi) outside town along the road to Viareggio, this restaurant prepares elegant renditions of Tuscan country-style cooking. Amid fine silver, linens, and crystal, you'll be treated to ingredients from the family farm in such dishes as *tagliolini con pernice rossa* (angel-hair pasta with partridge sauce). Ask for a piece of *buccellato,* Lucca's celebrated dessert bread. ✉ *San Macario in Piano,* ☎ *0583/59118. Reservations essential. AE, DC, MC, V. Closed Wed. and Jan. 7–15. No lunch Thurs.*

$$–$$$ ✗ **La Mora.** Detour to this former stagecoach station, now a gracious, ★ rustic country inn 9 km (5½ mi) outside Lucca, for local specialties—from *minestra di farro* (soup made with emmer, a grain that resembles barley) with beans to homemade *tacconi* (thin, short, and wide pasta) with rabbit sauce and lamb from the nearby Garfagnana hills. You'll be tempted by the varied crostini and delicious desserts. ✉ *Via Sesto di Ponte a Moriano 1748,* ☎ *0583/406402. AE, DC, MC, V. Closed Wed. and Oct. 10–30.*

$$ ✗ **Buca di Sant'Antonio.** This place has been around for more than two ★ centuries, and it's easy to see why. A white-walled interior adorned with copper pots, expertly prepared food, and an excellent staff make dining here a real treat. The menu offers something for everyone—from simple pasta dishes to more daring dishes such as the roast *capretto* (kid) with herbs. ✉ *Via della Cervia 3,* ☎ *0583/55881. AE, DC, MC, V. Closed Mon. and last 3 wks in July. No dinner Sun.*

$$ ✗ **Da Giulio in Pelleria.** A large trattoria that is quintessentially Tuscan in atmosphere, food, and clientele, this tavern is in one of Lucca's characteristic old neighborhoods near the ramparts and Porta San Donato, and handy to the Pinacoteca Nazionale. The menu features Lucca's specialties, including hearty barley or wheat soups and roasted meats—come hungry, the portions are generous. ✉ *Via delle Conce 47,* ☎ *0583/555948. AE, DC, MC, V. Closed Sun.–Mon. and Aug.*

$$ ✗ **Il Giglio.** Just off Piazza Napoleone, this restaurant has quiet, turn-of-the-century charm and classic cuisine. It's a place for all seasons, with a big fireplace for chilly weather and an outdoor terrace in summer. Among the local specialties are *farro garfagnino* (a thick soup made with emmer and beans), and *coniglio con olive* (rabbit stew with olives). ✉ *Piazza del Giglio 3,* ☎ *0583/494508. AE, DC, MC, V. Closed Wed. No dinner Tues.*

$$$$ ☷ **Locanda l'Elisa.** An intimate Relais & Châteaux hotel in a handsome blue neoclassical villa with white trim, this deluxe spin-off of the adjacent Villa La Principessa (☞ *below*) is a notch higher on the scale of style and comfort. ✉ *Via Nuova per Pisa, Massa Pisana, 55050,* ☎ *0583/379737,* ℻ *0583/379019. 10 suites. Restaurant, bar, pool, meeting room. EP, CP. AE, DC, MC, V.*

$$$$ ☷ **Villa La Principessa.** This exquisitely decorated 19th-century country mansion is 3 km (2 mi) outside of Lucca. Some rooms have handsome beamed ceilings, and doors are individually decorated; antique furniture and portraits impart an aura of gracious living. The grounds are well manicured, the pool large and inviting. ✉ *Massa Pisana, 55050,* ☎ *0583/370037,* ℻ *0583/379136. 40 rooms and suites. Restaurant, pool. EP, CP. AE, DC, MC, V. Closed Nov.–Mar. Restaurant closed Sun.*

$$ 🏨 **La Luna.** On a quiet, airy courtyard close to historic Piazza del An-
fiteatro Romano, this family-run hotel occupies two wings of an old
building. The bathrooms are modern, but some of the rooms still have
the atmosphere of Old Lucca. A parking lot for guests is a bonus. ⊠
Corte Compagni 12 (corner of Via Fillungo), 55100, ☎ *0583/493634,*
🗺 *0583/490021. 30 rooms. Free parking. EP. AE, DC, MC, V. Closed
last 3 wks in Jan.*

$ 🏨 **Piccolo Hotel Puccini.** Steps away from the busy square and church of
San Michele, this little hotel is quiet, calm, and handsomely decorated.
It also offers parking (which must be reserved in advance) at a reason-
able fee, which is a great advantage. ⊠ *Via di Poggio 9, 55100,* ☎ *0583/
55421,* 🗺 *0583/53487. 14 rooms. Parking (fee). EP. AE, DC, MC, V.*

Nightlife and the Arts

The **Estate Musicale Lucchese,** one of many music festivals throughout
Tuscany, runs throughout the summer in Lucca. Contact the Lucca tourist
office (⊠ Piazzale Verdi, ☎ 0583/419689) for details. The **Opera The-
ater of Lucca Festival,** sponsored by the Opera Theater of Lucca and
the music college of the University of Cincinnati, runs from mid-June
to mid-July; performances are staged in open-air venues. Call the
Lucca tourist office or **University of Cincinnati, College-Conservatory
of Music** (☎ 513/566–5662, 🗺 513/566–0202), for information.

Outdoor Activities and Sports

One of the best ways to get around this lovely medieval town is on a
bike. You can rent one at **Barbetti Cicli** (⊠ Via Anfiteatro 23, ☎ 0583/
954444) or at **Poli Antonio Biciclette** (⊠ Piazza Santa Maria 42, ☎ 0583/
493787).

Shopping

Chocolate Shop
Chocolate-lovers might think that they have died and gone to heaven
when they come to the chocolate shop **Caniparoli** (⊠ Via San Paolino
96, ☎ 0583/53456), closed in July and August.

Food Shop
Lucca's olive oil, available in food shops all over the city, is exported
throughout the world. Lucca is also famous for its farro. It's an an-
cient barley-like grain that has found its way into some regional spe-
cialties such as *zuppa (or minestra) di farro* (emmer soup). Buy some
at **Marsili Costantino** (⊠ Piazza San Michele 38, ☎ 0584/491751; ⊠
Via del Moro 18/22; Via dei Borghi 103) to take home, as it's hard to
find elsewhere.

Market
On the second Sunday of the month, there's a flea market in Piazza
San Martino.

Pasticceria
A particularly delicious version of buccellato—the sweet, anise-flavored
bread with raisins that is a specialty of Lucca—is baked at **Pasticceria
Taddeucci** (⊠ Piazza San Michele 34).

PISA

If you get beyond the kitschy atmosphere around the Leaning Tower,
you'll find Pisa has much to offer. Its cathedral-baptistery-tower com-
plex on Piazza del Duomo is among the most dramatic in Italy. Pisa's
treasures are more subtle than Florence's, to which it is inevitably com-

pared. Though it sustained heavy damage during World War II, Pisa and its many beautiful Romanesque structures are still preserved.

Exploring Pisa

Pisa, like many Italian cities, is best seen on foot, and most of what you'll want to see is within walking distance. The views along the Arno are particularly grand and shouldn't be missed—there's a feeling of spaciousness that doesn't exist along the Arno in Florence. A combination ticket of 10,000 lire allows entry to two sites on the Piazza del Duomo, and a ticket for 15,000 lire allows entry to all four sites.

A Good Walk

Start in the Campo dei Miracoli, exploring the piazza complex containing the **Torre Pendente** ⑬, **Duomo** ⑭, **Battistero** ⑮, **Camposanto** ⑯, **Museo dell'Opera del Duomo** ⑰, and the **Museo delle Sinopie** ⑱. After a coffee or gelato, walk down Via Santa Maria—the Campanile will be behind you. At Piazza Felice Cavallotti, go left on to Via dei Mille. On the right is the Romanesque church of **Santo Sisto** ⑲. Continue straight on Via dei Mille to **Piazza dei Cavalieri** ⑳, a study in Renaissance symmetry. Go straight through the piazza to Via Dini, and make a right on to Borgo Stretto, a major thoroughfare lined with cafés. On the left, before the river, is the church of San Michele in Borgo, with a wedding-cake feel to its early 14th-century Pisan Romanesque facade. Walk up to Piazza Garibaldi and turn left along the Lungarno Mediceo. Practically at the Ponte alla Fortezza, on the left, is the **Museo Nazionale di San Matteo** ㉑. Cross over the bridge and turn right on to Lungarno Galileo Galilei. Take a left on the little side street Vicolo Lanfranchi, which is at the corner of Palazzo Lanfranchi. At the end of the street is the church of San Martino. Make a right on to Via San Martino and walk until you reach Piazza XX Settembre where there is the large, freestanding Logge di Banchi (loggias) on the right. Go left on to Corso Italia, another major shopping thoroughfare.

TIMING

The walk takes a little more than an hour without stops—but there's lots to see along the way; it could take a couple of hours, depending upon how long you stay in the Museo Nazionale di San Matteo.

Sights to See

⑮ **Battistero.** The lovely Gothic Baptistery, which stands across from the Duomo's facade, is best known for the pulpit carved by Giovanni's father, Nicola, in 1260. Ask one of the ticket takers if he'll sing for you inside the baptistery. The acoustics are remarkable; a tip of 5,000 lire is appropriate. ⊠ *Piazza del Duomo,* ☎ *no phone.* 🎫 *10,000 lire combination ticket.* ☉ *Daily 10–7:40.*

⑯ **Camposanto.** The walled area on the northern side of the Campo dei Miracoli is the Cemetery, which is filled, according to legend, with earth brought back from the Holy Land during the Crusades. Its galleries contain numerous frescoes, notably *The Drunkenness of Noah,* by Renaissance artist Benozzo Gozzoli (1420–1498), and the disturbing *Triumph of Death* (14th century), whose authorship is disputed, but whose subject matter shows what was on people's minds in a century that saw the ravages of the Black Death. ⊠ *Campo dei Miracoli,* ☎ *050/560547.* 🎫 *10,000 lire combination ticket.* ☉ *Apr.–Sept., daily 8–7:40; Oct.–Mar., daily 9–5:40.*

⑭ **Duomo.** Pisa's cathedral was the first building to use the horizontal marble stripe motif (borrowed from Moorish architecture in the 11th century) common to Tuscan cathedrals. It is famous for the Romanesque panels on the transept door facing the tower, which depict the life of

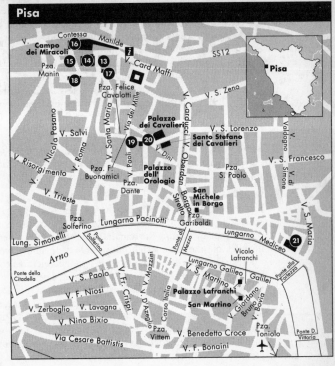

Christ, and for its beautifully carved 14th-century pulpit by Giovanni Pisano. ⊠ *Piazza del Duomo,* ☎ *no phone.* ☞ *2,000 lire (free Oct.–Mar.).* ☉ *Apr.–Sept., Mon.–Sat. 10–7:40, Sun 1–5; Oct.–Mar., daily 10–12:30 and 3–5:30.*

⑰ Museo dell'Opera del Duomo. At the southeast corner of the sprawling Campo dei Miracoli, the museum holds a wealth of medieval sculptures and the ancient Roman sarcophagi that inspired Nicola Pisano's (active circa 1258–1278) figures. ⊠ *Via Arcivescovado,* ☎ *050/560547.* ☞ *10,000 lire combination ticket.* ☉ *Apr.–Oct., daily 9–7:30; Nov.–Mar., daily 9–5:30.*

⑱ Museo delle Sinopie. The well-arranged museum on the south side of the Piazza del Duomo holds the *sinopie,* or preparatory drawings, for the Camposanto frescoes. ⊠ *Piazza del Duomo,* ☎ *050/560547.* ☞ *10,000 lire.* ☞ *10,000 lire combination ticket.* ☉ *Apr.–Oct., daily 8–7:40; Nov.–Mar., daily 9–5:40.*

㉑ Museo Nazionale di San Matteo. Along the northern side of the Arno, this museum contains some incisive examples of local Romanesque and Gothic art. ⊠ *Lungarno Mediceo,* ☎ *050/541865.* ☞ *8,000 lire.* ☉ *Tues.–Sat. 9–7, Sun. 9–1:30.*

....

NEED A BREAK? Even if you're not on your way to the Museo di San Matteo and are just strolling along the Arno, drop in to the **Drum and Bass** (⊠ Lungarno Pacinotti 1, ☎ 050/580580) for a cappuccino or *panini* (sandwich). Though it bills itself as an American bar, it feels downright Italian.

....

⑳ Piazza dei Cavalieri. The piazza, which holds the fine Renaissance **Palazzo dei Cavalieri, Palazzo dell'Orologio,** and **Santo Stefano dei Cavalieri,** was laid out by Giorgio Vasari in about 1560. The square was the seat of the Ordine dei Cavalieri di San Stefano (Order of the Knights of St.

Stephen), a military and religious institution that was meant to defend the coast from possible invasion by the Turks. Also in this square is the prestigious **Scuola Normale Superiore,** founded by Napoleon in 1810 on the French model. Here graduate students pursue doctorates in literature, philosophy, mathematics, and science. In front of the school is an oversize statue of Ferdinando de' Medici dating from 1596. On the extreme left is the tower where the hapless Ugolino della Gherardesca (died 1289) was imprisoned with his two sons; local legend holds that he ate them. Though Dante is reticent on the subject, he immortalized him in Canto XXXIII of *The Inferno.*

⑲ Santo Sisto. Dating from the 11th century, this church reveals a simple yet elegant arcaded colonnade and stone interior. ✉ *Piazza Francesco Buonamici,* ☎ *no phone.* 🎫 *Free.* ⏱ *Daily 8–7:30.*

⑬ Torre Pendente. The Leaning Tower was begun in 1174, the last of the three structures to be built, and the lopsided settling began when construction reached the third story. The tower's architects attempted to compensate by making the remaining floors slightly taller on the leaning side, but the extra weight only made the problem worse. The settling has continued, and a few years ago it accelerated to a point that led many to fear it would simply topple over, despite all efforts to prop the structure up. Now it has been firmly anchored to the earth. Legend holds that Galileo conducted an experiment on the nature of gravity by dropping metal balls from the top of the 187-ft-high tower; historians say this legend has no basis in fact (which is not quite to say that it is false). The tower is not open to the public, but you have a great view of its leanings from the outside. ✉ *Campo dei Miracoli.*

OFF THE   **LA CERTOSA DI PISA —** The Charterhouse of Pisa, a vast and sprawling
BEATEN PATH   complex begun in 1366, was home to the strict order of Carthusian monks. It was suppressed by Napoleon, and then again in 1866. Most of the art and architecture you see dates from the 17th and 18th centuries. Monks returned here, only to leave it definitely in 1969. The **Museo di Storia Naturale e del Territorio** is also housed within. ✉ *10 km (6 mi) east of Pisa,* ☎ *050/937751.* 🎫 *6,000 lire.* ⏱ *Tues.–Sat. 4–8, Sun. 10–11 and 4–8.*

Dining and Lodging

$$$ ✕ **Al Ristoro dei Vecchi Macelli.** The 17-year-old "Inn by the Old Slaughterhouse" got its name from being down the street from an old slaughterhouse, which is no longer in use. Such earthy connotations aside, the food is sophisticated and special, served in white-walled, white-tablecloth surroundings. You can order a fixed-price menu from either the sea or earth or choose dishes à la carte. The *gnochetti con broccoli e vongole veraci* (dumplings with broccoli and small clams) is a winner, as is the *coniglio disossato e farcito con salsa di tartufo* (boneless rabbit stuffed with truffle sauce). The place is calm and serene, a perfect backdrop for the food. Reservations are advised. ✉ *Via Volturno 49,* ☎ *050/20424. AE, DC, MC, V. Closed Wed. and Aug. 10–25. No lunch Sun. Closed Wed. and Sun. lunch, Aug. 10–25.*

$$ ✕ **Bruno.** A pleasant restaurant, with beamed ceilings and the look of a country inn, Bruno is just outside Pisa's old city walls, a short walk from the Campanile and Duomo. Dine on classic Tuscan dishes, from *zuppa alla pisana* (a thick vegetable soup) to *baccalà* (cod) served with leeks. ✉ *Via Luigi Bianchi 12,* ☎ *050/560818. AE, DC, MC, V. Closed Tues. No dinner Mon.*

$$ ✕ **Da Antonio.** Truckers originally came to this place to grab a bite to eat—probably because it's at the junction of two highly trafficked highways, a 10- to 15-minute drive from Pisa. They were on to something: The food here is good, sturdy, hearty Tuscan. Though the interior is nothing to write home about (except in the winter when they light their terrific fireplace), the food is: The grilled meats are delicious, as is the grilled pigeon and guinea hen. ⊠ *Via Arnaccia 15, Navacchio,* ☎ *050/742494. AE, DC, MC, V. Closed Fri. and 3 weeks in Aug.*

$$ ✕ **La Pergoletta.** On an old town street named for its "beautiful towers," this restaurant in a medieval tower is small and simple, with a shady garden for outdoor dining. The *signora* who is the owner-cook offers traditional Tuscan minestra di farro and *grigliata* (grilled beef, veal, or lamb). ⊠ *Via delle Belle Torri 36,* ☎ *050/542458. MC, V. Closed Mon. and Aug.*

$$ ✕ **Osteria dei Cavalieri.** This charming white-walled *osteria* (restau-
★ rant), a few steps from Piazza dei Cavalieri, is reason enough to come to Pisa. They can do it all here—serve up exquisitely grilled fish dishes, please vegetarians, and prepare *tagliata* (thin slivers of rare beef) four different ways. Three set menus, from the sea, garden, and earth, are put together for you, or you can order à la carte—which can be agonizing because everything sounds so good. And it is. Finish your meal with a lemon sorbet bathed in Prosecco (dry sparkling wine), and walk away feeling like you've eaten like a king at plebeian prices. ⊠ *Via San Frediano 16,* ☎ *055/580858. AE, DC, MC, V. Closed Sun. and July 25–Aug. 25. No lunch Sat.*

$$$ ▥ **Cavalieri.** Opposite the railway station, in an unremarkable 1950s building, this Jolly Group hotel offers functional, modern comforts in completely soundproof and air-conditioned rooms, all with color TVs and minibars. The restaurant specializes in homemade pasta and seafood and is open every day. ⊠ *Piazza della Stazione 2, 56100,* ☎ *050/43290,* ℻ *050/502242. 100 rooms. Bar, minibars. CP. AE, DC, MC, V.*

$$ ▥ **Fattoria di Migliarino.** Martino Salviati and his wife Giovanna have
★ turned their working farm (soy, corn, sugar beets) 15 minutes from Pisa into a working inn: Their *fattoria* (farmhouse) is now seven charming, spacious apartments (putting up from two to eight people), each complete with kitchen, and many have fireplaces. The pool is framed by fields, and the only sound you're likely to hear is the clucking of the hens they keep for eggs. The surrounding woods can be explored by horse or by mountain bike. There is a two-night minimum stay. Migliarino is convenient to Lucca and Florence, plus sandy beaches (five-minute drive) and horseback riding. ⊠ *Viale dei Pini 289, Migliarino Pisano, 10 km (6 mi) northwest of Pisa, 56010,* ☎ *050/ 803046,* ℻ *050/803170. 7 apartments. Pool. EP. MC, V.*

$$ ▥ **Royal Victoria.** In a pleasant palazzo facing the Arno, a 10-minute walk from the Campo dei Miracoli, this hotel is about as close as Pisa comes to old-world ambience. It's comfortably furnished, with antiques and reproductions in the lobby and in some rooms, whose style ranges from the 1800s, complete with frescoes, to the 1920s. ⊠ *Lungarno Pacinotti 12, 56100,* ☎ *050/940111,* ℻ *050/940180. 48 rooms, 40 with bath. Breakfast room. CP. AE, DC, MC, V.*

Nightlife and the Arts

The **Luminaria** feast day on June 16 honors San Ranieri, the patron saint of the city. Palaces along the Arno are lit with white lights, and there's plenty of fireworks; it's the city at its best.

EMPOLI AND CENTRAL HILL TOWNS

West to Livorno

Off the beaten track in Empoli, San Miniato, and the neighboring hill towns are fine examples of art—especially in Empoli and Castelfiorentino—and stirring views. San Vivaldo, an isolated Franciscan monastery, has changed since its tiny chapels were erected. The terrific restaurants here are less expensive than in the cities to the north.

Empoli

㉒ *50 km (31 mi) east of Pisa, 33 km (21 mi) west of Florence.*

Empoli, set along the Arno roughly halfway between Florence and Pisa, is a bustling town with a long history. References to the city first appear in documents of the 9th century. By 1182, it was completely aligned with Florence. In 1260, after the Battle of Montaperti, the Ghibelline Farinata degli Uberti made the decision while in Empoli not to burn Florence to the ground, which Dante immortalized in Canto X of *The Inferno*. Now Empoli is a sleepy little town only a half hour's train ride from Florence. If you're traveling in the summer, you might want to consider staying here and hopping on the train for day trips into Florence. But don't forget to see the sights in Empoli—they're worth it.

★ A woman who works at the **Collegiata di Sant'Andrea** describes it as a "little jewel" and she's completely right: In this museum, with its cloister filled with terra-cotta sculptures from the della Robbia school, is a magnificent 15th-century fresco of the *Pietà* by Masolino (circa 1383–1440); there's also a small Fra Filippo Lippi and a wonderful altarpiece by Francesco Bottincini (1446–1497) and Rossellino (1427–1479). ⊠ *Just off Piazza Farinata degli Uberti,* ☏ *0571/76284.* ☐ *5,000 lire, 8,000 lire combination ticket (including the Museo Leonardiano in Vinci and the Museo Archeologico e della Ceramica in Montelupo,* ☞ *below).* ۞ *Tues.–Sun. 9–12 and 3–6.*

Originally founded by the Augustines in the 11th century, **Santo Stefano** can be seen only by asking for a tour in the Collegiata (☞ *above*). It's worth the trip, as there are sinopie by Masolino depicting scenes from the *Legend of the True Cross*. He left without actually frescoing them—seems like the clergy was late in making payment. ⊠ *Via de' Neri,* ☏ *no phone.* ☐ *Free.* ۞ *Ask for entry at the Collegiata.*

NEED A   **Vinegar** (⊠ Piazza della Vittoria 36/37, ☏ 0571/74630) is a nice
BREAK?   bar near the train station that offers up a variety of panini as well as coffees and aperitifs of all sorts.

A short and not-too-scenic walk from the center of town will bring you to the little **San Michele in Pontorme,** chiefly notable for its gorgeous *St. John the Evangelist* and *Michael the Archangel,* two works dating from about 1519 by Jacopo Carrucci, better known as Pontormo. ⊠ *Piazza San Michele,* ☏ *no phone.* ☐ *Free.* ۞ *Ring for sacristan.*

OFF THE   **VINCI** –The small hill town from which Leonardo da Vinci derived his
BEATEN PATH   name is a short bus ride north from Empoli. It's worth the trip simply for the views. If you are interested in Leonardo or the history of science, the **Museo Leonardiano** has replicas of many of Leonardo's machines and gadgets. You can also see the baptismal font where he was baptized in the church in the town square; if you want to see the house where he was born you'll have to travel to Anchiano, 3 km (2 mi) north of Vinci. ⊠ *Vinci, 10 km (6 mi) north of Empoli,* ☏ *0571/56055.* ☐ *5,000 lire,*

8,000 lire combination ticket (includes Museo Archeologico e Della Ceramica in Montelupo, ☞ below, and Collegiata di Sant'Andrea in Empoli, ☞ above). ⊙ *Mar.–Oct., daily 9:30–7, Nov.–Feb., daily 9:30–6.*

MONTELUPO – The Museo Archeologico e Della Ceramica has some 3,000 objects devoted to majolica, a kind of glazed pottery that is native to this region and has been since the early 14th century. The collection ranges from the early 14th century to the late 18th. Most fascinating are the coats of arms sporting important Renaissance names such as Medici and Strozzi. ⊠ *Via Bartolomeo Sinibaldi 45, Montelupo, 7 km (4½ mi) east of Empoli,* ☎ *0571/51352.* ⊡ *5,000 lire, 8,000 lire combination ticket (includes Museo Leonardiano in Vinci and Collegiata di Sant'Andrea in Empoli, ☞ above).* ⊙ *Tues.–Sat. 8–12 and 2:30–7; Mon. and Sun. 2:30–7.*

Dining and Lodging

$$ ✕ **Il Galeone.** This place is known for its fish, so it makes sense to order
★ it, even though the meat dishes are equally as delicious. Pale-pink walls and pink tablecloths play off against the gray-and-white tiled floors. The atmosphere is relaxed and friendly. You'll have trouble deciding what to order, but give the *moscardini con fagioli e rucola* (little squidlets gently heated with cannellini beans, diced tomatoes, blessed with olive oil, and on a bed of arugula) a try; the *spiedini di seppioline e gamberoni* (kebabs of squid with shrimp) is terrific, too. If you're craving a pizza, it's served here as well. ⊠ *Via Curtatone e Montanara 67,* ☎ *0571/72826. AE, DC, MC, V. Closed Sun. and Aug.*

$$ ⌂ **Hotel Il Sole.** Conveniently located across the street from the railway station, this turn-of-the-century hotel has been in the hands of the Sabatini family since 1905. Each of the 12 rooms is different, an eclectic interpretation of the Victorian style. If you are on a budget, this is a good option instead of staying in Florence, about a half-hour train ride away. ⊠ *Piazza Don Minzoni 18, 50053,* ☎ *0571/73779,* FAX *0571/79871. 11 rooms, 9 with bath; 1 suite. Breakfast room. CP. AE, DC, MC, V.*

San Miniato

㉓ *9 km (5½ mi) west of Empoli, 43 km (27 mi) west of Florence.*

Dating from Etruscan and Roman times, San Miniato was so named when the Lombards erected a church here in the 8th century and consecrated it to San Miniato. The Holy Roman Empire had very strong ties to San Miniato; in fact, the castle was built in 962 under the aegis of Otto I (912–973). Matilde of Tuscany was born here in the mid-11th century. Eventually the town, with its Ghibelline sympathies, passed into the hands of the Florentines. Today the pristine, tiny hill town's narrow, cobbled streets are lined with austere 13th–17th century facades, some of them built over already centuries-old buildings. Its artistic treasures are somewhat limited in comparison with Florence, but it's well worth the trip simply because the town is so pretty.

St. Francis founded the 1211 **Convento e Chiesa di San Francesco** (Convent and Church of St. Francis), containing two cloisters and an ornate wooden choir. For a dose of monastic living, you can stay overnight (☞ Dining and Lodging, *below*). ⊠ *Piazza San Francesco,* ☎ *0571/43051.* ⊡ *Free.* ⊙ *Daily 9–noon and 3–7 (or ring bell).*

The **Convento e Chiesa di Santi Jacopo e Filippo** is also known as the church of San Domenico, which refers to the fact that the Dominicans took over the church in the 14th century. Most of the interior suffers from too much Baroque, but there is a lovely sculpted tomb by Bernardo Rossellino of Giovanni Chellini, a 15th-century doctor who died in 1461. ⊠ *Piazza del Popolo,* ☎ *0571/418739.* 🎟 *Free.* ⏱ *Daily 9–12 and 3–7.*

NEED A
BREAK?

Bar Cantini (⊠ Piazza del Popolo 27, ☎ 0571/43030) might be the meeting place for all San Miniatans; it serves some wonderful panini, in part because they bake their own bread. Try any *cazzotto* ("little punch"), a sandwich stuffed with a variety of fillings. They also serve pizza by the slice and homemade ice cream in the summer.

The only thing remarkable about the **Duomo,** set in a pretty piazza, is its 13th-century facade, which has been restored over the years. The interior is largely uninteresting; a moment of poignancy occurs when viewing the plaque commemorating the 55 citizens who were killed in this church in July 1944 (the Taviani brothers later made a movie *The Nights of San Lorenzo* about this). ⊠ *Piazza del Castello,* ☎ *no phone.* 🎟 *Free.* ⏱ *Daily 9–12 and 3–7.*

Although the **Museo Diocesano** is small, the modest collection incorporates a number of subtle and pleasant local works of art. Note the rather odd Fra Filippo Lippi *Crucifixion,* Verrocchio's (1435–1488) *Il Redentore,* and the small but exquisite *Education of the Virgin* by Tiepolo (1696–1770). ⊠ *Piazza del Castello,* ☎ *0571/418271.* 🎟 *2,000 lire.* ⏱ *Easter–Jan. 6, daily 9–noon and 2:30–5; Jan. 7–Easter, weekends 9–noon and 2:30–5.*

The **Torre di Federico II,** dating from around the time of Frederick II (1194–1250), was destroyed during World War II. A point of civic pride for the San Miniatans, it was rebuilt and reopened in 1958. If you're in shape, it's worth the climb to the top to see the fine view. The hapless ill-fated Pier della Vigna, chancellor and minister to Frederick II, was imprisoned here; Dante writes about him in Canto XIII of *The Inferno.* ⊠ *Piazza del Popolo,* ☎ *0571/42745.* 🎟 *Donation suggested.* ⏱ *Daily 9–12 and 3–7.*

Dining and Lodging

$$ ✕ Il Convio-Maiano. This charming restaurant 2 km (1 mi) from the
★ historic center, in San Miniato Basso, has stenciled walls, brightly colored tablecloths, and absolute calm, giving it a homey feel. Start with the *crostone al lardo e tartufato,* a gem of a *crostone* (big piece of grilled Tuscan bread) served with an amalgam of four cheeses, scented with tartufo, and speckled with lard. The menu is a bit different from standard Tuscan fare—check out the roast pork thinly sliced and chilled, served with oil and black peppercorns. Their *contorni* (vegetables) are also worth investigating; the *cavolfiore in umido* (cauliflower cooked with tomatoes) proves that cauliflower need not be a boring vegetable. ⊠ *Via San Maiano 2, San Miniato Basso,* ☎ *0571/408114. AE, DC, MC, V. Closed Wed.*

$$ ✕ L'Antro di Bacco. No one in San Miniato seems to know that this lovely restaurant is here, and it might be because its entrance is hidden within the confines of a well-stocked food shop. Nonetheless, it's right in the center of town and the food is very good. The chef has a deft touch with slightly odd combinations—the *involtini con pecorino tartufo* (flattened bits of stuffed rolled beef with truffled pecorino) is delicious. ⊠ *Via Quattro Novembre 5,* ☎ *0571/43319. AE, DC, MC, V. Closed Sun. and 1 wk in Aug. No dinner Wed.*

$$ 🏨 Miraville. The omnipresent blasting television in the lobby might be off-putting, but once you get past that, this hotel is the perfect place to park yourself for a few days. It's set in the middle of Piazza Castello, which houses the Duomo and the Museo Diocesano; the views of the hills are stellar and commanding. A restaurant is attached to the hotel, but it has no relationship with the innkeeper. ⊠ *Piazza Castello 3, 56020,* ☎ *0571/418075,* ℻ *0571/419681. 18 rooms. Breakfast room. EP. AE, DC, MC, V.*

$ 🏨 **Convento San Francesco.** For a complete change of pace, you can stay in this 13th-century monastery in the company of five Franciscan friars. Rooms are simple, bordering on spartan, but clean and quiet. You are given keys, so you're not expected home by a certain time. You can partake in some spiritual activities, or skip them altogether. All rooms have baths, and there are five rooms shared by groups. It's a short 10-minute walk from the center. ⊠ *Piazza San Francesco, 56020,* ☎ *0571/43051,* ℻ *0571/4398. 70 rooms. EP. No credit cards.*

Castelfiorentino

㉔ *12 km south (7 mi) of San Miniato, 50 km (31 mi) southwest of Florence.*

Like San Miniato, Castelfiorentino can claim Roman origins. During the Middle Ages, it was of strategic importance in the struggles between the Holy Roman Empire and the Papacy. Now it is a sleepy little town, the halfway point between Florence and Pisa.

Admirers of the Renaissance artist Benozzo Gozzoli will have much to see at the **Biblioteca Comunale,** as the detached frescoes and sinopie from two tabernacles executed by him are on display. The **Tabernacolo della Visitazione** shows scenes from the life of the Virgin; another tabernacle, *Madonna della Tosse* (literally Madonna of the Coughs), dating from 1484, shows important events exquisitely rendered from scenes from the life of the Virgin such as the *Dormition* and the *Assumption.* ⊠ *Via Tilli 41,* ☎ *0571/64019.* 🎟 *3,000 lire.* 🕙 *Tues., Thurs., Sat. 4–7; holidays 10–12 and 4–7; (at other hrs ring doorbell for custodian).*

San Vivaldo

㉕ *13 km (8 mi) south of Castelfiorentino, 63 km (39 mi) west of Florence.*

San Vivaldo, born around 1260, was a Franciscan hermit who lived in the woods here. After his death in 1320, a church was erected to honor him, and by 1500 Franciscan friars moved in. Thirty-two small chapels scattered throughout the woods, all decorated with terra-cotta sculptures by anonymous artists of the della Robbia school, were built shortly thereafter. Only 15 of the original chapels remain, as well as six that were built later. The chapels are arranged to evoke the places in Jerusalem where Christ spent his last days on earth. A restaurant (Le Focolare) is on the premises, and the grounds are an excellent place to have a picnic. ☎ *0571/6801.* 🎟 *Donation suggested.* 🕙 *Daily, 9–11:30 and 3–sunset.*

Certaldo

㉖ *9 km (6 mi) south of Castelfiorentino, 56 km (35 mi) west of Florence.*

Certaldo is probably most famous for having produced Giovanni Boccaccio (1313–1375), the witty and irreverent author of *The Decameron* (circa 1351), and it seems as if practically every shop in town has managed to incorporate his name into its title. The town was greatly damaged during World War II, and much of what you see of its brick buildings is postwar reconstruction.

The dimly lit church of **Santissimi Jacopo e Filippo,** begun in the 12th century, is where Boccaccio is buried. A tomb slab bearing his likeness is found in the center aisle, and a Latin epitaph is near it on the left wall. Also of interest are two terra-cotta tabernacles dated 1499 and 1502 from the school of the della Robbia. On the right wall is a stupendous, multicolored terra-cotta altarpiece attributed to one of the della Robbia depicting the *Madonna of the Snow.* ⊠ *Piazza Ss. Jacopo e Filippo,* ☎ *no phone.* ☎ *Free.* ☼ *Daily 8–12 and 4–8.*

Begun in the late 12th century, the **Palazzo Pretorio,** speckled with terracotta coats of arms on its facade, served as the city's town hall and also provided space for a women's prison. Now it houses a gallery for art exhibitions, a permanent display of Etruscan pottery, and fragments of 14th-century mural painting. Also in this complex is the church of **San Tommaso e Prospero,** which contains a Benozzo Gozzoli tabernacle depicting scenes from the life of Christ executed between 1466 and 1467. You can also view the sinopie, the preparatory drawings, which he executed for the tabernacle. ⊠ *Piazzetta del Vicariato,* ☎ *0571/661219.* ☎ *5,000 lire.* ☼ *Nov.–Mar., Tues.–Sun. 10–12:30 and 3–5; Apr.–Oct., Tues.–Sun. 8–8.*

At the **Casa di Boccaccio,** they say that the room in which he died is the only part of the house to have survived a World War II bombing. ⊠ *Via Boccaccio,* ☎ *0571/664208.* ☎ *Donation suggested.* ☼ *Daily 10–1 and 3–7.*

<table>
<tr><td>NEED A
BREAK?</td><td>**La Saletta di Dolci Follie** (⊠ Via Roma 3, ☎ 0571/668188), closed Tuesday, serves tasty light lunches and delectable sweets.</td></tr>
</table>

Livorno

 187 km (116 mi) west of Florence.

The ferry hub of Livorno is a gritty city with a long and very interesting history: In the early Middle Ages, it alternately belonged to Pisa and then to Genova. In 1421, Florence, seeking access to the sea, bought it. Cosimo I (1519-1574) started construction of the harbor in 1571, putting Livorno on the map. Ferdinando I Medici (1549–1609) proclaimed Livorno a free city, which meant that it became a haven for people suffering from religious persecution—Roman Catholics from England and Jews and Moors from Spain and Portugal, among others, settled here. The *Quattro Mori* (Four Slaves), also known as the Monument to Ferdinando I, commemorates this. (The statue of Ferdinand I dates from 1595, the bronze moors by Pietro Tacca from the 1620s.)

In the following centuries, and particularly in the 18th, Livorno boomed as a port. Its influence continued up to World War II, when, because of its importance, it was heavily bombed. Much of Livorno's architecture is therefore post–World War II construction, so it's somewhat difficult to imagine what it might have looked liked. Livorno has recovered from the war, however, as her influence in shipping—particularly container shipping—continues to this day. Tobias Smollett (1721–1771), the English novelist, is buried here; Percy Bysse Shelley (1792–1822) visited in 1819; and Lord Byron (1788–1824) visited in 1822. Livorno's most famous son may well be the 20th-century painter Amedeo Modigliani (1884–1920).

Most of Livorno's artistic treasures date from the 17th century, and aren't all that interesting unless you dote on obscure artists from the Baroque period. However, it's worth strolling around the city— the **Mercato Nuovo,** which has been around since 1894, sells all sorts of fruits, vegetables, grains, meat, and fish. Outdoor markets nearby are also chock-full of local color. The presence of Camp Darby, an American base just outside Livorno, accounts for the availability of many American products.

Dining

If you've got time, Livorno is at least worth a stop for lunch or dinner: Livornese restaurants capitalize on their close relationship with the sea. The fish is good, and of course it's fresh.

$$ ✕ **Antico Moro.** If you've never had *caciucco*, sample it here. Caciucco is Livornese for fish stew, and is absolutely delicious: It's got a tomato base, lots of fish (usually a combination of white fish and some shellfish), and is served with a slice of toast annointed with copious amounts of garlic and extra-virigin olive oil. The place is small and the decor tends to fishing nets, stuffed and mounted swordfish heads, and other marine paraphernalia—just to put you in the mood. ✉ *Via Bartelli 59,* ☎ *0586/884659. AE, MC, V. Closed Wed. and last wk in Aug.–first wk in Sept. No lunch (except Sun. and holidays).*

$$ ✕ **L'Arsella.** Arsella is Italian for snail, but there's nothing snail-like in the service at this family-run restaurant—it's always cheery, prompt, and efficient. The place is right on the water at Marina di Livorno, and if you're lucky you'll be able to see a splendid sunset. Everything the chef does here, from *insalata di mare* (cold marinated fish salad) to whole fish in *cartoccio* (baked in parchment paper) is delicious. Try the *risotto ai seppie neri* (risotto with squid ink)—it's a delight. ✉ *Via Padre Agostino 20 (on the Lungomare), Marina di Livorno,* ☎ *050/36615. AE, DC, MC, V. Closed Wed. No dinner Tues.*

CITIES WEST OF FLORENCE A TO Z

Arriving and Departing

By Bus

Most of these cities do have bus stations, but service is often sporadic or complicated; it's easier to take the train to Pisa, Prato, Pistoia, Lucca, Montecatini Terme, Livorno, and Empoli, where service is regular and trains run frequently. Pescia is an easy bus ride from the train station at Montecatini Terme; you can purchase bus tickets at the station at the news vendor. San Miniato and environs are best reached by car, as service is limited.

By Car

The A1 connects Florence to Prato; for Pistoia, Montecatini, and Lucca, follow signs for Firenze Nord, which connects to the A11. For Empoli, Pisa, and hill towns west, take the superstrada from Scandicci (just outside Florence).

By Plane

The largest airports in the region are Pisa's **Aeroporto Galileo Galilei** (☎ 050/500707) and Florence's **Aeroporto Peretola** (☎ 055/373498).

By Train

Trains from Rome and Milan run regularly to Florence, which serves as the hub for many connections (such as to Prato, Pistoia, Montecatini, Lucca, Empoli, Pisa, and Livorno). Empoli is easily reached via train, but the surrounding towns—Certaldo, Castlefiorentino, San Vivaldo, San Miniato—are not. For the state-run line (FS) **train information,** call ☎ 147/888088 toll-free.

Getting Around

By Bus
Cars are recommended for getting around the region, as bus connections rely on the main city hubs and service is limited.

By Car
Renting a car is the best way to see these cities west of Tuscany, as many of them are not on train lines or are served by buses that run sporadically. Prato, Pistoia, Montecatini Terme, Lucca, and Pisa are especially easy to travel among, since they are all off the A1. The other cities are along secondary two-lane roads.

By Train
Trains from the main station at Santa Maria Novella in Florence run regularly to Prato, Pistoia, Montecatini, and Lucca, which are all on the same line. Trains from Florence to Empoli and Pisa, on the same line, run frequently as well.

Contacts and Resources

Agritourist Agencies
For information, ☞ Chapter 2.

Car Rentals
Lucca (Avis, ✉ Sant'Anna, Via Luporini 1411/a, ☎ 0583/513614). **Montecatini Terme** (✉ c/o Garage Olimpia, Via Manin 8, ☎ 0572/72946). **Pisa** (Hertz, ✉ Aeroporto Galileo Galilei, ☎ 050/49187). **Prato** (Hertz, ✉ Via Valentini 60, ☎ 0574/611287; Autonoleggio Europa, ✉ Viale Vittorio Veneto 57, ☎ 0574/21055).

Emergencies
Ambulance (☎ 118). **Carabinieri** (☎ 112). **Emergencies** (☎ 113). **Fire** (☎ 115).

Late-Night Pharmacies
Many of the smaller towns post the name and address of late-night pharmacies, which are open on a rotating basis, in the windows of the tourist information centers as well as at individual pharmacies.

Travel Agencies
Montecatini Terme: Azienda Promozione Turistica Montecatini/Vadlinievole (✉ Viale Verdi 66/68, ☎ 0572/772244).

Visitor Information
Castelfiorentino (✉ Via Costituente, ☎ 0571/64602). **Certaldo** (☎ 0571/661211 or 0571/661241). **Lucca** (✉ Vecchia Porta San Donato, ☎ 0583/419689). **Montecatini Terme** (✉ Viale Verdi 66/68, ☎ 0572/772244). **Pisa** (✉ Piazza del Duomo 8, ☎ 050/560464). **Pistoia** (✉ Palazzo dei Vescovi, ☎ 0573/21622). **Prato** (✉ Via Cairoli 48, ☎ 0574/24112). **San Miniato** (✉ Piazza del Popolo, ☎ 0571/42745). **Vinci** (✉ Piazza Macelli, ☎ FAX 0571/568012).

5 Chianti

Blessedly compact, Chianti has hardly a hillside without something enriching—culturally, aesthetically, or gastronomically. The Chianti region, dotted with delightful villages and medieval castles, snuggles into the hills between Florence and Siena. It's graced with a combination of sun, soil, and slopes that has enabled farmers to produce some of Italy's best red wine and olive oil for thousands of years.

THE TWO SHAPES OF THE CHIANTI LANDSCAPE come into focus immediately. The country roads swirl around the hilltops that often appear to catch the passing clouds and hold on to them. And straight lines in the planted vineyards, fields, and orchards turn those curving hills into the patchwork of colors and textures that have inspired artists and delighted travelers for centuries. It's an enticing perspective that invites you to follow those roads to see where they go—maybe to a farmhouse where there is splendid olive oil or the region's Chianti Classico wine for sale, to a medieval country church (*pieve*), to an art-filled abbey (*badia* or *abbazia*), a fortress (*castello*), or a restaurant where there is outdoor dining on a covered patio that offers respite from the heat in the summer and a spectacular panorama.

By Nancy Hart

It's hard to imagine that this gentle area was once the battleground of the warring Sienese and Florentine armies, but until Florence finally defeated Siena in 1550, these enchanting walled cities were actually outposts in ongoing wars. Since the 1960s, many British and northern Europeans have relocated here, drawn to the unhurried life, balmy climate, and picturesque villages. They've bought and restored farmhouses, many given up by the young heirs who decided not to continue life on the farm and found work in the cities. There are so many Britons, in fact, that the area has been nicknamed Chiantishire. Still, it remains strongly Tuscan in character.

Pleasures and Pastimes

Biking

In the spring, summer, and fall, the spandex people are as much a part of the landscape as the cypress trees. A drive on any steep Chianti road will take you past groups of bikers peddling up and down the endless hills, seemingly biking from meal to meal. Many are on prearranged weeklong organized tours, but it's also possible to rent bikes for jaunts in the countryside or to find afternoon or day minitours. Most Italian roads are in excellent condition and Italian drivers are courteous and actually seem to enjoy the bikers. Remember though that the charming medieval hill towns that are often the destination of a bike trip usually only have one narrow winding road in and out, so it's important to remain cautious—especially considering that some of those drivers might be tourists too, who have just stopped at a vineyard for a tasting.

Dining

The menus in Chianti restaurants feature seasonal Tuscan dishes: Pizzerias have the classic thin-crust pizzas, bars and *pasticcerie* (bakeries) pile their *panini* (sandwiches) on the unsalted Tuscan bread—all similar to what you will find in Florence. Most restaurants in the countryside have terraces and patios for outside dining in good weather, and large picture windows that frame captivating views. But the views don't come cheap—restaurants here can be expensive but you can still find some bargains. The better restaurants take credit cards, but most of the village trattorias or roadside *taverne* (taverns) don't. Lunch is usually served from 1 to 3, and though city bars, taverns, and restaurants now offer a quick plate of pasta and salad for lunch, countryside restaurants still prepare the traditional hearty midday meal, which means you might want to operate on local siesta time, especially if you've tested a local Chianti. Dinner usually begins at 8. During the tourist season, advanced booking is *always* recommended.

CATEGORY	COST*
$$$$	over 110,000 lire
$$$	60,000 lire–110,000 lire
$$	35,000 lire–60,000 lire
$	under 35,000 lire

Prices are per person, for a three-course meal, house wine and tax included.

Lodging

Agriturismo (agritourism) offers a fresh alternative for those who want a more participatory holiday. "Agriturismo" facilities in the Chianti countryside can range from a farmer who rents a room of his farmhouse to entire medieval villages or grand villas that have been purchased by developers and turned into resorts with tennis courts, swimming pools, and gourmet restaurants. A stay on a real working farm can quickly immerse you in simple country life, while villas and village developments offer the joys of gentrified country living. Small hotels and pensions abound in the little Chianti villages, amid their small shops, street markets, and lively piazzas. But be prepared in your rambles, for many lodgings in Chianti are booked far in advance, especially in the height of summer—when you'll also discover air-conditioning is a rarity.

CATEGORY	COST*
$$$$	over 350,000 lire
$$$	220,000 lire–350,000 lire
$$	100,000 lire–220,000 lire
$	under 100,000 lire

Prices are for a double room for two, tax and service included.

Vineyards

Those picturesque vineyards on the Chianti hillsides are not cinematic backdrops; they are working farms, and when their grapes are harvested (in the fall) and processed, they become that world-famous *vino rosso* that has been complementing Tuscan food for ages. Chianti's heritage dates back thousands of years, but the borders that define Chianti Classico weren't officially drawn until 1932. The Chianti region is actually surprisingly large, as it includes all the areas where the various types of Chianti grapes are grown—stretching from Pistoia, north of Florence, to Montalcino, south of Siena. Chianti Classico is at the heart of the Chianti region. Its *Gallo Nero* (black rooster) logo dates from the 12th century, when the rooster was the symbol of the Chianti League that was a military alliance defending the Florentine border against Siena. Now that rooster logo signifies the highest-quality wines of the region that reaches from Florence to Siena.

Wine tasting lures travelers who want to relax their eyes after looking at all those halos in the churches and museums of Florence and Siena. Most of the vineyards have figured this out and offer direct sales and samplings of their products. Some have roadside stands, others have elaborate sampling rooms and serve snacks. Tourist information offices (☞ Visitor Information, *below*) in most Chianti towns have maps to guide you through an itinerary of vineyard hopping. For a rundown of local wines, *see* Close-Up: Bacchus in Tuscany, *below*).

Exploring Chianti

By far the best way to discover Chianti is by car, as its beauty often reveals itself along the route less traveled. Unfortunately, Chianti is not as spontaneous a place for exploration as it used to be. Even though area farmers are subdividing their barns and calling them *agriturismi,* there are a limited number of rooms. In the high season, which now spans from the end of March to mid-November, it is overflowing with people who have also come to take in the fresh air, inviting *enoteche* (wine bars), and fragrant trattorias. Surely you can rent a bicycle, stop the car at an interesting fork in the road, or go for a stroll. But don't count on taking off on bicycle, car, or foot in the morning and then being able to find a romantic hideaway to spend the night—reserve well in advance.

Numbers in the text correspond to numbers in the margin and on the Chianti map.

Great Itineraries

An itinerary can give you the big picture, but it's also important to look for the little picture, and to know that if you see something that looks interesting, turn the wheel, head down the road, and check it out. There are paths for walking, roads for biking, friendly residents for asking directions, and an abundance of fresh air and country smells.

IF YOU HAVE 3 DAYS

Leaving from Florence on day one, explore **San Donato in Poggio** ⑥ and surroundings, including **Badia a Passignano** ⑤ (even if the abbey is closed, it's set in stunning countryside), ▣ **Barberino Val d'Elsa** ⑦, and a ramble to the "cupola" and Sant'Appiano. Spend day two exploring the little hamlets and vineyards nestled in the hills off the Strada Chiantigiana (S222): ▣ **Greve in Chianti** ⑨, an attractive market town with a main pedestrian street lined with wine bars, cafés, and boutiques; tiny ▣ **Panzano** ⑩; ▣ **Castellina in Chianti** ⑪, a medium-size town with a lively center; ▣ **Radda in Chianti** ⑫, a crossroads of a wine town but no less enchanting; and Volpaia, a lost-in-time castle sitting on a hilltop.

On day three, go south to ▣ **Montalcino** ⑮ for some wine tasting and a walk through the streets; the Abbazia di Sant'Antimo (☞ Chapter 7); compact Pienza (☞ Chapter 7), a model Renaissance town commissioned by Pope Pius II, for lunch; and ▣ **Montepulciano** ⑯, another architectural gem. Return to Florence via the A1 or the S2, off of which is **Colle Val d'Elsa** ⑧, with some of the most impressive art in Chianti.

When to Tour Chianti

Summer is the peak season for visiting Chianti, when you'll find the road crammed with foreign licence plates and rental cars and full hotels and restaurants. But there's a reason for that. It's an absolutely glorious time to be driving in the hills, sitting on the terraces, biking on the trails. Spring and fall are also spectacular, when there may be more chance for rain, but the temperature is milder and there is more room for relaxing. In the winter, you wonder who invented the term "sunny Italy"; the panoramas, however, are still beautiful, even with overcast skies and chilling winds. Many hotels, agriturismi, wine estates, and restaurants close in the winter months (from after Christmas through March).

WESTERN CHIANTI

Just beyond Florence's reach are magnificently preserved country churches and abbeys and little-discovered towns that make for perfect jaunts from Florence—and quick art-stress relievers. But quick art fixes can be had, such as at Badia a Passignano, which shelters a 21-ft, 15th-century *Last Supper* by Domenico Ghirlandaio. The Western Chianti region also offers affordable, relaxed country lodging with easy access to Florence. The entrance to the region is through the Certosa interchange, with the choice of two roads—the Florence–Siena superstrada (no number), which is a four-lane, divided road with exits

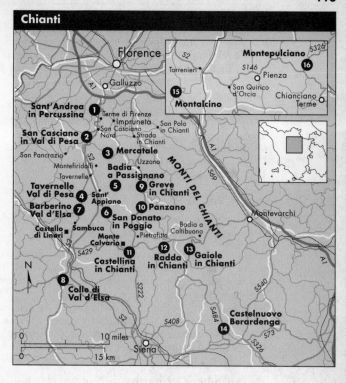

Chianti

Florence
S2
Montepulciano
S326
Torrenieri
S146
Pienza
16
Galluzzo
A1
San Quirico
d'Orcia
Chianciano
Terme
15
Montalcino

**Sant'Andrea
in Percussina**
1
Terme di Firenze
**San Casciano
in Val di Pesa**
2
Imprunета
San Casciano
Nord
San Polo
in Chianti
Strada
in Chianti
San Pancrazio
3 **Mercatale**
Montefiridolfi
Uzzano
**Badia
a Passignano**
MONTI DEL CHIANTI
Tavernelle
5
9 **Greve
in Chianti**
**Tavernelle
Val di Pesa**
4
Sant'
Appiano
S69
**Barberino
Val d'Elsa**
7
6
10 **Panzano**
**San Donato
in Poggio**
Montevarchi
Castello
di Linari
Sambuca
Badia a
Coltibuono
Monte
Calvario
Pietrafitta
S429
11
12 **13**
**Castellina
in Chianti**
**Radda
in Chianti**
**Gaiole
in Chianti**
A1
N
S222
S540
8
**Colle di
Val d'Elsa**
S2
S408
S484
**Castelnuovo
Berardenga**
0
10 miles
14
S73
0
15 km
Siena
S326

that allow you to weave in and out of the countryside, or the S2, the ancient Roman Via Cassia, which has been a paved road since 154 BC. The superstrada is more direct, but there is often a lot of traffic, especially on Sunday evening when all the Italians are returning from weekends in the countryside or at the beach, and there are no shoulders for stopping nor are there gas stations.

Sant'Andrea in Percussina

❶ *15 km (9 mi) south of Florence, 4 km (2½ mi) north of San Casciano in Val di Pesa.*

This tiny village is where Niccolò Machiavelli (1469–1527) lived when he was exiled from Florence in 1513 by the Medicis. The unassuming building—called **L'Albergaccio** (the rundown hotel) because of its humble origins—is where Machiavelli wrote *The Prince* and *Discourses*. A small, rarely open **Museo Machiavelli** shows his actual studio, kitchen, and bedroom just as they looked when he lived here. You might be able to gain entry at **Taverna Machiavelli**, across the road, where he went when in need of friendship and food. ⊠ *Via de Scopeti,* ☎ *no phone.* ▣ *Free.* ☼ *Key/tour through Taverna Machiavelli, (☞ below).*

The small Romanesque church of **Sant'Andrea,** perched on the nearby hillside, is worth a stroll for a closer look. ☎ *No phone.* ▣ *Free.* ☼ *Rarely open (view from outside).*

En Route If you continue on this road toward San Casciano in Val di Pesa, you will find the tiny hamlet of Spedaletto and the church of Santa Maria di Casavecchia, where works by the della Robbias are preserved, as well as a carved pulpit attributed to Desiderio da Settignano (1428–64).

Dining

$ ✕ **Taverna Machiavelli.** Across the road from Machiavelli's residence, this place was most certainly where he used to hang out, since it was the old neighborhood taverna. Now, it's a quality restaurant, with a typical Tuscan menu, big fires going in the kitchen, and a setup probably not so different from what Machiavelli saw—except perhaps for the credit-card machine. This is also a great place to stop by for a *merenda* (afternoon snack) of *bruschetta* (grilled bread rubbed with garlic, brushed with olive oil, and topped with fresh tomatoes) and a glass of wine (their own Chianti, of course). Proprietors of the restaurant will take patrons across the street to see the Museo Machiavelli (☞ *above*). ⊠ *Via de Scopeti, Sant'Andrea in Percussina,* ☏ *055/828471. DC, MC, V. Closed Mon.*

San Casciano in Val di Pesa

❷ *18 km (13 mi) south of Florence (take San Casciano exit, first exit south of Florence on Florence–Siena superstrada).*

Parts of the original walls and gates of San Casciano in Val di Pesa—one of the larger Chianti towns—are still standing and weave the old and new parts of the town together. A large wooded city park with parking is close to the city center. The Gothic church of **Santa Maria Sul Prato,** next to the remains of one of the city gates, dates from 1335. The church contains an altar crucifix by Sienese artist Simone Martini (1284–1344) and a carved marble pulpit by Giovanni Balducci da Pisa (1317–50), who was a student of Andrea Pisano (circa 1270–1348). ⊠ *Via Morrocchesi 19,* ☏ *055/820023.* 🎫 *Free.* ☉ *Daily 9–7.*

The **Museo d'Arte Sacra** in the church of **Santa Maria del Gesù** opened in 1989 and contains many works originally in the small country churches in the area. The pieces, including a Sienese wooden crucifix and four bronze crosses (circa 14th–15th centuries) and the carved pedestal of a marble baptismal font dating from the early 12th century, were brought to the museum for protection from the elements and thieves. ⊠ *Via Roma,* ☏ *055/820023.* 🎫 *Free.* ☉ *Sat. 4:30–7, Sun. and holidays 10–12:30 and 4–7.*

Dining and Lodging

$$$ ✕ **La Tenda Rossa.** This restaurant began as a pizzeria and as the owners have carefully added more touches, it has become one of Italy's top restaurants, with an extensive wine list. Try one of the house specialties, such as zucchini flowers stuffed with local mozzarella and topped with a saffron sauce. ⊠ *Cerbaia Val di Pesa, 5 km (3 mi) west of San Casciano in Val di Pesa,* ☏ *055/826132. AE, DC, MC, V. Closed Thurs. and Aug. No lunch Wed.*

$ ✕ **Tratoria Cantinetta del Nonno.** You walk through a front-room shop, where you can buy prosciutto or other cold cuts, then past an open kitchen, then into the small back dining room. Basic, but good, food is on offer. Try the *ravioli con burro salvia* (ricotta and spinach ravioli with butter and sage sauce) or the wonderfully salty spaghetti *al baccalà* (with codfish). ⊠ *Via 4 Novembre,* ☏ *055/820570. No credit cards. Closed Wed.*

$$ ✕🏨 **Hotel/Restaurant Antica Posta.** This is the old post house in San Casciano where travelers used to stop and exchange their horses as they traveled the old Roman road that connected Florence and Siena. The 400-year-old building has been a hotel and restaurant for more than 150 years. The rooms are basic and comfortable and all have private baths. Because the current owner's father is a butcher, you can count on the *bistecca alla fiorentina* (grilled local Chianina beef). ⊠ *Piazza*

Zannoni 1–3, ☎ *055/822313,* FAX *055/822278. 10 rooms. Restaurant. CP. AE, MC, V. Closed Tues. and 2nd and 3rd wks of Nov.*

$$ 🏠 **La Fattoressa.** The name La Fattoressa translates as "the farmer's wife," and in this case, it's the appropriate name for an agriturismo where La Signora attends to the needs of her guests—everything from cooking their meals to ironing the homemade bed linens, which she dries in the sun and sprinkles with lavender. The house and guest rooms are filled with "grandmother's antiques" and fresh flowers. She serves lunch and dinner (at an additional cost of 40,000 lire per meal) using only homegrown ingredients. ⊠ *Via Volterrana 58, 4 km (2½ mi) south of the Certosa autostrada interchange near Florence, 50124,* ☎ FAX *055/2048418. 6 rooms. Restaurant. CP. No credit cards.*

$ 🏠 **Castello Il Corno.** A 13th-century castle and Renaissance-style villa now offer the feeling of a luxury hotel in the middle of a farm. It's a fairy-tale setting, with two rooms in the castle plus 17 apartments in farm cottages with 19th-century furnishings. You can sign up for cooking classes in the fall, following family recipes and using fresh ingredients from the farm's garden. The farm itself has more than 10,000 olive trees and also produces wine, including a high-quality *vin santo* (sweet dessert wine). ⊠ *Via di Malafrasca 64, 50026,* ☎ *055/8248009,* FAX *055/8248035. 2 rooms, 17 apartments. Pool, mountain bikes. CP. V.*

$ 🏠 **Cigliano di Sopra.** You stay in farmhouses, decorated with rustic furniture and some with fireplaces, surrounding the main villa. The farm itself produces olive oil, wine, and fabulous honey—all grown and processed organically. ⊠ *Via Cigliano, 50026,* ☎ *055/820121,* FAX *055/2302693. 15 rooms. Restaurant, bar, pool. CP. No credit cards.*

$ 🏠 **La Ginestra.** If you want to take home a great memory of your Chianti vacation, why not a painting—your own! At La Ginestra, you can sign up for painting courses. This is a working farm that makes and sells pasta, salami, prosciutto, honey, wine, and olive oil. You stay in the small houses on the grounds, including Il Mandorlo, which has its own garden and can sleep 12 people. All rooms have typical rustic Tuscan trimmings. A large hay barn accommodates groups, ceremonies, and conventions. Horseback riding and tennis are available nearby. There is a one-week minimum stay. ⊠ *Via Pergolata 3, Località Santa Cristina a Salivolpe, 10 km (6 mi) south of San Casciano, 50026,* ☎ FAX *055/8249245. 15 rooms. Pool, convention center. CP. DC, MC, V.*

$ 🏠 **Mandorlo.** The exposed beams of a hay barn roof become an architectural focal point in this renovated agriturismo setting just outside San Casciano. The barn dates back to the 1700s; there are now four apartments, each with a living room, bedroom, bath, and cooking corner, and two have verandas. A huge porch invites relaxing. ⊠ *Via Borromeo 130, 1 km (½ mi) southwest of San Casciano in Val di Pesa, 50124,* ☎ *055/8244211,* FAX *055/8244382. 4 apartments. Pool. EP. No credit cards.*

Mercatale

❸ *25 km (16 mi) south of Florence, 6 km (4 mi) southeast of San Casciano in Val di Pesa.*

Mercatale, as the name implies, began in 1237 when the mayor of a neighboring town ordered the construction of a public square to serve as a marketplace for his court. The city center doesn't have much to offer in the way of important art, but it's roads lined with villas make for pleasant country strolls.

Lodging

$$–$$$ 🏠 **Castello il Palagio.** This is a unique opportunity to set up housekeeping just outside of Mercatale. The owners of this castle rent one of their country houses that sleeps up to 11 people by the week. You'll

find the surroundings very comfortable: The kitchen has a wood-burning fireplace; the bathrooms are new; the furniture is 19th-century country style; and the floors are the original terra-cotta. ⊠ *Via di Campoli 134, 1 km (½ mi) south of Mercatale, 50024,* ☎ *055/8244211.* FAX *055/8244382. 1 house. EP. MC, V.*

$$ 🏠 **Salvadonica.** There is a pervading friendly atmosphere at this place in Mercatale, with owners who will take their guests on tours of vineyards and olive groves in the area. Each well-cared-for apartment has a small kitchen. A communal room surrounded by glass functions as the lobby for all guests to enjoy. If you're interested in the real country Italian experience, there's even a boccie ball court. Another bonus: The pool has hydromassage. ⊠ *Via Grevigiana 82 50024,* ☎ *055/8218939,* FAX *055/8218043. 5 rooms, 11 apartments. Pool, tennis court, boccie, billiards. CP. AE, DC, MC, V.*

Tavarnelle Val di Pesa

❹ *28 km (15 mi) south of Florence, 12 km (7½ mi) south of San Casciano in Val di Pesa.*

The name Tavarnelle comes from *tabernulae,* which were the stopover villages between Florence and Siena for travelers on their way to Rome. Its location kept it out of the fierce battles between Florence and Siena, which explains the absence of towers and fortifications. Today Tavarnelle is a busy center—a good place to shop, as well as centrally located for side trips. **San Pietro in Bossolo,** one of the most beautiful country churches in the area, is just outside the city center. Dating from the 10th century, it has a 14th-century marble sanctuary and a 16th-century portico. The bell tower dates from the mid-1800s. Inside a small attached museum is an important 13th-century work, *Virgin Mary with Child and Saints,* by Coppo di Marcovaldo (active 1260–1280), one of the earliest painters from the Florence area. ⊠ *Via della Pieve 19,* ☎ *055/8077255.* 🎟 *Free.* ☉ *Church and museum: weekends 4:30–7:30.*

At the same spot where you see the sign for Sambuca near the superstrada, you will also see an unimposing monastery on the south side of the road near the tiny hamlet of Morrocco. This is the church of **Santa Maria del Carmine,** built in 1466, which contains a porcelain by Giovanni della Robbia (1400–82). But the main attraction of this church is the group of industrious Carmelite nuns from Australia who have been the proprietors since 1982. It's worth making sure you arrive at 5:30 any afternoon, when the nuns sing their vespers service with pure, beautiful voices. The pews are filled for Sunday and holiday masses with appreciative Italians and an English-speaking community who come from a wide area. The nuns also make and sell a range of products, such as perfumed candles and creams, using traditional formulas. ⊠ *Via di Morrocco 35, Tavarnelle Val di Pesa,* ☎ *055/8076067.* 🎟 *Free.* ☉ *Daily 9–7, vespers daily 5:30 PM.*

Dining and Lodging

$ ✕ **Borgo Antico.** Some restaurants have wine tastings; this one in Tavarnelle Val di Pesa offers olive oil tastings. The owner keeps several bottles of locally produced extra-virgin olive oil for you to sample, and it can be purchased at nearby farms. All the pasta is homemade, the ravioli is one of the prize choices, and the dessert cart will probably stay in your memory for quite a while, especially the tart lavished with figs and hazelnuts. ⊠ *Via Roma 55,* ☎ *055/8076180. AE, DC, MC, V. Closed Wed.*

$$$$ 🏠 **Castellare De'Sernigi.** There are six antiques-filled guest rooms with new large bathrooms and kitchens with restaurant appliances and marble counters in this perfectly restored 17th-century minivilla in Tav-

ernelle. It can be rented by the week or month in its entirety (six rooms), by a maximum of 14 people. All details for an elegant holiday will be taken care of, including complete office facilities for those who can't quite get away from it all. The owner will provide meals on request. ⊠ *Strada Palazzuolo 40, 50028,* ☎ FAX *055/8074213. 1 villa. Pool, mountain bikes, business services. EP. No credit cards.*

$$ ⊞ **Hotel Park Chianti.** Don't let the fact that it's close to the highway turn you off. This is a great place in Tavarnelle to stop if you've been in the car all day and want new-world amenities instead of old-world charm. Located at the Tavernelle exit of the Florence–Siena superstrada, this is an impeccable hotel, with predictable motel furniture and rooms, but a beautiful swimming pool and gardens and soundproof windows. ⊠ *Località Pontenuovo 50028,* ☎ *055/8070106,* FAX *055/8070121. 43 rooms. Restaurant, pool. EP. AE, DC, MC, V.*

$$ ⊞ **Sovigliano.** The owner of this 12th-century farmhouse in Tavarnelle has kept the agriturismo operation to a minimum, working to maintain the natural gardens filled with herbs, wildflowers, and pines. But, the orthopedic beds and new bathrooms are certainly a nice anachronism. During recent restoration, they uncovered logs from the original frame, which have been left exposed, covered with glass, and are now part of the decor. ⊠ *Strada Magliano 9, 50028,* ☎ *055/8076217,* FAX *055/8050770. 4 rooms, 3 apartments. CP. AE.*

$ ⊞ **Albergo Vittoria.** This wonderfully priced hotel is on a city street, but there are quadruple-paned soundproof windows covered with heavy drapes. Rooms are large, the furniture is modern, and the bathrooms are new. The hands-on owner works to make sure you are happy, provides all kinds of tourist tips, and even shares her computer with guests who need to send or receive E-mail. ⊠ *Via Roma 57 50028,* ☎ FAX *055/8076180. 7 rooms. CP. AE, DC, MC, V.*

$ ⊞ **La Villa.** You ring the bell at the front door, walk directly into a garden, and the hotel is actually in a restored 16th-century convent on the other side of a field. There's a rustic, country style to the six simply furnished apartments, which are situated around an enclosed courtyard filled with fruit trees. The young owners are enthusiastic about their work, happy to act as guides for you. ⊠ *Via Roma 396, 50028,* ☎ *055/8077041,* FAX *055/8077241. 6 apartments. Pool. CP. No credit cards.*

Sambuca

6 km (4 mi) east of Tavarnelle Val di Pesa, 25 km (15 mi) south of Florence, 1 km (½ mi) west of the San Donato exit off the Florence–Siena superstrada.

Cradled by the Pesa River, Sambuca itself is an unattractive industrial town, but its graceful arched bridge and riverside park make the 10-minute detour worth it. The **Ponte Romano** was built in 1069 as part of the Via Francigena that brought pilgrims from northern Europe to Rome. Written documents evidently prove that Leonardo da Vinci (1452–1519) himself once walked across this bridge.

Lodging

$ ⊞ **Hotel Torricelle Zucchi.** This hotel is in a commercial area of Sambuca and certainly has no eye appeal, but you're in central Chianti. The rooms and bathrooms are large, the price is low, and without too much begging, you might convince the owner to play a bit of Chopin on his baby grand piano in the lobby. ⊠ *Via Cellini 32 50028,* ☎ *055/8071780,* FAX *055/8071102. 22 rooms. EP. AE, DC, MC, V.*

Badia a Passignano

⑤ *4 km (2½ mi) east of Sambuca, 29 km (18 mi) south of Florence.*

One of the finest and best preserved works of art in Italy is in the dining room of the towering 11th-century Badia a Passignano: a 21-ft *Last Supper* (1476) by Domenico Ghirlandaio (1449–94). In the same room, a carved pulpit juts from the wall—this is where monks once stood to read from sacred books during their meals. Restorations are underway to uncover frescoes that were covered over with white paint when part of the Badia was used as a hospital. The church of **San Michele,** also called San Piaggio, contains a 10th-century statue of St. Michael, one of the oldest marble statues in Tuscany. All visitors are conducted on tours by the resident monks. Even if you can't be here during the limited hours (Sunday afternoon), it's worth a drive to see the Badia's fairy-tale setting and to walk in the beautiful hillsides. By the way, the areas beneath the monastery and church are rented by the neighboring Antinori vineyards, who store their wines here for aging. ⊠ *Badia a Passignano,* ☎ *055/8071622.* 🎟 *Free.* ☉ *Monastery and church: Sun. 3:30–5:30.*

Dining

$$ ✕ **La Scuderia.** Across the street from Badia a Passignano, this traditional Tuscan restaurant specializes in country cooking, especially roast chicken and duck and stewed rabbit. And, when you ask for house wine, that's what you're getting, because the owners make their own. ⊠ *Across from Badia a Passignano,* ☎ *055/8071623. Reservations essential Sun. No credit cards. Closed Wed.*

San Donato in Poggio

⑥ *5 km (3 mi) south of Badia al Passignano.*

Great care has been taken by the residents of San Donato in Poggio to ensure that this gem of a medieval city preserves its ancient ambience. No cars are permitted in this perfectly preserved walled village blissfully bereft of neon signs and advertising posters. A village has existed on this site since 1033 when a fortified castle was built high on the hill between San Casciano in Val di Pesa and Colle di Val d'Elsa. The original castle was destroyed in 1289. A new wall was constructed immediately after the fighting ended, and it still stands, enclosing the city with two gates—one facing Siena and one facing Florence. The only remains of the original castle walls can be seen in the base of the present-day municipal bell tower. The main square, **Piazza Malaspina,** is decorated with a 15th-century fresco. The **Pieve di San Donato,** just outside the wall, dates from 989, although the existing building is probably from the early 12th century. There is also a 13th-century cloister and a 16th-century ceramic baptismal font by Giovanni della Robbia. There are no set opening hours, but mass is held on Sunday mornings. ⊠ *Via della Pieve 25,* ☎ *055/8072934.* 🎟 *Free.* ☉ *Weekdays 1–6, Sat. 9–1.*

Lodging

$$ 🏨 **Le Filigare.** This was one of Chianti's pioneer agriturismo operations, set in the middle of a vineyard in San Donato in Poggio. It's actually an entire medieval village that's been converted into guest rooms and decorated with a combination of antique and modern furnishings. You can enjoy beautiful scenery in a mellow, extremely private atmosphere. Le Filigare is known throughout the area for its excellent wine and oil, grappa and vin santo, all of which can be tasted and purchased from their cellars. ⊠ *Località Le Filigare, 50020,* ☎ *055/8072796,* ℻ *055/755766. 7 apartments. Pool, tennis court, mountain bikes. EP. AE, DC, MC, V.*

Barberino Val d'Elsa

❼ *2½ km (1½ mi) southwest of Tavarnelle Val di Pesa, 28 km (17 mi) south of Florence.*

There are two gates in the medieval wall surrounding Barberino Val d'Elsa—one faces Florence, the other faces Siena. Via Francesco da Barberino connects the two gates and is the main street of this picturesque town, which offers glorious views of the surrounding hills and is a perfect jumping-off point for countryside explorations. The town dates from the 11th century, the walls from the 14th century. The 13th-century Renaissance **Palazzo Pretorio,** in Piazza Barberini, is decorated with the coats of arms of the *podeste* (mayors) who governed over the centuries. ⊠ *Piazza Barberini.*

A tiered walkway leads down to Via Vittorio Veneto, where the church of **San Bartolomeo** is worth a visit to admire the 14th- and 15th-century frescoes and the bronze bust by Pietro Tacca (1577–1664) in the rectory. ⊠ *Via Vittorio Veneto,* ☎ *no phone.* ⌖ *Free.* ☉ *Sun. 9–1.*

Dining and Lodging

$$$ ✕ **Il Paese dei Campanelli.** This is one of the top restaurants in Chianti, set in an old *cantina* (wine storage building) surrounded by glorious gardens, where meals are served in the summer. There are the typical Tuscan recipes but also some variations using exquisite ingredients, especially seasonal mushrooms, and beautifully presented plates. The duck comes rare, the salads are works of art. Make reservations well in advance. ⊠ *Località Petrognano, 4 km (2½ mi) south of Barberino,* ☎ *055/8075318. Reservations essential. AE, DC, MC, V. Closed Sun. No dinner Wed.*

$ ✕ **L'Archibugio.** This is inside the walls of the medieval hill town Barberino Val d'Elsa and is a great place for a thin-crust pizza. In the summer you eat outside and enjoy the respite from the heat; in the winter, you can eat inside next to a comforting fireplace. Residents from surrounding towns can be found here year-round. ⊠ *Via Vittorio Veneto 48,* ☎ *055/8075209. No credit cards. Closed Wed.*

$$$ ⊞ **La Spinosa.** The owners have organized a group of 17th-century farmhouses into an agriturismo destination and dedicate their lives to making sure their guests have perfect vacations. The buildings have been renovated, but maintain their original character, complete with a mix of Italian farmhouse furniture and antiques. The public spaces include a game room, library, and small bar. ⊠ *Via Le Masse 8 50021,* ☎ *055/ 8075413,* ℻ *055/8066214. 5 rooms, 4 suites. Bar, pool, archery, horseback riding, volleyball, library. MAP. AE, DC, MC, V.*

$$ ⊞ **Il Paretaio.** This peaceful, extremely private retreat attracts the horsey set, and offers riding lessons as well as trails for riding. A chef comes daily with fresh coffee cakes for breakfast and prepares excellent dinners for the guests who eat in the farmhouse dining room or outside in the garden. The six guest rooms are in the farmhouse. There is a week minimum stay. ⊠ *Località San Filippo, Barberino Val d'Elsa 50021,* ☎ *055/8059218,* ℻ *055/8059231. 6 rooms. Pool, horseback riding. MAP. No credit cards.*

$ ⊞ **Fattoria Casa Sola.** Near Barberino Val d'Elsa, this romantic agriturismo has views from each of its seven eclectically furnished apartments. Each apartment has its own garden or veranda. The owners are ready to supply information about local cultural events, and with a group of six or more, will also offer courses in painting, cooking, or photography. There is a week minimum for all stays. ⊠ *Località Le Cortine, Barberino Val d'Elsa 50021,* ☎ *055/8075028,* ℻ *055/8059194. 7 apartments. Pool. EP. MC, V.*

Sant'Appiano

8 km (5 mi) south of Barberino Val d'Elsa, 36 km (22 mi) south of Florence.

Taking the Via Cassia (S2) south from Barberino, signs will lead you to Sant'Appiano, the most important monument in the Barberino area. The road actually takes you to the back of the church, because the front of the church faces an intriguing set of ancient stone stairs that descends to the village below. Rising in a grass field in front of the church are four mystical sandstone pillars that remain from a 5th-century baptistry that was destroyed by an earthquake in the early 19th century. Paintings from the schools of Giotto and Ghirlandaio, as well as the skeletal remains of St. Appiano with dried flowers around his head, are inside the church. Also in the church is a two-room Etruscan museum, open weekends 3–6. ⊠ *Via Sant'Appiano 1,* ☎ *055/8075519.* ⊠ *Donations accepted.* ☼ *June–Sept., weekends 4–7:30; Oct.–May, Sat. 3–6.*

Castello di Linari

1 km (½ mi) south of Sant'Appiano, 38 km (24 mi) south of Florence.

On a wall beyond the Gothic entrance of this nearly abandoned village, commanding a position on top of a hill, is an Etruscan inscription (you'll find it on the wall across the street from Via Santa Maria 11). It translates as an ancient advertisement, inviting travelers and shepherds to stop at Linari, where they would find food and shelter. Today the castle in ruins makes for an interesting stop along the road for a walk.

En Route   Leaving Castello di Linari, if you return in the direction of Barberino (north), you will find a sign to Semifonte Petrognano that will lead you to the **Cappella di San Michele Arcangelo,** one of the biggest surprises in Tuscany. Just 2 km (1 mi) past Semifonte Petrognano you will see ahead of you what appears to be the Duomo of Florence. Here in the Chianti countryside is a 1-to-8-scale model of Brunelleschi's dome, built in 1597, using plans left by Tito and Gregorio Pagani. The "cupola" is in disrepair, but still a glorious sight, surrounded by cypress trees. The castle and village of Semifonte Petrognano were totally destroyed by the Florentines in the late 1200s and orders were given not to build any new buildings. More than 300 years passed before this small chapel, celebrating Florence, was built. ⊠ *2 km (1 mi) west of Semifonte Petrognano,* ☎ *no phone.* ⊠ *Free.* ☼ *Contact local tourist office for hours.*

Colle di Val d'Elsa

❽   *10 km (6 mi) south of Castello di Linari, 45 km (28 mi) south of Florence.*

Colle di Val d'Elsa, one of the most beautiful spots in Chianti, is really two cities. Colle Bassa, at the bottom of the hill, is mostly modern; Colle Alta, at the top of the hill, is lined with 16th- and 17th-century palaces (the family names of the original owners are displayed on plaques) and has a medieval center. There is bus service between the two, plus a surprisingly large car parking area (on the road that connects Colle Alta and Colle Bassa), both under and above ground. Colle di Val d'Elsa has been a manufacturing center for fine crystal since the middle of the 14th century. It was the scene of many battles between Florence and Siena, was "won" by the Florentines in 1333, but now, after all that bloodshed, is happily and peacefully a part of the Province of Siena.

The 8th-century **Romanesque Duomo** in Colle Alta, rebuilt in the early 17th century, contains a bronze crucifix designed by Giambologna

MCI Calling Card

123 456 7891 2345
J.D. SMITH

WorldPhone

Earn Miles With Your MCI Card.

Take the MCI Card along on this trip and start earning miles for the next one. You'll earn frequent flyer miles on all your calls and save with the low rates you've come to expect from MCI. Before you know it, you'll be on your way to some other international destination.

Sign up for MCI by calling 1-800-FLY-FREE

Earn Frequent Flyer Miles.

Is this a great time, or what? :-)

Easy To Call Home.

1. To use your MCI Card, just dial the WorldPhone access number of the country you're calling from.
2. Dial or give the operator your MCI Card number.
3. Dial or give the number you're calling.

# Austria (CC) ♦	022-903-012
# Belarus (CC)	
From Brest, Vitebsk, Grodno, Minsk	8-800-103
From Gomel and Mogilev regions	8-10-800-103
# Belgium (CC) ♦	0800-10012
# Bulgaria	00800-0001
# Croatia (CC) ★	0800-22-0112
# Czech Republic (CC) ♦	00-42-000112
# Denmark (CC) ♦	8001-0022
# Finland (CC) ♦	08001-102-80
# France (CC) ♦	0-800-99-0019
# Germany (CC)	0800-888-8000
# Greece (CC) ♦	00-800-1211
# Hungary (CC) ♦	00▼800-01411
# Iceland (CC) ♦	800-9002
# Ireland (CC)	1-800-55-1001
# Italy (CC) ♦	172-1022
# Kazakhstan (CC)	8-800-131-4321
# Liechtenstein (CC) ♦	0800-89-0222
# Luxembourg	0800-0112
# Monaco (CC) ♦	800-90-019
# Netherlands (CC) ♦	0800-022-9122
# Norway (CC) ♦	800-19912
# Poland (CC) ÷	00-800-111-21-22
# Portugal (CC) ÷	05-017-1234
Romania (CC) ÷	01-800-1800
# Russia (CC) ÷ ♦	
To call using ROSTELCOM ■	747-3322
For a Russian-speaking operator	747-3320
To call using SOVINTEL ■	960-2222
# San Marino (CC) ♦	172-1022
# Slovak Republic (CC)	00-421-00112
# Slovenia	080-8808
# Spain (CC)	900-99-0014
# Sweden (CC) ♦	020-795-922
# Switzerland (CC) ♦	0800-89-0222
# Turkey (CC) ♦	00-8001-1177
# Ukraine (CC) ÷	8▼10-013
# United Kingdom (CC)	
To call using BT ■	0800-89-0222
To call using C&W ■	0500-89-0222
# Vatican City (CC)	172-1022

#Automation available from most locations. (CC) Country-to-country calling available to/from most international locations. ♦ Public phones may require deposit of coin or phone card for dial tone. ★ Not available from public pay phones. ▼ Wait for second dial tone. ÷ Limited availability. ■ International communications carrier. Limit one bonus program per MCI account. Terms and conditions apply. All airline program rules and conditions apply. © 1998 MCI Telecommunications Corporation. All rights reserved. Is this a great time, or what? is a service mark of MCI.

(1529–1608) over the high altar that was a gift to the church from the grand-duchess Maria Maddalena of Austria in 1629, and (in the last chapel on the right) a bas-relief by Mino da Fiesole (1430–84) and a bronze lectern created by Giambologna's pupil, Pietro Tacca. ⊠ *Piazza del Duomo,* ☎ *no phone.* ⌦ *Free.* ☉ *Weekends 9–12:30 and 3:30–7.*

The **Antiquarium Etrusco** (Etruscan Museum) is also in the Piazza del Duomo, housed in the 14th-century **Palazzo Pretorio**. It contains a collection of 15th- and 16th-century frescoes and Etruscan pottery and bronze items excavated from the area. ⊠ *Piazza del Duomo,* ☎ *0577/ 922954.* ⌦ *4,000 lire.* ☉ *June–Sept., Tues.–Sat. 5–7 PM, Sun. and holidays 10–12 and 5–7; Oct.–May, Tues.–Sat. 3:30–5:30, Sun. and holidays 10–12 and 3:30–5:30.*

In Colle Bassa, the church of **Sant'Agostino** in Piazza Sant'Agostino, with a treasure of works by Bronzino, Cigoli, and Ghirlandaio, has a 13th-century unfinished facade but an ornate 16th-century Renaissance interior, designed by Antonio da Sangallo the Elder (1455–1537).

Dining and Lodging

$$$$ ✕ **Ristorante Arnolfo di Campio.** If you are looking for an exquisite
★ dining experience, this is it. One of the rooms at this small, elegant restaurant is filled with tables for two with oversized upholstered chairs, and there is a terrace overlooking the valley for summer dining. Specialties are *piccione* (pigeon) casserole and *agnello* (lamb) dishes topped with fresh herbs that vary with the season. The wine list is extensive and there is a fixed-price five-course menu (80,000 lire, not including wine) if your appetite can handle it. ⊠ *Via XX Settembre, Colle Alta,* ☎ *0577/920549. Reservations essential. AE, DC, MC, V. Closed Tues.*

$$$ ✕ **L'Antica Trattoria.** The homemade ravioli stuffed with leeks and ricotta cheese is worth the trip here, not to mention the refined decor and beautiful terrace where the meals are served in the summer. The *ribollita* (bread and vegetable soup) is wonderful when the weather is cold, or try the fillet served on a hot plate for an unusual treat. ⊠ *Piazza Arnolfo di Cambio 23, Colle Basso,* ☎ *0577/923747. Reservations essential weekends. AE, DC, MC, V. Closed Tues.*

$$ ✕ **Enoteca Cantina della Fortuna.** The name translates as "the lucky wine cellar," but this place is actually a cozy restaurant, featuring typical but very good Tuscan dishes. Try the well-prepared *pappardelle* (wide pasta) with *cinghiale* (wild boar) sauce. They stoke the fire in the winter, serve meals on the terrace in the summer. ⊠ *Via della Fontanelle 2,* ☎ *0577/923102. AE, D, MC, V. Closed Mon.*

$$ ✕ **Sapia Tea Room/Ristorante Sapia.** It's really two restaurants in the same spot. The tearoom serves light meals and antipasti, with live music in the evening. The small restaurant has an intimate garden for summer dining and bases its changing menus on fresh fish. ⊠ *Via del Castello 4, Colle Alta,* ☎ *0577/921453. D, MC, V. Closed Mon. (May–Sept.) and Mon–Wed (Oct.–Apr.).*

$ ✕ **Pisto Pub.** When it's finally time for a light meal, you'll know it. And this is the place to go. It features various types of bruschetta (perhaps topped with tomatoes or chicken liver pâté or garlic-flavored cheeses). There are also salads, sandwiches, good wines, and local and imported beer. ⊠ *V. Gracco del Secco, Colle Alta,* ☎ *0577/920055. AE, DC, MC, V.*

$$ ✕⌂ **Vecchia Cartiera Restaurant/Hotel.** The Vecchia Cartiera is located in a 14th-century paper factory that has been beautifully renovated to preserve the feeling of the old factory while providing comfortable rooms with *mobili in stile* (19th-century copies of 16th-century furniture), parquet floors, and a restaurant that serves typical Tuscan meals on dishes made by local potters. The restaurant features a special breakfast buffet (15,000 lire) complete with marmalade-filled tarts, home-cured meats, and local cheeses—a real treat in Italy, where the normal breakfast is a quick cappuccino and small sweet roll. ⊠ *Via Oberdan 5, 53034,* ☎ *0577/921107,* FAX *0577/923688. 38 rooms. Restaurant, bar. EP. AE, DC, MC, V. Restaurant closed Sun. No dinner Mon.*

$$–$$$ 🏨 **Villa Belvedere.** In addition to the pleasure of staying in a 17th-century villa that overlooks a formal Italian garden, here you can enjoy exquisite views of San Gimignano. The food extends beyond the Tuscan basics. The villa itself has been left with the feeling of a private home; the rooms are filled with period furniture, and several small and large rooms are for your use. A tennis court was planned at press time. ⊠ *Località Belvedere, Colle di Val d'Elsa 53034,* ☎ *0577/920966,* FAX *0577/924128. 15 rooms. Pool. CP. AE, DC, MC, V.*

$$ 🏨 **Arnoldo Hotel.** This is not a fancy hotel, but the location is excellent if you want to stay in a town. It's on the main street of Colle Alta, and there are views from the windows that face the valley (Val d'Elsa). The rooms have simple, modern furniture and new bathrooms. ⊠ *Via F. Campana 8, Colle Alta 53034,* ☎ *0577/922020,* FAX *0577/922324. 32 rooms. CP. AE, DC, MC, V.*

Shopping

Sandra Mezzetti (⊠ Via Oberdan 13, ☎ 0577/920395) is both a showroom and retail store for the best manufacturers of glass in Colle. **Mario Belli** (⊠ Via Armando Diaz 12, ☎ 0577/920784) is a workshop as well as showroom with shoppers invited to watch the artisans etch glass. At **Cristalleria Loreno Grassini** (⊠ Via di Spagna 124, ☎ 0577/922739) engravers will personalize any purchases.

STRADA CHIANTIGIANA FROM FLORENCE

The Strada Chiantigiana (Chianti Road, S222) cuts directly through the center of the Chianti region and is a much more rural drive than the S2 and certainly more rural than the superstrada. Here you are in the heartland, where both sides of the road are embraced by glorious panoramic views of vineyards, olive groves, the turrets of castles, and even an occasional flock of sheep waiting (or sometimes not waiting) to cross the road. It gets crowded during the high season, but no one is in a hurry, and the slow pace gives you time to soak up the beautiful scenery.

Greve in Chianti

❾ *28 km (17½ mi) south of Florence, 12 km (7½ mi) south of Impruneta.*

If there is a capital of Chianti, it is Greve, a friendly market town with no shortage of cafés, enoteche, and crafts shops along its pedestrian street. The sloping, asymmetrical **Piazza Matteotti** is attractively arcaded and has a statue of Giovanni da Verrazano (circa 1480–1527), the explorer who discovered New York harbor, in the center. At the small end of the piazza is the church of **Santa Croce,** with works from the school of Fra Angelico (1387–1455). ⊠ *Piazza Matteotti,* ☎ *no phone.* 🎟 *Free.* ☉ *Daily 9–1 and 3–7.*

Just a mile away, the tiny hilltop hamlet **Montefioralle** is the ancestral home of Amerigo Vespucci (1454–1512), the mapmaker, navigator, and explorer who named America and whose niece Simonetta was the model for Sandro Botticelli's (circa 1445–1510) *Birth of Venus.*

BACCHUS IN TUSCANY

USCANY IS ITALY'S CLASSIC wine country, and if you miss tasting this region's enological treasures, you're missing the point. In addition to the world-famous Chianti, one of Italy's top wine exports, Tuscan winemakers produce a host of other top-quality wines known to wine connoisseurs worldwide. Many of these are recognizable by the "DOCG" (Denominazione di Origine Controllata e Garantita) or "DOC" (Denominazione di Origine Controllata) on their labels, notations which identify the wine within not only as coming from the officially delineated wine regions, but also as adhering to rigorous standards of production and final product. Don't be afraid to sample something that doesn't bear this label, however; Tuscans have been making wine for 25 centuries, and DOC or not, most of the winemakers here seem to know what they're doing.

Vino Nobile di Montepulciano, "Noble Wine of Montepulciano," lays claim to its aristocratic title the old-fashioned way, by virtue of ancient history and royal patronage. The Etruscans were making wine here when ancient Rome was just a twinkle in mama wolf's eye, and centuries later, in 1669, William III of England sent a delegation to Montepulciano charged specifically with procuring for him this splendid wine. It was an appropriate choice, according to poet Francesco Redi, who wrote *"Montepulciano d'ogni vino è il re"* (Of all wine, Montepulciano is the king). Montepulciano is also home to a less noble but no less popular **Rosso di Montepulciano,** a light, fruity DOC red.

By Tuscan timelines, **Brunello di Montalcino** is a newcomer, but no less sophisticated, embodying velvety black berries and structured tannin. A strain of the Sangiovese grape variety used to make it was developed in 1870 by Ferruccio Biondi Santi, a local winemaker in need of a more resistant grape variety to cope with windy weather. It caught on quickly, however, and its first vintage

in 1888 was the first of many to have such success that 100 years later, Italy's then-president Francesco Cossiga presided over its centennial. Brunello has a younger sibling, the DOC **Rosso di Montalcino.**

Not all of Tuscany's great wines are reds; in fact, many give the region's highest honors to a white wine, **Vernaccia di San Gimignano.** This golden wine is made from grapes native to Liguria, and it's thought that its name is a corruption of Vernazza, a wine-making village that is part of the Ligurian coast's Cinque Terre. Pope Martin IV (1281–1285) used to like his with eels; you might try it with rabbit, sausage, or prosciutto and other cured meats.

To the foreigner, **Chianti** evokes Tuscany as readily as gondolas evoke Venice, but if you think Chianti is all straw-covered gallon jugs and deadly headaches, think again. This firm, full-bodied, and powerful wine pressed from mostly Sangiovese grapes is undoubtedly the region's most popular, and it's easy to taste why. Somewhat more difficult to understand is the difference between the many different kinds of Chianti: this DOCG region has seven sub-regions, including Chianti Classico, the oldest wine-growing area of the region, whose wines can be identified by the *gallo nero* (black rooster) on the label. Each of these (Chianti Classico, Colli Fiorentini, Colli Senesi, Colli Aretini, Colline Pisane, Montalbano, and Rufina) has its own particularities, but the most noticeable—and costly—difference to keep in mind is the difference between regular Chianti and the *riserva* (reserve) stock, which earns its title after four years of aging.

Dining and Lodging

$$$ ✕ **Trattoria del Montagliari.** Typical home-style cooking is a big draw for locals, who eat around a wood-burning fireplace in the winter and in the garden in the summer. Ravioli in walnut sauce and fragrant apple pie await. A small shop next door sells their oil, grappa, and the walnut sauce. ⊠ *Via Montagliari 29,* ☎ *055/852184. MC, V. Closed Mon. and Aug. 14–18.*

$$ ✕ **Il Camineto.** This is a small, cozy country restaurant with the usual Tuscan fare. The pasta is all homemade and the ravioli stuffed with porcini mushrooms is a real treat. There's a terrace for summer dining under the shade of lime trees. ⊠ *Via della Montagnola 52,* ☎ *055/8588909. MC, V. Closed Tues.*

$–$$ ✕ **Locanda Il Gallo.** This informal country restaurant has a wood-burning oven for making the specialty thin-crust pizza. The large dining rooms have stone walls and wood-beamed ceilings, and there's a veranda for dining outside in the summer. ⊠ *Via Lando Conti 16, Chiocchio,* ☎ *055/8572266. AE, DC, MC, V. Closed Mon.*

$$ ▦ **Albergo del Chianti.** Located at a corner of the main piazza, this hotel has modernized rooms with contemporary, functional furniture and views over the piazza or looking out over neighborhood terraces and rooftops toward surrounding hills. The swimming pool and terrace are a nice surprise, tucked behind the hotel. ⊠ *Piazza Matteotti 86 50022,* ☎ FAX *055/853763. 16 rooms. Restaurant, bar, pool. CP. DC, MC, V. Closed Nov.–Mar.*

$$ ▦ **Castello Vicchiomaggio.** This castle, now a prestigious wine estate with a tasting facility you can visit, can be traced to 956 and was rebuilt during the Renaissance. Throughout the seven apartments and two farmhouses is wonderful heavy wooden furniture, in keeping with the estate's history. The restaurant serves homemade pastas and specialties such as *stracotto,* meat cooked in the farm's own prize-winning Chianti Classico. The restaurant is closed weekdays April–November. ⊠ *Via Vicchiomaggio 4, 50022,* ☎ *055/854079,* FAX *055/853911. 9 apartments. Restaurant, pool. DC, MC, V.*

$$ ▦ **Il Cenobio/Villa Vignamaggio.** This historic estate has guest rooms and apartments in the villa as well as two small houses and a cottage on the grounds. The villa, surrounded by manicured classical Italian gardens, dates from the 14th century, but was restored in the 16th. It's reputedly the birthplace of Leonardo da Vinci's *Mona Lisa,* and was the setting for Kenneth Branagh's film *Much Ado About Nothing.* ⊠ *Greve in Chianti 50022,* ☎ *055/8544840,* FAX *055/8544468. 10 apartments, 2 rooms. Pool, tennis court. EP. AE, DC, MC, V.*

$ ▦ **Castello di Mugnana.** Medieval castle walls surround this *borgo* (small town), which has now been turned, in its entirety, into a dream escape. Rooms are inside the castle tower (yes, there's an elevator) and in small apartments on the grounds, all with spectacular views of the panorama outside the walls. Furnishings combine the antique and modern; bathrooms are new. Reservations are by the week. ⊠ *Via di Mugnana 106, 50022,* ☎ *055/8244211,* FAX *055/8244382. 7 apartments. Pool. EP. No credit cards.*

$ ▦ **Il Caseno.** The farm of Patrizia Falciani is 1 km (½ mi) from Greve in Chianti, surrounded by trees. The separate apartments are comfortable, well furnished in typical country Tuscan style. Signora Falciani speaks no English, but still manages to communicate with her guests. There's a small but delightful pool, and the owner's brother opens his olive oil and wine cellar for guests. Guests have the use of washing machines and a barbecue. ⊠ *Via di Melazzano 5, 1 km (½ mi) from Greve, 50022,* ☎ *055/8544505,* FAX *055/2301003. 7 apartments. Pool. EP. No credit cards.*

$ 🏠 **La Camporena.** The farmhouse of La Camporena, on the outskirts of Greve, dates from the 1200s. The rooms are rustic, decorated in typical farm furnishings. Here you can discover the joys of farm life, take walks in the countryside, and dine with the hosts. ⊠ *Via Figlinese 27, 3 km (2 mi) south of Greve 50022,* ☎ *055/853184,* 𝔽𝔸𝕏 *055/8544748. 20 rooms. Restaurant, bar. EP. AE, DC, MC, V.*

Shopping
One of the area's most famous butcher shops, **Antica Macelleria Falorni** (⊠ Piazza Matteotti)—you'll see the stuffed wild boar guarding the door—is definitely worth a stop for tastes of traditional salamis, hams, and other Tuscan specialties.

Panzano

🔟 *7 km (4½ mi) south of Greve, 40 km (25 mi) south of Florence.*

Panzano is easily one of the prettiest stops in Chianti, with its medieval walls and towers, magnificent views, and steep, narrow streets. The town centerpiece is the church of **Santa Maria Assunta,** where you can see an *Annunciation* attributed to Ghirlandaio. ⊠ *Panzano Alto,* ☎ *no phone.* ☑ *Free.* ☉ *Mass daily 6 PM.*

An ancient church even by Chianti standards, the hilltop church of **San Leolino** probably dates from the 8th century, but was completely rebuilt in the Romanesque style in the 12th century. The 3-km (2-mi) trip south of the village is well worth it for the church's exterior simplicity and 14th-century cloister. The16th-century terra-cotta tabernacles are attributed to Giovanni della Robbia, and there's a remarkable 13th-century altarpiece by Meliore di Jacopo. ⊠ *San Leolino,* ☎ *no phone.* ☑ *Free.* ☉ *Check with tourist office (☞ Visitor Information, below).*

Dining and Lodging
$$$ ✕ **Montagliari.** This pleasant little restaurant serves typical home-style cooking in a garden in the summer and in a cozy stone dining room with an open fireplace in cold weather. Menu items such as ravioli in walnut sauce and fragrant apple pie make this one of the most popular restaurants in the area. A small shop next door sells their oils, grappa, and that luscious walnut sauce. ⊠ *Via Montagliari 29,* ☎ *055/852184. Reservations essential. No credit cards. Closed Tues.*

$$$ ✕ **Oltre Il Giardino.** An ancient stone house has been converted into a tasteful dining area with a large terrace and spectacular views of the valley. Try to book a table in time to watch the sunset. The menu captures a little more fantasy than the typical Tuscan cuisine. ⊠ *Piazza G. Bucciarelli,* ☎ *055/852828,* 𝔽𝔸𝕏 *055/852465. Reservations essential weekends. MC. Closed Tues. No lunch Wed.*

$$$ ✕ **Vescovino.** This elegant restaurant is in a 13th-century palace with a terrace overlooking the Tuscan countryside. There is a choice of Tuscan dishes, plus homemade cakes, breads, and ice cream. Their fish is flown in fresh. There is a wine-tasting area in the cellar, where you can sample the Chianti before selecting wine for dinner, and a beautiful terrace for outdoor dining. ⊠ *Via Ciampolo da Panzano 9,* ☎ *055/ 852464. AE, DC, MC, V. Closed Tues.*

$$$$ 🏠 **Villa La Barone.** Once the family residence of the Tuscan family of Viviani della Robbia, this 16th-century villa was converted into an exclusive hotel by the Duchess Franca Visconti and has retained its old-world charm. It's nestled among vineyards and olive groves, with a pool, park, and tennis court. One of the joys of staying here is breakfast each morning on the terrace. Breakfast and dinner are included. ⊠ *Pieve di Panzano 50020,* ☎ *055/852621,* 𝔽𝔸𝕏 *055/852277. 30 rooms. Restaurant, pool, tennis court. MAP. AE, MC, V. Closed Nov.–Easter.*

$$ 🏨 **Albergo Sangiovese.** This simple and shipshape hotel right in the town square has terra-cotta tiled floors and an enclosed courtyard for dining during the summer. Country-style rooms are furnished with antiques; half of them look out over the hillside and the other half face the piazza. The restaurant, which features regional cooking, feels more like a hotel dining room than a restaurant, but the locals don't seem to care, as they come here in droves. ⊠ *Piazza G. Bucciarelli 5, 50020,* ☎ *055/852461,* FAX *055/852463. 16 rooms, 3 apartments. Restaurant, pool. CP. MC, V. Closed Wed. and Jan.–Feb.*

Shopping

BUTCHER

One of the highlights here is seeing the **Macelleria Cecchini** (⊠ Via XX Luglio 11, ☎ 055/852020), which could be the world's most dramatic butcher shop. Here, amidst the sound of classical music and lively conversation, the owner Dario Cecchini holds court on a pedestal, glancing into the small tasting room he built next door. He has researched recipes from the 15th century and offers pâtés and tureens you just won't find anywhere else, plus a library of cookbooks in several languages for customer use.

PRINTMAKING

Antique lead alphabets are still in use at **Rebis Press** (⊠ Piazza G. Bucciardelli 39, ☎ 0577/733653), a unique printmaking studio and gallery in a 15th-century vaulted cantina. Here you can watch the artisans create intricate etchings and visit exhibitions of local artists.

Castellina in Chianti

⓫ *59 km (35 mi) south of Florence, 20 km (12 mi) south of Greve.*

Castellina in Chianti, or simply Castellina, is on a ridge above the Val di Pesa, Val d'Arbia, and Val d'Elsa, and the panorama is bucolic no matter which direction you look. The strong 15th-century medieval walls and fortified town gate give a hint of the history of this village, which was an outpost during the continuing wars between Florence and Siena. If the view from the covered walkway that circles the city seems familiar to you, it could be because the panorama you are looking upon typifies the source for the pigment that Crayola called burnt sienna.

Dining and Lodging

$$$ ✕ **Albergaccio.** This small restaurant in town, limited to 35 diners at a time, features a mixture of traditional and creative cuisine with an excellent wine list. There is a garden for dining alfresco when weather permits. ⊠ *Via Fiorentina 63,* ☎ *055/741042. Reservations essential. No credit cards. Closed Sun.*

$$$ ✕ **Osteria all Piazza.** You dine in the middle of a vineyard 15 km (8 mi) from Castellina, with one of Chianti's most spectacular views. It's open for lunch and worth the drive into the countryside to relax in the garden, enjoy the sophisticated menu and, certainly, the delicious desserts. ⊠ *Locanda La Piazza,* ☎ *0577/733580. Reservations essential Sun. MC, V. Closed Mon.*

$$$ ✕ **Ristorante Le Tre Porte.** The specialty of the house is the thick Florentine steak. When they are in season, try the grilled fresh mushrooms that are harvested from the woods in the area. ⊠ *Via Trento e Trieste 4,* ☎ *0577/741163. Reservations essential in summer. AE, DC, MC, V. Closed Tues.*

$$$–$$$$ 🏨 **Villa Casalecchi.** This beautiful patrician villa is surrounded by glorious grounds and offers guests a choice of 16 rooms in the villa or three apartments in a nearby farmhouse. The villa is filled with antique furniture and has an intimate, wood-paneled restaurant. The farmhouse

apartments have a more rustic, country feeling. The pool ov_____
yards and a tennis court. ⊠ *Località Casalecchi in Chia____*
0577/740240, FAX *0577/74111. 16 rooms, 3 apartments. Restaurant,
pool, tennis court. CP. AE, DC, MC, V*

$$ 🏨 **Hotel Belvedere di San Leonino.** Wonderful gardens for strolling thread
through this restored country complex dating from the 14th century.
The guest rooms are in two country houses that look out upon vine-
yards to the north and upon Siena to the south. Homey rooms have
antique furniture and exposed beams. There is a restaurant with a fixed
menu, and in the summer, the guests can eat dinner in the garden by
the pool. ⊠ *Località San Leonino, Castellina in Chianti 53011,* ☎ *0577/
740887,* FAX *0577/740998. 28 rooms. Restaurant, pool. MAP, FAP. AE,
MC, V. Closed Nov. 10–Mar. 15.*

$$ 🏨 **Hotel Salivolpi.** This converted farmhouse is family run and offers a
very pleasant country atmosphere. The owners took special care not to
alter the feeling of the house when they converted it to accommodate
19 guest rooms. Each room is furnished with antiques and there is a
large pool reserved for the guests. ⊠ *Via Fiorentina 89, 53011,* ☎ *0577/
740484,* FAX *0577/740998. 19 rooms. Pool. CP. AE, DC, MC, V.*

$$ 🏨 **Palazzo Squarcialupi Albergo.** Rooms in this 14th-century farmhouse
are filled with antique furniture, air-conditioning, and satellite TV. There's
a wine cellar on the premises, and wine tastings are part of the daily
activities. You can relax in the three common rooms in the house, or
take a dip in the garden pool. ⊠ *Via Ferruccio 26, 53011,* ☎ *0577/
741186,* FAX *0577/740386. 15 rooms, 2 suites. Restaurant, bar, pool.
CP. AE, DC, MC, V.*

$ 🏨 **Il Querceto.** Each of the large, two-floor apartments has a fireplace.
There are games for children and a common living room. The kitchens
are all new, and some of the apartments have separate dining rooms;
all have private outside areas and antique furniture. You can taste and
buy the wine, olive oil, honey, jellies, and eggs that are produced here.
⊠ *Castellina in Chianti 53011.* ☎ *0577/733590.* FAX *0577/733636. 9
apartments. Pool, mountain bikes, library. MAP. AE, DC, MC, V.*

Radda in Chianti

⑫ *55 km (34 mi) south of Florence, 22 km (13 mi) east of Castellina in
Chianti.*

Radda in Chianti sits on a hill stretching between the Val di Pesa and
Val d'Arbia. It's another one of those tiny Chianti villages that invite
you to stroll through its steep streets and follow the signs that point
you toward the *camminamento,* a covered medieval road that circles
part of the city inside the walls. In Piazza Ferrucci, you'll find the **Palazzo
del Podesta,** or Palazzo Comunale, the city hall that has served the peo-
ple of Radda for more than four centuries and has 51 coats of arms
imbedded in the facade. ⊠ *Piazza Ferrucci.*

OFF THE
BEATEN PATH

VOLPAIA – Atop a hill 10 km (6 mi) north of Radda is this fairy-tale ham-
let, a military outpost from the 10th–16th centuries and once shelter for
religious pilgrims. Every July, for the Festa di San Lorenzo, people come
to Volpaia to watch for falling stars and a traditional fireworks display
put on by the family that owns the surrounding Castello di Volpaia (⊠
Piazza della Cisterna 1, 53017, ☎ 0577/738066), a wine estate and
agriturismo lodging.

Dining and Lodging

$ ✕ **La Bottega.** In the central piazza of Volpaia, this looks like a sand-
wich shop but there are a few tables inside (more outside when weather
permits) and some real surprises being prepared in the typical Tuscan

kitchen, including homemade pastas and salamis. ⊠ *Piazza della Torre 2,* ☎ *0577/738001. No credit cards.*

$ ✕▥ **Il Girarrosto Semplici.** This is like going to visit relatives for vacation. On the main street of Radda, this small, simply furnished hotel has a typical family restaurant that is one of the most popular in Chianti. This is true especially on Sunday, when there is a traditional feast at both lunch and dinner, with handmade pasta, an assortment of cheeses, and roasted game. ⊠ *Via Roma 41, 53017,* ☎ *0577/738010. 9 rooms. Restaurant. EP. No credit cards. Closed Wed.*

$ ✕▥ **Villa Miranda.** Five generations of the Miranda family have operated this hotel and restaurant in a fascinating post house dating from 1842, 2 km (1 mi), southeast of Radda in Chianti. The furniture is from the 1800s and some of the bathrooms have spa tubs. All the pasta is homemade, there is a charcoal fire for meats, and Signora Miranda is especially proud of her robust soups. Dining is in the garden in the summer. They serve the wine they produce as well as many others. Wines, meats, and jellies are all for sale. ⊠ *Località La Villa, Radda in Chianti 53017,* ☎ *0577/738021,* ℻ *0577/738668. 30 rooms. Restaurant, bar, pool, tennis court. CP. V.*

$$–$$$$ ▥ **Vescine.** Set on what was once an Etruscan settlement is this refined, secluded complex of low-slung medieval stone buildings connected by cobbled paths and punctuated by cypress trees. Unfussy white rooms have terra-cotta tile floors, attractive woodwork, and comfortable furnishings typical to Tuscany. ⊠ *Radda in Chianti 53017,* ☎ *0577/741144,* ℻ *0577/740263. 20 rooms, 5 suites. Restaurant, bar, breakfast room, wine shop, pool, tennis court, library. CP. AE, D, MC, V. Closed Dec. (except over Christmas)–Feb.*

$$$ ▥ **Podere Terreno.** One wing of this 16th-century farmhouse, about 5 km (3 mi) north of Radda in Chianti on the road to Volpaia, has been converted into seven double rooms, each with a bath and furnished with traditional furniture. Guests from all over the world come here to enjoy the quiet country life that attracts jet-setters and city folks. Austrian photographer Helmut Newton came here to shoot the calendar for Pirelli tires. All guests have breakfast and gourmet dinners with the friendly owners who enjoy cooking for their guests, serving the wine they make themselves, and surrounding themselves with friendly conversation at the dinner table. ⊠ *Via Della Volpaia, Radda in Chianti 53017,* ☎ ℻ *0577/738312. 7 rooms. Restaurant. MAP. AE, DC, MC, V.*

$$$ ✕▥ **Relais Fattoria Vignale.** Unadorned farmhouse on the main road on the outside, and comfortable English country house on the inside—with terra-cotta floors, sitting rooms, and exposed stone and woodwork—best sums up Fattoria Vignale. Rooms contain simple wood-and-iron-framed beds and country furniture, rugs and prints, a bedside candle to promote relaxation, and modern white-tile bathrooms. The grounds, lined with vineyards and plum and olive trees, are equally as inviting, with various lawns, terraces, and a pool. The cavernous and rustic Ristorante Vignale, under separate management, serves excellent wines and cold and warm Tuscan plates; it's perfect for a sampling of savory meats, pâtés, and cheeses at any time of day. ⊠ *Radda in Chianti 53017,* ☎ *0577/738300,* ℻ *0577/738592. 34 rooms. Restaurant, breakfast room, wine shop, pool, library. AE, MC, V. Closed early Dec.–Dec. 25 and early Jan.–late Mar.*

Shopping

If you're lucky enough to be here on the right day, the butcher at **Porciatti Alimentari** (⊠ Piazza IV Novembre 1) offers samples and will even walk you across the street to show you his spotless *laboratorio*, where his handmade salami and sausage are aging.

Gaiole in Chianti

⑬ *9 km (5½ mi) southeast of Radda in Chianti, 69 km (43 mi) south of Florence, 28 km (17 mi) northeast of Siena.*

Gaiole, undistinguished except for the stream that runs through its center, has been a market town since the year 1200 and now is a central location for touring the castle region of southern Chianti. (Castle, in this context, means fortified city.) These were the outposts and by definition are always perched on hilltops—which for you means the vistas are always dazzling. One loop suggested for castle-ing is from Gaiole to San Polo in Rose, to Montelucco, Ama, and Brolio.

★ A few miles outside Gaiole in Chianti, a turnoff on S408 leads to **Badia a Coltibuono,** owned by Lorenza de' Medici and her family for a century and a half. Founded by Vallombrosan monks in the 11th century, the Abbey of the Good Harvest has been producing wine from the very beginning; today the family continues the tradition, making Chianti Classico and other vintages, along with high-quality cold-pressed olive oil and various flavored vinegars and floral honeys. A small Romanesque church with campanile are surrounded by 2,000 acres of oak, fir, and chestnut woods threaded with walking paths—open to all—and dotted with two small lakes. Though the abbey itself, built between the 11th and 18th centuries, is the family's home, parts are open for tours spring through fall (in English, German, or Italian). Visits include the jasmine-draped main courtyard, the inner cloister with its antique well, the musty old aging cellars, and the Renaissance-style garden redolent of lavender, lemons, and roses. Groups of 10 or more may arrange tours and wine tastings by appointment. The shop, L'Osteria, sells Coltibuono's wine and other products, including beeswax hand lotion cakes in little ceramic dishes that make great gifts. A restaurant and cooking school are on site (☞ *below*). ⊠ *4 km (2½ mi) north of Gaiole in Chianti. Abbey:* ☎ *0577/749498,* FAX *0577/749235.* 🎫 *5,000 lire per person.* ☉ *Tours: May–July and Sept.–Oct. (except public holidays), Mon.–Sat. 2:30, 3, 3:30, 4. Shop:* ☎ FAX *0577/749479.* ☉ *Apr.–Nov. 5, daily 9:30–1 and 2–7; Nov. 6–mid-Jan and Mar., Mon. 2–6:30, Tues.–Sat. 9:30–1 and 2–6:30.*

Lorenza de' Medici—matriarch of the Stucchi Prinetti clan, who own the Badia, as well as descendant of those other Medici—is a well-known cook who has written more than 30 books. In spring and fall she opens the abbey up for five-day cooking courses (called **The Villa Table**) that include lodgings in nicely converted monks' cells, guided excursions, and dinners at her friends' villas and townhouses—a unique opportunity to observe sophisticated Tuscan culture. But it'll cost you. The course held during Siena's Palio includes prime seats in the stands, and costs even more. Prices include five nights' accommodations with private bath, all meals, and excursions. ⊠ *The Villa Table, Badia a Coltibuono, 53013 Gaiole in Chianti,* ☎ *0577749498,* FAX *0577749235. U.S. contact: Judy Ebrey* ⊠ *Box 25228, Dallas, TX 75225,* ☎ *214/373–1161,* FAX *214/ 373–1162.* 🎫 *Double $3,500 per person, single $4,100.*

OFF THE
BEATEN PATH

CASTELLO DI BROLIO – About 2 km (1 mi) southeast of Gaiole is the Castello di Brolio, one of the area's most impressive castles, replete with a winery. This is the castle to visit if you only have time for one. At the end of the 12th century, when Florence conquered southern Chianti from Siena and Brolio became Florence's most southern outpost, there was a saying, "When Brolio growls, all Siena trembles." Now, there's a sign at the Brolio gate that translates as "ring bell and be patient." You pull a rope and the bell above the ramparts bongs, and in a short time, the caretaker arrives to let you in. Although the manor house is not open, the grounds are amply entertaining, with the chance for a walk through a wooded area, past the formal Italian Renaissance garden, and along part of the rampart. Brolio was built about AD 1000 and owned by the monks of the Badia Fiorentina; the "new" owners, the Ricasoli family, have owned it since 1141. Bettino Ricasoli, The Iron Baron, was one of the founders of modern Italy, and also is said to have invented the present-day formula for Chianti vino. Brolio is one of Chianti's best-known labels, and the cellars may be visited by appointment. If it all looks a bit familiar to you, it's because this is the area where Bernardo Bertolucci's *Stealing Beauty* (1996) was filmed. You can rent one of the two apartments by the week. ⊠ *Località Brolio, 52013 Gaiole in Chianti,* ☎ *0577/7301.* 🎫 *5,000 lire.* ☺ *June–Sept., daily 9–12 and 2–6:30; Oct.–May, Sat.–Thurs. 9–12 and 2–6:30.*

Dining and Lodging

$$ ✕ **Badia a Coltibuono.** Just outside the abbey walls is Badia a Coltibuono's (☞ *above*) pleasant restaurant, with seating outside or in soft yellow rooms divided by ancient brick arches. Tuscan cuisine—featuring fresh pastas, local produce, goat's and sheep's milk cheeses, and the extraordinary Chianina beef—is served at lunch and dinner, along with the Coltibuono's and other good Tuscan wines. Between 2:30 and 7:30, a bistro menu featuring sandwiches, salads, appetizers, and desserts is available. ⊠ *Badia a Coltibuono, 4 km (2½ mi) north of Gaiole in Chianti,* ☎ *0577749031. MC, V.*

$$ ✕ **La Grotta della Rana.** A perfect stop for lunch while you're exploring Chianti's wineries, this trattoria features *cucina casalinga* (plain cooking) on a lovely outdoor patio (there's also indoor seating). Outstanding primi include ravioli in sage and butter and light as a feather mini-gnocchi in a rich mascarpone and spinach sauce. For secondi locals go straight for the *filetto al pepe verde* (Chianina beef in a creamy green peppercorn sauce). Homemade deserts such as torta della nonna and tiramisú round out the meal. ⊠ *San Sano, off S408, Gaiole in Chianti,* ☎ *0577/746020. AE, MC, V.*

$$$$ ✕🏨 **Castello di Spaltenna.** This fortified convent that dates from the 1300s has been transformed into a romantic country hotel and first-class restaurant. The hotel's minisuites have fireplaces and massage tubs. Dinners by candlelight feature Tuscan recipes, served in a flower-filled, cloistered garden in the summertime. The pool is tucked into a beautiful terrace. ⊠ *Pieve di Spaltenna, Gaiole in Chianti 53013,* ☎ *0577/749483,* 🄵🄰🄷 *0577/749269. 26 rooms. Restaurant, pool. CP. AE, DC, MC, V.*

$$ 🏨 **Borgo Argenina Bed & Breakfast.** Charming hostelry occupying a 1,000 year old villa which has been completely renovated by host and former interior designer Elena Nappa. Rooms have been lovingly decorated with antique quilts and furniture, but there is a slight nod to modern times with in-room telephones and minibars (gratis). A sunny breakfast room overlooks a neighboring vineyard and is the setting for a groaning board of local Tuscan delicacies and homemade cakes. Three resident dogs greet you at the steep drive upon your arrival, and are often companions during your stay. Elena is an authority on the surrounding Chianti area and happily draws maps and suggests wine tasting and touring routes for guests. ⊠ *MM 15 on S408, follow signs for San Marcellino Monti, Gaiole in Chianti, 53013,* ☎ *055/8077041,* ☎ 🄵🄰🄷 *0577/747117. 5 rooms, 2 apartments. CP. No credit cards.*

$$ 🏨 **Hotel Residence San Sano.** Housed in a renovated 13th-century fortress, this small hotel has retained the charm of the original structure, with an open hearth fireplace and hand-hewn stone porticoes, while adding a slew of modern amenities, including a beautiful outdoor

pool. Rooms are bright and spacious. ✉ *San Sano, L|
53010,* ☎ *0577/746130,* ℻ *0577/746156. 14 roc*
minibars, swimming pool. CP, MAP. AE, MC, V.

$–$$ 🏨 **Castello di Tornano.** If you'd like a bit of whimsy on your n
this may be the place for you. The agriturismo apartments are in a medieval tower, the unusual pool is sunk into the land, and the wine cellar once housed a prison. It all adds up to an unusual holiday experience
surrounded by woods and vineyards, with tennis courts and even a traditional Italian boccie ball court. ✉ *Gaioli in Chianti 53013,* ☎ *0577/
746067,* ℻ *0577/746067. 9 apartments. Pool, tennis court. CP. AE,
DC, MC, V.*

SOUTHEASTERN REACHES

Reaching southeast out of Chianti proper are the fortified hilltop villages of Montalcino and Montepulciano, where you can continue your
wine exploration with tasting the heady Brunello di Montalcino and
Vino Nobile di Montepulciano. Heading south of Siena and Chianti,
you'll notice a change in the landscape: Chianti's verdant, cypress-punc-
tuated hills give way to le Crete (also ☞ Chapter 6), the area around
Asciano marked by rich red earth and rolling vineyards.

Castelnuovo Berardenga

⑭ *23 km (14 mi) east of Siena, 90 km (56 mi) southeast of Florence.*

This is the southernmost village in the Chianti territory, and you know
southern hospitality abounds when you drive into the city and peek at
the gardens of **Villa Chigi,** a 19th-century villa built on the site of a 14th-
century castle (actually the "new castle" from which Castelnuovo got
its name). It is now home to a music academy, but it opens its manicured gardens for visitors on Sunday and holidays. ✉ *Castelnuovo Berardenga,* ☎ *no phone.* 🎫 *Free.* ◷ *Gardens: Apr.–Sept., Sun. and
holidays 10–8; Oct–Mar., Sun. and holidays 10–5.*

Inside the compact center of Castelnuovo Berardenga, the hilly, curv-
ing streets and plethora of piazzas invite wandering. The church of **San
Giusto e San Clemente** contains an important *Madonna and Child* by
Giovanni di Paolo (1403–82); this is all that remains of a dismantled
polyptych whose other parts are now in museums all over the world.
✉ *Piazza Matteotti 4,* ☎ *0577/355133.* 🎫 *Free.* ◷ *Daily 7:30–7.*

OFF THE
BEATEN PATH
SAN GUSMÈ – Perched quite jauntily on a hilltop 5 km (3 mi) north of
Castelnuovo Berardenga is the oldest and most interesting of the medieval villages that surround Castelnuovo Berardenga. This is because it
still retains its original layout, with arched passageways, gates topped
with coats of arms, narrow squares, and steep streets. You can walk
through the entire village in 20 minutes, but in those 20 minutes you will
feel as if you have stepped back in time 500 years.

Montalcino

⑮ *41 km (25 mi) south of Siena.*

Another medieval hill town with a special claim to fame, Montalcino
is home to Brunello di Montalcino, one of Italy's most esteemed reds.
You can sample it in wine cellars in town or visit a nearby winery for
a free guided tour and tasting; you must call ahead for reservations.
One such winery is Fattoria dei Barbi e del Casato (☞ *below*). Driving up to the town, you pass through the Brunello vineyards and ar-

rive at the 14th-century Sienese **La Fortezza,** which has an enoteca for tasting wines. From the fortress, you can wander down into the town where you'll have no problem finding a place to taste or buy the excellent-but-expensive red stuff. ⊠ , ☎ *0577/849211.* ☜ *3,500 lire.* ☉ *Apr.–Sept., Tues.–Sun. 9–1 and 2:30–8; Oct.–Mar., Tues.–Sun. 9–1 and 2–6.*

Dining and Lodging

$$$ ✕ **Poggio Antico.** One of Italy's renowned gourmet chefs, Roberto Minnetti, abandoned his highly successful restaurant in Rome a few years ago and moved to the country just outside Montalcino. Now he and his wife, Patrizia—who is also Poggio Antico's hostess—serve fine Tuscan cuisine, masterfully interpreted by Roberto, in a relaxed but regal dining room replete with arches and beamed ceilings. The seasonal menu might suggest ravioli *di castagne al burro e salvia* (with chestnut stuffing) or venison in a sweet-and-sour sauce. ⊠ *Località I Poggi, 4 km (2½ mi) outside Montalcino on road to Grossetto,* ☎ *0577/ 849200. V. Closed Mon. and 20 days in Jan. No dinner Sun.*

$$ ✕▥ **Fattoria dei Barbi e del Casato.** A meal at the taverna, set among
★ vineyards and mellow brick buildings on a family-owned winery estate, may well be a highlight of your journey through this part of Tuscany. The estate-produced Brunello is excellent. The rustic dining room features a beamed ceiling, huge stone fireplace, and arched windows. The estate farm produces many of the ingredients used in such traditional specialties as *stracotto nel brunello* (braised veal cooked with beans, in Brunello wine); big ravioli pillows filled with ricotta, swathed in butter, and dusted with Parmesan and herbs; and a dessert called *ricotta montata* (farm-fresh ricotta whipped with vin santo, sugar, and vanilla). Two comfortable, traditionally furnished agriturismo apartments right next to the taverna and above the cantina—where you can take a tour and buy the fattoria's different labels—each sleep three. Reservations for a meal or a stay are essential. ⊠ *Località Podernuovi, Podernovaccio 53024.* ☎ *0577/849357 taverna, 0577/849421 fattoria;* ℻ *0577/849356. 2 apartments. AE, DC, MC, V.* ☉ *Tours by appointment. Taverna closed Wed., last 2 wks Jan., and 1st 2 wks July.*

$$ ▥ **La Crociona.** This is a quiet and serene family-owned farm in the middle of a small vineyard with glorious views and all the comforts of home, including antique iron beds and 17th-century wardrobes in the rooms. There's a big terrace and you are invited to hang out around the pool and use the family barbecue as well as sample the owner's own wine supply. ⊠ *Località Croce di Mezzo, Montalcino 53024,* ☎ ℻ *0577/848007. 6 apartments. Pool, mountain bikes. AE, DC, MC, V.*

Montepulciano

★ ⑯ *12 km (7 mi) east of Pienza, 13 km (8 mi) west of the A1, 65 km (40 mi) south of Florence.*

Perched high on a hilltop, Montepulciano is made up of a pyramid of redbrick buildings set within a circle of cypress trees. At an altitude of almost 2,000 ft, it is cool in summer and chilled in winter by biting winds that sweep its spiraling streets. The town has an unusually harmonious look, the result of the work of three architects, Antonio Sangallo (il Vecchio 1455–1535), Giacomo da Vignola (1507–73), and Michelozzo (1396–1472), who endowed it with fine palaces and churches in an attempt to impose Renaissance architectural ideals on an ancient Tuscan hill town. The pièce de résistance is the beautiful **Piazza Grande,** where you will find the **Duomo,** which doesn't measure up to the external beauty of the neighboring palaces because it has no facade. On the inside, however, its Renaissance roots shine through. You can see fragments of the tomb of Bartolomeo Aragazzi, secretary to Pope Martin V (1368–1431), created by Michelozzo between 1427–36, parts of which have been dispersed to museums in other parts of the world. ⊠ *Piazza Grande,* ☎ *0578/757761.* ⊠ *Free.* ⊙ *Daily 9–12:30.*

Michelozzo's work can also be seen in the piazza named for him, **Piazza Michelozzo,** and in the tower he designed for the 13th-century Gothic **Palazzo Comunale.** You can climb up the tower to enjoy the views. ⊠ *Piazza Grande,* ☎ *no phone.* ⊠ *Free.* ⊙ *Daily 8–1.*

In the piazza is the church of **Sant'Agostino,** which he designed in 1427. He also carved the terra-cotta relief of the *Madonna and Child* above the door. ⊠ *Piazza Michelozzo,* ☎ *0578/757761.* ⊠ *Free.* ⊙ *Daily 9–12:30 and 3:30–7:30.*

On the hillside below the town walls is the **Tempio di San Biagio,** designed by Sangallo and a paragon of Renaissance architectural perfection considered his masterpiece. Inside this church, you'll find an image of a Madonna that, according to legend, was all that remained in an abandoned church when, on April 23, 1518, two young girls saw the eyes of the Madonna moving. That same afternoon, a farmer saw the same thing, as did his cow, who kneeled down in front of the image. In 1963 she was proclaimed the Madonna del Buon Viaggio (Madonna of the Good Journey), the protector of tourists in Italy. ⊠ *Via di San Biagio,* ☎ *0578/7577761.* ⊠ *Free.* ⊙ *Daily 9–12:30 and 3:30–7:30.*

Lodging

$$ 🏨 **Il Marzocco.** A 16th-century building within the town walls, this hotel is furnished circa 19th century, complete with dignified, old-fashioned parlors and a billiard room. Furnished in heavy turn-of-the-century style or in spindly white wood, some bedrooms have large terraces overlooking the countryside. Many rooms are large enough to accommodate extra beds. No breakfast is served. ⊠ *Piazza Savonarola 18, 53045,* ☎ *0578/757262,* 𝔽𝔸𝕏 *0578/757530. 16 rooms, 1 without bath. Restaurant. AE, DC, MC, V. Closed Jan. 20–Feb. 10.*

$$ 🏨 **La Bandita.** This attractive old farmhouse possesses great charm, with terra-cotta floors throughout, lace curtains and antiques in the bedrooms, and a fireplace and 19th-century Tuscan provincial furniture in a large, brick-vaulted living room. Some rooms can accommodate an extra bed. A garden and meals are available to guests. The restaurant is closed Tuesday. ⊠ *Via Bandita 72, Bettolle, 1 km (½ mi) from Valdichiana exit of A1 autostrada, 53048,* ☎ *0577/624649,* 𝔽𝔸𝕏 *0577/ 624649. 7 rooms. Restaurant. AE, DC, MC, V.*

Nightlife and the Arts

The **Cantiere Internazionale d'Arte,** held in July and August, is a multifaceted festival of figurative art, music, and theater, ending with a major theatrical production in Piazza Grande. Contact the Montepulciano tourist office (☞ Visitor Information, *below*) for info.

CHIANTI A TO Z

Arriving and Departing

By Bus

The best way to reach the region and to explore is by car. Several buses a day run from between Rome and Siena (2½ hrs), and there is frequent service between Florence and Siena (1 hr), with connections to Greve, Radda, Gaiole in Chianti, and Montepulciano. Contact **SITA** (☎ 0577/ 204211 or 0577/204270 in Siena, 055/483651 in Florence).

By Car

The area is easily reached by car on the **A1** autostrada (Autostrada del Sole), which runs between Rome and Florence (exit on S326 for Siena). The Strada Chiantigiana (**S222**) is the slower, scenic route, winding its way from Florence to Siena through Chianti's vineyards. The Via Cassia (S2) also connects Rome and Siena.

By Plane

The largest airports nearest to the region are Pisa's **Aeroporto Galileo Galilei** (☎ 050/500707), Florence's **Peretola** (☎ 055/333498), and Rome's **Fiumicino** (☎ 06/65953640).

By Train

The best way to get around the region is by car, as train connections in Chianti are limited. Trains run from Siena to Montepulciano, Radda, and Gaiole. For **state railway (FS) information,** call (☎ 147/888088) toll-free.

Getting Around

By Bus

A car is really the most efficient way to get around Chianti. SITA buses connect Greve, Radda, Gaiole in Chianti, and Montepulciano.

By Car

Local roads threading through the region, plus sensational vistas, make driving a joy in the region. The towns and landmarks are well signed, but you should arm yourself with a good map and nerves of steel to contend with speedy local drivers.

By Train

Train service from Siena is limited to Montepulciano, Radda, and Gaiole. You are best to rent a car or rely on buses if you must take public transportation.

Contacts and Resources

Agritourist Agencies

☞ Chapter 2.

Car Rentals

☞ Chapter 2.

Emergencies

Police, fire (☎ 113). **Ambulance,** medical emergency (☎ 118).

Guided Tours

I Bike Italy (✉ Borgo degli Albizi 11, ☎ FAX 055/2342371) offers one-day tours of the Florence countryside.

Late-Night Pharmacies

All pharmacies post the addresses of the nearest late-night pharmacies outside their doors.

Travel Agencies

Greve in Chianti: Vinea Viaggi (✉ Via Roma, 50022, ☎ 055/854352). **The Hillsland** (✉ Via Garibaldi 7, 50022, ☎ 055/8546058). **San Casciano in Val di Pesa: Machiavelli Viaggi** (✉ Via Machiavelli 49, 50026, ☎ 055/822324). **Tavarnelle Val di Pesa: Xtramondo Viaggi** (✉ Via Roma 238, 50028, ☎ 055/805023).

Villa Rentals

Chianti e Terre in Toscana (✉ Box 8, 50020 Montefiridolfi, ☎ 0577/8244211, FAX 0577/8244382) rents villas and country houses, most in vineyard estates.

Visitor Information

Castellina in Chianti (✉ Piazza del Comune 1, ☎ 055/740201). **Castelnuovo Berardenga** (✉ Via Roma 8, ☎ 0577/355500). **Greve in Chianti** (✉ Via Luca Cini 1, Palazzo della Torre, ☎ 055/8545243). **Impruneta** (✉ Via Mazzini 1, ☎ 055/2313729). **Montalcino** (✉ Costa del Municipio 8, ☎ 0577/849331). **Montepulciano** (✉ Via Ricci 9, ☎ 0578/758687). **Radda in Chianti** (✉ Piazza Ferrucci 1, ☎ 0577/738494; ☉ Mar.–Oct. only).

6   Siena and the Hill Towns

Once Florence's most fearsome rival, Siena remains the perfect medieval city to the south, rich with Gothic palaces and magnificent art. Proud of its past, Siena celebrates the Palio, with energy and emotion unchanged over the centuries. Siena is the perfect introduction to the celebrated hill towns, with the towers of San Gimignano and the Etruscan shadows of Volterra close at hand.

Revised by Jon Eldan and Carla Lionello

ITALY'S MOST ENCHANTING MEDIEVAL CITY, Siena is the one trip you should make in Tuscany if you make no other. Once there, you will undoubtedly be drawn to Italy's most famous hill town, San Gimignano, known as the "medieval Manhattan" because of the enormous towers, built by rival families, which still stand today. Like Siena, it benefitted from the commerce and trade along the pilgrimage routes, as the wonderful art in its churches and museums attests to. Equally intriguing is a visit to Volterra, an Etruscan town famous for its alabaster. Southern Tuscany is perhaps less familiar than the Chianti region to the north, but prestigious wines are made south of Siena, too, and the scenery is as classically Tuscan as anywhere. On your way down, don't miss a stop at the Abbazzia di Monte Oliveto Maggiore, sublimely decorated with Renaissance frescoes.

Pleasures and Pastimes

Dining

If you have already been eating in Tuscany, chances are you'll recognize much of what's on the menu in these towns. Some local specialties include *pici* (fat spaghetti almost as thick as a pencil); *zuppa alla volterrana* (a local version of *ribollita*, a soup with bread and vegetables); the white wine of San Gimignano (called San Gimignano and sold in every *enoteche*, or wine bar); and sweets in Siena such as *panforte* (traditional Sienese Christmas fruitcake with honey, hazelnuts, almonds, and spices). But despite their Tuscan heritage, Siena, San Gimignano, and Volterra are not known as especially good food towns. A recent article in a national newspaper declaring Siena as Italy's "most livable" city cited the lack of decent restaurants as its only drawback. Perhaps this is largely due to the proliferation of mediocre restaurants that cater to the incessant flow of day-trippers. Fortunately, the food scene in these towns is lately much improved. A quiet resurgence spurred on by the increasing interest in quality, local products and good wine (these days not just Chianti) means that it is no longer quite so hard to get a decent meal in town.

CATEGORY	COST*
$$$$	over 110,000 lire
$$$	60,000 lire–110,000 lire
$$	35,000 lire–60,000 lire
$	under 35,000 lire

Prices are per person, for a three-course meal, house wine and tax included.

Lodging

Siena, San Gimignano, and Volterra are among the most visited towns in Tuscany, so there is no lack of choice for hotels across the price range. The best accommodations, however, are often a few kilometers outside town. Every year there seem to be more old villas and monasteries converted into charming, first-rate hotels, as well as simpler *agriturismo* (agritourist) farmhouses, usually available on a weekly basis. The location makes a car necessary, but the splendor of the surroundings usually outweighs any problems getting in and out of town.

CATEGORY	COST*
$$$$	over 350,000 lire
$$$	250,000 lire–350,000 lire
$$	150,000 lire–250,000 lire
$	under 150,000 lire

Prices are for a double room for two, tax and service included.

Exploring Siena and the Hill Towns

As the smaller towns are a bit too far away from one another to make for easy coming and going, Siena makes the most sensible base from which to explore central Tuscany.

Numbers in the text correspond to numbers in the margin and on the Siena and the Hill Towns; Siena; and Volterra maps.

Great Itineraries

IF YOU HAVE 3 OR 4 DAYS

Spend a couple of days getting to know ⊞ **Siena** ①–⑨, exploring its medieval streets and neighborhoods as well as major sites like the Campo, Palazzo Pubblico, Duomo, and surrounding museums. Then make a day or overnight trip to see ⊞ **San Gimignano** ⑫ and its medieval towers or ⊞ **Volterra** ⑬–⑲ and its marvelous Museo Etrusco Guarnacci. Returning to Siena, take an excursion south through the countryside to the ⊞ **Abbazia di Monte Oliveto Maggiore** ㉑, with its remarkable frescoes and stunning scenery.

IF YOU HAVE 5 OR 6 DAYS

The itinerary above can be easily expanded to include an extra day in ⊞ **Siena** ①–⑨ and visits to ⊞ **San Gimignano** ⑫, ⊞ **Volterra** ⑬–⑲, and **Colle di Val d'Elsa** ⑪, and the drive south from Siena can be extended to take in the town of **Asciano** ⑳ and/or the thermal baths at Rapolano Terme on the way down to the ⊞ **Abbazia di Monte Oliveto Maggiore** ㉑.

When to Tour Siena and the Hill Towns

The region enjoys particularly sparkling weather in spring and fall. In summer, the same sun that makes the grapes grow can turn the packed streets unpleasantly hot—it is always easier to work with the local schedule than against it: If you get an early start, you can enjoy the sites in the cooler morning hours, and return to have an afternoon siesta while the sun is the highest. Make a point of catching the *passeggiata* (evening stroll), when the locals descend to the main street. Siena fills to the brim in the weeks surrounding the running of the Palio (☞ Close-Up: Il Palio, *below*) on July 2nd and August 16th, when prices, crowds, and commotion are at their highest. In the winter months you will probably have towns mostly to yourself, although the choices for hotels and restaurants can be a bit more limited than when the season is in full swing. Travel in winter is discouraged: from November to February, Siena is notably colder but less crowded; in Volterra and San Gimignano, it's hard to find a hotel open come January and February.

SIENA

The she-wolf and suckling twins on the city's emblem show Siena's claim to share common ancestry with Rome; the town's legendary founder, Senius, was a son of Remus, the twin brother of Rome's founder Romulus. Archaeological evidence suggests that there were prehistoric as well as Etruscan settlements here first, which undoubtedly made way for *Saena Julia,* the Roman town established by Augustus in the early 1st century.

Siena rose to prominence as an essential stop on that most important of medieval roads, the Via Francigena (or Via Romea), prospering from the yearly flow of thousands of Christian pilgrims coming south to Rome from Northern Europe. Siena developed a banking system (the first bank, Monte dei Paschi, is still very much in business) and dominated the wool trade, thereby establishing itself as a rival to Florence. The two towns became regional powers and bitter enemies, each town taking

Siena and the Hill Towns

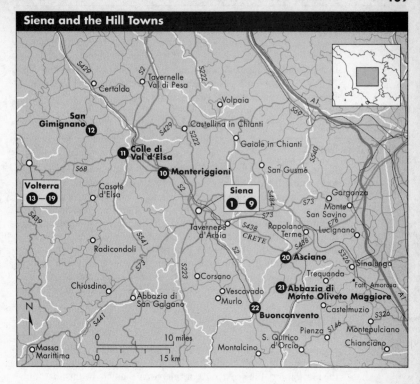

a different side in the struggle that divided the peninsula between the Guelph (loyal to the Pope) and Ghibellines (loyal to the Holy Roman Emperor).

Victory over Florence in 1260 marked the beginning of Siena's Golden Age. Even though the Florentines avenged the loss nine years later, Siena continued to prosper. Over the following decades, Siena erected its greatest buildings, including the Duomo and Palazzo Pubblico; established a model city government based on the Council of Nine; and became a great center of art, with painters at the forefront of the Renaissance. All of these achievements came together in the decoration of the Sala della Pace in Palazzo Pubblico.

That Siena was for centuries the great rival (in art, in trade, in textiles, in banking) to Florence, leaves us only to wonder what greatness the city might have gone on to achieve had its fortunes been different. But the Plague of 1348 decimated the population, brought an end to the Council of Nine, and left Siena economically weak and vulnerable to outside domination. After four centuries of conflict, Siena succumbed to Florentine rule in the mid-16th century, when a year-long siege virtually eliminated the native population. Ironically, it was precisely this decline which (along with the steadfast pride of the Sienese) prevented further development, to which we owe the city's marvelous condition.

With its redbrick streets and steep alleyways, stunning Gothic Duomo, bounty of early Renaissance art, and glorious Palazzo Pubblico overlooking its magnificent Campo, Siena is often described as Italy's best-preserved medieval city. But while much looks as it did in the early 14th century, Siena is no museum. Walk through the streets and you can witness a charming anachronism: The medieval *contrade*, the 17 neighborhoods into which the city has been historically divided, are vibrant and very much alive. Look up from just about any street and you will know the contrada—

Tartuca (turtle), *Oca* (Goose), *Istrice* (porcupine), *Torre* (tower)—you are walking in, as its symbol will likely be emblazoned on a banner or engraved in the street. Ask any Sienese and there will be no doubt—local identity is still very much defined by the *contrada* into which you were born and raised, baptized, and married, and loyalty and rivalry run deep. At no time is this more visible than during the centuries-old Palio, a yearly horse race through the main square (☞ Close-Up: Il Palio, *below*), but you need not visit during the wild festival to come to know the rich culture and enchanting pleasures of Siena.

Exploring Siena

If you come by car, you'll be better off leaving it in one of the parking lots around the perimeter of town, as access is restricted or just plain difficult in much of Siena. Practically unchanged since medieval times, Siena is laid out in a "Y" over the slopes of several hills, dividing the city into *terzi* (thirds). Although you will find the most interesting sites in a fairly compact area around the Campo at the center of town, be sure to leave some time to wander into the narrow streets that rise and fall steeply from the main thoroughfares. If your feet have had enough, there are usually cabs at the bottom of the Campo, and orange electric minibuses ply their way through the crowds and between the major sites.

A Good Walk

Try to avoid passing through Siena in less than a day, missing the opportunity to really explore the town, which is more than the sum of its most notable sites. Begin with a coffee on the **Piazza del Campo** ①, the focal point of the city, and considered by many to be the finest public square in Italy. Visit the **Palazzo Pubblico** ②, with its Museo Civico and adjacent tower, the Torre del Mangia. Cross the piazza and exit via the stairs to the left of the Fonte Gaia to Via di Città. Just to the left is the 15th-century Loggia della Mercanzia, where merchants and money traders once did business. Commerce is still pretty active along Via di Città, Siena's main shopping street, which climbs to the left. Up ahead on Via di Città is the enchanting Palazzo Chigi-Saracini, where concerts are often held. Step in to admire the especially well-preserved courtyard. Continue up the hill on Via di Città and take the next street on the right, Via del Capitano, which leads to Piazza del Duomo. The **Duomo** ③ is a must-see, along with the frescoes inside in the Libreria Piccolomini. Off to the side is the **Museo dell'Opera del Duomo** ④ and the **Battistero** ⑤ (around the other side of the Duomo), and across from the Duomo is the **Ospedale di Santa Maria della Scala** ⑥ and its Museo Archeologico. Chief among Siena's other gems is the **Pinacoteca Nazionale** ⑦, several blocks straight back down Via del Capitano (which becomes Via San Pietro). The church of **San Domenico** ⑧ lies in the other direction (you could take Via della Galluzza to Via della Sapienza) and nearby is the **Casa di Santa Caterina** ⑨, where one of Italy's patron saints was born.

TIMING

It is a joy to walk in Siena—hills notwithstanding—a rare opportunity to stroll through a medieval city rather than just a town (there is quite a lot to explore, unlike in tiny hill towns which can be crossed in minutes). The walk can be done in as little as a day, but plan on two days to really enjoy the various sites. If you only have one day in Siena, don't miss the Duomo, its museum, the Palazzo Pubblico, and the view from the top of the Torre del Mangia. Several of the sites have reduced hours on Sunday afternoon and Monday.

IL PALIO

JUST THREE LAPS around a makeshift track in Piazza del Campo, and it's all over in less than two minutes, but the spirit of Siena's Palio—which takes place every July 2 and August 16—lives all year long.

The first recorded race was run on August 16, 1310, and another on July 2 was added in 1649. Rules established soon after moved the event to the Campo—it had previously been run through the streets of the town—and set up the current system whereby 10 of Siena's 17 contrade are chosen at random to run in the July Palio. The August Palio is run with three of those 10 and the seven contrade left out the first time. Although the races are officially of equal importance, any Sienese will tell you that it is better to win the second Palio and have bragging rights for the rest of the year.

At first it might not seem like much of a race: There is barely room for the 10 horses along the course, so falls and collisions are inevitable. The competing contrade root emphatically for nameless horses (chosen at random three days before the race) and jockeys from other towns hired by each contrada. At stake is the respect or scorn of the neighboring and rival contrade, and the event is so important to the Sienese that almost nothing is too underhanded. Bribery, secret plotting, and betrayal are commonplace (so much so that the word for jockey in Italian, *fantino,* has come to mean untrustworthy in Siena). There have been incidents of drugging (the horses) and kidnapping (the jockeys); only sabotaging a horse's reins remains taboo.

Official festivities kick off three days prior to the Palio, with the selection and blessing of the horses, trial runs, ceremonial banquets, betting, speculation, and late-night celebrations. Residents don scarves with their contrada's colors and march in medieval costumes. The Campo is transformed into a racecourse lined with a thick layer of yellow sand. In the early afternoon of the race day, each horse is brought to the church of the contrada for which it will run, where it is blessed and told "Go little horse and return a winner." The piazza begins to fill in the mid-afternoon, and spectators crowd into every available space until bells ring and the piazza is sealed off. Processions of flag wavers in traditional dress march to the beat of tambourines and drums and the roar of the crowds. The palio itself, a banner dedicated to the Virgin Mary, makes an appearance, followed by the competitors and their jockeys.

The race is set off by one horse chosen to ride up from behind, but there are always a number of false starts, adding to the frenzied mood.

Finally the horses are off, and the race is over almost before the dust settles. The winning rider is carried back to the streets of the winning contrada, where in the past tradition dictated that the victory entitled him to the local girl of his choice. But the celebration is far from over. TV replays, winners, and losers go over the race from every possible angle, but only one contrada will celebrate long into the night, with long tables piled high with food and drink, the champion horse the guest of honor.

At a time when so many festivals in Europe are staged in a soulless attempt to impose charm on a town, the Palio is by and for the Sienese. Visitors are welcome, but keep in mind that the reserved seating in the stands is sold out six months in advance. The entire area in the center is free, but you'll need to show up early to secure a prime spot. For ticket information, *see* Outdoor Activities and Sports in Siena, *below.*

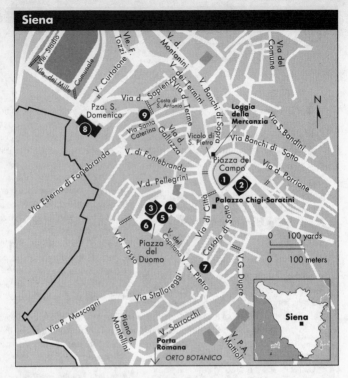

Siena

Sights to See

⑤ Battistero. Steps beneath the large archway between the cathedral and its museum lead down to the Baptistry, built to prop up one side of the Duomo. There are frescoes throughout, but the highlight is a large bronze 15th-century baptismal font, designed by Jacopo della Quercia (1374–1438) and adorned with bas-reliefs by various artists, including two by Renaissance masters who came down from Florence: Lorenzo Ghiberti (1378–1455, *The Baptism of Christ*) and Donatello (circa 1386–1466, *Herod Presented with the Head of St. John*). ⊠ *Piazza San Giovanni,* ☎ *0577/283048.* ▦ *3,000 lire, combination ticket 8,500 lire.* ☽ *Mid-Mar.–Sept., daily 9–7:30; Oct., 9–6; Nov.–mid-Mar., daily 10–1 and 2:30–5.*

NEED A BREAK?	Not far from the Duomo and the Pinacoteca, Siena's **Orto Botanico** (Botanical Gardens; ⊠ V. Via Pier Andrea Mattioli 4, ☎ 0577/298874) is a great place to relax and enjoy views of the countryside below. It's open weekdays 8–5:30, Saturday 8–noon.

⑨ Casa di Santa Caterina. Caterina Benincasa was born here in 1347, and although she took the veil of the Domenican Tertiary order at age eight, she lived in a cell here, devoting her life to the sick and poor in the aftermath of the devastating Plague of 1348. She had divine visions and received the stigmata, but is most famous for her writings and her argumentative skills (though she was unable to write—her letters, many of which are preserved in the Biblioteca Comunale, were dictated). She is credited with single-handedly convincing the pope (the Frenchman Gregory XI, 1329–1378) to return the papacy to Rome after 70 years in Avignon and French domination, partially ending the Great Schism that divided the Catholic Church. Catherine died in Rome in 1380 and was canonized in 1461. A few years later, she was made patron saint of Siena, and the city purchased the family house and turned it into a shrine, one of the first examples of its kind in Italy. The rooms of the house, including her cell and the kitchen, were converted into a series of chapels and oratories and decorated by noteworthy artists over the following centuries with scenes from Catherina's life. In 1939, she was made patron saint of Italy, along with St. Francis of Assisi. In 1970, she was elevated to Doctor of the Church, the highest possible honor in Christendom. ☒ *Entrance on Costa di San Antonio, off Via della Sapienza,* ☎ *0577/44177.* ☞ *Free.* ☉ *Apr.–Oct., daily 9–12:30 and 3:30–6; Nov.–Mar., daily 2:30–6.*

★ ❸ **Duomo.** Several blocks west of Piazza del Campo, Siena's Duomo is beyond question one of the finest Gothic cathedrals in Italy. The facade, with its multicolored marbles and painted decoration, is typical of the Italian approach to Gothic architecture, lighter and much less austere than the French. The cathedral as it now stands was completed in the 14th century, just as Siena reached its peak of power and prestige. But the Sienese had even bigger plans. They wanted to enlarge the building by using the existing church as a transept for a new church, with a new nave running toward the southeast, to make what would be the largest church in the world. But only the side wall and part of the new facade were completed when the Black Death struck in 1348, decimating Siena's population. The city fell into decline, funds dried up, and the plans were never carried out. (The dream of building the biggest church was actually doomed to failure from the start—subsequent attempts to get the project going revealed that the foundation was insufficient to bear the weight of the proposed structure.) The beginnings of the new nave, extending from the right side of the Duomo, were left unfinished, perhaps as a testament to unfulfilled dreams, and ultimately enclosed to house the Museo dell'Opera del Duomo (☞ *below*).

The amazingly detailed facade has few rivals in the region, although it is most similar to the Duomo in Orvieto. It was completed in two brief phases at the end of the 13th and 14th centuries (the gold mosaics are 18th-century restorations). The statues and decorative work were designed by the Pisano family, although most of what we see today are copies; the originals having been removed to the adjacent Museo dell'Opera del Duomo for protection. The Campanile (no entry) is central Italy's finest, with the number of windows increasing with each level.

The Duomo's interior, with its black-and-white striping throughout and finely coffered and gilded dome, is simply striking. Step in and look back up at Duccio's (circa 1255–1318) panels of stained glass that fill the circular facade window. Finished in 1288, it is the oldest example of stained glass in Italy. The Duomo is most famous for its unique and magnificent inlaid marble floors, which took almost 200 years to complete (beginning around 1370); more than 40 artists contributed to the work, made up of 56 separate compositions depicting biblical scenes, allegories, religious symbols, and civic emblems. The Duomo's carousel pulpit, also much appreciated, was carved by Nicola Pisano (circa 1220–1284) around 1265; the *Life of Christ* is depicted on the rostrum frieze. A striking contrast to all the Gothic decoration in the nave, the **Biblioteca Piccolomini** (off the left aisle) is painted with magnificent Renaissance frescoes by Pinturicchio (circa 1454–1513) completed in 1509, depicting events from the life of native son Aeneas Sylvius Piccolomini (1405–1464), who became Pope Pius II in 1458. The frescoes are in excellent condition and have a freshness rarely seen in work so old. ☒ *Piazza del Duomo,* ☎ *0577/283048.* ☞ *Biblioteca*

Piccolomini 2,000 lire; combination ticket 8,500 lire. ☉ *Mid-Mar.–Oct., daily 9–7:30; Nov.–mid-Mar., daily 10–1 and 2:30–5.*

❹ **Museo dell'Opera del Duomo.** Built into part of the unfinished nave of what was to have been the new cathedral, the museum contains the Duomo's treasury and some of the original decoration from its facade and interior. The first room on the ground floor displays weather-beaten 13th-century sculptures by Giovanni Pisano (circa 1250–after 1314) that were brought inside for protection and replaced by copies, as was a tondo of the *Madonna and Child* (now attributed to Donatello) that once hung on the door to the south transept. The masterpiece is unquestionably Duccio's *Maestà,* one side with 26 panels depicting episodes from the Passion, the other side with a *Madonna and Child Enthroned.* Painted around 1310 as the altarpiece for the Duomo (where it remained until 1505), it had an enormous influence on later painters. The second floor is divided between the treasury, with a crucifix by Pisano and several statues and busts of biblical characters and classical philosophers, and the Room of the Madonna with the Big Eyes, named after the namesake painting it displays by Maestro di Tressa, who painted in the early 13th century; the work was the original decoration of the high altar in the Duomo before being displaced by Duccio's *Maestà.* There is a fine view from the tower inside the museum. ✉ *Piazza del Duomo, next to the Duomo,* ☎ *0577/283048.* 🎟 *6,000 lire; combination ticket 8,500 lire.* ☉ *Mid-Mar.–Sept., daily 9–7:30; Oct., daily 9–6; Nov.– mid-Mar., daily 9–1:30.*

❻ **Ospedale di Santa Maria della Scala.** For more than a thousand years, this complex across from the Duomo was home to Siena's hospital, but the beds were recently moved out to make way for a major restoration. There are plans to move the Pinacoteca Nazionale here, but in the meantime several halls are being used to host traveling art exhibits. Restored 15th-century frescoes in the **Sala del Pellegrinaio** (once the emergency room) tell the history of the hospital, which was created to give refuge to passing pilgrims and those in need and to distribute charity to the poor. Incorporated into the complex is the church of the **Santissima Annunziata**, with a celebrated *Risen Christ* by Vecchietta (also known as Lorenzo di Pietro, 1410–1480). The curious will want to head down into the dark **Cappella di Santa Caterina della Notte,** where St. Catherine went to pray at night. A portion of the building is occupied by Siena's **Museo Archeologico,** right on the piazza, with an underrated collection. Assembled from various private collections and a few relics found locally, the displays—including the *bucchero* (dark, reddish clay) ceramics and the Bargagli and Chigi-Saracini collections—are clearly marked and can serve as a good introduction to the Etruscans. ✉ *Piazza del Duomo 2, opposite the Duomo front,* ☎ *0577/586410.* 🎟 *8,000 lire.* ☉ *May–Aug., daily 10–6:30; Sept.–Oct., daily 10–5:30; Nov.–Feb., daily 10:30–1; Mar.–Apr., daily 10:30–4:30.*

★ ❷ **Palazzo Pubblico.** Considered Italy's finest Gothic town hall, Palazzo Pubblico has been the symbol of the city and the seat of its government for almost 700 years. Several of the rooms are decorated with some of Italy's finest early Renaissance frescoes. The main doorway opens onto the Cortile del Podestà (Courtyard of the Podestà), at the left of which is the entrance to the Torre del Mangia (☞ *below*). The Magazzini del Sale (salt warehouses) where salt—once a precious commodity—was once kept safe, are now used for temporary exhibits. To the right is the entrance to the **Museo Civico.** The first room is the Sala del Risorgimento, with 19th-century panels telling the story of Italian Unification. Cut through to the main hall, the Sala del Mappamondo, named for a circular frescoed map of the Sienese state by Ambrogio

Lorenzetti (1290–1348), now lost. The room features Simone Martini's (circa 1284–1344) early 14th-century *Maestà* and *Portrait of Guidoriccio da Fogliano*. This interesting pair of subjects refers first to the Virgin, the guardian of good government—note that her cloak is shaped like the Campo—and the figure of Guidoriccio, thought to represent strong leadership.

The next room, the Sala della Pace, is decorated by the largest secular pictorial cycle of the Middle Ages and one of Italy's greatest paintings, the *Allegories of Good and Bad Government,* painted by Ambrogio Lorenzetti in 1338. The Council of Nine commissioned him to decorate the room in which they met, perhaps to be ever-reminded of the right thing to do. On the entrance wall is a city scene that depicts the effects of good government—easily identified as a utopian view of 14th-century Siena, of course. The painting is full of bright, vibrant colors, well-maintained buildings, happy, productive people, and a rich fertile landscape outside the town. Running across the foreground is the lifeblood of the city, the pilgrims of every sort who came through Siena on the Via Francigena (or Via Romea) on their way to or from Rome.

On the front wall is good government himself, the wise old man dressed in the colors of the *comune,* representing the town council. At his feet are the twin sons of Remus, one of which is the founder of Siena. Hovering above his head are the three holy symbols of Siena: Faith, Charity, and Hope. To his sides are the virtues of good government (left to right, Peace, Force, Prudence, Magnanimity, Temperance, and Justice), each holding corresponding symbols. To the left is the figure of Justice, looking up at Wisdom while balancing her scales: The left represents commutative justice (the distribution of wealth and power); the right represents distributive justice (the absolution of the innocent and punishment of the guilty). Down in the foreground are the town's 24 magistrates, who hold cords that connect them to the scales. Not left out of the scene are those who execute the orders of the government and those who oppose it, the soldiers and prisoners grouped to the right.

If good government served as an ideal to be aspired toward, the allegory of Bad Government on the opposite wall was a corresponding injuction against tyranny, the figure who takes the place of the wise old man in the adjacent wall. He is surrounded by a nasty bunch of negative attributes: Avarice, Pride, and Vanity hang in the air, while Cruelty, Deceit, Fraud, Fury, Discord, and War sit on either side, fondling strange animals. Interestingly, the bad government fresco is severely damaged, while the good government fresco is in terrific condition. You can barely make out the figure of Justice (all tied up), her scales lying on the ground, but the conditions in the town leave little doubt as to the results of bad government: buildings in ruin, mean soldiers everywhere, the landscape barren. Note that this was the view that visitors had on entering the room, only then turning to see the Council of Nine and the effects of their good government.

The next rooms feature more frescoes by Sienese artists from the 13th to 15th centuries, including ceiling frescoes by Lorenzetti (*San Michele Arcangelo*) and Neroccio di Bartolomeo (1447–1500, *Predica di San Bernardino*). Off the Sala del Mappamondo is the Antechapel, with frescoes by Taddeo di Bartolo (1363–1422) and the adjacent chapel with marvelous inlaid wood choir stalls. On a loggia upstairs are the original bas-reliefs by Jacopo della Quercia, which once decorated the fountain on the Campo, moved here to protect them from the elements.

Built to reach the height of the Duomo's Campanile, thereby asserting the power of temporal rule, the **Torre del Mangia** soars to a height of 330 ft, making it the second tallest in Italy. Its curious name comes from one of the tower's first bell ringers, Giovanni di Duccio (called Mangiaguadagni, or earnings eater). The climb up to the top is long and steep, but the superb view makes it worth every step. ⊠ *Piazza del Campo,* ☎ *0577/292263.* ⊠ *Museo Civico: 6,000; Torre del Mangia: 6,000 lire.* ⊘ *Torre del Mangia: Daily 10–1 hr before sunset. Museo Civico: Mar., Oct., and over Christmas Mon.–Sat. 9:30– 1:30, Sun. 9:30–1:30; Apr. and Sept., Mon.–Sat. 9:30–6:30, Sun. 9:30–1:30; Nov.-Feb., daily 9:30–1:30, Sun. 9:30–1:30; May-June, Mon.–Sat., 9–7, Sun. 9–1:30; July–Aug., Mon.–Sat. 9–7:30, Sun. 9–1:30.*

★ ❶ **Piazza del Campo.** Built in the 14th century on a market area that was originally the site of the Roman Forum, this fan-shape piazza is known simply as Il Campo (the Field). Unclaimed by any contrada, it was neutral ground, and thus the logical place to set up the town government. Strips in gray stone divide the brick pavement into nine sections—one for each of the medieval Council of Nine, which fan out from the Palazzo Pubblico. Now most associated with the running of the Palio (it's hard to walk very far in Siena without seeing a poster or calendar of the yearly event), the Campo remains the heart of Sienese life all year long, and is a pleasant place to take a rest and enjoy one of the greatest examples of medieval city planning. The surrounding buildings were restored in the 19th century with neo-Gothic facades to bring back the original appearance of the Campo, although the daily market was relocated. Several openings lead out to the main streets of the three wings of the city. At the top of the Campo is the **Fonte Gaia** decorated in the early 15th century by Siena's greatest sculptor, Jacopo della Quercia, with 13 reliefs of biblical events and virtues. The reliefs that now line the rectangular fountain are 19th-century copies; the originals are in the Museo Civico (☞ Palazzo Pubblico, *above*).

❼ **Pinacoteca Nazionale.** The superb collection of five centuries of local painting in Siena's national picture gallery will easily convince you that the Renaissance was by no means just a Florentine thing—Siena was arguably just as important a center of art and innovation as its rival to the north, especially at the beginning of the period. Accordingly, the most interesting part of the collection, chronologically arranged, is the initial part, which features several important "firsts." Room 1 contains a painting of the *Stories of the True Cross* (1215) by the so-called Master of Tressa, the earliest identified work by a painter of the so-called Sienese school, and is followed (in Room 2) by late-13th-century-artist Guido da Siena's *Stories from the Life of Christ,* one of the first paintings ever made on canvas (earlier painters used wood panels). Rooms 3 and 4 are dedicated to Duccio, a student of Cimabue (circa 1240– 1302) and considered to be the last of the proto-Renaissance painters. Ambrogio Lorenzetti's landscapes in Room 8 are the first truly secular paintings in western art. Among later works in the rooms on the floor above, keep an eye out for the preparatory sketches used by Domenico Beccafumi (circa 1486–1551) for the 35 etched marble panels he made for the floor of the Duomo. ⊠ *Via San Pietro 29,* ☎ *0577/281161.* ⊠ *8,000 lire.* ⊘ *Mon. 8:30–1:30, Tues.–Sat. 9–7, Sun. 8–1.*

❽ **San Domenico.** While the Duomo is celebrated as a triumph of 13th-century Gothic architecture, this church, built at about the same time, turned out as an oversized, hulking brick box that never merited a finishing coat in marble, let alone a graceful facade. Although named for the founder of the Domenican order, the church is now more closely associated with St. Catherine. Just to the right of the entrance is the chapel in which she received the stigmata. On the wall is the only known contemporary portrait of the saint, made in the late 14th century by Andrea Vanni (circa 1332–1413). Farther down is the famous **Cappella di Santa Caterina**, the church's official shrine to Catherine, although only her head is here (kept in a reliquary on the altar); revered throughout the country long before she was officially named patron saint of Italy in 1939, Catherine, or bits and pieces of her, was literally spread all over the country—a foot is in Venice, the rest of her body in Rome. On either side of the chapel are well-known frescoes by Il Sodoma (a.k.a. Giovanni Bazzi, 1477–1549) of *St. Catherine in Ecstasy.* Don't miss the view from the apse-side terrace onto the Duomo and town center. ⊠ *Piazza San Domenico,* ☎ *0577/280330.* ⊡ *Free.* ⊙ *Daily 9–12:30 and 3:30–6.*

NEED A BREAK?   Not far from the church of San Domenico, the **Enoteca Italica** (⊠ Fortezza Medicea, Viale Maccari, ☎ 0577/288497) is a fantastically stocked wine cellar in the bastions of the Fortezza Medici. Here you can taste wines from all over Italy and have a snack, too. It's open from noon to 1 AM.

Dining and Lodging

$$$ ✕ **Antica Trattoria Botteganova.** Just outside the city walls, along the road that leads north to Chianti, the Botteganova is arguably the best restaurant in Siena. Chef Michele Sonentino's cooking is all about clean flavors, balanced combinations, and inviting presentation—contemporary Italian food is rarely this successful. The interior, with high vaulting, is relaxed yet classy, and the service is first rate. The menu changes often, but a few dishes—delicious, light potato gnocchi with a sweet red onion sauce and delicate ravioli of pecorino cheese—frequently appear. The selection of wines is impressive, the prices fair. There is a small room reserved for nonsmokers. ⊠ *Strada Chiantigiana 29, 2 km (1 mi) north of Siena,* ☎ *0577/284230. AE, DC, MC, V. Closed Mon.*

$$ ✕ **Al Marsili.** This 900-year-old wine cellar is a marvelous place to dine, under broad, brick-vaulted ceilings. Tuscan and Italian specialties, among them homemade pastas such as *tortelloni burro e salvia* (large cheese-filled ravioli with a butter and sage sauce) are a delight to the palate. Various meat dishes are cooked in wine, and the wine list features the finest Tuscan and Italian labels, including stars from the nearby Chianti country. ⊠ *Via del Castoro 3, between Piazza del Campo and the cathedral,* ☎ *0577/47154. AE, DC, MC, V. Closed Mon.*

$$ ✕ **Le Logge.** Near Piazza del Campo, this is the classic Sienese trattoria, set in what was once an apothecary (there's also outside seating June–October). Tuscan dishes are the draw, such as *malfatti all'osteria* (ricotta and spinach dumplings in a cream sauce) and *anatra al finocchio* (roast duck with fennel). The owners proudly serve their own wine (along with a good selection of better-known Tuscan labels). ⊠ *Via del Porrione 33,* ☎ *0577/48013. Reservations essential. AE, DC, MC, V. Closed Sun., 2 wks in June, and Nov.*

$$ ✕ **Osteria Castelvecchio.** The menu at this cheerful little restaurant with modern decor, set in an old stall near the Pinacoteca, is an intriguing mix of rare dishes not seen for centuries and updated Sienese standards. The array of dishes is not ample, as chef Mauro prefers to select the choices—and he won't allow the same soup to boil for days on end. There's a solid selection of wines from Tuscany. ⊠ *Via Castelvecchio 65,* ☎ *0577/49586. AE, MC, V. Closed Tues.*

$$ ✕ **Tullio Tre Cristi.** This is a typical and historic neighborhood trattoria, still reliable and frequented by loyal customers. The paintings on the walls were executed by famous local artists of the 1920s, but the

culinary tradition here goes back even further. Try *spaghetti alle brici-ole* (a poor-man's dish of pasta with bread crumbs, tomato, and garlic), or veal *escalopes* (cutlets) subtly flavored with *dragoncello* (tarragon). You can eat outdoors in summer. ⊠ *Vicolo di Provenzano 1, take Via dei Rossi from Via Banchi di Sopra,* ☎ *0577/280608. MC, V. Closed Tues.*

$ ✕ **Enoteca I Terzi.** For a glass of wine from a list of several hundred, a little snack, or a full meal from mid-morning until after midnight, it's hard to beat I Terzi. A short walk from the Campo and the main shopping streets, this new *enoteca* (wine bar) offers hearty soups, well-selected cheeses, and tempting casseroles. Excellent desserts are home-made and beautifully presented. The service is fast and gracious. A small room toward the back is reserved for nonsmokers. ⊠ *Via dei Termini 7,* ☎ *0577/44329. AE, DC, MC, V. Closed Sun.*

$$$$ 🏨 **Certosa di Maggiano.** A former 14th-century monastery (replete with
★   working chapel) converted into an exquisite Relais & Châteaux country hotel, this haven of gracious living is a little more than about 1½ km (1 mi) south of the center, outside the Porta Romana gate, and worth the drive. The atmosphere is that of an exclusive retreat in which a select number of guests enjoy the style and comfort of an aristocratic villa. Guest rooms are a heavenly blend of taste and comfort, with classic prints and bold colors such as a happy daffodil yellow. Common rooms are luxurious, trimmed with fine woods, leathers, and traditional prints. In warm weather, breakfast is served on the patio next to the bucolic garden, aburst with roses, peonies, zinnias, and other blessed friends. ⊠ *Via Certosa 82, 53100,* ☎ *0577/288180,* 🄵🄰🅇 *0577/288189. 10 rooms, 7 suites. Restaurant, bar, pool, tennis court, horseback riding. CP. AE, DC, MC, V.*

$$$$ 🏨 **La Suvera.** This luxurious estate in the lovely valley of the River Elsa,
★   28 km (17 mi) west of Siena and 56 km (35 mi) south of Florence, was once owned by Pope Julius II. The papal villa and adjacent building accommodate guests in magnificently furnished rooms and suites appointed with antiques and modern comforts. With excellent facilities such as drawing rooms, a library, Italian garden, park, the Oliviera restaurant (serving estate wines), and even a helipad to use, guests find it hard to tear themselves away, though there is plenty to see in the vicinity. ⊠ *Pievescola (Casola d'Elsa), off S541, 53030,* ☎ *0577/960300,* 🄵🄰🅇 *0577/960220. 19 rooms, 13 suites. Restaurant, bar, pool, sauna, tennis court, horseback riding, meeting rooms. CP. AE, DC, MC, V. Closed Nov.–Easter.*

$$$$ 🏨 **Park.** Set among olive groves and gardens on a hillside just outside the city walls (you need a car), this hotel offers solid comfort and spacious double rooms with views of the grounds and countryside, which also includes a nine-hole golf course. Public rooms in the 16th-century villa lend an easy elegance and patrician antique charm. Comfortable guest rooms might seem familiar, with their bold, dark fabrics, mirrors, and modern appointments. The Olivo restaurant is known for fine regional cuisine. ⊠ *Via Marciano 18, 53100,* ☎ *0577/44803,* 🄵🄰🅇 *0577/49020. 63 rooms. Restaurant, bar, pool, 2 tennis courts. CP. AE, DC, MC, V.*

$$ 🏨 **Antica Torre.** A restored 17th-century tower within the town walls in the southeast corner of Siena, Antica Torre is a 10-minute walk from Piazza del Campo. With just eight small rooms, it has the feel of a simple bed-and-breakfast (without much breakfast). The old stone staircase, wooden beams, and original brick vaulted ceilings add charm, but the lack of an elevator might be reason to ask for a room on the lower floors. ⊠ *Via Fieravecchia 7, 53100,* ☎ 🄵🄰🅇 *0577/222255. 8 rooms. CP. AE, MC, V.*

$$ ☷ **Chiusarelli.** In a well-kept neoclassic villa, built in the early 1900s complete with caryatids, this hotel has functional rooms that are airy and reasonably quiet. A handy location—near the long-distance bus terminal and a parking area and only a 10-minute walk from the main sites—is the big plus here. The small garden invites reading; a downstairs restaurant caters to tour groups. ⊠ *Viale Curtatone 9, 53100,* ☎ *0577/280562,* 𝔽𝔸𝕏 *0577/271177. 50 rooms. CP. MC, V.*

$$ ☷ **Duomo.** Occupying the top floor of a 300-year-old building near Piazza del Campo, this quiet hotel is furnished in a neat contemporary style, with traces of the past showing in the artfully exposed brickwork in the breakfast room. Many bedrooms have superb views of the city's towers and the hilly countryside. Two rooms have balconies. ⊠ *Via Stalloreggi 38, 53100,* ☎ *0577/289088,* 𝔽𝔸𝕏 *0577/43043. 23 rooms. Breakfast room. CP. AE, DC, MC, V.*

$$ ☷ **Pensione Ravizza.** Don't let the name confuse you, the Ravizza is
★ a particularly elegant hotel. Rooms are large and furnished with antiques, rooms on the backside have great views over the garden and countryside. It's just a few minutes' walk from Piazza del Campo, the best choice in town for location, and the free parking is also a great plus. ⊠ *Pian dei Mantellini 34, 53100,* ☎ *0577/280462,* 𝔽𝔸𝕏 *0577/ 221597. 30 rooms, 4 suites. Free parking. CP. AE, DC, MC, V.*

$$ ☷ **Piccolo Hotel Oliveta.** This little hotel in a rejuvenated 18th-century brick farmhouse has lots of atmosphere. Just outside Porta Romana and only 10 minutes from Piazza del Campo on foot, it has simply furnished rooms and a garden overlooking olive groves and verdant hills. A Palio-time option includes tickets to the race (reserve far in advance). ⊠ *Via Piccolomini 35, 53100,* ☎ *0577/283930,* 𝔽𝔸𝕏 *0577/ 870009. 16 rooms. Free parking. CP. AE, MC, V.*

$$ ☷ **Santa Caterina.** Just outside Porta Romana—a 10-minute walk to
★ the Campo— the Santa Caterina is an extremely pleasant, well-run hotel. The owners are about as welcoming, hospitable, and enthusiastic about the town as you could ever imagine, and their attention to detail makes this one of Siena's little gems. Rooms are all nicely appointed with simple Tuscan furniture and firm beds; rooms on the back side look out onto the garden or the countryside in the distance, rather than the street below. Breakfast is served in a sunny enclosed patio or out in the garden. ⊠ *Via E. S. Piccolomini 7, 53100,* ☎ *0577/221105,* 𝔽𝔸𝕏 *0577/271087. 19 rooms. CP. AE, DC, MC, V.*

Nightlife and the Arts

The Arts

MUSIC

In late July and August, Siena hosts the **Settimane Musicali Senesi,** a series of concerts held in churches and courtyards with performances of local and other music.

Nightlife

There's music and dancing at **Al Cambio** (⊠ Via Pantaneto 48, ☎ 0577/ 43183) and at **L'Officina** (⊠ Piazza del Sale 3, ☎ 0577/286301). At press time, a live-music venue was about to open inside the **Fortezza Medicea** (⊠ Fortezza Medicea, Viale Maccari). The popular tea room **Porta Giustizia 11** (⊠ Via Porta Giustizia 11, ☎ 0577/222753) is open late. **Enoteca I Terzi** (☞ Dining and Lodging, *above*) is lively and open late.

Outdoor Activities and Sports

Siena's Palio horse race takes place every year on July 2 and August 16, but its spirit lives all year long. Three laps around the track in Piazza del Campo earn participants of the Palio the respect or scorn of the other 16 contrade (☞ Close-Up: Il Palio, *above*). Tickets are usually sold out eight months in advance of the events, but some hotels reserve a number of tickets for guests; call the **tourist office** (✉ Piazza del Campo 56, ☎ 0577/280551). It is possible you might luck out and get an unclaimed seat or two; of course, the center of the piazza is free to all on a first-come, first-serve basis, until just moments before the start.

Shopping

Local Specialties

The city is known for ceramics and for its delectable variety of cakes and cookies, their recipes of medieval origin: *cavallucci* (sweet spice biscuits), panforte, *ricciarelli* (almond paste cookies), and *castagnaccio*, a baked Tuscan treat made in the fall and winter from a batter of chestnut flour, topped with pine nuts and rosemary. Sweets from **Nannini**, Siena's major producer of cakes and cookies, are just about everywhere, and tend to obscure other brands.

Enoteca San Domenico (✉ Via del Paradiso 56, ☎ 0577/271181) has baskets full of artisanal panforte in various sizes, wrappings, and degrees of spiciness, as well as a rich selection of red wines from all over Tuscany. A good place to have a slice of castagnaccio is **Pizza al Volo** (✉ Via Pellegrini 19, ☎ 0577/280095).

HILL TOWNS WEST OF SIENA

Towards Volterra

From Siena, the road northwest to Florence (S2) leads up to two pretty towns, Monteriggioni and Colle di Val d'Elsa, both good places to take a break. From there it's a short climb to San Gimignano, known for its wine and medieval towers or a longer ride west to Volterra, city of the Etruscans. Although these two famous hill towns make easy day trips from Siena, each is interesting enough in its own right to be worthy of an overnight stay.

Monteriggioni

🔟 *20 km (12 mi) southeast of San Gimignano, 93 km (58 mi) southeast of Pisa, 55 km (34 mi) south of Florence.*

Tiny Monteriggioni makes a nice stop for a quiet walk around on the way north to Colle di Val d'Elsa, San Gimignano, or Volterra. It's hard to imagine that this little town surrounded by open countryside and poppy fields was ever anything but sleepy. But in the 13th century, Monteriggioni served as Siena's northernmost defense against impending Florentine invasion, so it's likely that the residents of the town spent many a sleepless night. The town's formidable walls are in good condition, although the 14 square towers are not as tall as in Dante's (1265–1321) time, when the poet likened them to the four giants who guarded the horrifying central pit of hell.

Dining and Lodging

$$ ✕ **Il Pozzo.** On the village square, this rustic tavern serves hearty Tuscan country cooking and savory wines. The specialties are homemade fresh pasta, main courses of fillet of Tuscan beef with porcini mushrooms and *piccione ripieno* (stuffed squab), and homey desserts. ✉ *Piazza Roma 2,* ☎ *0577/304127. AE, DC, MC, V. Closed Mon., Jan. 7–Feb. 7, and Aug. 1–7. No dinner Sun.*

$$$ ☒ **Residence San Luigi.** A bit more characterful than your typical Best Western hotel, the San Luigi occupies a 17th-century villa just outside Monteriggioni, lined with lavender bushes and cypress trees. The furnishings in the villa and the workers' quarters—converted into 10 apartments—are rustic, but you'll enjoy all the comforts of a four-star establishment. A poolside restaurant is open in the summer. ☒ *Via della Cerretta 38, Località San Luigi Strove, 53035, 4 km (2½ mi) from Monteriggioni on local road to Colle di Val d'Elsa,* ☎ *0577/301055,* 🆒 *0577/301167. 54 rooms, 10 apartments. Restaurant, bar. CP. AE, DC, MC, V.*

Colle di Val d'Elsa

⑪ *12 km (7 mi) west of Monteriggioni, 25 km (16 mi) northwest of Siena.*

Most people pass right through on their way to and from popular tourist destinations Volterra and San Gimignano—a shame, since Colle di Val d'Elsa has a lot to offer. Another town on the Via Francigena that benefitted from trade along the pilgrimage route to Rome, Colle got an extra boost in the late 16th century when it was given a bishopric, probably related to an increase in trade when nearby San Gimignano was cut off from the well-traveled road. From the 12th century onwards, the flat lower portion of town was given over to a flourishing paper-making industry; today it is mostly modern and efforts have shifted toward the production of fine glass and crystal. Buses arrive at Piazza Arnolfo, named after the town's favorite son, Arnolfo di Cambio (1245–1302), the early-Renaissance architect who designed Florence's Duomo and Palazzo Vecchio (but sadly nothing here). There is a convenient parking lot off S68, with stairs leading up the hill.

Make your way to the better-preserved upper part of town, arranged on two levels. The best views of the valley are to be had from Viale della Rimembranza, the road that loops around the west end of town, past the church of San Francesco. The early-16th century Porta Nuova was inserted into the preexisting medieval walls, just as several handsome Renaissance-style *palazzi* were placed into the medieval neighborhood to create what is now called the Borgo. Halfway down the main street Via Campana is the **Chiesa di Santa Caterina,** with life-size terra-cotta figures that make up the notable group of the *Lamentation.* The road passes through the facade of the surreal Palazzo Campana, an otherwise unfinished building that serves as a door connecting the two parts of the upper town. Via delle Volte, named for the arches that cover it, leads straight through to Piazza del Duomo.

Several redecoration projects have left little of the once-Romanesque **Duomo** to admire. Inside is the **Cappella del Santo Chiodo** (Chapel of the Holy Nail), built in the 15th century to hold a nail from the cross upon which Jesus was crucified (perhaps it inspired the locals to go into the nail-making business, which became another of the town's flourishing industries). ☒ *Piazza del Duomo,* ☎ *no phone.* 🆒 *Free.* ☉ *Daily 8–12 and 4–6.*

The **Museo Archeologico** in Palazzo Pretorio has a small group of Etruscan remains. ☒ *Palazzo Pretorio, Via Casolani,,* ☎ *0577/922954.* 🆒 *3,000 lire.* ☉ *Apr.–Sept., Tues.–Fri. 5–7, weekends, 10–12 and 4–7; Oct.–Mar., Tues.–Fri. 3:30–5:30.*

More interesting are the **Museo d'Arte Sacra** and the **Museo Civico,** both in the adjacent Palazzo del Priori. The latter features the town's tribute to Arnolfo di Cambio, with photos of the buildings he designed for other towns and some models of the town. Down the **Via del Castello** (No. 63) is the house-tower where Arnolfo was born in 1245.

✉ *Palazzo dei Priori, Via del Castello 31,* ☎ *0577/923888.* ▣ *5,000 lire.* ☉ *Nov.–Mar., Sat.–Sun. 10–12 and 3–6, Apr.–Oct., Tues.–Sun. 10–12 and 4–7.*

Dining

$$$–$$$$ ✕ **Ristorante Arnolfo.** Foodies should not miss Arnolfo, possibly one
★ of Tuscany's finest restaurants. In a tranquil location in the center of town, the restaurant sets high standards of creativity and intelligent uses of ingredients. Chef Gaetano Trovato's sublime dishes daringly ride the line between innovation and tradition, almost always with spectacular results. The menu changes frequently and features two fixed-price options, but you are always sure to find fish in the summer and lots of fresh vegetables and herbs. This is also the place to splurge on wine: the wine list is exhaustive and fairly priced. If you can't bear the thought of your next meal elsewhere, ask about the restaurant's four-room bed and breakfast (280,000 lire). ✉ *Piazza XX Settembre 52,* ☎ FAX *0577/920549. AE, DC, MC, V. Closed Tues., mid-Jan–mid-Feb, and 2 wks in Aug*

San Gimignano

★ ⑫ *14 km (9 mi) northwest of Colle di Val d'Elsa, 27 km (17 mi) east of Volterra, 38 km (24 mi) northwest of Siena, 54 km (34 mi) southwest of Florence.*

When you're high on a hill surrounded by crumbling towers in silhouette against the blue sky, it's difficult not to fall under the medieval spell of San Gimignano. Its high walls and narrow streets are typical of Tuscan hill towns, but it is the medieval "skyscrapers" that set the town apart from its neighbors and give it a uniquely photogenic skyline. Today 14 towers remain, but at the height of the Guelph-Ghibelline conflict there was a forest of more than 70, and it was possible to cross the town by rooftop rather than road. The towers were built partly for defensive purposes—they were a safe refuge and useful for pouring boiling oil on attacking enemies—and partly to bolster the egos of their owners, who competed with deadly seriousness to build the highest tower in town.

Arguably Tuscany's best-preserved medieval hill town, San Gimignano's relative proximity to Siena and Florence also makes it one of Italy's most visited. But the traffic is hardly a new thing; the Etruscans (a few scattered relics remain in the small museum) were here, and later the Romans made it an outpost at the intersection of the two main roads in the region—the Via Pisana that went west to the coast and the Via Francigena, which crossed the Alps. With the yearly flow of pilgrims to and from Rome in the Middle Ages, the town—then known as Castel di Selva—became a prosperous market center. When locals prayed to a martyred bishop from Modena for relief from invading barbarians, relief they got, and in gratitude they re-Christened the town in his honor as San Gimignano. Devasted by the Plague of 1348, the town subsequently fell under Florentine control. Things got going again in the Renaissance, with some of the best and brightest painters in the area—Ghirlandaio (1449–1494), Gozzoli (1420–1497), and Pinturicchio—coming to decorate, but soon after the main road moved, cutting San Gimignano off and sending it into decline.

Today, San Gimignano isn't much more than a gentrified walled city, amply prepared for its booming tourist trade, but still very much worth exploring. Unfortunately, tour groups arrive early and clog the wine-tasting rooms—San Gimignano is famous for its light white Vernaccia—and art galleries for much of the day, but most sights are open through late afternoon during summer. In the morning, you can enjoy

San Gimignano's exceptionally fine countryside and return to explore the town in the afternoon and evening, when things quiet down and the long shadows cast by the imposing towers take on fascinating shapes. A combination ticket (16,000 lire) for all the local sites (except the private Museo di Criminologia Medioevale) is available, but it's a good deal only if you plan on visiting all of them.

Porta San Giovanni opens in the medieval walls that surround the city, and Via San Giovanni leads the short way to the center of town, tracing the Roman Via Francigena. Touristy shops lining the way leave no doubt about the lifeblood of the town, but better things lie ahead. Pass under **Arco dei Becci,** a leftover from the city's Etruscan walls, to Piazza della Cisterna, named for the cistern at its center, and once the main piazza in town. To the right is the unusual **Museo di Criminologia Medioevale** (Museum of Medieval Criminology), a private museum (no state museum would be so bold). Just to let you know that the Middle Ages were about more than walled towns, praying monks, mosaics, and illuminated manuscripts, the museum presents what was once the cutting edge in medieval torture technology. Pretty much all the devices you see here were really used, and in case you have a hard time imagining just how, the no-nonsense descriptions give operating instructions and several illustrations reveal the intended effect. ⊠ *Via del Castello, just off Piazza della Cisterna,* ☎ *0577/942243.* ⊠ *15,000 lire.* ☉ *Mar.–Oct. and over Christmas, daily 10–1 and 2–7, Nov.–Feb., Fri.–Mon. 10–1 and 2–7.*

Beyond the twin towers built by the Ardinghelli family is the Piazza del Duomo, lined with San Gimignano's main civic and religious buildings. Behind the humdrum facade of the Romanesque **Collegiata,** the town's main church (not officially a *duomo* because San Gimignano has no bishop), is a treasure trove of fine frescoes, covering nearly every part of the interior. Bartolo di Fredi's 14th-century *Old Testament* scenes are painted in three levels along one aisle. Their distinctly medieval feel, with misshapen bodies, buckets of spurting blood, and skewed perspective, contrasts with the much more reserved scenes from the *Life of Christ* (attributed to 14th-century-artist Lippo Memmi), painted on the opposite wall just 14 years later. Taddeo di Bartolo's otherworldly *Last Judgment* (late 14th century), with its distorted and suffering nudes, reveals the great influence of Dante's horrifying imagery in the *Inferno,* and was surely an inspiration for later painters. Proof that the town had more than one protector, Benozzo Gozzoli's arrow-riddled *St. Sebastian* was commissioned in gratitude after the locals prayed to the saint for relief from plague. The Renaissance **Cappella di Santa Fina** is decorated with a fresco cycle by Domenico Ghirlandaio illustrating the unusual story of St. Fina. A small girl who suffered from a terminal disease, Fina repented for her sins—among them having accepted an orange from a boy—and in penance lived out the rest of her short life on a wooden board, tormented by mice. The scenes depict the arrival of St. Gregory, who appeared to assure her that death was near, the flowers which miraculously grew from the wooden plank, and the miracles that accompanied her funeral, including the healing of her nurse's paralyzed hand and the restoration of a blind choir boy's vision. ⊠ *Piazza del Duomo,* ☎ *0577/940316.* ⊠ *Cappella di Santa Fina: 3,000 lire.* ☉ *Daily 9:30–12:30 and 3–5:30.*

Even with all the decoration in the Collegiata, the fine collection of various religious articles at the **Museo d'Arte Sacra e Museo Etrusco,** through the pretty courtyard, is still worth a look. The highlight is a *Madonna and Child* by Bartolo di Fredi. Other pieces include several busts, wooden statues of Christ and the Virgin and the angel Gabriel, and several illuminated songbooks. The thin collection of Etruscan relics come up short of more interesting displays in other towns. ⊠ *Piazza Pecori,* ☎ *0577/942226.* ⊡ *7,000 lire.* ☉ *Mar.–Oct., daily 9:30–8, Nov.–Feb., Tues.–Sun. 9–1:30 and 2:30–5.*

Across the piazza is the **Palazzo Vecchio,** appropriately named as it is the "old" town hall (1239). Its tower was built by the municipality in 1255 to settle the raging "my-tower-is-bigger-than-your-tower" contest—as you can see a solution that just didn't last.

★ City government soon moved to the "new" Palazzo del Popolo, home to the impressive **Museo Civico** and the adjacent **Torre Grossa**. Dante visited San Gimignano for only one day as a Guelpf ambassador from Florence to ask the locals to join the Florentines in supporting the pope— just long enough to get the main council chamber named after him, which now holds a large *Maestà* (14th century) by Lippo Memmi. Off the stairway is a small room containing the racy frescoes by Memmo di Filippuccio (died 1324) depicting the courtship, shared bath, and wedding of a young, androgynous-looking couple. Recent scholarship indicates that this may actually be the story of a young man's initiation with a prostitute; either way, it's quite an unusual commission for a public palazzo and an entertaining break from the usual images.

Upstairs, famous paintings by Renaissance stars Pinturicchio (*Madonna Enthroned*), Gozzoli (*Madonna and Child*), and *Annunciation* tondoes by Filippino Lippi (circa 1457–1504) attest to the importance and wealth of San Gimignano. Also worth seeking out are Taddeo di Bartolo's *Life of San Gimignano,* with the saint holding a model of the town as it once appeared, and Lorenzo di Niccolò's gruesome martyrdom scene in the *Life of St. Bartholomew* (1401) and scenes from the *Life of St. Fina* (☞ Collegiata, *above*) on a tabernacle that was designed to hold her head. The admission price to Torre Grossa is steeper than the climb, but on a clear day the views are spectacular. ⊠ *Piazza del Duomo,* ☎ *0577/940008.* ⊡ *Museo: 7,000 lire; Torre: 8,000 lire; combination ticket: 12,000 lire available Mar.–Oct., daily 12:30–3 and 6–7:30.* ☉ *Mar.– Oct., daily 9:30–7:30; Nov.–Feb., Tues.–Sun. 9:30–1 and 2:30–5.*

If you can't make it all the way, or if you just want more of that quintessential Tuscan landscape, walk up to the **Rocca,** open daily sunrise–sunset. Built after the Florentine conquest to keep an eye on the town, and dismantled a few centuries later, it is now a public garden. From here, bird lovers will want to take the steps down to the **Museo Ornitologico,** set in an ex-church at the base of the former fortress. ⊠ *Via Quercecchio,* ☎ *0577/941388.* ⊡ *4,000 lire.* ☉ *Mar.–Oct., daily 9:30–12:30 and 3–6, Nov.–Feb., Tues.–Sun. 9:30–12:30 and 2:30–5.*

Via San Matteo is San Gimignano's most handsome street, framed by stout medieval buildings in excellent condition, with flowers here and there lightening up the otherwise heavy stone facades. The road ends at Porta San Matteo; just before, cut right into Piazza Sant'Agostino and make a beeline for Benozzo Gozzoli's superlative frescoes inside
★ the church of **Sant'Agostino.** This Romanesque-Gothic church holds Benozzo Gozzoli's stunning 15th-century fresco cycle of the *Life of St. Augustine.* Vastly overshadowed by St. Francis (at least in Italy), Augustine was essential to the early development of church doctrine. As thoroughly discussed in his autobiographical *Confessions* (an acute dialogue with God), Augustine, like many saints, sinned considerably in his youth before finding the way of God. But unlike other saints, where the story continues through a litany of miracles, deprivations, penitence, and often martyrdom, Augustine's life and work focused on philosophy and the reconciliation between faith and thought. Gozzoli's

17 scenes on the choir wall depict a man who traveled and taught extensively through the empire in the 4th–5th centuries. The 15th-century altarpiece by Piero del Pollaiolo (1443–1496) depicts the *Coronation of the Virgin* and the various protectors of the city. On your way out, stop in at the **Cappella di San Bartolo**, with a sumptuously elaborate tomb by Benedetto da Maiano (1442–1497). ⊠ *Piazza Sant'Agostino,* ☎ *0577/907012.* ⊡ *Free.* ☉ *Daily 7–12 and 3–7.*

NEED A BREAK?	As elsewhere in town, there is no shortage of places to try Vernaccia di San Gimignano, the justifiably famous white wine which the town would be singularly associated with—if it weren't for all those towers around. Get a bottle to accompany a picnic at **Enoteca Gustavo** (⊠ Via San Matteo 29, ☎ 0577/940057), or sit down and nibble on cheese and salami. On your way back into town, mosey on down to **Bar-Pasticceria Maria e Lucia** (⊠ Via San Matteo 55, ☎ 0577/940379) for some homemade gelato or desserts. **Antica Latteria di Maurizio e Tiziana** (⊠ Via San Matteo 19, ☎ 0577/941952), closed Sunday, serves up salads and *panini* (sandwiches) any way you want them, priced by weight.

Dining and Lodging

The **Cooperativa Hotels Promotion** (⊠ Via di San Giovanni 125, ☎ 0577/940809) offers commission-free booking services in local hotels and farmhouses.

$$–$$$ ✕ **Bel Soggiorno.** Italy is full of places called Belvedere, Bel Soggiorno, or Bellavista without the beautiful view or stay promised in the name, but San Gimignano's Bel Soggiorno does not disappoint. On the top floor of a 100-year-old inn, it has a wall of windows that look out onto the vineyards and olive trees that roll away in the distance. Tuscan specialties include *zuppa del granduca* (a medieval soup recipe of mushrooms, grain, and potatoes) and *sorpresa in crosta* (spicy rabbit stew with a bread crust). Don't miss the sweet *schiacciata di fichi e mandorle* (fig and almond bread) served as a dessert. ⊠ *Via San Giovanni 91,* ☎ *0577/940375. AE, DC, MC, V. Closed Mon. and Jan. 7–Feb.*

$$–$$$ ✕ **Le Terrazze.** Seasonal Tuscan classics are prepared in this restaurant in a time-honored inn in the heart of San Gimignano. A charming view of rooftops and the countryside and specialties like homemade pasta, a variety of grilled mushrooms, and grilled meats are in store. ⊠ *Piazza della Cisterna 23,* ☎ *0577/940328. AE, DC, MC, V. Closed Tues. and Nov.–Mar. 9. No lunch Wed.*

$$ ✕ **La Mangiatoia.** In this rustic trattoria, near the church of Sant Agostino, prices are more moderate than at places with a view, and the food is simple Tuscan country cooking. ⊠ *Via Mainardi 5, off Via San Matteo,* ☎ *0577/941528. MC, V. Closed Mon. and Nov. 4–25.*

$$ ✕ **Da Gustavo.** One look inside this enoteca on Via San Matteo and you'll know the owners mean business. Lined up behind a solid wooden counter is a complete hit parade of Tuscany's greatest wines (red and white). Take a seat in the more intimate room at the back for an informal sampling of local sausages and cheeses, homemade pickles and bruschetta (grilled Tuscan bread drizzled with olive oil, rubbed with garlic, and topped with tomatoes) to go along with your wine of choice—there are always at least 20 wines *in mescita* (by the glass) and several kinds of olive oil to try. ⊠ *Via San Matteo 29,* ☎ *0577/940057. AE, DC, MC, V. Closed Mon. and Nov.*

$ ✕ **Osteria delle Catene.** This popular restaurant shares its look and philosophy with many other Tuscan *trattorie* opened in the nineties by young food lovers. Expect to find the most traditional dishes—some of them almost a rarity these days—served in a stylish room with a vault. Standouts include *nana col cavolo nero* (duck with Tuscan kale) and *maiale con i gobbi* (pork loin with cardoons). A glass of *vin santo* is a better end to the meal than the less-than-exciting desserts. ⊠ *Via Mainardi 18,* ☎ *0577/941966. AE, DC, MC, V. Closed Wed. and Jan.*

$$$$ ⊞ **Collegiata.** After serving as a Franciscan convent and then residence of the noble Strozzi family, the Collegiata, about 1 km (½ mi) north of San Gimignano, has become one of the region's finest hotels, with no expense spared in the effort. Surrounded by a park, all the rooms (some with private balconies) are furnished with antiques and precious tapestries, and bathrooms in travertine feature whirlpool baths. A summer restaurant occupies the ex-church, with tables set out on the entrance. ⊠ *Località Strada 27, 53037,* ☎ FAX *0577/943201, 10 rooms, 4 suites. Restaurant, bar, pool, free parking. CP. AE, DC, MC, V. Closed Jan.*

$$$ ⊞ **Santa Chiara.** In a low contemporary building with a plethora of bal-
★ conies and terraces on a panoramic hillside just outside San Gimignano's walls, this hotel is an airy and spacious oasis, and an upscale base from which to explore the countryside and hill towns. The hotel has no restaurant but serves an ample buffet breakfast, and light meals in summer. ⊠ *Via Matteotti 15, 53037,* ☎ *0577/940701,* FAX *0577/942096. 41 rooms. Breakfast room, pool. CP. AE, DC, MC, V. Closed Jan. 10–Feb. 28.*

$$ ⊞ **Pescille.** This rambling farmhouse 4 km (2½ mi) outside San
★ Gimignano has been converted into a handsome hotel in which restrained contemporary and country classic motifs blend well. ⊠ *Località Pescille, Strada Castel San Gimignano, 53037,* ☎ *0577/940186,* FAX *0577/943165. 40 rooms. Pool, tennis court. CP. AE, DC, MC, V. Closed Nov.–Feb.*

Nightlife and the Arts

San Gimignano is one of the few small towns in the area that makes a big deal out of **Carnevale** festivities, with locals dressing up in colorful costumes and marching through the streets on the four Sundays preceding Shrove Tuesday from 3:30 to 6:30. If you visit in summer, check with the tourist office (⊠ Piazza del Duomo 1, ☎ 0577/940008) about concerts and performances related to the **Estate San Gimignanese,** one of Tuscany's oldest summer arts festivals (mid-June to August).

Outdoor Activities and Sports

HIKING AND WALKING

The pristine olive groves and vineyards outside the walls are easily accessible on foot, without unreasonably steep grades or ugly peripheries to pass through. The tourist office (☞ *above*) organizes three-hour walks in the countryside around town with English-speaking guides March–October, Wednesday, Friday, and Saturday afternoon, Sunday morning, or by appointment. Cost is 20,000 lire per person.

Shopping

The lovely countryside is so close and good ingredients so near at hand, it's hard to resist a picnic on a nice day in San Gimignano. The **grocery store** (⊠ Piazza Cisterna, ☎ no phone) stays open through the afternoon but is closed on Sunday. As everywhere else, the town brightens up a bit on **open-air market** mornings, every Thursday and Saturday in Piazza del Duomo. It's the place to pick up fresh fruits and veggies—then head for Via San Matteo (☞ Need a Break?, *above*) to fill up your basket.

VOLTERRA

As you make the dramatic climb up to Volterra through bleak, rugged terrain, you'll see that not all Tuscan hill towns rise above rolling fields of green, and also just how beautiful a change of scenery can be. It seems that most guidebooks introduce the town with a quote from the intrepid D. H. Lawrence, who made the trek here in 1927 on his quest to visit Italy's Etruscan ruins. The town began as the northernmost city of the 12 that made up the Etruscan league, and excavations in the 18th century revealed a bounty of relics now on exhibit at the impressive Museo Etrusco Guarnacci. Volterra's fortress, walls, and gates still stand mightily over *Le Balze,* a stunning series of gullied hills and valleys formed by erosion that has slowly eaten away at the foundation of the town, now considerably smaller than it was during its Etruscan glory days 25 centuries ago. The Romans and later the Florentines laid siege to the town to secure its supply of minerals and stones, particularily alabaster, which is still worked into handicrafts on sale in many of the shops around town.

Exploring Volterra

A combination admission ticket (12,000 lire) allows entrance to all three of Volterra's museums (Museo d'Arte Sacra, Pinacoteca, and Museo Etrusco Guarnacci). Volterra has several parking lots around the perimeter of the city walls, most conveniently in the underground parking lot at Piazza Martiri della Libertà.

A Good Walk

Begin in Piazza Martiri della Libertà and take Via Marchesi to Piazza dei Priori, lined with an impressive collection of medieval buildings, including the imposing **Palazzo dei Priori** ⑬, the seat of town government for more than seven centuries. Across the piazza is the Palazzo Pretorio topped by the Torre del Porcellino, named after the sculpted little boar mounted at the upper window. Walk down Via Turazza along the side of the **Duomo** ⑭ to the triangular Piazza San Giovanni, and head out the left corner of the piazza to steal a look at the ancient **Porta all'Arco Etrusco** ⑮. Return to the piazza and step inside the Duomo and its baptistry. Next to the Duomo is Palazzo Vescovile with the **Museo d'Arte Sacra** ⑯ (entrance around the corner), the first of Volterra's three worthwhile museums. From there proceed straight up Via Roma to the **Pinacoteca** ⑰. Via dei Sarti leads to Piazza San Michele, with the eponymous church decked out in black and white Pisan stripes. Via Guarnacci goes left to Porta Fiorentina and the ruins just outside the walls of the 1st-century BC **Teatro Romano** ⑱. Retrace your steps and continue across town on Via di Sotto, through Piazza XX Settembre to Via Don Minzoni and the **Museo Etrusco Guarnacci** ⑲. Farther along the street is the edge of the Rocca (fortress), one of the few still in use in the country, which serves as the town jail. Via del Castello leads back down the hill, along the Parco Archeologico, a pleasant public park with a few Etruscan stones here and there.

TIMING

The town can easily be seen in a day, although its distance from everything else makes it a good stopover as well. Allow at least three hours for the tour.

Sights to See

⑭ **Duomo.** Behind the textbook 13th-century Pisan Romanesque facade is proof that Volterra counted for something during the Renaissance, when many of the great Tuscan artists came to decorate the church. Stucco portraits of local saints stick out from Francesco Capriani's gold, red, and blue ceiling (1580), including St. Linus, the successor to St. Peter as pope, and claimed by the Volterrans to have been born here. The church is dedicated to Santa Maria Assunta, but local or patron saints are also venerated. Reliquary busts of St. Linus, St. Giusto, and St. Clement are locked away in the sacristy; out front a chapel contains the remains of St. Octavian (his empty head-shape reliquary was

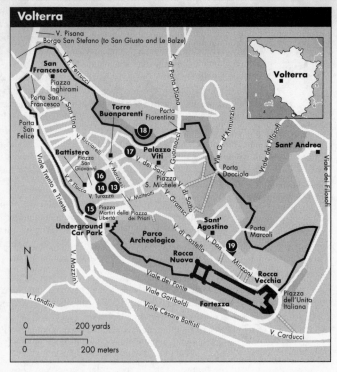

Volterra

moved to the Museo d'Arte Sacra), who became a patron saint of the town after prayers to him ended a plague in the early 16th century. The highlight of the Duomo is the harshly painted 13th-century wooden life-size *Deposition* (in the chapel of the same name), resembling those carried around in processions. The unusual Lady Chapel is decorated with two terra-cotta Nativity scenes, one with a background fresco by Benozzo Gozzoli. The 16th-century pulpit in the middle of the nave is lined with fine 14th-century sculpted panels, attributed to a member of the Pisano family. Across from the Duomo in the center of the piazza is the recently restored **Battistero** (Baptistry), with stripes that match the Duomo. Evidently the baptistry got a lot of use, as the small marble baptismal font carved by Sansovino in 1502 was moved to the wall to the right of the entrance in the mid-18th century to make room for a larger font. ✉ *Piazza San Giovanni,* ☎ *0588/87654.* ☞ *Free.* ⊙ *Duomo and Battistero: daily 7–12:30 and 2:30–6:30.*

OFF THE
BEATEN PATH

LE BALZE – From Piazza San Giovanni, take Via Franceschini (which becomes Via San Lino) to the church of San Francesco, well worth a look inside for the celebrated early 15th-century frescoes of the *Stories of the True Cross* by a local artist. It traces the history of the wood used to make the cross upon which Jesus was crucified back to the seed, and follows the cross to its return to Jerusalem. Continue along the road, through Porta San Franceso, and out Borgo Santo Stefano. This area was originally part of the Etruscan town (called Vlathri, as usual the current name is closer to the Roman name, Volaterrrae) as evidenced by walls that extend another kilometer toward the old Porta Menseri. Toward the end of the road, on the right, is the church of San Giusto (with terra-cotta statues of the town's patron saints). The church was built to replace an earlier church that disappeared into Le Balze—a desolate, undulating landscape of yellow earth drawn into crags and gullies, as if worn down by a desert torrent long past. Instead the haunting phenomenon is thought to have been created when rainwater collected and wore down the soil substructure. The bus for Borgo San Giusto, leaving from Piazza Martiri, goes through Le Balze (about 10 runs per day).

⑯ Museo d'Arte Sacra. Appropriately housed in the Bishop's Palace, this museum made up of religious art collected from local churches includes an unusual reliquary with the head of St. Octavian in silver resting on four golden lions by Antonio Pollaiolo and a fine terra-cotta bust of St. Linus by Andrea della Robbia (circa 1399–1482). Two paintings are also noteworthy, Rosso Fiorentino's (1494–1541) *Madonna di Villamagna* and Daniele da Volterra's *Madonna di Ulignano,* named for the village churches (now abandoned) in which they were originally placed. ⊠ *Palazzo Vescovile, Via Roma 1,* ☎ *0588/86290.* 🎫 *Combination ticket 12,000 lire.* ☉ *Mar. 16–Oct., daily 9–1 and 3–6; Nov.–Mar. 15, daily 9–1.*

★ **⑲ Museo Etrusco Guarnacci.** Although Etruscan sites are spread throughout Tuscany and Northern Lazio, the major relics have been assembled in state museums and the Musei Vaticani in Rome, leaving precious little for the towns closest to the excavations. Fortunately in the case of Volterra, an extraordinarily large and unique collection of relics remains close to home, made all the more interesting by clear explanations in English. The museum is large, laid out in 40 rooms over three floors. You will find the usual display of Attic vases, bucchero ceramics, jewelry, and household items, but the bulk of the collection is made up of roughly 700 carved funerary urns (as elsewhere in the northern portion of Etruria, the dead were cremated). The oldest, dating to the 7th century, were made from tufa (volcanic rock), a handful are of terracotta, and the vast majority—from the 3rd to 1st century BC—from alabaster. The urns are grouped by subject, and taken together form a fascinating testimony about Etruscan life and death. Some illustrate domestic scenes, others the funeral procession of the deceased, a journey typically made in one of four ways: on foot, on horseback, in a cart pulled by donkeys, and by four-horse chariots. Greek gods and mythology, by then adopted by the Etruscans, also figure prominently. The sculpted figures on many of the covers are thought to have been made in the image of the deceased, reclining and often holding the cup of life overturned. Particularly well known is *Gli Sposi* (Husband and Wife), a haunting portrait in terra-cotta. Another famous piece in the collection is a long, thin bronze votive statue called the *Ombra della Sera* (Shadow of the Evening). The museum also holds relics from the periods immediately preceding and following the Etruscan. Of particular interest are reconstructed tombs from the 10th–9th centuries BC, as well as Roman-era relics, the highlight of which is a colorful mosaic with a geometric pattern taken from the local baths, in excellent condition. ⊠ *Via Don Minzoni 15,* ☎ *0588/86347.* 🎫 *Combination ticket 12,000 lire.* ☉ *Mar. 16–Oct., daily 9–7; Nov.–Mar. 15, daily 9–2.*

⑬ Palazzo dei Priori. Palazzo dei Priori was built between 1208 and 1257, with a no-nonsense facade, fortresslike crenellations, and a five-sided tower. The first town hall in Tuscany, it was built when such fortifications were necessary and commonplace, and served as a model for other similar structures throughout the region, including Florence's Palazzo Vecchio (the Florentine medallions that adorn the facade here were added after the Florentines conquered Volterra). The town leaders still meet on the first floor in the Sala del Consiglio Comunale, open to the public, with a fresco on the wall of the *Annunciation* (1383) by Jacopo di Cione (died after 1398). ⊠ *Piazza dei Priori,* ☎ *0588/86050.* 🎫 *Free.* ☉ *Apr.–Oct., Mon.–Sat. 10–1 and 3–4; Nov.–Mar., Mon.–Sat. 10–1.*

⑰ Pinacoteca. Arranged in chronological order on two floors in one of Volterra's best-looking buildings, the Pinacoteca has an impressive collection of Tuscan paintings. Head straight for Room 12, where you will find Luca Signorelli's (circa 1450–1523) *Madonna and Child with Saints* and Rosso Fiorentino's *Deposition*. Both are masterpieces, and though painted just 30 years apart, they serve to illustrate the shift in style in the early 16th century from the late-Renaissance painting to all-out Mannerist style: The balance of Signorelli's composition becomes purposefully skewed in Fiorentino's painting, the colors go from vivid but realistic to emotive garish. Other important paintings in the small museum include Ghirlandaio's *Apotheosis of Christ with Saints*, and a polyptych of the *Madonna and Saints* by Taddeo di Bartolo which once hung in the Palazzo dei Priori. ⊠ *Via dei Sarti 1,* ☎ *0588/87580.* 🎫 *Combination ticket 12,000 lire.* ☉ *Mar. 16–Oct., daily 9–7; Nov.–Mar. 15, daily 9–2.*

⑮ Porta all'Arco Etrusco. Even if a good portion of the arch was rebuilt by the Romans, the three dark, weather-beaten 3rd-century BC heads carved in basaltic rock (thought to represent Etruscan gods) still face outward, greeting those who enter. A plaque recalls the efforts of the locals who saved the arch from destruction during the German withdrawal at the end of World War II by filling it with stones.

⑱ Teatro Romano. Just outside the walls past Porta Fiorentina are the ruins of the 1st-century BC Roman theater, one of the best preserved in Italy, with adjacent remains of the Roman *terme* (baths). ⊠ *Viale Francesco Ferrucci.* ☉ *May–Oct., daily 11–4. Closed when raining.*

Dining and Lodging

$$ ✕ **Da Badò.** This is the place in town to eat traditional food elbow-to-elbow with the locals. Da Badò is a typical family-run place (open only at lunch) and the chef's efforts concentrate on just a few dishes, so it won't take long to decide between the standards, all prepared with a sure hand: *zuppa alla volterrana* (a Tuscan soup made with vegetables and bread) and *pappardelle alla lepre* (wide fettuccine in a hare sauce), and a stew of either rabbit or wild boar. A slice of homemade almond tart is a must. ⊠ *Borgo San Lazzaro 9,* ☎ *0588/86477. AE, DC, MC, V. Closed Wed., 2 wks in July, and 10 days in Sept. No dinner.*

$$ ✕ **Etruria.** Turn-of-the-century frescoes on the walls and outdoor dining in the warm weather denote this restaurant on the town's main square. An array of local game is used in such specialties as pappardelle alla lepre and *cinghiale alla maremmana* (roast boar). ⊠ *Piazza dei Priori 8,* ☎ *0588/86064. AE, DC, MC, V. Closed Thurs.*

$$ 🏨 **San Lino.** In a former convent, this hotel has modern comforts and its own regional restaurant. Ask for a room on the second floor, as those below are short on space and amenities. There's a swimming pool at the center of the cloister. ⊠ *Via San Lino 26, 56048,* ☎ *0588/85250,* FAX *0588/80620. 43 rooms. Restaurant, pool, free parking. CP. AE, DC, MC, V. Closed Nov. 9–Feb.*

Nightlife and the Arts

On the first Sunday in September is the **Astiludio,** a festival with flag throwing and processions. Volterra's **Jazz Festival** lasts for three weeks between July and August.

Shopping

Market day in Volterra is Saturday morning in Piazza dei Priori (it moves just outside the walls to Viale Ferrucci May–October).

Alabaster

Volterra has a number of shops that sell boxes, jewelry, and other objects made of alabaster. The **Cooperativa Artieri Alabastro** (⊠ Piazza dei Priori 5, ☎ 0588/87590) has two large showrooms in a medieval building with an array of alabaster objects. In a former medieval monastery, the **Gallerie Agostiniane** showrooms (⊠ Piazza XX Settembre 3, ☎ 0588/86868) craft alabaster objects of all kinds. You can see a video on how the mineral is quarried and carved. At the **Rossi** (⊠ Via Lungo Mura del Mandorlo, ☎ 0588/86133), you can actually see the craftsmen at work; there are objects for all tastes and budgets.

THROUGH THE CRETE

Southeast of Siena

Van Gogh never saw the area south of Siena known as le Crete (*creta* means baked clay in Italian), but in the bare clay hills around Asciano— the rolling wheat fields, the warm light, the dramatic gullies and ravines cut by centuries of erosion—he would have perhaps found worthy subjects, as these landscapes seem carved into the earth much in the way that the furrows of paint layer his canvases.

Take the S73 southeast out of Siena toward Taverne d'Arbia, where the S438 branches off and goes 21 km (13 mi) to Asciano. About halfway you will notice a distinct change in landscape, from the farming valleys that surround Siena to much hillier Asciano. The road to the north goes to Rapolano Terme, one of several towns in the area known for its thermal baths. The road south passes through even more dramatic Crete countryside. At the Abbazia di Monte Oliveto Maggiore, the road turns west and leads down to Buonconvento and the Via Cassia, the Roman consular road that runs south to Rome. A good excursion can also be made to the east, passing through little-visited towns such as Trequanda, Sinalunga, and Montefollonico.

Asciano

 25 km (16 mi) southeast from Siena, 124 km (77 mi) southeast of Florence.

Another Etruscan-turned-medieval town, Asciano is only of passing interest, except for the surprisingly rich collection of Sienese painting in its **Museo d'Arte Sacra.** Unfortunately, only a portion of the collection, which includes works by Lorenzetti, Simone Martini, Sano di Pietro (1406–1481), and Taddeo di Bartolo, is on display. ⊠ *Next to the Collegiata Sant'Agata,* ☎ *0577/718207.* ⊡ *Free.* ☉ *By appointment only.*

If you do stroll through town, a few other museums are close at hand. Via Mameli leads left from the 13th-century Romanesque-Gothic **Collegiata di Sant'Agata** to the **Galleria Cassioli,** with portraits and drawings by the 19th-century artist Amos Cassioli (1832–1891). ⊠ *Via Mameli 36,* ☎ *no phone.* ⊡ *3,000 lire.* ☉ *May–Sept., Tues.–Sun. 10–12:30 and 4:30–6:30, Oct.–Apr., Tues.–Sun. 10–12:30,*

The **Museo Etrusco** in the close-by ex-church of San Bernardino (same hours as Galleria Cassioli) has relics from the nearby necropolis. ⊠ *Corso Matteotti 46,* ☎ *no phone.* ⊡ *5,000 lire combined ticket includes admission to Galleria Cassioli.* ☉ *May–Sept., Tues.–Sun. 10–12:30 and 4:30–6:30, Oct.–Apr., Tues.–Sun. 10–12:30.*

The local **Pharmacy De Munari** holds the town's most important Roman artifact, a polychrome Roman mosaic, in the basement. ⊠ *Corso*

Matteotti 82, ☎ *0577/718124.* ⌖ *Free.* ☉ *weekdays 9–1 and 4–8, Sat. 9–1.*

Abbazia di Monte Oliveto Maggiore

㉑ *9 km (5½ mi) south of Asciano, 36 km (22 mi) southeast of Siena.*

Monte Oliveto Maggiore, Tuscany's most visited abbey, sits in an oasis of olive and cypress trees amid the harsh landscape of le Crete. It was founded in 1313 by Giovanni Tolomei, a rich Sienese lawyer who, after miraculously regaining his lost sight, changed his name to Bernardo in homage to the saint, and created an order dedicated to the restoration of the founding principles of Benedictine monasticism. The order is named the White Benedictines, after a vision that Bernardo had in which Jesus, Mary, and his own mother were all clad in white, and also as the Olivetans, after the hill where the monastery was built. Famous for maintaining extreme poverty—their feast day meal consisted of two eggs—they slept on straw mats and kept a vow of silence. Although the monks look like they are eating a little better these days and are not afraid to strike up a conversation, the monastery still operates, and most of the area is off limits to visitors. One of Italy's most important book restoration centers is located here, and the monks still produce a wide variety of traditional liqueurs (distilled from herbs that grow on the premises), which are available in the gift shop along with enough food products to fill a pantry, all produced by monks in various parts of Italy.

From the La Torre restaurant (☞ *below*) at the entrance gate, a tree-lined lane leads down to the main group of buildings, with paths leading off to several shrines and chapels dedicated to important saints of the order. The church itself is not particularly memorable, but the exquisite choir stalls (1503) by Fra Giovanni of Bologna are among the finest examples of wood inlay in Italy. Forty-eight of the 125 stalls has inlaid decoration, each set up as a window or arched doorway that opens onto a space (a town, a landscape) or an object (a musical instrument, a bird), rendered in marvellous perspective. Check at the entrance for the schedule of masses, as the monks often chant the liturgy.

In the abbey's main cloister, frescoes by Luca Signorelli and Il Sodoma relate the *Life of St. Benedict,* unusual in its length (36 scenes) as well as the size of each panel. Signorelli began the cycle by painting scenes from the saint's adult life as narrated by St. Gregory the Great, and although his nine scenes are badly worn, the individual expressions are fittingly austere and pensive, full of serenity and religious spirit, and as individualized as those he painted in the San Brizio chapel in the Orvieto Duomo. Later Sodoma filled in the story with scenes from the saint's youth and the last years of his life. The results are also impressive, but here for the use of color and earthier depiction: note the detailed landscapes, the rich costumes and in a few scenes, the animals which Sodoma was known to keep as pets and the scantily clad boys he apparently preferred (for this he was called "the Sodomist" and described by Vasari as "a merry and licentious man . . . of scant chastity"). ✉ *S451 south from Asciano,* ☎ *0577/707611.* ⌖ *Free.* ☉ *Daily 9:15–noon and 3:15–5:45.*

Dining and Lodging

$–$$ ✕ **La Torre.** This pleasant restaurant and café in the massive tower at the abbey's entrance provides more than adequate sustenance for you. The local specialties—served in a cozy dining room in winter or on an attractive terrace under tall cypresses in good weather—include homemade *pici ai funghi* (thick, fat spaghetti with mushroom sauce) or *zuppa* *di funghi* (mushroom soup). The wine list is remarkably good, and the tourist menu is a good value. ⊠ *Entrance of Abbazia di Monte Oliveto Maggiore,* ☎ *0577/707022. AE, DC, MC, V. Closed Tues.*

$$$$ ✕⌘ **Locanda dell'Amorosa.** This "inn" is actually a four-star hotel
★ that occupies the 14th-century stone-and-brick hamlet of Amorosa, in the hills crowning the Val di Chiana, just south of Sinalunga. The stunning setting is matched by the gorgeous buildings, perfectly restored and superbly maintained. A lane lined with cypress trees brings you to the gateway of Amorosa, which still has its tiny little church and a group of farmers' houses for the staff. The bedrooms are handsomely decorated with antiques, the bathrooms seem like little sitting rooms. The restaurant, housed in the old stables, serves both traditional and contemporary dishes (stick to the former). ⊠ *Località Amorosa, Sinalunga, 10 km (6 mi) off the Valdichiana exit of A1,* ☎ *0577/679497,* ℻ *0577/ 632001. 17 rooms. Restaurant, bar. CP. AE, DC, MC, V.*

$$$–$$$$ ✕⌘ **La Chiusa.** This is just the kind of country inn you have been dream-
★ ing about: a beautifully restored farmhouse in nearby Montefollonico, lovingly run by an Italian couple, with first rate service and one of the best restaurants in the area, and best of all, total relaxation. A charming medieval hamlet is on hand should you feel the urge to explore, but the joy here is to eat and rest well. The 14 impeccable rooms are all a bit different, with prices varying accordingly. ⊠ *Via della Madonnina 88, Montefollonico, 53040, 25 km (15 mi) east of the abbey,* ☎ *0577/669668,* ℻ *0577/669593. 14 rooms. Restaurant, bar. CP. AE, DC, MC, V. Closed Dec. and mid-Feb.–mid-Mar.*

$–$$ ⌘ **Fattoria del Colle.** Set amid rolling vineyards and olive trees in Trequanda, 12 km (7 mi) east of Monte Oliveto Maggiore abbey and 8 km (5 mi) west of Sinalunga, is the agriturismo Il Colle, a *fattoria* (farmhouse) that produces fine Chianti and olive oil. The main stone farmhouse, surrounded by six apartments sleeping from two to 14 and a separate house sleeping 22, retains its enormous stone fireplace that warmed hunters centuries ago and a 16th-century family chapel next door. The simple, comfortable apartments have traditional Tuscan wood furniture, some antique, and full kitchens and linens; some have fireplaces. On the pastoral grounds are three pools, a tennis court, and access to hiking and biking trails. The owners, the Cinellis, offer lessons in olive oil and local cuisine, games for children, tastings of the Brunello di Montalcino from their Fattoria del Barbi in Montalcino (☞ Chapter 5), and more. ⊠ *15 km (9 mi) west of the A1, 53020 Trequanda* ☎ *0577/662108,* ℻ *0577/849356. 6 apartments, 1 farmhouse. Restaurant, 3 pools, 1 tennis court, mountain bikes, laundry service. EP.*

Buonconvento

㉒ *9 km (5½ mi) southwest of Abbazia di Monte Oliveto Maggiore, 27 km (17 mi) southeast of Siena.*

Buonconvento reached the height of its importance when it served as a major outpost along the Roman Via Cassia, although it is also remembered by the history books as the place where Holy Roman Emperor Henry VII was poisoned by a Eucharist wafer. Today quiet Buonconvento is worth a stop for a look at its tiny **Museo d'Arte Sacra** (closed for restoration), a two-room picture gallery with more than its fair share of works by Tuscan artists such as Duccio and Andrea di Bartolo. The highlight is a tryptych with the *Madonna and Saints Bernardino and Catherine* by Sano di Pietro. While there, have a look at the well-preserved **Porta Senese,** extra-fortified to make up for the town's lack of natural defenses when it served as the southern gate to Siena, and the handsome **Castello di Bibbiano** (6 km/4 mi to the west; call the tourist office in Siena for opening hours).

OFF THE
BEATEN PATH

MURLO – Instead of going straight back to Siena, stray 9 km (5½ mi) west of the main road (Via Cassia or S2) to Vescovado, and follow the signs from there 2 km (1 mi) south to Murlo, a tiny fortified medieval *borgo* (district) that has been completely restored. It consists of a cluster of houses and an imposing bishop's palace that holds the **Antiquarium Poggio Civitate** named after the nearby site from which most of the Etruscan relics were excavated. Although there are many more beautiful pieces on display, the almost entirely complete roof and pediment from a 5th-century BC Etruscan house is especially rare. ⊠ *Piazza della Cattedrale 4,* ☎ *0577/814099.* ⌷ *5,000 lire.* ☉ *Apr.–Sept., daily 9:30–12:30 and 3–7; July and Aug., daily 9:30–12:30 and 9 PM–11; Mar. and Oct., Tues.–Sun. 9:30–12:30 and 3–5:30; Nov.–Feb., Tues.–Sun. 10–12:30, weekends 10–12:30 and 2:30–5.*

SIENA AND THE HILL TOWNS A TO Z

Arriving and Departing

By Bus

Several buses a day run from between Rome and Siena (2½ hrs). There is frequent service between Florence and Siena (1 hr), Volterra (2 hrs), and San Gimignano (1 hr). **SITA** (☎ 0577/204211 or 0577/204270 in Siena, 055/483651 in Florence) runs from Siena to Florence, stopping in Poggibonsi. From Poggibonsi, **TRAI** (☎ 0577/978949) has service to San Gimignano, Volterra, and Colle di Val d'Elsa.

By Car

The area is easily reached by car on the **A1** Motorway (Autostrada del Sole), which runs between Rome and Florence (exit on S326 for Siena). From Florence, the fastest way to Siena and the hill towns is via the toll road through Poggobonsi. Alternatively, the Strada Chiantigiana (**S222**) is the scenic route through Tuscany's famous wine country.

By Plane

The airports nearest to the region are Pisa's **Aeroporto Galileo Galilei** (☎ 050/500707), Florence's **Peretola** (☎ 055/333498), and Rome's **Fiumicino** (☎ 06/65953640).

By Train

Frequent trains make the 80-minute trip between Florence and Siena. The train station is out of the old city, but cabs are readily available. Train service runs between Siena and Chiusi–Chianciano Terme (where you can make Rome–Florence connections), making many stops (Montepulciano, Sinalunga, and Asciano included). In many cases, bus trips are quicker. All stop in Poggibonsi; from there, buses go on to San Gimignano and Volterra. For **state railway (FS) information,** call (☎ 147/888088) toll-free.

Getting Around

By Bike

Hills pose a greater difficulty than distance, but all the towns are connected by roads that make for good cycling and rewarding panoramas.

By Bus

Buses connect San Gimignano and Volterra with Siena (changes in either Poggibonsi or Colle di Val d'Elsa). There is frequent bus service between Volterra and Colle di Val d'Elsa or Poggibonsi, and limited service between Volterra and San Gimignano. The nearest train station to Volterra is at Saline di Volterra (11 km/6 mi west), but makes for very slow connections to Cecina and the Rome–Pisa rail line along the coast.

By Car

Both the S2 and the A14 go through Monteriggioni and pass just east of Colle; the S68 runs from Colle to Volterra. The S2 runs to Rome and Florence, but it's much faster to go north to Florence via the Siena–Florence superstrada (no number) or down to Rome by taking the S73 east and the S326 toward Sinalunga to pick up the A1, the autostrada connecting Florence and Rome.

By Train

Train service through the region is limited. To and from Siena, trains run north to Poggibonsi and southeast to Sinalunga. Trains run from Chiusi–Chianciano Terme to Siena (1 hour) with stops to Montepulciano, Sinalunga, and Asciano. For state railway (FS) information, call (☎ 147/888088) toll-free.

Contacts and Resources

Agritourist Agencies

☞ Chapter 2.

Car Rentals

Siena: Avis (⊠ Via Simone Martini 36, ☎ 0577/270305). **General Car** (⊠ Viale Toselli 20, ☎ 0577/40518). **Hertz** (⊠ Viale Sardegna 37, ☎ 0577/45085).

Emergencies

In an **emergency,** dial 113 for paramedics, police, or the fire department.

Guided Tours

From Florence, **American Express** (⊠ Via Guicciardini 49/r, ☎ 055/288751) operates one-day excursions to Siena and San Gimignano. **CIT** (⊠ Via Cavour 56, ☎ 055/294306) has a three-day Carosello bus tour from Rome to Florence, Siena, and San Gimignano.

Late-Night Pharmacies

Pharmacies take turns staying open late or on Sunday; for the latest information, consult the list posted outside each pharmacy, or ask at the local tourist office.

Travel Agencies

Siena: Palio Viaggi (⊠ Piazza Gramsci 7, ☎ 0577/280828). **Balsina** (⊠ Via Montanini 73, ☎ 0577/285013). **Cotus** (⊠ Via Camollia 3, ☎ 0577/282011).

San Gimignano: Mundi Travel (⊠ Via San Matteo 74, ☎ 0577/940827). **Volterra: Pro-Volterra** (⊠ Piazza Priori, ☎ 0588/86150). **Atuv Viaggi** (⊠ Piazza Martiri della Libertà, ☎ 0588/86333).

Villa Rentals

Property International (⊠ Viale Aventino 79, 00153 Rome, ☎ 06/5743182) handles rentals of Tuscan villas. **Laura Cresti** (☎ 0577/282280 or 0330/750760), president of the local consortium of agriturismo operators, may also be of help in locating a rental.

Visitor Information

Asciano (⊠ Corso Matteotti 18, ☎ 0577/719510). **Buonconvento** (⊠ Via Soccini 32, ☎ 0577/806012). **Colle di Val d'Elsa** (⊠ Via Campana 18, ☎ 0577/920015). **Monteriggioni** (⊠ Strada Cassia 4, Località Colonna, ☎ 0577/304810). **San Gimignano** (⊠ Piazza del Duomo 1, ☎ 0577/940008). **Siena** (⊠ Piazza del Campo 56, ☎ 0577/280551). **Sinalunga** (⊠ Piazza Giuseppe Garibaldi 43, ☎ 0577/630364). **Volterra** (⊠ Via Turazza 2, ☎ 0588/86150).

7 Arezzo, Cortona, and Southern Tuscany

Antique architecture and artisan trades come together in a setting that's charming and off the beaten path. After touring perfect Pienza and the Val d'Orcia, lose yourself in the steep backstreets of Cortona, where local women hang out the wash, or peruse the monthly antiques fair in frescoed Arezzo. Rugged terrain marks the romantic, rough shores of Elba and Giglio and the crags of Monte Amiata.

SOUTHERN TUSCANY IS AS DIVERSE AS ITALY ITSELF, ranging from the cool mountain enclaves of Monte Amiata to the sandy beaches at Punta Ala. It contains the wildest parts of Tuscany—Maremma, once a malaria-ridden swampland where *butteri,* Italy's cowboys, rounded up their cattle, now a peaceful woodland fringed with beaches; Monte Amiata, a scruffy mountain landscape where goats gnaw at clumps of brown grass among scattered rocks; and the still-wild islands of Elba and Giglio. Some of Tuscany's best-kept secrets lie here in the south, among them the Abbazia di San Galgano, with its roof open to the sky, and the town of Pienza, built in just three years as Pope Pius II's dream town. This is Etruscan country, where the necropolis near Sovana hints at the mysterious pre-Roman civilization.

The lovely hill towns of Arezzo and Cortona carry on age-old local traditions—each September Arezzo's beautiful Franciscan, Gothic, and Romanesque churches are enlivened by the Giostra del Saracino, a costumed medieval joust. Since ancient times, Arezzo has been home to important artists: from the Etruscan potters who produced those fiery-red vessels to the poet Petrarch and Giorgio Vasari, writer, architect, and painter. Fine examples of the work of native painter Luca Signorelli are preserved in Cortona.

The road between San Quirico d'Orcia and Pienza, above the Val d'Orcia, lies along views of quintessential Tuscany: round, green knolls topped by a single stone house and a cluster of cypresses. In the region's deep south, near Saturnia and Sorano, the earth is pocked with gurgling hot springs, sulfur-smelling thermal baths, and natural geysers. The poppy or sunflower seasons in late spring and summer blanket the lands in vibrant colors, deepened by a backdrop of blue skies, earthy ochre hills, and emerald valleys.

Pleasures and Pastimes

Beaches
Though most Tuscan beaches are crowded in summer, this region offers wilder sandy beaches, such as those in the Parco dell'Uccellino, as well as cute and colorful old rocky ports reminiscent of Portofino (you can find these around Monte Argentario, as well as on Elba and Giglio).

Dining
Tuscan specialties and wines can be savored everywhere in this region. Traditional dishes are based around porcini mushrooms and game such as hare, rabbit, and *cinghiale* (wild boar). The Val d'Orcia has its own special pasta called *pici* (short, thick spaghetti) served with a tomato sauce, sometimes thickened with wild boar. On the coast and islands, you can feast on a bounty of delectably fresh seafood.

CATEGORY	COST*
$$$$	over 110,000 lire
$$$	60,000 lire–110,000 lire
$$	35,000 lire–60,000 lire
$	under 35,000 lire

Prices are per person, for a three course meal, house wine and tax included.

Lodging
Southern Tuscany is a great place to enjoy the *agriturismo* lifestyle, but here you will also find hotels: modern affairs in cities, surfside beach resorts, and stately, time-worn villas. For budget travelers, there are

nice, upscale campgrounds in the Punta Ala area. If you have a week to stay in a farmhouse, pick someplace central, such as Pienza, and explore the region from that base. It may be so relaxing and the food so good that you'll have trouble wandering away.

CATEGORY	COST*
$$$$	over 350,000 lire
$$$	220,000 lire–350,000 lire
$$	100,000 lire–220,000 lire
$	under 100,000 lire

Prices are for a double room for two, tax and service included.

Thermal Baths

Southern Tuscany is spotted with smokelike clouds of steam billowing out of natural geysers in the earth. There are also several outdoor naturally heated pools that smell of sulfur but are reputed to be therapeutic. Saturnia is the most famous; others are Venturina, near Piombino; Galleraie, near Montieri; Bagno Vignoni, near San Quirico d'Orcia; and Chianciano Terme, near Chiusi and not far from Lago Trasimeno in neighboring Umbria. But be aware that the baths can be crowded in summer.

Exploring Arezzo, Cortona, and Southern Tuscany

You can visit the whole region in about five days. This vast area can also be explored in bits and pieces, combined with visits to Chianti, the hill towns, and Umbria. Keep in mind that Southern Tuscany isn't well served by trains, so if you aren't renting a car you'll have to plan around sometimes difficult bus schedules, and the going will be slow.

Great Itineraries

Numbers in the text correspond to numbers in the margin and on the Arezzo, Cortona, and Southern Tuscany and Arezzo maps.

IF YOU HAVE 3 DAYS

Visit 🖼 **Arezzo** ①–⑦ and 🖼 **Cortona** ⑧–⑰ the first day, and stay overnight in Cortona. In the morning, head down to **Chiusi** ⑱, and wend your way along the Val d'Orcia to **Chianciano Terme** ⑲, 🖼 **Pienza** ⑳, stopping for lunch, **San Quirico d'Orcia** ㉑, and the **Abbazia di Sant'Antimo** ㉒. On your way, you can drop in on Montepulciano and Montalcino if you haven't already (☞ Chapter 5). Stay overnight in the Pienza or Montalcino (☞ Chapter 5) areas. The next day, head south to 🖼 **Pitigliano** ㉖ or 🖼 **Saturnia** ㉕, being sure to visit **Sovana** ㉗ and **Sorano** ㉘ too.

Alternatively, from Siena head southwest to the 🖼 **Abbazia di San Galgano** ㉙. Then make your way over to **Massa Marittima** ㉚ and spend the night there. The next day, visit the island of 🖼 **Elba** ㉛, taking the ferry from Piombino. On your third day, head south for **Monte Argentario** ㊱, seeing Porto Ercole and Porto Santo Stefano, where you can take a ferry to the island of 🖼 **Giglio** ㊲.

IF YOU HAVE 5 DAYS

Start your trip visiting 🖼 **Arezzo** ①–⑦ and 🖼 **Cortona** ⑧–⑰, overnighting in Cortona. On the second day, drive either north of Arezzo to the sunflower-blanketed Casentino or south to 🖼 **Pienza** ⑳, **San Quirico d'Orcia** ㉑, and the other towns in the Val d'Orcia. On day three, wander up **Monte Amiata** ㉔ and down to 🖼 **Pitigliano** ㉖, where you can spend the night. On day four, head west to **Monte Argentario** ㊱ and visit the island of 🖼 **Giglio** ㊲. Head back towards Siena on day five, taking time out to visit the 🖼 **Abbazia di San Galgano** ㉙ and the hill towns around it.

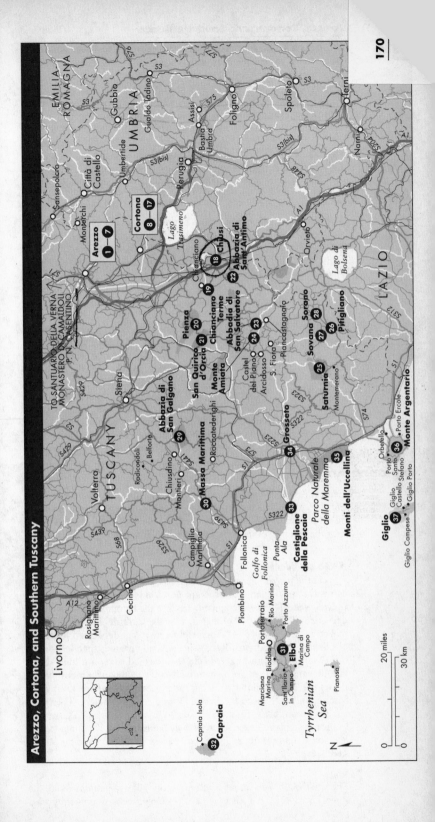

Arezzo, Cortona, and Southern Tuscany

When to Tour Arezzo, Cortona, and Southern Tuscany

Be prepared for steamy heat in the region in July and August. Coastal areas get crowded during this time, when Italians move en masse to their beach homes, especially in August. On the other hand, if you visit Southern Tuscany in July you'll see a spectacular explosion of sunflowers, creating an effect of blue sky over bright yellow fields. Spring and fall are the nicest seasons for southern sojourns, with relatively few tourists and pleasant temperatures, but beware of possible rainy seasons, especially in November and April. Winter can be fairly cold, and in the hilly areas near Umbria and especially Monte Amiata, it's freezing.

AREZZO

The birthplace of the poet Petrarch, the Renaissance artist and art historian Giorgio Vasari, and of Guido d'Arezzo, the inventor of musical notation, Arezzo is today best known for the magnificent, but very faint, Piero della Francesca frescoes in the church of San Francesco. Arezzo dates from pre-Etruscan times, when around 1000 BC the first settlers—who continue to puzzle scholars today—erected a cluster of huts. Arezzo thrived as an Etruscan capital from the 7th to the 4th centuries BC and was one of the most important cities in the Etruscans' anti-Roman 12-city Dodecapolis federation, resisting Rome's rule to the last. The city eventually fell, and in turn flourished under Roman rule. In 1248, Guglielmino degli Ubertini, a member of the powerful Ghibelline family, was elected bishop of Arezzo. This sent the city headlong into the enduring conflict between the Ghibellines (pro-emperor) and the Guelphs (pro-pope). In 1289, Florentine Guelphs defeated Arezzo in a famous battle. Among the Florentine soldiers was Dante Alighieri (1265–1321), who often referred to Arezzo in his *Divine Comedy*. Guelph-Ghibelline wars continued to plague Arezzo until the end of the 14th century, when Arezzo lost its independence to Florence.

Exploring Arezzo

Central Arezzo is pretty small, and you'll be able to explore it in a few hours, adding time to linger for some window shopping at Arezzo's many antiques shops. It's best to look for parking at the top of Arezzo, near the Duomo; otherwise, you'll have to park pretty far from the historic center of town.

A Good Walk

Start at the top of Arezzo with a visit to the **Duomo** ①. From here you can walk up Via San Domenico to **San Domenico** ② and the **Casa di Giorgio Vasari** ③. Retracing your steps to the Duomo, walk down Via dell'Orto off Piazza della Libertà, past the Casa del Petrarca (House of Petrarch, 1304–1374). Turn right down Via dei Pileati (note the old library covered with Renaissance family crests), then left under the Vasari loggia, and into **Piazza Grande** ④. Lovely antiques shops line this spacious square, which is also the center of a monthly antiques fair and an annual jousting event. Leave the square, taking Via Seteria, and visit **Santa Maria della Pieve** ⑤ on your right. Then turn left on Corso Italia, right on Via Cavour, and walk past Piazza San Francesco, visiting the church of **San Francesco** ⑥. If your taste for artifacts is not yet satiated, head to the lower part of town to the **Museo Archeologico** ⑦.

TIMING

The walk itself takes about a half hour, but allow a half day to see the sights and the city at a leisurely pace, and to squeeze in some shopping.

Sights to See

❸ Casa di Giorgio Vasari (Giorgio Vasari House). Giorgio Vasari (1511–1574), the region's leading Mannerist artist, art historian, and critic, designed and decorated the house after he bought it in 1540 for his own use. He may never have spent much time in the house, since he and his wife moved to Florence in 1554. Today the building houses archives on Vasari, and underwhelming works by the artist and his peers are on view. In the first room, which Vasari called the "Triumph of Virtue Room," a richly ornamented wooden ceiling shows Virtue combatting Envy and Fortune in a central octagon. Frescoes on the walls depict, among other things, Extravagance, Charity, the Fire of Troy, and a panorama of a Rome cow field. ⊠ *Via XX Settembre 55,* ☎ *0575/300301.* ☜ *Free.* ☉ *Mon.–Sat. 9–7, Sun. 9–1.*

❶ Duomo. Arezzo's medieval cathedral at the top of the hill contains an eye-level fresco of a tender *Magdalen* by Piero della Francesca (1420–1492); look for it in the north aisle next to the large marble tomb near the organ. Construction of the Duomo began in 1278, but twice came to a halt, and the church wasn't completed until 1510. The facade, designed by Arezzo's Dante Viviani, was added as late as 1900–1914. ⊠ *Via Ricasoli,* ☎ *0575/23991.* ☜ *Free.* ☉ *Daily 7–12:30 and 3–6:30.*

❼ Museo Archeologico. The Archaeological Museum, on the south side of Arezzo in the **Convento di San Bernardo,** just outside the Roman amphitheater, exhibits a fine collection of Etruscan bronzes. ⊠ *Via Margaritone 10,* ☎ *0575/20882.* ☜ *8,000 lire.* ☉ *Mon.–Sat. 9–2, Sun. 9–1.*

❹ Piazza Grande. With its irregular shape and sloping brick pavement, framed by buildings of assorted centuries, Arezzo's central piazza echoes Siena's Piazza del Campo. Though not so grand, it is lively enough during the outdoor antiques fair the first Sunday of the month and when the **Giostra del Saracino** (Joust of the Saracen), featuring medieval costumes and competition, is held here on the first Sunday of September.

❷ San Domenico. Just inside the northern city walls, the church was begun by Dominican monks in 1275 and completed in the 14th century. The walls were once completely frescoed and decorated with niches and chapels. Very little remains of the original works: a famous 13th-century crucifix by Cimabue (circa 1240–1302), a chapel, frescoes by Spinello (1350–1410) and Parri di Spinello and some 14th- and 15th-century paintings. ⊠ *Piazza Fossombroni, Piazza San Domenico,* ☎ *0575/22906.* ☜ *Free.* ☉ *Daily 7–1 and 3:30–6.*

★ ❻ San Francesco. The famous Piero della Francesca frescoes depicting *The Legend of the True Cross* (1452–1466) were executed on three walls of the choir of this 14th-century church. What Sir Kenneth Clark called "the most perfect morning light in all Renaissance painting" may be seen in the lowest section of the right wall, where the troops of the Emperor Maxentius flee before the sign of the cross. Unfortunately, part of the frescoes might still be hidden from view while restoration work takes place. ⊠ *Via Cavour, Piazza San Francesco,* ☎ *0575/20630.* ☜ *Free.* ☉ *Daily 2–7.*

NEED A BREAK? | The old-fashioned looking **Pasticceria Carraturo** (⊠ Corner of Corso Italia and Via Cavour, ☎ 0575/355757) has scrumptious pastries and cappuccinos, plus a tiny restaurant in the back.

❺ Santa Maria della Pieve (Saint Mary of the Parish). The curving, tiered apse on Piazza Grande belongs to one of Tuscany's finest Romanesque churches. Santa Maria della Pieve was originally a Paleo-Christian church built on the remains of an old Roman temple. It was redone in

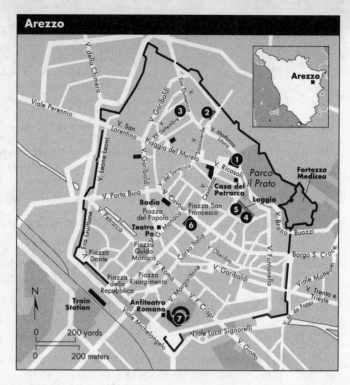

Romanesque style in the 12th century. The facade is original, dating back
from the early 13th century, but includes granite columns from the Roman
period. Inside, frescoes by Piero della Francesca, Lorenzo Ghiberti
(circa 1378–1455), and Pietro Lorenzetti (circa 1290–1348) were sadly
lost in the 16th, 17th, and 18th centuries. To the left of the altar, there
is a 16th-century Episcopal throne by Vasari. ⊠ *Via dei Pileati, end of
Corso Italia,* ☎ *0575/377678.* ⊠ *Free.* ☉ *Daily 8–1 and 3–7.*

Dining and Lodging

$$ ✕ **Buca di San Francesco.** A frescoed cellar restaurant in a historic build-
ing next to the church of San Francesco, this *buca* (literally "hole,"
figuratively "cellar") has a medieval atmosphere and serves straight-
forward local specialties, including *ribollita* (a thick soup of white beans,
bread, cabbage, and onions). Meat eaters will find the lean Chianina
beef and the *saporita di Bonconte* (a selection of several meats) suc-
culent treats. The owner says he'll give a free gift to those who come
with this guide in hand. ⊠ *Piazza San Francesco 1,* ☎ *0575/23271.
AE, DC, MC, V. Closed Tues. and 2 wks in July. No dinner Mon.*

$$ ✕ **Tastevin.** Tastevin has introduced creative cooking—penne Tastevin
(with cream of truffles) and seafood or meat carpaccio—to Arezzo, but
also remains true to tradition. Two of the dining rooms are done in a
warm provincial Tuscan style, one in more sophisticated bistro style.
At the small bar the talented owner plays and sings Sinatra and show
tunes, for which a 15% cover charge will appear on the *conto* (bill).
⊠ *Via dei Cenci 9, near San Francesco and Piazza Guido Monaco,* ☎
*0575/28304. AE, MC, V. Closed Sun. (except the 1st Sun. of every
month) and Aug. 1–20.*

$ ✕ **L'Agania.** The main reason for coming to this central *osteria* (up-
scale tavern), with plain wood paneling and rather cheap furniture, is
the good food for less. Its specialties include boar meat, roasted or grilled

as a second course and in a savory sauce with pasta. Also try the tasty *griffi* (veal cheek) with tomatoes and spices. ⊠ *Via Mazzini 10,* ☎ *0575/ 295381. AE, DC, MC, V. Closed Mon. and 2nd wk June.*

$$ 🏨 **Castello di Gargonza.** Enchantment reigns at this tiny 13th-century hamlet, with a castle, church, and cobbled streets, in the countryside near Monte San Savino. It is part of the fiefdom of the aristocratic Florentine Guicciardinis, restored by the modern Count Roberto Guicciardini as a way to rescue a dying village. Rooms are taken for a minimum of three nights. Cottages and apartments are for rent by the week; they have one to six rooms each, sleep two to seven people, and have as many as four baths. La Torre restaurant (closed Tuesday) serves solid local fare. ⊠ *Monte San Savino, 22 km (14 mi) southwest of Arezzo, 52100,* ☎ *0575/847021,* FAX *0575/847054. 7 rooms, 25 cottages and apartments. Restaurant, pool. CP. AE, DC, MC, V. Closed Jan. 10–31 and Nov.*

$$ 🏨 **Continental.** Centrally located near the train station and within walking distance of all major sights, the Continental has been a reliable and convenient place to stay since it opened in the 1950s. Bright white furnishings with yellow accents are throughout; gleaming bathrooms complete with hair dryers, air-conditioning (in most rooms), and a pleasant roof garden are welcome pluses. Breakfast is extra. ⊠ *Piazza Guido Monaco 7, 52100,* ☎ *0575/20251,* FAX *0575/350485. 74 rooms. CP. AE, DC, MC, V.*

Outdoor Activities and Sports

Horseback Riding

A well-reputed outfit is **Etruria Ippo Trekking** (⊠ Via Michelangelo da Caravaggio 34–36, just behind Piazza Giotto, Arezzo, ☎ 0575/ 300417).

Shopping

The first Sunday of each month, a colorful flea market selling antiques and not-so-antiques takes place in the **Piazza Grande.**

Antiques

La Belle Epoque (⊠ Piazza San Francesco 18, ☎ 0575/355495) collects antique lace and embroidered linens. For fine antique furniture and jewelery, peruse the objects at **La Nuova Chimera** (⊠ Via San Francesco 18, ☎ 0575/350155). **Grace Gallery** (⊠ Via Cavour 30, ☎ 0575/354963) deals in antique furniture and paintings. **Alma Bardi Antichità** (⊠ Corso Italia 97, ☎ 0575/20640) specializes in antique silver and jewelry.

Gold

Gold production here is on an industrial scale. **Uno-A-Erre** is the biggest of several factories. Big-time baubles can be purchased on a small scale in town center. For gold jewelry set with precious or semiprecious stones, try **Il Diamante** (⊠ Via Guido Monaco 69), **Borghini** (⊠ Corso Italia 126), **Prosperi** (⊠ Corso Italia 76), or **Aurea Monilia** (⊠ Piazza San Francesco 15).

Knitwear

A cottage knitwear industry is burgeoning in Arezzo. For sweaters, try **Maglierie** (⊠ Piazza Grande).

THE CASENTINO

East of Florence and north of Arezzo is the Casentino, a virtually unknown area of Tuscany that holds hidden treasures. In 1289 Dante fought here in the battle that ended the centuries-long struggle between the

Guelphs and the Ghibellines (the site of the battle—the Plain of Campaldino—is marked today by a column outside Poppi at the crossing of the S70 and the road to Stia). Later, exiled from Florence, he returned, traveling from castle to castle, and recorded his love of the countryside in passages throughout the *Divine Comedy*.

The sparsely populated region—defined as the upper valley of the Arno, which arises here as a spring on Mt. Falterona—contains enough castles and Romanesque parish churches and unspoiled villages to keep you happily exploring for days. But the jewels in its crown are contained within the Parco Nazionale Casentino, an 89,000-acre preserve of great beauty. The heart of the park, on an Apennine ridge between the Arno and the Tiber and straddling Tuscany and Emilia-Romagna, is the antique forest tended as a religious duty for eight centuries by the monks of the Abbazia Camaldoli, designers of the world's first forestry code. The result of their intelligent and diligent husbandry, which included planting 4,000–5,000 saplings every year, is that large tracts of original growth forest remain, and the whole preserve is probably more beautiful than ever. While they began by maintaining the mix of silver firs and beeches, eventually they planted only firs, creating vast, majestic stands of the deep green trees whose 150-ft-tall, straight black trunks were once floated down the Arno to be used for the tallest masts of warships.

Parco Nazionale Casentino

Pratovecchio 55 km (34 mi) north of Arezzo.

A drive through the park, especially on the very winding 34-km (21-mi) road between the Monastero di Camaldoli and Santuario della Verna, passing through the lovely abbey town of Badia Prataglia, reveals one satisfying vista after another, from walls of firs to velvety pillows of pastureland where sheep or white cattle may be spied picturesquely grazing. In autumn, the beeches add a mass of red-brown to the multigreen palate, and in spring, torrents of bright golden broom pour off the hillsides with a profusion and a fragrance that you're not likely to forget. Walking the forests—which also include sycamore, lime, maple, ash, elm, oak, hornbeam, and chestnut trees, and are laced with abundant brooks and impressive waterfalls—is the best way to see some of the wilder creatures, from deer and mouflon (wild sheep imported from Sardinia in 1872 and later) to eagles and many other birds, as well as 1,000 species of flora, including many rare and endangered ones and an orchid found nowhere else. *Headquarters,* ⊠ *Via Brocchi 7, 52015 Pratovecchio,* ☎ *0575/50301,* ℻ *0575/504497.*

Outdoor Activities and Sports
HIKING

The **Great Apennine Excursion** (GEA) hiking route runs along the winding ridge, and the park (☞ *above*) organizes theme walks in summer and provides English-speaking guides anytime with advance notice.

Monastero di Camaldoli

20 km (12 mi) east of Pratovecchio, 55 km (34 mi) north of Arezzo.

In 1012, St. Romualdo, scion of a noble Ravenna family, came upon the forests of the Casentino and found their remoteness, their beauty, and their silence conducive to religious contemplation. There he stayed to found a hermitage, Monastero Camaldoli (named for Count Maldoli, who donated the land), that became the motherhouse of a new, reformed Benedictine order, which, four centuries after its founding by St. Benedict, Romualdo felt had become too permissive. An important basis of the order was preserving the atmosphere of the place: "If the hermits are to be true devotees of solitude, they must take the greatest care of the woods." When the flow of pilgrims began to threaten that solitude, Romualdo had a monastery and hospital built 1 km (2 mi) down the mountain to create some distance. Today the hermitage, **Sacro Eremo di Camaldoli**—where the monks live in complete silence in 20 separate little cottages, each with its own walled garden—can be seen through gates, and the church and original cell of Romualdo, the model for all the others, can be visited. The church, rebuilt in the 13th century and transformed in the 18th to its present appearance, strikes an odd note in connection with such an austere order and the simplicity of the hermits' cells, because it is done up in the gaudy Baroque style, complete with gilt cherubs and frescoed vault. Its most appealing artwork is the glazed terra-cotta relief *Madonna and Child with Saints* (including a large figure of Romualdo and a medallion of his fight with the devil) by Andrea della Robbia.

In the monastery complex, the church (rebuilt repeatedly) features 14th-century frescoes by Spinello Aretino, seven 15th-century Mannerist paintings on wood by Giorgio Vasari, and a quietly lovely monastic choir with 18th-century walnut stalls, more Vasari paintings, and a serene fresco (by Santi Pacini) of St. Romualdo instructing his white-robed disciples. In a hospital built for sick villagers in 1046 is the 1543 **Antica Farmacia**, complete with original carved walnut cabinets. Here you can buy herbal teas and infusions, liqueurs, honey products, and natural toiletries made by the monks from the old recipes as part of their daily routine balancing prayer, work, and study (the monastery is entirely self-supporting). In the back room is an exhibit of the early pharmacy's alembics, mortars, and other equipment with which they made herbs into medicines. In accordance with the Benedictine rule, simple rooms ($ with meals) are available in the *foresteria* (guesthouse) for people of any faiths seeking "spiritual nourishment." ⊠ *S71 to Serravalle then follow signs, 52010 Camaldoli,* ☏ *Monastero: 0575/ 556012; Foresteria Monastero: 0575/556013,* ☎ *0575/556001.* ⊠ *Free.* ☉ *Daily 9–1 and 3:30–6.*

Santuario della Verna

34 km (21 mi) southeast of Monastero di Camaldoli, 65 km (40 mi) north of Arezzo.

A hill or two away, dramatically perched atop a sheer-walled rock surrounded by firs and beeches, is the monastery of La Verna, founded by St. Francis in 1214 on land given to him by a count who heard him speak and was moved by his holiness. Ten years later, after a 40-day fast, St. Francis—who had dedicated his life to following as closely as possible in Christ's footsteps—had a vision of Him on the cross, and when it passed, he was marked with the stigmata. As Dante rendered it: "On the crag between Tiber and Arno then, in tears of love and joy, he took Christ's final seal, the holy wounds." A stone in the floor of the 1263 Chapel of the Stigmata marks the spot, and the Chapel of the Relics in the basilica contains a cloth stained with the blood that issued from his wounds. A covered corridor through which the monks pass, chanting, in a solemn procession each afternoon at 3 PM on the way to mass is lined with simple frescoes of the *Life of St. Francis* by a late 17th-century Franciscan. The true artistic treasures of the place, though, are 15 della Robbia glazed terra-cottas, including some of the finest works of Andrea, the most talented of his family. Some were commissioned, like the huge *Crucifixion* scene in the Chapel of the Stigmata; others have been donated through the centuries by the faithful.

Most, like a heartbreakingly beautiful *Annunciation,* are in the 14th-to 15th-century basilica, whose 5,000-pipe organ sings out joyously at masses.

There are several chapels, each with its own story, to visit, as well as some natural and spiritual wonders. A walkway along the edge of the cliff leads to the indentation in the rock said to have miraculously melted away to receive St. Francis's body when the devil tried to hurl him off the precipice, 230 ft above the valley below. Most touching are the enormous Projecting Rock, detached on three sides and surrounded with mossy rocks and trees, where St. Francis would meditate; and St. Francis's Bed, a slab of rock in a cold, damp cave with an iron grate on which he prayed, did penance, and sometimes slept. A 40-minute walk through the woods to the top of Mt. Penna passes some religious sites and ends in panoramic views of the Arno Valley, but those from the wide, cliff-edge terrace are equally impressive, including the tower of the castle in Poppi, the Prato Magno (great meadow), the olive groves and vineyards on the lower slopes, and a changing skyscape that seems to echo the mystical feel of the monastery and the woods that surround it. Santuario della Verna's foresteria also offers travelers simple but comfortable rooms with or without bath. A restaurant with basic fare is open to the public, and a shop sells souvenirs and the handiworks of the monks. ✉ *S208 east from Bibbiena; Santuario della Verna, 52010 Chiusi della Verna* ☎ *0575/5341 and 534211,* FAX *0575/599320.* ✉ *Free.* ☉ *Daily 9–1 and 3–6.*

As you leave La Verna, be glad you needn't do it as Edith Wharton (1862–1937) did on a 1912 visit during a drive across the Casentino. As she wrote, her car "had to be let down on ropes to a point about ¾ of a mile below the monastery, Cook steering down the vertical descent, and twenty men hanging on to a funa that, thank the Lord, didn't break."

Lodging

$–$$ Fattoria di Celli. For less austere lodgings than those the monasteries provide, this former *fattoria*—a farm where owners and workers lived side by side—is a great choice. Set on a gentle rise in the countryside outside the castle town of Poppi, it is a tranquil place with wide lawns sprinkled with flowers and good modern sculptures for a sculpture-garden effect, play areas for children with swings and climbing things, and picnic tables placed to appreciate distant views of the mountains. Best of all are the beautifully situated and landscaped pools. Apartments, which sleep two to eight, have working fireplaces and are cozily done up, preserving the old farmhouses in details like stone walls left uncovered in some bedrooms. The villas, independent restored farmhouses with private gardens, accommodate four to six. In July and August, rentals are only by the week (Sat.–Sat.). (The owners also have another, similar property, the Fattoria di Corsignano, not far away, with 10 fireplaced apartments and houses, better views, and fields with sheep and sunflowers, but no sculpture.) ✉ *52013 Poppi,* ☎ *0335/6056104 or 0575/529917,* FAX *0575/500191. 10 apartments, 3 villas. 2 pools, tennis court, basketball. EP. No credit cards.*

CORTONA

Magnificently situated, with olives and vineyards creeping up to its walls, one of Tuscany's prettiest villages commands sweeping views over Lake Trasimeno and the plain of the Valdichiana. Its two fine galleries and scattering of churches are blessedly free of tourists; its delightful medieval streets are a pleasure to wander for their own sake.

Cortona may be one of Italy's oldest towns—"Mother of Troy and Grandmother of Rome" in popular speech. Tradition claims that it was founded by Dardanus, the founder of Troy (after whom the Dardanelles are named). He was fighting a local tribe, so the story goes, when he lost his helmet (*corythos* in Greek) on Cortona's hill. In time a town grew up that took its name (Corito) from the missing headgear. By the 4th century BC the Etruscans had built the first set of town walls, whose cyclopean traces can still be seen in the 3-km (2-mi) sweep of the present fortifications. As a member of the Etruscans' 12-city Dodecapolis, it became one of the federation's leading northern cities. An important consular road, the Via Cassia, which passed the foot of its hill, maintained the town's importance under the Romans. Medieval fortunes waned, however, as the plain below reverted to marsh. After holding out against neighbors like Perugia, Arezzo, and Siena, the *comune* was captured by King Ladislas of Naples in 1409 and sold to the Florentines two years later.

Exploring Cortona

Cortona is very steep and it's easy to get winded. Take it slowly and stop frequently to visit sights and for a gelato.

A Good Tour

Start in Piazza della Repubblica, Cortona's heart, where the **Palazzo Comunale** ⑧ stands. Move on to the adjacent Piazza Signorelli, and stroll into the courtyard of the picturesque **Palazzo Pretorio** ⑨, which houses the Museo dell'Accademia Etrusca and its important collection of Etruscan bronzes. Across Via Casali is the Teatro Signorelli; walk north on Via Casali towards the Piazza del Duomo and the **Duomo** ⑩, pinned against the city wall. Visit the Duomo, built in Florentine Renaissance style, and the **Museo Diocesano** ⑪ opposite. Then walk past the **Chiesa del Gesù** ⑫ down Via Jannelli and turn left on Via Roma to head back to Piazza della Repubblica. From Piazza della Repubblica, if you're in shape for another climb and have the time, head behind the Palazzo del Capitano del Popolo up into Via Santucci to the 13th-century church of **San Francesco** ⑬ (at press time closed for restoration) and the 1441 Ospedale di Santa Maria della Misericordia. From Piazza San Francesco climb up the steep Via Berrettini, turn right on Via San Marco, and walk until you get to the church of **San Niccolò** ⑭. From there, it's just a little farther along Via Santissima Trinità to Via Santa Margherita, the road on the edge of town that leads all the way to the church of **Santa Margherita** ⑮ and the Fortezza Medicea behind it. On your way back, complete the circle by taking Via Santa Croce to the church of **San Cristoforo** ⑯, and pass by the convent of Santa Chiara on your way back down Via Berrettini. The 3-km (2-mi) drive downhill along Via Guelfa to the fine Renaissance **Santa Maria delle Grazie al Calcinaio** ⑰, a church dedicated to medieval tanners, could well be your most rewarding stop in Cortona. You could also see the church on your way in or out of the city.

TIMING

It takes about an hour to complete the tour as far as San Niccolò, which does not include the detours to Santa Margherita and Santa Maria delle Grazie al Calcinaio. The whole tour, adding time to see the sights, takes the good part of a day.

Sights to See

⑫ **Chiesa del Gesù.** Below the Museo Diocesano is the Chiesa del Gesù, reachable by descending the 1633 staircase opposite the Duomo. The church was built between 1498 and 1505 and restructured by Giorgio Vasari in 1543. Vasari divided it into two floors and painted the frescoes of the *Transfiguration, Jesus in the Inferno,* and *The Conversion* *of St. Paul.* The upper floor, which used to be the baptistery, is now one of the rooms of the Museo Diocesano. The church houses a crucifix by Pietro Lorenzetti. ⊠ *Piazza del Duomo,* ☎ *0575/62830.* ⊇ *Free.* ⊙ *Daily 9–1 and 3–6:30.*

🔟 **Duomo.** Cortona's cathedral stands on an outside edge of the city, next to what's left of the Etruscan and medieval walls that run from Porta Santa Maria to Porta Colonia. It was built on the site of an old Romanesque church, but the present Renaissance church was begun in 1480 and finished in 1507. An arcade along the outside wall was erected in the 16th century. Inside, the Duomo is a mixture of Renaissance and Baroque styles, with a 14th-century *Pietà* and a Baroque high altar by Francesco Mazzuoli. ⊠ *Piazza del Duomo,* ☎ *0575/603712.* ⊇ *Free.* ⊙ *Daily 8–12 and 3–6:30.*

★ ⑪ **Museo Diocesano** (Diocesan Museum). The museum houses an impressive number of large and splendid paintings by native son Luca Signorelli (1441–1523), as well as a beautiful *Annunciation* by Fra Angelico (1387–1455), a delightful surprise to find in this small town. ⊠ *Piazza del Duomo 1,* ☎ *0575/62830.* ⊇ *5,000 lire.* ⊙ *Apr.–Sept., Tues.–Sun. 9–1 and 3–6:30; Oct.–Mar., Tues.–Sun. 9–1 and 3–5.*

⑧ **Palazzo Comunale.** This edifice on Piazza della Repubblica, with its broad staircase and turreted bell tower, dates from 1241 but was restored and changed substantially in the late 19th century. ⊠ *Piazza della Repubblica.*

⑨ **Palazzo Pretorio.** Wander into the courtyard of the picturesque *palazzo,* also called Palazzo Casali after the family that built and lived in it until 1409. The side of this building that faces Via Casali maintains its 13th-century style, and the front, facing the piazza, was redone in 1608. Today the building houses the Accademia Etrusca with an extensive library, the **La Biblioteca Municipale,** and the **Museo dell'Accademia Etrusca.** Beyond the museum's centuries-old stone staircase is an eclectic mix of Egyptian objects, Etruscan and Roman bronzes and statuettes, and Renaissance-era painters such as Luca Signorelli and Pinturcchio (1454–1513). ⊠ *Piazza Signorelli 9,* ☎ *0575/ 630415.* ⊇ *5,000 lire.* ⊙ *Apr.–Sept., Tues.–Sun. 10–1 and 4–7; Oct.–Mar., Tues.–Sun. 9–1 and 3–5.*

NEED A BREAK? **Caffe degli Artisti** (⊠ Via Nazionale 18, ☎ 0575/601237) is a pleasant place to stop for a cappuccino or snack.

⑯ **San Cristoforo.** In the 12th-century church of St. Christopher is a 14th-century fresco by unknown artists of the Umbro-Sienese school depicting the *Crucifixion,* the *Annunciation,* and the *Ascension.* ⊠ *Piazza San Cristoforo,* ☎ *0575/603741.* ⊇ *Free.* ⊙ *Daily 9–1 and 3–6:30.*

⑬ **San Francesco.** In the early 13th century this Gothic-style church was built on the site of Etruscan and Roman baths. It contains frescoes dating from 1382, a big crucifix by Giuseppe Piamontini of Florence, and the *Relic of Santa Croce,* a crucifix relic brought over from Constantinople in the early 13th century. The church had a beautiful organ, built in 1466, that was almost completely destroyed during World War II. ⊠ *Piazza San Francesco.* ⊇ *Free. Closed for restoration.*

⑭ **San Niccolò.** On the main altar of this delightful, country-style 15th-century Romanesque church is a fresco by Luca Signorelli depicting the *Deposition of Jesus,* painted around 1510. On the left wall is another fresco by Signorelli of the *Madonna and Child,* which was plastered over in 1768 and rediscovered in 1847. ⊠ *Via Santissima Trinità,* ☎ *0575/604591.* ⊇ *Free.* ⊙ *Daily 9–12 and 3–7.*

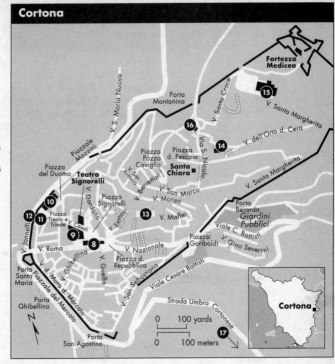

⑮ Santa Margherita. Not as charming as Cortona's other churches from
the outside, the large 19th-century basilica was completed as recently
as 1897. What makes the walk worthwhile, however, is the richly decorated interior. The body of the 13th-century saint, Margherita—
clothed but with skull and bare feet clearly visible—is displayed on the
main altar. ⊠ *Piazzale Santa Margherita,* ☎ *0575/603116.* 🎫 *Free.*
🕙 *Daily 8:30–12 and 3–7.*

★ **⑰ Santa Maria delle Grazie al Calcinaio.** Down the hill, about 3 km (2
mi) from town center, is a Renaissance sanctuary most likely designed
by Sienese architect Francesco di Giorgio Martini (1439–1502) and
built between 1485 and 1514. Legend has it that the image of the
Madonna appeared on a wall of a medieval *calcinaio* (tannery), the
site on which the church was then built. The linear gray-and-white interior recalls the neo-Gothic Duomo in Florence. ⊠ *Località Calcinaia
227,* ☎ *0575/62537.* 🎫 *Free.* 🕙 *Daily 4:30–7.*

Dining and Lodging

$$ ✕ **La Loggetta.** Above Cortona's main medieval square, this attractive
restaurant is housed in a 16th-century wine cellar. In good weather you
can eat outdoors, overlooking the 13th-century town hall, dining on
regional dishes and such specialties as *ravioli gnudi,* "naked ravioli,"
made with spinach and ricotta but without pasta, and *tagliata* (thin
slivers of rare beef). The owners pride themselves on their selection of
Tuscan wines. ⊠ *Piazza Pescheria 3,* ☎ *0575/630575. AE, DC, MC,
V. Closed Nov. 5–20 and Mon. Sept.–June.*

$$ ✕ **Tonino.** It must be host Tonino's own *antipastissimo*—an incredible variety of delectables—that make this large modern establishment
noisy and crowded at times. But it is very satisfactory indeed when not,
when you can enjoy the view of the Chiana valley and savor a Chian-

ina steak. ⊠ *Piazza Garibaldi,* ☎ *0575/630500. AE, DC, MC, V. Closed Tues.*

$$$ ✗🍽 **Il Falconiere.** A charming old villa less than 3½ km (2 mi) outside Cortona, this once belonged to an early 19th-century poet and has been lovingly restored and impeccably furnished in the local style as an upscale inn. The winter garden and terrace have been transformed into a restaurant that features Tuscan dishes and seasonal specialties. The restaurant is closed Monday from November to March. ⊠ *Località San Martino, 52044,* ☎ *0575/612679,* 🖷 *0575/612927. 12 rooms. Restaurant, bar, pool. AE, DC, MC, V. Closed 1st 3 wks in Nov.*

Shopping

For nice ceramics, many depicting the brilliant sunflowers that blanket local fields, go to **Il Cocciaio** (⊠ Via Nazionale 54, ☎ 0575/604405).

PIENZA AND THE VAL D'ORCIA

The Val d'Orcia is a sumptuous green river valley with breathtaking views unfolding over the River Orcia. It's a pleasure to drive through, a good place to get a delicious meal for a reasonable price, and blessedly undiscovered by fellow visitors.

Chiusi

⑱ *2½ km (1½ mi) east of the A1, 67 km (42 mi) south of Arezzo, 84 km (50 mi) southeast of Siena, 126 km (78 mi) southeast of Florence.*

Known for the frescoed tombs that date from the 5th century BC in its necropolis, Chiusi was one of the most powerful of the 12 ancient cities in the Etruscan federation. It's a transportation hub accessible from either the main north–south rail line or by car or bus from the A1 autostrada.

Chianciano Terme

⑲ *11 km (7 mi) northwest of Chiusi, 73 km (44 mi) southeast of Siena, 132 km (79 mi) southeast of Florence.*

The small medieval town of Chianciano, surrounded by walls, has billboards proclaiming that the restorative waters of its *terme* (spa) are indispensable for a *fegato sano* (healthy liver, ☞ Close Up: Terme: Wrath of the Gods, *below*). Outside the old walls is the well-attended, top-of-the-line modern spa, Chianciano Terme, with neat parks and a host of hotels. The spa has grabbed attention away from the old city center, which nevertheless is worth a visit, mainly for its castle, Castello di Chianciano.

Pienza

⑳ *22 km (14 mi) west of Chianciano Terme, 52 km (31 mi) southeast of Siena, 120 km (72 mi) southeast of Florence.*

Pienza owes its appearance to Pope Pius II (1405–1464), who had grand plans to transform his home village of Corsignano—the town's former name—into a compact model Renaissance town. The man entrusted with the transformation was Bernardo Rossellino (1409–1464), a protégé of the great Renaissance architectural theorist Leon Battista Alberti (1404–1474). His mandate was to create a cathedral, a papal palace, and a town hall (plus miscellaneous buildings) that adhered to the vainglorious pope's principles. Gothic and Renaissance styles were fused, and the buildings were decorated with Sienese and Florentine paintings. The net result was a project that expressed Renaissance ideals of art, ar-

chitecture, and civilized good living in a single scheme: It
exquisite example of the architectural canons that Albert
in the early Renaissance and which were utilized by later a
cluding Michelangelo, in designing many of Italy's finest buildings and
piazzas. Today the cool nobility of Pienza's center seems almost surreal
in this otherwise unpretentious village, known locally for *pienzino,*
also called *cacio,* the smooth sheep's-milk pecorino cheese.

Pius II commissioned Rossellino in 1459 to design the perfect palazzo
for his papal court. The architect took Florence's Palazzo Rucellai by
Alberti as a model, and designed the **Palazzo Piccolomini** with exactly
100 rooms. Three sides of the building fit perfectly into the urban plan
around it, while the fourth, looking over the valley, has a beautiful loggia uniting it with the gardens in back. You can visit the papal apartments, including a beautiful library, the Sala delle Armi, with an
impressive weapons collection, and the music room, with its extravagant wooden ceiling forming four letter "P"s, for Pope, Pius, Piccolomini, and Pienza. ⊠ *Piazza Pio II,* ☎ *0578/748503.* ⊠ *Free.* ☉
*June–Oct., Tues.–Sun. 10–12:30 and 4–7 and Nov.–May, Tues.–Sun.
10–12:30 and 3–6.*

The 16th-century **Duomo** was also built by Rossellino under the influence of Alberti. The facade is divided in three parts with Renaissance
arches under the Pope's coat of arms encircled by a wreath of fruit.
Inside, the cathedral is simple but richly decorated with Sienese paintings. But the Duomo wasn't as perfect as it was supposed to be—the
first cracks appeared immediately after the building was completed,
and its foundations have shifted slightly ever since, as rain erodes the
hillside behind. You can see this effect if you look closely at the base
of the first column as you enter the church and compare it with the
last. ⊠ *Piazza Pio II.* ⊠ *Free.* ☉ *June–Oct., Tues.–Sun. 10–12:30
and 4–7; Nov.–May, Tues.–Sun. 10–12:30 and 3–6.*

The **Museo Diocesano** is in the clerical building to your left as you face
the Duomo. It is small, but has a few interesting papal treasures and
rich Flemish tapestries. The most precious piece is a rare mantle woven
in gold with pearls and embroidered religious scenes that belonged to
Pope Pius II. ⊠ *Piazza Pio II,* ☎ *0575/628390.* ☉ *Nov.–May, Tues.–
Sun. 10–12:30 and 3–6, June–Oct., Tues.–Sun. 10–12:30 and 4–7.*

Part of the acclaimed 1996 film *The English Patient* was filmed at
Sant'Anna in Camprena, an abandoned Benedictine monastery in the
open country 7 km (4½ mi) north of Pienza. Il Sodoma (1477–1549)
frescoes can be seen in the common eating areas, along with the room
where the "English Patient" lay in bed. It is best reached by car or bicycle (no public transportation available). ☎ *0578/748303 or Pienza
tourist office (☞ Visitor Information, below).* ⊠ *Free.* ☉ *Easter–mid-
October, Thurs.–Sun. 5 PM–7, or by appointment.*

Dining and Lodging

$ ✕ **La Chiocciola.** This restaurant offers typical Pienza fare, including
the homemade local pasta, pici, with hare or boar sauce, and pienzino
cheese baked in a thin crust. It has a nice summer garden. ⊠ *Via del-
l'Acero 2,* ☎ *0578/748063. No credit cards. Closed Wed. and for about
10 days in mid-Nov.*

$ ✕ **Osteria Sette di Vino.** This tiny restaurant in a pleasant square in
central Pienza is a good place to get a cheap meal with some good wine,
perhaps a savory Brunello di Montalcino. It specializes in dishes with
the local cheeses and a starter of radicchio, quickly baked to just
brown at the edges. ⊠ *Piazza di Spagna 1,* ☎ *0578/749092. No credit
cards. Closed Wed., July 1–15, and Nov.*

$$ ⊞ **Corsignano.** This comfortable, modern hotel is just outside the old city walls. Two light-beige buildings, the older one right on the road, are connected by a hallway in between. The rooms in the newer half of the hotel in the back are quieter, larger, and more recently furnished—all have carpeting except a few in the older front rooms, which have tile floors. Rooms are furnished with plain, modern wood furniture. ⊠ *Via della Madonnina 11, 53026,* ☎ *0578/748501,* FAX *0578/748166. 36 rooms. CP. AE, DC, MC, V.*

$ ⊞ **Camere di Pienza.** This tiny hotel with only four rooms is in a Renaissance building on Pienza's main street. The rooms have particularly nice ceilings—three with wood beams and one with a fresco. ⊠ *Corso Il Rossellino 23, 53026,* ☎ *0578/748500. 4 rooms. EP. No credit cards.*

San Quirico d'Orcia

㉑ *9½ km (5½ mi) southwest of Pienza, 43 km (26 mi) southeast of Siena, 111 km (67 mi) southeast of Florence.*

San Quirico d'Orcia, on the Via Cassia (S2) south from Siena towards Rome, has almost-intact 15th-century walls topped with 14 turrets. The pleasantly crumbling appearance of the town recalls days of yore, and the town is best suited for a stop for a gelato in a local bar or a meal and to see its 13th-century Romanesque **Collegiata** church with its three majestic portals, one possibly the work of Giovanni Pisano (circa 1250–after 1314). Against the walls is the **Horti Leonini,** a public park with Italian-style gardens retaining merely a shimmer of their past opulence. Near it stands **Palazzo Chigi,** named after the family to whom the Medicis gave San Quirico in 1667. Just outside the town are the thermal baths of **Bagno Vignoni** and the **Castello di Vignoni** (Castle of Vignoni), which offers nice views of the valley.

Dining and Lodging

$$ ✕ **La Taverna del Barbarossa.** The Hotel Casanova's restaurant is housed in its own separate typically Tuscan country house dating back to 1800. Its name commemorates a meeting held here in medieval times between papal messengers and Frederick I (circa 1123–90), called Il Barbarossa. The dining rooms have stone arches and wooden beams, and there's a spacious outdoor dining terrace. Special dishes include the *cappelli del prete,* ravioli-like pasta with various sauces to choose from. All dishes are served with excellent Tuscan wines like Brunello di Montalcino and Vino Nobile di Montepulciano. ⊠ *S146 Località Casanova, 53027 San Quirico d'Orcia,* ☎ *0577/898177. AE, DC, MC, V.*

$$ ✕ **Trattoria Al Vecchio Forno.** A meal here is truly delicious. Specialties include dishes accented with porcini mushrooms, such as the excellent mushroom soup, pici with tomato and/or boar sauce, and roast boar and game, all rounded out by the good wine selection. There's a nice garden out back. ⊠ *Via Piazzola, 8,* ☎ *0577/897380. No credit cards. Closed Wed. and for about 10 days in mid-Nov. and 2 wks in mid-Jan.*

$$ ⊞ **Hotel Residence Casanova.** This country hotel is 300 meters from the city walls of San Quirico d'Orcia. It has been converted from a lovely old villa, and has plenty of grounds and views of the Orcia valley. The rooms are nicely decorated in solid Tuscan furniture. The pool is Olympic size, and there are various game rooms and a tennis court. ⊠ *S146 Località Casanova, 53027 San Quirico d'Orcia,* ☎ *0577/898177,* FAX *0577/898190. 11 rooms and 26 junior suites. Restaurant, bar, breakfast room, pool, sauna, tennis court, exercise room, recreation room. CP. AE, DC, MC, V.*

Abbazia di Sant'Antimo

㉒ *20 km (13 mi) southwest of San Quirico d'Orcia, 10 km (6 mi) south of Montalcino, 31 km (19 mi) south of Siena, 100 km (60 mi) south of Florence.*

It's well worth your while to visit this abbey, a 12th-century Romanesque gem of pale stone set in the silvery green of an olive grove. The exterior and interior sculpture is outstanding, particularly the nave capitals, a combination of French, Lombard, and even Spanish influences. The **sacristy** (rarely open) forms part of the primitive Carolingian church (founded in AD 781), its entrance flanked by 9th-century pilasters. The small **vaulted crypt** dates from the same period. Above the nave runs a *matroneum* (women's gallery), an unusual feature once used to separate the congregation. Equally unusual is the ambulatory, whose three radiating chapels (rare in Italian churches) were probably copied from the French model. ⊠ *Castelnuovo dell'Abate,* ☎ *0577/ 835659.* 🎟 *Free.* ☉ *Apr.–Sept., daily 9–noon and 2–7; Oct.–Mar., daily 10–noon and 2–4.*

HEART OF THE SOUTH

Monte Amiata is the wildest part of Tuscany, and once across the mountains the landscape is still full of cliffs, like the one Pitigliano perches on. The deep south offers good wine, especially in Pitigliano, thermal baths at Saturnia, and archaeological wonders, such as the Etruscan necropolis outside Sovana.

Abbadia di San Salvatore

㉓ *41 km (25 mi) southwest of Chiusi, 73 km (44 mi) southeast of Siena, 143 km (86 mi) southeast of Florence.*

This thousand-year-old town has grown into a fairly unattractive mountain town of furniture makers, but its tiny medieval village is still intact. The abbey was rebuilt in the 11th century but retains its 8th-century crypt.

Monte Amiata

㉔ *13½ km (8 mi) west of the Abbadia di San Salvatore, 86½ km (52 mi) southeast of Siena, 156½ km (94 mi) southeast of Florence.*

At 5,702 ft high, the benign volcano Monte Amiata is one of Tuscany's few ski resorts, but it's no match for the Alps or the Dolomites. Its main attraction is a wide-open view of Tuscany. From here, you can meander along panoramic mountaintop roads in your car and visit Castel del Piano, Arcidosso, Santa Flora, and Piancastagnaio, towns dating from the middle ages.

Saturnia

㉕ *47 km (30 mi) south of Monte Amiata, 129 km (77 mi) south of Siena, 199 km (119 mi) south of Florence.*

Etruscan and pre-Etruscan tombs cut into the local rock remain in this town, a lively center in pre-Etruscan times. Today it is known for its hot sulphur thermal baths. There is a modern spa with hotel called **Terme di Saturnia** (☞ Dining and Lodging, *below*), or you can bathe for free at the tiered natural pools of Cascate del Gorello by the road to Montemerano.

According to an oft-repeated local legend, the 3,000-year-old thermal baths were created when Saturn, restless with earth's bickering mor-

TERME: WRATH OF THE GODS

IN A COUNTRY KNOWN FOR MILLEN-NIA as a hotbed of seismic activity, Tuscany seems to have gotten a lucky break. While Campania and Sicily are famous for violent volcanoes, and Umbria and the Marches stand on notoriously shaky ground, Tuscany's underground activity makes itself known in the form of steamy and sulfurous hot springs that have earned the region a name as a spa goer's paradise.

Tuscany is dotted throughout with small *terme,* or thermal baths, whose hot waters flow from natural springs deep under the earth's surface. Since the time of the Etruscans, Tuscany's first rulers, these hot springs have been valued for their curative properties; the Romans, in their turn, attributed the springs' origins to divine thunderbolts which split the earth open and let flow the miraculous waters. Although modern geology robs the springs of some of their mystery, their appeal endures, as bear witness the thousands of people who take the waters in Tuscany each year.

For the thermal spring connoisseur, each of the terme has different curative properties, attributable to the various concentrations of minerals and gases that individual water flows pick up on their way to the earth's surface. Carbon dioxide, for example, is said to promote drainage and strengthen the immune system, while sulphur, its characteristic rotten-egg smell notwithstanding, is said to relieve pain and aid in relaxation. Although customs and conventions vary between spa establishments, visitors generally pay an admission fee to swim in baths that range from hot natural lakes and waterfalls (with all the accompanying mud) to giant limestone swimming pools distinguishable from the garden variety only by their cloudy, bright blue and steaming water. Larger establishments then offer a wide variety of treatments based on the springs, which can range from mineral mud baths to doctor-supervised steam inhalations, all with much-touted curative effects. Believers swear that Tuscany's hot springs have a positive effect on everything from skin disorders to back pain to liver function to stress, and spa personnel will gladly offer up case histories and scientific studies to prove their point. Whatever your opinion, a good soak in a Tuscan spring is a relaxing way to take a break, and as far as geological phenomena go, it beats an earthquake or a volcano any day.

A few of the region's spas, notably the world-famous Montecatini Terme (☞ Chapter 4), are already well-known outside of Tuscany. For the most part, however, the local establishments that run the springs are not well publicized; this can mean a more local flavor, lower prices, and fewer crowds than you'll find at the big spas. Places like the **Terme di Bagni di Lucca** (✉ Bagni di Lucca, ☎ 0583/87221), near Lucca (☞ Chapter 6); **Terme di Chianciano** (✉ Chianciano Terme, ☎ 0578/68111), near Grosseto; and **Terme di Saturnia** (✉ Saturnia, ☎ 0564/601061) like many other smaller spa establishments, offer the experience of a visit to the waters without the accompanying overkill of a famous spa town. Local tourist offices have the most up-to-date information on many of these smaller springs, many of which are only open for part of the year; contact an APT or Pro Loco in the area you plan to visit for recommendations on where to go for a nice, hot bath.

tals, threw down a thunderbolt and created a hot spring whose miraculously calming waters created peace among them. Today, these mythic magnesium-rich waters bubble forth from the clay at a purported perfect 98.6°F, drawing Italians and Germans seeking relief for skin and muscular ailments as well as a bit (well, a lot) of relaxation. Unlike better-known spa centers like Montecatini Terme, nature still has her place here; just outside of the town's medieval center, the hot, sulfurous waters cascade over natural limestone shelves, affording bathers a sweeping view of the open countryside with not a nightclub in sight.

Dining and Lodging

$$$ ✕ Da Caino. This excellent restaurant in the nearby town of Montemerano (on the road to Scansano) is at the high end of the category. Its specialties include tomatoes and peppers on crisp phyllo dough, lasagna with pumpkin, and hearty roast boar meat dishes. ⊠ *Via della Chiesa 4, Montemerano, 7 km (4½ mi) south of Saturnia,* ☎ *0564/ 602817. Reservations essential. AE, DC, MC, V. No dinner Wed.; no lunch Thurs.*

$$$ ✕ I Due Cippi–Da Michele. This is one of the region's most popular
★ restaurants, and a reservation is a must. It serves Maremman cuisine, which includes roast or grilled boar and other locally hunted animals such as venison and pheasant. Eating in the garden can be enjoyed in good weather. The proprietors also run a lovely hotel, Villa Garden ($$; ☎ *0564/ 601182).* ⊠ *Piazza Veneto 26/a,* ☎ *0564/601074. Reservations essential. AE, DC, MC, V. Closed Tues. (except July–Sept.) and Dec. 10–24.*

$$$$ 🏨 Terme di Saturnia. Cure-takers looking for a more refined approach
★ can don their bathrobes here, at the region's premier resort. The hotel, an elegant stone building, wraps around three tufa-rock pools built over the hot springs' source. Every imaginable type of health and beauty treatment is available here, supplemented by decidedly unspalike meals in the hotel restaurant. Half-pension prices are a good deal. ⊠ *Saturnia 58050,* ☎ *0564/601061,* 𝐅𝐀𝐗 *0564/601266. 82 rooms, 8 suites. Restaurant, bar, piano bar, in-room safes, minibars, in-room VCRs, 4 pools, beauty salon, sauna, spa, steam room, health club. CP, EP. AE, MC, V.*

$$$ 🏨 Albergo La Stellata. Sitting prettily on a hilltop with views of neighboring fields, this rustic stone farmhouse is a low-key base for a visit to Saturnia's baths and the Maremman countryside. The natural hot waterfall is less than 2 km (1 mi) away, as is the Terme di Saturnia complex, use of whose facilities is 25,000 lire/day for La Stellata guests. ⊠ *Località Pian del Bagno, Saturnia 58050,* ☎ 𝐅𝐀𝐗 *0564/602978. 14 rooms. Restaurant, bar. MAP. MC, V.*

$$ 🏨 Villa Acquaviva. This elegant villa painted antique rose is at the end of a long tree-lined driveway and perched on top of a hill on the main road 1 km (½ mi) from Montemerano. It has lovely views and quintessential Tuscan charm, with tastefully decorated rooms both in the main villa and in a guest house. The farm that fans out around it produces both wine and olive oil. ⊠ *Strada Scansanese, Montemerano 58050,* ☎ *0564/602890,* 𝐅𝐀𝐗 *0564/602895. 16 rooms. CP. AE, DC, MC, V.*

Pitigliano

㉖ *33 km (21 mi) east of Saturnia, 147 km (92 mi) southeast of Siena, 217 km (136 mi) southeast of Florence.*

From a distance the medieval stone houses of Pitigliano look as if they melt into the cliffs of soft tufa rock they are perched on. Etruscan tombs, which locals use to store wine, are connected by a network of caves and tunnels. At the beginning of the 14th century, the Orsini family moved their base from Sovana to the more naturally fortified Pitigliano. They built up the town's defenses, and fortified their home,

Palazzo Orsini. Later, starting in 1543, Antonio da Sangallo the Younger added more to the town's fortress aspect, building bastions and towers throughout the town, and adding the acqueduct as well.

Savory local specialties include the famous Pitigliano white wine, olive oil, cold cuts, and cheeses; local restaurants serve up good food at modest prices. Note the 16th-century **acqueduct** below the fortress. Wander down the narrow streets of the old **Jewish Ghetto,** where Jews took refuge from 17th-century Catholic persecution.

The 18th-century Baroque **Duomo** has a single nave with chapels and various paintings on the sides. There are two Zuccarelli altarpieces. ⊠ *Piazza S. Gregorio,* ☎ *0564/616090.* ☛ *Free.* ☉ *Daily 9–7.*

Inside the **Palazzo Orsini** is the **Museo Zuccarelli,** featuring paintings by local artist Francesco Zuccarelli (1702–1788), as well as a Madonna by Jacopo della Quercia (1374–1438), a 14th-century crucifix, and other works of interest. ⊠ *Piazza della Repubblica,* ☎ *0564/615568.* ☛ *5,000 lire.* ☉ *Mar. 21–Dec., Tues.–Sun. 10–1 and 3–6.*

Lodging

$ ☷ **Hotel Guastini.** This central hotel in a plain beige three-story building is actually the only show in town. It is comfortable enough, with brick floors and wooden furniture dating to the 1960s. Rooms have nice views of the town center. ⊠ *Piazza Petruccioli 4, 58017,* ☎ *0564/616065,* ☎ *0564/616652. 27 rooms. Restaurant. CP, EP. AE, DC, MC, V.*

Sovana

❷ *5 km (3 mi) north of Pitigliano, 155 km (97 mi) southeast of Siena, 225 km (141 mi) southeast of Florence.*

This town of Etruscan origin was once the capital of the area in southern Tuscany ruled by the Aldobrandeschi family, whose reign was at its height in the 11th and first half of the 12th centuries. One member of the family, Hildebrand, was the 11th-century Catholic reformer Pope Gregory VII (circa 1020–1085). The 13th- to 14th-century Romanesque fortress known as the **Rocca Aldobrandesca** is now in ruins. The town extends from the fortress on one end to the imposing **Duomo** on the other, almost outside the town. **Via di Mezzo,** its stones arranged in a fishtail pattern, is the main street running the length of the town. It leads to the central **Piazza del Pretorio,** with the 13th-century **Palazzo Pretorio** whose facade is adorned with crests of Sovana's captains of justice, and the Renaissance **Palazzo Bourbon dal Monte.** A little farther along is the little 14th-century church of **Santa Maria,** which has frescoes of the late 15th-century Siena and Umbria schools. About 2 km (1 mi) from Sovana is an **Etruscan Necropolis,** with rock tombs dating from the 2nd–3rd centuries BC.

Dining

$$ ✗ **Scilla.** This restaurant, in a medieval palazzo close to the central square, serves simple Tuscan cuisine. Try the *zuppa di ricotta,* a thick vegetable soup with ricotta cheese, or, if you like a strong garlic flavor, the thick local pici with a tomato and garlic sauce. The restaurant also has the usual Maremman roast or grilled boar meat dishes. It has a nice terrace with a garden underneath. ⊠ *Via del Duomo 5,* ☎ *0564/616531. AE, DC, MC, V. Closed Tues. and Nov.*

Sorano

❷ *10 km (6 mi) east of Sovana, 138 km (86 mi) southeast of Siena, 208 km (130 mi) southeast of Florence.*

Sorano is another cliff-top village, with brown houses jutting from tufa and surrounded by intense green wooded hills. The village was built around a 15th-century castle-fortress. Walking down the narrow streets and alleyways from one end of town to the other, you can see old-style artisans at work—here a blacksmith, there a potter. Looking up, you'll note gracefully decorated window and door frames.

SOUTH TO ELBA AND THE MAREMMA

The area between Siena and the Mediterranean coast is yet another expanse of lovely Tuscan hill towns, less traveled than the Chianti area. Chiusdino, Radicondoli, Belforte, and Montieri are all old towns worth a drive, and the spectacular Abbazia di San Galgano makes a meander through the area truly unforgettable. But the Maremma is mostly known for its beaches and islands. These are more rugged than in northern Tuscany, and in some cases exclusive playgrounds of the wealthy set.

Abbazia di San Galgano

㉙ *33 km (20 mi) southwest of Siena, 101 km (63 mi) southwest of Florence.*

Time has had its way with this Gothic cathedral without a rooftop, truly a hauntingly beautiful sight to see. The church was built in the 13th century by Cistercian monks, who designed it after churches built by their order in France. But starting in the 15th century it fell into ruins, declining gradually over centuries. Grass has grown through the floor, and the roof and windows are gone. What's left of its facade and walls makes a grandiose and desolate picture. Behind it, a short climb up a hill brings you to the charming little **Chiesa di San Galgano**, with frescoes by 14th-century painter Ambrogio Lorenzetti (1290–1348), and a sword in stone. Legend has it that Galgano, a medieval warrior, was struck by a revelation on this spot to give up fighting. He thrust his sword into stone, where it remains to this day.

Lodging

$$ ✕ **Il Granaio.** The Tuscan owner and his Sardinian wife transformed this old stone granary at the entrance to Radicondoli into a restaurant and pizzeria in late 1996, and word of it spread fast. Tuscan specialties include *penne alla boscaiola,* with porcini mushrooms sauce, and *bistecca* or thinner sliced *tagliata* made with the top-quality Chianina beef raised right in the area. Sardinian specialties include *gulugiones,* or long pasta stuffed with cheese, potato, and spices (something like long ravioli). ✉ *Via G. di Vittorio 1, Radicondoli,* ☎ *0577/790611. AE, DC, MC, V. Closed Wed. and Jan. 15–Feb. 15.*

$$ ▥ **Fattoria Solaio.** This is an elegant farm near Radicondoli with sculpted gardens and a swimming pool. The rooms are plain, with baked clay floors and simple furniture. The owners are friendly and the scenery is breathtaking, making this perfect for a quiet country *agriturismo* (agritourist) vacation. ✉ *Radicondoli (Siena) 53030,* ☎ *0577/761029,* 🖷 *0577/761029. 14 rooms, 2 cottages. Restaurant, pool. EP. No credit cards.*

$$ ▥ **Rifugio Prategiano.** Horse lovers can have an ideal agritourist getaway here. Just outside the town of Montieri, beyond Chiusdino, this property has a pool, tennis courts, idyllic views, and above all, horseback-riding tours. ✉ *Via dei Platani 3/b, Località Prategiano, Montieri (Siena) 58026,* ☎ *0566/997703,* 🖷 *0566/997891. 24 rooms. Restaurant, pool, tennis court, horseback riding. CP, EP. MC, V.*

Massa Marittima

③⓪ *32 km (20 mi) southwest of Abbazia di San Galgano, 62 km (39 mi) southwest of Siena, 132 km (82 mi) southwest of Florence.*

Massa Marittima is a charming medieval hill town that, despite its name (which means maritime hill), isn't on the sea and for its landscape might as well be in the middle of Chianti country. The town has a rich mining and industrial heritage, thanks to the surrounding Colline Metallifere rich in ores. The central Piazza Garibaldi, dating from the 13th to early 14th centuries, contains the Romanesque **Duomo,** with sculptures of the life of patron saint St. Cerbone above the door. ⊠ *Piazza Garibaldi,* ☎ *0566/902237.* ☞ *Free.* ☉ *Daily 8–noon and 3–6.*

Also on the Piazza Garibaldi is the 13th-century **Palazzo Pretorio,** home to the **Museo Archeologico,** with plenty of Etruscan artifacts. The most famous painting in the **Pinacoteca,** also housed in the palace, is the *Maestà* by Lorenzetti. ⊠ *Piazza Garibaldi,* ☎ *0566/902289.* ☞ *5,000 lire (combined admission to both museums).* ☉ *Sept.–July 15, Tues.–Sun. 10–12:30 and 3:30–7; July 16–Aug., daily 10–12:30 and 3:30–10:30.*

The **Museo Arte e Storia della Miniera** (Museum of the Art and History of Mining), in the upper part of town, shows how dependent Massa Marittima was, since Etruscan times, on copper, lead, and silver ore mining. Exhibits illustrate how the local mining industry worked. ⊠ *Palazzetto delle Armi, Corso Diaz.* ☞ *5,000 lire.* ☉ *Tues.–Sun. 10– 11 and 5–6:30.*

You can see an old olive oil press, called the **Antico Frantoio,** in a small stone farm building next to the palace. ⊠ *Corso Diaz, next to Palazzetto delle Armi.* ☞ *5,000 lire.* ☉ *Sept.–July 15, Tues.–Sun. 11–1 and 3:30–5; July 16–Aug., Tues.–Sun. 11–1 and 4–7.*

Nightlife and the Arts

On the first Sunday after May 22, and again on the first Sunday in August, Massa Marittima's three traditional neighborhood groups dress in medieval costumes, parade throught the town, and then compete in the **Balestro del Girifalco,** where contestants try to shoot down a toy falcon.

Elba

③① *Portoferraio, 22 km (14 mi) by sea southwest of Piombino, 183 km (114 mi) southwest of Florence.*

The largest island in the Tuscan archipelago, ringed with pristine beaches and marked with rugged vegetation, Elba is an hour by ferry or a half hour by hovercraft from Piombino, or a short hop by air from Pisa. Its main port is Portoferraio, fortified in the 16th century by the Medici Grand Duke Cosimo I (1519–1574). The island is full of surprises, like the picturesque inland mountain towns of Poggio Terme and Sant'Ilario in Campo. Local wines include Moscato and Aleatico.

Lively **Portoferraio** is the best base for exploring the island. Be sure to visit **Rio Marina,** a charming town with a dark mineral-rich pebble beach. Other good beaches are at **Biodola, Procchio,** and **Marina di Campo.** From Elba, private visits can be arranged to the other islands in the archipelago, including **Montecristo,** which inspired Alexander Dumas's (1824–1895) 19th-century best-seller *The Count of Monte Cristo,* and is now a wildlife refuge.

Victor Hugo (1802–1885) spent his boyhood in Portoferraio, and Napoleon (1769–1821) his famous exile in 1814–1815, when he built out of two windmills the **Palazzina Napoleonica dei Mulini,** which

still contains furniture from the period. The ⬚
side town, became the **Villa San Martino,** Na⬚
with a classical facade added later by a Ru⬚
Via del Padiglione, Portoferraio, ☎ *0565/9*⬚
San Martino, ☎ *0565/914688.* ⬚ *8,000 lire*⬚
day. Both: ⊙ *Apr.–Sept., Mon.–Sat. 9–*⬚
Mon.–Sat. 9–4, Sun. 9–1; possible evening⬚

The **Museo Archeologico** reconstructs the island's ancient history through a display of Etruscan and Roman artifacts recovered from shipwrecks. ⊠ *Calata Buccari, Portoferraio,* ☎ *0565/937370.* ⬚ *4,000 lire.* ⊙ *Apr.–June and Sept., Fri.–Wed. 9:30–12:30 and 4–7; July–Aug., Fri.–Wed. 9:30–12:30 and 6–midnight.*

Dining and Lodging

$$$ ✕ **La Canocchia.** In the center of Rio Marina, across the street from a public garden, this restaurant serves such specialties as fish-stuffed ravioli with a red shellfish sauce, and *tagliolini* (thin spaghetti) with fresh shrimp. Reservations are essential in summer. ⊠ *Via Palestro 3, Rio Marina,* ☎ *0565/962432. DC, MC, V. Closed Mon. Nov.–Apr.*

$$$ ✕ **Trattoria da Lido.** In the historic center of Portoferraio, at the beginning of the road heading up to the old Medici walls, this restaurant serves specialties such as *gnocchetti di pesce* (bite-size potato and fish dumplings) with a white cream sauce, and *pesce all'elbana* (fresh white fish baked with vegetables and potatoes). A lovely terrace seats about 20. Reservations are encouraged. ⊠ *Salita del Falcone 2, Portoferraio,* ☎ *0565/914650. AE, DC, MC, V. Closed Mon. Nov.–Apr. and Dec. 15–Feb. 15.*

$$$–$$$$ ⌂ **Hermitage.** Cradled by the most exclusive bay on Elba, Biodola, this
★ hotel is heavenly. It is composed of a central building with rooms and several little cottages, each with six to eight rooms with their own separate entrances. Hotel guests have private access to a white sandy beach, and there are a bar and restaurant on the beach, all part of the hotel. ⊠ *Biodola, 8 km (5 mi) west Portoferraio, 57037,* ☎ *0565/ 936911,* FAX *0565/969984. 110 rooms. Restaurant, bar, 3 pools, 6-hole golf course, 9 tennis courts, soccer, volleyball, beach, meeting rooms. EP. AE, DC, MC, V. Closed Nov.–Apr.*

$$–$$$ ⌂ **Hotel Rio.** A comfortable, modern hotel is in the town center of Rio
★ Marina and 100 meters from the gravel and sand beach. All the rooms have views of the sea. The hotel provides beach chairs and umbrellas. ⊠ *Via Palestro 34, Rio Marina 57038,* ☎ *0565/924225,* FAX *0565/ 924162. 37 rooms. Restaurant. CP, EP. AE, DC, MC, V. Closed Oct.– Mar.*

$$–$$$ ⌂ **Riva del Sole.** On the beach in an enchanting bay, with a mountain
★ looming as a backdrop, is this bright, pleasantly appointed hotel. The rooms are modern and spacious and have nice terraces. ⊠ *Viale degli Eroi 11, 57034,* ☎ *0565/976316,* FAX *0565/976778. 53 rooms, 4 suites. Restaurant, tennis court. EP. AE, DC, MC, V. Closed Nov.–Easter.*

$$ ⌂ **Park Hotel Napoleone.** This is a late 19th-century villa, in a park
★ right next to Napoleon's Villa San Martino, with sumptuous interiors. It is 5 km (3 km) outside the center of Portoferraio, and 5 km (3 km) from the sandy beach of Biodola. Buses run often from the hotel to the port in Portoferraio, and the airport runs its own shuttle buses back and forth to Biodola. ⊠ *Località San Martino, Portoferraio 57037,* ☎ *0565/918502,* FAX *0565/917836. 64 rooms. 2 pools, miniature golf, 2 tennis courts, mountain bikes. CP, EP. DC, MC, V. Closed Nov.–Easter.*

Outdoor Activities and Sports

There are seven places to rent bikes, scooters, motorcycles or cars in Portoferraio, including **Chiappi** (⊠ *Calata Italia 30,* ☎ *0565/916779*).

50 km (31 mi) by sea northwest of Elba, 165 km (103 mi) southwest of Siena, 233 km (145 mi) southwest of Florence.

Only a handful of people actually live on the island of Capraia, which is frequented mainly by sailors. It's a rocky and hilly unspoiled national park, with only one sandy beach, **Cala della Mortola,** on the northern end of the island. The ferry pulls in at the town of **Capraia Isola,** dominated by the Fortezza di San Giorgio up above. Nearby, an archway leads to an area that was once a prison. Call the Elba information office in Portoferraio (☎ 0565/914671) for information on Capraia and its national park.

Castiglione della Pescaia

③③ *70 km (44 mi) east of Elba (via Piombino), 94 km (59 mi) southwest of Siena, 162 km (101 mi) southwest of Florence.*

Castiglione della Pescaia is a modern beach town capped by the Castello di Castiglione perched on a hill. The lovely port has a good fresh fish market. You'll be disappointed with this part of Tuscany if you're looking for something out of the last century—everything but the castle is new. Wealthy Italians vacation in the stretch between Castiglione and Punta Ala, and hotels must be booked early. Punta Ala, just down the road, has a newly refurbished port with chic shops and pubs on the waterfront. There are some very nice campgrounds in the area.

Lodging

$$$$ 🏨 **Roccamare.** This is an expensive, exclusive modern hotel, with cottages and a private beach, about halfway between Castiglione della Pescaia and Punta Ala. You can stay in either the hotel or a cottage. The restaurant is reliable, and the hotel provides umbrellas and beach chairs, as well as windsurfing equipment. ✉ *Strada Provinciale, Rocchette, 5 km (3 mi) west of Castiglione della Pescaia, 58043 Grosseto,* ☎ *0564/941124,* 📠 *0564/941133. 51 rooms, 101 cottages. Restaurant, bar, pool, tennis court. CP, EP. AE, DC, MC, V. Closed Nov. 1–Easter.*

$$ 🏨 **Miramare.** This hotel close to the center is about as good as it gets in town. Although one side of the hotel is on the main street going into town, the other side is on a private beach—a must in August. As good as it gets here amounts to standard, modern, and clean digs. ✉ *Via Vittorio Veneto 35, Castiglione della Pescaia 58043 Grosseto,* ☎ *0564/933524,* 📠 *0564/933695. 29 rooms. Restaurant, bar, private beach. CP, EP. AE, DC, MC, V. Closed Nov.–Mar.*

Outdoor Activities and Sports

Check with the **tourist information office** (✉ Piazza Garibaldi, ☎ 0564/933678) for information on horseback riding, sailing, and windsurfing.

Grosseto

③④ *23 km (14 mi) east of Castiglione della Pescaia, 73 km (45 mi) southwest of Siena, 141 km (88 mi) southwest of Florence.*

The central core of Grosseto is attractive and it has a nice cathedral, but otherwise it's a sprawling city best avoided. There are trains and buses to and from Florence and Siena here, and you can use Grosseto as a starting point to visit the southern Tuscan coast.

Monti dell'Uccellina

③⑤ *15 km (10 mi) south of Grosseto, 88 km (55 mi) southwest of Siena, 156 km (97 mi) south of Florence.*

This wild national park is characterized more by dunes than mountains. Be sure to walk along its rugged sandy beaches covered with driftwood.

Monte Argentario

36 *30½ km (19 mi) south of Monti dell'Uccellina, 118½ km (74 mi) southwest of Siena, 186½ km (116 mi) southwest of Florence.*

Monte Argentario is almost an island—it's connected to the mainland by three thin strips of land. Monied Italians vacation here, and some of the villas they've built are spectacular (Sofia Loren's castlelike abode is perched on one mountain peak). **Porto Santo Stefano** and **Porto Ercole** are colorful and charming old towns built into opposite sides of the mountain. You can take a ferry to the island of Giglio (☞ *below*) from Porto Santo Stefano.

Dining and Lodging

$$$ ✕ **Gambero Rosso.** This super seafood restaurant in Porto Ercole is right on the port and from its terrace you can dine with a nice view. Try the *antipasto sorpresa del gambero,* an assortment of four or five seafood starters. There's a variety of seafood dishes on the menu, some unusual and all worth trying. There are also yummy Tuscan soups if you don't want seafood. ⊠ *Lungomare Andrea Doria, Porto Ercole,* ☎ *0564/ 832650. AE, DC, MC, V. Closed Wed.; Nov. 5–20; and Feb. 1–20.*

$$ ✕ **Armando.** This family-run restaurant is on the main road as you enter Porto Santo Stefano, and isn't romantic or right on the beach, but it has a great cook. You can eat outside under a white awning, or inside, amid wooden decor designed to look like a boat. The dish the restaurant is most famous for, spaghetti *alle briciole* (literally spaghetti with crumbs), tastes better than it sounds—it's a very rich, original invention by Armando's chef made with crisp bread crumbs, garlic, oil, hot peppers, and anchovies. The restaurant also has lots of good seafood. ⊠ *Via Marconi 1/3, Porto Santo Stefano,* ☎ *0564/812568. AE, DC, MC, V. Closed Wed. and Dec. 1–25.*

$$ ✕ **La Fontanina di San Pietro.** This restaurant is up on a hill 3 km (2 mi) south of Porto Santo Stefano (on the road winding up to Monte Argentario), in a country setting overlooking the port. The scene is romantic, with grape vines climbing on a trellis and cherry trees. Specialties include scampi with vegetables and spaghetti *al scoglio* (literally spaghetti of the rocks), in a light tomato sauce with clams and mussels. There's a good wine selection. Reservations are suggested. ☎ *0564/ 825261,* FAX *0564/817620. AE, DC, MC, V. Closed Wed. and Jan.*

$$$ ☷ **Don Pedro.** This is a reasonable, modern hotel in Porto Ercole with a private beach. Rooms are spacious but unexciting—they have tile floors and sturdy and standard wooden furniture. The good restaurant offers a half-pension plan if you want to eat one meal in. The hotel also has a bar on the beach and provides beach chairs and umbrellas to its guests. There's no pool, however. ⊠ *Via Panoramica 7, Porto Ercole 58018,* ☎ *0564/833914,* FAX *0564/833129. 49 rooms. Restaurant. CP, EP. AE, DC, MC, V. Closed Nov. 1–Easter.*

$$ ☷ **Vittoria.** This hotel is a steep walk up the hill from the port of Porto Santo Stefano. It has a gorgeous view, and is very comfortable, not to mention the pool and tennis court. Ten of the rooms are suites with small living rooms attached, and seven of the double rooms that aren't suites have terraces with sea views. The hotel dates from the 1970s and has tile floors and simple wooden furniture. ⊠ *Strada del Sole 65, Porto Santo Stefano 58019,* ☎ *0564/818580,* FAX *0564/818055. 26 rooms. Restaurant, pool, tennis court. CP, EP. AE, DC, MC, V. Closed Nov.–Mar.*

Giglio

③⑦ *20 km (12.5 mi) west of Porto Santo Stefano (Monte Argentario), 138½ km (86 mi) southwest of Siena, 206½ km (129 mi) south of Florence.*

Giglio is a romantic island less savage than Capraia and smaller than Elba. You can visit it in a day from Porto Santo Stefano (the ferry takes about an hour). It has three towns—**Giglio Porto,** where the ferry arrives, **Giglio Castello,** at the top of the island's little mountain, and **Giglio Campese,** on the other side of the island. The cluster of 18th- and 19th-century houses that greets the ferry is truly charming. You can take a bus to Giglio Campese and sunbathe on its sandy beach with a romantic view of an old lighthouse tower.

Lodging

$$$ 🏨 **Arenella.** This hotel is on the mountain road leading away from Giglio Porto, 3 km (2 mi) out of town but unfortunately not on the bus route to Giglio Castello—to get here you need a car or the hotel will send one to pick you up at the ferry. The hotel is isolated and quiet, crowned above the sea with great views, and has a private beach reachable by a steep 60-ft walk down. Rooms in the main building are larger and nicer and include suites and rooms for families; more ordinary double rooms are in a smaller building, but they have verandas. Ask for a sea view. The beige stone hotel was built and furnished in the 1970s and rooms are in modest style with stone floors and simple new wood furniture. ⊠ *Località Arenella, Giglio Porto 58013,* ☎ *0564/809340,* 🆁🅰🆇 *0564/809443. 27 rooms. Restaurant, private beach. MAP. AE, MC, V. Closed Nov.– Easter.*

AREZZO, CORTONA, AND SOUTHERN TUSCANY A TO Z

Arriving and Departing

By Bus

There are buses from Florence and Siena to Arezzo, from Siena to San Quirico d'Orcia, and from Florence and Siena to Grosseto and Castiglione della Pescaia.

By Car

The **A1** Autostrada del Sole, running from Florence to Rome, passes close to Arezzo; Cortona is just off the highway linking Perugia to the A1. You can reach Pienza and the Val d'Orcia easily from the A1 or from the Siena–Rome route, which passes through San Quirico d'Orcia. There is also a good road (S223) linking Siena and Grosseto. From Genoa or the northern Tuscan coast, you can drive down the coastal highway (A12), which is being extended south, to reach the coastal towns and islands.

By Plane

The largest airports nearest to the region are Pisa's **Aeroporto Galileo Galilei** (☎ 050/500707), Florence's **Peretola** (☎ 055/333498), and Rome's **Fiumicino** (☎ 06/65953640).

By Train

There are FS trains from Florence to Arezzo and from Siena to Chiusi or Buonconvento, where you can change to buses for smaller towns. For information, call ☎ 147/888088 toll-free. There are also local FS trains that run up and down the Mediterranean coast, from Genoa or Livorno to Piombino (where you can get a ferry to Elba) and Grosseto.

Getting Around

By Boat

Boat services link the islands of Tuscany's archipelago with the mainland. Passenger and car ferries leave from Piombino and Livorno for Elba. **Navarma Line** (✉ Piazzale Premuda, 57025 Piombino, ☎ 0565/225211). **Elba Ferries** (✉ Viale Regina Margherita, Piombino 57025, ☎ 0565/220956; ✉ Nuova Stazione Marittima Calata Carrara, Livorno 57100, ☎ 0586/898979; ✉ Portoferraio 57037, ☎ 0565/930676). **Toremar** (✉ Porto Mediceo, Piombino 57025, ☎ 0565/31100; ✉ Porto Mediceo, Livorno 57123, ☎ 0586/896113, ☎ 0586/886273; ✉ Piazzale A. Candi, Porto Santo Stefano 58019, ☎ 0564/818506). The ferry to Giglio leaves from Porto Santo Stefano on the Argentario peninsula (☞ Toremar, *above*).

By Bus

There are bus routes linking many Tuscan towns, some by private lines and some run by the state-owned railway FS (call La Ferroviaria Italiana, ☎ 0578/91174). Check with tourist offices for more information (☞ Visitor Information, *below*).

By Car

The best way to see southern Tuscany, making it possible to explore tiny hill towns and country restaurants, is by car. But the roads are better north–south than east–west, so allow time for excessively windy roads when heading east or west. Sometimes it's faster to go a little out of your way and get on one of the bigger north–south routes.

By Train

There aren't many good train routes between towns in Southern Tuscany; it's best to use the trains for arriving and departing and then switch to buses.

Contacts and Resources

Car Rentals

Cars are for rent in the airports and in Florence and Siena (☞ Chapters 2 and 6). In Arezzo, try **Avis** (✉ Piazza della Repubblica 1/a, Arezzo, ☎ 0575/354232).

Emergencies

Police, fire (☎ 113). **Ambulance, medical emergency** (☎ 118).

Late-Night Pharmacies

All pharmacies post the addresses of the nearest late-night pharmacies outside their doors.

Visitor Information

Tourist offices are generally open 9–12:30 and 3:30–6 or 7. **Arezzo** (✉ Piazza della Repubblica 28, ☎ 0575/377678). **Capraia** (contact Elba office: ✉ Calata Italia 26, Portoferraio, ☎ 0565/914671). **Castiglione della Pescaia** (✉ , ☎ 0564/933678). **Chianciano Terme** (✉ Piazza Italia 67, ☎ 0578/63167). **Cortona** (✉ Via Nazionale 72, ☎ 0575/630352). **Elba** (✉ Calata Italia 26, Portoferraio, ☎ 0565/914671). **Grosseto** (✉ Via Monterosa 20/b, ☎ 0564/22534). **Monte Amiata** (✉ Via Mentana 97, La Piazzetta, Abbadia San Salvatore, ☎ 0577/778608).

Monte Argentario (⊠ Corso Umberto 55/a, Porto Santo Stefano, ☎ 0564/814208). **Pienza** (⊠ Piazza Pio II, ☎ 0578/749071). **Pitigliano** (⊠ Via Roma 6, ☎ FAX 0564/614433). **Portoferraio** (Elba, ⊠ Calata Italia 26, ☎ 0565/92671). **San Quirico d'Orcia** (⊠ Via Dante Alighieri 33, ☎ 0577/897211).

8 Perugia and Northern Umbria

Majestic art, architecture, and landscapes come together in perfect harmony in the land of Perugino and his pupil Raphael. After the simple geometry of Tuscan architecture, the palaces of Perugia and Urbino, in the nearby Marche region, appear more grandiose. This corner of the world is a fantasy land, where you can almost picture dukes and duchesses and costumed revellers at every turn.

PERUGIA IS A LIVELY CITY, majestic, handsome, and wealthy. Students from local universities keep the streets buzzing with music and activity year-round, and an important jazz festival every July adds to the mix. With its glamorous designer shops, refined cafés, and grandiose architecture, Perugia doesn't try to hide its affluence.

It is the capital of a region rich in history, art, tradition, and breathtaking landscapes. The northern end of Umbria is squeezed between eastern Tuscany—notably Arezzo and Cortona—and the Marches, where the fairy-tale Palazzo Ducale of Urbino sets the stage. The landscapes are those depicted by Perugino in his paintings: hills with a few sparse trees, flat land, and lakes.

Gubbio climbs straight up a mountain, filling the bottom half with its houses and churches. Every May, costumed runners ascend to the top, to the church of Sant'Ubaldo, during Gubbio's bizarre Festa dei Ceri. From here, you can take side trips to Urbino or up to the Republic of San Marino, which claims to be the oldest and smallest independent state in the world.

In Etruscan times, Perugia and Gubbio were among the last to bow to Roman rule, but were eventually conquered by the Romans in the 3rd century BC. Attesting to its importance in Roman times, Gubbio has a Roman theater that could seat around 12,000 spectators. Perugia was caught in the middle of a power struggle between two Roman rulers, and burned, sacked, and destroyed in 140 BC. The city was slowly built back up, and during the medieval period gave its allegiance to the popes.

After winning a war with Assisi in 1202, Perugia flourished. Churches and government buildings were erected, and the university was founded in 1308. In the 15th century, noble families became more powerful and the Baglioni family briefly ruled the city, but it quickly returned to the Papal States. In 1540 the Perugians rebelled against a tax on salt imposed by Pope Paul III (1468–1549), and won the so-called Salt War, but the Pope's son, Pier Luigi Farnese (1503–1547), quickly reconquered the area. Perugia didn't become independent of the church's rule until 1860, when the troops of Victor Emmanuel II of Savoy (1820–1878) conquered it and unified the entire Italian peninsula.

Gubbio, so close by, followed a different path. Its destiny was intertwined with that of Urbino, and the city was ruled by the Montefeltro and Della Rovere families of Urbino during the Renaissance. Like Perugia, in 1631 it fell under the rule of the Papal States and didn't become independent until the unification of Italy.

Pleasures and Pastimes

Dining

Northern Umbria is mountainous, and the food is sturdy and essential, with a hearty quality necessary to sustain artisans and hardworking farmers. Italians are generally thought not to eat much meat, but this is untrue of Italy in general and of Umbria in particular. Novelist Anthony Burgess once observed that a beefsteak in Italy is never "*una bistecca*" but always "*una bella bistecca*"—a beautiful steak—and a simple steak in Umbria is almost always *bella*. You'll find plenty of mushrooms and exquisite *tartufi neri*, black truffles, on the menus in this region. The local pasta specialty, thick, homemade spaghetti called *stringozzi*, is good *al tartufo*, with a sauce of truffles and excellent local olive oil.

A meal of fresh fish pulled from Lago Trasimeno is enough to warrant a detour on your way from Tuscany to Perugia. In the coastal Marches, fish in various forms is also the thing to look for. One of the characteristic dishes in Ancona is *brodetto,* a rich fish chowder containing as many as nine types of Adriatic saltwater fish. Ascoli Piceno, inland, is known for two dishes: *olive ascolane* (olives stuffed, rolled in batter, and deep fried) and *vincisgrassi* (lasagna with a plentiful sauce, enriched with innards and sometimes perfumed with black truffles), far richer than you're likely to find elsewhere in Italy. Ascoli Piceno is also the home of the licorice-flavored liqueur anisette.

CATEGORY	COST*
$$$$	over 110,000 lire
$$$	60,000 lire–110,000 lire
$$	35,000 lire–60,000 lire
$	under 35,000 lire

Prices are per person, for a three course meal, house wine and tax included.

Lodging

Virtually every historic town in Umbria has some kind of hotel, no matter how small the place may be. But be sure to reserve—traveling in high season to Perugia or Urbino without advance bookings is a chancy proposition. Northern Umbria also abounds with *agriturismi,* farmhouses with guest rooms ranging from bed-and-breakfast accommodation to full apartments; note that proprietors often prefer that you stay at least one week.

CATEGORY	COST*
$$$$	over 350,000 lire
$$$	220,000 lire–350,000 lire
$$	100,000 lire–220,000 lire
$	under 100,000 lire

Prices are for a double room for two, tax and service included.

Hiking

Magnificent scenery makes Northern Umbria fine hiking and mountaineering country. Check with local tourist offices for itineraries of walks or climbs.

Shopping

Pottery and wine are the two most famous Umbrian exports, and examples of both commodities are excellent and unique to this region. Torgiano, south of Perugia, is one of the best-known centers of wine making, where you can watch the process and buy the product; you can find some of the best ceramics in Gubbio, Perugia, and nearby Assisi. Those with the most flair are found in Deruta, south of Torgiano. The red glazes of Gubbio pottery have been famous since medieval times. The secret of the original glaze died with its inventor some 500 years ago, but there are contemporary potters who produce a fair facsimile.

Swimming

Lago Trasimeno offers safe and clean bathing facilities. Castiglione del Lago has a public beach, with no strong undercurrents or hidden depths.

Exploring Perugia and Northern Umbria

The steep hills and deep valleys that make Umbria so picturesque also make it difficult to explore. Driving routes must be chosen carefully to avoid tortuous mountain roads, and major towns are not necessarily linked to each other by train, bus, or highway. But Perugia is a convenient base for exploring the region, and you can get around fairly quickly by car. You might want to combine your trip with a southern Tuscany itinerary that includes Arezzo and Cortona (☞ Chapter 7), or with visits to Assisi, Spoleto, and Southern Umbria (☞ Chapter 9). You can reasonably visit the area around Perugia, see Gubbio and Città di Castello, and take a side trip to Urbino, in four days. You would be shortchanging a trip to this region if you skipped Urbino (in the adjoining Marches region) and its storybook palace.

Great Itineraries

Covering distances in this area can take longer than it might look on the map, due to winding mountain roads. Between sightseeing, you might want to set aside extra time for lounging near the lake or shopping for pottery in Deruta. But if you're in the area, try not to skip Perugia or Urbino.

Numbers in the text correspond to numbers in the margin and on the Northern Umbria and the Marches and Perugia maps.

IF YOU HAVE 2 DAYS

Spend a day in ⛫ **Perugia** ①–⑪ and stay overnight. The next day, visit ⛫ **Gubbio** ㉑ in the morning and ⛫ **Urbino** ㉒ in the afternoon. On your way to or from Perugia, a stop at ⛫ **Lago Trasimeno** ⑮–⑯ for a meal of fresh fish is highly recommended.

IF YOU HAVE 5 DAYS

Spend your first day exploring ⛫ **Perugia** ①–⑪ and stay overnight. The next day, visit **Torgiano** ⑫ and ⛫ **Deruta** ⑬, and then head back to Perugia and around ⛫ **Lago Trasimeno** ⑮–⑯ to **Castiglione del Lago** ⑯. If you're interested in art, an alternative route is via **Fontignano** ⑲, **Panicale** ⑱, and **Città della Pieve** ⑰ to see Perugino's works. Return to your hotel in Perugia for the second night. On the third day, visit first **Città di Castello** ⑳ and then ⛫ **Gubbio** ㉑, where you can stay overnight. The next morning, take a daylong side trip to ⛫ **Urbino** ㉒. From here, you can spend a fifth day exploring more of the Marches: ⛫ **Ancona** ㉔ and the Parco del Conero just south of Ancona, **Loreto** ㉕, and ⛫ **Ascoli Piceno** ㉖.

When to Tour Perugia and Northern Umbria

Unlike many other parts of Italy, Northern Umbria is fairly free of tourist hordes, even in summer, when you might welcome the lush greenness of these interior tracts. In August much of the local population shifts to such Adriatic resorts as Rimini to enjoy their vacation—though just as enticing is the Parco del Conero, south of Ancona. The forested hills also ensure beguiling colors in the fall and an explosion of greenery in the spring, two seasons when the tourist count is especially low and the temperature usually comfortable (but beware of possible rainy seasons in November and April).

The predominantly hilly terrain of Northern Umbria means that winters can be bitterly cold, and snow is not uncommon. Since many destinations here are hilltop towns, including Perugia itself, you should be prepared for harsh conditions and possible hazardous driving if you're traveling at this time of year. From the point of view of the region's cuisine, however, winter is best: January through April is the season to sample the truffles for which the area is famous (though of course truffles are dried and can be had at any time of year), and wild mushrooms are picked fresh October to December.

PERUGIA

Perugia, the largest and richest of Umbria's cities, is an old and elegant place of great character. Despite a rather grim crust of modern suburbs, Perugia's location on a series of hills high above the suburban plain has ensured that the medieval city remains almost completely intact. Perugia is the best preserved hill town of its size, and few other places in Italy illustrate better the concept of the self-contained city-state that so shaped the course of Italian history.

Exploring Perugia

The best approach to the city is by train—the station is in the unlovely suburbs, but there are frequent buses running directly to Piazza d'Italia, the heart of the old town. If you are driving to Perugia, it is best to leave your car in one of the parking lots near the station and then take the bus or the escalator, which passes through fascinating subterranean excavations of the Roman foundations of the city, to town center.

A Good Walk

Starting in Piazza Italia, stroll down **Corso Vannucci** ① to the **Duomo** ② in Piazza IV Novembre, and visit the **Palazzo dei Priori** ③ and the **Collegio del Cambio** ④. If you want to see museums, detour back to Piazza Italia and down Corso Cavour to the **Galleria Nazionale d'Umbria** ⑤ and **Museo Archeologico Nazionale** ⑥. Return to Piazza IV Novembre, breaking for lunch or an espresso at a café. Walk down Via dei Priori, and you'll pass the Sant'Agata church on your left. Continuing down the hill, you'll reach another church, the Baroque **San Filippo Neri** ⑦ in Piazza Ferri. Farther down the street, past the escalator, note the **Torre degli Sciri** ⑧, the only antique tower that survives in its original state. Walk around the tower to the Oratorio della Confraternità di San Francesco, another example of Baroque architecture. After you pass the Porta Trasimena on your left, head to the right down Via San Francesco to the church of San Francesco al Prato. The *prato* (lawn) is a nice grassy square that students enjoy in nice weather. From the lawn, you can see the small **Oratorio di San Bernardino** ⑨, connected to San Francesco by an archway in the middle that spans the entrance to a former convent, now the Accademia delle Belle Arti (Academy of Fine Arts), with a museum that contains Antonio Canova's (1757–1822) plaster casts. Walk back up the hill along Via del Poggio, turn right on Via Armonica, and walk along the Etruscan walls to Piazza Cavallotti. Turn left on Via Cesare Battisti, past a 13th-century aqueduct, and at the end of the street you'll find the **Arco di Augusto** ⑩, right next to Perugia's Università per Stranieri (University for Foreigners). Down some steps to your right, wind around to Piazza Michelotti, take a left on Via dell'Aquila, and you arrive at the church of **San Severo** ⑪.

TIMING

A thorough walk through Perugia takes about an hour, and if stopping at all sites along this whole walk, you should plan on a full day with a stop for lunch.

Sights to See

⑩ **Arco di Augusto** (Arch of Augustus). Dating from the 3rd century BC, this arch was the entrance to the Etruscan and Roman acropolis. In the same square is the **Università per Stranieri** (University for Foreigners). ✉ *Piazza Fortebraccio.*

★ ④ **Collegio del Cambio** (Bankers' Guild Hall). The series of elaborate rooms of the Collegio del Cambio housed the meeting hall and chapel of the guild of bankers and money changers. The walls were frescoed from 1496 to 1500 by the most important Perugian painter of the Renaissance, Pietro Vannucci, better known as Perugino (1450–1523). The iconography prevalent in the works includes common religious themes such as the *Nativity* and the *Transfiguration* (on the end walls), but

Northern Umbria and the Marches

also figures intended to inspire the businessmen who congregated here. On the left wall are female figures representing the virtues, beneath them the heroes and sages of antiquity. On the right wall are the prophets and sibyls—said to have been painted in part by Perugino's most famous pupil, Raphael (1483–1520), whose hand, the experts say, is most apparent in the figure of *Fortitude*. On one of the pilasters is a remarkably honest self-portrait of Perugino, surmounted by a Latin inscription and contained in a faux frame. The Collegio is attached to Palazzo dei Priori (☞ *below*), but entered by way of Corso Vannucci. ⊠ *Corso Vannucci 25,* ☎ *075/5728599.* ⊡ *5,000 lire.* ☉ *Mar.–Oct., Mon.–Sat. 9–12:30 and 2:30–5:30, Sun. 9–12:30; Nov.–Feb., Tues.–Sat. 8–2, Sun. 9–12:30. (Dec. 20–Jan. 6., museum follows Mar.–Oct. timetable).*

❶ **Corso Vannucci.** This is the nerve center of the city, a broad, stately pedestrian street that runs from Piazza d'Italia to Piazza IV Novembre. As evening falls, Corso Vannucci is filled with Perugians out for their evening *passeggiata,* a pleasant pre-dinner stroll that may include a pause for an aperitif at one of the many bars that line the street.

NEED A
BREAK?

You can enjoy the lively comings and goings on Corso Vannucci from the vantage point of the **Bar Sandri** (⊠ Corso Vannucci 32). This fine old bar is a 19th-century relic with wood-paneled walls and an elaborately frescoed ceiling.

---

❷ **Duomo.** Otherwise known as the Catttedrale di San Lorenzo, this church is a large and rather plain building dating from the Middle Ages but with many additions from the 15th and 16th centuries. The interior is vast and echoing, with little in the way of decoration. There are some elaborately carved choir stalls, executed by Giovanni Battista Bastone in 1520. The treasure of the church—the wedding ring of the Virgin Mary that the Perugians stole from the nearby town of Chiusi—is kept in a chapel

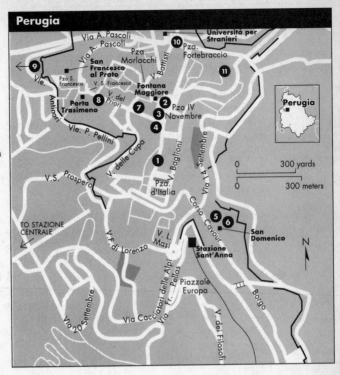

in the left aisle. The ring is the size of a large bangle and is kept under lock (15 locks, actually) and key every day of the year except July 30, when it is exposed to view. Outside the Duomo is the elaborate **Fontana Maggiore**, decorated with Perugian symbols like the griffin, the lion, and the eagle, as well as with agricultural scenes. It is currently being restored but can be glimpsed through Plexiglas. ⊠ *Piazza IV Novembre,* ☎ *075/ 5723832.* 🎟 *Free.* 🕐 *Daily 8–noon and 4–7:30.*

⑤ Galleria Nazionale d'Umbria. The region's most comprehensive art gallery is housed on the fourth floor of the Palazzo dei Priori (☞ *below*). Enhanced by skillfully lit displays and computers allowing you to focus on details of the works and background information on them, the collection in 33 rooms includes work by native artists—most outstandingly Pinturcchio (1454–1513) and Perugino—and others of the Umbrian and Tuscan schools, including Gentile da Fabriano (1370–1427), Duccio (circa 1255–1318), Fra Angelico (1387–1455), Fiorenzo di Lorenzo (1445–1525), and Piero della Francesca (1420–1492). In addition to paintings, the gallery has frescoes, sculptures, and some superb examples of crucifixes from the 13th and 14th centuries; other rooms are dedicated to the city of Perugia itself, showing how the medieval city evolved. ⊠ *Palazzo dei Priori, Corso Vannucci 19, Piazza IV Novembre,* ☎ *075/5741247.* 🎟 *8,000 lire.* 🕐 *Mon.–Sat. 9–7, Sun. 9–1. Closed 1st Mon. of each month.*

⑥ Museo Archeologico Nazionale. A 10-minute walk south of the center along Corso Cavour leads to this museum, next to the imposing church of San Domenico. It contains an excellent collection of Etruscan artifacts from throughout the region. Perugia was a flourishing Etruscan site long before it fell under Roman domination in 310 BC. (Other than this collection, little remains of Perugia's mysterious ancestors, although the Gate of Augustus, in Piazza Fortebraccio, the northern entrance to the city, is of Etruscan origin.) ⊠ *Piazza Giordano Bruno*, ☎ *075/ 5727141.* ☞ *4,000 lire.* ☉ *Mon.–Sat. 9–1:30 and 2:30–7, Sun. 9–1.*

OFF THE
BEATEN PATH   **LA CITTÀ DELLA DOMENICA –** Umbria's attraction aimed directly at the younger set is La Città della Domenica, a Disney-style playground in the town of Montepulito, 8 km (5 mi) west of Perugia on the secondary road that leads to Corciano. The 500 acres of parkland contain a variety of buildings based on familiar fairy-tale themes—Snow White's House, the Witches' Wood—as well as a reptile house, a medieval museum, an exhibit of shells from all over the world, game rooms, and a choice of restaurants. ⊠ *Località Montepulito*, ☎ *075/5054941.* ☞ *16,500 lire (17,500 lire Sun. and holidays).* ☉ *Apr.–mid-Sept., daily 10–7; mid-Sept.–Oct., weekends and holidays 10–7; Nov.–mid-Mar. (aquarium and reptile house only), Sat. 2–7, Sun. 10–7.*

★ ⑨ **Oratorio di San Bernardino.** This lovely little Renaissance church with a pink-and-blue lacey stone facade was designed 1457–1461 by Agostino di Duccio (circa 1418–1481). ⊠ *Piazza San Francesco*, ☎ *075/5733957.* ☞ *Free.* ☉ *Daily 8–12:30 and 3:30–6.*

★ ❸ **Palazzo dei Priori.** This imposing building, begun in the 13th century, has an unusual staircase that fans out into the square. The facade is decorated with symbols of Perugia's pride and past power: The griffin is the city's symbol; the lion denotes Perugia's allegiance to the Guelph (or papal) cause. Both figures support the heavy chains of the gates of Siena, which fell to Perugian forces in 1358. On the fourth floor is the **Galleria Nazionale d'Umbria** (☞ *above*). ⊠ *Corso Vannucci 19, Piazza IV Novembre*, ☎ *075/5741247.* ☞ *8,000 lire.* ☉ *Mon.–Sat. 9– 7, Sun. 9–10. Closed 1st Mon. of each month.*

❼ **San Filippo Neri.** With its grandiose facade dating from 1665, this church is an interesting piece of Baroque architecture. Inside there are frescoes by various 18th-century artists, as well as a 1662 altarpiece by Pietro da Cortona (1596–1669) depicting the *Conception of Mary.* ⊠ *Piazza Ferri*, ☎ *075/5725472.* ☞ *Free.* ☉ *Daily 7:30–12 and 4–7.*

⓫ **San Severo.** This tiny church houses the only Raphael fresco in Perugia, painted in 1505–1508. The lower part (six saints) was added in 1521 by Raphael's teacher, Perugino. ⊠ *Piazza Raffaello*, ☎ *075/ 5733864.* ☞ *3,500 lire.* ☉ *Oct.–Mar., weekdays 10:30–1:30 and 2:30–4:30, weekends 10:30–1:30 and 2:30–5:30; Apr.–Sept., daily 10–1:30 and 2:30–6:30.*

❽ **Torre degli Sciri** (Sciri Tower). This 12th- to 13th-century tower is the only one of its time left standing. At a height of 46 meters (151 ft), it proclaimed to the neighborhood the wealth of the family that built it. ⊠ *Via dei Priori.*

Dining and Lodging

$$ ✕ **Il Falchetto.** Here you'll find exceptional food at reasonable prices, making this Perugia's best restaurant bargain. The service is smart but relaxed in the two medieval dining rooms, with the kitchen and chef on view. The house specialty is *falchetti* (homemade gnocchi) with spinach and ricotta cheese. ⊠ *Via Bartolo 20*, ☎ *075/5731775. Reservations essential. AE, DC, MC, V. Closed Mon.*

$$ ✕ **La Rosetta.** This restaurant, in the hotel of the same name, is a peaceful, elegant spot. In the winter you dine inside under medieval vaults; in summer, in the cool courtyard. The cuisine is simple but reliable and flawlessly served. ⊠ *Piazza d'Italia 19*, ☎ *075/5720841. Reservations essential. AE, DC, MC, V.*

$$ ✕ **La Taverna.** Medieval steps lead to this rustic restaurant on two levels, where lots of wine bottles and artful clutter heighten the *taverna* (tavern) atmosphere. The menu features regional specialties and better-known Italian dishes. Good choices include *chitarrini* (extra-thick spaghetti), with either *funghi* (mushrooms) or *tartufi* (truffles), and grilled meats. ⊠ *Via delle Streghe 8, next to the Teatro Pavone, off Corso Vannucci,* ☎ *075/5724128. Dinner reservations essential. AE, DC, MC, V. Closed Mon.*

$$$$ ⊞ **Brufani Hotel.** The two hotels (this one and the Palace Hotel Bellavista, ☞ *below*) in this 19th-century palazzo were once one. The Brufani's public rooms and first-floor guest rooms have high ceilings and are done in the grand belle epoque style. The second-floor rooms are more modern, and many on both floors have a marvelous view of the Umbrian countryside or the city. ⊠ *Piazza d'Italia 12, 06121,* ☎ *075/5732541,* FAX *075/5720210. 24 rooms. Restaurant, bar, meeting rooms. CP. AE, DC, MC, V.*

$$$ ⊞ **Locanda della Posta.** This luxuriously decorated small hotel in the
★ center of Perugia's historic district is a delight, from its faux-marble moldings, paneled doors, and tile bouquets in the baths to the suede-upholstered elevator and fabric-covered walls. Architectural details of the 18th-century palazzo are beautiful, with windows and balconies framing views of the city rooftops. ⊠ *Corso Vannucci 97, 06121,* ☎ *075/5728925,* FAX *075/5732562. 39 rooms. Breakfast room, lobby lounge. CP. AE, DC, MC, V.*

$$$ ⊞ **Palace Hotel Bellavista.** Though the hotel's entrance is unimpressive, the public rooms are palatial, with antiques imparting a discreet tone of turn-of-the-century grandeur. Guest rooms are spacious, unfussy, and mostly with stupendous views. Prices are at the lower end of the category, and weekly rates are available. ⊠ *Piazza d'Italia 12, 06121,* ☎ *075/5720741,* FAX *075/5729092. 74 rooms. Bar, meeting rooms. CP. AE, DC, MC, V.*

$$ ⊞ **Priori.** On an alley leading off the main Corso Vannucci, this unpretentious but refined hotel has spacious and cheerful rooms with modern furnishings. There is a panoramic terrace where breakfast is served in summer. The hotel is difficult to find if you're driving, and a car is an encumbrance wherever you are in Perugia's historic center—though there is a garage you can pay extra for. ⊠ *Via Vermiglioli 3, 06123,* ☎ *075/5723378,* FAX *075/5723213. 50 rooms. Bar, parking (fee). CP. V.*

$ ⊞ **Rosalba.** This is a bright and friendly choice on the fringes of Perugia's historic center. Rooms—each equipped with telephones and TVs—are scrupulously clean, and the ones at the back enjoy a view. Although somewhat out of the way, the hotel is only a matter of minutes from Corso Vannucci by virtue of the nearby escalator stop, saving a good deal of legwork. Parking is easy, too. ⊠ *Via del Circo 7, 06121,* ☎ *075/5728285,* FAX *075/5720626. 11 rooms. CP. No credit cards.*

Nightlife and the Arts

Summer sees two music festivals in Perugia: the **Jazz Festival of Umbria** (July) and the **Festa della Musica Sacra** (Festival of Sacred Music) in September. Events and ticket information for both festivals can be obtained, year-round, from the **Perugia tourist office** (⊠ Piazza IV Novembre 3, ☎ 075/5736458).

Shopping

Perugia is a well-to-do town, and judging by the array of expensive shops on Corso Vannucci, the Perugians are not afraid to part with their money.

Chocolate

The best and most typical thing to buy in Perugia is, of course, some of the famous and sumptuous Perugina chocolate. *Cioccolato al latte* (milk chocolate) and *fondente* (dark chocolate) are sold all over town in tiny jewel-like boxes and giant gift boxes the size of serving trays. The most famous chocolates made by Perugina are the round chocolate- and hazelnut-filled candies called Baci (kisses), which come wrapped in silver paper and, like fortune cookies, contain romantic sentiments or sayings.

Clothing and Accessories

The main streets of the town are lined with clothing shops selling the best-known Italian designers, either in luxurious boutiques or shops— such as Gucci, Ferragamo, Armani, and Fendi—run by the design firms themselves.

AROUND PERUGIA

The area around Perugia is rich countryside where pleasant agriturismi abound. Highlights are Torgiano, for its excellent wine; Deruta for its ceramics tradition; and Lago Trasimeno, for good fish and lakeside views.

Torgiano

⑫ *16 km (10 mi) southeast of Perugia, 27 km (17 mi) southwest of Assisi.*

Wine aficionados are certain to want to visit this home to the **Cantina Lungarotti,** a winery best known for delicious Rubesco Lungarotti, San Giorgio, and chardonnay. ⊠ *Torgiano 06089,* ☎ *075/9880348.* ☉ *Tours weekdays by appointment only.*

The fascinating **Museo del Vino** (Wine Museum) has a large collection of ancient wine vessels, presses, documents, and tools that tell the story of viticulture in Umbria and beyond. The museum traces the history of wine in all its uses—for drinking at the table, as medicine, and in mythology. At the **Osteria del Museo** (☎ FAX 075/9880069), you can taste and buy Lungarotti's award-winning reds or whites. ⊠ *Corso Vittorio Emanuele 11,* ☎ *075/9880200.* ✑ *5,000 lire.* ☉ *Apr.–Sept., daily 9–1 and 3–7; Oct.–Mar., daily 9–1 and 3–6.*

Dining and Lodging

$$$ ✕ **Le Melagrane.** The hotel restaurant in Le Tre Vaselle (☞ *below*)— a comfortable affair with red tablecloths, wood-beamed ceilings, arches, and fireplaces—offers exquisite local specialties. The *tagliata di manzo,* for example, is served with a balsamic red grape sauce produced at Le Tre Vaselle. In summer, you can dine alfresco on a terrace between the two buildings that make up the hotel. ⊠ *Via Garibaldi 48,* ☎ *075/ 9880447. AE, DC, MC, V.*

$$$ ⊞ **Le Tre Vaselle.** This 17th-century hotel housed in a charming stone ★ building in the center of Torgiano is composed of four separate buildings linked underground. Its rooms are spacious, especially the most expensive suites, some of which have fireplaces. The floors have typical Tuscan red-clay tiles; ceilings are wood beamed. The outdoor pool is surrounded by olive groves, and the indoor pool is complete with whirlpool and currents to swim against. There's also a fitness center and sauna. You can park outside for free or in the garage for 20,000 lire per day. ⊠ *Via Garibaldi 48, 06089,* ☎ *075/9880447,* FAX *075/ 9880214. 61 rooms. Restaurant, bar, indoor and outdoor pools, sauna, exercise room, meeting room, parking (fee). CP. AE, DC, MC, V.*

Deruta

13 *7 km (4½ mi) south of Torgiano, 19 km (11 mi) southeast of Perugia.*

Deruta has been distinguished since the 16th century for its ceramics. The local tradition began towards the end of the 13th century and continues today. But Deruta is most famous for its gold-painted metallic outline, the *Lustro* technique dating from the Renaissance period and of Middle Eastern origin. Notable in the medieval hill town are the 14th-century **San Francesco** and the **Palazzo Comunale,** but its main attraction is the magnificent ceramics collection in the **Museo delle Ceramiche.** The museum has two parts—an historic exposition of Deruta ceramics, with panels explaining (in Italian and English) history, artistic techniques, and production processes, and Italy's largest collection of modern Italian ceramics. There is a so-called didactic room, as well as a large ceramics library. There are nearly 8,000 pieces displayed in the museum altogether, and the most notable are the Renaissance vessels using the Lustro technique. ⊠ *Piazza dei Consoli 1,* ☎ *075/9711000.* 🖃 *5,000 lire.* ⊙ *July–Sept., daily 10–1 and 3:30–7; Oct.–Mar., Wed.– Mon. 10:30–1 and 2:30–5; Apr.–June, daily 10:30–1 and 3–6.*

Lodging

$$$ 🏨 **Nel Castello.** This little turretted castle, which the owner says dates from the 5th century, has nine guest rooms and a good Umbrian restaurant. Atop a hill 5 km (3 mi) outside Deruta, it is surrounded by grass and trees, and is a quiet, peaceful place to stay. The restaurant serves local specialties like roast boar meat and dishes infused with the local truffles. Guests usually eat out at lunch and come back to the castle for dinner. At press time, the hotel was closed for renovation and due to open spring, 1999 (call ahead). ⊠ *Castelleone, Deruta 06503,* ☎ *075/9711302. 9 rooms. Restaurant, pool. AE, DC, MC, V.*

$$ 🏨 **Melody.** This is a plain, comfortable, modern hotel on the road just
★ outside the center of Deruta, with a reasonably priced restaurant and a big parking area surrounded by pine trees. Rooms are very spacious, some with carpeting, the newer ones with nice wooden floors and wood furniture. All have balconies. Rooms in the back are quiet, with nice views of the surrounding hills. ⊠ *Strada statale 3 bis (on the south side of Deruta), 06053,* ☎ *075/9711186,* 📠 *075/9711018. 47 rooms. Restaurant, bar, breakfast room. CP, EP. AE, DC, MC, V.*

Shopping

CERAMICS

There are about 70 ceramics workshops and shops in and around this small town. Keep your eyes peeled for quality, handcrafted pieces, as some of the merchandise is mass produced and of lesser quality. Start your browsing in the central Piazza dei Consoli, where you can find a nice selection at **Maioliche Cintia** (⊠ Piazza dei Consoli, ☎ 075/ 9711255), specializing in reproductions of antique Deruta ceramics, **Maioliche Fanny** (⊠ Piazza dei Consoli, ☎ 075/9711064), **Ceramiche Michela Cavallini** (⊠ Piazza dei Consoli 2, ☎ 075/9711772), and **Ceramiche El Frate** (⊠ Piazza dei Consoli 29, ☎ 075/9711435). If you want to visit a workshop, try **Fabbrica Maioliche Tradizionali** (⊠ Via Tiberina Nord 37, ☎ 075/9711220), or ask for a suggestion at the tourist information office in Piazza dei Consoli 4.

Corciano

14 *13 km (8 mi) northwest of Perugia, 97 km (60 mi) east of Siena.*

Corciano is a nicely preserved medieval hilltop village, with a view of the valley that stretches as far as Lago Trasimeno. Visit the **Museo della Casa Contadina** (Farmhouse Museum) to see what a typical Corciano home was like before the industrial era. ⊠ *Via Tarracone,* ☎ *075/5188254 city hall.* 🎫 *Free.* ⊙ *Check with the city hall for hrs. Generally you can see the museum on request.*

Lago Trasimeno

Passignano sul Trasimeno: 16 km (10 mi) northwest of Corciano, 30 km (18 mi) northwest of Perugia; Castiglione del Lago: 22 km (13 mi) southwest of Passignano, 52 km (31 mi) west of Perugia.

⑮ **Passignano sul Trasimeno** is a picturesque town on the northern shore of Lago Trasimeno (Lake Trasimeno), complete with castle ruins and medieval walls. There are very nice beaches in Passignano and in Castiglione del Lago and the lake is clean enough for swimming. On the ⑯ western shore is **Castiglione del Lago,** also with castle ruins, where the **Palazzo della Corgna** is worth a visit for its Renaissance frescoes. ⊠ *Piazza A. Gramsci 1.* ☎ *075/96581 city hall.* 🎫 *3,000 lire.* ⊙ *April–Oct., daily 10–1 and 3–7; Nov.–Mar., weekends and holidays 10–4.*

In both towns you can sail, windsurf, or take a ferry to **Isola Maggiore,** a little island on the lake, with a pleasant little fishermen's town. Houses date from the 15th century and a church from the 14th. The local men fish and the women still craft handmade lace.

Dining and Lodging

$$$ ✕ **Cacciatori–Da Luciano.** Here you'll find exceptional fresh fish straight from the lake, along with delectable *antipasti* (starters) and good wine. The menu is truly sumptuous. ⊠ *Via Nazionale 11, Passignano sul Trasimeno,* ☎ *075/827210. Reservations essential. AE, DC, MC, V. Closed Wed.*

$$ ✕ **Kursaal.** This hotel restaurant decorated in pastel colors is located right on the lakefront in Passignano sul Trasimeno, a blessing when in summer the outdoor veranda gets in full swing. Of the dishes featuring seafood and fish from the lake, try the *pasta al sapore di lago con tinca affumicata,* or pasta with smoked tench. ⊠ *Via Europa 41, Passignano sul Trasimeno,* ☎ *075/828085. Reservations essential. V. Closed Mon. Nov.–Apr..*

$$ ✕ **La Fontana.** The hotel restaurant at Hotel Miralago in Castiglione del Lago offers good fish and a nice view of the lake. Special dishes include *tegamaccio,* a fish stew with onions, beet greens, tomato sauce, and all kinds of fish. Sit outside in the flowered garden with its quaint gazebo and picturesque vista of the lake. ⊠ *Piazza Mazzini 6, Castiglione del Lago,* ☎ *075/9653235. AE, DC, MC, V. Closed Thurs. in winter; closed Nov.–mid-Dec. and Jan. 20–Mar.*

$$ 🏨 **Kursaal.** Every room in this pink two-story hotel has a balcony, and most have views of the lake. Rooms and furniture are in pastel colors, sage green, salmon, and light blue. There's a swimming pool outside not far from the lake, a private beach for hotel guests, and a nice garden. ⊠ *Via Europa 41 (800 m from the center of Passignano), Passignano Sul Trasimeno 06065,* ☎ *075/828085,* 🖷 *075/827182. 18 rooms. Restaurant, pool. CP. V. Closed Nov.*

$ 🏨 **Albergo Sauro.** This reasonable, quiet hotel is on the tiny island of Isola Maggiore, reachable by ferry from both Castiglione del Lago and Passignano sul Trasimeno. Its rooms are rustic, but it is harmoniously perched right on the lakefront. You can relax on the beach, sit in the garden, or wander down to the little boat dock. The hotel offers a choice of just breakfast, half pension, or full pension. The hotel's owner fishes for carp and other fish for his private stock and for serving in the hotel restaurant. ⊠ *Isola Maggiore, Lago Trasimeno 06060,* ☎ *075/826168,* 🖷 *075/825130. 10 rooms, 2 miniapartments. Restaurant. CP, MAP, FAP. DC, MC, V. Closed Nov., Jan., and Feb.*

$ ⚏ **Locanda del Galluzzo.** This reasonable hilltop agriturismo has both
rooms and apartments with kitchens, and there's no minimum stay. It
is 650 meters above lake level and has beautiful views of the lake and
countryside, amid absolute quiet. A new swimming pool is set among
the olive groves, where walks here are idyllic. The rooms are simple,
with dark wood furniture. The restaurant turns out delicious repasts,
and in summer guests dine on a pretty veranda under a pergola. But
no fish is served here—the menu is typically Umbrian, with rich dishes
such as *papardelle al capriolo* (flat noodles in a red venison sauce) or
cinghiale alle ulive nere (roast boar with black olives). ⊠ *Via Castel
Rigone 12/A, Località Trecine (5 km/3 mi east of Passignano Sul Trasimeno), Passignano Sul Trasimeno 06065,* ☎ ﬀ︁ *075/845352. 4 rooms,
6 apartments. Restaurant, pool. CP. No credit cards. Closed Nov.*

ON THE PERUGINO TRAIL

Studying under Verrocchio (1435–1488), native Umbrian Pietro Vannucci, known as Il Perugino, developed his artistic career in Florence
and then Rome, where he helped paint the Cappella Sistina. He out-
lived his star pupil, Raphael Sanzio (1483–1520), a native of Urbino.
A visit to Perugino's major works in the area around Perugia is not only
a way to reconstruct the evolution of his career, but is also a way of
seeing in person just how much the artist was affected by—and re-cre-
ated—the environment he grew up in. Don't forget that the Collegio
del Cambio in Perugia (☞ *above*) is a must for any Perugino itinerary.

Città della Pieve

⑰ *26 km (16 mi) south of Castiglione del Lago, 43 km (26 mi) southwest of Perugia.*

Perugino was born in this small Etruscan town of plain redbrick buildings, flat-topped towers and churches, so it makes sense churches here
are chock-full of his frescoes, some in better condition than others. Perugino's *Baptism of Christ* and *Madonna in Glory* in the 17th-century
Duomo (⊠ Piazza Plebiscito), transformed from an old Romanesque
church, are examples of his later works. The *Adoration of the Magi*
in **Santa Maria dei Bianchi,** painted in 1504, is particularly well restored.
It depicts the nativity scene in perfect Renaissance court style on a spring
day, with the Perugian countryside in the background. At a time when
Leonardo da Vinci (1452–1519) and Michelangelo (1475–1564) were
embarking into new scientific and religious territory, Perugino reaffirmed
a classical, humanistic Renaissance style. ⊠ *Via Vannucci,* ☎ *0758/
299696.* ▦ *Free.* ☉ *Mon.–Sat. 10:30–12:30 and 3:30–6, Sun. 10–
1 and 3–6.*

Also worth a peek for its Perugino frescoes are the churches of **Santa
Maria dei Servi** and **San Pietro,** outside the city walls near the hospital (follow signs).

Panicale

⑱ *21 km (13 mi) northeast of Città della Pieve, 34 km (20 mi) southwest
of Perugia.*

On the drive from Città della Pieve to Panicale, a wide open view of
Lake Trasimeno appears, with islands on the lake and mountains on
its far shore. Once you've reached Panicale, head straight for the
church of **San Sebastiano,** where Perugino painted his famous fresco
depicting the *Martyrdom of St. Sebastian.* This was executed in 1505,
only one year later than the *Adoration of the Magi* in Città della Pieve

(☞ *above*), but it is much more abstract and geometric. The painting is almost dreamlike, with St. Sebastian on a strange classical terrace, and God appearing fatherlike above. The landscape in the background, though, is the same Perugian countryside found in the *Adoration*. ⊠ *Outside city walls, off Piazza Vittoria,* ☎ *0758/37602.* 🎫 *Free.* ☉ *Daily 10–12 and 4–6.*

Fontignano

⑲ *12 km (7 mi) east of Panicale, 22 km (13 mi) southwest of Perugia.*

Just one year before he died in Fontignano of the plague, Perugino painted the almost naif-looking *Madonna and Child* in the church of the **Annunciation.**

NORTH TOWARDS URBINO

The trip north from Perugia to Città di Castello and Gubbio, and across to Urbino, passes through rugged, mountainous terrain. Città di Castello can be combined with San Sepolcro in an itinerary, possibly also including Arezzo.

Città di Castello

⑳ *54 km (32 mi) north of Perugia, 42 km (26 mi) east of Arezzo.*

This noble-looking town is still surrounded in part by 16th-century walls. The town is centered around Piazza Matteotti, dominated by the 14th-century **Palazzo del Podestà.** The **Duomo** dates from the 6th century, but was renovated between 1466 and 1529, and in the 17th century received an unfinished Baroque face lift. ⊠ *Piazza del Duomo,* ☎ *0758/521647.* 🎫 *Free.* ☉ *Daily 10–12 and 4–6.*

Inside the 16th-century **Palazzo Vitelli alla Cannoniera,** built by Sangallo the Younger (1483–1546) with a facade by Giorgo Vasari (1511–74), is the **Pinacoteca Comunale,** second only to Perugia's art gallery for Umbrian painting. It houses paintings by Raphael, including *The Creation of Eve,* Luca Signorelli (1441–1523), Neri di Bicci, and Ghirlandaio (1449–1494). ⊠ *Via della Cannoniera 22,* ☎ *0758/554202.* 🎫 *7,000 lire.* ☉ *Mar.–Oct., daily 10–1 and 3:30–7; Nov.–Feb., Tues.–Sun. 10–1 and 3:30–6.*

Dining and Lodging

$$$ ✕ **Il Postale di Marco e Barbara.** Friendly owners Marco and Barbara
★ turned this old bus depot into a stellar restaurant. They did a nice job preserving the original structure—details include old wooden beams in the ceiling and an antique gas pump outside—while creating a pleasant environment. Every two weeks the chefs reinvent new recipes with the freshest local vegetables, fish, and meat. Artistic and tasty antipasti might be bite-size marinated veal with sprouts and lemon cream, or little tarts of mussels and vegetables. Entrées include roast quail with cherry tomatoes and beans, and lots of delicious fish and seafood. Throughout the year, you can order a *degustazione* (tasting) menu, where the chef decides which two antipasti, first, and second courses you receive. ⊠ *Via De Cesare 8,* ☎ *075/8521356. Reservations essential. AE, DC, MC, V. Closed Mon. No lunch Sat.*

$$ 🏨 **Le Mura.** This comfortable, modern hotel in the center of town is attached to the old city walls. It was built in 1993 and has carpeting, wooden furniture, satellite TV, and is nicely air-conditioned in the summer. Price includes a good buffet breakfast. ⊠ *Via Borgo Farinario 24/26, 06012,* ☎ *075/8521070,* 🖷 *075/8521350. 34 rooms. CP. Restaurant, bar, meeting room. AE, DC, MC, V.*

Nightlife and the Arts

The **Festival delle Nazioni di Musica da Camera** (Chamber Music Festival of Umbria), is held every August and September. For information, contact the tourist office (✉ Piazza Fanti, ☎ 075/8554922).

Gubbio

㉑ *39 km (24 mi) northeast of Perugia, 92 km (57 mi) east of Arezzo.*

There is something otherworldly about this small jewel of a medieval town tucked away in a mountainous corner of Umbria. Even at the height of summer, the cool serenity and quiet of Gubbio's streets remain intact. The town is perched on the slopes of Monte Ingino, and the streets are dramatically steep. Gubbio's relatively isolated position has kept it free of hordes of high-season visitors, but even during the busiest times of year the city lives up to its Italian nickname, La Città del Silenzio (City of Silence). Parking in the central Piazza dei Quaranta Martiri—named for 40 hostages murdered by the Nazis in 1944—is easy and secure, and it is wise to leave your car there and explore the narrow streets on foot.

★ The striking Piazza Grande is dominated by the medieval **Palazzo dei Consoli,** attributed to a local architect known as Gattapone—a man still much admired by today's residents (hotels, restaurants, and bars have been named after him), though studies have suggested that the palazzo was in fact the work of another architect, Angelo da Orvieto. In the Middle Ages the Parliament of Gubbio met in this palace, which has become a symbol of the town.

The Palazzo dei Consoli houses a small museum, famous chiefly for the **Tavole Eugubine,** seven bronze tablets written in the ancient Umbrian language, employing Etruscan and Latin characters, and providing the best key to understanding this obscure tongue. Also in the museum are a fascinating miscellany of coins, medieval arms, paintings, and majolica and earthenware pots, not to mention the exhilarating views over Gubbio's roofscape and beyond from the lofty loggia. For a few days at the beginning of May, the palace also displays the famous *ceri*, the ceremonial pillars at the center of Gubbio's annual festivities. ✉ *Piazza Grande,* ☎ *075/9274298.* ✍ *5,000 lire.* ☉ *Apr.–July and Sept., daily 10–1:30 and 3–6; Aug., daily 10–1:30 and 3–7; Oct.–Mar., daily 10–1 and 2–5.*

The **Duomo,** on a narrow street on the highest tier of the town, dates from the 13th century, with some Baroque additions—in particular, a lavishly decorated bishop's chapel. The Duomo was damaged in a 1997 earthquake and is closed indefinitely for restoration. ✉ *Via Ducale.* ☉ *Daily 8–12:45 and 3–7:30.*

The **Palazzo Ducale** is a scaled-down copy of the Palazzo Ducale in Urbino (Gubbio was once the possession of that city's ruling family, the Montefeltro). Gubbio's palazzo contains a small **museum** and a **courtyard.** There are magnificent views from some of the public rooms. ✉ *Via Ducale,* ☎ *075/9275872.* ✍ *4,000 lire.* ☉ *Mon.–Sat. 9–1:30 and 2:30–7, Sun. 9–1:30.*

Just outside the city walls at the eastern end of town (follow Corso Garibaldi or Via XX Settembre to the end), is a **funicular** (☉ July and Aug., daily 8:30–7:30; Sept.–June, Thurs.–Tues. 10–1:15 and 2:30–5; ✍ one way 5,000 lire, round-trip 6,500 lire) that provides a bracing ride to the top of Monte Ingino. Aside from the spectacular views, the mountain commands the basilica of **Sant'Ubaldo,** repository of Gubbio's famous ceri, three 16-ft-high pillars crowned with statues of

Saints Ubaldo, George, and Anthony. The pillars are transported to the Palazzo dei Consoli on the first Sunday of May to honor the Festa dei Ceri. ⊠ *Top of Monte Ingino,* ☎ 075/9273872. 🎫 *Free.* ☉ *Daily 9– noon and 4–7.*

Dining and Lodging

$$$ ✕ **Taverna del Lupo.** The "Tavern of the Wolf" is one of the city's best *taverne,* and one of the largest—it seats 200 people and can still get a bit hectic during the high season. Lasagna made in the Gubbian fashion, with ham and truffles, is the best pasta. You'll also find excellent desserts and an extensive wine cellar here. ⊠ *Via G. Ansidei 21,* ☎ *075/9274368. Reservations essential. AE, DC, MC, V. Closed Mon. Oct.–July.*

$$ ✕ **Bosone Garden.** This restaurant, underneath the Hotel Bosone, has a summer garden that seats 200. It is in the former stables of the palace that houses the Hotel Bosone (☞ *below*), as you can see from the stone arches inside. The menu features a mushroom salad with two kinds of mushrooms, plus risotto *alla porcina* (with porcini mushrooms, sausage, and truffles) and leg of pork. ⊠ *Via XX Settembre 22,* ☎ *075/ 9220688. AE, DC, MC, V. Closed Jan.*

$$ ✕ **Grotta dell'Angelo.** This rustic trattoria is in the lower part of the old town, near the main square and tourist information office. The menu features simple local specialties, including *capocollo* (a type of salami), stringozzi pasta, and lasagna *tartufate* (with truffles). A few tables welcome outdoor dining. Inexpensive guest rooms are also available. ⊠ *Via Gioia 47,* ☎ *075/9273438. Reservations essential. AE, DC, MC, V. Closed Tues. and Jan. 7–Feb. 7.*

$$ ✕ **Porta Tessenaca.** This atmospheric restaurant occupies what used to be the stables of the Palazzo Ducale. The brick vaulted setting is perfect, if somewhat touristy, and the food is excellent Umbrian fare; there are three fixed-price menus. If possible, opt for the stringozzi *ai porcini* (with porcini mushrooms) for starters, and the duck for the next course. There is a good wine selection. ⊠ *Via Piccardi 21,* ☎ *075/ 9272765. AE, DC, MC, V.*

$$ 🛏 **Hotel Bosone.** Occupying the old central Palazzo Raffaelli, the Hotel Bosone has many rooms decorated with frescoes from the former palace. The suites furnished with period pieces are particularly lavish. ⊠ *Via XX Settembre 22, 06024,* ☎ *075/9220688,* ℻ *075/9220552. 30 rooms. Bar. AE, DC, MC, V. Closed Jan.*

$$ 🛏 **Hotel Gattapone.** Right in the center of town is this spiffy hotel with wonderful views of the sea of rooftops. It is casual and family run, with good-size, modern, comfortable rooms, some with well-preserved timber-raftered ceilings. ⊠ *Via Ansidei 6, 06024,* ☎ *075/9272489,* ℻ *075/ 9271269. 18 rooms. AE, DC, MC, V. Closed Jan.*

$$ 🛏 **Residence Cortevecchio.** A truly special agriturismo vacation can be had here, where the energetic owners have plenty organized for you. Apartments are available in the 19th-century castle (12 units) and its guest houses (four units), with minimum stay of a week in summer. The castle stands in the middle of a vast wooded park with a pool, stables (replete with its own English riding instructor and lodging for your horse), tennis courts, and a small soccer field. In the truffle season, October and November, the owners take guests truffle hunting with specially trained dogs. Mountain bikes are available for guests. The rooms are nicely furnished in simple elegant castle style in wood and marble, with beamed ceilings and clay tile floors. ⊠ *Località Nogna, 06024,* ☎ *075/9241017,* ℻ *075/9241079. 10 double rooms (by March, 1999), 16 apartments. Restaurant, bar, pool, 2 tennis courts, boccie, horseback riding, soccer. AE, DC, MC, V. Closed mid-Jan.–Feb. 10.*

Nightlife and the Arts

Every May 15th teams of Gubbio's young men, dressed in medieval costumes, race up the steep slopes to the basilica of Sant'Ubaldo carrying the heavy pillars crowned with saints, called ceri, in the **Festa dei Ceri.** This festival, enacted faithfully every year since 1151, is to thank the town's patron saints for their assistance in a miraculous Gubbian victory over a league of 11 other towns.

Outdoor Activities and Sports

Among the region's other historical pageants, Gubbio's costumed **Palio della Balestra** (crossbow tournament) takes place on the last Sunday in May; contact the Gubbio tourist office (⊠ Piazza Oderisi 6, ☎ 075/9220693) for details.

THE MARCHES
Including San Marino

An excursion from Umbria into the region of the Marches gets you off the beaten track to see a part of Italy rarely visited by foreigners. Not as wealthy as Tuscany or Umbria, the Marches has a diverse landscape of mountains and beaches, and marvelous views. Like its neighbors to the west, Le Marche's patchwork of rolling hills is stitched with grapevines and olive trees, bearing luscious wine and olive oil.

Traveling in the Marches is not as easy as in Umbria or Tuscany. Beyond the narrow coastal plain and away from major towns, the roads are steep and twisting. There's an efficient bus service from the coastal town of Pésaro to Urbino, the other principal tourist city of the region. Train travel in the region is slow, and stops are limited, although you can reach Ascoli Piceno by rail.

Urbino

65 km (40) mi north of Gubbio, 170 km (106 mi) northeast of Perugia, 190 km (119 mi) east of Florence.

Majestic Urbino, atop a steep hill with a skyline of towers and domes, is something of a surprise to come upon—it's oddly remote—and it is even stranger to reflect that it was once a center of learning and culture almost without rival in western Europe. The town looks much as it did in the glory days of the 15th century, a cluster of warm brick and pale stone buildings, all topped with russet-color tiled roofs. The focal point is the immense and beautiful Palazzo Ducale.

Urbino's fame rests on the reputation of three of its native sons: Duke Federigo da Montefeltro (1422–1482), the enlightened warrior-patron who built the Palazzo Ducale; Raphael, one of the most influential painters in history and an embodiment of the spirit of the Renaissance; and the architect Donato Bramante (1444–1514), who translated the philosophy of the Renaissance into buildings of grace and beauty. Why three of the greatest men of the age should have been born within a generation of one another in this remote town has never been explained. Oddly enough, there is little work by either Bramante or Raphael in the city, but the duke's influence can still be felt strongly, even now, some 500 years after his death.

★ The **Palazzo Ducale** (Ducal Palace) holds the place of honor in the city, and in no other palace of its era are the principles of the Renaissance stated quite so clearly. If the Renaissance was, in ideal form, a celebration of the nobility of man and his works, of the light and purity of the soul, then there is no place in Italy, the birthplace of the Renaissance, where these tenets are better illustrated. From the moment you enter the peaceful courtyard, you know that you are in a place of grace and beauty, the harmony of the building reflecting the high ideals of the men who built it.

Today the palace houses the **Galleria Nazionale delle Marche** (National Museum of the Marches), with a superb collection of paintings, sculpture, and other objets d'art, well arranged and properly lit. It would be hard to mention all the great works in this collection—some originally the possessions of the Montefeltro family, others brought to the museum from churches and palaces throughout the region—but there are a few that must be singled out. Of these, perhaps the most famous is Piero della Francesca's enigmatic work, long known as *The Flagellation of Christ*. Much has been written about this painting, and few experts agree on its meaning. Other masterworks in the collection are Paolo Uccello's *Profanation of the Host*, Piero della Francesca's *Madonna of Senigallia*, and Titian's *Resurrection* and *Last Supper*. Duke Federigo's study is an astonishingly elaborate but tiny room decorated with inlaid wood, said to be the work of Botticelli. ⊠ *Piazza Duca Federico,* ☎ *0722/2760.* ⊡ *8,000 lire.* ☉ *Mon.–Sat. 9–7, Sun. 9–1.*

La Casa di Raffaello really is the house in which Raphael was born and where he took his first steps in painting (under the direction of his artist father). There is some debate about the fresco of the Madonna that adorns the house. Some say it is by Raphael, others attribute it to the father—with Raphael's mother and the young painter himself standing in as models for the *Madonna and Child*. ⊠ *Via Raffaello,* ☎ *0722/ 320105.* ⊡ *5,000 lire.* ☉ *Mar.–Sept., Mon.–Sat. 9–1 and 3–7, Sun. 9–1; Oct.–Jan., Thurs.–Sat. and Mon.–Tues. 9–2, Sun. 10–1.*

Dining and Lodging

$$$ ✕ **Vecchia Urbino.** This simple yet elegant wood-panelled restaurant in the center of Urbino has views of the hills from the windows. Try the *vincisgrassi*, a meat lasagna named after an Austrian captain who brought the recipe to Urbino more than 100 years ago, or *spaghetti alla Vecchia Urbino*, with bacon and pecorino cheese. A particularly good second course is the *coniglio al coccio* (literally, rabbit in earthenware), or rabbit cooked in milk on the stovetop in an earthenware casserole and then oven baked. ⊠ *Via dei Vasari 3/5,* ☎ *0722/4447. AE, DC, MC, V. Closed Tues.*

$$ ✕ **La Vecchia Fornarina.** These two small rooms just down from Urbino's central Piazza della Repubblica are often filled to capacity. The trattoria specializes in meaty country fare, such as rabbit and *vitello alle noci* (veal cooked with walnuts) or ai porcini. There is also a good range of pasta dishes. ⊠ *Via Mazzini 14,* ☎ *0722/320007. Reservations essential. AE, DC, MC, V.*

$$$ 🏨 **Hotel Bonconte.** Dating from the beginning of the century, this classic hotel is just inside the city walls and close to the Palazzo Ducale. The rooms are elegantly decorated with antique furniture and display a great attention to detail—for example, every room has a bathroom scale. The rooms have views of the valley below Urbino and the Dukes' mausoleum. ⊠ *Via delle Mura 28, 61029,* ☎ *0722/2463,* 𝖥𝖠𝖷 *0722/ 4782. 25 rooms. CP. AE, DC, MC, V.*

$ 🏨 **Hotel San Giovanni.** This hotel is in the Old Town and is housed in a renovated medieval building. The rooms are basic, clean, and comfortable—with a wonderful view from Nos. 18–21 and 24–31—and there is a handy restaurant-pizzeria below. ⊠ *Via Barocci 13, 61029,* ☎ *0722/2827,* 𝖥𝖠𝖷 *0722/329055. 33 rooms, 21 with shower. CP. No credit cards. Closed July and Christmas wk.*

San Marino

㉓ *45 km (28 mi) northwest of Urbino, 168 km (104 mi) northeast of Florence.*

Legend has it that the town climbing up the side of Monte Titano in the Appenines was founded at the beginning of the 4th century by Marino, a humble Christian stonecutter escaping from persecution by Diocletian together with his friend Leo (who is said to have founded the nearby town of San Leo). Somehow San Marino, which is known to have been independent in the 11th century, managed to remain so and was recognized by Napoleon and the Council of Vienna.

The Republic of San Marino, which has its own currency (the San Marino lira, equivalent to the Italian lira, which is accepted here) and postage stamps, measures only 61 square km (23 square mi). The town of San Marino is the capital but there are eight more villages, known as the San Marino castles. Each of them is run by a council called the Consiglio del Castello, presided over by a Capitano del Castello.

In San Marino, the church of **San Francesco** was originally built in the 13th century but renovated in the 17th and 18th. On the three cliffs of Monte Titano are three towers. The second, called the **Cesta,** which dates from the 13th century, houses an antique weapons museum. It was built on a cliff 2,421 ft above sea level and offers great views.

Shopping

San Marino's legislation is looser than Italy's, and the tiny Republic is a tax haven that resembles a large duty free shopping center. In addition to shops selling products with known brand names, you'll find plenty of stores stocked with imitations, from perfumes to cheap stereos with labels like Panaphonic. All this may change, however; the Italian government is beginning to tire of its lax little neighbor and is stepping up border controls and pressure on San Marino to change.

Ancona

㉔ *87 km (54 mi) southeast of Urbino, 139 km (87 mi) northeast of Perugia, 262 km (164 mi) east of Florence.*

Ancona was probably once a lovely city. It is set on an elbow-shape bluff (hence its name; *ankon* is Greek for "elbow") that juts out into the Adriatic. But Ancona was the object of serious aerial bombing during World War II—it was, and is, an important port city—and was reduced to rubble. The city has been rebuilt in the unfortunate postwar poured-concrete style, practical and inexpensive but not aesthetically pleasing. Unless you are taking a ferry to Venice, there is little reason to visit the city—with a few exceptions. Once in a while, glimpses of old architectural detail are redeeming, as seen in the **Duomo San Ciriaco** and the **Loggia dei Mercanti.** In addition, Ancona can be the base for an excursion to Loreto or to Ascoli Piceno, farther south along the Adriatic coast.

Dining and Lodging

$$ ✕ **La Moretta.** This family-run trattoria is on the central Piazza del Plebiscito. In summer there is dining outside in the square, which has a fine view of the Baroque church of San Domenico. Among the specialties here are *stoccafisso all'Anconetana* (stockfish baked with capers, anchovies, potatoes, and tomatoes) and the famous brodetto fish stew. ⊠ *Piazza del Plebiscito 52,* ☎ *071/202317. Reservations essential. AE, DC, MC, V. Closed Sun.*

$$$ ⊡ **Grand Hotel Palace.** In town center, near the entrance to the port of Ancona, and widely held to be the best in town, this is an old-fashioned place well run by a courteous staff. ⊠ *Lungomare Vanvitelli 24, 60100,* ☎ *071/201813,* 🖷 *071/2074832. 41 rooms. Bar, free parking. AE, DC, MC, V.*

Loreto

❷❺   *31 km (19 mi) south of Ancona.*

Loreto is famous for one of the best-loved shrines in the world, that
★ of the **Santuario della Santa Casa** (House of the Virgin Mary), within the **Basilica.** The legend is that angels moved the house from Nazareth, where the Virgin was living at the time of the Annunciation, to this hilltop in 1295. The reason for this sudden and divinely inspired move was that Nazareth had fallen into the hands of Muslim invaders, not suitable landlords, the angelic hosts felt. More recently, following archaeological excavations made at the behest of the Church, evidence has come to light proving that the house did once stand elsewhere and was brought to the hilltop by human means around the time the angels are said to have done the job.

The house itself consists of three rough stone walls contained within an elaborate marble tabernacle; built around this centerpiece is the giant basilica of the Holy House, which dominates the town. Millions of visitors come to the site every year (particularly at Easter and on the Feast of the Holy House, December 10), and the little town of Loreto can become uncomfortably crowded with pilgrims. Many great Italian architects, including Bramante, Antonio Giamberti da Sangallo (the Younger, 1483–1546), Giuliano da Sangallo (circa 1445–1516), and Sansovino (1467–1529), contributed to the design of the basilica. The basilica was begun in Gothic style in 1468 and continued in Renaissance style through the late Renaissance. The bell tower is by Luigi Vanvitelli (1700–73). Inside the church are a great many mediocre 19th- and 20th-century paintings but also some fine works by Renaissance masters such as Luca Signorelli and Melozzo da Forlì. ⊠ *Piazza della Maddona.* ☉ *June–Sept., daily 8–8; Oct.–May, daily 6 AM–7 PM.*

If you're a nervous air traveler you can take comfort in the fact that the Holy Virgin of Loreto is the patroness of air travelers and that Pope John Paul II has composed a prayer for a safe flight—available in the church in a half dozen languages.

Ascoli Piceno

❷❻   *105 km (65 mi) south of Ancona.*

Ascoli Piceno is not a hill town; rather, it sits in a valley ringed by steep hills and cut by the fast-racing Tronto River. The town is almost unique in Italy, in that it seems to have its traffic problems—in the historic center, at any rate—pretty much under control; you can drive *around* the picturesque part of the city, but driving *through* it is most difficult. This feature makes Ascoli Piceno one of the most pleasant large towns in the country for exploring on foot. True, there is traffic, but you are not constantly assaulted by jams, noise, and exhaust fumes the way you are in other Italian cities.

★   The heart of the town is the majestic **Piazza del Popolo,** dominated by the Gothic church of **San Francesco** and the **Palazzo del Popolo,** a 13th-century town hall that contains a graceful Renaissance courtyard. The square itself functions as the living room of the entire city. At dusk each evening the piazza is packed with people strolling and exchanging news and gossip—the sweetly antiquated ritual called the passeggiata, done all over the country.

☺ Ascoli Piceno's **Giostra della Quintana** (Joust of the Quintana) takes place on the first Sunday in August. Children should love this medieval-style joust and the richly caparisoned processions that wind through the streets of the old town. Contact Ascoli's tourist office (⊠ Piazza del Popolo, ☎ 0736/257288) for details.

Dining and Lodging

$$ ✕ **Ristorante Tornasacco.** In this family-run restaurant with modern
★   decor, you can sample Ascoli's specialties, like olives ascolane (here, stuffed with minced meat), as well as *maccheroncini alla contadina* (a homemade pasta in a thick meat sauce). ⊠ *Piazza del Popolo 36,* ☎ *0736/254151. AE, DC, MC, V. Closed Fri. and July 1–15.*

  $ ▥ **Piceno.** This modest hostelry is one of the few lodgings in the historic center. It offers clean, basic amenities—no frills at all here. The staff is helpful and courteous, and the setting is perfect. ⊠ *Via Minucia 10,* ☎ *0736/252553. 32 rooms, 14 without bath. No credit cards. Closed Jan.*

PERUGIA AND NORTHERN UMBRIA A TO Z

Arriving and Departing

By Bus

Buses leave from Florence, Siena, Assisi and Rome for Perugia. Contact a tourist information office for details.

By Car

A highway (75 bis) connects Perugia to the Florence–Rome Autostrada del Sole (A1), Italy's main north–south highway—making Perugia easy to reach.

By Plane

The small airport of Sant'Egidio, 12 km (7 mi) east of Perugia, has flights to and from Milan.

By Train

From Florence, take a train headed for Chiusi and Rome and change at Terontola for Perugia. The Florence-Terontola-Chiusi train stops at Castiglione del Lago, on Lake Trasimeno, and a few even stop at Città della Pieve. From Rome, take the Ancona train and change at Foligno for Perugia. Gubbio isn't reachable by train, but it's reachable by bus from Perugia. For the state-run line (FS) train information, call ☎ 147/888088 toll-free.

Getting Around

By Bus

Buses connect Perugia to Città di Castello and San Sepolcro, Perugia to Todi via Deruta, and Perugia to Gubbio.

By Car

Umbria has a good road network, and the highway (75 bis) connecting Perugia to Tuscany (to Siena via S326 and E76) is excellent and goes right by Lake Trasimeno. However, getting across the mountains to Urbino can be a bit treacherous due to winding mountain roads; plan for plenty of travel time.

By Train

A small, privately owned railway runs from Città di Castello in the north to Terni in the South.

Contacts and Resources

Agritourist Agencies

Agriturist (⊠ Via Savonarola 38, Perugia 06100, ☎ 075/36665). **Terranostra** (⊠ Via Campo di Marte 10, Perugia 06100, ☎ 075/5009559). **Turismo Verde** (⊠ Via Campo di Marte 14/1, Perugia 06100, ☎ 075/5002953).

Car Rentals

Avis (⊠ Egido airport, ☎ 075/6929796; ⊠ Stazione Fontivegge, ☎ 5000395). **Hertz** (⊠ Piazza Vittorio Veneto 4, ☎ 075/5002439).

Emergencies

Perugia: Police (⊠ Piazza dei Partigiani, ☎ 113); **Fire department** (☎ 115); **Red Cross** (ambulance service, ☎ 075/5721111). **Gubbio: Police** (☎ 113).

Late-Night Pharmacies

All pharmacies post the addresses of the nearest late-night pharmacies outside their doors.

Visitor Information

The **Umbria regional tourist office** is in Perugia (⊠ Corso Vannucci 30, ☎ 075/5041). **Città di Castello** (⊠ Piazza Fanti, ☎ 075/8554922). **Città di Pieve** (⊠ Piazza Matteotti 4). **Deruta** (⊠ Piazza dei Consoli 4, 06053, ☎ 075/9711559). **Gubbio** (⊠ Piazza Oderisi 6, 06024, ☎ 075/9220693). **Lago Trasimeno** (⊠ Piazza Mazzini 10, Castiglione del Lago, ☎ 075/9652484). **Perugia** (⊠ Piazza IV Novembre 3, ☎ 075/5723327). **Urbino** (⊠ Piazza Rinascimento 1, 61029, ☎ 0722/2613).

9 Assisi, Spoleto, and Southern Umbria

Legends linger in smiling Umbria, ethereal birthplace of the saints. Here await Gothic treasures—Assisi's Basilica di San Francesco and Orvieto's awe-inspiring cathedral. Southern Umbria's wealth of hill towns, connected by sinuous roads lined with olive groves and vineyards, will be enough to convince you that central Italy doesn't begin and end with Tuscany.

Revised by Jon
Eldan and
Carla Lionello

IN DISCOVERING THE PEACE AND TRANQUILLITY of the green Umbrian plains, perhaps we are all just catching up with the pilgrims who have been crossing the serene valleys for centuries to pay homage to Italy's most important religious figure, St. Francis of Assisi. His town is the area's big draw, often overflowing with tour buses and crowds, but nonetheless worth a visit if only to see the famous Basilica di San Francesco, which contains some of the most important paintings in Western art. Farther down the Valle Umbra are great little hill towns like Spello, Montefalco, Trevi, Narni, and Amelia. Spoleto, world famous for its Festival dei Due Mondi held every summer, is a medieval jewel at the end of the valley, but there is plenty more to see, east through the lush mountainous terrain toward Norcia or west through the shadowy walled towns of Narni and Amelia to stunning Orvieto and Todi.

Few other regions pack so many fascinating, different places into such a compact and compelling terrain—all very much waiting to be discovered. And while these towns don't offer the vast wealth of art and architecture you will find in Florence or Rome, this will actually work in your favor. Individual towns can be experienced whole, the way people live in them today, rather than as a forced march through a series of museums and churches; in Southern Umbria, art and history come in small bites, with plenty of good meals and relaxing walks in between.

Pleasures and Pastimes

Dining

The food of Southern Umbria is typically hearty and straightforward, with a stick-to-the-ribs quality that sees hardworking farmers and artisans through a long day's work and helps them make the steep climb home at night. You will never be far from a rotisserie grill or fireplace, or a bowl of hot *ciriole* (rough-shape, thick spaghetti, often made in-house) or *stringozzi* (pasta like ciriole, *above*) laced with a light tomato or meat sauce. The local delicacy is truffles, which are generously shaved over pasta, pounded into sauces, or used to flavor meat (☞ Close-Up: Truffle Trouble, *below*). The tiny town of Norcia deserves special mention for its cured pork meat products, famous throughout Italy yet difficult to find out of their native Norcia; they go wonderfully well with the bread of the region, which is often made without salt. The nearby town of Castelluccio is renowned for a variety of tiny, tender, and tasty lentils. Umbria is landlocked, but freshwater fish from the lakes and streams play a limited role in local cooking—a famous dish is the *carpa in porchetta,* made with giant 40-pound carps dressed and roasted like suckling pigs.

Essential to the local cuisine, Umbrian olive oil is every bit as good as the more famous Tuscan olive oils. The basic cheese of the region is a soft *pecorino* (sheep's milk cheese), often flavored with truffles or herbs, eaten as a spread or stirred into hot pasta. Cheeses from neighboring Tuscany and Lazio also make their way to the Umbrian table. The monasteries and convents throughout the region produce a wide variety of multicolored *rosolii* (sweet liqueurs) and digestive bitters, sold in all manners of gift bottles. Desserts are strictly local, usually made with fruit, nuts, honey, and spices.

Wine making is nothing new to Umbria, where Sagrantino di Montefalco and Orvieto Classico are among Italy's oldest varieties, but mass commercialization has left them with middling reputations, and decisively overshadowed by Tuscan varieties. Renewed attention in the region to top-quality wine making has produced full-bodied winners like Rubesco and Torre di Giano, definitely worth seeking out.

CATEGORY	COST*
$$$$	over 110,000 lire
$$$	60,000 lire–110,000 lire
$$	35,000 lire–60,000 lire
$	under 35,000 lire

Prices are per person, for a three-course meal, house wine and tax included.

Hiking and Outdoor Activities

Magnificent scenery makes Umbria a great place to enjoy the outdoors. There is excellent hiking, mountaineering, rock climbing, and horseback riding throughout the region, and most tourist offices have maps of nearby trails and itineraries of walks and climbs to suit all ages and levels of ability.

Lodging

The main towns in Southern Umbria generally have one or two hotels in a high price category, and a few smaller, basic hotels in the inexpensive-to-moderate ($–$$) range, often family run. A recent and popular trend is the conversion of old villas and monasteries into small, first-class hotels. These tend to be out in the countryside, but the splendor of the settings often outweighs the problem of getting into town. If you are planning on staying in the area for a few days or more, you could stay in a cottage or apartment in the countryside (*agriturismo*), which offer excellent value and an interesting alternative to the usual hotels. Reservations are always advisable, and essential if you plan to visit Spoleto during the Festival dei Due Mondi (late June–early July) or Assisi from Easter through October.

CATEGORY	COST*
$$$$	over 350,000 lire
$$$	220,000 lire–350,000 lire
$$	100,000 lire–220,000 lire
$	under 100,000 lire

Prices are for a double room for two, tax and service included.

St. Francis

Born to a noblewoman and a well-to-do merchant in 1181, Francis led a troubled youth and spent a year in prison. Although he planned on a career in the military, after a long illness he heard the voice of God, publicly renounced his father's wealth, and began a life of austerity. His mystical approach to poverty, asceticism, and the beauty of man and nature struck a responsive chord in the medieval mind, and he quickly attracted a vast number of followers. Without actively seeking power, as did many clerics in his day, he became very influential and changed the history of the Catholic Church. In 1209, his order was recognized by Pope Innocent III (circa 1161–1216), and St. Francis later traveled widely throughout the Mediterranean to spread the word of God. He was the first saint to receive the stigmata (wounds on the hands, feet, and sides, corresponding to the torments of Christ on the cross). He died on Oct. 4, 1226, in the Porziuncola, the secluded chapel in the woods where he had first preached the virtue of poverty to his disciples.

The Franciscans are the largest of all Catholic orders. Among the mass of clergy at Assisi, you can identify the saint's followers by their simple, coarse brown habits bound by sashes of knotted rope. St. Francis was made the patron saint of Italy in 1939, and is remembered as the gentle man who spoke to the birds. His *Canticle to the Creatures*, one of the first written examples of the Italian vernacular, is still taught in schools today.

TRUFFLE TROUBLE

UMBRIA IS RICH WITH truffles—more are found here than anywhere else in Italy, and those not consumed fresh are processed into pastes or flavored oils. The primary truffle areas are around Spoleto (signs warning against unlicensed truffle hunting are posted at the base of the Ponte delle Torri) and the hills around the tiny town of Norcia, which holds a truffle festival every February. Even if they grow locally, the rare delicacy can nonetheless cost a small fortune, up to $200 for a quarter pound (fortunately, a little goes a long way). At such a price, there is great competition among the nearly 10,000 registered truffle hunters in the province, who use specially trained dogs to sniff them out among the roots of several trees, including oak and ilex. Although there have been recent incidences of poisoning truffle-hunting dogs and the importing of inferior tubers from China, you can be reasonably assured that the truffle shaved onto your pasta has been unearthed locally. The kind of truffle you taste will depend on the season: In summer, there's the *scorzone* (rough-skinned, dark gray-brown tuber); the fall rains bring out the *bianchetto* (small-sized, smoother, and dirty-white truffle variety); and the prized black *tartufo nero* (black truffle) appears from December through March. Out of season, restaurants rely on preserved truffles (in olive oil, vacuum sealed, frozen, or ground into a paste).

Swimming and Water Sports

Lago di Piediluco (Lake Piediluco) is a safe, clean place to swim, and there is river rafting in the Valnerina, in the Nera River, below the waterfalls at Marmore. Southern Umbria has several famous *terme* (thermal springs), which have long been visited by travelers for their soothing, curative powers.

Exploring Southern Umbria

The main towns in the region are easily accessible from Rome and Florence by road or rail, and despite the hilly terrain, getting around Southern Umbria is actually a snap. The main highways run southeast from Perugia through or very near the main towns of the region, which are almost all linked by fairly frequent train and bus service. Distances are relatively short from one town to the next, although Assisi and Spoleto make the most sensible bases from which to explore the rest of the region. A car is a must, and a bit of Italian will be very helpful throughout the region.

Numbers in the text correspond to numbers in the margin and on the Assisi, Spoleto, and Southern Umbria; Assisi; Spoleto; and Orvieto maps.

Great Itineraries

Southern Umbria is particularly well suited to touring in a limited time, as you can easily hop from one town to the next with a minimum of distance or difficulty. Alternatively, any of the towns, with the exception of Norcia to the east, can be covered in day trips from Perugia.

Begin in 🖼 **Assisi** ①–⑥ with the Basilica di San Francesco, seeing the town's other major sites, including the tiny Museo Civico and fortress. Spend the following day south of Assisi, visiting some of the delightful hill towns in the Valle Umbra, such as 🖼 **Spello** ⑦ or **Montefalco** ⑩. Devote the third day to good walks through the narrow streets of **Spoleto** ⑫–㉒, including a walk across the Ponte delle Torri and around the pretty Monteluco. The next morning, go east to **Norcia** ㉓ for a day hike and to try the savory local sausage, or south to the towns of **Narni** ㉗ and **Amelia** ㉘. On the fifth day visit quaint 🖼 **Todi** ㉚ and the stunning Duomo and museums in nearby 🖼 **Orvieto** ㉛–㉠.

Spend the first day discovering 🖼 **Assisi** ①–⑥. The next day, make your way through the Franciscan sites outside the walls, like Eremo delle Carceri and the church of San Damiano, before moving south to 🖼 **Spello** ⑦ and **Foligno** ⑧. The third day can be spent in the remaining hill towns in the Valle Umbra. On the fourth day move on to 🖼 **Spoleto** ⑫–㉒. The following day, go east to **Norcia** ㉓ for a day hike, being sure to try the savory local sausage. The sixth day could be spent between the towns of **Terni** ㉖, **Narni** ㉗, and **Amelia** ㉘, or at the waterfalls at Marmore and the lovely Lake Piediluco. On the final day, visit 🖼 **Todi** ㉚ and the stunning Duomo and museums in nearby 🖼 **Orvieto** ㉛–㉠.

When to Tour Southern Umbria

The forested hills of Southern Umbria ensure beguiling colors in the fall and an explosion of greenery and flowers in spring. Keep in mind that winters can be especially cold, and that many hotels and restaurants close for some portion of the winter. Book accommodations far in advance if you are planning to visit Spoleto in June or July during the Festival dei Due Mondi. Assisi is especially crowded during Christmas, Easter, the Festa di San Francesco (October 4) and the Calendimaggio festival (early May).

ASSISI

The legacy of St. Francis, founder of the Franciscan monastic order, pervades the rose-color hills of Assisi. Each year, several million pilgrims come here to pay homage to the man who made God accessible to commoners. But not even the steadily massive flow of visitors to this town of just 3,000 residents can spoil the singular beauty of Italy's most significant religious center, which can also claim some of the greatest frescoes ever painted. The hill on which Assisi sits rises dramatically from the flat plain, and the town is dominated at the top of the mount by a medieval castle; on the lower slopes of the hill is the massive Basilica di San Francesco, rising majestically on graceful arched supports. From a distance, St. Francis's birthplace looks—to use an evocative phrase of travel essayist James Reynolds—"calm, white, pure as the fresh-washed wool from the Pascal Lamb."

Like most towns in the region, Assisi began as an Umbri settlement in the 7th century, and was conquered by the Romans four hundred years later. The town was christianized by St. Rufino in AD 238, but it is the spirit of St. Francis, patron saint of Italy and founder of the Franciscan monastic order, that is felt throughout its narrow medieval streets. The famous 13th-century basilica built in his honor was decorated by the greatest artists of the period. Assisi is pristinely medieval in architecture and appearance, due in large part to relative neglect from the 16th century until 1926, when the celebration of the 700th anniversary of St. Francis' death brought more than 2 million visitors.

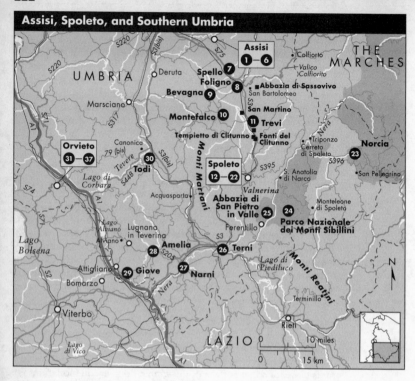

Assisi, Spoleto, and Southern Umbria

Since then, Assisi has become one of the most important pilgrimage sites in the Christian world.

A series of severe earthquakes in late September and early October 1997 did extensive damage to Assisi and many towns in Umbria and neighboring Le Marche. Particularly hard hit was the Basilica di San Francesco; frescoes by Giotto (1266–1337), widely held to be masterpieces of Western art, were destroyed when the vaulting over the entrance doorway and the main altar of the Upper Basilica collapsed, tragically killing four people. The Upper Basilica will be closed until the year 2000, but the rest of the town has made a quick recovery. With the exception of the Upper Basilica and other Basilica di San Francesco sites, in Assisi only the Pinacoteca Comunale remains closed at press time; other sites scattered throughout Umbria were also still closed due to earthquake damage.

Exploring Assisi

Assisi lies on the Terontola-Foligno rail line, with almost hourly connections to Perugia, and direct trains to Rome and Florence several times per day. The train station is 4 km (2½ mi) from town, with bus service about every half hour. Assisi is easily reached from the A1 Motorway (Rome–Florence) and the S75b highway. The walled town is closed to outside traffic, so cars must be left in the parking lots at Porta San Pietro (the gate just below Porta San Francesco), near Porta Nuova, or beneath Piazza Matteotti. It's an easy walk into the center of town, but frequent minibuses (buy tickets from a newsstand or tobacconist) make the rounds for weary pilgrims.

A Good Walk

Much of your visit to Assisi will likely be spent in churches and walking through the cobblestone streets. You'll want to set aside a good portion of your time for the **Basilica di San Francesco** ①, even if only the Lower Basilica is currently accessible. Via San Francesco leads downhill from the basilica, past storefronts overflowing with souvenirs, several attractive facades, and a fine public fountain. Up ahead is Piazza del Comune, the town square built in the Middle Ages over Roman remains, which can be visited in the adjacent **Museo Civico** ②. To the left is the beautiful **Tempio di Minerva** ③, among the best-preserved Roman-era facades in Italy. Across the piazza is the Palazzo dei Priori, with the **Pinacoteca Comunale** ④ (closed indefinitely at press time). From the piazza, Via di San Rufino leads to the **Duomo di San Rufino** ⑤, which houses the remains of the martyred 3rd-century bishop who brought Christianity to Assisi. To the side is the small Museo Capitolare, with detached frescoes and artifacts from the church, and includes admission to the 11th-century crypt. Double back to Piazza del Comune and take Corso Mazzini to **Santa Chiara** ⑥, then continue through Porta Nuova to the church of San Damiano, a 1½ km (1 mi) walk outside the walls. Also of interest outside the walls are the Eremo delle Carceri, east of the center along Via Santuario delle Carceri, and the church of Santa Maria degli Angeli, near the train station.

TIMING

Although the itinerary can be done in as little as a half day, it is a shame to be in a rush in a place as peaceful as Assisi. An especially pleasant way to work up an appetite for dinner is to take part in the *passeggiata* (evening stroll) along the long streets (Via Fontebella, Via San Francesco) which cross the hill, where you can catch glimpses of the valley below and plenty of local color.

Sights to See

★ ❶ **Basilica di San Francesco.** The basilica was begun by the followers of St. Francis in 1228, two years after his death. They finished what is now the Lower Basilica in just a few years. But less than half a century later, Franciscan leaders from Northern Europe crossed the Alps and arrived in Assisi. They built a second church on top of the first, in French Gothic style, with soaring arches and stained glass, in stark contrast to the Lower Basilica and its dark and somber Romanesque-Lombard style. The two levels are brought together by a 13th-century campanile and Romanesque facade. Inside, the walls and ceilings are decorated with masterpieces by the greatest artists of the period. At first, the splendor and grandeur of the basilica might seem at odds with the tenets of the Franciscan order, expressed in the credo "Carry nothing for the journey, neither purse nor bag nor bread nor money." But it is important to consider the essential role that this church served for pilgrims as far back as the 14th century, and that great works of art and elaborate decoration were seen as an homage to saintliness, aimed at elevating—as well as intimidating—the soul.

The **Upper Basilica** suffered extensive structural damage when portions of the vaulted ceiling collapsed during several earthquakes in the fall of 1997. Extensive efforts to restore and rebuild the basilica are underway, and it is expected to reopen before the year 2000. The highlight among many great works in the Upper Basilica, and unfortunately severely damaged by the quakes, is Giotto's 28-panel fresco cycle of the *Life of St. Francis,* a landmark in the history of Western painting. Giotto broke away from the stiff, unnatural styles of earlier generations and moved toward a realism and grace that reached its peak in the Renaissance. The paintings are viewed left to right, starting in the transept; the narration closely follows the biography of the saint given by San Bonaventura (St. Bonaventure). Although St. Francis' days were mostly filled with miracles and mystic visions, Giotto doesn't dwell

Assisi

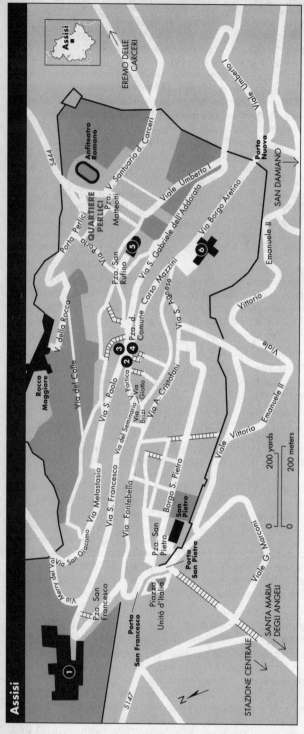

Basilica di
San Francesco, **1**
Duomo di San
Rufino, **5**
Museo Civico, **2**
Pinacoteca
Comunale, **4**

Santa Chiara, **6**
Tempio di
Minerva, **3**

much on the myth of the fragile, pure, and holy poor man. Instead, he portrays a powerful, good friar who actively worked in behalf of his "brothers" and "sisters" and was deeply committed to his community. Giotto's St. Francis is a robust man busy meeting people in front of real buildings and trees; rather than floating through the clouds, St. Francis' feet are firmly set on the ground.

The first four episodes are a prelude to the fifth, in which St. Francis renounces his worldly goods. Episodes 6 to 20 depict St. Francis' supernatural deeds: the most beloved scene of all is *The Sermon to the Birds,* a touching image that seems to sum up the gentle spirit of the saint. It stands in marked contrast to *St. Francis Appearing before Pope Innocent III in a Dream,* in which the pope dreams of a humble monk who will steady the church. Sure enough, in the panel next to the sleeping pope, you see a strong St. Francis supporting a church that seems to be—bitterly ironic today—on the verge of tumbling down. Other famous scenes include: *St. Francis Appearing to His Companions in a Flaming Chariot*; *St. Francis Proposing Trial by Fire before the Sultan*; and *St. Francis Chasing the Devils from Arezzo.* The 19th and 20th panels solemnly illustrate St. Francis receiving the stigmata, followed by his death and funeral. Aside from the scene in which St. Clare mourns the loss of her friend, the last eight episodes refer to the cannonization of St. Francis (24) and the miracles he performed after his death. In the transept are frescoes (in poor condition) by Giotto's master Cimabue (circa 1240–1302). Note the inlaid choir, a 16th-century masterpiece made up of 105 stalls decorated with episodes from the lives of famous Franciscan friars, and the 13th-century stained-glass windows (also used in the lower church), among the oldest in existence.

Around the left side of the facade and beneath a Renaissance porch is the entrance to the **Lower Basilica.** The low ceilings and dimly lit interior contrast sharply with the soaring, airy space above, but it seems an appropriate shrine for the tomb of St. Francis, beneath the main altar. Stairs at the sides of the nave lead down to the crypt. The saint's body was once visible through a window, but was hidden away in the 15th century when rival towns threatened to steal it. In 1818, after a 52-day search, the simple stone coffin containing St. Francis' remains was found again, and reinterred in the center of the crypt, with the sepulchres of his four closest disciples placed at the corners.

The frescoes on the four sections of the cross-vaulting above the main altar are attributed to a student of Giotto, and represent allegories of the Franciscan virtues (*Poverty, Chastity,* and *Obedience*) and the *The Triumph of St. Francis.* In the right transept is Cimabue's *Madonna and Child Enthroned, with Four Angels and St. Francis,* which features one of the best-known images of the saint. Just below are the tombs of five of St. Francis' early followers, with their portraits on the wall above by Pietro Lorenzetti (circa 1280–1348). By the same artist, in the left transept, is a moving group of frescoes depicting the *Passion of Christ* with particular expressiveness and tension. The staging of the crucifixion is totally innovative, involving three crosses instead of one and a crowd rendered more real than ever before by its size and the perspective, which shows figures and horses from behind.

Also worthy of a look is the **Cappella di San Martino** (first on the left of the nave), with frescoes of the *Life of St. Martin* (1322) by Sienese master Simone Martini (circa 1284–1344). The cycle begins at the lower left, with a famous scene in which St. Martin shares his cloak with Christ disguised as a poor man (realistically portrayed as barefoot, in torn garments, covering himself from the cold), and continues with the saint's knighthood, and his renouncing of the sword. The frescoes along the walls on either side of the nave, by an unknown artist, present the lives of Christ and St. Francis, and served as inspiration to Giotto's more famous *Life of St. Francis* cycle in the Upper Basilica. The **Cappella della Maddalena** (last chapel in the right nave) features frescoes of the life of St. Mary Magdalen by Giotto and assistants.

The adjacent **Chapter House, Treasury,** and **Cloister** were closed indefinitely at press time. The basilica is run by monks, who often give tours in English. In addition to normal services, there are special celebrations throughout the year. On October 4th, the anniversary of St. Francis' death, a ceremony is held in which oil is offered for the lamp that burns above his tomb. Masses are sung during Easter week, and special ceremonies during Lent re-create the life of St. Francis and Jesus. ⊠ *Piazza di San Francesco,* ☎ *075/819001.* ▧ *Treasury: 3,000 lire.* ☉ *Lower Basilica Easter–Oct., daily 7–7; Nov.–Easter, daily 7– 12:30 and 2–6. Upper Basilica closed indefinitely. Note: Dress code (no bare shoulders or bare knees) strictly enforced.*

❺ Duomo di San Rufino. St. Francis and St. Clare were among those baptized in Assisi's Duomo, which was the principal church in town until the 12th century. The baptismal font has since been redecorated, but it is possible to see the crypt of San Rufino, the martyred 3rd-century bishop who brought Christianity to Assisi. Admission to the crypt includes a look at the small **Museo Capitolare,** which features detached frescoes and artifacts. ⊠ *Piazza San Rufino,* ☎ *075/81228.* ▧ *Crypt 2,500 lire; Museo Capitolare 2,500 lire; combined ticket 4,000 lire.* ☉ *Daily 10–noon and 3–8.*

OFF THE BEATEN PATH **EREMO DELLE CARCERI –** Just 4 km (2½ mi) east of Assisi is a monastery set in dense wood against Monte Subasio. In the caves on the slope of the mountain, St. Francis and his followers established their first home, to which he returned often during his lifetime to pray and meditate. The only site in Assisi that remains essentially unchanged since St. Francis' times, the church and monastery is the kind of oasis of tranquility that St. Francis would have appreciated. The walk out from town is very pleasant, and many trails lead from here across the wooded hillside of Mt. Subasio (now a protected forest), with beautiful vistas across the Umbrian countryside. True to their Franciscan heritage, the friars here are entirely dependent on alms from visitors. ⊠ *Eremo delle Carceri,* ☎ *075/812301.* ▧ *Donations accepted.* ☉ *Daily dawn–dusk.*

❷ Museo Civico. Several dozen interesting Umbrian and Roman relics line the walls of this one-room museum, set in the crypt of an ex-church. Down a hallway to the right is an excavated gallery under Piazza del Comune; once thought to be the remains of the Roman-era forum, it is now believed to have been a sacred site in front of the Tempio di Minerva. ⊠ *Via Portica 2,* ☎ *075/813053.* ▧ *4,000 lire.* ☉ *Mid-Mar.–mid-Oct., daily 10–1 and 3–7; mid-Oct.–mid-Mar., daily 10–1 and 2–5.*

❹ Pinacoteca Comunale. The Palazzo dei Priori, which has been the seat of city government for more than six centuries, contains this gallery, with early paintings by local artists. ⊠ *Piazza del Comune,* ☎ *075/ 812579.* ▧ *4,000 lire.* ☉ *Closed for restoration.*

❻ Santa Chiara. The stunning red and off-white striping on the facade makes this 13th-century church the best looking in town. It is dedicated to St. Clare, one of the earliest and most fervent of St. Francis's followers and the founder of the order of the Poor Ladies, or Poor Clares, based on the Franciscan monastic order. The church contains the body of the saint, and in the **Cappella del Crocifisso** (on the right) is the cross that spoke to St. Francis. A heavily veiled nun of St. Clare's order is usually stationed before the cross in adoration of the image. ✉ *Piazza Santa Chiara,* ☎ *075/812282.* ✉ *Free.* ☉ *Daily 8–noon and 2:30–sunset.*

OFF THE
BEATEN PATH

SAN DAMIANO – It was here that a crucifix (now in the church of Santa Chiara (☞ *above*) spoke to St. Francis, saying *"Vade, Francisce, et repara domum meam"* ("Go, Francis, and repair my house"). Taking the phrase literally, he had the church restored. After taking the Franciscan vows, St. Clare lived out her life in the convent of this church, and attracted a wide following and fame for her piety. She was often bedridden from illness, sustained only by divine providence. Shortly before death, she reported having "seen" the Easter celebrations being held in the Basilica di San Francesco. Such abilities earned her the title of the patron saint of television in the 1950s. In a Papal Bull in 1253, Pope Innocent IV (died 1254) confirmed her order, the Poor Clares, and she died the next day. St. Francis returned here to compose the *Canticle of the Creatures.* Pleasantly situated in an olive grove, the simple, austere church and convent give a far better idea of St. Francis and his movement than the great basilica across town. ✉ *Località San Damiano, 1½ km (1 mi) south, outside the walls,* ☎ *075/812273.* ✉ *Free.* ☉ *Daily 10–noon and 2–6.*

❸ **Tempio di Minerva.** Dating from the time of Augustus, the structure was used as a monastery and prison before being converted into a church in the 16th century. The expectations raised by the perfect classical facade are not met by the interior, subjected to a thorough Baroque assault in the 17th century. ✉ *Piazza del Comune,* ☎ *no phone.* ✉ *Free.* ☉ *Daily 7–noon and 2:30–sunset.*

OFF THE
BEATEN PATH

ROCCA MAGGIORE– Even if there's not much to see inside the 14th-century fortress, the views are well worth the walk up to the peak, day or night. On the way, pass through the Quartiere Perlici, a little neighborhood with narrow streets that follow a symmetrical Roman layout; in one part the houses and street trace the elliptical plan of the 1st-century Anfiteatro Romano (Roman amphitheater) that stood on the site. ✉ *End of Via della Rocca,* ☎ *075/815292.* ✉ *5,000 lire.* ☉ *Daily sunrise–sunset.*

SANTA MARIA DEGLI ANGELI–Down by the train station, 8 km (5 mi) south of town, this hulking Baroque church restored in the 19th century was built over the **Porziuncola,** St. Francis' little chapel in the forest. The shrine is much venerated because it was in the adjacent **Cappella Transito,** then a humble cell, that St. Francis died on the bare earth, wearing a borrowed tunic. ✉ *Località Santa Maria degli Angeli,* ☎ *075/ 80511.* ✉ *Free.* ☉ *Daily 9–12:30 and 2:30–sunset.*

Dining and Lodging

Assisi is not a late-night town, so don't plan on any midnight snacks. You can count on the ubiquitous stringozzi pasta. A local specialty— strange in light of St. Francis' famous rapport with birds—is *piccione all'assisana* (roasted pigeon with olives and liver). The locals eat *torta al testo* (a dense flatbread, often stuffed with vegetables or cheese) with their meals, which explains why Assisi has no bakeries (bread is imported from surrounding towns). There are, however, several pastry shops around town, featuring (of course) *pane di San Francesco* (an egg bread sweetened with raisins and sugar) and *rocciata di Assisi* (the local version of strudel, filled with apples, nuts, raisins, and dried fruit). Good places to try these goodies are **Bottega del Pasticcere** (✉ Via Portica 9, ☎ 075/812392) and **Fratelli Sensi** (✉ Corso Mazzini 14 and Via Fontebella 20, ☎ 075/812529).

It is hard to overemphasize the importance of reserving a room in Assisi if you are visiting between Easter and October or over Christmas, especially since hotels in the town itself are the first to fill up. Latecomers are often left to choose from those in modern Santa Maria degli Angeli, 8 km (5 mi) out of town; Spello (☞ *below*) might be a more pleasant option. Until not long ago, pilgrim hostels outnumbered the ordinary hotels in Assisi, and they present an interesting alternative to conventional lodgings. Rooms are usually on the spartan side, but you are virtually assured of a peaceful stay. Check with the **tourist office** (⊠ Piazza del Comune, ☎ 075/812534) for a list.

$$$ ✕ **La Buca di San Francesco.** This is one of Assisi's busiest restaurants, with a cozy dining room in the cellar and additional seating outside in the garden. The restaurant belongs to an association that prides itself on authentic regional cooking, and the wine list is among the best in town. The *filetto al rubesco* (fillet steak cooked in a heady red wine) is a specialty of the house. Reservations are recommended. ⊠ *Via Brizi 1,* ☎ *075/812204. AE, DC, MC, V. Closed Mon. and July.*

$$$ ✕ **La Fortezza.** Parts of the walls of this modern, family-run restaurant were built by the Romans. The service is personable and the kitchen is reliable. A particular standout is *anatra al finocchio selvatico* (duck cooked with wild fennel). La Fortezza also has seven simple but clean guest rooms available. Reservations are recommended. ⊠ *Vicolo della Fortezza 19/b,* ☎ *075/812418. AE, DC, MC, V. Closed Thurs. and Feb.*

$$$ ✕ **San Francesco.** Here's your chance to dine in front of the Basilica di San Francesco, but you'll certainly do better than bread and water. The cuisine is the fanciest in town, with creative Umbrian dishes based on local ingredients and aromatic herbs. The menu changes periodically, but might include dishes like eggplant gnocchi and goose stuffed with wild fennel. ⊠ *Via di San Francesco 52,* ☎ *075/812329. AE, DC, MC, V. Closed Wed.*

$$ ✕ **La Stalla.** A kilometer or two outside the town proper, this onetime stable has been turned into a simple and rustic restaurant. In summer, lunch and dinner are served outside under a trellis shaded with vines and flowers. In keeping with the decor, the kitchen turns out hearty country fare, with meats grilled in the fireplace at the center of the room. ⊠ *Via Eremo delle Carceri 8,* ☎ *075/812317. No credit cards. Closed Mon. Oct.–June.*

$–$$ ✕ **La Pallotta.** The women do the cooking and the men serve the food
★ in this cozy, honest family-run trattoria, which may very well be the best place to eat in town. All the local dishes are excellently prepared and reasonably priced—try the *menu degustazione* (tasting menu) or the stringozzi *alla pallotta* (with a pesto of olives and mushrooms). The interior is cozy, with a fireplace and stone walls. ⊠ *Via San Rufino 4,* ☎ *075/812317. AE, DC, MC, V. Closed Tues. and 2 wks in Jan.–Feb.*

$ ✕ **Osteria Piazzetta dell'Erba.** This new osteria is a great change of pace
★ in a town with more than its fair share of stodgy tourist eateries, and it's an excellent place to come for an informal meal or light snack. There are two different *primi piatti* (first courses) on offer every day, along with various salads and a good selection of toppings to go with the ever-present torta al testo. The "imported" goat cheese is from Sardinia and is a delicious surprise. There are tables outside in the summer. ⊠ *Via San Gabriele dell'Addolorata 15b,* ☎ *075/815352. AE, DC, MC, V. Closed Mon. and 3 wks. in Jan.*

$$$–$$$$ 🛏 **Hotel Subasio.** A little rough around the edges, but by far the fanciest hotel in town, the Subasio is a stone's throw from the Basilica di San Francesco. Housed in a converted monastery, some of the rooms remain a little cell-like, but others are very spacious and furnished with antiques. Most rooms have views of the valley, as do the comfortable

old-fashioned sitting rooms, flowered terraces, and lovely garden. ⊠ *Via Frate Elia 2, 06081,* ☎ *075/812206,* 𝖥𝖠𝖷 *075/816691. 61 rooms. Restaurant, bar. CP. AE, DC, MC, V.*

$$$ 🏨 **Fontebella.** Between Piazza del Popolo and the Basilica di San Francesco, the Fontebella has spacious lounges and comfortable rooms (with rather small bathrooms), decorated with cheerful tapestries. The breakfast is especially ample, the welcome warm. ⊠ *Via Fontebella 25, 06081,* ☎ *075/816456,* 𝖥𝖠𝖷 *075/812941. 46 rooms. Breakfast room. CP. AE, DC, MC, V.*

$$$ 🏨 **Le Silve.** Not exactly the kind of hermitage in the forest that St. Francis had in mind, Le Silve is a well-restored medieval manor house in the Subasio reserve, just 8 km (5 mi) out of town. Rooms are different from one another, but always well appointed, and the common areas have fireplaces and antiques. The restaurant serves traditional Umbrian fare. There is a swimming pool and horseback riding is available. ⊠ *Località Armenzano, 06081,* ☎ *075/8019000,* 𝖥𝖠𝖷 *075/8019005. 15 rooms. Restaurant, pool, horseback riding. CP. AE, DC, MC, V.*

$$$ 🏨 **San Francesco.** You can't beat the location—some of the rooms look out onto the facade of the Basilica di San Francesco, which is just opposite the hotel. Rooms are rather basic, but with nice touches like slippers and a goodnight piece of chocolate. This is also one of the few hotels with air-conditioning in every room. The breakfast is first rate, and features homemade desserts, fruit, savory tarts, and fresh ricotta. ⊠ *Via di San Francesco 48, 06082,* ☎ *075/812281,* 𝖥𝖠𝖷 *075/816237. 44 rooms. Restaurant, bar. CP. AE, DC, MC, V.*

$$ 🏨 **Hotel Umbra.** A 16th-century town house is home to this family-
★ run hotel, which is in a tranquil part of the city near Piazza del Comune. The rooms, all different and simply appointed, are arranged as small apartments, each with a tiny living room and terrace. In the warm season breakfast is served under the arbor on the patio. The restaurant in the garden serves regional cuisine; it's closed Sunday at lunch and Tuesday. ⊠ *Via degli Archi 6, 06081,* ☎ *075/812240,* 𝖥𝖠𝖷 *075/ 813653. 25 rooms. Restaurant. CP. AE, DC, MC, V. Closed mid-Jan.–mid-Mar. and Dec. 1–20.*

$ 🏨 **La Pallotta.** Just above a great family-run restaurant (☞ *above*), this
★ hotel is one of the best in its category. The beds are firm, and some of the rooms look out across the rooftops of town, but the real attraction is the reading room in the *torretta* (small tower), with a 360-degree panoramic view. There is no breakfast, but a self-service bar is available to guests. ⊠ *Via di San Francesco 48, 06082,* ☎ *075/812281,* 𝖥𝖠𝖷 *075/816237. 44 rooms. CP. AE, DC, MC, V.*

Nightlife and the Arts

Concerts are occasionally held in the various churches around town; check with the tourist office. All the major Catholic holidays are celebrated with particular enthusiasm in Assisi. **Calendimaggio,** a three-day medieval pageant, begins the first Thursday after May 1. It includes a procession in medieval costume and the singing of madrigals to celebrate spring. **Corpus Domini** (the ninth Sunday after Easter) is celebrated with an *infiorata*, during which the streets are decorated with flower petals. In the **Festa del Perdono** (Forgiveness Day), crowds of pilgrims walk to the church of Santa Maria degli Angeli on August 1 and 2 to ask for forgiveness. **St. Clare,** the patron saint of television, is remembered on August 11 with solemn masses. The last Sunday in August brings celebrations in honor of San Rufino, which include processions in historical dress and the **Palio della Balestra,** a crossbow competition. The high point of the year comes every October 4, with the **Festa di San Francesco,** commemorating the anniversary of St. Francis' death.

Shopping

In addition to just about everything imaginable connected with the image of St. Francis, from key chains and lighters to Franciscan sandals to tiny "blessed" olive trees, Assisi is also well known for white-and-blue *ricamo a punto,* a traditional style of embroidery kept alive by religious institutions over the centuries. A good shop for ricamo items is **Rossi** (⊠ Via Frate Elia 1, ☎ 075/812555). If you will not be passing through Deruta (☞ Chapter 8), Assisi has a number of shops that sell ceramics from the town.

FROM ASSISI TO SPOLETO
Through the Valle Umbra

The main road (SS75) runs straight down the Valle Umbra from Assisi to Spoleto, but you'll do well to stop and smell the flowers in the towns that line the valley.

Spello

❼ *12 km (7 mi) southeast of Assisi, 33 km (21 mi) north of Spoleto.*

Although it's half the size of Assisi and has more than twice as many inhabitants, chances are you'll find Spello relatively empty, perhaps a welcome relief after where you have just been. Just a few minutes from Assisi by car or train, this hill town at the edge of Mt. Subasio makes an excellent base from which to explore the surrounding towns. But Spello has its own charm, too, with first-rate frescoes by Pinturicchio (1454–1513) and fine Roman ruins. The Romans called the town Hispellum, and traces remain of their walls, gates, amphitheater, and theater. The town is 1 km (½ mi) from the train station, and buses run every 30 minutes for Porta Consolare, the dilapidated Roman gate at the south end of town and the best place to enter.

From Porta Consolare continue up the steep main street that begins as Via Consolare and changes names several times as it crosses the little town, following the original Roman *cardo maximus* (main street). As it curves around, notice the medieval alleyways to the right and the more uniform Roman-era blocks to the left. Just up ahead is the basilica of **Santa Maria Maggiore,** with vivid frescoes by Pinturicchio in the Cappella Baglioni (1501). Striking in their rich colors, finely dressed figures, and complex symbolism, the *Nativity, Dispute at the Temple* (on the far left side is a portrait of Troilo Baglioni, the prior who commissioned the work), and the *Annunciation* (with a self-portrait, on the far right) were painted after the artist had already won great acclaim for his work on the Palazzi Vaticani in Rome, and are among his finest works. Two pillars on either side of the apse are decorated with frescoes by Perugino (circa 1450–1523), the other great Umbrian artist of the 16th century. ⊠ *Piazza Matteotti 18,* ☎ *0742/301792.* ☞ *Free.* ☉ *May–Sept., daily 8–12:30 and 2:30–7; Oct.–Apr., daily 8–12:30 and 2:30–6.*

Adjacent is the new **Pinacoteca Civica,** inside Palazzo dei Canonici, which holds a rich assortment of art that once adorned the church, including several unusual wooden statues that were carried during Easter processions in centuries past. ⊠ *Palazzo dei Canonici, Piazza Matteotti,* ☎ *0742/301497.* ☞ *5,000 lire.* ☉ *June–Aug., Tues.–Sun. 10–1 and 4–7; Sept.–May, Tues.–Sun. 10–1 and 3–6.*

The Gothic church of **Sant' Andrea** has a fresco of the *Madonna and Child with Saints* by Pinturicchio, as well as the mummified remains of the church's namesake, who was an early follower of St. Francis. ✉ *Via Cavour,* ☎ *no phone.* ✉ *Free.* ☉ *May–Sept., daily 8–12:30 and 2:30–7; Oct.–Apr., daily 8–12:30 and 2:30–6.*

Piazza della Repubblica sits at the center of town, with the 13th-century **Vecchio Palazzo Comunale,** one of the oldest town halls in the region, and a small **Museo Emilio Greco** (☎ 0742/30001) inside. Leave some time for strolling around town and a stop at the *belvedere* (viewpoint) at the top of Via Torre del Belvedere, with the shabby remains of the Roman amphitheater just below and the surrounding towns in the distance.

OFF THE BEATEN PATH

VILLA COSTANZI – The road out of town leads past the crumbling remains for the 1st century AD Anfiteatro Romano (closed indefinitely at press time) on the left, and the pleasant 12th-century church of San Claudio on the right. Up ahead is Villa Costanzi, an 18th-century mansion modeled on Villa Madama in Rome, surrounded by a beautiful garden. It is now home to the small, eclectic Collezione Straka-Coppa, set amid the antique furnishings of the villa. You'll find paintings and manifestos from the Italian Futurist movement on the ground floor, an assemblage of early painting on the second floor, and various contemporary pieces on display. ✉ *Via Centrale Umbra,* ☎ *0742/301866.* ✉ *5,000 lire.* ☉ *Apr.–June and Sept., Thurs.–Sun. 10:30–1 and 3:30–6:30, July–Aug., daily 10:30–1 and 3:30–6:30; Oct.–Mar., Sat.–Sun. 10:30–1 and 3–5:30.*

Dining and Lodging

$$ ✕ **Il Cacciatore.** This trattoria-inn run by several generations of the Cruciani family won't win awards for its decor (if weather permits, try the view from the terrace), but the food might be enough to make you check in to the family's adjacent inn and have another meal. The pasta is rolled fresh every day; try the *pappardelle con sugo d'oca* (ribbons of pasta dressed in goose sauce) or tagliatelle with peas and prosciutto, then select from the usual array of grilled and roasted meats and truffles (in season). Round off your meal with a homemade dessert. ✉ *Via Giulia 42,* ☎ *0742/651141, 0742/301603. AE, MC, V. Closed Mon., 3 wks. in Nov., and 2 wks. in July.*

$$ ✕ **La Cantina.** As its name implies, this place right on the main street is definitely the place to come for wines from all over the country. The menu features a good variety of pasta dishes, many with refreshing seasonal dressings such as wild asparagus (in spring) or artichokes (in fall and winter). Although the specialty of the house is grilled meat (the prized Tuscan Chianina beef and baby lamb chops), you might be tempted by the pigeon casserole or roasted baby pork. For dessert there's homemade *rocciata* (strudel) or the unusual house specialty, "*sweet maccheroni.*" ✉ *Via Cavour 2,* ☎ *0742/651775, 0742/652122. AE, DC, MC, V. Closed Wed.*

$$ 🛏 **La Bastiglia.** Here's your chance to sleep in a renovated grain mill, but there's no grist lying around this tidy, cozy hotel. Sitting rooms and bedrooms are comfy, done in soft, light colors with a mix of antique and modern pieces. Rooms on the top floor have views. A separate building, with seven additional rooms, is surrounded by a cheerful garden. Breakfast includes (appropriately) homemade bread. The terrace looks out onto the valley and is used by the hotel restaurant, which serves solid local fare. ✉ *Via dei Molini 17, 06081,* ☎ *0742/651277,* FAX *0742/301159. 22 rooms. Restaurant. CP. AE, DC, MC, V.*

Nightlife and the Arts

If you happen to be in the area, don't miss the infiorata on **Corpus Domini** (the ninth Sunday after Easter), when the streets are decorated with flower petals, or the **Festa dell'Olio,** an olive oil festival, on the last Sunday of Carnevale (February).

Shopping

Olives and hemp have always grown around Spello, so it's a good place to find good olive oil, carved olive wood, and hemp (*canapa*) crafts— try the **Frantoio Cianetti** (✉ Via Bulgarella 10, ☎ 0742/652781), **Angelo Passeri** (✉ Via Giulia 18, ☎ 0330/282104), and **Le Ali di Paldina** (✉ Via Sant'Angelo 26, ☎ no phone).

Foligno

❽ *5 km (3 mi) southeast of Spello, 18 km (11 mi) southeast of Assisi, 28 km (17 mi) north of Spoleto.*

The third-largest town in Umbria, Foligno has been an important commercial center since the 14th century, known especially for ceramics, miniatures, ironwork, carving, and embroidery (some small workshops can still be found around town). This made the city a target for heavy Allied bombing in World War II, and reconstruction and flourishing light industry now obscure what must have once been a charming town. The historic center retains the old Roman street grid and a medieval feel, as well as several churches worthy of a stop. Sadly, the town suffered some of the worst damage wrought by the 1997 earthquakes. The most evocative part of town is the area between the piazza and the river, still very much as it was centuries ago. Via delle Conce and Via dei Molini are pleasant streets to stroll along, with views onto the canals. The main shopping street is Corso Cavour.

Find your way to Piazza della Repubblica, the central square in the old part of town. The two-faced 12th-century **Duomo** shows its better side here—with fine Cosmatesque mosaics lining the doorway and fantastic carvings of animals all around. The other facade, renovated in the early years of this century, is around the corner. The interior got a thorough dressing up in the 18th century. The two busts in the sacristy are attributed to Bernini. ✉ *Piazza della Repubblica.* 🎫 *Free. Closed indefinitely at press time.*

The facade of **Palazzo Trinci** is neoclassical, but the mostly Gothic interior features an early 15th-century fresco cycle of the personification of the liberal arts by Benozzo Gozzoli (1420–1497). The building houses the **Museo Archeologico**, with Roman-era relics found in the area, and the **Pinacoteca Civica**, with works by local painters who made Foligno an important art center in the Renaissance. At press time the Museo Archeologico had opened a small exhibit of its works and the Pinacoteca Civica was scheduled to reopen by late 1999, the earliest. ✉ *Piazza della Repubblica,* ☎ *0742/350734.* 🎫 *All sites: 5,000 lire.* ☉ *Tues.–Sun. 10–6.*

At the other end of town, straight down Via Mazzini, is the Romanesque church of **Santa Maria Infraportas,** with several cycles of votive frescoes in the three naves and 12th-century frescoes in the Byzantine style in the **Cappella dell'Assunta.** ✉ *Piazza San Domenico,* ☎ *0742/ 2350517.* 🎫 *Free.* ☉ *Open for mass Sun.; call ahead for schedule).*

OFF THE
BEATEN PATH

ABBAZIA DI SASSOVIVO – Take S77 east out of Foligno (towards Colfiorito). Just after crossing the superstrada (S3), take the local road to the right (no number, not the S77), which is indicated as the road for the Abbazia di Sassovivo. After a few km, the church of San Bartolomeo will appear on the right. The abbey is another 2 km (1 mi) farther up the road. Founded by Benedictines in the 11th century, the abbey's church was rebuilt in the 19th century (the remains of the original church are visible, about 100 yards farther up). The real attraction is the beautiful Romanesque cloister, almost perfectly intact, with paired columns, rounded arches, and polychromatic marble decoration. ⊠ *6 km (4 mi) east of Foligno,* ☎ *0742/356397.* ⊠ *Free, donations accepted. Closed indefinitely at press time.*

Dining and Lodging

$ ✕ **Il Bacco Felice.** Probably the only smoke-free *enoteca* (wine bar) in the entire country, the "Happy Baccus" is just perfect for a light meal and a wonderful glass of wine. The owner personally selects not only the prosciutto and cheeses, but even the bread, brought from the best bakeries in the valley. Hot vegetable soups (lentil, fava, barley) and rabbit casseroles are tasty standards. ⊠ *Via Garibaldi 73–75,* ☎ *0742/ 341019. AE, DC, MC, V. Closed Mon.*

$$$ ▦ **Le Mura.** Right in the center of town, this quiet hotel offers well-appointed rooms and cozy corners to read or to sip a cup of tea. The restaurant has a good reputation even among locals, and breakfast includes freshly baked cakes. ⊠ *Via Mentana 25,* ☎ *0742/357344,* FAX *075/353327. 29 rooms. Restaurant. CP. AE, MC, V.*

$$$ ▦ **Villa Roncalli.** You won't have to put up with the creaking and squealing of old floors and fixtures in this late 16th-century villa on the outskirts of town. The 10 rooms feature terra-cotta floors and modern furniture. An ample buffet breakfast with homemade bread, jams, and cakes make it hard to leave. ⊠ *Località Sant'Eraclio, Via Roma 25,* ☎ *0742/391091,* FAX *0742/391001. 10 rooms. CP. AE, DC, MC, V.*

Nightlife and the Arts

If you are in the area on the second or third Sunday in September, check out the **Giostra della Quintana,** a 17th-century joust held in the stadium among the town's 10 neighborhoods, with the participants and several hundred cheering locals in traditional dress.

Bevagna

🟢 *9 km (5½ mi) west of Foligno, 27 km (17 mi) south of Assisi.*

Built right on the Via Flaminia, an important consular road, Bevagna was a prosperous Roman outpost (they called it Mevania) until the road was diverted and the town dried up. As a result, Bevagna shows more evidence of its Roman past than other towns that were successively built up and torn down over the centuries by various conquering forces.

Enter through **Porta Foligno** and walk along the main road, Corso Matteotti, which follows the old path of the Via Flaminia. Just to the right, a pretty group of trees traces the elliptical bowl where the amphitheater once stood. Via Crescimbeni goes off to the right toward another Roman-era gate, leading to more Roman ruins: to the right, the church of **San Francesco** is built over the remains of a 2nd-century AD temple. Down Via di Porta Guelfa are what's left of the baths, mostly a wonderful marine mosaic visible from a walkway that passes over it.

Aside from a small collection of relics in the **Museo Archeologico,** a small Roman house (ask at the tourist office) and more vague ruins outside the walls, that's it for the Roman part; uncharacteristically, the medieval city was built next to (rather than right above) its Roman predecessor. ⊠ *Palazzo del Municipio, Corso Matteotti 70,* ☎ *0742/ 360031.* 🎫 *5,000 lire.* ☉ *Sept.–May, Tues.–Sun. 10:30–1 and 2:30– 5; June–Aug., Tues.–Sun. 10:30–1 and 4–7.*

Retrace your steps to the Corso and continue to the asymmetrical **Piazza Silvestri** at the center of town. It's handsome in a medieval sort of way, bordered by three Romanesque churches (closed indefinitely).

Ask at the tourist office (☞ Visitor Information, *below*) about a visit to the exquisite **Teatro Torti,** the 19th-century theater built inside the Gothic **Palazzo dei Consoli,** with cast-iron decorations adorning the fronts of the seating boxes and frescoes in the entrance, bar, and foyer. ⊠ *Piazza Silvestri,* ☎ *0742/361667.* ☎ *Donations accepted.* ☉ *Mon.– Sat. 9:30–12:30.*

Shopping

Leading from Piazza Silvestri, **Via di Porta Mulini** is a street where the art of rope making still survives in a few shops from the times when hemp and flax were mainstays of the local economy. At the end of June, the town holds the **Mercato delle Gaite,** a medieval market with arts and crafts and vendors in traditional dress.

Montefalco

🔟 *6 km (4 mi) southeast of Bevagna, 34 km (21 mi) south of Assisi..*

Nicknamed the "balcony of Umbria" for its high, spectacular vantage point over the valley, Montefalco began as an important Roman settlement. It owes its current name—Falcon's Mount—to Emperor Frederick II (1194–1250), who was, unfortunately, a greater fan of falconry than Roman architecture and destroyed the town. Aside from a few fragments incorporated in a private house just round the corner of Borgo Garibaldi, there are no traces left of the old Roman center, but Montefalco has more than its fair share of interesting art and architecture, well worth the drive up the hill.

It won't take long to walk around the town. A good starting point is from the 14th-century **Porta Sant'Agostino,** one of five gates that open in the medieval walls. Take the main street, Corso Goffredo Mameli, and head straight for the 13th- to 14th-century Gothic church of **Sant'Agostino** (closed indefinitely), with frescoes by Ambrogio Lorenzetti, who also decorated part of Siena's Palazzo Pubblico. At the end of the Corso is the **Piazza del Comune,** surrounded by several Renaissance buildings, including the 15th-century **Palazzo Comunale.** Ask the custodian to let you in to the tower, from which you get the falcon's-eye view of Southern Umbria; on a clear day you can see as far as Perugia to the north and Lake Piediluco to the south.

The highlight of Montefalco is the ex-church of **San Francesco.** In tribute to the Franciscan order and the religious significance of the region, Perugino painted a *Nativity* scene in an Umbrian setting; Benozzo Gozzoli decorated the church apse with medallions bearing portraits of eminent Franciscans, and a vivid fresco cycle of the *Life of St. Francis* (1452), a highly original work that compares favorably with those by Giotto in Assisi. The small **Pinacoteca** upstairs contains religious paintings and altarpieces by local artists; in the basement, there is a small collection of sculpture and fragments from various periods. ⊠ *Via Ringhiera Umbra,* ☎ *0742/379598.* ☎ *5,000 lire.* ☉ *Nov.–Feb, Tues.–Sun. 10:30–1 and 2:30–5; Mar.–May and Sept.–Oct., daily 10:30–1 and 2–6; June–Aug., daily 10:30–1 and 3–7:30.*

If you like Gozzoli's work, there's more, although in less pristine condition, in the **Convento di San Fortunato,** a 15-minute walk outside the town walls: Look for the *Madonna with Saints and Angels* in the lunette over the doorway of the cloister chapel (left side) and the fresco of *San Fortunato* on the altar. More impressive perhaps, is Tiberio d'Assisi's *Life of St. Francis* (1512), also in the cloister chapel. ⊠ *Follow signs,* ☎ *no phone.* ☎ *Free.* ☉ *Daily 9–12:30 and 3–6.*

Nightlife and the Arts

The local wine Sagrantino di Montefalco (☞ Shopping, *below*) is celebrated during the **grape harvest festival** in September and a **Wine Week** during Easter.

Shopping

The town is known for Sagrantino di Montefalco, a strong, full-bodied red wine much appreciated by connoisseurs but little known outside the region. Among the various types, the most interesting is the *passito*, made with grapes that have been picked and left to dry to half their original volume. The high concentration of sugar yields a sweet, complex flavor that might remind you of good sherry. Adanti, Caprai, and Paolo Bea are among well-known producers.

Trevi

⓫ *5 km (3 mi) southeast of Spello, 16 km (10 mi) southeast of Assisi.*

If you aren't in a hurry to get to Spoleto, Trevi—no relation to the famous fountain in Rome, which takes its name from the three streets (*tre vie*) that once met in front of it—makes a pleasant stop. The especially well-preserved town has no Roman ruins to hunt down, but a small **Raccolta d'Arte San Francesco** contains a good little collection of paintings by local artists, including Lo Spagna (circa 1450–1528) and Perugino. ⊠ *Convento di San Francesco, Largo Don Bosco,* ☎ *0742/381628.* ☞ *5,000 lire.* ⊙ *Apr.–May and Sept., Tues.–Sun. 10:30–1 and 2:30–6; June–July, Tues.–Sun., 10:30–1 and 3:30–7, Aug., daily 10:30–1 and 3–7:30; Oct.–Mar., Fri.–Sun. 10:30–1 and 2:30–5.*

The best works, as usual, are in the local churches. **San Martino** (for entry, ring the bell at the monastery next door) and **Madonna delle Lacrime** (ring the bell at the convent next door), are pleasantly set 1 km (½ mi) north and south of the town, respectively, along the main road that leads up the steep hill from the highway below.

OFF THE BEATEN PATH

TEMPIETTO E FONTI DEL CLITUNNO – About 2 km (1 mi) south of Trevi is the so-called Tempietto del Clitunno, an early-Christian church built from bits and pieces of Roman temples in the area. The badly worn frescoes, some of the earliest in the region, date from the 7th century. Farther down the road are the Fonti del Clitunno, named after the Roman river god and famous in the ancient world. The remains of the Roman-era Tempio del Clitunno are also nearby. The waters flow from fissures in the rocks and collect in a shallow pond before passing on to an artificial basin. The springs were created when the Romans diverted several rivers upstream, and were used until the last century to supply water to run the mills in the nearby town of Pissignano. ⊠ *About 2 km (1 mi) south of Trevi.* ☞ *Free.* ⊙ *Apr.–Oct., daily 9–8; Nov.–Mar., daily 9–2.*

Dining

$$ ✕ **Taverna del Pescatore.** Even if you don't intend to stop at the nearby Fonti del Clitunno, this is a restaurant definitely worth a detour. Meals are served out on the terrace with the Clitunno river flowing below. The menu changes daily, but is always based on fresh fish from local streams and lakes, such as trout and shrimp, a welcome change in carnivorous Umbria (although there's plenty of meat on the menu, too). Preparations are clean and simple and mirror the seasons. The more adventurous might go for the superb *fritturina di rane* (fried frogs), but there are plenty of more familiar items to choose from. The wine list is notably deep and fairly priced. ⊠ *Statale Flaminia, km 139,* ☎ *0742/780920. AE, DC, MC, V. Closed Wed. Sept.–May, and 1 wk in Jan.*

SPOLETO

If you have heard of Spoleto before, chances are it's because of its famous annual Festival dei Due Mondi (Festival of Two Worlds), a three-week-long art extravaganza in late June–early July, when the sleepy town is swamped with visitors who come to enjoy world-class plays, operas, concerts, and avant-garde paintings and sculpture. But there is good reason to visit Spoleto during the rest of the year. A solid collection of Roman and medieval attractions and superb natural surroundings make it one of Umbria's most inviting towns. Spoleto also makes a good base from which to explore all of Southern Umbria, since Assisi, Orvieto, and the towns in between are all within easy reach.

Umbri tribes were the first to settle here, probably taking advantage of the protection provided by the steep and narrow gorge that runs along the back side of Spoleto's hill. As usual, the Romans were not far behind, fortifying the city walls and building an acqueduct across the gorge, which serves as a foundation to Spoleto's most amazing sight, the Ponte delle Torri. By all accounts an important city, *Spoletum* turned away Hannibal in the 2nd century BC. Ancient churches set in silvery olive groves below either side of town testify to Spoleto's importance in the early-Christian period, when it ruled over a sizable independent duchy. In the 14th century, the town fell under church control, and the Rocca was built at its summit to enforce papal rule.

Exploring Spoleto

It is unwise to arrive during the festival period without confirmed hotel reservations. The walled city is set on a slanting hillside, with the most interesting sites clustered toward the upper portion. Good parking options inside the walls include Piazza Campello (just below the Rocca), Via del Trivio, Piazza della Vittoria, and at Piazza San Domenico. There are also several well-marked larger lots just outside Porta San Matteo and near the train station. If you arrive by train, the station is 1 km (½ mi) from Piazza Garibaldi and the entrance to the lower town. There are good bus connections to Piazza della Libertà, where you'll find the tourist office. Like most towns made up of narrow, winding streets, Spoleto is best explored on foot. Several pedestrian walkways cut across Corso Mazzini, which zigzags up the hill. A 5,000-lire combination ticket allows you entry to the Pinacoteca Comunale, Casa Romana, and the Galleria d'Arte Moderna.

A Good Walk

Begin your day at Piazza della Libertà, with a visit to the adjacent **Teatro Romano** ⑫ and Museo Archeologico (enter on Via Apollinare). From the ancient ruins it's a short jump to the **Galleria d'Arte Moderna** ⑬, a five-room collection with paintings and small sculpture that has won awards in past festivals. Return to Piazza della Libertà and walk up Via Brignone to Piazza Fontana and go left on Via Arco di Druso, named for the **Arco di Druso** ⑭. Up ahead is Piazza del Mercato, built on the site of the Foro Romano, and today is where the small open-air produce market takes place daily. Take the street that leads up out of the piazza and make a quick left onto Via Visiale, crossed by several arches. On the right is the entrance to the **Casa Romana** ⑮. Go back around to the pretty Piazza del Municipio and visit the **Pinacoteca Comunale** ⑯ (same combination ticket as Casa Romana) inside the Palazzo Comunale, with a 13th-century tower and an unusual sundial. Leave the Pinacoteca through the other side of the building, which opens onto Via Saffi. Just opposite is Palazzo Arcivescovile, with the church of **Sant'Eufemia** ⑰ in the courtyard and a small museum. Via Saffi leads uphill to Via dell'Arringo, which descends to **Piazza del Duomo** ⑱. The **Duomo** ⑲ stands against a backdrop of hill and sky with **La Rocca** ⑳ towering overhead. After lunch, proceed up to Piazza Campello and take Via del Ponte, which loops around the base of La Rocca, passing the magnificent **Ponte delle Torri** ㉑. Walk across the bridge, and either circle back around the Rocca or continue along the shady paths of Monteluco and down to the church of **San Pietro** ㉒. From there, return the way you came or cross the highway and take Via Monterone back up into town.

TIMING

Spoleto is small, and its noteworthy sites are clustered in the upper part of town; allow a full day for a thorough exploration, including time to stroll around town and across the Ponte delle Torri. Note that the Casa Romana is closed on Monday.

Sights to See

⓮ **Arco di Druso** (Arch of Drusus). This structure was built in AD 23 by the Senate of Spoleto to honor the Roman general Drusus (circa 13 BC–AD 23), son of the emperor Tiberius. It once marked the entrance to the Foro Romano (Roman Forum), and excavations to the side reveal the original street level. ✉ *Piazza del Mercato.*

⓯ **Casa Romana.** Spoleto became a Roman colony in the 3rd century BC, but the best excavated remains date to the 1st century AD. Excavated in the late 9th century, the Casa Romana was probably not your typical Roman residence—according to an inscription, it belonged to Vespasia Polla, the mother of the Emperor Vespasian—but it does give an interesting look at a Roman noble home in the center of a town. The rooms have intricate mosaics that are still mostly intact, and were arranged around a large central atrium built over an *impluvium* (rain cistern). Although difficult to imagine now, there was once a sizable garden surrounded by a peristyle, which faced the valley. ✉ *Via Visiale 9,* ☎ *0743/2181.* ✆ *5,000 lire combination ticket.* ☉ *May–Sept., Tues.–Sun. 4–7; Oct.–Apr., Tues.–Sun. 10–1 and 3–6.*

★ ⓳ **Duomo.** The church's facade consists of a rather dour 12th-century Romanesque background, lightened up by the addition of a Renaissance loggia, eight rose windows, and an early-13th-century gold mosaic of the Benedictory Christ. A stunning contrast in styles, it is one of the finest in the region. The original pavement dates from an earlier church that was destroyed by Frederick I (circa 1123–1190). Above the entrance wall is Bernini's bust of Pope Urban VIII (1568–1644), who had the rest of the church redecorated in 17th-century Baroque; fortunately he didn't touch the 15th-century frescoes in the apse by Fra Filippo Lippi (circa 1406–69). Be ready with a 500-lira coin to illuminate the immaculately restored masterpieces, which tell the story of the life of the Virgin—the *Annunciation, Nativity,* and the *Death of Mary.* The *Coronation of the Virgin,* adorning the half dome, is the literal and figurative high point. Portraits of Lippi and his assistants are on the right side of the central panel. The Florentine artist died shortly after completing the work, and his tomb—designed by his son, Filippino Lippi (circa 1457–1504)—lies in the church's right transept. Another fresco cycle, including work by Pinturicchio, can be seen in the **Cappella Eroli** off the right aisle. In the left nave, not far from the entrance, is the well restored 12th-century Crucifix by Alberto Sozio, the earliest known example of this kind of work, with a painting on parchment attached to a wood cross. To the right of the presbytery is the *Cappella della Santissima Icona* (Chapel of the Extremely Holy Icon), which contains a small Byzantine painting of a Madonna given to the town by Frederick Barbarossa as a peace offering in 1185, having destroyed the cathedral and town

238

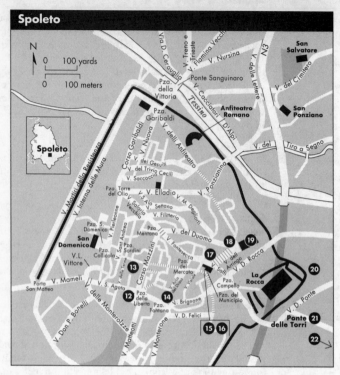

three decades earlier. ✉ *Piazza Duomo,* ☎ *0743/44307.* 🎫 *Free.* ☉
Daily 8–1 and 3–6:30 (3–5:30 in winter).

⓭ Galleria d'Arte Moderna. This five-room gallery contains the winning
paintings and sculptures from the first 13 years of the festival, including
the original preparatory sketches for Alexander Calder's (1898–1976)
Teodelapio (1962). There are also several more recent pieces by contemporary Italian artists, such as Alberto Burri and Arnaldo Pomodoro.
✉ *Palazzo Rosari-Spada, Corso Mazzini, Vicolo III,* ☎ *0743/45940.*
🎫 *5,000 lire combination ticket.* ☉ *Tues.–Sun. 10–1 and 3–6.*

★ ⓴ La Rocca. Built in the mid-14th century for Cardinal Egidio Albornoz,
the Rocca served as a seat for the local pontifical governors, a tangible sign of the restoration of the papacy after the exile in Avignon. Several popes spent time here, as did Lucrezia Borgia (1480–1519). The
plan is long and rectangular, with six towers and two fine courtyards
inside. The Gubbio-born architect Gattapone (14th century) used the
ruins of a Roman acropolis as a foundation, and took materials from
many Roman-era sites, including the Teatro Romano. Until 1982, the
Rocca was in use as a high-security prison, but since then it has been
undergoing restoration and is expected to open as a cultural complex
in 1999, with a museum about the history of Spoleto, an art restoration center, and an exhibition space. Until then you can admire its exterior from the road that circles around it. ✉ *Take Via Saffi (off Piazza
del Duomo) to Via del Ponte.*

⓲ Piazza del Duomo. The piazza, restored in 1998, is surrounded by fine
buildings, including the small Teatro Caio Melisso, one of the first the-
aters built in Italy, and used during the Festival, and the Duomo.

⓰ Pinacoteca Comunale. Right around the corner from the Casa Romana,
this museum contains a small collection of works from the 12th to the

18th centuries. Highlights include two 16th-century frescoes by a local artist known as Lo Spagna, which were detached from the Rocca, the *Magdalene* by Il Guercino (1591–1666), and the view of the Duomo from the window in the second room. ⊠ *Palazzo del Municipio, Via A. Saffi,* ☎ *0743/2181.* 🎫 *5,000 lire combination ticket.* ☉ *May–Sept., Tues.–Sun. 4–7; Oct.–Apr., Tues.–Sun. 10–1 and 3–6.*

★ ㉑ **Ponte delle Torri** (Bridge of the Towers). Spoleto's most famous monument is this massive, 750-ft-long bridge built by Gattapone over the foundations of a Roman-era aqueduct. It stands 262 ft above the forested gorge at its highest point—taller than the dome of the Basilica di San Pietro in Rome. The bridge is open to pedestrians, and a walk over it affords marvelous views, especially at night. ⊠ *Take Via Saffi (off Piazza del Duomo) to Via del Ponte.*

㉒ **San Pietro.** A walk to the church of San Pietro, at the foot of Monteluco, is a pleasant jaunt from town, either across the Ponte delle Torri and down the path to the right, or out Porta Monterone and across the highway. The church was rebuilt in the 13th century over earlier Christian, Roman, and Umbri holy sites. It is rarely open, but the real attraction here are the puzzling decorations on the facade, among the best Romanesque carvings in the region. Beneath the tympanum is an empty square frame, which presumably once held a mosaic, flanked by reliefs of St. Andrew and St. Peter, with a bull beneath each. Paired reliefs in the panels around the doors represent allegories of work and the Eternal life, and typical Christian scenes. If it wasn't clear to them already, the fate of the just and the sinner were written on the church wall: the former being saved by St. Peter, with the devil held at bay, the latter being abandoned by the Archangel Michael to a pair of demons who torture him to death. ⊠ *Beginning of the Strada di Monteluco, 1 km (1//2:mi) south of town center,* ☎ *0743/44882 custodian.* 🎫 *Free.* ☉ *Hrs vary; call the custodian.*

⑰ **Sant'Eufemia.** Set in the courtyard of the archbishop's palace with a partial view of the Duomo over the back wall, this austere ancient church dates from the 12th century. Built on the site of a Roman-era *insula* (city block), the plain Romanesque interior features a Cosmatesque altar and frescoes on the pillars. The most interesting part is the gallery above the nave where female worshippers were required to sit—a holdover from the Eastern Church—one of the few such galleries in this part of Italy. On the courtyard, the **Museo Diocesano d'Arte Sacra** has paintings that are far more interesting than those in the nearby Pinacoteca (☞ *above*), but the museum is closed indefinitely due to damage sustained in the 1997 earthquake. ⊠ *Via Saffi, between Piazza del Duomo and Piazza del Mercato,* ☎ *0743/231021.* 🎫 *Church 3,000 lire.* ☉ *Daily 10–7 (closed indefinitely for restoration).*

⑫ **Teatro Romano.** The small 1st-century Roman theater was used as a quarry for building materials for centuries, so the most intact portion is the hallway that passes under the *cavea* (stands). The rest was heavily restored in the early 1950s and serves as a venue for Spoleto's festival. It was the site of one of the town's most macabre incidents. During the Middle Ages, Spoleto took the side of the Holy Roman Emperor in the interminable struggle between Guelph (papal) and Ghibelline (imperial) factions over the question of who would control central and northern Italy. Four hundred of the pope's supporters were massacred in the theater, and their bodies were burned in an enormous pyre. The Guelphs were triumphant in the end and Spoleto was incorporated into the states of the Church in 1354. Through a door in the west portico of the adjoining building is the **Museo Archeologico,** with assorted relics found in the theater and around the town. The collection contains mostly busts and devotional epigrams found around the theater, although one room features Umbrian and pre-Roman pieces. The highlight is the pair of tables inscribed with the *Lex Spoletina* (Spoleto Law) tablets. Dating from 315 BC, this legal document prohibited the destruction of the *Bosco Sacro* (Sacred Forest), a pagan prayer site on nearby Monteluco sacred to Jupiter, later frequented by St. Francis of Assisi. Interestingly, the punishment was more lenient for violators who were ignorant of the law (required to pacify the god by sacrificing an ox) than for those who were aware of it (who had to pay a fine in addition to making a sacrifice). ⊠ *Via Apollinare, southern end of Corso Mazzini,* ☎ *0743/223277.* 🖾 *4,000 lire.* ⊙ *Mar.–Oct., Mon.–Sat. 9–1:30 and 2:30–7, Sun. 9–1; Nov.–Feb., Mon.–Sat. 9–1:30 and 2:30–5, Sun. 9–1.*

OFF THE
BEATEN PATH

SAN SALVATORE – The church and cemetery of San Salvatore seem very much forgotten, ensconced in solitude and cypress trees on a peaceful hillside, with the motorway rumbling below. One of the oldest churches in the world, it was built by eastern monks in the 4th century, largely of Roman-era materials. The facade dates from a restoration in the 9th century and has hardly been touched since. The highlight is the facade, with three exquisite marble doorways and windows, one of the earliest and best preserved in Umbria. Inside is a 9th-century cross, studded in gems. On the way back, have a look at **San Ponziano** (⊠ 250 yards down Via del Cimitero), open daily 10–1 and 2:30–5, or ring next door for the custodian, with a crypt containing the remains of the the patron saint of Spoleto. Walking back to town you'll pass **Ponte Sanguinario** (⊠ Piazza della Vittoria), named for the waters that flowed red with blood during the games in the **Anfiteatro Romano** just upstream. The amphitheater is now part of the local military barracks; its stones were stripped away and used to build the Rocca. ⊠ *Via della Basilica di San Salvatore, just out of town on the Via Flaminia.* ⊙ *Nov.-Feb., daily 7–5; Mar.-Apr. and Sept.-Oct., daily 7–6; May-Aug., daily 7–7.*

Dining and Lodging

Spoleto's contribution to the regional cuisine comes in the form of truffles found in the vicinity, served locally with abandon and shipped all over the country. Dishes like stringozzi *alla spoletina* (with tomato, parsley, garlic, and hot red pepper flakes) and the delicious *crescionda* (a flanlike dessert, with a base of crushed almond cookies) stay closer to home. Much harder to find is the mix of wild herbs that make up *insalatina di campo*. Sow, thistle, and burnet—whose names are all strange to us now—are picked in the fields at dusk and served at lunch the following day with excellent local olive oil. Unfortunately, Spoleto's restaurants for the most part reflect the mass tourism of the festival year-round. The hotel scene is a little better, with a good selection of medium-size hotels and small family-run *pensioni*. Because Spoleto is known for nature sports and hiking, there are a good number of *agriturismi* (agritourist properties) here as well.

$$$ ✕ **Il Tartufo.** As the name suggests, this is Spoleto's shrine to the truffle, a restaurant that prides itself on using only the finest seasonal truffles available (and the best quality preserved truffles when there are no fresh truffles to be found). Preparations vary from the traditional and simple (stringozzi *al tartufo*—with truffles) to the creative and elaborate (pheasant breast stuffed with truffles and potatoes, served on a bed of wild asparagus). There is also a nontruffle menu if you're not wild about these wild tubers. Don't miss the original Roman brick floor in the cellar dining room. ⊠ *Piazza Garibaldi 24,* ☎ *0743/40236. Reservations essential. AE, DC, MC, V. Closed Wed. and mid-July–1st wk Aug.*

$$–$$$ ✕ **Apollinare.** Low wooden ceilings and candlelight make Apollinare the more romantic of the restaurants in Spoleto, and definitely the in spot in town. The food is a slightly sophisticated, innovative approach to local cooking, with good-size portions; here the usual stringozzi take on cherry tomatoes, mint, and a touch of red pepper. Try the *caramella* (light puff pastry roll filled with local cheese, served on a Parmesan fondue). In late spring and summer there is dining under a pergola on the piazza. ⊠ *Via Sant'Agata 14,* ☎ *0743/223256. AE, D, MC, V. Closed Tues.*

$$ ✕ **Il Pentagramma.** If it weren't for the festival, chances are the menu wouldn't group first courses as "symphonies" and the grilled dishes as "ballets," but the food strikes good notes just the same and the bill won't sound like a requiem. Try the *ravioli alle noci* (fresh ravioli stuffed with walnuts and dressed with butter and sage) and lamb in a truffle sauce. If you happen by in springtime, ask about the wild-herbed in-salatina di campo. Reservations are recommended. ⊠ *Via Martani 4,* ☎ *0743/223141. DC, MC, V. Closed Mon.*

$ ✕ **Pecchiarda.** There's barely a sign out in front of Pecchiarda, but the Spoletini seem to find their way there anyway, seeking the simple cooking and good value at this family-run trattoria. There are plenty of tables outside on an enclosed lawn, or inside in the plain dining rooms. There are usually four primi piatti on offer, including first-rate stringozzi and potato gnocchi filled with ricotta. Second courses are mostly grilled, and the house specialty is a ground chicken and artichoke loaf. Save room for the crescionda, the best in town, and the home-distilled grappa makes for a nice finish. ⊠ *Vicolo San Giovanni 1,* ☎ *0743/221009. MC, V. Closed Thurs. in winter.*

$ ✕ **Trattoria Panciolle.** In the heart of Spoleto's medieval quarter, this restaurant has one of the most pleasant settings you could wish for. Dining outside in summer is a welcome respite, in a small piazza filled with lime trees. Specialties include stringozzi with mushroom sauce and *agnello scottadito* (grilled lamb chops). Seven guest rooms are also available here. ⊠ *Via del Duomo 3,* ☎ *0743/45598. Reservations essential. AE, MC, V. Closed Wed.*

$$–$$$ 🏨 **San Luca.** A brand new hotel built to old-world standards, the San
★ Luca is the finest hotel in Spoleto, thanks to commendable attention to details. Rooms are spacious, bathrooms elegantly appointed, beds comfortable enough to reconsider the day's plans. An ample breakfast buffet, including homemade cakes, is served in a pretty room facing the central courtyard, while afternoon tea can be sipped in oversize armchairs in front of the fireplace. Service is cordial and prices are surprisingly modest. ⊠ *Via Interna delle Mura 21, 06049,* ☎ *0743/223399,* FAX *0743/223800. 35 rooms. Breakfast room. CP. AE, DC, MC, V.*

$$ 🏨 **Dei Duchi.** This excellent, well-run hotel is a favorite among performers in the festival. It's in the center of town, near the Roman amphitheater. Some rooms have fine views of the city. ⊠ *Viale Matteotti 4, 06049,* ☎ *0743/44541,* FAX *0743/44543. 49 rooms. Restaurant, bar, meeting rooms, free parking. CP. AE, DC, MC, V.*

$$ 🏨 **Hotel Gattapone.** The Gattapone sits in an enviable position; just a few hundred yards from the Ponte delle Torri, it is very close to the center of town and at the same time nicely secluded. Wake up to wonderful views of the ancient bridge and the wooded slopes of Monteluco, and go for a morning walk around the Via del Ponte, which circles the base of the Rocca above. The modern decor is understated and tasteful, with beautiful wooden floors and comfortable leather furniture. ⊠ *Via del Ponte 6, 06049,* ☎ *0743/223447,* FAX *0743/223448. 16 rooms. Bar, breakfast room. CP. AE, DC, MC, V.*

$$ 🏨 **Nuovo Clitunno.** A renovated 18th-century building houses this pleasant hotel, a five-minute walk from the town center. Some bedrooms have lovely wood-beamed ceilings, wrought-iron beds, and Oriental carpets; others a mixture of period as well as less-charming modern furniture. ☒ *Piazza Sordini 6, 06049,* ☎ *0743/223340,* FAX *0743/222663. 38 rooms. Restaurant, bar. CP. AE, DC, MC, V.*

$ 🏨 **Aurora.** Right on Piazza della Libertà, there's not much to say about the Aurora, a simple little hotel with basic, clean rooms, run by the owners of the Apollinare restaurant below. ☒ *Via Apollinare 3, 06049,* ☎ *0743/220315,* FAX *0743/221885. 15 rooms. Breakfast room. CP. AE, DC, MC, V.*

$ 🏨 **Azienda Agrituristica Bartoli.** Just 13 km (8 mi) southeast of Spoleto, this agriturismo offers simple rooms with private baths in a converted farmhouse, with common kitchen and TV rooms. There is also an apartment that sleeps six. Rooms look out onto the green valleys below Monte di Patrico, with many hiking trails in the area. Rent by the night or the week, with half- or full-board. There are ample hiking trails in the area, and horses are available with or without guides. ☒ *Località Patrico, 06049,* ☎ *0743/220058. 6 double rooms, 1 apartment which sleeps 6. Horseback riding. FAP, MAP. No credit cards.*

Nightlife and the Arts

In 1958, composer Gian Carlo Menotti chose Spoleto for the first **Festival dei Due Mondi** (Festival of Two Worlds), a gathering of artists, performers, and musicians intended to bring together the "new" and "old" worlds of America and Europe (there was once a corresponding festival in Charleston, South Carolina, but it is no longer connected to Spoleto's festival). The annual event (late June–early July) soon became one of the most important cultural happenings in Europe, attracting big names in all branches of the arts—particularly music, opera, and theater—and drawing thousands of visitors. With so much activity, the small town gives itself over entirely to the festival—events are staged in every possible venue, from church cloisters to the Roman Theater, street performers abound, and prices rise considerably. The closing concert (always free) takes place on the Piazza del Duomo.

At any other time of year, you will notice the changes brought by the festival—Spoleto is far more cosmopolitan than other towns in the region, its people more welcoming—and undoubtedly you will see traces of past festivals; old promotional posters hung in virtually all the shops and hotels, and modern sculptures left to the city in its art gallery, or on permanent display outdoors. These include Alexander Calder's enormous bronze *Teodolapio* sculpture in front of the train station, Anna Mahler's *Sitting* in Piazza della Signoria, and a *Geodesic Dome* by Buckminster Fuller (1895–1983) in the Parco della Passeggiata. Tickets for all performances should be ordered in advance from the **festival's box office** (☒ Piazza Duomo 9, ☎ 0743/44325 during festival; call 0743/45028 or 0743/220320 year-round), which has full program information starting in April.

In addition to the festival, Spoleto hosts a prestigious vocal competition at the Teatro Lirico Sperimentale Adriano Belli from mid-August to mid-September. Check with the tourist office (☞ Visitor Information, *below*) about special concerts, exhibitions, and cultural events.

Outdoor Activities and Sports

Biking

Bicycles can be rented at **Scocchetti Cicli** (☒ Via Marconi 82, ☎ 0743/44728), open Monday–Saturday 9–1 and 3:30–8, but call ahead to reserve.

Hiking

Pick up a map of local roads and trails from the tourist office and head out for a hike. Trails on Monteluco (just across the Ponte delle Torri), among others, are especially nice.

Horseback Riding

Horses can be rented with English-speaking guides at the **Centro Ippico La Somma** (✉ Frazione Aiacugigli-Montebibico, about 15 km/9 mi south of Spoleto, ☎ 0743/54370), open daily 9:30–12 and 3:30–7.

Shopping

Spoleto's main shopping street begins as **Via Fontesecca** (near Piazza del Mercato), and continues down the hill, changing names several times. **Aracne** (✉ Vicolo Primo di Corso Mazzini 2, ☎ 0743/46085) specializes in fine lace and embroidery. **Mobilia** (✉ Via Filitteria 3, ☎ 0743/45720) is one of many antiques shops. Spoleto's tiny open-air **produce market,** open Monday–Saturday 8–1:30, is held in Piazza del Mercato, near the Arco di Druso.

SPOLETO ENVIRONS AND NORCIA

Spoleto is the obvious starting point for a visit to the eastern edges of Umbria, as few roads cut across the rugged mountainous terrain that quickly rises from the Valle Umbra. Roads narrow and the towns get smaller and farther apart as you break out off the well-traveled path from Spoleto to Assisi, but great rewards await. Spring is the best time of year to venture east from Spoleto, as the climate and wildflowers are at their finest. The main attractions are Norcia, a town famous for its culinary delights and the road you take to get there, full of breathtaking views across unspoiled verdant mountain landscapes. Beyond Norcia is the Parco Nazionale dei Monti Sibillini, one of Italy's best nature reserves.

No less inviting is the Valnerina (valley of the Nera River), also home to a protected nature area, and its own array of stunning scenery. At press time, long-standing plans to make a regional park in the Valnerina were finally nearing completion. Lest any part of Italy be without an intresting church, the Abbazia di San Pietro della Valle sits like a gem amid the lush greenery of the valley.

Norcia

㉓   *48 km (31 mi) east of Spoleto, 99 km (62 mi) southeast of Perugia.*

En Route   The road east from Spoleto (S395) goes east 19 km (12 mi) to the Nera river, then turns north (S209). As you climb higher, the olive groves that produce Spoleto's fine oil give way to chestnut trees and forests populated by wolves, porcupines, and owls. When you reach Cerreto di Spoleto, take the long way around to the S320, passing Triponzo, for the best views. Most minor roads are not in the best of shape, but reward you with the dramatic mountain scenery.

For most Italians, Norcia is synonymous with fabulous sausages and prosciutto and the great tradition of butchers who produce them, so much so that from Rome to Rimini a *norcineria* is a place where sausages are made and sold and a *norcino* is a pork butcher. (Under the circumstances, it is no wonder that the locals call themselves *nursiani*.) There is, however, more to life in Norcia than pork products—here you'll also find the finest truffles in Umbria, a solid tradition of cheese making, plenty of good baked goods, and chocolate. If all this weren't enough to put Norcia on the map, it is also the birthplace of

St. Benedict, the founder of Christianity's first monastic order, and the town is surrounded by stupendous, lush mountainous terrain.

If you arrive on a full stomach, head for the local sites, clustered around Piazza San Benedetto, with a monument and church dedicated to the hometown saint. The 14th-century church of **San Benedetto** was built over the supposed birthplace of the saint and his twin sister St. Scolastica. Both are represented in statues set into the facade, which in turn must have been constructed over the remains of a Roman house, visible in the church crypt. ⊠ *Piazza San Benedetto,* ☎ *0743/ 817125.* 🎫 *Free.* ⊙ *Daily 8:30–12:30 and 3:30–6:30.*

Off to the side, the **Duomo** (⊠ Piazza San Benedetto) bears the scars of repeated redecoration necessitated by frequent earthquakes over the centuries (the locals now adhere to strict building codes and height limitations). More interesting is the superb **Castellina,** the sturdy papal palace that has been recently restored. Inside, the **Museo Civico** offers more than the usual drab collection of local work. The Della Robbia terracotta of the Madonna, a rare example in this region of the work of the masterful Florentine family, and a 13th-century *Deposition,* made up of several wooden statues, are worth the admission alone. ⊠ *Piazza San Benedetto,* ☎ *0743/817030.* 🎫 *5,000 lire.* ⊙ *Oct.–May, Tues.–Sun. 10–12:30 and 3:30–5; June–Sept., Tues.–Sun. 10–12:30 and 4:30–7.*

Another museum worth seeking out is the **Mostra Permanente della Civiltà Contadina,** a good look at clothes, tools, and personal items from the local farming culture. ⊠ *Piazza Sergio Forti 9,* ☎ *075/802145.* 🎫 *Donations accepted.* ⊙ *Weekends 8–1 and 3–6.*

Dining and Lodging

$$ ✕🏠 **Granaro del Monte.** This is your typical restaurant in Norcia, and guess what's on the menu—a feast of pork prepared every which way, but also famous lentils from nearby Castelluccio and mushrooms and truffles from the local forests. The family also runs a simple but comfortable hotel next door, the Grotta Azzurra. ⊠ *Via C. Battisti,* ☎ *0743/ 816504. AE, DC, MC, V. Closed Tues.*

Parco Nazionale dei Monti Sibillini

㉔ *About 46 km (29 mi) east of Spoleto.*

Norcia actually lies within the boundaries of the Parco Nazionale dei Monti Sibillini. Just south of town is **San Pellegrino,** source of one of the country's most famous mineral waters. The main road that winds its way through the mountains, eventually crossing the border into the Marche region, passes through **Castelluccio,** a pretty town famous through Italy for its extraordinary lentils. But it isn't the towns you have come this far to see, but the park, which, weather permitting, offers some of the country's best hiking and outdoor activities. A good resource are the maps issued by the Club Alpino Italiano (CAI), available at newsstands.

The **Cooperativa Monte Patino** (☎ 0743/817487 reservations), open weekdays 9:30–1:30 and 3:30–6, offers guided tours in English, including excursions to villages and isolated churches and hiking in the Parco dei Sibillini. A food-shopping tour called "Sentiero Sapori" (path of the taste) focuses on visits to artisanal workshops and cheese and sausage producers. For those who like to hear just the sound of their own steps, the **Casa del Parco** (⊠ Via Solferino 22, Norcia, ☎ 0743/817090; ⊠ Via Santa Caterina, Preci Alto, ☎ 0743/99145), a sort of "green" tourist office, both open daily 9:30–12:30 and 3–6, has free maps and brochures about the Umbrian side of the National Park.

Lodging

$ **⚄ Rifugio Perugia.** You won't have a private room in this *rifugio di montagna* (mountain refuge)—in fact you'll have to share with three more people. But if you like the cozy atmosphere and the getting together over a last bottle of wine typical of these high inns, do join in and get the seat near the guy with the guitar. You don't need to pack tuna fish and chocolate either for your day's excursion, since the Perugia has a restaurant done up, of course, in wood and stone. The rate of 30,000 lire a person includes sheets and bath towels. ⊠ *Località Canapine, about 22 km (14 mi) southeast of Norcia,* ☎ *0743/823015 or 0337/640415. 35 beds in about 7 rooms. Restaurant. No credit cards. Closed Oct.–Nov. and Mar.*

Abbazia di San Pietro in Valle

㉕ *35 km (22 mi) southeast of Spoleto, 44 km (27 mi) southwest of Norcia.*

It's hard to believe that this remote building once served as one of the centers of Christianity in the region, but the remnants of one of the fortresses that once protected it, still visible in the distance, testify to its earlier importance. Capitals in the apse and a 1st-century BC altar near the back door seem to suggest that the 8th-century abbey was built over the ruins of a Roman temple. Sacked by the Saracens, the abbey was rebuilt in the 12th century and a perfectly graceful cloister and Lombard-style campanile were added, as well as the stunning frescoes in the side naves representing scenes from the Old and New Testament. The unknown artist who painted them preceded Giotto by more than a hundred years in his attempt to break away from rigid Byzantine models. The frescoes have been recently restored, and the best-preserved scenes overflow with realistic and vivid details that bring the stories to life. The skillful use of light and shadow can be considered as an early, tentative step toward the techniques of perspective that were developed in the Renaissance. The main altar is a rare 8th-century artifact with unusual reliefs, among which are the lord who commissioned the piece and the artist himself, a certain Ursus. To the right is a handsome Roman sarcophagus containing the bones of Duke Faroald II of Spoleto (who built the abbey after having a vision of St. Peter). ⊠ *S209,* ☎ *0744/780316. ▣ Donations accepted. ☉ Oct.–Apr., daily 10:15–12:30 and 2–5; May–Sept., daily 10:15–12:30 and 2–6. If closed, ring at the custodian's house, about 1 km (½ mi) south of the abbey.*

En Route You can take the minor road that goes southeast to Monteleone di Spoleto, cutting across the main mountain ridge and climbing toward Mt. Coscerno (5,527 ft). The road continues to Cascia, an unremarkable town where the only attraction is a famous (modern) sanctuary dedicated to Santa Rita da Cascia, the powerful protector of all women in serious trouble. The road proceeds along the path of the Corno and Sordo rivers, leading up towards Norcia.

Dining

$$ **✕ Piermarini.** In the tiny town of Ferentillo, 4 km (1½ mi) south of the abbey, this is a great place to have your Umbrian truffle experience (especially between the months of November and February). The dishes are traditional and no-nonsense: truffles are often served with eggs, which bring out the full flavor of the tuber without obscuring its. Second courses are excellent as well, and include the usual grilled meats, plus kid, lamb, and roasted pork. There is a pleasant garden for outside dining in good weather. ⊠ *Via della Vittoria 53, Ferentillo (18½ km/11 mi northeast of Terni, 31 km/19 mi southeast of Spoleto),* ☎ *0744/780714. AE, MC, V. Closed Mon. and 1 wk in Jan.*

Shopping

To get your fill of the local sausages, here are some worthwhile addresses. **Norcineria Ercole Ulivucci** (⊠ Via Mazzini 4, ☎ 0743/816661), closed Monday in even years, Tuesday in odd years. **Norcineria Fratelli Ansuini** (⊠ Via Anicia 105, ☎ 0743/816643), closed Tuesday. Pick up some cheese at the **Boutique del Pecoraro** (⊠ Via San Benedetto 7, ☎ 0743/816453), which also has truffles in season, as do the folks at **Tartufi Moscatelli** (⊠ Via Dante 14b, ☎ 0743/817388), closed Sunday. For something sweet, try the shop at **No. 13 Corso Sertorio** (☎ 0744/816623), closed Sunday.

SOUTHERN UMBRIA AND ORVIETO

It's a short drive from Spoleto to Terni, but tempting diversions along the way include one of central Italy's finest abbeys and the refreshing Lake Piediluco. Hold your breath while river rafting at the foot of the tallest falls in Europe, then recover while driving through olive groves to sleepy Amelia—Umbria's oldest town—before stepping into the medieval past of Todi. Finish off your visit to the province in Orvieto, with its unforgettable Duomo and wine made from the same grapes that made the Etruscans tipsy.

Terni

㉖ *33 km (21 mi) southwest of Spoleto, 70 km (45 mi) southeast of Orvieto.*

There's not much to attract you to Terni, which was heavily bombed by the allies in World War II on account of its weapons industry and metalworks—not the kind of place you would associate with St. Valentine, who was martyred here in AD 273. Although a church just outside of town marks his burial place, his heart was presciently removed and taken to Venice, that most romantic of cities. If you happen to find yourself here, Terni is not bereft of art, and the local **Pinacoteca** has Benozzo Gozzoli's *The Marriage of St. Catherine,* as well as several noteworthy modern paintings. ⊠ *Via Frattini 55,* ☎ *0744/400290.* 🎫 *2,500 lire.* ⊙ *Mon.–Sat., 10–1 and 4–7.*

Just a few blocks down is the round church of **San Salvatore,** open daily 9–12 and 4–6, once thought to have been a Roman temple on account of its dome and open oculus.

OFF THE BEATEN PATH

CASCATA DEL MARMORE – East of Terni the road leads 10 km (6 mi) to the waterfalls at Marmore, which at 541 ft are the highest falls in Europe. They were created by the Romans to prevent flooding in the nearby agricultural plains. Nowadays the waters are often diverted to provide hydroelectric power for the town of Terni, so check with Terni's tourist office (⊠ Viale C. Battisti 5, ☎ 0744/423047) before heading there. On summer evenings, when the falls are in full spate, the cascading water is floodlit to striking effect.

LAGO DI PIEDILUCO – The road continues east to Lake Piediluco, a nice spot to rest and get your feet wet. The lake is the prettiest in the region, surrounded by steep forested hillsides. There are facilities for boat and canoe rental, as well as waterskiing and sailing.

Outdoor Activities and Sports

Rapids near the Cascata del Marmore make for good water rafting for all skill levels; inquire at the **Centro Rafting Le Marmore** (⊠ Belvedere Inferiore, ☎ 0330/753420 or 0337/729154), open daily mid-March–

October. Rafting is available to those 15 to 55 years old and weighing under 220 pounds. A descent, with a brief class beforehand, takes about two hours.

Narni

27 *13 km (8 mi) west of Terni, 46 km (29 mi) southeast of Orvieto.*

For centuries Narni was protected from invasion by its lofty perch at the top of a gorge over the Nera river valley and by its imposing **Rocca,** open two weeks between April and May, built by Gattapone. These days there is only the wind and the occasional tourist to invade the otherwise peaceful hill town. Modern development is kept at bay (and out of sight) in the new town of **Narni Scalo** below, which means you will find the old part safely preserved behind its sturdy walls. Sunday is the best day to visit Narni, when the excavated Roman sites are open. Otherwise, call the Associazione Culturale Subterranea (☎ 0744/722292) a week in advance to set up a tour in English during the week.

The **Duomo** originally had three naves, but a fourth nave was added to the right of the church to incorporate a 6th-century shrine of San Giovenale, the patron saint of the town. As a result the Via Flaminia passes through the church. A 9th-century mosaic over the shrine is partially visible. ⊠ *Piazza Cavour,* ☎ *0744/722610.* ☞ *Free.* ⊙ *Daily 8– 12:30 and 3–7.*

Piazza Garibaldi, the town's main square, is built over the **Lacus,** a large late-medieval cistern with vaulting and remains of the Roman-era stone pavement. The town's big artistic attraction is an altarpiece by Domenico Ghirlandaio (1449–1494), the *Coronation of the Virgin,* in the Sala del Consiglio of the **Palazzo Comunale,** opposite a loggia by Gattapone. The palazzo was being restored at press time, scheduled to reopen mid-1999. ⊠ *Piazza dei Priori,* ☎ *0744/715362.* ☞ *Not available at press time. Closed for restoration.*

Farther along, the 12th-century church of **Santa Maria in Pensole** is well worth a visit for the finely carved facade. Under the church, excavations have revealed an 8th-century church with three naves and two aisles, built over a Roman temple which was converted into a crypt for the church above. There are also two Roman cisterns, one of them in especially good condition. ⊠ *Via Mazzini,* ☎ *0744/722292, 0744/ 715362.* ☞ *Free.* ⊙ *Daily 8–12:30 and 4–6:30.*

The ex-**Monastero di San Domenico** is now the town library. Around the back, underneath the monastery, an entrance leads to a Romanesque church with frescoes from the 13th to 15th centuries. In the adjacent remains of a Roman building with a cistern is a cell used during the Inquisition, decorated with graffitti left by prisoners. ⊠ *Via Mazzini,* ☎ *0744/747203.* ☞ *Free.* ⊙ *weekdays 9–12.*

Dining

$ ✕ **Il Cavallino.** When it comes to eating out, many Narniani head 2 km (1 mi) out of town to Il Cavallino, for first-rate, home-style cooking in this trattoria run by the third generation of the Bussetti family. There are always lots of pastas to choose from, truffle in season, and the specialty of the house, *palombaccio alla leccarda* (roasted pigeon). ⊠ *Via Flamina Romana 220,* ☎ *0744/722683. AE, D, MC, V. Closed Tues. and in July.*

Nightlife and the Arts

The town celebrates the **Festa di San Giovenale** in May, with two weeks of special festivities that culminate in the **Corsa all'Anello,** in which a ring is strung up across Via Maggiore and contestants from the town's neighborhoods try to put a lance through it.

Amelia

28 *50 km (31 mi) southeast of Orvieto.*

Amelia has the distinction of being the oldest town in the region, with archaeological evidence going back as far as 1100 BC. The bulky walls that still surround the little town show that the Umbri knew a thing or two about fortifications—the walls are over 20 ft thick at some points. There are no museums of interest, but it's a pleasure just to walk around the town. Admire the walls from a path that leads from Porta Romana around the perimeter of the town, or walk up the main road to the brick **Duomo,** open daily 10–1 and 4–6:30, at the top of the town. The interior, redone in the 19th century, is decorated with two Turkish flags won in the Battle of Lepanto. Although it now serves as its bell tower, the unusual **Torre Civica** (1050) predates the Duomo, its 12 sides thought to represent the signs of the zodiac or the 12 apostles. There are fine views from the top of the hill.

En Route The road northwest (S205) passes first through **Lugnano in Teverina,** with its important Collegiata di Santa Maria Assunta. The facade is the region's best piece of Romanesque architecture. The interior is mostly undecorated, apart from a handsome Cosmatesque floor. Just a few kilometers ahead is the town of **Alviano.** The pretty Rocca is the focal point of the town, and inside the fortress is the Museo della Civiltà Contadina (☎ 0744/904421), open Monday–Saturday 8–2, with an interesting collection of relics that trace the history of farming in the area. In the courtyard is the Cappella dei Rondini (Chapel of the Swallows), with frescoes recounting St. Francis' miraculous silencing of the swallows, who were disturbing his preaching. Alviano is nonetheless an important nature reserve with good bird-watching around the lake below. The road continues through Baschi, westward (13 km/8 mi) toward Orvieto, and east (28 km/17 mi) to Todi.

Dining

$$ ✕ **Il Carleni.** This pleasant restaurant in the center of Amelia offers very good value, as well as special menus for children and vegetarians, a particular rarity in Umbria. The cuisine is Italian with some French influence (the owner's wife is French), so you can have *manfricoli a l'aioli* (homemade rustic spaghetti with garlic mayonnaise). There's also a pleasant garden for outside dining. ✉ *Via P. Carleni 21, Amelia,* ☎ *0744/983925. AE, MC, V. Closed Tues. Sept.–July.*

Giove

29 *12½ km (8 mi) southwest of Amelia, 9½ km (6 mi) south of Lugnano in Teverina, 24 km (15 mi) west of Terni.*

The little town of Giove was named for the Roman god Jupiter and a famous temple in his honor that once stood here. Just outside the town is a convent with a Madonna by Perugino. The town also has an interesting 16th-century **Palazzo Ducale** (✉ Piazza XXIV Maggio, ☎ 0744/992928), open by appointment, with 365 windows for the days of the year and a peculiar spiral ramp large enough to allow horse-driven carts to enter the building through the front door and reach the upper floors. The road continues to **Attigliano,** where the modern church of San Lorenzo the Martyr gives an idea of how all the churches in the region might look if they were built in this century.

Todi

🚇 *34 km (22 mi) south of Perugia, 34 km (22 mi) east of Orvieto.*

Standing on Piazza del Popolo, looking out onto the Tiber valley below, it's easy to see how Todi is often described as Umbria's prettiest hill town. Legend has it that the town was founded by the Umbri, who followed an eagle who had stolen a tablecloth to this lofty perch. They liked it so much that they settled here for good. The eagle is now perched on the insignia of the medieval palaces in the main piazza. But historical evidence suggests that the Umbri didn't find an empty nest; Iron-Age remains dating from 2700 BC make it the oldest settled area in the region. The usual Etruscan to Roman progression continued, and Todi rose to prominence in the 13th century, when it ruled over a *comune* that included Amelia and Terni. Aside from the view and charm of the streets, two small but worthwhile museums have recently opened after lengthy restoration. Todi is best reached by car, as the town's two train stations are way down the hill and connected to the town by infrequent bus service. The lack of any real accommodations makes the town day-trip material.

Built above the Roman Forum, **Piazza del Popolo** is Todi's high point, a model of spatial harmony with stunning views onto the surrounding countryside. In the best medieval tradition, the square was conceived to house both the temporal and spiritual centers of power. On one end is the 12th-century Romanesque-Gothic **Duomo,** with a simple facade enriched by a finely carved rose window. There's not much to draw you inside, as Ferraù da Faenza's copy of Michelangelo's *Last Judgment* only serves to illustrate the gap between the two artists. The severe, solid mass of the Duomo is mirrored by the Palazzo dei Priori across the way. ⊠ *Piazza del Popolo,* ☎ *075/8943041.* 🎟 *Church free; crypt 1,500 lire.* ☉ *May–Sept., daily 8:30–12:30 and 2:30–6:30; Oct.–Apr., daily 8:30–12:30 and 2:30–4:30.*

A staircase on the square leads to Palazzo del Popolo and the entrance to the **Museo Etrusco-Romano and Pinacoteca.** The first room is devoted to the history of Todi; the collection includes religious garments, local coins, Roman relics, Etruscan pottery, and more recent ceramics from Deruta. The highlight of the Pinacoteca is the *Coronation of the Virgin* by Lo Spagna. ⊠ *Palazzo del Popolo, Piazza del Popolo,* ☎ *075/ 8944148.* 🎟 *6,000 lire.* ☉ *Oct.–Feb., Tues.–Sun. 10:30–1 and 2– 4:30; Mar. and Sept., Tues.–Sun. 10:30–1 and 2–5; Apr., daily 10:30– 1 and 2:30–6; May–Aug., Tues.–Sun. 10:30–1 and 4:30–6.*

Via di Santa Prassede heads down to the northern part of town; although called the *borgo nuovo* (new quarter), it includes two 14th-century churches and many well-preserved old buildings. Piazza del Popolo is thought to have been built over the remains of the town's Foro Romano, but the only ancient ruins that are visible are the so-called **Nicchioni** (large niches) that make up one side of Piazza del Mercato Vecchio, now used as a parking lot. Follow the signs from Corso Cavour. From there, continue down to the **Fontana di Scarnabecco,** a good stop for a sip of cool spring water with benches nearby.

Return to Piazza del Polpolo (there are stairs from Piazza del Mercato Vecchio), this time taking Via Mazzini up to Piazza Jacopone. At the top of the grass-lined grade is the **Tempio di San Fortunato.** Had it been completed, it might have looked like a small version of the Duomo in Orvieto. But the project was never realized (legend has it that Lorenzo Maitani (circa 1275–1330) was given the job, but was murdered by the jealous Orvietanis to ensure that no other town's Duomo could rival their own). Aside from the carved doorway and captivating angels attributed to Jacopo della Quercia (circa 1371–1438), the church remains more impressive for its sheer mass than its makeup. The whitewashed interior is remarkably free of any Gothic atmosphere. Under the main altar is the crypt of the local saint Jacopone da Todi (circa 1230–1306), who was no stranger to sin when he experienced a severe conversion, becoming so extreme in self denial that at first even the Franciscans didn't accept him. ⊠ *Piazza Umberti I,* ☏ *no phone.* 🎫 *Free.* ⊙ *Oct.–Mar., Tues.–Sun. 9:30–12:30 and 3–5, Mon. 9:30–12:30; Apr.– Sept., Tues.–Sun. 9:30–12:30 and 3–7, Mon. 9:30–12:30.*

Follow the lane to the left of the exit leading to a public garden, where you'll find a few benches and all that's left of the Rocca, the papal fortress. Follow the signs for the winding path that descends to the unexpected Renaissance treasure of Todi, the church of **Santa Maria della Conso- lazione.** Thought to have been inspired by designs by Bramante, it was begun in 1508 but not finished for another hundred years, its perfect symmetry heightened by an almost neoclassical purity of form and pro- portions. ⊠ *Piazza della Consolazione,* ☏ *075/8943120.* 🎫 *Free.* ⊙ *Apr.–Sept, daily 9–1 and 3–6; Oct.–Feb., daily 10–12.*

Dining and Lodging

$$ ✕ **Ristorante Umbria.** Todi's most popular restaurant for more than four decades, Umbria is a reliable address for sturdy country food with a wonderful view from the terrace. There's always a hearty soup simmering away, as well as homemade pasta with truffles, game, and the specialty of the house, *palombaccio alla ghiotta* (roasted pigeon). ⊠ *Via San Bonaventura 13,* ☏ *075/8942390. AE, D, MC, V. Tues. and in July*

$ ✕ **La Mulinella.** If it weren't for all the other tables around, you'd think you were a guest at the home of Signora Irma, who has been making bread and pasta for 35 years. Beware of the primi piatti: if you intend to go on to *secondi* (second courses)—such as *tacchino farcito d'uva* (turkey stuffed with grapes) or stewed wild boar—because portions are enough for three and the waiters fear the wrath of Irma if they don't bring back an empty serving platter. So share a dish of her light-as-a- feather *gnocchetti* or tagliatelle in a goose sauce. Save room for the sim- ple desserts. Service is quick and friendly, prices are particularly modest. ⊠ *Via Pontenaia 2,* ☏ *075/8944779. No credit cards. Closed Wed.*

$$ 🏠 **Tenuta di Canonica.** The affable hosts, Daniele and Maria Fano, scoured Tuscany and Umbria and returned to the first place they saw, a turn- of-the-century brick farmhouse and medieval tower (with a foundation dating from the Roman period) in the Tiber Valley 5 km (3 mi) north- west of Todi. The Fanos have tastefully retained the architectural in- tegrity: you're bound to marvel at the exposed stone walls, high-beamed ceilings, and terra-cotta tiles, all soothed by cool colors and handsome lighting. Guest rooms, which have access to a working ancient well, are filled with family antiques, Oriental rugs, candelabra, and fresh fruit and flowers. You can hike or horseback ride among the olive groves, orchards, and forest on the grounds, which also includes two apartments that each sleep 2–3 people. ⊠ *Località La Canonica, 75–76 06059,* ☏ *075/8947545,* 📠 *075/8947581. 11 rooms, 2 apartments. Dining room, pool, library. CP, MAP. No credit cards (at press time).*

Shopping

Todi is full of little shops, a surprising number of them selling fresh fruit. The local sweet, available in most pastry shops, is *panpolenta* (a coffee cake made with corn flour and ground almonds). Local ceram- ics are available from several boutiques along Corso Cavour. The town also hosts one of Italy's most important annual antique fairs (usually two weeks around Easter time, call the tourist office for exact dates and venue).

ORVIETO

The natural defenses offered by an enormous plateau rising 1,000 ft above the flat valley proved very attractive to settlers in central Italy as far back as the Bronze Age, making Orvieto among the oldest cities in the region. The Etruscans developed the town considerably, carving a network of 1,200 wells and storage caves out of the soft tufa (volcanic stone). By 283 BC, the Romans had attacked, sacked, and destroyed the city, by then known as *Volsinii Veteres*. Perhaps they were attracted by the golden Orvieto Classico made from grapes grown in the rich volcanic soil of the valley below—a wine the town is still famous for today.

Charlemagne (742–814) changed the name to Urbs Vetus, from which the modern name derives. The town rose steadily as an independent comune in the late Middle Ages, and the construction began on the Duomo in the 13th century after the Miracle at Bolsena (☞ Duomo, *below*). When the Guelphs won decisively over the Ghibellines in the 14th century, Orvieto passed under the control of the papacy, and was subsequently used by the popes as a refuge from enemies or the summer heat of Rome.

In addition to wine and some of the best restaurants in the region, Orvieto has great things in store: The much celebrated Duomo, with Italy's best Gothic facade, is worth the trip alone. Inside are masterful frescoes (stunningly restored) by Luca Signorelli (circa 1450–1523), perhaps the most underrated in the entire country. A couple of good museums and some excavations round out the sites.

The festival highlight of the year is without a doubt the Festa della Palombella on Pentecost Sunday (the seventh Sunday after Easter), with the Orvietanis' weird take on a fireworks show: a tabernacle with images of the Madonna and the Apostles is set up on the steps in front of the central doorway of the Duomo. A white dove attached to a cable strung across the piazza slides down and ignites the fireworks.

A much mellower scene is the Festa del Corpus Domini (the ninth Sunday after Easter), begun by Pope Urban IV in 1264. Each year the famous *corporale* (square linen cloth) is taken out of the chapel and led around town in a solemn procession, preceded by a rich court in sumptuous period costumes. Between Christmas and the first days of January, the Umbria Jazz Festival comes to Orvieto. Plan on big crowds and high season rats in the hotels, but plenty of music flowing through the streets.

Exploring Orvieto

Orvieto is well connected by train to Rome, Florence, and Perugia, and adjacent to the A1 superstrada that runs between Florence and Rome. Parking areas in the upper town tend to be crowded. There is ample parking in the lower town, near the railway station, and on the other side of town, in Campo della Fiera (at the end of S71). The steep grade led the Orvietanis to build an ingenious funicular in the 19th century that runs from the train station up the side of the hill and through the fortress to Piazzale Cahen. It runs every 20 minutes, daily 7:15 AM–8:30 PM, and costs 1,200 lire. Although the workings have been modernized, there are a few pictures in each station of the old cog railcars, which were once run hydraulically. Keep your funicular ticket, as it will get you a discount on admission to the Museo Claudio Faina. Bus 1 makes the same trip from 8 AM to 11 PM. From Piazzale Cahen, bus A runs to Piazza del Duomo in town center. A new *biglietto unico* (uni-

fied ticket) is a great deal; for 20,000 lire, you get admission to the
four major sites in town—Cappella di San Brizio (Duomo), Museo Claudio Faina, Torre del Moro, and Orvieto Underground—plus a combination bus-funicular pass or five hours of free parking.

A Good Walk

Piazzale Cahen, with a large parking lot and the funicular station, is
a good place to begin. A quick walk around the Rocca will give you
an idea of just how far you have come from the valley floor. The
fortress is now a public garden with great views from its battlements.
Nearby is the so-called **Pozzo di San Patrizio** ㉛ and the ruins of an Etruscan Temple. Cross Piazzale Cahen and walk up Corso Cavour, which
cuts through to the center of town. Only about halfway up, as the streets
narrow and plaster and stucco are replaced by stone, does Orvieto begin
to resemble the other hill towns in the region. Off to the right, Via San
Leonardo leads to Piazza del Popolo, home to a good little market on
Thursday and Saturday mornings, as well as Orvieto's most handsome
civic building, the 13th-century Romanesque-Gothic **Palazzo del
Popolo** ㉜.

Return to the Corso and take Via del Duomo to the left, which leads
past several gift shops selling local ceramics and curves toward Piazza
del Duomo. The spires of the **Duomo** ㉝ just come into view, along with
a glimpse of the marvelous multicolored facade that extends skyward,
an effect that is heightened once you arrive at the wide, narrow piazza.
Stop in at the nearby tourist office for tickets to the Duomo's Cappella
di San Brizio to marvel at the fresco cycle by Luca Signorelli, one of
the great masterpieces of Italy. Around the corner is the **Museo Archeologico** ㉞, a disappointingly sparse collection that is poorly maintained; only a must for hard-core Etruscan fans, who by now will
probably have seen much better relics elsewhere. In the part of the building at the far right that juts out is the **Museo Emilio Greco** ㉟, a worthwhile collection of bronze sculptures and sketches by the contemporary
Sicilian sculptor, who made the doors of the Duomo. The **Museo Claudio Faina** ㊱, directly across from the entrance to the Duomo, is another story. Its excellent collection is beautifully arranged, and it's worth
the admission price just for the views of the facade of the Duomo from
the second-floor hallway. Back on the Corso is the 14th-century **Torre
del Moro** ㊲, with a bell at the top with the 24 symbols of the arts practiced in Orvieto. With all the activity focused around Piazza del Duomo,
you're likely to find the rest of Orvieto relatively quiet, except during
the passeggiata (evening stroll), which is particularly thick along the
Corso in the evenings. Before you leave Orvieto, don't miss the chance
to have a look at the carved-out bowels of its mighty tufa mount (☞
Orvieto Underground, *below*).

TIMING

The main sites in town can be seen in a full day; allow plenty of time
for the Duomo and the Cappella di San Brizio, although a day and a
half might do just as well, especially because Orvieto has several great
restaurants. Thursday and Saturday are especially good for the market in Piazza del Popolo.

Sights to See

★ ㉝ **Duomo.** In a country with so many churches to marvel at, hyperbole
should be reserved for a select few. But no matter how you cut it, Orvieto's Duomo is simply stunning. Your first glimpse of the facade will
likely be a partial view, perhaps of the gray spires against the sky or
the gold mosaics shimmering in the light. Even when you get to the
center of the piazza, you'll find that it's too shallow to allow the monumental facade to be taken in with a single glance. It is thought that

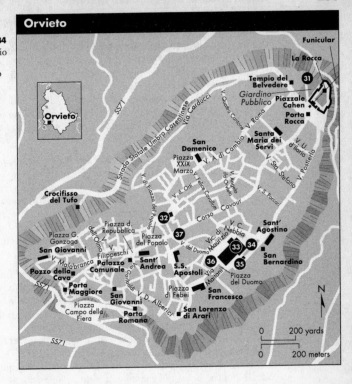

Arnolfo di Cambio (circa 1245–1302), the famous builder of the Duomo in Florence, was given the initial commission. But the project was soon taken over by Lorenzo Maitani (circa 1275–1330), who consolidated the structure and designed the facade. Maitani also made the bas-relief panels between the doorways, which graphically tell the story of the Creation (on the left) and the Last Judgment (on the right). The lower registers, now protected by Plexiglas, succeed in conveying the horror of hell as few other works of art manage to do, an effect made all the more powerful by the worn gray marble.

Above are bronze statues of an eagle, lion, angel, and bull, representing the four evangelists, also by Maitani. The bare lunette above the central doorway marks the place of Andrea Pisano's (circa 1270–1348) *Maestà,* which has been removed for restoration. Gold mosaics, framed by finely detailed Gothic decoration, lead up to a sensational rose window by mid-14th-century-artist Orcagna. The mosaics were remade in the 17th and 18th centuries. Before completion, the Duomo passed into the hands of dozens of architects, artists, and artisans, but the die had essentially been cast. For a building designed by committee, the results are surprisingly harmonious and balanced.

The origins of the church itself go back to the Miracle at Bolsena. In 1263, a young priest who questioned the miracle of transubstantiation (that the Eucharist elements become the blood and flesh of Christ) was saying mass at nearby Lago di Bolsena. His doubts were put to rest, however, when a wafer he had just blessed suddenly started to drip blood, staining the linen covering the altar. The cloth and the host were taken to the pope, who proclaimed a miracle and a year later provided for a new religious holiday—the Feast of Corpus Domini. Thirty years later, construction began on a *duomo* to celebrate the miracle and house the stained altar cloth.

Step inside the vast and rather empty interior, and head straight to the transept. To the left is the **Cappella del Corporale,** where the famous square linen cloth (corporale) is kept in a golden reliquary modeled on the cathedral, inlaid with enamel scenes of the miracle. The cloth is removed for public viewing on Easter and on Corpus Domini (the ninth Sunday after Easter). On the right wall is the miracle scene as imagined by mid-14th-century artist Ugolino di Prete Ilario, opposite are scenes of past miracles involving the Eucharist. Also in the chapel is the fine *Madonna dei Raccomandati* by 14th-century-artist Lippo Memmi, which has been recently restored.

In the right transept is the **Cappella di San Brizio,** or Cappella Nuova, which features one of Italy's greatest fresco cycles, important for its influence on Michelangelo's *Last Judgment,* as well as the extraordinary beauty of the figuration. Along with Giotto's frescoes in Assisi, these are the most important paintings in Umbria. The frescoes have emerged from a recent restoration with colors that are nothing short of shocking in their brilliance, made all the more powerful by the relatively short distance from which they are viewed.

Several great masters, including Benozzo Gozzoli and Fra Angelico, were called to decorate the chapel, but none got very far and what we admire today is almost entirely the work of Luca Signorelli, who painted here between 1499 and 1504. The choice of the Last Judgment as a subject was likely related to the Counter-Reformation, when the classical ideals of the Florentine Renaissance had come under fire and Italy had been invaded from the north by Charles VIII (1470–98). In this context, Signorelli frescoes can be seen as an affirmation of classical ideals and the beauty of the human form.

The story begins on the left wall with the *Sermon of the Antichrist,* in which Chistians are martyred in the background as Signorelli and Fra Angelico (1387–1455) look on from the left side. On the archway over the entrance wall, the story continues with the scene of the *End of the World,* closely tied to the description in the New Testament: we see the young and old fleeing in fear, tumbling out of the scene as the sun darkens, the stars fall from the sky, earthquakes bring buildings to the ground, and demons appear, breathing fire and blood. In the *Resurrection of the Body* on the right wall, two angels summon skeletons from the ground to be recomposed for Judgment Day. It is here we begin to see Signorelli's genius. The notable absence of children and the elderly suggests that Signorelli followed the interpretation that the dead would be resurrected in perfect health and to age 33, the same age as Christ when he was crucified, a notion that undoubtedly appealed to the classical ideals of the perfection of man. Here we see Signorelli's tremendous fascination with the male body, a hallmark of the Renaissance; but rather than dozens of different figures, it seems that the artist has painted a single perfected human form, seen from a thousand angles and iterated across a glorious scene in a fugue of flesh and bones. Michelangelo (1475–1564) was an admirer, while Leonardo (1452–1519) thought otherwise, complaining that the figures' bulky musculature looked like a "sack full of nuts." The following scene, the *Casting out of the Damned,* features an impressive tangle of bodies and demons flying above, picking up sinners and dropping them into the gates of hell. On the wall behind the altar, the *Angels Drive the Sinners to Hell and Guide the Elect to Paradise* are scenes heavily influenced by the imagery in Dante's (1265–1321) *Divine Comedy.* The cycle finishes on the left wall with a majestic final scene of the *Blessed Entering Heaven* as they are serenaded by angels on the rise. In this case the bodies reinforce the classical pairing of goodness and beauty.

As if the fresco cycle did not do enough to link the contemporary with the classical, Signorelli chose to decorate the lower registers with medallions of great classical personages such as Homer (circa 9th–8th centuries BC), Virgil (70–19 BC), and Horace (65–8 BC), and show the link to his day by including Dante, and other great Italian thinkers. ⊠ *Piazza del Duomo,* ☎ *0763/342477.* ☒ *Cappella di San Brizio: 3,000 lire (buy tickets at tourist office across the piazza).* ☉ *Daily 7–1 and 2:30–sunset.*

NEED A BREAK?

Orvieto doesn't lack good places to stop for a quick bite to eat. **Gastronomia Carraro** (⊠ Corso Cavour 101, ☎ 0763/342870), closed Sunday, has an excellent selection of local cheeses and sausages. Farther up the street is the **Pasticceria Montanucci** (⊠ Corso Cavour 21, ☎ no phone), with sweets of every kind. For a more low-key snack or coffee and tables outside, continue up a bit farther to the Piazza della Repubblica to **Bar Sant'Andrea** (⊠ Piazza della Repubblica, ☎ 0763/343285). Across the piazza is the odd-looking 12-sided bell tower of the church of Sant'Andrea. Wonderful gelato in large scoops is to be had at **L'Archetto** (⊠ Piazza del Duomo 14, ☎ 0763/341034), closed mid-December–February, its outdoor tables shaded by ivy.

㉞ Museo Archeologico. With its Etruscan roots, one might expect that Orvieto would have a first-rate archaeological museum, but it seems that the best relics and enthusiasm for displaying them were put into the private collection across the piazza (☞ Museo Claudio Faina, *below*). Greek vases and some interesting relics found in excavations nearby, including pieces of soldier's armor, have been set out in four rooms of the 13th-century **Palazzo del Popolo**, but the items are poorly presented and the descriptions incomplete. If you do go, ask the sleepy staff to turn the lights on in the two reconstructed Etruscan tombs with detached frescoes from the Necropolis of Settecamini. ⊠ *Piazza del Duomo,* ☎ *0763/341039.* ☒ *4,000 lire.* ☉ *Mon.–Sat. 9–1:30 and 2:30–7, Sun. 9–1.*

★ ㊱ Museo Claudio Faina. This superb private collection, beautifully arranged and presented, goes far beyond the usual museum with a scattering of remains found in the area. The collection is particularly rich in several different types of Greek- and Etruscan-era pottery, from large Attic amphorae (6th–4th century BC), to Attic black-and-red figure pieces, to Etruscan *bucchero* (dark, reddish clay) vases. The collection shows how the Etruscans were slowly influenced by Greek culture, first importing their pottery, then the craftsmen themselves, eventually taking on the Greek notion of gods of the afterlife—as shown in several pots found nearby with the figure of Vanth, a winged Etruscan goddess. Other interesting pieces in the collection include a 6th-century sarcophagus with traces of polychromatic decoration, gold jewelry, and masks, and a substantial display of Roman-era coins. Don't miss the view of the facade of the Duomo from the windows in the hallway on the second floor. ⊠ *Piazza del Duomo 29,* ☎ *0763/341511.* ☒ *7,000 lire, 4,000 lire with funicular or bus ticket.* ☉ *Apr.–Sept., Tues.–Sun. 10–1 and 2–6; Oct.–Mar., Tues.–Sun. 10–1 and 2:30–5.*

㉟ Museo Emilio Greco. Another medieval building built by a pope on leave here from Rome, 13th-century Palazzo Soliano was for many years home to the Museo dell'Opera del Duomo, a fine collection that includes a work by Signorelli and other notable names like Simone Martini, Pisano, and Arnolfo di Cambio. But the art treasures have been locked away during an interminable restoration. Meanwhile, the ground floor has been made into the Museo Emilio Greco, a good-looking space filled with sculpture and sketches that the prolific Sicilian artist Emilio Greco (born 1913)—who also made the doors for the Duomo in the 1960s—donated to the city. ⊠ *Piazza del Duomo, Palazzo Soliano,* ☎ *0763/ 344605.* 🎟 *5,000 lire.* ☉ *Apr.–Sept., Tues.–Sat. 10:30–1 and 3–7; Oct.–Mar., Tues.-Sat. 10:30–1 and 2–6.*

㉜ Palazzo del Popolo. Built in tufa and basaltic rock, this was once the town hall. Restoration work in the late 1980s revealed the remains of an Etruscan temple underneath, and it is now used as a conference center and home to the state archives. ⊠ *Piazza del Popolo.*

㉛ Pozzo di San Patrizio (St. Patrick's Well). When Pope Clement VII (1523–34) took shelter in Orvieto during the Sack of Rome in 1527, he saw the need to ensure a safe water supply in the event that Orvieto were to come under siege. Many wells and cisterns were built, and the pope commissioned one of the great architects of the day, Antonio da Sangallo the Younger (1493–1546), to build the well adjacent to the Rocca. After nearly a decade of digging, water was found at a depth of 203 ft. The pope had since died, but the well was finished as planned, with a double-helicoidal stairway that allowed donkey-driven carts to descend and climb back out without running into one another. Windows open onto the shaft, providing natural light in the stairwells. There are 248 steps down to the bottom, but you'll probably get the idea after just a few. Somebody once likened the well to St. Patrick's Well in Ireland. The name stuck, and in Italian the phrase "*pozzo di san patrizio*" has come to represent an inexhaustible source of wealth. ⊠ *Via Sangallo, off Piazza Cahen,* ☎ *0763/343768.* 🎟 *6,000 lire.* ☉ *Mar.–Sept., daily 9:30–7; Oct.–Feb., daily 10–6.*

<table>
<tr><td valign="top">OFF THE
BEATEN PATH</td><td>

CROCIFISSO DEL TUFO – This Etruscan necropolis, about 2 km (1 mi) down Viale Crispi, doesn't have the frescoes that other Etruscan tombs are famous for, and the relics that were buried within have long since been taken away. But it is still a pleasant walk, and interesting to see the type of site from which nearly all our knowledge of Etruscans comes; like the Egyptians, they equipped the dead with everyday items to ease their journey to the next world. The relative lack of pictorial decoration and the standard size of these tombs has led some to speculate that these were not tombs of aristocratic families or warriors. ⊠ *1½ km (1 mi) from Piazzale Cahen, down Viale F. Crispi (SS 71),* ☎ *0763/343611.* 🎟 *4,000 lire.* ☉ *Daily 9–dusk.*

ORVIETO UNDERGROUND – In a way, Orvieto has more than any other town grown from its own foundations—if one were to remove from present-day Orvieto all the building materials that were dug up from below, there would hardly be a building left standing. The Etruscans, the Romans, and those who followed dug into the tufa (the same soft volcanic rock from which catacombs were made), and over the centuries created more than a thousand separate cisterns, caves, secret passages, storage areas, and production areas for wine and olive oil. The tufa they removed was partly used as building blocks for the city we see today, and partly ground into *pozzolana*, which was made into mortar. The most thorough tour (in English, about an hour long) is run daily at 11 AM and 4 PM out of the **tourist office** (⊠ Piazza del Duomo 24, ☎ 0763/344891); admission is 10,000 lire. More frequent (and slightly shorter) tours begin at the **Grotta dell'Hotel Italia** (⊠ Via del Popolo, ☎ 0763/344784). Guided visits are at 9:45 and 11:15 AM and 3:45 and 5:15 PM, and admission is 9,000 lire. If you are short on time but still want a look at what it was like down there, head for the **Pozzo della Cava** (⊠ Via della Cava 28, ☎ 0763/342373), open Wednesday–Monday 8–dusk; admission is 2,500 lire.

</td></tr>
</table>

③⑦ **Torre del Moro.** Perhaps the extraordinary attention lavished on the Duomo left the locals indifferent about the tower in the center of their town; it's hard to imagine a simpler, duller affair. It took on a little more character in the 19th century, when the large, white-faced clock was added along with the fine 14th-century bell, marked with the symbols of the 24 arts-and-crafts guilds then operating in the city. The views, however, are worth the climb. ⊠ *Corso Cavour at Via del Duomo,* ☎ *0763/344567.* ☜ *5,000 lire.* ☯ *May–Aug., daily 10–8; Mar.–Apr. and Sept.–Oct., daily 10–7, Nov.–Feb., daily10:30–1 and 2:30–5.*

Dining and Lodging

\$\$ ✕ **Le Grotte del Funaro.** This restaurant has an extraordinary setting,
★ deep in a series of caves within the volcanic rock beneath Orvieto. Once you have negotiated the steep steps, typical Umbrian specialties such as tagliatelle *al vino rosso* (with red wine sauce) and grilled beef with truffles await. Sample the fine Orvieto wines, either the whites or the lesser-known reds. ⊠ *Via Ripa Serancia 41,* ☎ *0763/343276. Reservations essential. AE, DC, MC, V. Closed Mon.*

\$\$ ✕ **Maurizio.** In the heart of Orvieto, just opposite the cathedral, this
★ warm and welcoming restaurant gets its share of tourists and has a local clientele as well. The decor is unusual, with wood sculptures by Orvieto craftsman Michelangeli. The menu offers hearty soups and homemade pastas such as *tronchetti* (a pasta roll with spinach and ricotta filling). ⊠ *Via del Duomo 78,* ☎ *0763/341114. Reservations essential in summer. AE, MC, V. Closed Tues.*

\$\$\$ ⛉ **Hotel La Badia.**This is one of the best-known country hotels in Umbria. The 700-year-old building, a former monastery, is set in rolling parkland that provides wonderful views of the valley and the town of Orvieto in the distance. The rooms are well appointed. ⊠ *Località La Badia, 4 km (2½ mi) south of Orvieto, 05018,* ☎ *0763/90359,* ⅿ *0763/92796. 26 rooms. Restaurant, bar, pool, 2 tennis courts, meeting rooms. CP. AE, MC, V. Closed Jan.–Feb.*

\$\$\$ ⛉ **Hotel Maitani.** In a 17th-century Baroque palazzo, this hotel has rather ugly public rooms and no restaurant. On a better note, parquet and marble grace the floors and there's a deluxe roof terrace. The rooms are old-fashioned but comfortable. ⊠ *Via Maitani 5, 05018,* ☎ *0763/342011,* ⅿ *0763/342012. 39 rooms. Bar. AE, DC, MC, V.*

\$\$–\$\$\$ ⛉ **Grand Hotel Reale.** The best feature of this hotel is its locale in the center of Orvieto, across a square that hosts a lively market. Facing the impressive Gothic-Romanesque Palazzo del Popolo, rooms are spacious and adequately furnished, with a traditional accent. ⊠ *Piazza del Popolo 25, 05018,* ☎ *0763/341247,* ⅿ *0763/341247. 32 rooms. Bar, breakfast room. CP. MC, V.*

\$\$ ⛉ **Virgilio.** The modest Hotel Virgilio is right in Piazza del Duomo, and the rooms with views of the cathedral are wonderful. The rooms are small but nicely furnished. ⊠ *Piazza del Duomo 5, 05018,* ☎ *0763/341882,* ⅿ *0763/343797. 13 rooms. Bar, breakfast room. CP. MC, V. Closed Feb.*

Enoteche

Orvieto has since its beginnings been synonymous with white wine. There is evidence that the Etruscans grew grapes in the rich volcanic soil in the valley below, and then fermented their wine in the cool caverns dug out of the tufa atop the hill. The Romans made special efforts to bring the local wine down to Rome, which they blended with water and spices. Things had not changed by the early 16th century, when Signorelli was paid in part with wine for his work on the Cappella di San Brizio. Today, wine (along with tourism) is an essential part of the local economy. Although it is the best-known wine in the region, it is no longer one of the Italy's best. However, it is drinkable and pleasantly so, and chances are that the Orvieto Classico you find in the town itself will be better than those exported in large quantities. You will also have the chance to taste different types of Orvieto, from the well-known dry Orvieto Classico to the less-commercialized *abboccato* (semisweet) and *muffato* (made in the style of sauterne).

Here are a few good *enoteche* (wine bars) and producers places to begin your investigations. At **Cantina Foresi** (⊠ Piazza del Duomo 2, ☎ 0763/341611), closed Tuesday November–February, hundreds of bottles are stored in the cool earth of the cellar. In addition to wine served all day long, **L'Asino d'Oro** (⊠ Vicolo del Popolo 1, ☎ 0763/344406, closed October–March) serves lunch and dinner, with a different soup and first course every day and plenty of cold snacks between meals. **La Bottega del Buon Vino** (⊠ Via della Cava 26, ☎ 0763/342373), closed Tuesday, serves meals on tables with a window in the floor that looks down into the caves. Two wine producers in the area worth visiting are **Rocca Ripesana** (call Signore Dubini, ☎ 0763/344166) and the more famous **Castello della Sala** (owned by the Antinori group, Signore Cotarella, ⊠ Località Sala, 20 km/12 mi north of Orvieto, ☎ 0763/86051).

Nightlife and the Arts

If in Orvieto on Pentecost Sunday (the seventh Sunday after Easter), don't miss the **Festa della Palombella,** with its Duomo fireworks show set off by a dove.

Shopping

Ceramics

As with other towns in the region, Orvieto has its fair share of pottery resellers, along with a few genuine shops selling Orvietan-style pottery, bright-white vessels with hand-painted motifs. **La Torreta** (⊠ Corso Cavour 283, ☎ 0763/340248) has a kiln right in the shop and will custom paint something for you on the spot. Far more sophisticated is **L'Arte del Vasaio** (⊠ Via Pedota 3, ☎ 0763/342022), whose copies of ancient ceramics were good enough to fool the curators of a famous museum, who put them out as the real thing.

Embroidery and Lace

Minor arts, such as embroidery and lace making, flourish in Orvieto. Two of the best shops for *merletto* (lace) are **Duranti** (⊠ Corso Cavour 107, ☎ no phone) and **Ditta Moretti Merletti** (⊠ Via Duomo 55, ☎ 0763/41714).

Liqueurs

Gli Svizzeri Drogheria (⊠ Corso Cavour 35, ☎ 0763/341233) makes their own digestives and bitters, as well as *rosolio* (a sweet liqueur, mildly alcoholic) flavored with almond.

Market

A good time to experience an outdoor market in Orvieto is Thursday and Saturday morning, when a small but good market bustles at **Piazza del Popolo.** You'll find a few stalls selling crafts, but mostly vegetable stands and the usual variety of clothing, housewares, and junk.

Woodwork

Orvieto is a center of woodworking, particularly fine inlays and veneers. Corso Cavour is lined with a number of artisan shops specializing in woodwork, the best known being the **Michelangeli family**

studio (✉ Corso Cavour, ☎ 0763/342377), crammed with a variety of imaginatively designed objects ranging in size from a giant *armadio* (wardrobe) to a simple wooden spoon.

ASSISI, SPOLETO, AND SOUTHERN UMBRIA A TO Z

Arriving and Departing

By Bus
Private bus lines such as Lazzi, Sulga, and Spoletina run from Rome and Florence to the major cities in the region (Assisi, Spoleto, Orvieto, and Terni). Check with the local tourist offices (☞ Visitor Information, *below*) for timetables.

By Car
The region is easily reached from the Rome–Florence autostrada (A1), with exits at Orvieto and Perugia.

By Plane
Aeroporto Sant'Egidio (☎ 075/6929447), 12 km (7 mi) east of Perugia, serves the region.

By Train
Slow trains on the Rome–Ancona line make stops in Narni-Amelia, Terni, Spoleto, Trevi, and Foligno; slow trains on the Rome–Florence line stop in Orvieto. For information for the state-run line (FS), dial 147/888088.

Getting Around

By Bus
A multitude of private companies such as ASP, Sulga, and Spoletina offer bus service between the towns in southern Umbria, but offices are often difficult to reach on the phone. Check with the local tourist office for the latest information.

By Car
The main highways run south from Perugia (E45) to Todi and Terni or southeast from Perugia to Assisi, Spello, Foligno, and Spoleto (via S75) and Terni (via S3). Orvieto lies above the Rome–Florence autostrada (A1), and is also connected to Todi by a country road (79 bis).

By Train
Three train lines connect most of the towns, but most are a few kilometers from their respective stations. Slow trains on the Rome–Ancona line make stops in Narni-Amelia, Terni, Spoleto, Trevi, and Foligno, while the Terontola-Foligno line connects Foligno, Spello, Assisi, and Perugia. Slow trains on the Rome–Florence line stop in Orvieto. For information for the state-run line (FS), dial ☎ 147/888088.

Contacts and Resources

Agritourist Agencies
☞ Chapter 8.

Car Rentals
Orvieto/Spoleto: Hertz (✉ Via Cerquiglia 36, Spoleto, ☎ 0743/47217; ✉ Strada dell'Arcone 13, Orvieto, ☎ 0763/301303). **Terni: Avis** (✉ Via XX Settembre 80/d, Terni, ☎ 0744/287170); **Europcar Italia** (✉ Lungonera Savoia 12/c, Terni, ☎ 0744/282652).

Emergencies

In an **emergency,** dial 113 for paramedics, police, or the fire department.

Guided Tours

Associazione Guide Turistiche dell'Umbria (☎ 075/815228).

Hiking and Climbing

Club Alpino Italiano (☎ 075/220433).

Hotels

Assisi Hoteliers Association (☎ 075/816566).

Late-Night Pharmacies

Pharmacies take turns staying open late or on Sunday; for the latest information, consult the list posted outside each pharmacy, or ask at the local tourist office.

Thermal Springs

Terme di Santo Raggio (✉ Via P. A. Giorgi 6, near Assisi, ☎ 075/816064), closed November–mid-May. **Terme di San Gemini** (✉ 05029 San Gemini, near Terni, ☎ 0744/630426), closed October–April. **Terme Amerino** (✉ Via San Francesco 1, 05021 Acquasparta, between Terni and Todi, ☎ 0744/943921), closed November–April.

Travel Agencies

Agenzia Stoppini (✉ Corso Mazzini 31, Assisi, ☎ 075/812597). **Agenzia Jazz Viagi e Vacanze** (✉ Piazza della Libertà 11, Spoleto, ☎ 0743/221818). **Orvietur Viaggi e Turismo** (✉ Via Duomo 23, Orvieto, ☎ 0763/341555).

Visitor Information

Assisi (✉ Piazza del Comune, kiosk, ☎ 075/812534). **Bevagna** (✉ Piazza Silvestri, ☎ 0742/361667). **Foligno** (✉ Porta Romana 126, ☎ 0742/354459). **Montefalco** (✉ Via Ringhiera Umbra, ☎ 0742/379598). **Narni** (✉ Piazza del Popolo 18, ☎ 0744/715362). **Orvieto** (✉ Piazza del Duomo 24, ☎ 0763/341772). **Spello** (✉ Piazza Matteotti 3, ☎ 0742/301009). **Spoleto** (✉ Piazza della Libertà 7, ☎ 0743/220311). **Terni** (✉ Viale C. Battisti 5, ☎ 0744/423047). **Todi** (✉ Piazza del Popolo 38, ☎ 075/8943867).

10 Portraits of Florence, Tuscany, and Umbria

Florence, Tuscany, and Umbria at a Glance: A Chronology

Artistically Speaking: A Glossary

Books and Videos

FLORENCE, TUSCANY, AND UMBRIA AT A GLANCE: A CHRONOLOGY

ca. 1000 BC	Etruscans arrive in central Italy.
ca. 800	Rise of Etruscan city-states.
510	Foundation of the Roman republic; expulsion of Etruscans from Roman territory.
ca. 350	Rome extends rule to Tuscia (Tuscany), the land of the Etruscans.
ca. 220	Umbria, the land of the Umbri and later Etruscans, come under Roman sway.
133	Rome rules entire Mediterranean Basin except Egypt.
49	Julius Caesar conquers Gaul.
46	Julian calendar introduced; it remains in use until AD 1582.
44	Julius Caesar is assassinated.
27	Rome's Imperial Age begins; Octavian (now named Augustus) becomes the first emperor and is later deified. The Augustan Age is celebrated in the works of Virgil (70 BC–AD 19), Ovid (43 BC–AD 17), Livy (59 BC–AD 17), and Horace (65 BC–AD 27).
AD 14	Augustus dies.
65	Emperor Nero begins the persecution of Christians in the empire; Saints Peter and Paul are executed.
117	The Roman Empire reaches its apogee.
165	A smallpox epidemic ravages the Empire.
ca. 150–200	Christianity gains a foothold within the Empire, with the theological writings of Clement, Tertullian, and Origen.
212	Roman citizenship is conferred on all nonslaves in the Empire.
238	The first wave of Germanic invasions penetrates Italy.
293	Diocletian reorganizes the Empire into West and East.
313	The Edict of Milan grants toleration of Christianity within the Empire.
410	Rome is sacked by Visigoths.
476	The last Roman Emperor, Romulus Augustus, is deposed. The Empire of Rome falls.
552	Eastern Emperor Justinian (527–565) recovers control of Italy.
570	Lombards gain control of much of Italy, including Rome.
590	Papal power expands under Gregory the Great.
ca. 600–750	Lucca is chief city of Tuscany.
774	Frankish ruler Charlemagne (742–814) invades Italy under papal authority and is crowned Holy Roman Emperor by Pope Leo III (800).
ca. 800–900	The breakup of Charlemagne's (Carolingian) realm leads to the rise of Italian city-states.
1077	Pope Gregory VII leads the Holy See into conflict with the Germanic Holy Roman Empire.

1152–1190   Frederick I (Barbarossa) is crowned Holy Roman Emperor (1155); punitive expeditions by his forces (Ghibellines) are countered by the Guelphs, creators of the powerful Papal States in central Italy. Guelph–Ghibelline conflict becomes a feature of medieval life.

ca. 1200   Lucca appears strongest of Tuscan cities. Religious revival in Umbria centers around activities of St. Francis of Assisi and the foundation of the Franciscan order. Umbria takes the lead in art and architecture, attracting Pisano, Cimabue, Giotto, Simone Martini, and Lorenzetti.

ca. 1250   Florence takes the cultural and financial lead.

1262   Florentine bankers issue Europe's first bills of exchange.

1264   Charles I of Anjou invades Italy, intervening in the continuing Guelph–Ghibelline conflict.

1290–1375   Tuscan literary giants Dante Alighieri (1265–1321), Francesco Petrarch (1304–1374), and Giovanni Boccaccio (1313–1375) give written imprimatur to modern Italian language.

1309   The pope moves to Avignon in France, under the protection of French kings.

1376   The pope returns to Rome, but rival Avignonese popes stand in opposition, creating the Great Schism until 1417.

ca. 1380–1420   Umbrian cities ruled by *condottieri*.

1402   The last German intervention into Italy is repulsed by the Lombards.

1443   Brunelleschi's (1377–1446) cupola is completed on Florence's Duomo.

1469–1492   Lorenzo "Il Magnifico" (1449–1492), the Medici patron of the arts, rules in Florence.

1498   Girolamo Savonarola (1452–1498), the austere Dominican friar, is executed for heresy after leading Florence into a drive for moral purification, typified by his burning of books and decorations in the "Bonfire of Vanities."

1504   Michelangelo's (1475–1564) *David* is unveiled in Florence's Piazza della Signoria.

1513   Machiavelli's (1469–1527) *The Prince* is published.

1521   The Pope excommunicates Martin Luther (1483–1546) of Germany, precipitating the Protestant Reformation.

1540   Pope Paul III consolidates rule of Umbria with other Papal States.

1545–1563   The Council of Trent formulates the Catholic response to the Reformation.

ca. 1700   Opera develops as an art form in Italy.

1720–1790   The Great Age of the Grand Tour: Northern Europeans visit Italy and start the vogue for classical studies. Among the famous visitors are Edward Gibbon (1758), Jacques-Louis David (1775), and Johann Wolfgang von Goethe (1786).

1796   Napoleon begins his Italian campaigns, annexing Rome and imprisoning Pope Pius VI four years later.

1801   Tuscany is made kingdom of Etruria within French domain.

1807–1809 Tuscany is a French département.

1808 Umbria annexed to French empire as département of Trasimeno.

1815 Austria controls much of Italy after Napoleon's downfall.

1848 Revolutionary troops under Risorgimento (Unification) leaders Giuseppe Mazzini (1805–1872) and Giuseppe Garibaldi (1807–1882) establish a republic in Rome.

1849 French troops crush rebellion and restore Pope Pius IX.

1860 Garibaldi and his "Thousand" defeat the Bourbon rulers in Sicily and Naples.

1861 Tuscany and Umbria join Kingdom of Sardinia, which becomes Kingdom of Italy.

1870 Rome is finally captured by Risorgimento troops and is declared capital of Italy by King Vittorio Emanuele II.

1900 King Umberto I is assassinated by an anarchist; he is succeeded by King Vittorio Emanuele III.

1915 Italy enters World War I on the side of the Allies.

1922 Fascist "black shirts" under Benito Mussolini (1883–1945) march on Rome; Mussolini becomes prime minister and later "Il Duce" (head of Italy).

1929 The Lateran Treaty: Mussolini recognizes Vatican City as a sovereign state, and the Church recognizes Rome as the capital of Italy.

1940–1944 In World War II, Italy fights with the Axis powers until its capitulation (1943), when Mussolini flees Rome. Italian partisans and Allied troops from the landings at Anzio (January 1944) win victory at Cassino (March 1944) and force the eventual withdrawal of German troops from Italy.

1957 The Treaty of Rome is signed, and Italy becomes a founding member of the European Economic Community.

1966 November flood damages many of Florence's artistic treasures.

1968–1979 The growth of left-wing activities leads to the formation of the Red Brigades and provokes right-wing reactions. Bombings and kidnappings culminate in the abduction and murder of Prime Minister Aldo Moro (1916–1978).

1992 The Christian Democrat Party, in power throughout the postwar period, loses its hold on a relative majority in Parliament.

1993 Italians vote for sweeping reforms after the Tangentopoli (Bribe City) scandal exposes widespread political corruption, including politicians' collusion with organized crime. A bomb outside the Galleria degli Uffizi in Florence kills five, but spares the museum's most precious artwork; authorities blame the Cosa Nostra, flexing its muscles in the face of a crackdown.

1994 A center-right coalition wins in spring elections, and media magnate Silvio Berlusconi becomes premier—only to be deposed within a year. Italian politics seem to be evolving into the equivalent of a two-party system.

1995 Newly appointed Lamberto Dini takes hold of the government's rudder and, as president of the Council of Ministers, institutes major reforms and replaces old-line politicians.

1996 A league of center-left parties wins national elections and puts together a government coalition that sees the Democrats of the Left (PDS), the former Communist party, into power for the first time ever in Italy.

1997 Political stability and an austerity program put Italy on track toward the European Monetary Union and adoption of the single Euro currency. A series of earthquakes hit the mountainous interior of central Italy, severely damaging villages and some historic towns. In Assisi, portions of the vault of the Basilica di San Francesco crumble, destroying frescoes by Cimabue.

1998 In October the center-left prime minister, Romano Prodi, loses a Parliament confidence vote by one ballot and is forced to resign. At press time, Massimo D'Alema, a former Communist and leader of Democrats of the Left, is reaching a center-left coalition. In Rome, public works projects designed to take some of the snarls out of Jubilee Year traffic in the year 2000 get under way.

ARTISTICALLY SPEAKING: A GLOSSARY

THE ELOQUENCE of the world's greatest masterpieces can be deafening, and Italy's treasures—their message made manifest in marble, pigment, and precious metals—instill a spirit of awe. The privilege of enjoying this bounty of the ages can be greatly deepened and enhanced by a familiarity with the language and terms of art-speak. Here is a limited glossary for the interested layman. Many of these Italian words are now part of the basic art history vocabulary.

Acanthus: Sculptural ornamentation from antiquity; it's based on the foliage of the acanthus plant.

Apse: A semicircular terminus found behind the altar in a church.

Atrium: The courtyard in front of the entrance to an ancient Roman villa or an early church.

Badia: Abbey.

Baldacchino: A canopy—often made of stone—above a church altar, supported by columns.

Baptistery: A separate structure or area in a church where rites of baptism are held.

Baroque: A 17th-century European art movement in which dramatic, elaborate ornamentation was used to stir viewers' emotions. The most famous Italian Baroque artists were Carracci and Bernini.

Basilica: A rectangular Roman public building divided into aisles by rows of columns. Many early churches were built on the basilican plan, but the term is also applied to some churches without specific reference to architecture.

Belvedere: Usually a lookout point for vistas; the word means "beautiful view."

Campanile: A bell tower of a church.

Capital: The crowning section of a column, usually decorated with Doric, Ionic, or Corinthian ornament.

Chiaroscuro: Meaning "light/dark;" refers to the distribution of light and shade in a painting, either with a marked contrast or a muted tonal gradation.

Cinquecento: Literally "five-hundred," used in Italian to refer to the 16th century.

Contrapposto: A dramatic pose of a sculpted figure in which the upper portion of the body is placed in opposition to the lower portion.

Cortile: Courtyard.

Cupola: Dome.

Duomo: Cathedral.

Fresco: A wall-painting technique, used in Roman times and again in the early Renaissance, in which pigment was applied to wet plaster.

Gothic: Medieval architectural and ornamental style featuring pointed arches, high interior vaulting, and flying buttresses to emphasize height and via symbolism, an ascension to heaven. The term is also used to describe the painting style made famous by Giotto and Simone Martini.

Grotesques: Decorations of fanciful human and animal forms, embellished with flowers; first used in Nero's Golden House and rediscovered during the Renaissance.

Loggia: Roofed balcony or gallery.

Maestà: Majestic image of the Virgin Mary enthroned and surrounded by angels.

Mannerism: Style of the mid-16th century, in which artists—such as Bronzino and Il Rosso—sought to replace the warm, humanizing ideals of Leonardo and Raphael with super-elegant, coldly emotional forms. Portraits in the Mannerist style feature florid colors, high-fashion anatomies, and frosty demeanors.

Nave: The central aisle of a church.

Palazzo: A palace, or more generally, any large building.

Perspective: The illusion of three-dimensional space that was obtained in the early 15th century with the discovery that all parallel lines running in one direction meet at a single point on the horizon known as the vanishing point. Leonardo da Vinci later perfected aerial perspective, in which gradations of *sfumato* (haze) and color can be used to create the illusion of distance.

Piano nobile: The main floor of a palace (the first floor above ground level).

Pietà: Literally "piety," refers to an image of the Virgin Mary holding the crucified body of Christ on her lap.

Polyptych: A painting—often an altarpiece—on multiple wooden panels that are joined. A three-paneled painting is a tryptych.

Predella: A series of small paintings found below the main section of an altarpiece.

Putti: Cherubs, cupids or other images of infant boys in painting.

Quattrocento: Literally "four-hundred;" refers to the 15th century.

Renaissance: Major school of Italian art, literature, and philosophy (14th century–16th century) that fused innovations in realism with the rediscovery of the great heritage of classical antiquity. After Giotto introduced a new naturalism into painting in the 14th century, Florentine artists of the 1430s, such as Masaccio and Fra Filippo Lippi, paved the way for the later 15th-century realism of Botticelli and Signorelli. While reaching first flower in Florence, the movement culminated in Rome with the High Renaissance (circa 1490–1520) and the masterpieces of Leonardo, Raphael, and Michelangelo.

Rococo: Light, dainty 18th-century art and architectural style created in reaction to heavy Baroque. Tiepolo is the leading painter of the Rococo style.

Romanesque: Architectural style of the 11th and 12th centuries that reworked ancient Roman forms, particularly barrel and groin vaults. Stark, severe, and magisterial, Romanesque basilicas are among Italy's most awe-inspiring churches.

Sacra conversazione: The motif of the "holy conversation," showing the Madonna and Child in the midst of and/or interacting with saints.

Tondo: Circular painting or sculpture.

Trompe l'oeil: An artistic technique employed to "fool the eye" into believing that the object or scene depicted is actually real.

Veduta: A painting of a city or landscape as viewed from afar, popular in the 18th century.

BOOKS AND VIDEOS

Books

The musings of some well-known travelers who visited Tuscany and Umbria when travel was as much ordeal as vacation make for entertaining reading. Many keen observations by Henry James's *Italian Hours* (offered in many editions, including *Traveling in Italy with Henry James: Essays,* William Morrow) and D. H. Lawrence's *Etruscan Places* (Penguin) still hold true, and their experiences put modern travel into an interesting perspective.

For background, Luigi Barzini's *The Italians* is the classic analysis of the Italian national character, still worthy reading although published in 1964 (Atheneum). More recent reflections on Italian life include *Italian Days,* by Barbara Grizzuti Harrison (Ticknor & Fields), and *That Fine Italian Hand,* by Paul Hofmann (Henry Holt), for many years *New York Times* bureau chief in Rome. If you are looking for a general historical and art history framework, Harry Hearder's *Italy, A Short History* (Cambridge) cuts right to the chase, with two thousand years covered in less than 300 pages, and Michael Levey's clear and concise treatment of the Renaissance (*Early Renaissance* and *High Renaissance,* Penguin) are good places to begin. The history of the Renaissance, the great artists and political figures and turbulent power struggles throughout the region make great reading when told by Christopher Hibbert (*The House of Medici: Its Rise and Fall,* Willliam Morrow).

Novels and historical fiction often impart a greater sense of a place than straight history books: Irving Stone's best-selling *The Agony and the Ecstasy* (NAL) romanticizes the life of Michelangelo, but paints an enduring picture of Renaissance Florence; Umberto Eco's *The Name of the Rose* (Harcourt Brace) is a gripping murder mystery that will leave you with tremendous insight into monastic life in Italy. On the lighter side, Florence is the setting for two of Magdalen Nabb's entertaining thrillers: *Death in Autumn* and *Death of a Dutchman.*(HarperCollins).

English and American expatriates have preferred everything Tuscan (and more recently, Umbrian) for decades now, and many writers have chronicled their experiences restoring a farmhouse and making sense of the local culture and color. Among the better examples of what is becoming a genre unto itself are Matthew Spender's *Within Tuscany: Reflections on a Time and Place* (Viking), *Under the Tuscan Sun: At Home in Italy* by Frances Mayes (Broadway Books), and Lisa St. Aubin de Terán's *A Valley in Italy: The Many Seasons of a Villa in Umbria* (HarperCollins).

Whet your appetite with a survey of some of the beautiful buildings and gardens within easy reach: Harold Acton's *Great Houses of Tuscany: The Tuscan Villas* (Viking) or Carey More's *Views from a Tuscan Vineyard* (Pavillion). The glories of historic Italian gardens are caught in the ravishing photographs in Judith Chatfield's *Gardens of the Italian Lakes* (Rizzoli) and Ethne Clark's *Gardens of Tuscany* (Weidenfeld & Nicolson, out of print).

Although every year there are more and more cookbooks on Tuscan food, Waverley Root's *Food of Italy* (Vintage), published in 1977, is still a handy (if not infallible) reference. Take Faith Heller Wilinger's newly revised *Eating in Italy* (Morrow) to guide you to the good food and restaurants, and Burton Anderson's *Pocket Guide to Italian Wines* (Little Brown) to sort your way through the wine lists.

Videos

You'll recognize the idyllic scenery of central Italy in numerous films, recent among them Miramax's *The English Patient* (1996), Kenneth Branagh's *Much Ado About Nothing* (1993), Bernardo Bertolucci's *Stealing Beauty* (1996), and the sights of Florence in Merchant/Ivory's *A Room with a View* (1986).

INDEX

NOTES

NOTES

Fodor's
ESCAPE

One-of-a-kind Italian experiences

The perfect companions to **Fodor's** Gold Guides, these exquisite full-color guidebooks will inspire you with their unique vacation ideas, help you plan with detailed contact information, and safeguard your memories with their gorgeous photographs.

WHEREVER YOU TRAVEL, $\mathcal{H}$ELP IS NEVER FAR AWAY.

From planning your trip to

providing travel assistance along

the way, American Express®

Travel Service Offices are

always there to help

you do more.

www.americanexpress.com/travel

American Express Travel Service Offices
are located throughout Florence, Tuscany and Umbria.